Lecture Notes in Artificial Intelligence 10207

Subseries of Lecture Notes in Computer Science

More information about this series at http://www.springer.com/series/1244

Natalia Criado Pacheco · Carlos Carrascosa
Nardine Osman · Vicente Julián Inglada (Eds.)

Multi-Agent Systems and Agreement Technologies

14th European Conference, EUMAS 2016
and 4th International Conference, AT 2016
Valencia, Spain, December 15–16, 2016
Revised Selected Papers

 Springer

Editors
Natalia Criado Pacheco
King's College London
London
UK

Carlos Carrascosa
Polytechnic University of Valencia
Valencia
Spain

Nardine Osman
Artificial Intelligence Research Institute
(IIIA-CSIC)
Barcelona
Spain

Vicente Julián Inglada
Polytechnic University of Valencia
Valencia
Spain

ISSN 0302-9743 ISSN 1611-3349 (electronic)
Lecture Notes in Artificial Intelligence
ISBN 978-3-319-59293-0 ISBN 978-3-319-59294-7 (eBook)
DOI 10.1007/978-3-319-59294-7

Library of Congress Control Number: 2017943035

LNCS Sublibrary: SL7 – Artificial Intelligence

Printed on acid-free paper

This Springer imprint is published by Springer Nature
The registered company is Springer International Publishing AG
The registered company address is: Gewerbestrasse 11, 6330 Cham, Switzerland

Preface

This volume contains revised versions of the papers presented at the 14th European Conference on Multi-Agent Systems (EUMAS 2016) and the 4th International Conference on Agreement Technologies (AT 2016), which were both held in Valencia during December 15–16, 2016. EUMAS 2016 followed the tradition of previous editions (Oxford 2003, Barcelona 2004, Brussels 2005, Lisbon 2006, Hammamet 2007, Bath 2008, Agia Napa 2009, Paris 2010, Maastricht 2011, Dublin 2012, Toulouse 2013, Prague 2014, and Athens 2015) in aiming to provide the prime European forum for presenting and discussing agents research as the annual designated event of the European Association of Multi-Agent Systems (EURAMAS). AT 2016 was the fourth instalment in a series of events (after Dubrovnik 2012, Beijing 2013, and Athens 2015) that focus on bringing together researchers and practitioners working on computer systems in which autonomous software agents interact, typically on behalf of humans, in order to come to mutually acceptable agreements. A wide scope of technologies can help provide the support needed for reaching mutually acceptable agreements, such as argumentation and negotiation, trust and reputation, computational social choice, coalition and team formation, coordination and distributed decision-making, and semantic alignment, to name a few.

This year, for the second time, both events were co-located and run as a single, joint event. This joint organization aimed to encourage and continue cross-fertilization among the broader EUMAS and the more specialized AT communities, and to provide a richer and more attractive program to participants. While the technical program was put together by their independent committees into conference-specific thematic sessions, they shared keynote talks and aligned their schedules to minimize overlap and enable participants to make the best possible use of the combined program of the two conferences. Traditionally, both conference series have always followed a spirit of providing a forum for discussion and an annual opportunity for primarily European researchers to meet and exchange ideas. For this reason, they have always encouraged submission of papers that report on both early and mature research. The peer-review processes carried out by both conferences put great emphasis on ensuring a high quality of accepted contributions. The EUMAS Program Committee accepted 17 submissions (32.7%) as full papers and another 16 submissions (30.8%) as short papers out of a total of 52 submissions. The AT review process resulted in the acceptance of seven full (43.8%) and three short papers (18.8%) out of 16 submissions overall. This volume is structured as follows: In the first part, we present the two invited papers; in the second, we present the EUMAS papers, and in the third we present the AT papers. The papers of each part are then grouped into thematic areas, where we first present full papers, followed by short papers. For the EUMAS papers, the thematic areas are:

- Agent and Multi-agent System Models
- Algorithms
- Applications
- Simulations
- Theoretical Studies

For AT, the thematic areas are:
- Algorithms and Frameworks
- Applications
- Philosophical and Theoretical Studies

The editors would like to thank all authors for submitting to EUMAS and AT, all participants, the invited speakers, the members of the Program Committees, and the additional reviewers for putting together strong programs. We also thank the local organizers for their hard work organizing the events. Finally, we would like to express our gratitude to the sponsors of the conferences, the European Association for Artificial Intelligence (EurAi), the Universitat Politecnica de Valencia, the Escuela Técnica Superior de Ingeniería Informática, and the *Artificial Intelligence* journal for their generous support, without which this event would not have been possible.

March 2017   Natalia Criado
                                                                                Carlos Carrascosa
                                                                                Nardine Osman
                                                                                Vicente Julian

Organization

EUMAS 2016 Co-chairs

Natalia Criado   King's College London, UK
Carlos Carrascosa   Universitat Politècnica de València, Spain

AT 2016 Co-chairs

Nardine Osman   Artificial Intelligence Research Institute, Spain
Vicente Julian   Universitat Politècnica de València, Spain

EUMAS 2016 Program Committee

Alessandro Ricci   University of Bologna, Italy
Alessio Lomuscio   Imperial College London, UK
Amal El Fallah   Pierre and Marie Curie University, France
  Seghrouchni
Andrea Omicini   Università di Bologna, Italy
Aniello Murano   Università di Napoli Federico II, Italy
Brian Logan   University of Nottingham, UK
Cristiano Castelfranchi   Institute of Cognitive Sciences and Technologies (CNR),
                            Italy
Christopher Frantz   Otago Polytechnic, New Zealand
Christopher Hampson   King's College London, UK
Dominique Longin   IRIT-CNRS, France
Edith Elkind   University of Oxford, UK
Emiliano Lorini   IRIT-CNRS, France
Emilio Serrano   Technical University of Madrid, Spain
Emma Norling   Manchester Metropolitan University, UK
Estefania Argente   Universitat Politècnica de València, Spain
Felipe Meneguzzi   Pontifical Catholic University of Rio Grande do Sul, Brazil
Franziska Kügl   Örebro University, Sweden
Frederic Moisan   Carnegie Mellon University, USA
George Vouros   University of Piraeus, Greece
Ingo J. Timm   University of Trier, Germany
Ingrid Nunes   Universidade Federal do Rio Grande do Sul, Brazil
João Leite   NOVA LINCS, Universidade Nova de Lisboa, Portugal
John-Jules Meyer   Utrecht University, The Netherlands
Jörg P. Müller   TU Clausthal, Germany
Jose M. Such   Lancaster University, UK
Josh Murphy   King's College London, UK
Julian Padget   University of Bath, UK

Laurent Vercouter	LITIS lab, INSA de Rouen, France
Lina Barakat	King's College London, UK
Louise Dennis	University of Liverpool, UK
Marija Slavkovik	University of Bergen, Norway
Massimo Cossentino	National Research Council of Italy, Italy
Mehdi Dastani	Utrecht University, The Netherlands
Michael Rovatsos	University of Edinburgh, UK
Natasha Alechina	University of Nottingham, UK
Neil Yorke-Smith	American University of Beirut, Lebanon
Nicoletta Fornara	Università della Svizzera Italiana, Lugano, Switzerland
Nils Bulling	Delft University of Technology, The Netherlands
Nir Oren	University of Aberdeen, UK
Olivier Boissier	ENS Mines Saint-Etienne, France
Pablo Noriega	Artificial Intelligence Research Institute (IIIA-CSIC), Spain
Paolo Turrini	Imperial College London, UK
Paolo Torroni	University of Bologna, Italy
Pavlos Moraitis	LIPADE, Université Paris Descartes, France
Pinar Yolum	Bogazici University, Turkey
Rubén Fuentes-Fernández	Universidad Complutense de Madrid, Spain
Samhar Mahmoud	King's College London, UK
Sanjay Modgil	King's College London, UK
Serena Villata	Laboratoire d'Informatique, Signaux et Systèmes de Sophia-Antipolis (CNRS), France
Sofia Ceppi	University of Edinburgh, UK
Stella Heras	Universitat Politècnica de València, Spain
Thomas C. King	Lancaster University, UK
Vicent Botti	Universitat Politècnica de València, Spain
Victor Sanchez-Anguix	Coventry University, UK
Wamberto Vasconcelos	University of Aberdeen, UK

AT 2016 Program Committee

Alberto Fernandez	CETINIA, Rey Juan Carlos University, Spain
Alexander Artikis	National Centre of Scientific Research Demokritos, Greece
Carles Sierra	Artificial Intelligence Research Institute (IIIA-CSIC), Spain
Carlos Chesñevar	Universidad Nacional del Sur, Argentina
Cristiano Castelfranchi	Institute of Cognitive Sciences and Technologies (CNR), Italy
Denis Trcek	University of Ljubljana, Slovenia
Elena Cabrio	University of Nice Sophia Antipolis, France
Elise Bonzon	LIPADE, Universite Paris Descartes, France
Elizabeth Sklar	King's College London, UK
Emiliano Lorini	IRIT-CNRS, France

Contents

EUMAS 2016: Applications

Invited Speakers

Autonomy and Roles of Intelligent Social Agents in Our Hybrid and Mixed World: Some Hints

Cristiano Castelfranchi[✉]

ISTC-CNR, Rome, Italy
cristiano.castelfranchi@istc.cnr.it

1 Introduction

Ag-MAS community created autonomous and proactive intelligent entities (which will become 'presences' and 'roles' in our *hybrid* (human and artificial agents) society and *mixed* reality (combined virtual and 'real' world). Now a question will be: are we able to manage these autonomous and too informed and intelligent agents?

It is not only a problem of level of delegation (open vs. restricted and specified) or of the possibility of initiative in cooperation with 'over-help', 'critical-help', and even with functional norms violations. It is not only a matter of 'adjustable autonomy' and negotiation of the degree of control based on trust and self-trust. It is a matter of: which roles will those material or immaterial, visible and invisible 'entities' play in our life and environment? Will they be our 'Guardian angel' with a 'tutelary' role? Or our tempting Devil (for the benefit of some marketing strategy)? Or will they be an influencing and manipulating manager for hidden political or economic powers? Or our supervisor and exploiter in the ICT-Panopticon we live in?

Which interests they will care of? Of the interests of sellers or of us as consumers? Of the interests of dominant groups or of submitted and discriminated people? Which political and moral view will orient them: I mean not our 'car drivers' but our 'society drivers' and our 'life navigator'.

Shouldn't we develop not only useful 'agreement technologies' but also some 'disagreement' supporting technologies?

Intelligent Agents will decide "for us", but in which sense? "Instead of" us or also "for our good"? Robots and Intelligent Ags will not govern for their own interests, but in whose interests?

2 Some of the Real Risks and Challenges

We – AAMAS community – are responsible for the introduction of "Agents" as "autonomous" (proactive, with initiative, with their own learning, reasoning, evolution, …) and "social", cooperating with human by following true "norms" (but also – in case –

© Springer International Publishing AG 2017
N. Criado Pacheco et al. (Eds.): EUMAS 2016/AT 2016, LNAI 10207, pp. 3–12, 2017.
DOI: 10.1007/978-3-319-59294-7_1

violating them), and critically adopting our goals (not just "executing"), with *over-help*, *critical-help*, …[1]

And this was a *correct* and unavoidable solution, for a real "Intelligence" interacting with and usable from humans. And also for "science": for modeling and understanding human intelligence and sociality.

I'm not repented at all, of modeling *artificial* intelligence and sociality… However this obliges you/us to become aware of possible appropriation of such creation, of possible unacceptable uses of these instruments.

There are *dangers* in AI and in particular in Autonomous Agent and Augmented/Hybrid Intelligence. Are we missing the control? Not of our Autonomous Agents, Robots, etc. but of their possible uses?

Are we ready for the anthropological revolution grounded on Intelligent Technologies and artificial mixed society? Which also is *an economic, social, and political revolution*.

Following the mass media, the problems mainly are: *Privacy*; *Security* (*on WEB, … on access …*); *Hackers' attacks*; *Anthropomorphism*; *War and Artificial soldiers/arms*; *Ethics inside Artificial creatures and algorithms*.

These are problems, for sure. Just a couple of examples of this focus on.

(i) **War and Artificial soldiers/arms:** Subra Suresh, Carnegie Mellon's president, said "injecting ethical discussions into A.I. was necessary as the technology advanced. While the idea of "Terminator" robots still seems far-fetched, the United States military is studying autonomous weapons that *could make killing decisions on their own*—a development that war planners think would be unwise."
Finally solved the problem of the poor general![2] Finally generals no longer need a (human) driver or mechanic! The AI driver can think, yes; but we/generals can *decide and control how it will think*!

(ii) **"Engineering Moral Agents":** Dagstuhl Seminar 2017: "Imbuing robots and autonomous systems with *ethical norms and values* is an increasingly *urgent challenge*, given rapid developments in, for example, driverless cars, unmanned air vehicles (drones), and care assistant robots."

Two immediate problems:

- the *formalization of ethics* in a format that lends itself to machine implementation;
- the actual *implementation of moral reasoning and conduct in autonomous systems*.

---

[1] "Proactive" means that the Ag can anticipate us, takes the initiative; has its own information, and understanding, and learning, and abilities, …; "Goal-Adoption" is not "execution", "obedience"; and there are different levels of delegation, reliance, adjustability, etc. And there is a "spontaneous" (not requested!) help, and help beyond request and even violating request, but "for our good", with a "tutelary" role.

[2] The famous poem of Bertolt Brecht: "General, your tank is a powerful vehicle/ It smashes down forests and crushes a hundred men./ *But it has one defect:/ It needs a driver./* General, your bomber is powerful./ It flies faster than a storm and carries more than an elephant./ *But it has one defect:/ It needs a mechanic./* General, man is very useful./ He can fly and *he can kill./ But he has one defect:/ He can think.*"

2.1 Not Less Serious Problems

For me there are not less serious problems, like:

Is our Intelligent Technology research *only business oriented* just because it needs money?

Consider these relevant recent examples:

"Meeting of *the minds* for machine intelligence. *Industry leaders, computer scientists* and students, and *venture capitalists* gather to discuss *how smarter computers are remaking our world.* ...savvy machines can help us evaluate (social) policies." (MIT News, Oct 2016)

Are only these the right subjects/minds to involve for discussing about ethical and political and social consequences of machine intelligence and hybrid society? What about other subjects to be involved like: moral and political philosophers, trade unions, social democratic movements (like women movement, like "occupy Wall Street", ...), poor countries, etc.

Why such alliance only between academy, scientists, and capitalists and businessmen?

Is this so obvious and undisputable in current culture to become *invisible*?

"Carnegie Mellon University plans to announce on Wednesday that *it will create a research center that focuses on the ethics of artificial intelligence.* The ethics center, called the 'K&L Gates Endowment for Ethics and Computational Technologies', is being established at a time of growing international concern about the impact of A.I. technologies. That has already led to an array of academic, governmental and private efforts to explore a technology that until recently was largely the stuff of science fiction. ... Peter J. Kalis, chairman of the law firm, said the potential impact of A.I. technology on the economy and culture made it essential that as a society we make thoughtful, ethical choices about how the software and machines are used."

(*New Research Center to Explore Ethics of Artificial Intelligence.* By John Markoff NYTimes - NOV. 1, 2016)

Just another example of this obvious alliance:

The ex-CEO (Chief Executive Officer) of Google and current President of Google CdA, Eric Schmidt, has been nominated by Ash Carter, USA Defense Secretary, chairman del DoD Innovation Advisory Board of Pentagon. The aim of DoD Innovation organization is the *full exploitation of Silicon Valley "best practices" for military purposes.*

Again: Why an alliance only between academy, scientists, and capitalists and businessmen, (and war powers)? Is this really undisputable in current culture?

3 Hidden Interests and Powers

The bad results and government of societies is not mainly due to ignorance (lack of data and models) and technical problems, now perhaps solved by the ICT explosion and Digital Revolution. It is mainly due to the dominance of class interests, which are paradoxically guaranteed by "spontaneous" and self-organizing "order", the market-society, and the "invisible" managing hand.

¡Error! No se encuentra el origen de la referencia. Security, Privacy, War, Ethics, … are for sure very relevant issues, we have to reflect on, but not the most or the only relevant ones from the moral and political point of view.

Hidden interests, *manipulation of us* (users and programmers), exploitation, … emptying democracy, etc., are not less important.

We have to be conscious *not just manipulated,*[3] *unaware although genial servants* of those forces and interests.

Democracy is not a formal and misinformed voting ritual. It also is up to us to foster a real understanding and power of people on the hybrid societies evolution. We should build not only an *improved and collective intelligence* but an improved and *collective awareness*, which is a crucial form of "intelligence", of understanding what we are doing and _why_ we are doing that.

Intelligent Agent and algorithms have to help us to understand not only our Goals and how to decide (by revealing us and correcting our rational & affective biases) but help us to understand our "finalities"/"aims", which go much beyond our mental Goals.

3.1   Functions and Interests

This is the crucial issue of "functions" and of "interest" beyond our intended goals.

"Functions" are "external (non represented) goals" impinging on us and on our minds and conducts. *Non intended "purposes"* of our behavior. We follow them _without understanding them_, or deciding about them, although they not only "emerge" from our collective behaviors, but feedback and "immerge" in our minds.[4]

Also the Goals of our Agents and Robots (or just their rules and procedures) *serve to "functions"*: external, not chosen and understood Goals. Will they be explicit, transparent at least for us?

They will favor some interest. *Is this intended or not-intended by us?* To which *values* do they respond? Perhaps do not shared by us but at least clear, transparent! Or obscure?

"Interest" is what is better for me and my goals but… I do not understand or intentionally pursue it.

"Tutelary Role": X takes care of my "interests", of my good, even in conflict with me, with my current goals; X helps me or pushes me or obliges me!

In a lot of circumstances Agents (or Agent sellers?) will decide *for us* (delegated or not by us), in a "tutelary" role. Even if they would just use hints and prompts or just a little push (the celebrated liberal (sic!) "nudges") *like in marketing*, by exploiting how the stimulus is presented, the elicited impulses or associations…

---

[3] Our notion of "manipulation" is: X influences Y's behavior by communication or action, by changing Y's goals, by changing his/her beliefs and feelings, but in a hidden way. That is, without communicating his intention of influencing Y, of changing Y's mind.

[4] "Immergence" theory (Conte and Castelfranchi, Cognitive and Social Action, UCL Press, 1995); Castelfranchi, C. (2001). The theory of social functions. Challenges for multi-agent-based social simulation and multi-agent learning. *Journal of Cognitive Systems Research* 2, 5–38. Elsevier. http://www.cogsci.rpi.edu/~rsun/si-mal/article1.pdf.

1. Does really this make us **more** "free" than an explicit recommendation or an imperative?

   Moreover:

2. For whose benefit/advantage?

   Who is judging what is better for me, for us? Is this really "in *our* interest" or primarily in the interest of financial and informational dominant powers? Or (in many countries) of the political regime?

4   The "Mouth of Truth" Algorithm

Clearly we are developing algorithms for ascertaining the "truth" in that mess of data, of assertions, hoaxes, and news, which will be diffused and accessible through the WEB. An algorithm for deciding about *reliable sources, credible information*: what is "true" among so many different claims and data. There is no alternative on that. However:

- On which base such algorithm will "ascertain what is true"? Only on the basis of reliable and convergent sources? Of their number and net topology? On direct or indirect access to the "fact"?
- Also on the basis of the "values" and on the sharing and acceptability of the values of the source?

   Even for 'official' science: is it always capturing or saying the truth?

- And there will be dogmatic truths and undisputable authorities, like in any culture?
- And which culture and values will be assumed as the "right" ones?

   How will we allowed to distinguish between a *conflict of values or of interests* from a mere conflict between more or less credible data, more or less grounded, direct, controlled, reliable, ...?

5   'Presences' in Our Mixed Reality Society

The autonomous and proactive intelligent entities that Ag-MAS community created will become 'presences' and 'roles' in our *hybrid* society (human and artificial agent) and *mixed* and *augmented* reality (combined *virtual and 'real'*, *'natural'* and *automatic/prosthetic* world).[5]

   Now the problem will be:

- Are we able to manage these *autonomous* and too informed and intelligent agents?

---

[5] Alessandro Ricci, Michele Piunti, Luca Tummolini and Cristiano Castelfranchi, The Mirror World: Preparing for Mixed-Reality Living. *PERVASIVE COMPUTING*, 1536-1268/15/2015 IEEE.

As we said, it is not only a matter of <u>level of delegation</u> (open vs. restricted and specified) or of the possibility of <u>initiative</u> in cooperation and "over-helping" and even "critical-help", and even functional <u>norms violations</u>; or a matter of <u>adjustable autonomy</u> and negotiation of the degree of power based on <u>trust</u> and self-trust (see note 1).

It is a matter of:

(A) Which *roles* will those material or immaterial, visible and "entities" play in our life and environment?

Will they be our Guardian angel with a 'tutelary' role? Or – less religiously – our Jiminy Cricket (The Talking Cricket) with its recommendations? Or our supervisor in the ICT-Panopticon we live in? Or some tempting Spirit, or a tempting Devil for the benefit of some marketing policy or monopoly; or the influencing and manipulating manager for hidden political or economic powers?

It is a matter of:

(B) Which *interest* they will care of?

Of the interest of the seller or of us as consumers? Of the interests of the dominant groups or of the submitted or discriminated people? Which political and moral views will orient them: not our "car driver" but the "society drivers"! And our *life-navigator*.

They will decide "for us", but this expression is ambiguous: "instead of" us or also "for our good"?

Social Robots and Intelligent Agents *will NOT govern in their own interest* (science fiction!) but… in the interest of whom? And will we be able to monitor and understand that? And to make that "transparent" for people?

5.1   Mixed Reality, Mixed Body and Mind

Will we "incorporate", feel them as *part of "us"*, our *"mental prosthesis"*? Will we listen to that moral or rational "voice" as *our own* mental or consciousness voice, our (expanded) SuperEgo.

Or will our SuperEgo be "externalized"? Not "me". Will we listen to "her" as to the voice of our mother, our teacher? Or will we become "voice hearers"?

Will it be a boring "Talking Cricket" trying to correct us: *wooden marionettes*? But with the advantage that we could turn off that voice!

Both solutions will be probably there:

- The "social" one: Externalized voices and Agents.
- The "reflexively social" one: an augmented internalized Self and Consciousness.

Will I prefer to maintaining my judgment and to discuss with some friend or advisor, and listen to him/her or do not pay attention to? And has s/he to have my own values and character?

Or will I change and acquire a new Self with new introjected conflicts, values and style?

6 Disagreement Technologies

It is obviously very relevant to support the "agreement" technologies, a real strategic challenge for ICT and in particular for MASystems.[6]

Intelligent systems for:

- Rational and effective argumentation, negotiation, compromises, fair business practices, ...
- Norms, commitments, and value management, ...
- Consumer protection, transparency, trust, etc.

However, Agreement Technologies implicitly have two sides; let's look more directly at the other important side: the *Disagreement Technologies*.

There is a too strong ideology and rhetoric about society as cooperation, collaboration, common intent, collective advantages, ... how to reach convenient agreements and equilibrium, etc.

Moreover, the web is (non accidentally) favoring a deviating political feeling: *"we" against "them"* (governors, political caste, centralized powers). This perception of "we" is completely misleading: there is no a "we" with common values and goals and interests, which has to be unified against the political power as such (in case against the real power (financial power) that has usurped the political power).

- *Making conflicts to emerge and become aware, making express disagreement, making transparent which interests are hidden and prevailing, ...* should be (in democracy) one of the main tasks of intelligent social technologies.

Sometimes in order to facilitate a balanced conflict resolution, agreement; sometimes just for supporting the opposition and expressed disagreement that is the ground of democracy.

- Using WEB technologies for organizing "movements" it is OK; but not so good without *promoting critical consciousness, understanding* of real social interests and hidden powers and conflicts.
- To provide new environment, contexts, and instruments for *promoting motivated/grounded conflicts*, for making them well grounded and effective, for solving them not just by persuasion but by some achievement.

6.1 The Need for Conflicts

No Conflicts No Democracy
Conflicts are the presupposition of Democracy. Democracy is not only a "response" to them and for moderating them; it would be a way of encouraging, growing (and solving) them.

---

[6] See for example the remarkable results of the Project on "Agreement Technologies":
http://www.agreement-technologies.org/project.

Conflicts are not only to be governed, reduced, reconciled: they should even be *promoted* and this is in fact the role/function of specific forces and organizations, like trade-unions, parties, group of interests, association, movements, etc. These are crucial stakeholders of democracy, but also definitely responsible of the typical social, cultural, economic "progress" of western countries in the last centuries and now of the rest of the world.

Of course conflicts might be dangerous conducing us to fighting, violence, war, … So it is true that societies and groups need "rules" for governing them, to avoid degeneration. Centralized state was one of these solutions: the state monopolizes violence; private or group violence is forbidden.

Conflicts are not just conflicts of views or opinions, or due to different conceptions, information, reasoning. There are conflicts of "interests": if you realize your goal I cannot realize my goal or loose something I have.

So the problem is conflicts between interests of group or classes, or conflicts between "private" interests vs. common interests, the "commons" and public goods.

Social conflicts in fact *do not* have a "verbal/cognitive" or a "technical" solution, just based on data and technical principles; they need a "political" solution; it is a matter of "power" and of prevailing interests and compromises (equilibrium, partitions/shares).

Conflicts - with their *disagreements and agreements* - are thus the motor and principle of Democracy and of its possible effectiveness in changing society in favor of the submitted subjects, disadvantaged classes and groups, etc. Viva conflict! And its information technology.

6.2 "Life Navigator"

As already said, ICT and cognitive technologies are strongly submitted to the private interest of marketing; they are used for recognize our profile and interests in order to propose/*induce us to "buy" something* (goods, ideas, …) They are monitoring and analyzing us in order to manipulate us and influence our choices.

We need *anti-manipulation* AI technologies:

I would like to have not so much a personal virtual or robotic psychotherapist or physiotherapist; I would like much more a "life navigator" in my main "social role" (consumer!), but not a navigator just saying "turn right, turn left", "buy that; do not buy this"… But a tutor, a trainer, inducing me to understand and to reflect about why I'm oriented in that direction, why I'm choosing that product; worrying if I have the right information, or I have wrong beliefs, etc. A tutor making me conscious of who and how is persuading or just unconsciously manipulating me; and so on.

Mixed reality not only with some 'tempting devil' – as we said – but with some virtual 'guardian angel'.

We need environments and Agents for:

- learning and developing a "*critical thinking*" attitude;
- to manage our *cognitive and motivational biases*; etc.

- to support us in argumentation and discussion, and in understanding the tricky arguments of the others;
- to resist to the prevalence of "audience" against "quality", of self-marketing and indexes (like in research) against originality and quality; etc.

And so on, about propaganda, Academy, gender models, fanaticism, superstition, urban legends, ...

We have impressive possibilities with new intelligent and interacting technology, big data, etc. They shouldn't be just used for selling and for dominating.

Why creation, design, and diffusion of ICT Technologies should just service capital and not workers and people? How could we create or use technology in order to defend subjects, poor, marginalized, exploited people?

It is enough that capital puts money in research and university for being unaware of its domination and for accepting to be a-critical instruments of its logics?

7 Concluding Remarks

(A) *Self-Organization = Out of Minds*

Society works thanks to our *partial* intelligence. We cooperate and jointly act not just in spite of but *thanks to the fact that we do not (fully) understand and intend what we are jointly doing*. And even if we disagree. Society is governed by the "Invisible hand", since it is a "market-society".

Obviously there are also very dysfunctional and undesirable results of our stupidity/blindness. For example, since we do not understand or forget, and thus *do not learn* from the worse tragedies of our History, that's why we repeat them as farces.

This is part of our political "alienation": We are *dominated* by our own 'delegated' (emergent) (social and intellectual) *powers*, we are not aware of; we do not realize and we do not decide/intend to create such collective or such institutional powers impinging on us.

Can We Overcome Our Alienation?

Will the Leviathan become a giant *connected and informed community of agents*, managing their Collective Power? I'm skeptical about that (also for cognitive reasons); and I also worry about possible net-Demagogy.

Could we, by exploiting *collective, distributed, hybrid intelligence* and *big data*, and run-time feedbacks and information from local stakeholders and intelligent sensors and computational learning and predicting and computer (agent-based) social simulation, and virtual reality and serious games, etc...., could we to *make visible the invisible hand* and to (partially) govern it?[7]

---

[7] Castelfranchi, C. (2014) Making Visible "the Invisible Hand". The Mission of Social Simulation. In Adamatti, D.F., Pereira Dimuro, G., Coelho, H. (eds.) *Interdisciplinary Applications of Agent-Based Social Simulation and Modeling.* IGI Global, 2014.

In the Digital Society Artificial Intelligence may either exploit or overcoming our natural stupidity.

As for Democracy let's remind Mark Twain's is brilliantly sentence: *"If voting made any difference they wouldn't let us do it."* But… the problem is much harder; it is not just a complot, is that <u>we</u> vote in a self-defeating way, and, in general, our collective stupidity.

Might political "education" and education to "commons" & Digital society and <u>participatory democracy</u> be enough, and solve this "cognitive" and social problem?

I wish they will help; but given the immediate local perception of the conflicting interests and competition and the *blindness to common interests* among different countries and poor classes and ethnic groups, and affiliation and identity feelings, conformism, and in-group vs. out-group psychology, … I have some doubt. In a couple of centuries they will see.

(B) *Pessimism of the Intellect but Optimism of the Will*

Let's give two ironic perspectives of the realistic pessimism we should challenge, just by citing a real expert of power and a philosopher:

"When a government depends on bankers for money, they and not the heads of government control matters. *The hand that gives holds sway over the hand that receives*. Money has no homeland and financiers have no patriotism or decency - their only objective is gain" (Napoleon Bonaparte).

Thrasymachus' pessimism: "Justice is nothing more than whatever is advantageous to the stronger".

Can we build some Artificial Intelligence and some Hybrid and Mixed Sociality & Reality <u>smarter than us but on our side</u>, for our collective interests and commons, such that we can eventually face Thrasymachus' "unavoidable" result?

Competence and ideas are there, in our scientific community: What about means?

Acknowledgments. This contribution is in memory of Rosaria Conte (Social Simulation LABSS Group). I like to thank my research group in Cognitive Science at ISTC: the '*GOAL group*' http://www.istc.cnr.it/group/goal.

I'm also in debt with our community of Ag and MAS, in particular with EUMAS, and with the scholars of the Agreement Technologies project.

An Introduction to the Pocket Negotiator: A General Purpose Negotiation Support System

Catholijn M. Jonker[1(✉)], Reyhan Aydoğan[2], Tim Baarslag[3],
Joost Broekens[1], Christian A. Detweiler[5], Koen V. Hindriks[1],
Alina Huldtgren[4], and Wouter Pasman[1]

[1] Technical University of Delft, Delft, The Netherlands
{c.m.Jonker,d.j.broekens,k.v.hindriks,w.pasman}@tudelft.nl
[2] Özyeğin University, Istanbul, Turkey
reyhan.aydogan@ozyegin.edu.tr
[3] Centrum Wiskunde & Informatica, Amsterdam, The Netherlands
T.Baarslag@cwi.nl
[4] Technical University of Eindhoven, Eindhoven, The Netherlands
a.huldtgren@tue.nl
[5] De Haagse Hogeschool, Den Haag, The Netherlands
C.A.Detweiler@hhs.nl

Abstract. The Pocket Negotiator (PN) is a negotiation support system developed at TU Delft as a tool for supporting people in bilateral negotiations over multi-issue negotiation problems in arbitrary domains. Users are supported in setting their preferences, estimating those of their opponent, during the bidding phase and sealing the deal. We describe the overall architecture, the essentials of the underlying techniques, the form that support takes during the negotiation phases, and we share evidence of the effectiveness of the Pocket Negotiator.

1 Introduction

Negotiation is a complex emotional decision-making process aiming to reach an agreement to exchange goods or services. Although a daily activity, few people are effective negotiators [38]. Fisher and Ury, Raiffa and Thompson, and others, emphasize that negotiation is not just about money. Good relationships, awareness of all issues (domain model), personal preferences (user and opponent model), and knowledge of your alternatives (if no deal is reached), are all important, see e.g., [20,21,36,38]. In negotiation four major stages can be discerned: private preparation, joint exploration, bidding, and closing (see the upper bar of Fig. 1).

Existing automated negotiating agents could make a significant improvement if the negotiation space is well-understood, because computers can better cope with the computational complexity. However, the negotiation space can only

---

Author ordering: Jonker as overall initiator and coordinator as first author, other authors in alphabetical ordering as their contribution is hard to quantify.

© Springer International Publishing AG 2017
N. Criado Pacheco et al. (Eds.): EUMAS 2016/AT 2016, LNAI 10207, pp. 13–27, 2017.
DOI: 10.1007/978-3-319-59294-7_2

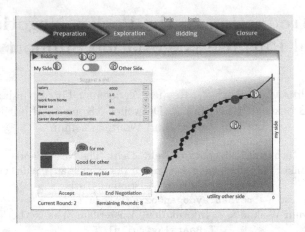

Fig. 1. The Pocket Negotiator can suggest possible bids to the user and preview their placement in the estimated outcome space. Support for the four negotiation phases can be reached by clicking on the phase intended. (Color figure online)

be properly developed if the human parties jointly explore their interests. The inherent semantic problem and the emotional issues involved make that negotiation cannot be handled by artificial intelligence alone, and a human-machine collaborative system is required.

Based on our long-standing experience in automated negotiation, see e.g., [9,10,14–16,27,31], we decided to use our knowledge of negotiation strategies to offer negotiation support to human users. For this purpose we developed a prototype system called the Pocket Negotiator. It offers a qualitative preference elicitation tool that is inspired by Harvard's approach for addressing underlying concerns, often called interest-based negotiation. As almost all bidding strategies are utility-based we decided to map the qualitative profiles of the user and the opponent to additive linear utility functions. Furthermore, the user receives bidding advice and an advice of when to accept a bid of the other party.

The organization of the paper is as follows. Section 2 describes the architecture. The interests underlying the negotiation and all other profiling tools are the topic of Sect. 3. The bidding phase is detailed in Sect. 4. Before we implemented the Pocket Negotiator we investigated the acceptability and possible usability of such a device, see Sect. 5. Once the Pocket Negotiator was on its feet we started experimenting, and here we present some of our results in Sect. 6. Our is not the only effort to develop negotiation support systems. A brief review of related work can be found in Sect. 7. In Sect. 8 we discuss the current state of the Pocket Negotiator and draw conclusions about its future use.

2   Architecture and Negotiation Phases

The Pocket Negotiator is set up as a modular system to allow an efficient connection to the repositories of the GENIUS framework [31], which is an automated negotiation simulation framework that supports a variety of agents, scenarios, and protocols. A simplified picture of the architecture is presented in Fig. 2. It has two repositories; one for domains that also includes preference profiles for the roles mentioned in the domains, and a repository for the strategies used to provide advice to the user.

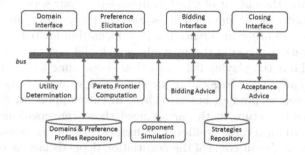

Fig. 2. The architecture of the Pocket Negotiator

Through the domain interface, the user obtains information about the available domains, and picks the appropriate one. Furthermore, this interface allows the user to inform the PN about his experience in negotiation, how badly a deal is needed, and what kind of negotiation personality he has. The same is asked about the opponent (in as far as the user knows about this). In the preference elicitation interface the user sets all his preferences: domain related, strategic, and procedural. The specifications of domains and preference profiles are stored in a dedicated repository.

For the strategies, all bilateral bidding strategies, the opponent modeling strategies and the strategies for when to accept bids as available in the GENIUS strategies repository can, with small moderations, be used in the PN, see [3]). More information on each of these aspects can be found in the next sections.

The Pareto Frontier Computation component approximates the Pareto Optimal Frontier for the preference profile of the user and the estimated profile of the opponent.

The Utility Determination component determines a utility function for both negotiation participants based on the information gathered in the preference elicitation interface. Furthermore, it keeps a tab on all bids exchanged between the parties, and, if appropriate, updates the profile of the opponent. The automated opponent modeling strategy uses a frequency analysis approach as described in, e.g., [7].

The Opponent Simulation is a component that is active in the variants of PN designed for experiments and training. In these variants human participants negotiate against a bot.

The Pocket Negotiator distinguishes and emphasizes the four phases of negotiation identified in Sect. 1 by design: the Preparation, Exploration, Bidding and

Closing phases. Each of theses phases is supported through a set of dedicated interfaces. The list of phases is always available at the top of all PN interfaces, see e.g., Fig. 1.

The Preparation phase supports the choice of domain and strategic choices and information, as described in Sect. 3. For reasons of security, the domain editor is not directly linked to the Pocket Negotiator. It is provided as an independent program, the output of which is uploaded by our server administrators upon request. Both the Preparation phase and the Exploration phase give access to the interests and other preference profile information for both roles.

The Exploration phase is the phase in which the negotiators get to know each other, feel out the playing field, and thus spend time to deepen and adapt their profiles. The Pocket Negotiator specifically urges users to not only model their own preferences profiles, but also those of their opponent. As preferences are constructive in nature, both parties need those conversations and private contemplations to form these profiles. The literature of human negotiation shows that the quality of the outcome of the negotiation depends largely on the quality of the preparation and exploration phase, see e.g., [20,21,37,38].

The Bidding phase is supported by the bidding interface which presents the Pareto Optimal Frontier as provided by the Pareto Frontier Computation component, and specific interface elements to let the user enter his bid and see how good that is for himself and for the opponent. It presents an overview of the bidding history. It gives access to the bidding support agent to suggest bids, and offers advice on whether to accept the bid of the opponent. More information can be found in Sect. 4.

The Closing interface supports the closing phase by summarizing the agreement, and offering to either print or email the outcome for further processing.

The next sections provide more information on the essential components and technology that underly the Pocket Negotiator. No further information is provided on the Closing interface.

3   Profiling

This section discusses the essentials of the tools and techniques used in the Pocket Negotiator for profiling the domain, the user and the opponent. Next to domain preferences that explain which negotiation outcomes are to be preferred as described in Sect. 3.3, the profiling also addresses strategic preferences and background information for the negotiation, see Sect. 3.2.

3.1   Domain Editor

With respect to domains a small number of domains is standardly made available, and new domains can easily be loaded or designed using a dedicated domain editor. The domain editor enables the specification of the domain in terms of the roles in negotiation typically taken (e.g., seller vs buyer, or consumer vs provider), the interests, the most commonly negotiated issues with their value ranges, example outcomes, and initial profiles for each of the roles. The domain editor requires a good understanding of modeling domains, preference profiles and utility functions. For security reasons it is disconnected from the PN.

By now there are a number of negotiation domains available in the PN. Most elaborated are the *Jobs* scenario and real estate, where also the link between the interests-based profile and the utility-based profile has been validated. Other available domains are: Energy contracts and Water management.

3.2 Strategic Preferences and Background Information

In terms of strategic information and choices, the user can choose which agent will offer support and how many rounds he expects to negotiate. He enters information about the expertise in negotiation for both parties, see Fig. 3.

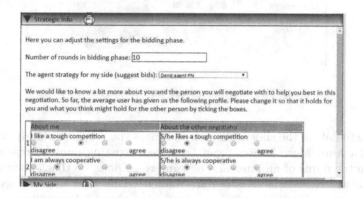

Fig. 3. The domain interface of the Pocket Negotiator

The expertise and expectation questions are about the user and what user beliefs about his opponent. The questions are about how competitive they are, how cooperative, how much they need a deal, and how experienced they are in negotiation. The answers to each of these questions can be used to fine tune the strategies for bidding and accepting offers. More information on cooperative vs competitive negotiation strategies can be found in, e.g., [5].

3.3 Interest-Based Preference Elicitation

As the way people prepare for a negotiation determines to a large extent the quality of the outcome of the negotiation, preference elicitation is of fundamental importance to a negotiation support systems. For that purpose we investigated various ways of elicitation, see e.g., [33,35]. In the first paper, we set up a compositional design approach for the creation of preference elicitation interfaces that takes into account that preference elicitation requires the user to undergo a constructive process. The constructive nature of preferences refers to the fact that humans typically don't know their preferences; they have to figure these out by engaging with the topic. In the second paper, we applied the method of the first paper, to study the effectiveness of elicitation methods in relation to the cognitive effort required and preference detail. Based on our results and given recommendations to use interest-based negotiation, we decided to use the Value-Sensitive Design approach, see e.g., [22], to develop the preference elicitation tools for the PN. This led to a system in which the user is first asked to reflect on the interests that for him underly the negotiation, see Fig. 4.

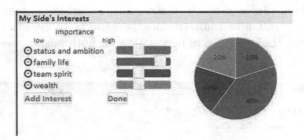

Fig. 4. The interests underlying the negotiation

By manipulating the sliders the user indicates the relative importance of the interests for him. More interests can be added, existing ones be removed. By clicking on the name of an interest a new interface pops up that allows the user to indicate which negotiable issues are influenced by that interest, see Fig. 5. The examples presented come from a negotiation about job conditions, and are discussed from the point of view of the new employee. By doing a user study amongst young ICT specialists, we found that these were the most commonly encountered interests.

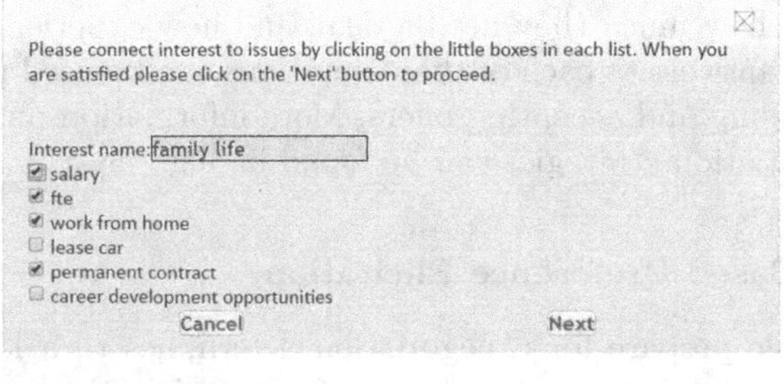

Please connect interest to issues by clicking on the little boxes in each list. When you are satisfied please click on the 'Next' button to proceed.

Interest name: family life
☑ salary
☑ fte
☑ work from home
☐ lease car
☑ permanent contract
☐ career development opportunities
                Cancel   Next

Fig. 5. How an interest links to negotiable issues

In this interface the check-boxes indicate which of the issues are influenced by the interest. The link is made from the interest in family life to salary (as that is necessary to pay for e.g., children), fte (which stands for "full time equivalent", and is relevant for being able to care for children yourselves), work from home (as that makes you more flexible with respect to e.g., children and school), and a permanent contract (as that gives security). By clicking on the "next" button, the user is presented with a new interface, see Fig. 6.

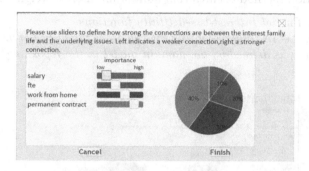

Fig. 6. The impact of an interest on the weights of negotiable issues

We chose as much as possible the same interface type so as to make them easy to understand for the user. As in Fig. 6 we are again asking for a relative impact, we chose the same format as for the interests. In this case we are asking for the relative influence of the interest in family life on the importance (called weight) of the issues.

3.4   Utility Functions

The preference elicitation method of the PN as described above, defines a qualitative preference structure. To be able to use the state-of-the-art negotiation strategies from automated negotiation research, we need to transform this to a linear additive utility function. We do this in two steps. We first define a utility function U by taking the settings of the sliders from the preference elicitation tools as numbers. Even though the user only entered this as relative notions and not concrete values, this direct translation certainly respects the rankings make by the user. Then we define a our target linear additive utility function U'. The final step is to prove that these two functions give the same utility for any bid. This requires the introduction of some notation:

IN is the collection of interest items; e.g., $\{sparetime, wealth, status\}$
IS is the collection of negotiable issues; e.g., $\{salary, fte, leasecar\}$
V_i is the collection of value items for issue $i \in IS$; e.g., $V_{fte} = \{0.6, 0.8, 1.0\}$
$B : \Pi_{i \in IS}(V_i)$ is the set of all possible bids. For any $b \in B$, let b_i denote the
    projection of b on V_i, i.e., the value for issue i in the bid.

Definition 1. *Weights of an Interest-based Utility function*
Let $w_n \in \langle 0, 1]$ denote the weight of interest $n \in IN$. Let $w : IN \times IS \rightarrow [0, 1]$ denotes the weight of an issue as part of an interest in the profile.
The weights w_n and $w(n, i)$ are defined by what the user entered in the corresponding interfaces, see Figs. 4 and 6 respectively.

The elicitation method ensures that sum of all interest weights is 1.

Definition 2. *Partial Interest-based Utility functions*
For any $i \in IS$, $n \in IN$, and $v \in V_i$, $u_i(n, v)$ denotes the utility of v. Each partial utility function u_i is defined by the domain model in the repository[1].

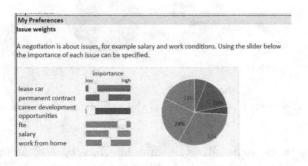

Fig. 7. The weights of negotiable issues

Definition 3. *Interest-based Utility*
We define the interest-based utility function $U : B \rightarrow [0, 1]$ as follows:

$$U(b) = \sum_{n \in IN} w_n \sum_{i \in IS} w(n, i) u_i(n, b_i) \tag{1}$$

Definition 4. *Intended utility function*
The intended linear additive utility function $U' : B \rightarrow [0, 1]$ is defined by

$$w'_i = \sum_{n \in IN} w_n w(n, i) \tag{2}$$

$$u'_i(b_i) = \sum_{n \in IN} \frac{w_n w(n, i)}{w'_i} u_i(n, b_i) \tag{3}$$

$$U'(b) = \sum_{i \in IS} w'(i) u'_i(b_i) \tag{4}$$

where U' refers to the overall utility function, $w'(i)$ to the weight of issue i, and $u'_i : V_i \rightarrow [0, 1]$ refers to the partial utility function of issue i. The deeper part of the preference elicitation interfaces present these weights w'_i and functions u'_i to the user. For the weights the format of relative importance is used, see Fig. 7. The pictures for u'_i are left out for reasons of space.

---

[1] Functions are not visible in the interfaces of PN.

Theorem 1. *The interest-based utility function U and the intended utility function U' give the same results for all bids in B:*

$$\forall b \in B : U(b) = U'(b) \tag{5}$$

4 Bidding Phase

The PN offers support for making the right proposals during the bidding phase (see Fig. 1). To make the PN aware of bids that have been offered by the opponent (in real-life), the user can enter their bid into the system. By clicking *Suggest a bid*, the PN can recommend a counter-proposal and highlight a preview of this bid in the outcome space (i.e. the red dot in Fig. 1). The user has the opportunity to refine the suggestion by tweaking the desired values for each individual issue. Finally, the user can choose to send out the offer to the opponent (in real-life) and signal this to the PN by pressing *Enter my bid*.

For every contemplated offer, the PN also provides an estimate of the utility for the user and for the opponent, which, at the start of the bidding phase, is determined by the information provided during the preparation and exploration phase. Similarly, it shows the estimated outcome space, in which the red area signifies lose-lose outcomes that are to be avoided, while the green area indicates the win-win outcomes, including, in particular, the estimated Pareto optimal offers, which the PN will aim for.

The bid recommendations by the PN are performed by a negotiation agent, which is designed as a modular component of the system. The negotiation model of the Pocket Negotiator is in principle compatible with all repository items from Genius [31]. This means the bidding strategies (including the ability to accept [13]) contained in Genius can all be integrated into the Pocket Negotiator with only minor adjustments; examples include [1,17,18,25,28,40].

During the bidding phase, the agent has the opportunity to learn more about the opponent through the exchanged bids [2,7,8], which involves three different aspects: the opponent's *type*, *preference*, and *strategy* [9]. The agent that is used in conjunction with the PN determines which type of learning method is employed. The PN supports a separate bidding, opponent modeling, and accepting architecture [4,12], whereby any established concession strategy (e.g. time-dependent tactics [19]) can be recombined with established components for learning (e.g. Bayesian learning [18,26]) and acceptance (c.g. optimal stopping [11]).

Currently the (type of) bidding strategies that are available are the Bayesian agent [26], the Conceder Agents [19], the Simple Agent, and the Simple Tit for Tat Agent, see [5,10] for their descriptions. The default bidding strategy is the Deniz agent, which is an extension of the optimal bidding strategy as described in [6]. In the practice versions of the Pocket Negotiator, where an agent plays the user's opponent, Deniz is also the strategy for the opponent.

5 Acceptability

Before implementing the Pocket Negotiator, we decided to first to perform some acceptability studies to make sure we would be making something that would be to the interest of people. This study is reported in [34], where we asked people to reflect on the possible use of negotiation support systems (NSS) in different social contexts and the consequences for their design. We conducted focus groups sessions separately with negotiation experts and potential users. This resulted in the idea that we should design a mobile NSS, and some design guidelines.

We used an online survey to establish the following. Our first goal was to find out in which situations people consider a NSS socially acceptable. The second goal was to find the factors and relationships that influence this acceptance in the different situations and social contexts. The last goal was to investigate the consequences of people's attitudes toward NSS for the system's design.

The data showed that subjective norm is an important factor influencing the intention to use the system and that the acceptance of NSS depends on the use context. We concluded that our NSS should be designed not only merely as a tool for actual negotiations, but also as a social device harnessing social networks to provide support in all negotiation phases. These were promising results, that motivated us to implement our ideas for the Pocket Negotiator.

6   Experiments

In order to assess to what extent the Pocket Negotiator successfully supports people in their negotiation, we conducted a user experiment. We prepared two variations of the Pocket Negotiator: *No-support* and *PN-support*. In both versions, the opponent of the human participant is played by the Deniz agent. In all experiments exactly the same domains and preference profiles are used in the two variants. The only difference between the variants is that the PN-support version provides all the support as presented in the previous sections, while the No-support version does not provide any of them.

We asked half of the participants to negotiate with the PN-support and the other half to negotiate with the No-support version. During their negotiation, we logged their actions and the negotiation outcome they reached. The results show that the participants with the PN-support gained higher utilities/or at least high utility as the participants with the No-support version received in most of the cases. According to the questionnaire filled in by the participants after their negotiation, it can be said that most of the participants found the Pocket Negotiator useful in their negotiation.

7   Related Work

This section discusses research reports of other Negotiation Support Systems, but also a bit about research into human-agent negotiations. The last category is where we see a possible line of future research work.

According to the classification of negotiation support systems in [23] into (1) real-life applications, (2) systems used in business, research and training, and (3) research results, the Pocket Negotiator is intended for real-life applications, but needs to specialize to business systems. The variants we initially created for our research in which you can play against an bot-opponent are actually already used for training students (psychology students of Leiden University, business and computer science students of TU Delft and Erasmus University, and computer science students of Özyeğin University. Similarly, their listing of key constructs in Negotiation Support Systems is still useful and has also helped us in determining what we wanted to focus on in developing the PN. Their discussion of successful and unsuccessful cases makes it clear to us that our PN still has to pass this test. The Aspire system [30] has been an inspiration from the start. We decided to focus on complete bids, and avoid free text interaction.

The work of Vahidov and co-authors, see [39], studies the prospects of agent-to-human negotiations using experiments with human subjects. In particular, they studied how humans use analytical support tools in making their decisions. The strategies used in the agents that played their opponents show the same types of strategies we offer to the user: conceder, individualistic, and tit-for-tat. Their findings confirm those of similar experiments of the past, see e.g., [14]: Overall, the findings speak in favor of agent-managed negotiations.

The Shaman systems as introduced in [29] is a framework for the construction and operation of heterogeneous systems enabling business interactions such as auctions and negotiations between software and human agents across those systems. The Pocket Negotiator could be linked to Shaman to support humans in their negotiations. It would be interesting to see how the PN could largely do the negotiations on behalf of the human and every now and then discuss the progress with the human user before concluding the negotiations. As automated negotiating agents can easily exchange some 3000 bids for normal-sized domains, such a bounded interaction with human users could improve the overall outcomes over agent-agent negotiations and agent-human negotiations.

Gratch et al. studied how virtual agents can be used in practicing negotiation skills [24]. They observed that the participants in their experiments were more comfortable to negotiate with a tough computer agent rather than a tough human opponent. Mell and Gratch developed a human-agent negotiation environment namely IAGO, which studies of human-agent negotiations with the aim to improve the negotiation skills of humans by teaching and practicing with IAGO, see [32]. Future research is to see what difference a NSS, in particular, the PN can make for these negotiations.

8 Discussion and Conclusion

The Pocket Negotiator is a negotiation support system that provides support for negotiations in all negotiation phases. It's key contributions are the unique way of eliciting preference profiles over interests and automatically translating the profiles to linear additive utility functions.

The second key contribution is that the PN encourages the user to also model a preference profile for the opponent. This further improves the preparation of the user for the negotiation, and furthermore enables the PN to support the user with tools developed for automated negotiations and their performance analysis. The bidding support is therefore equiped with a picture of the bidding space that includes an estimation of the Pareto Optimal Frontier, depicts the bidding history and allows the user to pick elements of the Pareto Optimal Frontier for reaching efficient outcomes.

The last key contribution is the access to the richness of the state-of-the-art in bidding-, opponent modeling, and acceptance strategies for bilateral negotiations for arbitrary domains.

To prepare for a negotiation you start it with the domain you need and a strategy that fits the needs and wishes of a stakeholder. It encourages the user to also consider the position and preferences of the party he will negotiate with. For professional negotiators this is easier than for the layperson, but if the domain model has been well researched, also the layperson can take advantage of studying the profile that comes with the domain description. However, we feel that for a commercialization of the PN, it would be better to specialize this part further and connect it to the Internet to automatically update and enhance the domain model. Domains that might lend themselves well for the PN are conflict resolution, customer retainment, and contract renewal for e.g., energy providers, Internet providers and so on.

The preference elicitation strategy is based on the interest-based negotiation approach. It is unique in deriving a standard utility function automatically from the user's reflection on the relative importance of typical interests underlying negotiations in the given domain. The user can iteratively deepen his investigation of his preferences, by linking the interests to the negotiable issues and indicating the relative impact of an interest to those issues. When continuing the reflection of his preferences brings the user to the more often seen of ranking the possible outcome elements per issue. More research is needed to add explanation of these matter to the system.

In case the domain of negotiation needed is not included in the Pocket Negotiator, a domain editor is available to create a new domain description. However, improvements to this domain editor would be necessary to make it suitable for a layperson. Due to its modular architecture plug-ins can be added that automatically extract domain knowledge from the Internet. For example, for a second hand car dealer, current prices for a car model and mileage can be easily added. The car dealer can update the domain model with all accessories, and services that are negotiable.

Acknowledgement. This research was supported by the Dutch Technology Foundation STW, applied science division of NWO and the Technology Program of the Ministry of Economic Affairs. It is part of the Pocket Negotiator project with grant number VIVI-project 08075.

References

1. An, B., Lesser, V.R.: Yushu: a heuristic-based agent for automated negotiating competition. In: Ito, T., Zhang, M., Robu, V., Fatima, S., Matsuo, T. (eds.) New Trends in Agent-Based Complex Automated Negotiations. Studies in Computational Intelligence, vol. 383, pp. 145–149. Springer, Heidelberg (2012)

2. Aydoğan, R., Yolum, P.: Learning opponent's preferences for effective negotiation: an approach based on concept learning. Auton. Agents Multiagent Syst. **24**(1), 104–140 (2012)
3. Baarslag, T.: What to bid and when to stop. Dissertation, Delft University of Technology, September 2014
4. Baarslag, T., Dirkzwager, A.S., Hindriks, K.V., Jonker, C.M.: The significance of bidding, accepting and opponent modeling in automated negotiation. In: 21st European Conference on Artificial Intelligence. Frontiers in Artificial Intelligence and Applications, vol. 263, pp. 27–32 (2014)
5. Baarslag, T., Fujita, K., Gerding, E.H., Hindriks, K., Ito, T., Jennings, N.R., Jonker, C., Kraus, S., Lin, R., Robu, V., Williams, C.R.: Evaluating practical negotiating agents: results and analysis of the 2011 international competition. Artif. Intell. **198**, 73–103 (2013)
6. Baarslag, T., Gerding, E.H., Aydogan, R., Schraefel, M.C.: Optimal negotiation decision functions in time-sensitive domains. In: Proceedings of the 2015 IEEE/WIC/ACM International Conference on Web Intelligence and Intelligent Agent Technology (WI-IAT), WI-IAT 2015, vol. 1, pp. 190–197. IEEE Computer Society (2015)
7. Baarslag, T., Hendrikx, M., Hindriks, K., Jonker, C.: Measuring the performance of online opponent models in automated bilateral negotiation. In: Thielscher, M., Zhang, D. (eds.) AI 2012. LNCS, vol. 7691, pp. 1–14. Springer, Heidelberg (2012). doi:10.1007/978-3-642-35101-3_1
8. Baarslag, T., Hendrikx, M.J., Hindriks, K.V., Jonker, C.M.: Predicting the performance of opponent models in automated negotiation. In: 2013 IEEE/WIC/ACM International Joint Conferences on Web Intelligence (WI) and Intelligent Agent Technologies (IAT), vol. 2, pp. 59–66 November 2013
9. Baarslag, T., Hendrikx, M.J., Hindriks, K.V., Jonker, C.M.: Learning about the opponent in automated bilateral negotiation: a comprehensive survey of opponent modeling techniques. Auton. Agents Multi-Agent Syst. **30**(5), 849–898 (2016)
10. Baarslag, T., Hindriks, K., Jonker, C.M., Kraus, S., Lin, R.: The first automated negotiating agents competition (ANAC 2010). In: Ito, T., Zhang, M., Robu, V., Fatima, S., Matsuo, T. (eds.) New Trends in Agent-based Complex Automated Negotiations. Studies in Computational Intelligence, pp. 113–135. Springer, Heidelberg (2012)
11. Baarslag, T., Hindriks, K.V.: Accepting optimally in automated negotiation with incomplete information. In: Proceedings of the 2013 International Conference on Autonomous Agents and Multi-agent Systems, AAMAS 2013, pp. 715–722. International Foundation for Autonomous Agents and Multiagent Systems, Richland (2013)
12. Baarslag, T., Hindriks, K.V., Hendrikx, M.J., Dirkzwager, A.S., Jonker, C.M.: Decoupling negotiating agents to explore the space of negotiation strategies. In: Marsa-Maestre, I., Lopez-Carmona, M.A., Ito, T., Zhang, M., Bai, Q., Fujita, K. (eds.) Novel Insights in Agent-based Complex Automated Negotiation. Studies in Computational Intelligence, vol. 535, pp. 61–83. Springer, Tokyo (2014)
13. Baarslag, T., Hindriks, K.V., Jonker, C.M.: Effective acceptance conditions in real-time automated negotiation. Decis. Support Syst. **60**, 68–77 (2014)
14. Bosse, T., Jonker, C., Treur, J.: Experiments in human multi-issue negotiation: analysis and support. In: Proceedings of the Third International Joint Conference on Autonomous Agents and Multi-Agent Systems (AAMAS 2004), pp. 671–678. IEEE Computer Society Press, New York (2004)

15. Bosse, T., Jonker, C.M., van der Meij, L., Robu, V., Treur, J.: A system for analysis of multi-issue negotiation. In: Unland, R., Calisti, M., Klusch, M. (eds.) Software Agent-Based Applications, Platforms and Development Kits. Whitestein Series in Software Agent Technologies. Birkhäuser, Basel (2005)
16. Brazier, F., Cornelissen, F., Jonker, C., Treur, J.: Compositional design and verification of a multi-agent system for one-to-many negotiation. In: Proceedings of the Third International Conference on Multi-Agent Systems. ICMAS 1998, pp. 49–56. IEEE Computer Society Press, Paris (1998)
17. Chen, S., Weiss, G.: OMAC: a discrete wavelet transformation based negotiation agent. In: Marsa-Maestre, I., Lopez-Carmona, M.A., Ito, T., Zhang, M., Bai, Q., Fujita, K. (eds.) Novel Insights in Agent-based Complex Automated Negotiation. Studies in Computational Intelligence, vol. 535, pp. 187–196. Springer, Tokyo (2014)
18. Şerban, L.D., Silaghi, G.C., Litan, C.M.: AgentFSEGA - time constrained reasoning model for bilateral multi-issue negotiations. In: Ito, T., Zhang, M., Robu, V., Fatima, S., Matsuo, T. (eds.) New Trends in Agent-Based Complex Automated Negotiations. Series of Studies in Computational Intelligence, pp. 159–165. Springer, Heidelberg (2012)
19. Faratin, P., Sierra, C., Jennings, N.R.: Negotiation decision functions for autonomous agents. Robot. Auton. Syst. 24(3–4), 159–182 (1998)
20. Fisher, R., Shapiro, D.: Beyond Reason: Using Emotions as You Negotiate. Random House Business Books, New York (2005)
21. Fisher, R., Ury, W., Patton, B. (eds.): Getting to Yes: Negotiating Agreement Without Giving In. Penguin Books, London (2003)
22. Friedman, B., Kahn, P.J., Borning, A.: Value Sensitive Design and Information Systems, pp. 348–372 (2006)
23. K, G., Lai, H.: Negotiation support and e-negotiation systems: an overview. Group Decis. Negot. 16, 553–586 (2007)
24. Gratch, J., DeVault, D., Lucas, G.: The benefits of virtual humans for teaching negotiation. In: Traum, D., Swartout, W., Khooshabeh, P., Kopp, S., Scherer, S., Leuski, A. (eds.) IVA 2016. LNCS, vol. 10011, pp. 283–294. Springer, Cham (2016). doi:10.1007/978-3-319-47665-0_25
25. Hao, J., Leung, H.: ABiNeS: an adaptive bilateral negotiating strategy over multiple items. In: Proceedings of the 2012 IEEE/WIC/ACM International Joint Conferences on Web Intelligence and Intelligent Agent Technology, WI-IAT 2012, vol. 2, pp. 95–102. IEEE Computer Society, Washington, DC, December 2012
26. Hindriks, K.V., Tykhonov, D.: Opponent modelling in automated multi-issue negotiation using bayesian learning. In: Proceedings of the 7th International Joint Conference on Autonomous Agents and Multiagent Systems, AAMAS 2008, vol. 1, pp. 331–338. International Foundation for Autonomous Agents and Multiagent Systems, Richland (2008)
27. Jonker, C., Treur, J.: An agent architecture for multi-attribute negotiation. In: Proceedings of the 17th International Joint Conference on AI, IJCAI 2001, pp. 1195–1201. Morgan Kaufman (2001)
28. Kawaguchi, S., Fujita, K., Ito, T.: AgentK: compromising strategy based on estimated maximum utility for automated negotiating agents. In: Ito, T., Zhang, M., Robu, V., Fatima, S., Matsuo, T. (eds.) New Trends in Agent-Based Complex Automated Negotiations. Studies in Computational Intelligence, vol. 383, pp. 137–144. Springer, Heidelberg (2012)

29. Kersten, G.E., Kowalczyk, R., Lai, H., Neumann, D., Chhetri, M.B.: Shaman: Software and Human Agents in Multiattribute Auctions and Negotiations, pp. 116–149. Springer, Heidelberg (2008)

30. Kersten, G.E., Lo, G.: Aspire: an integrated negotiation support system and software agents for e-business negotiation. Int. J. Internet Enterp. Manag. 1(3), 293–315 (2003)

31. Lin, R., Kraus, S., Baarslag, T., Tykhonov, D., Hindriks, K., Jonker, C.M.: Genius: an integrated environment for supporting the design of generic automated negotiators. Comput. Intell. 30(1), 48–70 (2014)

32. Mell, J., Gratch, J.: IAGO: interactive arbitration guide online. In: Proceedings of the 2016 International Conference on Autonomous Agents and Multiagent Systems, pp. 1510–1512. International Foundation for Autonomous Agents and Multiagent Systems, Singapore, May 2016

33. Pommeranz, A., Broekens, J., Wiggers, P., Brinkman, W.-P., Jonker, C.M.: Designing interfaces for explicit preference elicitation: a user-centered investigation of preference representation and elicitation process. User Model. User-Adapt. Interact. 22(4), 357–397 (2012)

34. Pommeranz, A., Wiggers, P., Brinkman, W.-P., Jonker, C.M.: Social acceptance of negotiation support systems: scenario-based exploration with focus groups and online survey. Cogn. Technol. Work 14(4), 299–317 (2012)

35. Pommeranz, A., Wiggers, P., Jonker, C.M.: Towards compositional design and evaluation of preference elicitation interfaces. In: Kurosu, M. (ed.) HCD 2011. LNCS, vol. 6776, pp. 586–596. Springer, Heidelberg (2011). doi:10.1007/978-3-642-21753-1_65

36. Raiffa, H.: The Art and Science of Negotiation, How to Resolve Conflicts and get the best out of Bargaining. Belknap Press of Harvard University Press, Cambridge (1982)

37. Raiffa, H., Richardson, J., Metcalfe, D.: Negotiation Analysis: The Science and Art of Collaborative Decision Making. Belknap Press of Harvard University Press, Cambridge (2002)

38. Thompson, L.: The Heart and Mind of the Negotiator. Pearson Prentice Hall, Upper Saddle River (2005)

39. Vahidov, R., Kersten, G., Saade, R.: An experimental study of software agent negotiations with humans. Decis. Support Syst. 66, 135–145 (2014)

40. Williams, C.R., Robu, V.E., Gerding, H., Jennings, N.R.: LAMhaggler: a negotiation agent for complex environments. In: Ito, T., Zhang, M., Robu, V., Fatima, S., Matsuo, T. (eds.) New Trends in Agent-Based Complex Automated Negotiations. Studies in Computational Intelligence, pp. 151–158. Springer, Heidelberg (2012)

EUMAS 2016: Agent and Multi-agent System Models

A Concise Review on Multiagent Teams: Contributions and Research Opportunities

Ewa Andrejczuk[1,2]([envelope]), Juan A. Rodriguez-Aguilar[1], and Carles Sierra[1]

[1] Artificial Intelligence Research Institute (IIIA-CSIC), Barcelona, Spain
{ewa,jar,sierra}@iiia.csic.es
[2] Change Management Tool S.L., Barcelona, Spain

Abstract. The composition and formation of effective teams is crucial for both companies, to assure their competitiveness, and for a broad range of emerging applications exploiting multiagent collaboration (e.g. human-agent teamwork, crowdsourcing). The aim of this article is to provide an integrative perspective on team composition, team formation and their relationship with team performance. Thus, we review and classify the contributions in the computer science literature dealing with these topics. Our purpose is twofold. First, we intend to identify the strengths and weaknesses of the contributions made so far. Second, we pursue to identify research gaps and opportunities. Given the volume of the existing literature, our review is not intended to be exhaustive. Instead, we focus on the most recent contributions that broke new ground to spur innovative research.

1 Introduction

In the last decades, there has been increasing interest in team-based work structures together with a focus on organisational efficiency [16]. On that account, team composition and formation research is of interest to many fields of science, also of computer science, especially within the area of multiagent systems (MAS). In this paper, our understanding of team composition and formation differentiates from the definitions provided by the multiagent field. We define *team composition* as the process of deciding which agents will be part of a team. We understand *team formation* as the process undertaken by agents to learn to work together in a team, and through this learning decide the roles and internal organisation of the team. Our definition of team formation is in line with the organisational psychology literature, which differentiates between the team composition and formation processes [16, p. 16].

The aim of this article is: (i) to determine dimensions that will help to classify MAS literature; (ii) to survey the most recent contributions in the literature on

Work supported by Collectiveware TIN2015-66863-C2-1-R (MINECO/FEDER), CollectiveMind (MINECO TEC2013-49430-EXP), SMA (201550E040), and Gencat 2014 SGR 118. Ewa Andrejczuk is supported by an Industrial PhD scholarship from the Generalitat de Catalunya.

N. Criado Pacheco et al. (Eds.): EUMAS 2016/AT 2016, LNAI 10207, pp. 31–39, 2017.
DOI: 10.1007/978-3-319-59294-7_3

team composition and formation according to identified dimensions; and (iii) to identify research gaps and opportunities by classifying the current state-of-the-art on team composition and formation.

In order to structure our analysis, we have identified several dimensions that will help us dissect the contributions in the literature:

1. *WHO is concerned?* The properties of the agents involved.
2. *WHAT is the problem?* The features of the task to complete by a team.
3. *WHY do we do it?* The objective function to optimise when composing/forming a team.
4. *HOW do we do it?* The organisation and/or coordination structure adopted by the team in charge of performing a particular task.
5. *WHEN do we do it?* The dynamics of the stream of tasks to be completed by agent teams.

Overall, our analysis of the literature indicates that MAS research focuses on building systems whose agents interact to achieve a common objective or exploit features of one another to achieve self-interested goals. The concept of agent teams is quite simplistic and it does not include the whole complexity of aspects considered by the organizational psychology (OP) literature. For instance, OP assumes that human capabilities are necessarily dynamic [17] (evolve along time) so that teams can successfully perform tasks in dynamic real-world scenarios and in a variety of contexts. Furthermore, OP observes that the quality of human resources (e.g. motivation, satisfaction, commitment), the ability of individuals to learn new capabilities, and the context constraining a team significantly influence its performance [11,12,25,26]. The MAS literature has typically disregarded significant organizational psychology findings, with the exception of several recent, preliminary attempts (such as [3,10,13]). However, our analysis of the literature indicates that Computer Science (CS) and OP exhibit also some similarities. One of the crucial findings in CS that has been confirmed by organizational psychology studies [32] is that team members have to be heterogeneous to maximize team performance. When modeling agents, similarly to OP, the Computer Science (CS) literature considers two main approaches: either there is complete information about the properties of each agent; or agents are capable of learning about their teammates through repeated interactions. We believe that further analysis of the OP literature could be beneficial to CS.

For a long version of this article, containing both a review of the OP literature review and a detailed description for each dimension above, we refer the reader to [4].

2   Dimensions to Analyse the State of the Art

In this section we describe the meaning of each of the dimensions identified in the introduction above.

2.1   WHO Is Concerned?

MAS research mainly focuses on the interaction among intelligent agents. In the team composition and formation literature, the focus is on the interaction of cooperative and heterogeneous agents. That is, agents who share a common goal, but have different individual properties. Here we classify the literature depending on the agents' individual properties along two dimensions: capacity and personality.

2.1.1   Capacity: Individual and Social Capabilities of Agents

In many domains, a capability is defined as a particular skill required to perform an action. The capacity dimension has been exploited by numerous previous works [2,6–8,18,23,24,28]. The majority of these approaches represent capabilities of agents in a Boolean way (i.e., an agent either has a required skill or not). When modeling agents' properties, many existing approaches typically assume extensive a-priori information about teammates (e.g. [2,8,15,28] just to name a few). This is a strong limitation for real-life settings. Notice that in many companies there is no central and extensive knowledge about all employees' capabilities.

2.1.2   Personality: Individual Behaviour Models

Very recently some MAS contributions have started to consider the notion of personality, i.e. individual behaviour model, to compose heterogeneous teams [1,3,5,9,10,13,20–22]. We observe an increasing interest in building more realistic models considering agents' behavioural patterns.

2.2   WHAT is the Problem? The Notion of Task

In its most general sense, a task is a course of action to achieve a goal. The execution of a task is then usually equated to the execution of an action plan. In the team composition and formation literature it is often the case that simplifying assumptions are made and tasks are assumed to be solved by simple action plans. For instance, an action plan can be seen as a set of actions, or even as a set of competences. Thus, we identify two main approaches: *individual-based* and *plan-based*.

2.2.1   Individual-Based Approaches

Given a task, it is generally assumed that if the joint capabilities of agents in a team fulfill those required by the task, then the team is capable of solving the task. Existing work on team composition focuses on two categories of individual properties: capacity and personality. Regarding capacity, there are many models in the MAS literature that define a task as a set of requirements on agents' capacities. These requirements are either direct (a task makes explicit a set of demanded capabilities [2,7,8,23]), or indirect (sub-tasks are matched to agents' capacities [24] or task complexity levels are matched to graded agents' capabilities [6]). Regarding personality, some works define task types and match them with different personalities [9,10]. Others highlight the importance of diversity in personalities within a team [3] or communication style (associated with personality type) [13].

2.2.2 Plan-Based Approaches

The notion of task in plan-based approaches is normally understood either as a set of actions or as a sequence of actions that are assigned to the individual members of a team. Some authors [1,5] employ an indirect planning method driven only by the most informed agents to solve a set of actions. Other approaches consider a task as a sequence of actions and let all agents in a team jointly vote on the possible alternatives from a discrete set of possible actions [20–22].

2.3 WHY Do We Do It? The Objective(s)

The motivation of individual efforts or actions is to attain or accomplish a certain state of affairs: a goal. A large body of the literature proposes team composition and formation algorithms to attain at least one of the following team objectives: minimizing overall cost (e.g. cooperation cost, team cost), maximizing social utility, or maximizing the quality of an outcome. Regarding the first objective, there are various costs associated with team composition and formation problems (e.g. communication costs, or agent service costs). The reviewed models in the MAS literature *minimizing overall cost* [8,15,23] compose teams based on individual competences, though do not take into account individual motivations to complete some assigned task. A second objective considered in the team composition and formation literature is *maximizing social welfare*. That is, maximizing the utility function of a team. Typically, the utility obtained is then allocated to the individual members of the team [1,6,7,10,30]. The literature focusing on maximizing social welfare considers both agent competences and motivation. Motivation increases by making agents compete (like in crowdsourcing teams [30]), or by giving agents the freedom to select their collaborators (like in [6] or [1]). Finally, researchers in MAS propose a number of methods where agents try to maximize the quality of solutions whilst minimizing the time to achieve them, namely to *maximize team performance* [3,13,18–20,24,29]. To do this, one of the crucial findings in CS is that team members must be heterogeneous. Further variables that have been used by computer scientists in the area of MAS to compose teams are: agent reputation [24], personality of humans and agents [3,10,20], synergy between team members [19], and feeling of fairness among team members [29].

2.4 HOW Do We Do It? The Organisation

There are two aspects to be considered while discussing the societal structure of teams, that is: which agents will be members of a team, and how teams will be organized to solve tasks.

2.4.1   Team Composition

Team composition is the process of deciding which agents will be part of a team. Although team composition in MAS has mainly focused on building teams of software agents, that is, agent teams, there is a growing number of works considering either mixed teams [13], where agents and humans cooperate to achieve common goals [27], or human environments, where people are supported by software [14]. In MAS, we distinguish between two groups of methods (or processes) to compose teams: exogenous and endogenous. Exogenous team composition is when there exists an algorithm external to the agents that determines the composition of teams. The majority of reviewed works focuses on these methods to compose either the best team for a given task [7,8,19,23,28] or a set of teams to solve an incoming set of tasks [2,3,9,31]. Endogenous methods for organizing teams incorporate algorithms enabling agents to decide on team composition by themselves. In detail, agents are equipped with negotiation and decision-making mechanisms that they employ to agree among themselves on a team structure [6,10,24]. Therefore, team composition occurs without explicit external command and in a distributed manner.

2.4.2   Team Formation

Team formation is the process of deciding the roles and internal organisation of a team. This organisation can be imposed or be the result of self-organisation. The resulting organisations can be categorized as hierarchical or egalitarian. A hierarchical structure considers a team leader who is responsible for and makes the decisions affecting the team. This organisation type is imposed by defining two or more types of agents (such as requesters and contributors [10], mediators and workers [24], or best-response agents and ad-hoc agents [1]). An egalitarian structure assumes that all workers in a team are equally informed and have the same rights. The leadership within a team is shared and existing team roles result from the team's task requirements. We find this team structure in Groupsourcing [30], Robust Teams [8,23], *Ad-hoc* teams [5–7], Mixed Teams [13], Learning Teams [18,19] or Voting Teams [20–22].

2.5   WHEN Do We Do It? The Dynamics

The literature on team composition and formation mostly considers that tasks are static in the sense that their requirements do not change during their execution. However, some works consider that there is a stream of tasks that dynamically appear to be completed. Thus, there could be multiple tasks to be solved concurrently and new tasks may arrive in an asynchronous, localized manner. The different works in the literature consider different issues in this dynamic process. For instance, the number of tasks to be serviced, task and team members localization, team size per task or time limitations. Hence, the literature can be classified depending on two main aspects: the succession of tasks and the concurrency of tasks.

The simplest case is represented by a one-shot task. There is neither succession nor concurrency, and hence the problem of team composition is normally reduced to finding the best team for the only task [8,15,23,28]. When tasks come in sequence without concurrency, then the problem can be reduced to finding the best team for each task while using the learned experiences in the composition of each new team [2,19]. If tasks come in succession and can be simultaneous, the need for dealing with multiple teams acting at the same time becomes the key issue. Finally, the succession of possibly simultaneous tasks represents the most complex scenario [6,7,10,24]. Here memory becomes a crucial element as it lets agents learn from the past experiences and build their beliefs based on this knowledge.

3 Discussion

The aim of this article is to review the most recent, representative and relevant literature on team composition and formation and identify research gaps and opportunities for further research. In this final section, we focus on identifying research opportunities:

- **Establish a connection with the OP literature.** A goal of organizational psychology is to improve organizational performance by placing the right people in the right jobs, thus enhancing the fit between the individual and the organization. This includes the methods for building effective teams. Nevertheless, research on team composition and team formation in CS and OP has evolved separately. The MAS literature has typically disregarded significant OP findings, with the exception of several recent, preliminary attempts (like [3,10] or [13]). This body of research has focused on algorithms that help automate team formation and composition. Heuristics for team composition and formation investigated by the OP literature have much potential for MAS research.
- **Exploration of complex agents.** The CS literature is in need of analysing more complex examples where humans are modeled as agents. While some of the human properties may not make sense in an agent context, some do. For instance, the dynamics of competences through learning and experience and the cultural values could be used to program more sophisticated agents, specially when interacting in mixed teams involving humans. Additionally, OP research highlights motivation as an important factor for team performance [12]. The majority of MAS literature on team composition and teamwork assumes that agents always behave according to their capabilities and knowledge. While in MAS research it is shown that motivation increases by introducing competition mechanisms (like in crowdsourcing teams [30]), or by giving agents freedom when selecting their collaborators (like in ad-hoc teams [1]), there are only early attempts to include agents' motivation as an important factor for team performance.
- **Study of plan-based approaches.** Regarding the tasks that are executed by agent teams, CS focuses on team members' properties required to perform

a task rather than on a detailed planning of task execution. The majority of approaches assume that the joint capabilities of agents in a team are enough to solve a given task. There are some preliminary attempts to include planning, though they are very simplistic. The majority of methods do not consider time constraints, action dependencies, action failure, plan robustness, task dynamic changes and hence, the vast literature on planning has not yet been integrated into team formation methods.

- **Exploration of complex approaches for task execution.** Since in CS agents can be engineered depending on the needs (i.e. agents can be designed with different properties, such as personality or memory, depending on the whole system design), researchers can study different settings depending on the dynamics of task arrival (one task or many, one time or many). The CS literature uses complex scenarios to let agents build their beliefs based on past experiences and compose new teams according to these learned beliefs. However, while executing tasks, there are no contributions that explore successive or simultaneous settings. Hence, the state of the importance of agent learning when executing tasks.
- **The study of team properties.** Although individuals' properties have been extensively studied and considered, there is still a need for modeling the global properties of agent teams. Such modeling should go beyond considering simple properties such as the sum of the agents' individual capabilities or the Boolean representation of whether the team can perform a task or not.

References

1. Agmon, N., Barrett, S., Stone, P.: Modeling uncertainty in leading ad hoc teams. In: Proceedings of the 13th International Conference on Autonomous Agents and Multiagent Systems (AAMAS), May 2014
2. Anagnostopoulos, A., Becchetti, L., Castillo, C., Gionis, A., Leonardi, S.: Online team formation in social networks. In: Proceedings of the 21st World Wide Web Conference 2012, WWW 2012, Lyon, France, 16–20 April 2012, pp. 839–848 (2012)
3. Andrejczuk, E., Rodríguez-Aguilar, J.A., Sierra, C.: Optimising congenial teams. In: International Workshop on Optimisation in Multi-Agent Systems (OPTMAS), 10 May 2016 (2016)
4. Andrejczuk, E., Berger, R., Rodriguez-Aguilar, J.A., Sierra, C., Marín-Puchades, V.: The composition and formation of effective teams. computer science meets psychology. arXiv preprint arXiv:1610.08804 (2016)
5. Barrett, S., Stone, P., Kraus, S., Rosenfeld, A.: Teamwork with limited knowledge of teammates. In: Proceedings of the Twenty-Seventh AAAI Conference on Artificial Intelligence, July 2013
6. Chalkiadakis, G., Boutilier, C.: Sequentially optimal repeated coalition formation under uncertainty. Auton. Agents Multi-Agent Syst. **24**(3), 441–484 (2012)
7. Chen, B., Chen, X., Timsina, A., Soh, L.: Considering agent and task openness in ad hoc team formation. In: Proceedings of the 2015 International Conference on Autonomous Agents and Multiagent Systems, AAMAS 2015, Istanbul, Turkey, 4–8 May 2015, pp. 1861–1862 (2015)

8. Crawford, C., Rahaman, Z., Sen, S.: Evaluating the efficiency of robust team formation algorithms. In: International Workshop on Optimisation in Multi-Agent Systems (2016)
9. Farhangian, M., Purvis, M., Purvis, M., Savarimuthu, T.B.R.: Agent-based modeling of resource allocation in software projects based on personality and skill. In: Koch, F., Guttmann, C., Busquets, D. (eds.) Advances in Social Computing and Multiagent Systems. CCIS, vol. 541, pp. 130–146. Springer, Cham (2015). doi:10.1007/978-3-319-24804-2_9
10. Farhangian, M., Purvis, M.K., Purvis, M., Savarimuthu, B.T.R.: Modeling the effects of personality on team formation in self-assembly teams. In: Chen, Q., Torroni, P., Villata, S., Hsu, J., Omicini, A. (eds.) PRIMA 2015. LNCS (LNAI), vol. 9387, pp. 538–546. Springer, Cham (2015). doi:10.1007/978-3-319-25524-8_36
11. Guzzo, R.A., Dickson, M.W.: Teams in organizations: recent research on performance and effectiveness. Annu. Rev. Psychol. 47(1), 307–338 (1996)
12. Hackman, J.R.: Groups that Work (and Those That Don't): Creating Conditions for Effective Teamwork. Jossey-Bass, San Francisco (1990). Number 10–H123
13. Hanna, N., Richards, D.: Do birds of a feather work better together? The impact of virtual agent personality on a shared mental model with humans during collaboration. In: Proceedings of the 3rd International Workshop on Collaborative Online Organizations, COOS 2016, co-located with the 14th International Conference on Autonomous Agents and Multi-Agent Systems, AAMAS 2015, Istanbul, Turkey, 4 May 2015, pp. 28–37 (2015)
14. Jennings, N.R., Moreau, L., Nicholson, D., Ramchurn, S., Roberts, S., Rodden, T., Rogers, A.: Human-agent collectives. Commun. ACM 57(12), 80–88 (2014)
15. Kargar, M., An, A., Zihayat, M.: Efficient bi-objective team formation in social networks. In: Flach, P.A., Bie, T., Cristianini, N. (eds.) ECML PKDD 2012. LNCS, vol. 7524, pp. 483–498. Springer, Heidelberg (2012). doi:10.1007/978-3-642-33486-3_31
16. Kozlowski, S.W.J., Bell, B.S.: Work groups and teams in organizations. In: Handbook of Psychology. Wiley Online Library (2003)
17. Laal, M., Salamati, P.: Lifelong learning; why do we need it? Procedia-Soc. Behav. Sci. 31, 399–403 (2012)
18. Liemhetcharat, S., Veloso, M.: Team formation with learning agents that improve coordination. In: Proceedings of the 2014 International Conference on Autonomous Agents and Multi-Agent Systems, AAMAS 2014, Richland, SC, pp. 1531–1532. International Foundation for Autonomous Agents and Multiagent Systems (2014)
19. Liemhetcharat, S., Veloso, M.M.: Modeling and learning synergy for team formation with heterogeneous agents. In: International Conference on Autonomous Agents and Multiagent Systems, AAMAS 2012, Valencia, Spain, 4–8 June 2012 (3 Volumes), pp. 365–374 (2012)
20. Marcolino, L.S., Jiang, A.X., Tambe, A.: Multi-agent team formation: diversity beats strength? In: Proceedings of the 23rd International Joint Conference on Artificial Intelligence, IJCAI 2013, Beijing, China, 3–9 August 2013 (2013)
21. Soriano Marcolino, L., Xu, H., Gerber, D., Kolev, B., Price, S., Pantazis, E., Tambe, M.: Multi-agent team formation for design problems. In: Dignum, V., Noriega, P., Sensoy, M., Sichman, J.S.S. (eds.) COIN 2015. LNCS, vol. 9628, pp. 354–375. Springer, Cham (2016). doi:10.1007/978-3-319-42691-4_20
22. Nagarajan, V., Marcolino, L.S., Tambe, M.: Every team deserves a second chance: identifying when things go wrong (student abstract version). In: Proceedings of the Twenty-Ninth AAAI Conference on Artificial Intelligence, Austin, Texas, USA, 25–30 January 2015, pp. 4184–4185 (2015)

23. Okimoto, T., Schwind, N., Clement, M., Ribeiro, T., Inoue, K., Marquis, P.: How to form a task-oriented robust team. In: Proceedings of the 2015 International Conference on Autonomous Agents and Multiagent Systems, AAMAS 2015, pp. 395–403. International Foundation for Autonomous Agents and Multiagent Systems (2015)
24. Peleteiro, A., Burguillo-Rial, J.C., Luck, M., Arcos, J.L., Rodríguez-Aguilar, J.A.: Using reputation and adaptive coalitions to support collaboration in competitive environments. Eng. Appl. Artif. Intell. **45**, 325–338 (2015)
25. Podsakoff, P.M., MacKenzie, S.B., Ahearne, M.: Moderating effects of goal acceptance on the relationship between group cohesiveness and productivity. J. Appl. Psychol. **82**(6), 974 (1997)
26. Quijano, S., Navarro, J., Yepes, M., Berger, R., Romeo, M.: Human system audit (HSA) for the analysis of human behaviour in organizations. Papeles del Psicólogo **29**(1), 92–106 (2008)
27. Rangapuram, S.S., Bühler, T., Hein, M.: Towards realistic team formation in social networks based on densest subgraphs. In: Proceedings of the 22nd International Conference on World Wide Web, pp. 1077–1088. ACM (2013)
28. Rangapuram, S.S., Bühler, T., Hein, M.: Towards realistic team formation in social networks based on densest subgraphs. CoRR, abs/1505.06661 (2015)
29. Rochlin, I., Aumann, Y., Sarne, D., Golosman, L.: Efficiency and fairness in team search with self-interested agents. Auton. Agent. Multi-Agent Syst. **30**(3), 526–552 (2016)
30. Rokicki, M., Zerr, S., Siersdorfer, S.: Groupsourcing: team competition designs for crowdsourcing. In: Proceedings of the 24th International Conference on World Wide Web, WWW 2015, Florence, Italy, 18–22 May 2015, pp. 906–915 (2015)
31. Spradling, M., Goldsmith, J., Liu, X., Dadi, C., Li, Z.: Roles and teams hedonic game. In: Perny, P., Pirlot, M., Tsoukiàs, A. (eds.) ADT 2013. LNCS (LNAI), vol. 8176, pp. 351–362. Springer, Heidelberg (2013). doi:10.1007/978-3-642-41575-3_27
32. Wilde, D.J.: Teamology: The Construction and Organization of Effective Teams. Springer, London (2009)

A Modeling Language for Adaptive Normative Agents

Marx Viana[1(✉)], Paulo Alencar[2], and Carlos Lucena[1(✉)]

[1] Laboratory of Software Engenieer (LES), Informatics Department,
Pontifical Catholic University – PUC-Rio, Rio de Janeiro, RJ, Brazil
{mleles,lucena}@inf.puc-rio.br
[2] University of Waterloo, Waterloo, ON, Canada
palencar@uwaterloo.ca

Abstract. Agent-based software engineering has been proposed as a means of mastering the complexity associated with the development of large-scale distributed systems. However, agent-oriented software engineering has not been widely adopted, mainly due to lack of modeling languages that are expressive and comprehensive enough to represent relevant agent-related abstractions and support the refinement of design models into code. Most modeling languages do not define how these abstractions interact at run-time, but many software applications need to adapt their behavior, react to changes in their environments dynamically, and align with some form of individual or collective normative application behavior (e.g., obligations, prohibitions). In this paper, we propose a conceptual framework to developing adaptive normative agents. We believe the proposed approach will advance the state-of-the-art in agent systems so that software technologies for dynamic, adaptive, norm-based applications can be developed and implemented.

Keywords: Multiagent systems · Software modeling · Software adaptation · Normative systems

1 Introduction

Agent-Oriented Software Engineering (AOSE) emerged as a new technology for building complex systems. These systems are characterized by being distributed and composed of autonomous entities that interact with each other [17]. Multiagent Systems (MASs) are societies in which these heterogeneous and individually designed entities (agents) work to accomplish common or independent goals [12]. Thus, the use of agents for constructing such complex systems is considered a promising approach in many areas [18]. However, the successful and widespread deployment of large-scale MASs requires a unifying set of agent-related abstractions to support modeling languages and respective methodologies. Furthermore, there is still a poor understanding about some MAS abstractions such as those used to define different forms of adaptation and to represent concepts involving normative behavior. In addition, most modeling languages do not define how these abstractions interact at run-time [2], but many

© Springer International Publishing AG 2017
N. Criado Pacheco et al. (Eds.): EUMAS 2016/AT 2016, LNAI 10207, pp. 40–48, 2017.
DOI: 10.1007/978-3-319-59294-7_4

software applications need to change their behavior and react to changes in their environments dynamically.

Self-adaptive software systems are software programs that monitor themselves and their operating environment and take appropriate measures when circumstances change [13]. One of the main advantages of self-adaptive software is its ability to manage the complexity arising from highly dynamic and non-deterministic operating environments. According to [11], for software to be considered self-adaptive it needs to: (i) have the ability to observe changes in its operating environment; (ii) have the ability to detect and diagnose changes in the operating environment and assess its own behavior; (iii) have the ability to change its own behavior in order to adapt to the new changes; and (iv) support dynamic behavior, i.e., its internal and external behavior should be able to be changed intentionally and automatically. Although various approaches [11, 13] describe how agent-oriented systems can perform self-adaptive, they do not focus on modeling and implementing software agents. Thus, properties related to agents and considered important for self-adaptive systems such as autonomy, learning, reasoning and proactivity, are not explicitly addressed in these approaches [10].

Norms are understood as mechanisms to regulate the behavior of agents, representing the way in which agents understand the responsibilities of other agents [12]. Norms have several properties [14]. These properties include: Addressee, Condition (e.g., Activation, Expiration), Motivation (e.g., Rewards, Punishments), Deontic Concept and State. The description of each property is provided as follows: (i) Addressee is used to specify the agents or roles responsible for fulfilling a norm; (ii) Activation is the activation condition for a norm to become active, (iii) Expiration is the expiration condition for a norm to become inactive; (iv) Rewards are used to represent the set of rewards to be given to an agent for fulfilling a norm; (v) Punishments are the set of punishments to be given to an agent for violating a norm; (vi) Deontic Concept is used to indicate if a norm states an obligation, a permission or a prohibition; and (vii) State is used to describe the set of states being regulated. Several authors observed that most modeling languages do not represent some important concepts present in MASs such as those related to adaptation and norms [2]. Nevertheless, norms and adaptation are relevant and indispensable to the internal and external design and run-time models of the MAS. Many types of practical applications of multiagent systems, such as [4, 6, 8, 9], need to support adaptive and normative mechanisms in design and run-time. The paper is organized as follows. Section 2 discusses the proposed metamodel. Section 3 presents the ANA modeling language. Section 4 presents related work. Section 5 presents our conclusions and future work.

2 A Conceptual Framework

The ANA metamodel (Adaptive Normative Agent) enables the structural and adaptive behavior of agent-based software to support norms. Based on the distinction proposed by Beydoun et al. [2] about design and run time, the proposed metamodel aims to represent the relationships and entities internal and external to the software agent.

Figure 1 shows the external agent design-time representation, which aims to represent how agents relate to each other and to other entities of the environment in which they reside. This metalevel representation was adapted from TAO [16] and FAML [2].

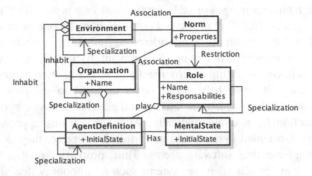

Fig. 1. External agent design-time representation.

Agents transform the environment, so it is necessary to consider the environment state and the "mental states" of each agent to understand how they work. The agent behavior is characterized by its plans, actions, reasoning type and active norms in the environment. These features are related to general agent characteristics such as interaction, autonomy and adaptation [10, 14, 15]. In addition, agents can interact by sending and receiving messages from other agents within the environment. Agents are adaptive entities, since they can adapt their status and behavior with respect to the changes and constraints of the environment. When it executes actions, the agent can change its mental state, introducing new perceptions about the environment by sending and receiving messages from other agents. These concepts were included in the metamodel to make it possible to use the BDI architecture for the reasoning about the agent.

An agent role guides and constrains the agent behavior by describing the goals it needs to reach when playing a certain role [10]. TAO [15] has introduced the concepts of duty and right related to the role an agent is playing. However, these concepts are not enough to show that an agent needs to comply with the goals of the role, because the agent has no advantage if it decides to fulfill or violate the duties of that role. If an agent does not see any advantage in achieving the goals of the role, it will only fulfill its individual goals. For this reason, the concept of norms has been introduced in the ANA metamodel, in order to restrict the behavior of agent roles. Norm properties include rewards and punishments, leaving to the agent the task of deciding its interest in complying with the goals of that role.

An organization in turn divides the agents of a multiagent system into groups and roles, both defining the structure of different groups of agents and sub-groups within an organization [3]. Establishing an organization involves the specifications of social plans, objectives and norms. TAO defines the concept of axiom, which agents and sub-organizations must satisfy. In FAML, the concept of convention has been established as an agreement between the organization and the agent. However, the concepts used by TAO and FAML are not provided to regulate the behavior of agents without removing their autonomy.

Figure 2 shows the internal agent design-time representation which explicitly describes the agent internal properties and how they relate to each other. To express the mental state of an agent the model needs to capture its mental components such as beliefs, goals, intentions, plans and actions [14]. MentalState is responsible for checking how a norm can affect the beliefs and desires of an agent and its used to capture the state and behavior of the agent at a moment in time. The AgentDefinition entity function initializes all agents in the system and to specifies a function of the role to be used when an agent intends to play a certain role.

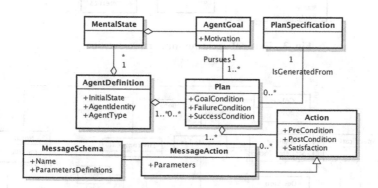

Fig. 2. Internal agent design-time representation.

A Plan is composed of actions and is related to a set of goals that the agent can access and execute. The GoalCondition attribute characterizes the goals for which the plans can be applied. The FailureCondiction attribute characterizes when a plan will not be able to achieve the desired goal. The SucessCondition attribute describes when a plan can be deemed to have successfully achieved a goal. An Action entity comprises the following attributes: (i) PreCondition refers to the conditions (system events) that must be performed before an action; (ii) PosCondition defines the conditions (system events) that most hold after the execution of the action; and (iii) Satisfaction attribute describes the level of satisfaction that the agent will have by performing a given action. For agents to support adaptive plans, a PlanSpecification entity, we can set plans on how to monitor, analyze, decide and effect internal changes of the agent so that it can reasoning about norms. In AgentGoal, the Motivation attribute describes the level of motivation that an agent has to accomplish a specific goal.

Figure 3 shows the classes related to the Enviroment where agents "live" at run-time. These classes coexist with instances of the agent design-time representation, that is, those shown in Figs. 1 and 2. The classes related to Enviroment focus on features that exist only in the run-time environment. Finally, Fig. 4 shows the classes related to the internal agent run-time representation. These classes include: (i) plans and actions; (ii) relationships between actions and messages; (iii) communication and the relationship between messages and protocols; (iv) mental states and the relationship with the BDI architecture; (v) the relationship between the previous abstractions and the states of the environment; and (vi) the adaptive reasoning performed by the agent to adapt the norm-related activities in the system.

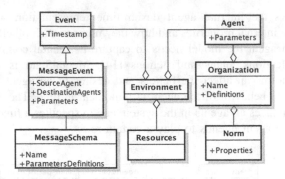

Fig. 3. External agent run-time representation.

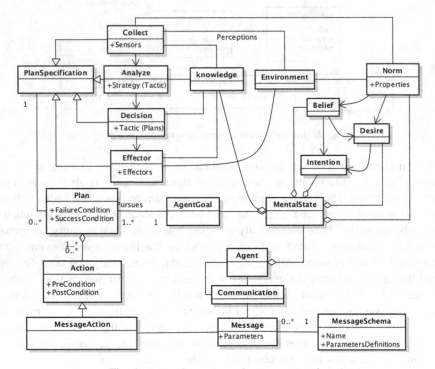

Fig. 4. Internal agent run-time representation.

3   ANA-ML

This section proposes a modeling language, ANA-ML (Adaptive Normative Agent Modeling Language), to support the development of adaptive normative agents. This metamodel enables structural and behavioral software agent adaptations able to reason about norms. ANA-ML was proposed to introduce adaptation and norm-related abstractions in the modeling language MAS-ML [15]. The mechanisms adopted in

ANA-ML were the creation of a profile that focuses onthe definition of new classes, restrictions and stereotypes based on the MAS-ML. The ANA-ML metamodel is presented in Fig. 5. The metaclass Element is a superclass of the metaclass Classifier, which in turn is a superclass, for example, of the metaclass Class. This allows the metaclasses Norm and EnvironmentClass to be used by any sub-metaclass of Classifier. Further, the metaclasses AgentCollect, AgentAnalyze, AgentDecision and AgentEffector are related to the metaclass AgentBehavior, being a sub-metaclass of BehavioralFeature, which allows us to model behavioral entities. The metaclass Classifier is related to the meta-classes StructuralFeature and BehavioralFeature. A structural characteristic is a characteristic of a classifier used to represent the structure of an instance itself. A behavior characteristic is a characteristic of a classifier that specifies a behavioral aspect of the instances. So, the metaclass StructuralFeatures is a generalization of the metaclass Property, where the class attributes are represented with instances of Property, and the metaclass BehavioralFeatures is a generalization of the metaclass Operation, defined in [15]. The metaclass AgentClass was created to represent agents. Furthermore, we created stereotypes for an agent to understand the responsibilities and restrictions addressed to it by norms. To represent, beliefs the stereotype <<belief>> was created. New stereotypes were created to represent the mental state of the agent, such as: (i) <<desire>> to represent the set of desires; (ii) <<intention>> to represent the set of intentions, and are instantiated as attributes.

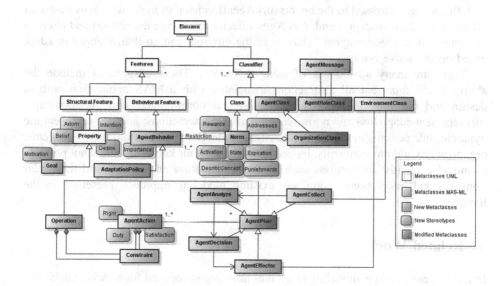

Fig. 5. ANA-ML diagram.

An action is represented through the metaclass AgentAction that extends AgentBehavior. The agent plans are represented by AgentPlan, which extends AgentBehavior. AgentBehavior extends BehavioralFeature and was created to represented all agent behavior. The AgentBehavior has the stereotype <<Importance>>, which defines the level of an agent motivation to realize a goal or of an agent satisfaction to execute an action [12]. A new metaclass called Norm that extends the Class metaclass has been created to specify the restrictions imposed by the environment. A norm is related to the metaclass AgentBehavior through the relationship Restriction. Futhermore, a norm is related to the OrganizationClass through the relationship Agregation. The metaclass AgentPlan is associated with the metaclass AdaptationPolicy. This metaclass was created to verify that the plan started by an agent is in accordance with the system adaptation policies, since an unpredictable behavior could cause the system to fail.

Organizations extend the notion of agents, but there are other properties and relationships. The change we made in the MAS-ML metaclass OrganizationClass was the incorporation of the concept of norms, which represent in a more precise and restrictive way normative behavior than axioms limited to represent the overall organizational constraints [15]. On the order hand, norms such as obligations, permissions or prohibitions were incorporated to represent agent behaviors linked to their roles in an organization [12]. The role of the agent is defined by the AgentRoleClass metaclass. However, roles have been incorporated into a set of norms and the agents decide how to deal with them. It is important to mention that intentions, desires and plans are internal properties of an agent and not part of its role. New metaclasses are created to specify the adaptive behavior of an agent, and include: (i) AgentCollect to monitor the norms in the environment; (ii) AgentAnalyze to analyze what possible plans can deal with the norms addressed to the agent; (iii) AgentDecision to make decisions based on differents kinds of strategies and; (iv) AgentEffector to execute the actions and plans in the setting of a specific agent behavior in the environment so that agents can adapt based on the active norms.

There are many advantages of using ANA-ML. These advantages include the ability to: (i) represent all abstractions associated with a MAS application both at design and run-time; (ii) specify adaptation and norm-related static relationships; (iii) represent adaptation and norm-related dynamic interactions; and (iv) represent the dynamic interactions involving abstractions related to adaptation, norms, agents, organizations and environments. Indeed, to the best of our knowledge, it is not possible to model explicitly abstractions such as agent adaptation and norms, and their relationships and interactions, using any existing modeling approach presented in the literature.

4   Related Work

In recent years, various modeling languages have been proposed for MASs: Adelfe [1], FAML [2], AML [5], NormML [7], MAS-ML [14] and Gaia [18]. However, there is still a need for a modeling language that describes concepts related to adaptation and norms and: (i) supports these concepts as first-class citizen abstractions; (ii) supports these concepts through an explicit description of a MAS metamodel; (iii) can be used to model the structural and dynamic aspects often described in MASs for these concepts; and (iv) promotes the refinement of these models from design into code.

Some modeling languages and methodologies such as, AML [5], MAS-ML [14], Adelfe [1], FAML [2] and Gaia [18] do not support the modeling of norms. Approaches such as NormML [7] also make the modeling of several elements of a norm possible. From the set of modeling languages [5, 7, 14], and methodologies [1, 2, 18] we have reviewed just one of them (NormML) is able to model all the properties of the elements described in the Sect. 1. However, NormML does not support the representation of adaptation-related abstractions. Further, in terms of abstractions for adaptation, although only Adelfe [1] supports representing adaptive agents using adaptive workflows, it does not introduce the atomic elements an agent needs to adapt its behavior.

5   Conclusions and Future Work

This paper proposes a metamodel approach to developing adaptative normative agents. This work assumes that introducing abstractions related to adaptation and norms in MAS representation languages results in a new metamodel that supports these abstractions. We are in the process of defining a multiagent system modeling language based on the proposed structural and dynamic properties presented in the ANA metamodel. ANA-ML addresses specific norm and adaptation-related MAS characteristics that are not explicitly addressed in a satisfactory way in the models available in the literature, which include Adelfe [1], FAML [2], AML [5], NormML [7], MAS-ML [15] and Gaia [18].

References

1. Bernon, C., Gleizes, M.P., Peyruqueou, S., Picard, G.: ADELFE: a methodology for adaptive multi-agent systems engineering. In: Petta, P., Tolksdorf, R., Zambonelli, F. (eds.) ESAW 2002. LNCS, vol. 2577, pp. 156–169. Springer, Heidelberg (2003). doi:10.1007/3-540-39173-8_12
2. Beydoun, G., Low, G., Henderson-Sellers, B., Mouratidis, H., Gomez-Sanz, J.J., Pavon, J., Gonzalez-Perez, C.: FAML: a generic metamodel for MAS development. IEEE Trans. Softw. Eng. 35(6), 841–863 (2009)
3. Boissier, O., et al.: Multi-agent oriented programming with JaCaMo. Sci. Comput. Program. 78(6), 747–761 (2013)
4. Cerqueira, S.L.R., et al.: Plataforma GeoRisc Engenharia da Computação Aplicada à Análise de Riscos Geo-ambientais. PUC-RIO, Rio de Janeiro (2009)
5. Cervenka, R., Trencansky, I.: The Agent Modeling Language-AML: A Comprehensive Approach to Modeling Multi-Agent Systems. Springer Science & Business Media, Heidelberg (2007)
6. Cook, D.J.: How smart is your home? Science 35, 1579–1581 (2012)
7. da Silva Figueiredo, K., Torres da Silva, V., de Oliveira Braga, C.: Modeling norms in multi-agent systems with normML. In: De Vos, M., Fornara, N., Pitt, J.V., Vouros, G. (eds.) COIN -2010. LNCS, vol. 6541, pp. 39–57. Springer, Heidelberg (2011). doi:10.1007/978-3-642-21268-0_3

8. Gubbi, J., et al.: Internet of things (IoT): a vision, architectural elements, and future directions. Future Gener. Comput. Syst. **29**(7), 1645–1660 (2013)
9. Janssen, M., et al.: Advances in multi-agency disaster management: key elements in disaster research. Inf. Syst. Front. **12**(1), 1–7 (2010)
10. Jennings, N.R., Wooldridge, M.: Agent-Oriented Software Engineering. Handbook of Agent Technology. AAAI/MIT Press, Cambridge (2000)
11. Kalareh, M.A.: Evolving software systems for self-adaptation. Ph.D. thesis, University of Waterloo (2012)
12. López, F.L.: Social power and norms. Ph.D. thesis, University of Southampton (2003)
13. Nallur, V., Bahsoon, R.: A decentralized self-adaptation mechanism for service-based applications in the cloud. IEEE Trans. Softw. Eng. **39**(5), 591–612 (2013)
14. Neto, S.: A deontic approach for the development of autonomous normative agents. Pontifical Catholic University - Technical report. PUC-Rio, Rio de Janeiro (2012)
15. Silva, V.T., Choren, R., De Lucena, C.J.P.: MAS-ML: a multi-agent system modeling language. Int. J. Agent-Oriented Softw. Eng. **2**(4), 381–421 (2008)
16. Silva, V.T.: Uma Linguagem de Modelagem para Sistemas Multi-agentes Baseada em um Framework Conceitual para Agentes e Objetos. PUC-Rio, Rio de Janeiro (2004)
17. Wooldridge, M.: An Introduction to Multiagent Systems. Wiley, Hoboken (2011)
18. Zambonelli, F., Jennings, N.R., Wooldridge, M.: Developing multiagent systems: the Gaia methodology. ACM Trans. Softw. Eng. Methodol. (TOSEM) **12**(3), 317–370 (2003)

An MDE Approach for Modelling
and Reasoning About Multi-agent Systems

Fazle Rabbi[1,2(✉)], Yngve Lamo[1], and Lars Michael Kristensen[1]

[1] Western Norway University of Applied Sciences, Bergen, Norway
{Fazle.Rabbi,Yngve.Lamo,Lars.Michael.Kristensen}@hvl.no
[2] University of Oslo, Oslo, Norway

Abstract. Epistemic logic plays an important role in artificial intelligence for reasoning about multi-agent systems. Current approaches for modelling multi-agent systems with epistemic logic use Kripke semantics where the knowledge base of an agent is represented as atomic propositions, but intelligent agents need to be equipped with formulas to derive implicit information. In this paper, we propose a metamodelling approach where agents' state of affairs are separated in different scopes, and the knowledge base of an agent is represented by a propositional logic language restricted to *Horn clauses*. We propose to use a model driven approach for the diagrammatic representation of multi-agent systems knowledge (and nested knowledge). We use a message passing for updating the state of affairs of agents and use belief revision to update the knowledge base of agents.

Keywords: Model-driven engineering · Epistemic logic · Modal logic · Knowledge base

1 Introduction

Our approach for modelling multi-agent system is based on combining metamodelling and epistemic logic with diagrammatic specifications and logic statements. We use the *basic modal system* **K** [5] for epistemic logic and enhance the modelling with the use of model-driven engineering techniques. Traditionally, Kripke structures have been used to give the semantics of epistemic logic by representing the information state of several agents [5]. Although Kripke structures can be used to model the cognitive states of other agents but the knowledge representation of different agents in a Kripke model are not structured. In our approach, agents' information states are modularized into scopes. Scopes include states where the knowledge base of a state is represented by horn clauses making agents capable of deducing new information. We propose to use metamodels for specifying the information state of agents. Using metamodels for defining domain specific modelling languages has potential as languages can be easily customized. However, model-driven engineering using metamodels has not been explored for modelling multi-agent systems.

© Springer International Publishing AG 2017
N. Criado Pacheco et al. (Eds.): EUMAS 2016/AT 2016, LNAI 10207, pp. 49–57, 2017.
DOI: 10.1007/978-3-319-59294-7_5

Our work is closely related to the deductive model of belief proposed by Konolige [8] where agents' beliefs are described as a set of sentences in a formal language together with a deductive process for deriving consequences of those beliefs. Deductive model of belief provides a model for agents' problem solving ability based on the reasoning about other agents' problem solving ability. Konolige introduced the concept of *belief subsystem* which can model fairly complicated and confusing situations where agents believe that other agents have belief subsystems of varying capabilities. Some of these scenarios would be useful in representing situations where agents have different beliefs. In real-life, different sources will expose agents to different information, which can naturally lead to disagreement. In our approach, we use several distinct elements to represent and to reason about knowledge in a MAS setting. We use Diagram Predicate Framework [11] for the diagrammatic representation of agents' state of affairs where the knowledge base is represented using Horn clauses. We apply category theory for structuring the knowledge of different agents and combine our approach with Delgrande's inconsistency-based contraction [3] for knowledge base revision. Our proposed approach of modular information states can be used to represent different knowledge of agents, and leads to a simple mechanism to update the knowledge base of agents. We introduce the application of category theoretical operations for extracting the local and global knowledge base of agents which opens up a new formal way of modelling multi-agent systems.

The paper is organized as follows. In Sect. 2, we present a language for representing the knowledge base of agents. Section 3 presents the modelling artifacts for specifying multi-agent systems. Section 4 provides details of how agents communicate information and update their knowledge base, Sect. 5 concludes the paper with a direction for future work.

2   Knowledge Representation of Multi-agent Systems

Unlike Kripke models, states in our multi-agent model are associated with knowledge bases (KB). The knowledge base is given by a restricted form of the propositional logic language $\mathcal{L}_{\mathcal{HC}}$ based on a finite set of atoms (atomic propositions) $\mathbf{P} = \{\bot, p, q, r, \ldots\}$, where $\mathbf{P}$ includes the distinguished atom $\bot$ (false). The language $\mathcal{L}_{\mathcal{HC}}$ over $\mathbf{P}$ is given by a set of horn clauses as defined in [3]. A horn clause can be written as a rule in the form $\alpha_1 \wedge \alpha_2 \wedge \ldots \wedge \alpha_n \rightarrow \alpha$, where $n \geq 0$, and α, α_i $(1 \leq i \leq n)$ are distinct atoms and $\rightarrow$ represents implication. Let φ be a horn clause in $\mathcal{L}_{\mathcal{HC}}$, if $n = 0$ then φ represents a ground atom and $\rightarrow \alpha$ is written as α. We will use $body(\varphi)$ to refer to the set of atomic propositions to the left of $\rightarrow$ and $head(\varphi)$ to refer to the consequence of φ. We use $\bot$ in the consequence of a clause to represent an *integrity constraint* [3]. In other words, a clause with $\bot$ in the consequence represents an impossible situation. A horn clause φ can be derived from a set of horn clauses Φ, written $\Phi \vdash \varphi$ if φ can be obtained by the inference relation given in [3]. A set of horn clauses Φ is inconsistent if $\Phi \vdash \bot$. We use the notation $\Phi^* = \mathtt{Cn}(\Phi) = \{\varphi : \Phi \vdash \varphi\}$ to represent the set of all logical consequences of Φ. A *scope* of an agent consists of one or

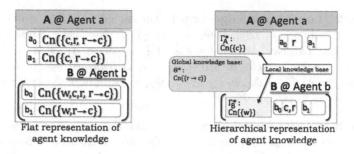

Fig. 1. An example model of an agent a and its scopes

more states representing epistemic alternatives. To express what an agent know in its states or about other agents, we need a language of epistemic logic $\mathcal{L}_k$ which is defined as: $\varphi ::= p \,|\, \neg\varphi \,|\, (\varphi \wedge \varphi) \,|\, (\varphi \vee \varphi) \,|\, (\varphi \rightarrow \varphi) \,|\, K_a\varphi$. Here p is an atomic proposition and K_a is a knowledge operator. For an agent a, $K_a\varphi$ is interpreted as "agent a knows φ".

Figure 1(left) shows an example where the knowledge of an agent a is represented diagrammatically. The example illustrates a scope **A** of agent a consisting of two states a_0 and a_1. These two states are representing two epistemic alternatives of agent a. We use $\text{KB}(a_0)$ and $\text{KB}(a_1)$ to refer to the knowledge bases of states a_0 and a_1, respectively. In scope **A**, agent a knows that it is cloudy (represented by the ground atom c) and rain implies cloudy (represented by horn clause: $r \rightarrow c$), but agent a does not know if it is raining or not. Therefore, he cannot distinguish between states a_0 and a_1 where $r \in \text{KB}(a_0)$ and $r \notin \text{KB}(a_1)$ (i.e., uncertain about r). What agent a knows about agent b's epistemic alternatives are represented in the internal scope **B**. The internal scope **B** represents the information state of agent b where agent b knows that it is windy (represented by the ground atom w) but he cannot distinguish between b_0 and b_1 where $c \in \text{KB}(b_0), r \in \text{KB}(b_0)$ and $c \notin \text{KB}(b_1), r \notin \text{KB}(b_1)$. Figure 1(right) illustrates this model with hierarchically structured information. Distinguished clauses that are true only in a particular state are represented inside the rectangular box representing the state. Horn clauses that are commonly known among all the agents are represented in a global knowledge base Θ. Horn clauses that are commonly known among all the states in a scope are visualized in a local knowledge base (e.g., Γ_A, Γ_B in Fig. 1). For brevity we will not display all the logical consequences inside the boxes. Note that local knowledge bases implicitly include the global knowledge base. Therefore in Fig. 1(right), $\Gamma_A^* = \text{Cn}(\{r \rightarrow c, c\})$ and $\Gamma_B^* = \text{Cn}(\{r \rightarrow c, w\})$. We apply a pullback operation for extracting the local and global knowledge bases of agents which is a very common construction in category theory [1]. Below we formalize the notion of local and global knowledge base of agents. In order to apply category theory, we need to constitute a category for *knowledge base* where the objects are sets of horn clauses and morphisms are given by the inclusion mapping of horn clauses.

Definition 1 (Inclusion mapping of horn clauses). *Let Φ and Ψ be two sets of horn clauses. An inclusion mapping $f : \Phi \rightarrow \Psi$ exists if $\forall \varphi \in \Phi$, $\Psi \vdash \varphi$.*

Definition 2 (Local knowledge base). *Let s_0, s_1, ...s_n be states of agent a in scope A_1 and $\Phi_0 = KB(s_0)$, $\Phi_1 = KB(s_1)$,... knowledge bases comprised of horn clauses. The local knowledge base Γ_{A_1} of scope A_1 is the information commonly known by agent a in scope A_1 and is obtained by the limit of the inclusion mappings $\Phi_0 \to \Phi_C, \Phi_1 \to \Phi_C, ... \Phi_m \to \Phi_C$ where Φ_C is the combined knowledge base of $\Phi_0, \Phi_1, ... \Phi_m$.*

Definition 3 (Global knowledge base). *Let $\Gamma_{A_1}, \Gamma_{A_2}, ... \Gamma_{An}$ be the local knowledge bases of scopes $A_1, A_2, ... A_n$. The global knowledge base Θ is the information commonly known in scopes $A_1, A_2, ... A_n$ and is obtained by the limit of the inclusion mappings $\Gamma_{A_1} \to \Gamma_C, \Gamma_{A_2} \to \Gamma_C, ... \Gamma_{A_n} \to \Gamma_C$ where Γ_C is the combined knowledge base of all the local knowledge bases.*

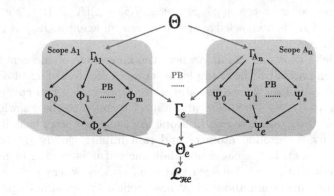

Fig. 2. Local and global knowledge base

Figure 2 shows the knowledge bases of different agents and their local and global knowledge bases. All the arrows in the figure represent inclusion mappings of horn clauses.

Theorem 1. *The limit of a set of inclusion mappings of horn clauses $\{\Phi_0 \to \Psi, \Phi_1 \to \Psi, ... \Phi_m \to \Psi\}$ is a consistent knowledge base if at least one of $\Phi_0, \Phi_1, ... \Phi_m$ are consistent.*

Proof: Let Γ be the limit of the inclusion mappings and $\Phi_i (0 \leq i \leq m)$ be a consistent knowledge base. Since $\forall \gamma \in \Gamma$, $\Phi_i \vdash \gamma$, it is not possible that Γ is an inconsistent knowledge base while Φ_i is a consistent knowledge base.   □

In Fig. 2 the colimit Θ_C represents the combined knowledge base of all the agents and the colimit Γ_C represents the distributed knowledge of a set of agents. There exists an inclusion mapping from Θ_C to the language $\mathcal{L}_{\mathcal{HC}}$. It is possible that the colimits might be inconsistent. However, a consistent Γ_C supports collaboration of the agents' knowledge.

3   Metamodelling with DPF

We use Diagrammatic Logic [4] and the Diagram Predicate Framework (DPF) [11] for the formal development of metamodel specifications. A metamodel specifies the abstract syntax of a modelling language that often includes a set of modelling concepts, their attributes and their relationships, as well as the rules for combining these concepts to specify valid models. In the context of this paper we develop a metamodel for hierarchical representation of agents' knowledge. In DPF, a (meta)model is represented by a diagrammatic specification $\mathfrak{S} = (S, C^{\mathfrak{S}} : \Sigma)$ consisting of an underlying graph S together with a set of *atomic constraints* $C^{\mathfrak{S}}$ specified by a *predicate signature* Σ. A predicate is used to specify constraints in a model by means of graph homomorphisms. DPF provides a formalization of multi-level metamodelling by defining the conformance relation between models at adjacent levels of a metamodelling hierarchy [10].

The graph in Fig. 3(b) represents the specification of a multi-agent model $\mathfrak{S}_1 = (S_1, C^{\mathfrak{S}_1} : \Sigma)$. Constraints are added into the structure by predicates. Figure 3(a) shows the predicates used for constraining the model $\mathfrak{S}_1$. Each predicate has a name p, a shape graph (arity) $\alpha(p)$, a visualization, and a semantic interpretation. For instance, the intended semantics of $<mult(n,m)>$ is that for each instance of X, f must have at least n and at most m instances. The predicates are constraining the model $\mathfrak{S}_1$ by means of a graph homomorphism $\delta : \alpha(p) \to S_1$ from the arity of the predicate p to the graph of the model $\mathfrak{S}_1$. The model $\mathfrak{S}_1$ specifies that an agent may have a scope consisting of a number of states. An agent's scope may have internal scopes of other agents. An instance (I, ι) of $\mathfrak{S}_1$ is shown (represented in abstract syntax) in Fig. 3(c). The instance (I, ι) of $\mathfrak{S}_1$ is given by a graph I together with a typing graph homomorphism $\iota : I \to S_1$ that satisfies the constraints $C^{\mathfrak{S}_1}$. The diagram shown earlier in Fig. 1 is the concrete syntax of this instance. The semantics of the predicates are provided in a fibred manner [4]. That is, the semantics of a predicate p is given by the set of its instances. The multiplicity predicate $<mult(n,m)>$ is used to add an atomic constraint on edge 'contains' in Fig. 3. This atomic constraint specifies that every Scope instance must contain at least one State instance. The irreflexive predicate $<irreflexive>$ is used to add an atomic constraint on edge 'internal'. The atomic constraint specifies that a Scope instance cannot have reflexive reference of type 'internal'.

We use the concept of a single 'State' in the multi-agent model to represent the condition of an agent and use the word 'information state' to represent an instance of a multi-agent model. An instance of an agent's state is valid if the associated knowledge base is consistent. Let (M, ι) be a multi-agent model instance consisting of a set of agents $\mathcal{A}$ (instances of Agent) and $\Phi = \text{KB}(s_a)$ be a set of horn clauses representing the knowledge base of a state s_a in scope $\mathbf{A}$ of an agent $a \in \mathcal{A}$. The state s_a is consistent or satisfiable if $\Phi \nvdash \bot$. We define that a propositional logic formula φ is true in s_a, written as $(M, \iota), s_a \models \varphi$, as follows:

$(M, \iota), s_a \models p$ iff $p \in \Phi^*$ (Φ^* is the set of all logical consequences of Φ)
$(M, \iota), s_a \models \neg p$ iff $p \notin \Phi^*$

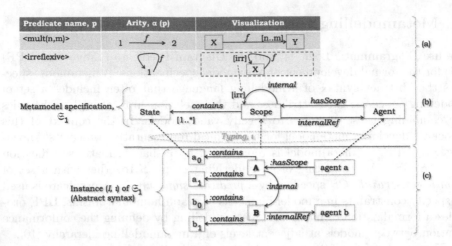

Fig. 3. A DPF specification $\mathfrak{S}_1$ for multi-agent model

$(M, \iota), s_a \models (\varphi \wedge \psi)$ iff $(M, \iota), s \models \varphi$ and $(M, \iota), s \models \psi$
$(M, \iota), s_a \models (\varphi \vee \psi)$ iff $(M, \iota), s \models \varphi$ or $(M, \iota), s \models \psi$

Let us consider that a scope **A** contains a set of states, **S**. Any formula φ generated by the language of epistemic logic $\mathcal{L}_k$ is true in scope **A** (written as $(M, \iota), \mathbf{A} \models \varphi$) or in a state $s_a \in \mathbf{S}$ (also written as $(M, \iota), s_a \models \varphi$) as defined below:

$(M, \iota), \mathbf{A} \models p$ iff $\forall s \in \mathbf{S}$ $(M, \iota), s \models p$
$(M, \iota), \mathbf{A} \models \neg p$ iff $\exists s \in \mathbf{S}$ $(M, \iota), s \not\models p$
$(M, \iota), \mathbf{A} \models (\varphi \wedge \psi)$ iff $\forall s \in \mathbf{S}$ $(M, \iota), s \models \varphi$ and $(M, \iota), s \models \psi$
$(M, \iota), \mathbf{A} \models (\varphi \vee \psi)$ iff $\forall s \in \mathbf{S}$ $(M, \iota), s \models \varphi$ or $(M, \iota), s \models \psi$
$(M, \iota), \mathbf{A} \models K_a\varphi$ iff $\forall s \in \mathbf{S}$ $(M, \iota), s \models \varphi$
$(M, \iota), \mathbf{A} \models K_b\varphi$ $(b \in \mathcal{A} \wedge b \neq a)$ iff $(M, \iota), \mathbf{B} \models \varphi$ where agent b's scope **B** is an internal scope of **A**
$(M, \iota), s_a \models K_a\varphi$ iff $(M, \iota), \mathbf{A} \models K_a\varphi$
$(M, \iota), s_a \models K_b\varphi$ $(b \in \mathcal{A} \wedge b \neq a)$ iff $(M, \iota), \mathbf{A} \models K_b\varphi$

An instance of a multi-agent model (i.e., an information state of an agent) is valid if it satisfies all the domain constraints specified in the DPF specification and contains only valid states for agents.

4   Message Passing Communication

We envision a system where agents collaborate with each other by exchanging messages which include epistemic information. These messages are used to update the knowledge bases of agents and their information states. The agents have their own knowledge base, and in addition they are aware of other agents' knowledge bases.

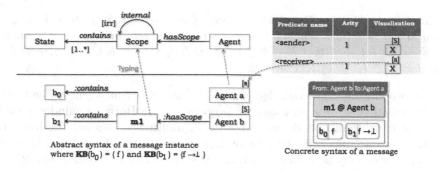

Fig. 4. Predicates for annotating message instance

A message is an instance of the multi-agent model where the agents are anno-tated with [S] and [R] (<sender> and <receiver> predicates). Figure 4 shows the predicates and the abstract and concrete syntax of a message. A message contains a scope of an agent with a set of states. The states have an associated knowledge base which contains a set of propositional horn clauses. An incom-ing message from the sender agent is used to update the internal scope of the receiver agent. Two kinds of update operations are performed in order to update the internal scope of the receiver agent: (i) product of states (in the category of sets), and (ii) knowledge base revision. The product operation deals with the higher order information and the revision operation updates the knowledge base of states. Figure 5 illustrates an agent b sending a message to agent a. Agent b informs agent a that he does not know if it is foggy (represented by f) or not. The figure shows the effect of an update operation where a product is formed to update the information states of the internal scope **B**. After performing the product operation, the knowledge base of the states are revised based on the knowledge base from the message.

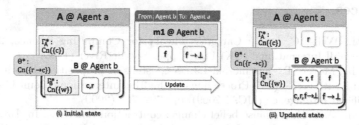

Fig. 5. Example effect of an update

We consider Delgrande's inconsistency based contraction [3] for knowledge base revision. The purpose of this type of revision is to modify the knowledge base in such a way that adding new horn clauses from the message does not result in an inconsistent knowledge base. While modifying the knowledge base we want to retain as much as possible from the old knowledge base. We use Delgrande's definition of i-reminder set for the horn language:

Definition 4 (Horn i-Reminder Sets). *Given a knowledge base Φ in $\mathcal{L}_{\mathcal{HC}}$ and a set of new horn clauses Ψ, Horn i-reminder sets of Φ w.r.t. Ψ, written $\Phi \downarrow_i \Psi$ is the set such that $K \in \Phi \downarrow_i \Psi$ iff (i) $K \subseteq \Phi$, (ii) $K \cup \Psi \nvdash \bot$, (iii) $\nexists K'$ such that $K \subset K' \subseteq \Phi$, $K' \cup \Psi \nvdash \bot$.*

While updating the knowledge base Φ of a state s of an agent a due to the new information Ψ of a message, we propose to use Horn i-reminder sets. If there are more than one element in $\Phi \downarrow_i \Psi$, multiple states are produced by replacing s containing different possibilities of revised knowledge base. However other strategies may be followed to revise Φ such as Horn i-Contraction [2].

5   Conclusion and Future Work

Epistemic logic was first introduced by Hintikka in [7] and later on used by numerous researchers for modelling multi-agent systems where the information state of multi-agent systems are given by Kripke semantics [5,6]. One issue with this approach is that models become very big in size as the number of epistemic alternatives increases. In this paper, we presented a model driven approach where the states are modularized in scopes which clearly represents agents dimension of epistemic alternatives. To extract the local and global knowledge base of agents, we use pullback, limit and colimit operations.

In future, we will investigate reasoning algorithms to rule out uncertainty. Reasoning about uncertainty may play an important role in optimizing resources via strategies. In [9], we introduced a categorical approach for metamodelling epistemic game theory. As part of the future work, we will investigate how game theoretic concepts can be applied in a multi–agent system environment using model driven engineering approaches.

References

1. Barr, M., Wells, C. (eds.): Category Theory for Computing Science, 2nd edn. Prentice Hall International (UK) Ltd., Upper Saddle River (1995)
2. Booth, R., Meyer, T., Varzinczak, I.J.: Next steps in propositional horn contraction. In: Boutilier, C. (ed.) Proceedings of the 21st International Joint Conference on Artificial Intelligence (IJCAI 2009), pp. 702–707 (2009)
3. Delgrande, J.P.: Horn clause belief change: contraction functions. In: Brewka, G., Lang, J. (eds.) Proceedings of the Eleventh International Conference on Principles of Knowledge Representation and Reasoning, KR 2008, pp. 156–165. AAAI Press (2008)
4. Diskin, Z., Wolter, U.: A diagrammatic logic for object-oriented visual modeling. Electron. Notes Theoret. Comput. Sci. **203**(6), 19–41 (2008). Proceedings of the Second Workshop on Applied and Computational Category Theory (ACCAT 2007)
5. Van Ditmarsch, H., van Der Hoek, W., Kooi, B.: Dynamic Epistemic Logic, 1st edn. Springer, Heidelberg (2007)

6. Gerbrandy, J.: Dynamic epistemic logic. In: Logic, Language and Computation, Stanford, CA, USA, vol. 2, pp. 67–84. Center for the Study of Language and Information (1999)
7. Hintikka, J.: Knowledge and Belief: An Introduction to the Logic of the Two Notions. Texts in Philosophy, King's College Publications (2005)
8. Konolige, K.: A deductive model of belief. In: Proceedings of the Eighth International Joint Conference on Artificial Intelligence - Volume 1, IJCAI 1983, San Francisco, CA, USA, pp. 377–381. Morgan Kaufmann Publishers Inc. (1983)
9. Rabbi, F., Lamo, Y., Yu, I.C.: Towards a categorical approach for meta-modelling epistemic game theory. In: Proceedings of the ACM/IEEE 19th International Conference on Model Driven Engineering Languages and Systems, MODELS 2016, pp. 57–64. ACM. New York (2016)
10. Rabbi, F., Lamo, Y., Yu, I.C., Kristensen, L.M.: WebDPF: a web-based metamodelling and model transformation environment. In: MODELSWARD 2016 - Proceedings of the 4th International Conference on Model-Driven Engineering and Software Development, Rome, Italy, 19–21 February 2016, pp. 87–98. SciTePress (2016)
11. Rutle, A.,: Diagram predicate framework: a formal approach to MDE. Ph.D. thesis, Department of Informatics, University of Bergen, Norway (2010)

LightJason
A BDI Framework Inspired by Jason

Malte Aschermann, Philipp Kraus$^{(\boxtimes)}$, and Jörg P. Müller

Department of Informatics, Clausthal University of Technology,
Julius-Albert-Str. 4, 38678 Clausthal-Zellerfeld, Germany
{malte,philipp}@lightjason.org, joerg.mueller@tu-clausthal.de
http://lightjason.org

Abstract. Current BDI agent frameworks often lack necessary modularity, scalability and are hard to integrate with non-agent applications. This paper reports ongoing research on *LightJason*, a multi-agent BDI framework based on *AgentSpeak(L)*, fine-tuned to concurrent plan execution in a distributed framework; *LightJason* aims at efficient and scalable integration with existing platforms. We state requirements for BDI agent languages and corresponding runtime systems, and present the key concepts and initial implementation of *LightJason* in the light of these requirements. Based on a set of requirements derived for scalable, modular BDI frameworks, the core contribution of this paper is the definition of a formal modular grammar for *AgentSpeak(L++)*, a modular extension of *AgentSpeak(L)*, and its underlying scalable runtime system. A preliminary validation of *LightJason* is given by means of an example evacuation scenario, an experimental analysis of the runtime performance, and a qualitative comparison with the Jason platform.

Keywords: Agent programming language · Scalability · Multiagent-based simulation

1 Introduction

Agent-oriented programming (AgOP) [18] is about building systems consisting of *software agents* maintaining mental states, based on declarative logical languages. The Belief-Desire-Intention (BDI) paradigm [16] has become the prevalent approach to AgOP and multi-agent systems (MAS). Such agent programs consist of statements in first-order logic, allowing agents to deduce new facts, commit to plans and eventually execute actions. A very popular language for programming BDI agents is *AgentSpeak(L)* [15]. *Jason* [4] has been instrumental to the popularity of *AgentSpeak(L)* by providing a BDI agent framework that

---

M. Aschermann—Parts of this work were supported by the German Research Foundation (DFG) through the Research Training Group *SocialCars: Cooperative (De-) centralized Traffic Management (GRK 1931)*.

© Springer International Publishing AG 2017
N. Criado Pacheco et al. (Eds.): EUMAS 2016/AT 2016, LNAI 10207, pp. 58–66, 2017.
DOI: 10.1007/978-3-319-59294-7_6

combines an extension of *AgentSpeak(L)* with an interpreter and provides integrated development environment (IDE) plugins for JEdit and Eclipse. However, analysing the level of usage of BDI agent frameworks in software engineering practice reveals a sobering picture. A look at the major programming indices Tiobe [20], Redmonk [17] and PopularitY [13], which measure the popularity of programming languages, shows that the world of practice is still dominated by imperative and object-oriented languages. Only Tiobe lists any logic-based languages: The major proponent *Prolog* is ranked 33rd. AgOP languages are not represented at all. Furthermore, in their study of MAS application impact, [12] show that among the agent languages, the only 'true' BDI language with some application impact is Jack, a proprietary language, while the use of languages like *Jason* or *GOAL* is restricted to academic prototypes. The hypothesis underlying our research is that part of the reasons for this dire state are elementary shortcomings of AgOP languages regarding modularity, maintainability, software architecture interoperability, performance, and scalability. This paper reports ongoing research on a multi-agent framework based on *AgentSpeak(L)* which aims at an efficient and scalable integration into existing platforms, enabling non-agent-aware systems to incorporate agent-based optimisation techniques to solve distributed problems. We present the initial version of *LightJason*, a BDI agent framework fine-tuned to concurrent plan execution in a distributed environment.[1]

2   Requirements and State of the Art

Requirements. Over the past years, we have gained experience in modelling and engineering multi-agent applications based on the BDI paradigm (most notably in domains of traffic and industrial business processes), but also with developing agent programming languages and runtime platforms. While we consider the BDI abstraction appealing and intuitive for modelling sociotechnical systems, we were often confronted with the limitations of today's agent platforms. From these limitations, we derived a number of requirements for BDI agent platforms, which extend the list of general requirements from [4, p. 7]) and are summarised as follows: (1) Integrability in existing software architectures. (2) Modularisation of agents and underlying data structures. (3) Agent scripting language with strict language syntax. (4) Action checking during parsing time, not during run time. (5) Avoid *action-centric* reasoning cycle as argued by [1]. (6) Parallel execution of plans in separated execution tasks. (7) Agent generation mechanism for easy instantiation of large numbers of agent. (8) Hierarchically structured belief bases and actions in semantic groups.

Discussion of State of the Art. The main concepts of BDI frameworks are mostly based on the Procedural Reasoning System (PRS) [7,8] and the first robust implementations such as dMARS [6]. As [10] and subsequent surveys

---

[1] For a much more comprehensive version of this short paper, we refer to [2].

point out, virtually all existing multi-agent frameworks are not designed for productive use (performance, scalability) and easy integration with specific domains. The design of agent-based scripting languages leads to challenges in maintainability; e.g. Bordini et al. [3, p. 1300] state that: *"[T]he AgentSpeak(L) code is not elegant at all. The resulting code is extremely clumsy because of the use of many belief addition, deletion, and checking (for controlling intention selection) [...] [and] thus a type of code that is very difficult to implement and maintain."* Though this is a paper from 2002, the situation has not changed much. MAS platforms like *Jason* provide a separate runtime system, these approaches raise issues regarding scalability and consistency, especially when combining existing systems with MAS. In the case of *Jason*, this also can lead to ill-defined execution behaviour of agents, especially regarding clarity when an iteration of the agent control cycle has ended (see requirement 2 above).

In this paper, we focus on the comparison with *AgentSpeak(L)/Jason* as the most prominent (open-source) representative of BDI languages/platform. We compared the legacy *Jason* 1.4 branch, which is still in use in our research group for small-scale agent-based traffic simulation (e.g. [5]), and the quite recently published *Jason* 2.0 branch with our requirements. *Jason* 1.4 lacks support for all the above-mentioned requirements except a partially support for modular agents (requirement 2), due to its `include` functionality. *Jason* 2.0 additionally supports a hierarchical structuring of agents (requirement 2), but this feature is limited to beliefs and plans[2]. Also, one new feature of *Jason* 2.0 is parallel execution of plans [22], which addresses requirement 2. However, like *Jason* 1.4, *Jason* 2.0 still heavily relies on synchronised data structures in their architecture design, implying slow-downs due to locking and CPU context switches during each agent cycle. In their approach adding concurrency to the reasoning cycles in *Jason*, [22] provided benchmark results regarding scalability; their test setup with only two CPU cores and synthetic benchmarks (e.g. nested for-loops and Fibonacci sequence) resulted in a linear increase in execution time for up to 500 agents, which would also be expected for single-thread applications.

In order to tackle the above requirements, we start from the architecture design of Multi-Agent Scalable Runtime platform for Simulation (MASeRaTi) [1], as an attempt to tackle the scalability issues in modern MAS. We created a modified, light version of *AgentSpeak(L)* (named *AgentSpeak(L++)*) and build a Java-based implementation of the MASeRaTi architecture.

3 *LightJason* Architecture and Data Model

There is broad agreement in the AgOP literature that *"[a] multi-agent system is inherently multithreaded, in that each agent is assumed to have at least one thread of control [21, p. 30]"* meaning that agents should be able to pursue more than one objective at the same time. To implement this conceptual notion of concurrency at the technical level, we refer to the basic notion of a thread [19] as a *"lightweight process"*, and that all threads are running within the same process.

---

[2] https://git.io/vXqup.

Thus, in *LightJason*, an agent is be controlled by a thread during the reasoning process and stores all data for the reasoning internally, by following the thread-local-storage model. Our general approach in *LightJason* is to conceive *AgOP* as a combination of *Imperative, Object-Oriented* and *Logic Programming*, see [2, p. 6]. To get into a more detailed view, an agent is not one single software component but it is split up into two different elements, i.e. *agent-mind* and *agent-body*. This approach is a reverence to the Mind-Head-Body model proposed by Steiner in [9]. The symbolic representation of an agent's mind is stored as *logic literals*, as in *Prolog* or *AgentSpeak(L)*. All literals of *LightJason*'s agents are stored within a belief base for getting access during runtime. During execution the agent asks for particular literals, initiating a *unification* process. As this process is run many times, we optimised the internal data structure representing the logic elements for parallel execution and avoiding cost-intensive back-tracking. The *Imperative Programming* paradigm is used to describe the execution behaviour of agents in *LightJason* (similar to the Patterns of Behaviour (PoBs) in the INTERRAP architecture [11]). In contrast, to INTERRAP, we provide for parallel execution of PoBs, so that actions, assignments or expressions can be run or evaluated in parallel. Finally, *LightJason* is Java-based; the internal representation of agents is written in an Object-Oriented Programming (OOP) style with *concurrent data structures*, allowing us to create inheritable agent objects running in a multithreading context and easier integration with domain-specific software systems. To further parallelise execution and gain more scalability, we made extensive use of state-of-the-art Java techniques, such as lambda-expressions[3] and streams[4].

4 *AgentSpeak(L++)* Language Definition

We regard an agent as a hybrid system, which combines different programming language paradigms, allowing programmers to describe complex behaviour. This abstract point of view allows a flexible structure – also for non-computer scientists – to parameterise or specify a software system. The whole syntax was designed as a *logic programming language*, by which all elements could be reduced to *terms*[5] and *literals*[6], defining a symbolic representation of behaviour and (environment) data. This allows modelling a generalised multi-agent system, which can later be concretised for different applications, i.e. scenarios and supports the agent programmer to design the behaviour by scripting beliefs, rules, plans and actions. Our first contribution is the definition of a *scripting language* based on a modified and extended *AgentSpeak(L)* grammar. We modularised the grammar into subgrammars to obtain a more abstract structure of the agent programming language. The main grammar definition of *LightJason* is hierarchically structured into the modules depicted in Fig. 1 and is explained in

---

[3] http://www.webcitation.org/6lfbGeOlc.
[4] http://www.webcitation.org/6lfbNP7nX.
[5] Term: https://git.io/viKWQ, EBNF: https://git.io/viKWx.
[6] Literal: https://git.io/viKlt, EBNF: https://git.io/viKll.

Fig. 1. Modular grammar structure

detail in [2, p. 7ff.]. This allowed us to get a more flexible parsing component, which could be split up into a layer-based structure.

Built-in Actions. The language structure and the underlying architecture of our implementation allows to create a flexible action interface. In comparison to *Jason*, we can detect the agent is running, if the agent source code is syntactically correct and all actions can be executed. If the action does not exist, the parsing process will fail. The built-in actions are organised in packages. In our framework we support actions related to various types of computation. For a complete overview of these actions and how they can be implemented, we refer to [2, p. 14] and our unit test agent `complete.asl`[7], published in the appendix of [2].

5   Evaluation and Discussion

Evacuation Scenario. In this section we illustrate the capabilities of *Light-Jason* on a grid-based evacuation scenario, where agents needed to reach an exit to leave the grid. The *AgentSpeak(L++)* code for the corresponding walking agent is displayed in the listing below. For finding a route to the exit the agent used the *Jump Point Search (JPS+) with Goal Bounding* [14] algorithm, which, after an initial $O(n^2)$ preprocessing of the grid, outperforms A^* by two to three orders of magnitude in speed. To demonstrate the clarity of *LightJason*'s grammar, we grouped all *plans* and respectively *actions* describing a `moving` behaviour, e.g.

```
+!movement/walk/forward <-        +!movement/walk/right <-
   move/forward();                    move/right();
   !movement/walk/forward.            !movement/walk/forward.
```

The concrete agent with its source code is available in [2].

Preliminary Validation. To validate our results, we conducted first tests with *LightJason* implementation of the evacuation scenario. The goal was to investigate whether the design and implementation of *LightJason* leads to good scalability and cycle consistency regarding the routing model, and number of concurrent running agents. We chose a grid-based scenario with 250×250 cells on an iMac with an Intel® Core™ i7-3770 and 16 GB RAM. Each agent received the same

---

[7] https://git.io/vi67u.

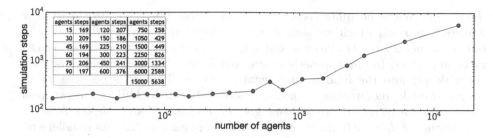

agents	steps	agents	steps	agents	steps
15	169	120	207	750	258
30	209	150	186	1050	429
45	169	225	210	1500	449
60	194	300	223	2250	826
75	206	450	241	3000	1334
90	197	600	376	6000	2588
				15000	5638

Fig. 2. Number of agents plotted against cycles until all agents left the scenario.

exit destination $(140, 140)$; it disappeared once it reached the approximate destination (± 10 cells). Figure 2 illustrates the run-time behaviour of the agents. It (not surprisingly) shows that with an increasing number of agents, each agent needs more cycles to complete its task. This can be attributed to additional invocations of repair plans when an agent's path got obstructed by other agents. This scales sub-linearly up to roughly 1000 agents. After that point, the mainly egoistic approach of each agent prevents them to find a free path to the exit, resulting in plan-failures and necessary re-routing. From a technical perspective we also observed that the CPU utilisation is constantly at around 70% for 15000 agents (for detailed plots we refer to [2]). The constant CPU load shows that the workload induced by agents is distributed fairly and evenly, avoiding spikes and idle times. Furthermore we observed a low utilisation of the JVM's *survivor space* (roughly 3.5 MB after the initialisation spike), reflecting the design in relying on *lazy bindings* and *LightJason*'s ability to share references to concurrently used data structures, e.g. plans, which only differ in their context and parameters.

Discussion. In this paper we presented our design and implementation of an agent framework, introducing *LightJason*, an *AgentSpeak(L)* variant. The key aspects we focused on were modularity, flexibility, scalability and deterministic execution behaviour. The *AgentSpeak(L++)* language supported by *LightJason* reflects *AgentSpeak(L)* as implemented by [4], we differ on a number of aspects, in terms of the language features and – to a larger extent – in the software architecture underlying the implementation. Among others the most notable additions to *AgentSpeak(L)* are lambda-expressions, multi-plan definitions, explicit repair-planning, multi-variable assignments, parallel execution and thread-safe variables. When considering to port an existing *Jason* code to *LightJason* it is important to understand, that by design in *LightJason* all plans which conditions evaluate to *true* get instantiated. Here we argue, that in comparison to *Jason*, a non-synchronised system's behaviour results in a considerably more plausible multi-agent system, considering the requirements formulated by [21].

Additional Features. Most of the *AgentSpeak(L)* expressions find their equivalents in *LightJason*'s *AgentSpeak(L++)*. Major additions are expressions for parallel execution and unification (@). As it is in general possible to design an agent to run plans sequentially, we argue, that for performance reasons it is sensible to make use of parallel execution whenever possible.

Jason 2.0. With the quite recent release of *Jason* 2.0, there now exist new features[8] in *Jason* which are similar, but independently developed, to some of our own. *Jason* 2.0 introduces *modules and namespaces* to modularise beliefs, goals and plans. In our approach we go even further by integrating those concepts deeply into the fundamental agent grammar. Thus it is possible for us to, for example, modularise actions, functions or beliefs by building hierarchical structures in arbitrary depth allowing greater flexibility than in *Jason*. Another new feature of *Jason* 2.0 are *concurrent courses of actions* [22]. As parallel execution is a fundamental aspect of scalability, we made this an integral part of *LightJason*'s architecture by mainly using state-of-the-art Java 1.8 developing techniques and features to enable concurrency at a very fine granularity.

6 Conclusion and Outlook

The contribution of this paper is a flexible agent programming framework *Light-Jason*, which can be easily integrated into existing systems. The key features of *LightJason* are the simplification of the agent's reasoning cycle and the support of some important requirements including modularity, maintainability, and scalability, combined with state-of-the-art techniques in software development. At the core of *LightJason* is *AgentSpeak(L++)*, a declarative agent scripting language extending *Jason*. We provide a formal grammar definition describing the features of *AgentSpeak(L++)*. For the sake of usability, *LightJason* supports many built-in actions and a structure to load actions in a pre-processing step of the parser. Thus, by parsing the agent's source code it is possible to check that the agent is syntactically correct and can be executed. We further provide generator structures that enable automated creation of large numbers of agents which can be further customised by the user. We also support a fully concurrent and parallel agent execution model of an agent. This paper describes ongoing work. Our next steps will involve a formal definition of the semantics of *AgentSpeak(L++)*. The reader will have noticed that *AgentSpeak(L++)* does not contain language elements for communication. This is intentional, because in our view, communication is a matter of the runtime system rather than of the compilation mechanism. Yet, agent communication is one of the next features to be added to *LightJason*. Also, while we performed an initial qualitative comparison with *Jason*, a thorough experimental benchmarking remains to be performed. Our project can be found under http://lightjason.org providing further documentation[9] and source code[10].

References

1. Ahlbrecht, T., Dix, J., Köster, M., Kraus, P., Müller, J.P.: An architecture for scalable simulation of systems of cognitive agents. Int. J. Agent-Oriented Softw. Eng. 5(2–3), 232–265 (2016)

[8] https://git.io/vXmeK.
[9] http://lightjason.github.io/AgentSpeak/index.html.
[10] https://github.com/LightJason/AgentSpeak.

2. Aschermann, M., Kraus, P., Müller, J.P.: LightJason: a BDI framework inspired by Jason. IfI Technical Report Series IfI-16-04, Department of Informatics, Clausthal University of Technology (2016)
3. Bordini, R.H., Bazzan, A.L., de O Jannone, R., Basso, D.M., Vicari, R.M., Lesser, V.R.: AgentSpeak(XL): efficient intention selection in BDI agents via decision-theoretic task scheduling. In: Proceedings of the 1st International Joint Conference on Autonomous Agents and Multiagent Systems: Part 3, pp. 1294–1302. ACM (2002)
4. Bordini, R.H., Hübner, J.F., Wooldridge, M.: Programming Multi-agent Systems in AgentSpeak Using Jason. Wiley, Hoboken (2007)
5. Dennisen, S., Müller, J.P.: Iterative committee elections for collective decision-making in a ride-sharing application. In: Bazzan, A.L.C., Klügl, F., Ossowski, S., Vizzari, G. (eds.) Proceedings of the 9th International Workshop on Agents in Traffic and Transport (ATT 2016) at IJCAI 2016, pp. 1–8. CEUR, New York, USA, July 2016. Electronic proceedings
6. d'Inverno, M., Luck, M., Georgeff, M., Kinny, D., Wooldridge, M.: The dMARS architecture: a specification of the distributed multi-agent reasoning system. Auton. Agents Multi-agent Syst. 9(1/2), 5–53 (2004)
7. Georgeff, M.P., Lansky, A.L.: Reactive reasoning and planning. In: Proceedings of the 6th National Conference on Artificial Intelligence, AAAI 1987, vol. 2, pp. 677–682. AAAI Press (1987)
8. Georgeff, M., Lansky, A.: Procedural knowledge. Proc. IEEE 74(10), 1383–1398 (1986)
9. Lux, A., Steiner, D.: Understanding cooperation: an agent's perspective. In: ICMAS, pp. 261 268 (1995)
10. Mascardi, V., Demergasso, D., Ancona, D.: Languages for programming BDI-style agents: an overview. In: WOA, pp. 9–15 (2005)
11. Müller, J.P.: The Design of Intelligent Agents. LNAI, vol. 1177. Springer, Heidelberg (1996)
12. Müller, J.P., Fischer, K.: Application impact of multi-agent systems and technologies: a survey. In: Shehory, O., Sturm, A. (eds.) Agent-Oriented Software Engineering: Reflections on Architectures, Methodologies, Languages, and Frameworks, pp. 27–53. Springer, Heidelberg (2014)
13. PopularitY: http://pypl.github.io/. Accessed 27 June 2016 (archived by WebCite® at http://www.webcitation.org/6iZxjsbBs)
14. Rabin, S., Sturtevant, N.: Combining bounding boxes and JPS to prune grid pathfinding. In: AAAI Conference on Artificial Intelligence (2016)
15. Rao, A.S.: AgentSpeak(L): BDI agents speak out in a logical computable language. In: Velde, W., Perram, J.W. (eds.) MAAMAW 1996. LNCS, vol. 1038, pp. 42–55. Springer, Heidelberg (1996). doi:10.1007/BFb0031845. http://dl.acm.org/citation.cfm?id=237945.237953
16. Rao, A.S., Georgeff, M.P.: BDI agents: from theory to practice. In: Proceedings of the 1st International Conference on Multi-agent Systems, 12–14 June 1995, pp. 312–319, San Francisco, California, USA (1995)
17. RedMonk: http://redmonk.com/sogrady/2016/02/19/language-rankings. Accessed 27 June 2016 (archived by WebCite® at http://www.webcitation.org/6iZxPEb9K)
18. Shoham, Y.: Agent-oriented programming. Artif. Intell. 60(1), 51–92 (1993)
19. Tanenbaum, A., Bos, H.: Modern Operating Systems: Global Edition. Pearson Education Limited, London (2015)

20. TIOBE: http://www.tiobe.com/tiobe_index. Accessed 27 June 2016 (archived by WebCite® at http://www.webcitation.org/6iZwpVq0y)
21. Wooldridge, M.J.: An Introduction to Multiagent Systems. Wiley, Hoboken (2009)
22. Zatelli, M.R., Ricci, A., Hübner, J.F.: A concurrent architecture for agent reasoning cycle execution in jason. In: Rovatsos, M., Vouros, G., Julian, V. (eds.) EUMAS/AT-2015. LNCS (LNAI), vol. 9571, pp. 425–440. Springer, Cham (2016). doi:10.1007/978-3-319-33509-4_33

Paffin: Implementing an Integration of Agents and Workflows

Thomas Wagner, Dennis Schmitz$^{(\boxtimes)}$, and Daniel Moldt

Department of Informatics, Faculty of Mathematics,
Informatics and Natural Sciences, University of Hamburg, Hamburg, Germany
wagner@informatik.uni-hamburg.de
http://www.informatik.uni-hamburg.de/TGI/

Abstract. Modelling with agents focusses on the structure of a software system, while modelling with workflows focusses on the behaviour. Our research aims to combine and integrate the strengths of each of these concepts in a unified modelling approach. This current paper presents a technical implementation and proof-of-concept of that approach in the so-called PAFFIN (PROCESSES AND AGENTS FOR A FULL INTEGRATION) system. An application scenario is also discussed.

Keywords: Agents · Workflows · Modelling · Integration · High-level Petri nets

1 Introduction

Agents, as autonomous components of a software system, emphasise the structure of the system. Workflows, though, are processes, which emphasise the behaviour of a system. The strengths of each concept lie in the ability to easily model and represent the focussed aspect, even in large and complex scenarios.

In previous work [14,17] we presented a conceptual approach of how to combine and integrate agents and workflows. The goal of that approach is to provide and unify the strengths of **both** agents and workflows. The approach does not assume the main modelling abstraction to be either exclusively agent or workflow, but instead considers an entity. That entity can, at run- and modelling-time, dynamically act and be interacted with as agent, workflow, both or something in between. This current paper now presents the actual, technical implementation and proof-of-concept of the approach, the PAFFIN system, as well as an application of it to our software engineering teaching project.

The paper is structured in the following way. Section 2 shortly describes the concepts, before Sects. 3 and 4 present the PAFFIN system and its application respectively. Section 5 discusses the results and Sect. 6 concludes the paper.

2 The Agent Activity

Agents represent a system as a structural abstraction of components. Workflows, on the other hand, represent a system as a behavioural abstraction of

© Springer International Publishing AG 2017
N. Criado Pacheco et al. (Eds.): EUMAS 2016/AT 2016, LNAI 10207, pp. 67–75, 2017.
DOI: 10.1007/978-3-319-59294-7_7

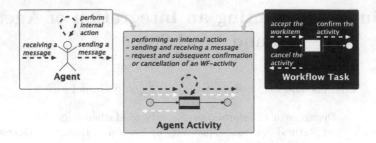

Fig. 1. AGENT ACTIVITY concept. (modified from [17])

processes[1]. Together, structure through agents and behaviour through workflows capture the essential and primary aspects of any software system.

The conceptual approach to integrate and combine these aspects considers the most basic level. Agent actions can be classified as either send message, receive message or execute some internal action. These are the *fundamental agent actions*. Workflows consist of tasks. Workitems[2] can be requested by a resource, which then confirms or cancels the associated activity. These are the *basic workflow operations*. Fundamental agent actions describe what agents can do and basic workflow operations describe what can happen in a workflow. In order to create something that is both agent and workflow, that something needs to be able to execute both. The AGENT ACTIVITY (AGAC) is a modelling abstraction that integrates agent actions and workflow operations.

Conceptually, an AGAC represents an abstract activity consisting of a number of agent actions and workflow operations. The concept is illustrated in Fig. 1. AGACs are conceptually atomic, meaning that they, and all actions and operations within them, are treated as a single management element that either happens fully or not at all. By merging actions and operations into a single construct the AGAC enables the description of an *integrated entity* that can alternate between agent and workflow and also act as a hybrid of both. Examples of possible hybrid behaviour include communicating workflow processes (i.e. processes that communicate to solve problems through data exchange or negotiation), task-based interactions between agents (i.e. agents interacting as engines and resources based on tasks, cf. [18]) and agent-enhanced workflow tasks (i.e. tasks containing complex agent functionality to better facilitate user support). For more details on the AGAC concepts please refer to [17].

3   Processes and Agents for a Full Integration

The PAFFIN system (**P**rocesses and **A**gents **F**or a **F**ull **IN**tegration) is a proof-of-concept for the conceptual approach described above. It implements the AGAC

---

[1] Note that, while traditionally associated with business processes, we consider workflows to represent *any* kind of processes, including those inside a software system.

[2] We use the terminology from [16] to distinguish between task states, i.e. workitems as tasks available for execution and activities as currently executing tasks.

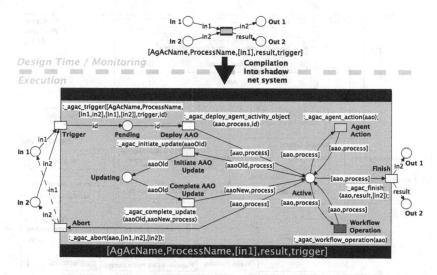

Fig. 2. Compilation of the AGENT ACTIVITY transition.

as a full fledged framework for the creation of integrated agent/workflow applications. The PAFFIN system is implemented with reference Petri nets [11] in RENEW[3]. The majority of the code are Petri nets inscribed with Java.

From a technical point of view, the PAFFIN system is a straightforward extension of the CAPA agent framework (Concurrent Agent Platform Architecture, [8]). The PAFFIN system is currently still actively being developed. In its current form, the prototype already supports the full functionality defined by the AGAC concept. The following describes the implementation of the AGAC and the overall system architecture.

The AGENT ACTIVITY *Transition:* The AGAC is implemented as a standardised Petri net structure. The AGAC net structure represents an AGAC in the behaviour of PAFFIN integrated entities, called process-protocols. Within it, the AGENT ACTIVITY OBJECT (AAO, another reference net) encapsulates the state of an instance of an AGAC, including the internal process of actions and operations. The AGAC net structure implemented in the PAFFIN system is shown, with all technical inscriptions, in the lower part of Fig. 2.

An AGAC models an abstract, singular activity. During modelling a special AGAC transition, shown in the upper part of Fig. 2, is used within the process-protocols. During compilation of the system a custom compiler is used to translate all AGAC transitions into AGAC net structures. Figure 2 illustrates this compilation process. Elements of the inscription tuple on the AGAC transition are parsed onto the net structure transitions for triggering, aborting and finishing the AGAC. During runtime, the system executes the AGAC net structure, while maintaining the singular AGAC transition as representation for monitoring.

---

[3] **Reference Net Workshop.** Available at www.renew.de.

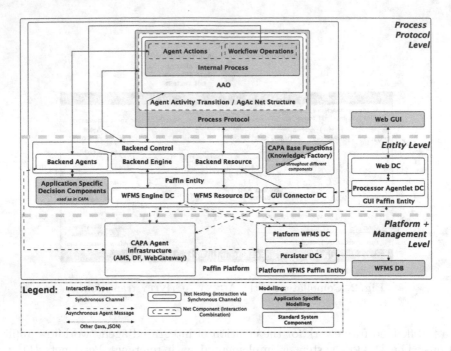

Fig. 3. PAFFIN architecture.

The PAFFIN *Architecture:* The architecture of the PAFFIN system is illustrated in Fig. 3. The figure showcases the different components of the architecture and how they are related to one another.

Process-protocols (topmost level of Fig. 3) and the AGACs contained in them are executed by PAFFIN integrated entities. Each PAFFIN entity contains a technical backend and additional components to facilitate agent and workflow management. CAPA base functionality provides mechanisms of the CAPA agent basis that are adopted without change. These include the knowledge base and (process-)protocol factory. Application specific decision components (DCs) are custom components that describe continuous, proactive entity behaviour. The *WFMS Engine DC* and *WFMS Resource DC* are standardised DCs. They facilitate the connection between the corresponding backends and the management system on the platform level. Finally, the *GUI Connector DC* realises the connection to a graphical user interface (GUI) for a human workflow user. For a clear encapsulation and separation between functionality and GUI, the control of the GUI was moved to a specialised PAFFIN entity.

The platform/management level of the PAFFIN architecture largely adopts the infrastructure for CAPA agents. A special, platform-specific PAFFIN entity is added to that infrastructure, which realises global workflow management aspects. That WFMS PAFFIN entity also controls the database for the platform, which contains additional data for workflow tasks inside AGACs.

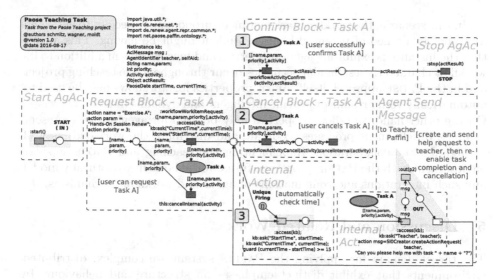

Fig. 4. Example: internal AGAC process for an extended task.

4   Application Example

In previous work [15], the processes of our yearly teaching project have been modelled as workflow Petri nets [16]. The processes serve as a model for the content and the structure of the exercise's descriptions. The results are process-oriented worksheets that explicitly represent the control flow of the teaching processes. These worksheets prepare the students for using the PAOSE methodology (**P**etri net-based, **A**gent-**O**riented **S**oftware **E**ngineering, [5]) to build complex multi-agent systems in the teaching project.

Currently, we are developing a technical environment to execute and support the worksheets, and in future work development with PAOSE itself, in a computer-facilitated way. This environment supports the communication between the teachers and the students. If a student, for example, needs more time than anticipated to solve a task, help from a teacher may be required. In such a situation the workflow instance should notify a teacher.

In Fig. 4 the internal process of an AGAC for a task from the above mentioned situation is shown. If the student needs more time than expected the AGAC automatically asks for help. The AGAC of Fig. 4 starts on the left, followed directly by the request of the workitem. After this point there are three possibilities: (1) The student finishes the activity and confirms it, which correctly terminates the AGAC. (2) The student cancels the activity, which reenables the task as a workitem so it can be requested again. (3) The student exceeds the predefined work time and may require help to solve the activity. This is determined as an internal action through the knowledge of the executing PAFFIN entity. If the working time is in excess, a help request is sent to the teacher.

In this scenario, the workflow task instance autonomously decides to act when a teacher is notified of potential issues a student might be having. This means that the instance is exhibiting agent properties and mechanisms in addition to its workflow characteristics. Similar scenarios occur throughout the teaching project and in the PAOSE approach itself. Agent properties for workflows may be used to automatically verify results or provide intelligent and dynamic hints for exercises. On the other hand, workflow properties may be used for agents that represent complex development processes to divide and distribute the workload, as well as organise the collaboration. Implementing the teaching and PAOSE support environment with the PAFFIN prototype framework allows us to naturally model any such integrations and combinations of agent and workflow mechanisms.

5   Discussion and Related Work

The target domain for applying the PAFFIN system are complex, distributed environments that exhibit distinct emphases on structure and behaviour. In inter-organisational contexts, for example, organisations are both their part (sub-workflow) of the overall inter-organisational workflow, as well as an actor and interaction partner. This duality is perfectly captured by PAFFIN entities executing AGACS. The AGACS executed by the PAFFIN entity model the organisation as an actor (agent actions), a workflow (workflow operations) or as a hybrid (mix of agent actions and workflow operations). The PAFFIN entity can consequently represent itself both as the actor and as the inter-organisational subworkflow.

As mentioned in the previous section, distributed software development, especially with PAOSE [5], is another target domain. PAOSE arranges, designs and implements multi-agent systems according to roles and interactions. This correlates well with an arrangement through structure/agents and behaviour/workflows. Furthermore, PAOSE considers not only the emerging system as a multi-agent system, but the development teams as well. This creates a complex web of relations between actors/roles/agents and processes/interactions/workflows on multiple levels of abstraction. PAFFIN entities are capable of exploiting these relations between structure and behaviour through the use of AGACS.

Generally, the PAFFIN system enables system modellers to explicitly incorporate both structural and behavioural aspects on the same abstraction level when developing a system. This incorporation allows for AGACS to directly and natively model the complex correlations and interdependencies between structure and behaviour. This is a major strength of the AGAC approach and PAFFIN system, which allows them to realise a "full" integration of agents and workflows. A "partial" integration only emphasises either agents or workflows and enhances the chosen concept with properties and mechanisms from the other one (see discussion about related work). A "full" integration, as provided by AGACS and the PAFFIN system, doesn't emphasise one concept over the other, while still providing the capability to exploit any mechanism from either concept wherever it is best suited. Beyond that, the "full" integration also makes combinations of these mechanisms available, as illustrated in the previous section.

Overall, AGACS and the PAFFIN system are quite expressive and powerful. Still, first evaluations have shown that this expressiveness and power are difficult to handle and utilise in modelling. Consequently, modelling tool support is a research focus. Currently, the PAFFIN system mostly utilises established tools from CAPA and PAOSE. These tools are specialised for agents. This means that the agent aspects within the PAFFIN system are suitably covered, but some of the AGAC and workflow aspects are not. Improving these tools to better represent and model all aspects within the PAFFIN system is an important focus of future work. Beyond that, the adaption of the PAOSE methodology itself is also being considered and will help to support system modelling by providing suitable practices for integrated agent/workflow development.

Related Work. Agents have often been used to implement and enhance workflows, e.g. in [2,6,10]. [7] provides an extensive survey on this topic. Using workflows to implement and enhance agents is more rare but can be found in e.g. [9,12,13]. These combinations utilise properties from agents or workflows to enhance and improve the other concept. This represents only a "partial" integration (see above), as modellers are still provided with only *one* of the concepts. The AGAC approach provides modellers with the abilities to use both agents and workflows as equal, fully integrated modelling abstractions.

There is some research that exhibits a larger degree of integration. Jadex Active Components [3] combine agents, active objects and components into a novel modelling abstraction. Active components can implement workflows while maintaining agent mechanisms, but do not offer the same kind of modelling flexibility as AGACS w.r.t. the dynamic integration in the same modelling artefact.

Another approach providing a larger degree of integration is the WADE platform [1], on which agents can execute workflow tasks. Similarly, [4] utilises BDI agents and mental concepts to emphasise process flexibility. These works rely heavily on agents and their properties, but still emphasise workflow modelling.

6 Conclusion

This paper presented the PAFFIN system. The PAFFIN system is a technical implementation and proof-of-concept of the conceptual AGENT ACTIVITY approach. AGENT ACTIVITIES allow the modelling of hybrid entities, which can act and be interacted with as agent, workflow, both or something in between.

Ongoing work focusses on modelling support. For example, the employment of meta-modelling techniques can simplify modelling of AGACS. Suitable meta-concepts could conceal low-level technical details of Petri nets modelling. The teaching project support system mentioned in Sect. 4 is one application focus for future work. Beyond that, the system is set to be extended to fully support distributed software development in PAOSE.

In conclusion, the PAFFIN system already confirmed that the AGENT ACTIV-ITY could be implemented as envisioned. The applications we are currently building with the framework, will enable us to further evaluate modelling with these integrated hybrid entities.

References

1. Bergenti, F., Caire, G., Gotta, D.: Interactive workflows with WADE. In: IEEE 21st International Workshop on Enabling Technologies: Infrastructure for Collaborative Enterprises (WETICE 2012), pp. 10–15. IEEE (2012)
2. Both, F., Hoogendoorn, M., van der Mee, A., Treur, J., de Vos, M.: An intelligent agent model with awareness of workflow progress. Appl. Intell. **36**(2), 498–510 (2012)
3. Braubach, L., Pokahr, A.: Developing distributed systems with active components and Jadex. Scalable Comput. **13**(2), 100–120 (2012)
4. Burmeister, B., Arnold, M., Copaciu, F., Rimassa, G.: BDI-agents for agile goal-oriented business processes. In: AAMAS 2008, Proceedings: Industrial Track, pp. 37–44. IFAAMAS, Richland (2008)
5. Cabac, L.: Modeling Petri Net-Based Multi-agent Applications. Agent Technology - Theory and Applications, vol. 5. Logos Verlag, Berlin (2010)
6. Czarnul, P., Matuszek, M., Wójcik, M., Zalewski, K.: BeesyBees - efficient and reliable execution of service-based workflow applications for BeesyCluster using distributed agents. In: Proceedings of IMCSIT 2010, pp. 173–180 (2010)
7. Delias, P., Doulamis, A., Matsatsinis, N.: What agents can do in workflow management systems. Artif. Intell. Rev. **35**(2), 155–189 (2011)
8. Duvigneau, M., Moldt, D., Rölke, H.: Concurrent architecture for a multi-agent platform. In: Giunchiglia, F., Odell, J., Weiß, G. (eds.) AOSE 2002. LNCS, vol. 2585, pp. 59–72. Springer, Heidelberg (2003). doi:10.1007/3-540-36540-0_5
9. Ebadi, T., Purvis, M., Purvis, M.K.: A colored petri net model to represent the interactions between a set of cooperative agents. In: Beneventano, D., Despotovic, Z., Guerra, F., Joseph, S., Moro, G., Pinninck, A.P. (eds.) AP2PC 2008-2009. LNCS, vol. 6573, pp. 141–152. Springer, Heidelberg (2012). doi:10.1007/978-3-642-31809-2_13
10. Elhasnaoui, S., Iguer, H., Medromi, H., Moussaid, L.: A multi agent architecture for communication workflow management system integrated within an IT GRC platform using sharing information mode. In: IT4OD 2016, pp. 1–5, March 2016
11. Kummer, O.: Referenznetze. Logos Verlag, Berlin (2002)
12. Mislevics, A., Grundspenkis, J.: Workflow based approach for designing and executing mobile agents. In: Second International Conference on Digital Information Processing and Communications (ICDIPC), pp. 191–203, July 2012
13. Purvis, M., Savarimuthu, S., de Oliveira, M.: Mechanisms for cooperative behaviour in agent institutions. In: IEEE/WIC/ACM International Conference on Intelligent Agent Technology. IAT 2006, pp. 121–124, December 2006
14. Reese, C.: Prozess-Infrastruktur für Agentenanwendungen. Agent Technology - Theory and Applications, vol. 3. Logos Verlag, Berlin (2010)
15. Schmitz, D., Moldt, D., Cabac, L., Mosteller, D., Haustermann, M.: Utilizing petri nets for teaching in practical courses on collaborative software engineering. In: ACSD 2016, Toruń, Poland, 19–24 June 2016, pp. 74–83. IEEE (2016)

16. Aalst, W.M.P.: Verification of workflow nets. In: Azéma, P., Balbo, G. (eds.) ICATPN 1997. LNCS, vol. 1248, pp. 407–426. Springer, Heidelberg (1997). doi:10.1007/3-540-63139-9_48

17. Wagner, T., Moldt, D.: Integrating agent actions and workflow operations. In: Müller, J.P., Ketter, W., Kaminka, G., Wagner, G., Bulling, N. (eds.) MATES 2015. LNCS (LNAI), vol. 9433, pp. 61–78. Springer, Cham (2015). doi:10.1007/978-3-319-27343-3_4

18. Wagner, T., Moldt, D.: Workflow management principles for interactions between petri net-based agents. In: Devillers, R., Valmari, A. (eds.) PETRI NETS 2015. LNCS, vol. 9115, pp. 329–349. Springer, Cham (2015). doi:10.1007/978-3-319-19488-2_17

EUMAS 2016: Algorithms

A Decentralized Approach to Solve Group AHP with Agreements by Consensus

Miguel Rebollo[(⊠)], Alberto Palomares, and Carlos Carrascosa

Universitat Politècnica de València, Camino de Vera s/n, 46022 Valencia, Spain
{mrebollo,apalomares,carrasco}@dsic.upv.es

Abstract. The analytical hierarchical process (AHP) is a multi-criteria, decision-making process that has demonstrated to be of a high utility to achieve complex decisions. This work presents a method to apply it in grupal decisions, where the weights that each user assigns to the criteria are different and private. A combination of consensus process and gradient ascent is used to reach a common agreement that optimizes the utility of the decision using the information exchanged in the local neighborhood exclusively.

The AHP problem is modeled through a multilayer network. Each one of the criteria are negotiated by consensus with the direct neighbors on each layer of the network. Furthermore, each node performs a transversal gradient ascent and corrects locally the deviations from the personal decision to keep the best option.

The process locates the global optimal decision, taking into account that this global function is never calculated nor known by any of the participants. If there is not a global optimal decision where all the participants have a not null utility, but a set of suboptimal decisions, they are automatically divided into different groups that converges into these suboptimal decisions.

Keywords: Complex networks · Consensus · Gradient descent · Analytical hierarchical process · Agreement

1 Introduction

The Analytic Hierarchical Process (AHP) is a muli-objective optimization method. The decision makers provide subjective evaluations regarding to the relative importance of the different criteria and the preference of each alternative for each criteria [12]. The result is a ranking of the considered alternatives that includes the relative score assigned to each one of these alternatives. The main advantage of this process is that it allows (i) to organize the information in a efficient and clear way, even for complex problems; and (ii) synthesize and visualize the effects of changes in the levels or preferences. Furthermore, it is possible to measure the consistency of the model, since a perfect consistency is very difficult to be achieved due to the subjectivity introduced to judge the relative importance of each criteria.

© Springer International Publishing AG 2017
N. Criado Pacheco et al. (Eds.): EUMAS 2016/AT 2016, LNAI 10207, pp. 79–91, 2017.
DOI: 10.1007/978-3-319-59294-7_8

The AHP can be used for a single used to take a decision, but also for a group of people, such as a committee or a group of experts, to achieve a common agreement. There are works that extends the original AHP problem. But these approaches assume that all the actors are able to exchange information. This work proposes a method for group decision making based on AHP, where the participants are connected though a network and they interact exclusively with their direct neighbors. A combination of consensus [17] and gradient ascent is used as optimization method [21].

The proposed solution considers each criterion as a layer in a multiplex network. A consensus process is performed in each layer, trying to achieve a common decision for the corresponding criteria for all the participants. Simultaneously, a gradient ascent is executed across the layers, trying to keep the preferred value for each one of the participants in the decision. This joint process converges to the desired, agreed decision. This decision is the optimal decision of the group if some conditions are fulfilled.

The rest of the paper is organized as follows. Section 2 explains the related techniques that have been combined and used to define the final proposed method to solve AHP in a decentralized and distributed way. The method is detailed and analyzed in Sect. 3 and, finally, Sect. 4 shows the results. Section 5 closes this work with the conclusions.

2   Related Works

2.1   The AHP Process

The AHP begins with the definition of the criteria used to evaluate the alternatives, organized as a hierarchy. The importance of each criteria is defined through its weight $w^\alpha \in [0, 1]$. For example, let's assume that a new leader has to be chosen among three candidates: Tom, Dick and Harry. To evaluate them, their age, experience, education and charisma are going to be considered. The criteria hierarchy and the weights associated to each criterion α are show in Fig. 1.

Once the criteria are defined, a pairwise matrix is created, assigning a relative judgement or preference value to each pair of alternatives. The value a_{ij} represents the preference of the alternative i over the alternative j for the considered criteria, and $a_{ij} = 1/a_{ji}$ (Table 1).

From this pairwise matrix, the local priority l_i^α is calculated, which defines the preference of the alternative i for the criterium α. The local priority is calculated as the values of the principal right eigenvector of the matrix.

Finally, all the local priorities are synthesize across all the criteria in order to calculate the final, global priority p_i for each alternative. There exist many methods to calculate the priorities. The most usual ones are the mean of the rows of he pairwise matrix to calculate l_i^α, and the weighted average $p_i = \sum w^\alpha l_i^\alpha$ for the global priority.

There are approaches to extend AHP into grupal decision problems, but they are centralized solutions and use complete information. In this work, the

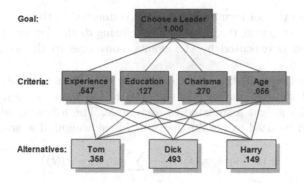

Fig. 1. Example of criteria hierarchy for a AHP

Table 1. (Left) Local priority matrix with the relative importance of each candidate regarding to their experience. (Right) Final priorities for the selected candidates. Dick is selected candidate, with the higher global value

	Tom	Dick	Harry	Priority (l_i^a)	Candidate	Exp	Edu	Char	Age	Goal
Tom	1	1/4	4	**0.217**	Tom	0.119	0.024	0.201	0.015	*0.358*
Dick	4	1	9	**0.717**	Dick	0.392	0.010	0.052	0.038	**0.492**
Harry	1/4	1/9	1	**0.066**	Harry	0.036	0.093	0.017	0.004	*0.149*

participants are connected through a network that bounds the possible information exchanges. An agreement in the final decision is reached through a combination of a consensus process and a gradient ascent (see Fig. 2).

2.2   Consensus on Networks

Consensus means reaching an agreement on the value of a variable which might
represent, for example, a physical quantity, a control parameter, or a price.
Agents are connected through an acquaintances network whose topology constraints the possible interaction between them. This is one of the most promising
research subjects in the MAS area that is currently emerging [8,9,11,13,20].

The theoretical framework for solving consensus problems in agent networks
was formally introduced by Olfati–Saber and Murray [16,17]. Let G be a graph
of order n with the set of entities E as nodes. Let (G, X) be the state of a
network, where $X = (x_1, \ldots, x_n)^T \in \mathbb{R}^n$ and x_i is a real value that is associated
with the node $e_i \in E$. A consensus algorithm is an interaction rule that specifies
the information exchange between the agents and all of their neighbors in the
network in order to reach the agreement. Consensus is reached in the network
when $x_1 = \ldots = x_n$. It has been demonstrated that a convergent and distributed
consensus algorithm in discrete-time exists and it converges to the average of
their initial values.

$$x_i(t + 1) = x_i(t) + \varepsilon \sum_{j \in N_i} (x_j(t) - x_i(t)) \tag{1}$$

where N_i denotes the set formed by all nodes connected to the node i (neighbors of i) and ε is the step size, $0 < \varepsilon < \min_i 1/d_i$, being d_i the degree of node i. This expression, when is executed by the agents, converges to the average of their initial values.

An interesting modification of the consensus introduces weights in the agents, which represent their importance in the system. Let $w = (w_1, w_2, \ldots, w_n)^T$ be a vector with the weight associated to each node. The following algorithm (see [16], p. 225) can be used to obtain the value of the weighted average consensus

$$x_i(t+1) = x_i(t) + \frac{\varepsilon}{w_i} \sum_{j \in N_i} (x_j(t) - x_i(t)) \tag{2}$$

where N_i denotes the set formed by all nodes connected to the node i (neighbors of i) and ε is the step size. The algorithm converges to the weighted average of the initial values of the state of each agent $x_i(0)$ if $\varepsilon < \min_i d_i/w_i$, being d_i the degree of node i [18].

Other works have extended the consensus algorithm for its application in large-scale systems [5], for its usage as a clustering technique [14], for treating problems derived from a failure in communications [10], or for applications in arbitrary directed graphs [7]. However, the application of the consensus algorithm to dynamic networks, where participants may enter and leave during the consensus process, is still an open issue.

2.3 Distributed Gradient Descent

Consensus leads to the average value of the network. But agreement processes frequently involve the optimization of some global utility function. Centralized methods usually require data fusion and distribution along the network, which supposes a high computational and communication cost when the systems scale. Decentralized approaches take advantage of scalability, adaptation to dynamic network topologies and can handle data privacy. Coupled optimization problems can be solved using a variety of distributed algorithms. A classical way is to iteratively refine an estimate of the optimizer using incremental subgradient methods [1]. It is used in static networks, where the topology does not change during the process. Matei [15] studies how the degree distribution in random networks affects the optimal value deviation, defining some metrics to evaluate the quality of the approximated solution. One way of accelerating the consensus process has been proposed by Pereira [19]. This new method is applied to random sensor networks. It is based on the study of the network spectral radius, requiring a complete view of the network to obtain that radius. The relation among the connection probabilities in a random network and the convergence speed has also been studied [19]. This relation also determines the optimal ε value that minimizes the convergence time. The work of Zanella [2] applies the Newton–Raphson method to distributed convex optimization problems. To minimize the optimization function, it uses a consensus process that converges to the exact solution in contrast to the subgradient–based methods. This last work has been extended to consider asynchronous transmission [3] and the multi-dimensional case in order to optimize an n-dimensional function [4].

The combination of consensus and gradient models can be expressed as a two step process [21]

$$x_i(t+1) = \sum_j w_{ij} x_j(t) - \alpha \nabla f_i(x_i(t)) \tag{3}$$

where $W = [w_{ij}]$ is a symmetric, double stochastic matrix (note that it has the same properties demanded to the consensus process to converge) and $\nabla f_i(x_i(t))$ performs a gradient descent to minimize a cost function.

2.4 Multilayer Networks

Multilayer networks are a recent formalism created to model the phenomena that appears in complex networks in a more realistic way. Usually, relations do not occur isolated in one network and notions such as network of networks, multilayer networks, multiplex networks or interdependent networks are defined. In multilayer networks, links of different type exist among the nodes. For example, in a group of people, links representing friendship, working relations or family ties can be defined. Or in a communication model, different media, such as phone and mail, can be considered. Each one of this different links form a network in one layer. The interdependence among layers is defined through cross links between the nodes that represent the same entity in each network. These cross links models the transference of information that passes from one layer to the others.

A multilayer network (see Fig. 2, left) is formally defined [6] as a pair $M = (G, C)$ where $G = \{G^1, \ldots, G^p\}$ is a family of graphs $G^\alpha = (E^\alpha, L^\alpha), \forall \alpha \in [1, p]$ called layers, and $C = \{L^{\alpha\beta} \subseteq E^\alpha \times E^\beta, \forall \alpha, \beta \in [1, p], \alpha \neq \beta\}$ is the set of connections between two different layers G^α and G^β. The elements of each L^α

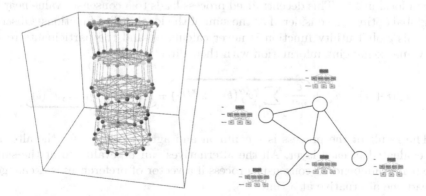

Fig. 2. (Left) Multilayer network example with 20 agents and 5 layers. (Right) Example of network, where each agent has its own values for the criteria an a preferred option.

are called *intralayer* connections and the elements of C are the *interlayer* ones or *crossed layers*. The characteristic of the multilayer network is that all the layers have the same set of nodes $E^1 = \ldots = E^p = E$ and the cross layers are defined between equivalent nodes $L^{\alpha\beta} = \{(e^\alpha, e^\beta), \forall e \in E; \alpha, \beta \in [1, p]\}$.

In the present work, multilayer networks are used to represent the different criteria that form the decision. Each criterion will be negotiated in one layer.

3   Decentralized AHP Using Consensus in Multiplex Networks

Lets consider the participants connected in an undirected network. The topology is not relevant, but all the nodes must be connected in one component. Lets consider only the criteria that are the leafs of the hierarchy defined for the AHP problem, with $\sum w^\alpha = 1$, different and private for each one of the participants. Lets create a multilayer network, where each layer represents one of the final criteria. Each layer is weighted using the weight defined for the criteria. For example, the problem exposed in Fig. 1 has 4 criteria: experience, education, charisma and age. Therefore, a network with 4 layers is created. Furthermore, the weights associated to each one of them are 0.547, 0.127, 0.270 and 0.056 respectively. An utility function can be defined for each preference of the participants using a gaussian function with mean l_i^α and standard deviation $1 - w_i^\alpha$ (see Sect. 3.1). This function is used by the participant to perform the gradient ascent, trying to keep as near as possible to its preferred distribution.

Each participant has its own criteria and the goal of the system is to agree the best candidate according to all the agents involves in the decision. Therefore, a consensus process is executed in each layer in order to find the weighted average. But this process considers the criteria as independent and it does not converge in the value that optimize the decision. The combination of the consensus process with a gradient ascent, as it is defined in Eq. 4, corrects the deviation produced by the consensus and each participant tries to maintain the decision that maximizes its own local utility. This decentralized process leads to a consensus value near to the global optimum, considered as the sum of the local utility functions. Observe that this global utility function is never calculated and the participants reach this value exchanging information with their direct neighbors.

$$x_i^\alpha(t+1) = x_i^\alpha + \overbrace{\frac{\varepsilon}{w_i^\alpha} \sum_{j \in N_i^\alpha} (x_j^\alpha(t) - x_i^\alpha(t))} + \underbrace{\varphi \nabla u_i(x_i^1(t), \ldots, x_i^p(t))} \tag{4}$$

The result of the process is a common and agreed priority for the alternative evaluated in each layer. All the alternatives can be evaluated at the same time using independent consensus process if a vector of preferences is exchanged instead one alternative at a time.

If the global utility function is a smooth one and all the participants have an utility $u_i > 0$ for any final decision, the proposed method converges to the optimal decision for the group. But if there is no point in which all the participants have a positive utility, the resulting global utility function will have one (or more that one) local maximum that may alter the convergence process. In those cases, we allow the nodes to break the links with those neighbors that are pulling them to an undesired area. To do that, it is enough with breaking the communications and stopping exchange information with them. In this case, the network can be split in several groups and each one of them will reach a different decision.

The advantage of this distributed approach is that avoids the bottlenecks problems that arise in mediated solutions. Individual agents are not conscious of a final, global solution, but of the convergence to an agreed compromise among its near neighbors. Furthermore, the system is scalable since new nodes can be added without additional notifications to the rest of the network.

3.1   Utility Function

Utility functions have some common properties in any optimization problem: independence, completeness, transitivity and continuity. As we propose a model with cooperative agents, we'll assume that the utility functions have a maximum and this maximum will be the starting point for all the agents. Furthermore, the function must be a decreasing one. The normal distribution fulfills all this properties. Therefore, it has been the selected one for the utility function u_i of the agents. We can assume that agents are initially situated in its maximum value, which corresponds with the mean value of the utility function. The weight assigned to the term can be used in the dispersion measure. An agent does not desire changes in its more relevant term. Therefore, any change in its value must decrease drastically its utility. On the other hand, the agents would allow changes in terms with low importance, which might slightly decrease their utilities. In the case of a normal distribution, the standard deviation is the parameter that rules this behavior. If we use $\sigma_i^\alpha = 1 - w_i^\alpha$ we obtain the desired behavior. The utility function is defined as follows:

$$u_i^\alpha(x_i^\alpha) = e^{-\frac{1}{2}\left(\frac{x_i^\alpha - l_i^\alpha}{1 - w_i^\alpha}\right)^2} \tag{5}$$

All this individual functions are combined in one unique utility function for the agent.

$$u_i(x_i) = \prod_\alpha u_i^\alpha(x_i^\alpha) \tag{6}$$

This definition corresponds to a renormalized multi-dimensional gaussian distribution such that the maximum utility for the agent i is $u_i(x_i(0)) = 1$.

The global utility of the system is the sum of the individual utilities of the agents. This value is never calculated in the system directly and the function is known by none of the participants in the agreement.

$$U = \sum_i u_i(x_i) \tag{7}$$

4   Application Example

Lets consider a group of 9 agents that are going to take a decision using AHP. A bi-dimensional example has been chosen to be able to represent it graphically, so just 2 criteria will be considered. Figure 3 shows the utility function calculated from the initial preferences of each participant.

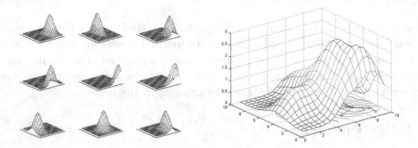

Fig. 3. (Left) Local utilities $u_i(x_i)$ as defined in Eq. 6 from the AHP criteria for each of one the 9 participants. (Right) Final global utility function U (Eq. 7) to locate the optimal decision, defined as the sum of the individual, local utility functions. These functions is not calculated, nor known by the participants, but the process converges to the maximum of this function.

Figure 4 shows the initial and final status of the process. When the combined process stops, all the participants have reached the same point, which corresponds to the common decision agreed by the agents. For this solution to exist, the only condition is that all the participants have a positive utility $u_i > 0$ along the complete solution space.

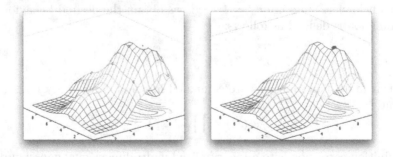

Fig. 4. Initial and final states for a decision in a group of 9 participants using two criteria. An agreed solution exists and it is located correctly by the group using local information only.

Figure 5 shows the evolution of the value for each criterion (left and right) for each one of the participants (in a different colour) along the process. It converges to the final decision. If these values are considered as the x and y coordinates, it matches with the point that corresponds to the solution in Fig. 4.

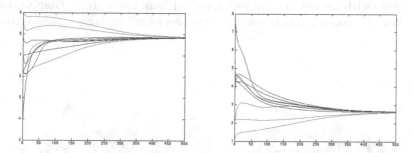

Fig. 5. Evolution of the values for each criteria for each one of the participants. The convergence is guaranteed if $\forall i \ u_i > 0$ in all the solution space (Color figure online)

Nevertheless, when this condition is not fulfilled when some of the participants has an utility equal to zero in some areas of the solution space. In that case, the shape of the global utility function will show peaks and valleys, with local optimal values. Then, the convergence to the optimal solution is not guaranteed and, as it is shown in Fig. 6, the process halts on any value, depending on the initial preferences and the distribution of the utility functions over the solution space.

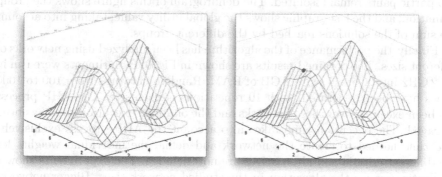

Fig. 6. Example of convergence to a suboptimal solution because participants refuses to move towards the best solution for the group since its has zero-utility for some individual agent.

Our proposal to solve this additional problem is to allow break links among the participants. When a participant detects that the solution guides towards a point with zero-utility, the agent can decide to break the link to those neighbors who are pulling from the preferences. As Fig. 7 shows, in this case the network is broken into groups, each one of them converges to a different agreement. The optimal decision is located by the group formed by those participants whose utility function is positive in the best solution. Actually, this solution is reached if the agents with zero-utility are just removed from the system. Despite doing so, we allow this participants to reach another decision forming a separate group.

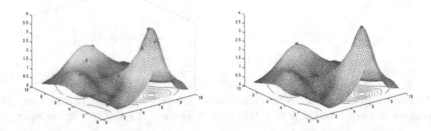

Fig. 7. Initial and final states for an AHP process allowing to break links and reconnect to near neighbors. This solutions guarantees the convergence of a subgroup to the best possible decision, along with another agreements around suboptimal solutions.

Figure 8 shows the evolution of the criteria in such a case. It can be clearly observed how more that one decision is taken. In this case, the network is divided into 4 groups: the bigger one arrives to the best decision, and another group formed by two agents arrives to another private agreement. Finally, another two participants remain isolated. The dendrogram of this figure shows the group formation, and the last graphic shows the global utility value, taking into account the sum of the solutions reached by the different groups.

Finally, the performance of the algorithm has been analyzed using networks of different sizes. The obtained results are shown in Fig. 9. Experiments were run in a 3.2 GHz Intel Core i5, with 8 GB of RAM. Random networks from 100 to 1000 nodes have been generated, with 10 repetitions of each size. The AHP process has been executed over these networks and the obtained execution time has been averaged. The execution time takes into account the AHP process exclusively. The time needed to create the network and define the individual weights for the different criteria and alternatives are not included. The experiments show a quadratic cost for the algorithm in the studied network sizes. Bigger networks need to be analyzed. The main drawback of the current implementation is that the calculation of the φ parameter (see Eq. 4) to guarantee the convergence of the method is a centralized one (the φ parameter is related with the value of the Lipschitz constant for each utility function) and the cost is too high to be calculated in bigger networks (beyond 4 magnitude orders with respect to the execution time).

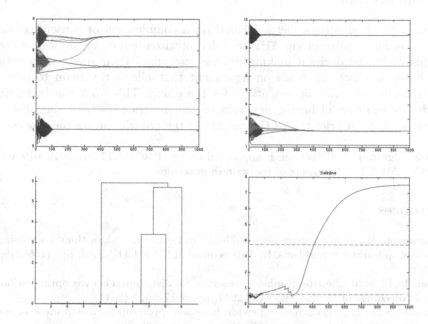

Fig. 8. (Top) Evolution of the criteria and convergence into separated groups. (Bottom) Group division and global utility obtained by this process

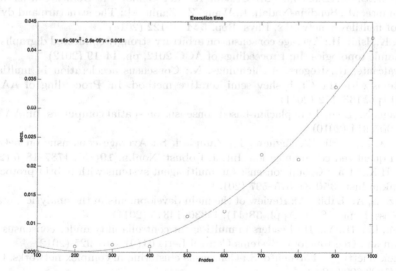

Fig. 9. Execution time of the algorithm with different network sizes

5   Conclusions

This work has presented a method based on a combination of consensus and gradient ascent to solve group AHP in a decentralized environment, where the participants in the decision making process exchanges their preferences with their direct neighbors to reach an agreement that allows the team to select the alternative with the highest utility for the group. This work can be easily extended to the case of having networks of preferences (ANP) or the case of changes in the local priorities or the weights of the criteria during the process.

Acknowledgements. This work is supported by the PROMETEOII/2013/019 and TIN2015-65515-C4-1-R projects of the spanish government.

References

1. Johansson, B., et al.: Subgradient methods and consensus algorithms for solving convex optimization problems. In: Proceedings of IEEE CDC 2008, pp. 4185–4190 (2008)
2. Zanella, F., et al.: Newton-Raphson consensus for distributed convex optimization. In: Proceedings of IEEE CDC-ECC 2011, pp. 5917–5922 (2011)
3. Zanella, F., et al.: Asynchronous newton-Raphson consensus for distributed convex optimization. In: Proceedings of IFAC NecSys 2012 (2012)
4. Zanella, F., et al.: Multidimensional newton-Raphson consensus for distributed convex optimization. In: Proceedings of ACC 2012, pp. 1079–1084 (2012)
5. Askari-Sichani, O., Jalili, M.: Large-scale global optimization through consensus of opinions over complex networks. Complex Adapt. Syst. Model. **1**(1), 11 (2013)
6. Boccaletti, S., Bianconi, G., Criado, R., del Genio, C., Gómez-Gardeñesi, J., Romance, M., Sendiña-Nadalj, I., Wang, Z., Zanin, M.: The structure and dynamics of multilayer networks. Phys. Rep. **544**, 1–122 (2014)
7. Cai, K., Ishii, H.: Average consensus on arbitrary strongly connected digraphs with dynamic topologies. In: Proceedings of ACC 2012, pp. 14–19 (2012)
8. Cavalcante, R., Rogers, A., Jennings, N.: Consensus acceleration in multiagent systems with the Chebyshev semi-iterative method. In: Proceeding of AAMAS 2011, pp. 165–172 (2011)
9. Elhage, N., Beal, J.: Laplacian-based consensus on spatial computers. In: AAMAS, pp. 907–914 (2010)
10. Frasca, P., Carli, R., Fagnani, F., Zampieri, S.: Average consensus on networks with quantized communication. Int. J. Robust. Nonlin. **19**(16), 1787–1816 (2009)
11. Hu, H.X., et al.: Group consensus in multi-agent systems with hybrid protocol. J. Franklin Inst. **350**(3), 575–597 (2013)
12. Ishizaka, A., Labib, A.: Review of the main developments in the analytic hierarchy process. Expert Syst. Appl. **38**(11), 14336–14345 (2011)
13. Ji, Z., Lin, H., Yu, H.: Leaders in multi-agent controllability under consensus algorithm and tree topology. Systems Control Lett. **61**(9), 918–925 (2012)
14. Lancichinetti, A., Fortunato, S.: Consensus clustering in complex networks. CoRR abs/1203.6093 (2012)
15. Matei, I., Baras, J.: Performance evaluation of the consensus-based distributed subgradient method under random communication topologies. IEEE Sig. Proc. **5**(4), 754–771 (2011)

16. Olfati-Saber, R., Fax, J.A., Murray, R.M.: Consensus and cooperation in networked multi-agent systems. Proc. IEEE **95**(1), 215–233 (2007)
17. Olfati-Saber, R., Murray, R.M.: Consensus problems in networks of agents with switching topology and time-delays. IEEE TAC **49**(9), 1520–1533 (2004)
18. Pedroche, F., Rebollo, M., Carrascosa, C., Palomares, A.: On the convergence of weighted-average consensus. CoRR [math.OC] (2013). arXiv:1203.6093
19. Pereira, S., Pages-Zamora, A.: Consensus in correlated random wireless sensor networks. IEEE Sig. Proc. **59**(12), 6279–6284 (2011)
20. Salazar-Ramirez, N., Rodríguez-Aguilar, J.A., Arcos, J.L.: Robust coordination in large convention spaces. AI Commun. **23**, 357–372 (2010)
21. Yuan, K., Ling, Q., Yin, W.: On the convergence of decentralized gradient descent. Technical report, 13–61, UCLA CAM (2014)

Efficient Multi-criteria Coalition Formation Using Hypergraphs (with Application to the V2G Problem)

Filippos Christianos and Georgios Chalkiadakis[(✉)]

School of Electronic and Computer Engineering,
Technical University of Crete, Chania, Greece
{fchristianos,gchalkiadakis}@isc.tuc.gr

Abstract. This paper proposes, for the first time in the literature, the use of *hypergraphs* for the efficient formation of effective coalitions. We put forward several formation methods that build on existing hypergraph pruning, transversal, and clustering algorithms, and exploit the hypergraph structure to identify agents with desirable characteristics. Our approach allows the near-instantaneous formation of high quality coalitions, adhering to multiple stated quality requirements. Moreover, our methods are shown to scale to *dozens of thousands* of agents within fractions of a second; with one of them scaling to even *millions* of agents within seconds. We apply our approach to the problem of forming coalitions to provide *(electric) vehicle-to-grid (V2G)* services. Ours is the first approach able to deal with *large-scale, real-time* coalition formation for the V2G problem, while taking *multiple criteria* into account for creating the electric vehicle coalitions.

1 Introduction

Coalition formation (CF) is a paradigm widely studied in multiagent systems and economics, as means of forming teams of autonomous, rational agents working towards a common goal [2]. One domain where the formation of coalitions comes naturally into play is the so-called *vehicle-to-grid (V2G)* problem. In V2G, battery-equipped *electric vehicles (EVs)* communicate and strike deals with the electricity Grid in order to either lower their power demands, or return power back to the network when there is a peak in the request for power. This helps the Grid to maintain a balanced power load [13]. G2V is V2G's "sister" problem, where EVs connect and draw power from the Grid without overloading it [14]. In both cases, the coordination of EVs efforts, is essential.

As such, several recent approaches have called for the formation of EV coalitions in order to tackle the V2G problem [9–11]. The existing approaches, however, typically exhibit the following characteristics: *(a)* they attempt to form *optimal* coalitions or coalition structures; and *(b)* they either attempt to form coalitions with respect to a single criterion, or employ lengthy negotiation protocols in order to capture various coalitional requirements while respecting the constraints of individual agents.

© Springer International Publishing AG 2017
N. Criado Pacheco et al. (Eds.): EUMAS 2016/AT 2016, LNAI 10207, pp. 92–108, 2017.
DOI: 10.1007/978-3-319-59294-7_9

The inherent hardness of the optimal coalition structure generation problem [12], however, and the fact that negotiation protocols can be lengthy and thus highly time consuming, severely restricts the practicality and scalability of such algorithms: they can handle at most a few hundred EVs. In reality though, there exist hundreds of thousands of EVs that connect to the Grid, and could potentially offer their services; any formed coalition would be required to possess *a multitude of desirable characteristics* (e.g., high collective storage capacity, and high collective discharge rate); and, if the aim is to balance electricity demand in real time, any such service should be offered by the appropriate coalition almost instantaneously.

In this paper, we overcome the aforementioned difficulties by employing, for the first time in the literature, *hypergraphs* to achieve the timely formation of coalitions that satisfy *multiple criteria*[1]. In our approach, EV agents that share specific characteristics are organised into *hyperedges*. Then, building on the existing hypergraphs literature [6,17], we propose algorithms for *(i)* hypergraph *pruning*, to focus on interesting parts of the search space; *(ii)* hypergraph *transversal* to identify sets of vertices (agents) that combine several desirable characteristics; and *(iii)* hypegraph *clustering*, that allows the identification of clusters of high quality agents. Moreover, we put forward *(iv)* a heuristic formation algorithm that benefits from pruning and generates high quality coalitions near-instantaneously, while scaling linearly with the number of agents.

In contrast to existing approaches, we do not attempt to generate an optimal coalition structure, nor do we attempt to compute a single optimal coalition. Instead, we exploit the hypergraph representation of our problem in order to select agents and form highly effective coalitions, while being able to scale to *dozens of thousands* of agents within fractions of a second; and, in the case of our heuristic method, even to *millions* of EV agents in seconds.

Though here we apply it to the V2G problem, our approach is generic and can be used in *any* coalition formation setting. It is perhaps surprising that a powerful model like hypergraphs has not been so far exploited for devising efficient coalition formation methods, despite its intuitive connections to the concept of coalitions. Regardless, we are not aware of any work to date that has exploited hypergraphs and related algorithms in order to perform *real-time*, *large-scale*, *multi-criteria* coalition formation, as we do in this paper.

2   Related Work

Here we review related work, and highlight its differences to our approach. To begin, Valogianni *et al.* [14] propose an *adaptive smart charging algorithm* that adjusts *the power drawn* from the Grid for charging EVs, based on each EV owner's utility from charging. The approach employs *reinforcement learning* for capturing agent needs and behaviour; and an optimization module schedules the charging of each EV to maximise its utility subject to network constraints. Though effective, it does not focus on the problem of feeding the network with

---

[1] A sketch of these ideas appeared in a short ECAI-2016 paper [5].

power drawn from EVs in a coordinated fashion, and as such there is no mentioning of EV coalitions in that work.

By contrast, an attempt to explicitly sell power in the regulation market via the formation of EV coalitions is presented in [10]. In that work, EV coalitions provide the following service to the Grid every few seconds: they either *scale down* their power draw (or discharge); or they *scale it up*, and request more power. The approach is quite effective, but there is a need for a complicated EV selection process by an aggregator agent, and simulations presented in that paper involved a pool of 300 vehicles only.

A paper adopting a game-theoretic perspective on the formation of coalitions in the Smart Grid is [15]. It constitutes an attempt to solve the optimal coalition structure generation problem (CSG). Forming *virtual energy consumer coalitions*, manages to flatten the demand in order to get better prices in what could be a G2V arrangement. By solving the CSG, it finds the best VEC for every consumer on the market; and guarantees a core-stable payoff distribution outcome. Unfortunately, this solution is shown to work on social graphs with only a handful of agents. By contrast, our approach manages to produce high quality solutions in milliseconds, and scales to the millions.

Two recent papers which study *cooperative games* defined *over graphs* that impose constraints on the formation of the coalitions, are [3,4]. Specifically, they assume that the environment possesses some structure that forbids the creation of individual coalitions, due to limited resources and existing physical or even legal barriers. This is captured by an undirected graph providing a path connecting any two agents that can belong to the same coalition. Both of these papers, however, do not employ hypergraphs in any way. Hypergraphs have in fact been used for modelling agent interactions in cooperative game settings where agents can simultaneously belong to multiple coalitions [8,18]. Nevertheless, all of these papers [3,4,8,18] focus on studying the theoretical problem of achieving *coalitional stability* via appropriately distributing the payoff among the agents; rather than providing algorithms for large-scale coalition formation in real-world settings, as we do in this work. By contrast, two papers that study the generation of optimal coalition structures while focusing on stability are [1,16]. These approaches scale to thousands of agents - but not to millions, as ours (which does not form optimal coalitions), and do not tackle multiple formation criteria.

A paper that is more related to our work here, in the sense that it exploits constraints among vehicles for coalition formation, is the work of Ramos *et al.* [11]. They propose the dynamic formation of coalitions among EVs so that they can function as *virtual power plants* that sell power to the Grid. However, that work also attempts to tackle the optimal CSG problem. The method relies heavily on a inter-agent negotiations protocol; and is empirically shown to produce solutions that are close to optimal (98%), but this is when tested in scenarios with a few dozens of agents only. Moreover, there is only a single criterion for the formation of a coalition—namely, the *physical distance* among the EVs. Physical distance, however, is not a very natural criterion; and, in any case, it is imperative that a multitude of criteria is taken into account—such as capacity, discharge power, and perceived reliability (see, e.g., [9]). Our approach, by contrast, is able to take into account any number of natural criteria to form EV coalitions.

3 Our Approach

In order to develop multi-criteria coalition formation algorithms that generate coalitions efficiently, we employ the concept of *a hypergraph*. A hypergraph $H = (V, E)$ is a generalization of a graph, where each *hyperedge* $e \in E$ can contain any number of *vertices (or nodes)* in the set V. Vertices in H correspond to agents; while we view a hyperedge as corresponding to some particular *attribute* or *characteristic* possessed by the agents in the hyperedge. In the V2G setting, the agents correspond to EVs (i.e., an EV is represented by a node in our hypergraph); while the hyperedges correspond to vehicle characteristics. More specifically, a hyperedge corresponds to a "quality level" of some EV attribute, as we explain below.

In order to represent the different *quality* of the various hyperedges, and utilize it in our algorithms, we mark each hyperedge with a weight.[2] These weights define the *degree* of a node: *The degree $deg(u)$ of a node u is the sum of the weights of its edges*. Intuitively, *a high degree node is a high quality one*. This fact is exploited in our algorithms below. A hyperedge (of a given quality) will be also called a *category*. The (quality of the) categories to which an EV belongs will be influencing the decisions of our *hypergraph pruning* algorithm, which we describe in Sect. 3.2 below. A node that belongs to a hyperedge characterizing the quality of a given agent attribute, cannot belong to some other hyperedge characterizing the quality of the same attribute.

To illustrate the use of hypergraphs in our setting, consider for example the hypergraph of Fig. 1, which contains the hyperedges $e_{1...6}$ and vertices $u_{1...7}$.

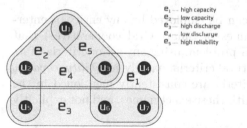
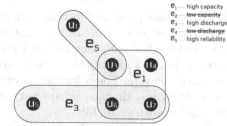

Fig. 1. A simple hypergraph   **Fig. 2.** Pruning a simple hypergraph

---

[2] In our implementation, the weight of the edges, according to the quality of each attribute (capacity, reliability and discharge), are as follows: { *extremely-high: 8, very-high: 7, high: 6, medium-high: 5, medium-low: 4, low: 3, very-low: 2, extremely-low: 1* }. Thus we have 24 edges + 1 containing commitment of EVs.

It is clear in this example that vertices may belong to multiple hyperedges: the hyperedge e_1 contains the vertices $u_{3,4,6,7}$, while the vertex u_1 belongs in the hyperedges e_2, e_5, e_4. Vertices in Fig. 1 correspond to EVs; while the hyperedges correspond to the "quality" of the following EV attributes: *capacity, discharge rate* and *observed reliability*. The meaning of these attributes is intuitively straightforward, but will be nevertheless explained in Sect. 3.1 below. Each attribute is related to at least one hyperedge in the hypergraph. For instance, in Fig. 1, the *capacity* attribute is represented by three hyperedges in the hypergraph: *low-capacity, medium-capacity*, and *high-capacity*. As noted above, no node can belong in more than one capacity-related hyperedges. In our figure,

- the hyperedge $e1$ represents the nodes which have high capacity;
- the hyperedge $e2$ contains nodes that have low capacity;
- $e3$ and $e4$ include the vehicles with high and low discharge rate, respectively;
- finally, $e5$ contains nodes that are expected to the *highly reliable*.

For example, node $u1$ is a *low-capacity, low-discharge* but *highly reliable* vehicle—while node $u3$ is a *high-capacity, low-discharge* and *highly reliable* one.

Organizing the information relating to specific agent attributes using hyperedges, enables us to both access this information efficiently, and keep it organized. Moreover, in many settings, agent characteristics captured by hyperedges, naturally correspond to criteria according to which we can form coalitions. For example, it is conceivable that we want to use agents with *high capacity* from the respective *high-capacity* edge, if our goal is to form coalitions with *high capacity*. Our approach of using hypergraphs is even more generic than what implied so far, since we can easily define hyperedges that contain agents which are or are not *permitted* to connect with each other, for various reasons; and since we can exploit the hypergraph to allow the formation of coalitions according to a multitude of criteria.

3.1   Criteria for Forming Coalitions

The algorithms presented in this work can be employed by any entity or enterprice (such as the Grid, utility companies or Smart Grid cooperatives) that wants to form EV coalitions for the V2G problem, using any set of criteria of its choosing. Here we identify three such natural criteria, namely *reliability, capacity* and *discharge rate*. These formation criteria are consistently mentioned in the related literature, though perhaps not with these exact names, and not explicitly identified as such [9,10,14].

First of all, a coalition has to be consistently *reliable*, i.e. it should be able to serve the power that has been requested without any disruptions. For a coalition to be reliable, its members must be reliable too, and gaps in reliability must be met with backup agents. We define *agent reliability* as *the estimated probability that an agent will fulfill its promises*. The *promise* of an agent is its *commitment* on being connected to the Grid during a specific time slot in order to contribute via providing energy to the Grid, if so requested. Such slots naturally correspond to electricity trading intervals.

In addition, a coalition must fulfill a *capacity* requirement. The *capacity* of a coalition is the amount of electricity (measured in kWh) the coalition will be offering to the Grid; while the capacity of en EV is, similarly, the amount of electricity (in kWh) the EV will be offering to the Grid. In fact, gathering enough EV capacity to cover the Grid needs during high demand periods, is the main objective of any V2G solution.

Another factor in the V2G problem is the *discharge rate* of a coalition (or, of a single EV)—the rate by which the coalition (resp., the EV) is able to provide (electrical) energy to the Grid over a specified time period. Discharge rate is measured in kW. A high coalitional discharge rate could be required in cases where capacity should be offered within a small amount of time, for example when the Grid is under a heavy demand load. Naturally, a coalition has a high discharge rate if its members discharge rates are high; for our purposes, we assume that the discharge rate is additive, i.e., the discharge rate of a coalition is the sum of its EVs discharge rates. In Sect. 4, we will be forming coalitions in order to meet specific capacity and discharge rate targets; and observing how reliable the coalitions meeting these targets are.

Now, the hypergraph used in our current implementation was designed so that it could easily satisfy requests pertaining to these particular criteria. As such, there was a total of 25 hyperedges in the hypegraph—{*extremely-high, very-high, high, medium-high, medium-low, low, very-low, extremely-low*} × {*capacity, discharge rate, reliability*}; and a *committed* one, containing EVs that have stated they will be connecting to the Grid during the particular slot.

In our model, we assume that, at any time step that this is required—due to a consumption peak, an unplanned event, or the need to regulate frequency and voltage—the Grid (or some other entity) advertises its demand for a V2G coalition with several desirable characteristics. As noted in [9], individual EVs are well-suited for providing services at short notice. What we show in this paper, is that we can select agents from a huge pool of EVs to form *coalitions* that are able to provide large amounts of power at short notice, and with high reliability.

3.2 Pruning the Hypergraph

An important aspect of using hypergraphs for dealing with large state-spaces, is the resulting ability to perform node and edge pruning. Since dozens or hundreds of thousands of our EVs populate the hypergraph, and each one is a member of several hyperedges, running the algorithms without pruning would require an enormous amount of computing power. However, due to the nature of the hypergraph, and the way we store our vehicles and their attributes, it is extremely easy and effective to narrow down the number of vehicles and edges used, by leaving out EVs that are less promising as coalition members. For example, if achieving a high capacity for the to-be-formed coalition is a key goal, then, intuitively, we can narrow down our search for coalition members by focusing only on nodes belonging to the set of hyperedges (or "categories") *highcapacity* ∪ *veryhighcapacity* ∪ *exhighcapacity*.

To illustrate pruning, Fig. 1 shows a hypergraph that contains all EVs. In order to reduce the size of the hypergraph and thus the computing requirements, we could keep only EVs belonging to at least one high quality edge, as shown in Fig. 2.

Algorithm 1. Pruning the hypergraph

1: **procedure** PRUNING(H, $CategoriesKept$)
2:      **for** Hyperedge $\in$ H **do**
3:          **if** $Hyperedge \in CategoriesKept \cap Committed$ **then**
4:              $NewHEdges \leftarrow NewHEdges \cup HyperEdge$
5:              $NewNodes \leftarrow NewNodes \cup HyperEdge.nodes$
6:          **end if**
7:      **end for**
8:      $NewHGraph \leftarrow Hypergraph(NewNodes, NewHEdges)$
9: **end procedure**

Algorithm 1 is our implementation of pruning. The algorithm iterates over all hyperedges in the given hypergraph H, and keeps only the nodes belonging to hyperedges that correspond to the specified "categories of interest" (*CategoriesKept* in Algorithm 1).

In our implementation, the *CategoriesKept* are heuristically selected, and depend on the algorithms. For instance, the *minimal transversal* algorithm requires a more aggressive pruning, since its complexity is sensitive to the number of nodes used as input (cf. Sect. 3.3), and we therefore empirically feed it with as few hyperedges as possible.

Our experimentation indicates that the use of pruning can lead to a significantly smaller hypergraph, and to vast improvements in terms of execution time for our algorithms. In our simulations, the hypergraphs are pruned to about 1/20 of the initial size of the EVs pool, without sacrificing the methods' performance (cf. Sect. 4.1). Moreover, pruning using Algorithm 1 is almost instantaneous.

3.3   Minimal Transversal Algorithm

Using hypergraphs allows to use an intuitive approach for locating agents for coalitions: to generate the set of *minimal transversals* for the *high-value hyperedges* [6]. A *transversal* (or *hitting set*) of a hypergraph H, is a set $T \subseteq V$ with hyperedges X where $X = E$ (i.e., vertices in T belong to *all* hyperedges in E). A *minimal transversal* is a set that does not contain a subset that is a hitting set of H. As such[3], generating several minimal transversal sets for *high-quality* hyperedges is expected to identify agents which are high-quality and should be used in the formation of a coalition. Subsequently, we join those agents together until our criteria are met.

---

[3] Of course there can be more than one minimal transversals, and it is not necessary that they have the same cardinality.

Our approach with the minimal transversal set is to prune all edges but those of extremely high quality that are also "committed", as seen in Algorithm 2. Then we generate progressively the minimal hitting sets, using an algorithm similar to [6]. That is, we first generate the minimal hitting sets containing one node, then those with two, and so on. Then we randomly pick agents belonging to those minimal transversals, until the coalitions requirements are met. If the requirements are met during the progressive minimal transversal generation process, no further minimal transversals are generated.

To illustrate this concept with the help of Fig. 1, we prune the hypergraph to keep only the high-quality edges e_1, e_3, e_5, leaving us with the nodes $u_1, u_3 \ldots u_7$ and edges e_1, e_3, e_4, as seen in Fig. 2. Then we generate all minimal transversals. Those generated first are the ones with two nodes (since there are no minimal transversals with one) i.e. the following $\{u_3, u_5\}$, $\{u_1, u_7\}$, $\{u_6, u_1\}$, $\{u_3, u_7\}$, $\{u_3, u_6\}$. Last, we generate the final minimal transversal with three nodes, $\{u_1, u_5, u_4\}$.

This method creates a set of agents with uniformly distributed high-quality characteristics. Though this is desirable in theory, in practice the results vary depending on the generated minimal transversal set. There are characteristics which might be of higher importance than others and this cannot be taken into account by the transversal algorithm due to its nature. Regardless, this method could be of much use for creating a base of quality agents; for uniformly improving the quality of an already formed coalition by adding agents from the minimal transversal sets, and for creating versatile coalitions without focusing on specific attributes.

Line 6 of Algorithm 2 is our implementation of minimal transversal [6]. Though there is no known polynomial time algorithm for the general hypergraph transversal problem, the algorithm given was shown experimentally to behave well in practice, and its memory requirements are polynomially bounded by the size of the input hypergraph, though it comes without bounds to its running time.

Algorithm 2. Coalition formation using minimal transversal

1: **procedure** MINIMALTRANSVERSAL(H)
2:      $H \leftarrow Prune(H, exhigh)$ ▷ exhigh signifies all hyperedges with exhigh qualities
3:      $T = \emptyset, C = \emptyset$ ▷ Start with an empty coalition
4:      **for** i=1 to $|E|$ **do**   ▷ where $|E|$ is the number of edges in the (pruned) H
5:           Create the union U of minimal transversal sets with size i, generated from H.
6:           $T = T \cup U$
7:           **while** C does not meet the criteria **do**
8:                Randomly select an *unselected* node $\in T$ and add it to C
9:           **end while**
10:         **if** criteria have been met **then**
11:              return formed coalition C
12:         **end if**
13:    **end for**
14: **end procedure**

3.4   Clustering Algorithm

The second approach is to create clusters of agents. After creating said clusters, we efficiently calculate the best cluster and then sample EVs from that group until our coalition criteria are met.

In more detail, we first generate a hypergraph of EV agents with the characteristics described previously. Then, hypergraph clustering is performed. The hypergraph clustering itself is an implementation of that proposed in [17], and is conducted as follows.

We begin by implementing functions that calculate

- *the Incidence Matrix*: A matrix H with entries $h(u, e) = 1$ if $u \in e$ and 0 otherwise.
- *the Weight Matrix*: A diagonal matrix W containing the weights of the hyperedges.
- D_u and D_e: Matrices containing the node and hyperedge degrees respectively.
- *the Adjacency Matrix*: A matrix defined as $A = HWH^T - D_u$.

The matrices above are used for the final calculations of the hypergraph *Laplacian matrix*. This a matrix representation of a graph, that has information on the degrees of the nodes, and their connections with the hyperedges (cf. [17], Sect. 5).

As explained in [17], having the Laplacian, enables us to calculate the Φ eigenvectors $[\Phi_1 \dots \Phi_k]$ corresponding to the k lowest eigenvalues. These can then define $X = [\Phi_1 \dots \Phi_k]$, a matrix that can be employed for k-way partitioning to cluster our agents. This is achieved via running the *k-means* algorithm [7] on the row vectors of X [17]. As explained in [17], the rows of X are representations of the hypergraph vertices in the k-dimensional Euclidean space. Of course, choosing a value for k has to be decided empirically. In Sect. 4.4 we will be testing different values for k. After generating the clusters, we are given the task to locate the "best" cluster among them. To do this efficiently, we simply sort them by looking at *the average of the node degrees*. This provides us with a cluster that is better than the rest. We then sample nodes from the best cluster until our criteria are met. Algorithm 3 summarizes the method.

Algorithm 3. Coalition formation using hypergraph clustering

1: **procedure** CLUSTERING(H)
2:     $H \leftarrow Prune(H, (vhigh \cup exhigh))$ ▷ exhigh and vhigh signify the sets of extremely high and very high quality hyperedges respectively
3:     Generate k clusters using the algorithm described in 3.4 [17]
4:     $C = \emptyset$ ▷ Start with an empty coalition
5:     Find the best cluster, A, by comparing the sum of node degrees of each cluster.
6:     **while** C does not meet the criteria **do**
7:         Randomly select a node $\in A$ and add it in C
8:     **end while**
9: **end procedure**

3.5 A Heuristic Algorithm

While using a minimal transversal generates quality sets of agents, computing the
degree of a node can identify single agents with many quality attributes. As an
example, when we have a reliable coalition as a base but we require more capacity,
we can use the sorted list we have generated, to pick agents with high capacity.
Intuitively, this approach will result to picking high overall quality agents for our
coalition. We can also create coalitions by using only the best available agents.
Moreover, we can use the aforementioned sorted-by-degree list of nodes in order
to "fill gaps" and improve on the quality of already formed coalitions.

Thus, our heuristic method operates as follows. *(1)* First, we prune the
hypergraph to include only "promising" nodes and hyperedges. For instance,
we exclude nodes not in *extremely high* or in *very high* hyperedges. *(2)* Then
we sort the remaining nodes based on their node degree. *(3)* Finally, we pick
the highest degree nodes from the list until the coalition criteria are met. By
starting at the top of the list, we can guarantee that agents have many positive
characteristics.

We can see at step *(1)* above, that this algorithm, like the rest of our methods,
employs pruning. As such, it does exploit the hypergraph structure. However,
in practice the algorithm can deliver excellent results without much pruning. In
our experiments in Sect. 4 below, the heuristic approach is shown to outperform
the rest while pruning only the non-committed nodes in the hypergraph. In
fact, one strength of this approach is that it does not *rely* on pruning, since
its complexity is low: essentially, that of the algorithm employed for sorting
(i.e., $O(nlogn)$, since we use with Python's built-in *Timsort* algorithm). By not
relying on pruning, the algorithm can focus on promising nodes with high node
degree (and, therefore, quality), irrespective of the exact hyperedges to which
they belong.

3.6 A Simple Sampling Method

For interest, and in order to have a benchmark for the rest of our algorithms,
a simple sampling algorithm was also developed. The algorithm takes random
samples until the specified goals are achieved.

4 Experiments and Results

In this section we present the evaluation of our algorithms. First we explain
how the EV population is generated, and the time this generation process takes.
Then, the performance of the algorithm is evaluated in terms of the quality of
the formed coalition and also in terms of execution time and scaling behavior.
All figures and tables present average values over multiple runs. Specifically, we
generated 20 hypergraphs with 20,000 EVs each, and then ran each algorithm
on every hypergraph 10 times, and took the averages (and the average of those
averages). Our experiments were run on a Sandy Bridge i7-2600K at 4.2 GHz.
All the tests were running on a single thread on Python, meaning that there is
a lot of room for optimization.

4.1   Generating the EV Population

To generate the population for each type of experiment we create the vehicles one by one, by first generating its properties as follows. The capacity of each vehicle is generated from a Gaussian distribution with mean value 100 and $\sigma = 80$. The discharge rate of each vehicle is generated from a Gaussian distribution with mean value 10 and $\sigma = 5$. The reliability of each vehicle is picked from a Gaussian distribution with mean value 0 and $\sigma = 1$. Each EV's commitment of being connected to the Grid is a *true/false* variable, with a 0.9 probability of being *true*. If *true*, then the EV is inserted in the *committed* hyperedge. When a vehicle has its properties created, it is added in the pool of available EVs. The computational complexity of generating the hypergraph is, as expected, $O(n)$.

The coalition requirements are set to values which are commonly used in the regulation market [9], namely the following two. First, each coalition must have a total capacity of at least $10MWh$. The discharge rate must also be at least $1MW$ [9] These values are kept constant throughout all experiments—except when we test scaling against an increasing capacity goal, where capacity is treated as a variable.

Creating the hypergraph is a problem that scales linearly with time. Specifically, generating the hypergraph, including the vehicles and distributing them to hyperedges, takes a very small amount of time and scales linearly up to a million within a minute (Table 2). As mentioned above, the initial EV population was 20,000 nodes. However, before feeding the nodes to the algorithms, we pruned the hypergraph to keep promising nodes. Table 1 shows the average hypergraph size finally fed to the algorithms.

Table 1. Pruning results

Algorithm	Nodes after pruning	Edges after pruning
Transversal	1148.4	4
Clustering	1218.8	7
Heuristic	18012.6	25

4.2   Forming the Coalitions

We now proceed to evaluate the performance of our algorithms. Our evaluation will examine *(a)* how fast and *(b)* by selecting how many vehicles they can meet the set requirements. Naturally, the faster an algorithm forms a coalition that meets all the requirements, the better. Moreover, coalitions with fewer vehicles are preferable, since intuitively, this allows for a more efficient allocation of resources, and also means that fewer EVs will share the payoff associated with forming the coalition (exactly how this payoff allocation will occur, is a problem we do not deal with in this paper).

To begin, in all Figs. 3, 4, 5 and 6:

- In all subfigures, the horizontal axis depicts the progression of the coalition size.

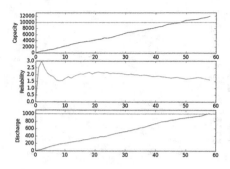
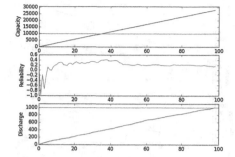

Fig. 3. Coalition formation with the heuristic algorithm

Fig. 4. Coalition formation with the clustering algorithm

- *Capacity subfig.* On the first graph of each figure, the capacity of the coalition is displayed. We can see how it is increased by selecting the appropriate agents until the goal (horizontal line) is reached.
- *Reliability subfig.* The second graph displays the mean reliability of our coalition.
- *Discharge subfig.* The third and last graph displays the discharge rate of the coalition. The goal of 1,000 kW is shown as a horizontal line.

Heuristic Algorithm. As explained in Sect. 3.5, this algorithm attempts (in a rather "greedy" manner) to identify the best EVs from the hypergraph. As we can observe in Fig. 3, it takes on average only 58.5 vehicles to reach the goal requirements, which is the most efficient use of resources observed across all our methods. The reliability achieved is also high, reaching a value of more than 1.5. We remind the reader that the mean reliability of our pool of EVs is 0. This approach is also the most time and memory efficient of all. Specifically the algorithms average completion time is only 25 ms for these experiments, and it also scales linearly into the millions as seen in Fig. 9 below.

Clustering Algorithm. This method performs clustering, as explained in Sect. 3.4, and then takes random samples from the best cluster. Figure 4 depicts its performance when using $k = 3$ clusters. Unfortunately, we cannot control how exactly the clusters are formed, so we do not have a guarantee that high quality vehicles will be clustered together. This leads to a mediocre result with an increased average coalition size, and a slightly-over-the-average reliability. The average size of coalitions meeting both requirements is 98. The average time required for the method's completion is 709 ms. In Sect. 4.4, we show how different k values affect our results.

Transversal. Using the transversal algorithm and taking nodes from a list of minimal hitting set. Figure 5 shows its performance. The transversal algorithm appears to work quite well since the average coalition size is only 64, slightly higher than that achieved by the heuristic approach. The reliability of the

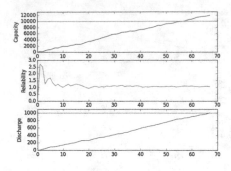
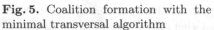

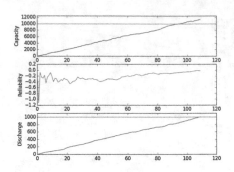

Fig. 5. Coalition formation with the minimal transversal algorithm

Fig. 6. Coalition creation with the simple sampling algorithm

coalition is high, reaching values over 1.1. It can also scale quite well, reaching thousands of vehicles (cf. Fig. 7), but not as well as the heuristic approach. The average time to completion was 120 ms.

Simple Sampling. Figure 6 depicts our results for the Simple Sampling method. The average coalition size achieved with this algorithm is 109.3. The average completion time was 24 ms. As expected, this algorithm achieves the weakest results among all our algorithms. The algorithms' performance is summarized in Table 2 for convenience.

Table 2. Summarizing the performance results

Algorithm	Heuristic	Clustering	Transversal	Simple sampling
Mean coalition size (# EVs)	58.5	98	64	109.3
Mean running time (*ms*)	25	709	120	24
Mean generat. + Run. time (*ms*)	1041	1725	1136	1040

4.3   Scaling Behaviour

We now test the scaling behaviour of our algorithms. First, we show how our algorithms scale with time when the *capacity* goal is increased. Then, we show how they scale as the number of EVs under consideration increases.

In Fig. 8 we can see how the transversal, heuristic and clustering algorithm scale against an increasing capacity goal (assuming any other goal remains fixed). The starting size of the available agents was kept constant at 20,000 EVs for this experiment. We observe that the scaling behaviour of the heuristic algorithm against an increasing capacity goal is superlinear. Nevertheless, its total required execution time is low, since it takes the algorithm 0.9 s to reach the goal capacity of 300,000 kWh. The transversal algorithm scales with steps. The main reason for this is that the minimal transversal sets are generated before we select the agents of a coalition. If a minimal transversal set does not achieve the goal capacity, we generate a new one with more agents, till we reach the set capacity goal. This generates a step pattern, the first stages of which are shown in Fig. 8. In Fig. 8 we actually manage to see only one step because generating the minimal transversals with 3 EVs is enough to find good coalitions for all goals from 40,000 kWh onwards (while it was enough to generate the minimal transversals with 2 EVs to cover the 10,000 kWh capacity goal).

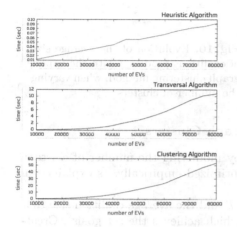

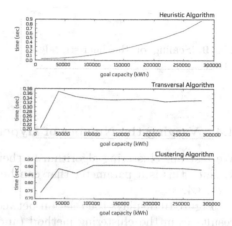

Fig. 7. Scaling against an increasing EV population

Fig. 8. Scaling against an increasing "capacity" goal

Now, the running time of the hypegraph clustering algorithm is largely independent of the size of the stated capacity goal. This is because the clustering itself, which is the part of the algorithm that requires the most processing power, takes place regardless of the final coalition requirements. Indeed, we observe in Fig. 8 that after an initial jump due to increased sampling requirements (cf. lines 6–8, Algorithm 3) when moving from a goal of 10,000 to 40,000 kWh, the algorithm's running time remains largely unaltered.

Figure 7 displays scaling against the initial EV population. The coalition goals were kept constant, and the same for all algorithms. The heuristic algorithm shows a linear scaling in time as the agent size grows. Specifically, the heuristic algorithm can scale *up to a million agents* within an acceptable time.

Figure 9 demonstrates this behaviour, starting from 50,000 EVs. Of course, one expects that when the population reaches several millions, the complexity of the sorting algorithm will kick in, creating bottlenecks. Regardless, the fact that linear scalability is maintained up to 1,000,000 agents is reassuring. By contrast, looking at Fig. 7, we observe that the transversal and clustering algorithms scale superlinearly.

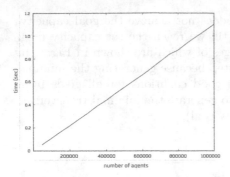

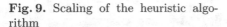

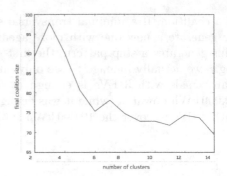

Fig. 9. Scaling of the heuristic algorithm

Fig. 10. Evolution of the average size of coalitions produced with the hypergraph clustering method, when varying the number of clusters

4.4 Varying the Number of Hypergraph Clusters

We test our clustering algorithm further by modifying the number of clusters, k, since this is a parameter that can be optimized empirically, as explained in Sect. 3.4.

Figure 10 displays the relation between k and the average coalition size that results from the clustering method (and which achieves the set goals). Creating a larger number of clusters results in smaller, and thus better, coalitions. Regardless, even when $k = 15$, the clustering algorithm still produces coalitions with more EVs than the heuristic one.

5   Conclusions and Future Work

In this paper, we demonstrated how to employ hypergraphs for creating coalitions based on multiple criteria. The existence of several hypergraph transversal and clustering algorithms makes hypergraphs easy to work with. Moreover, the ability to select almost instantaneously parts of the hypergraph that are interesting, offers a significant advantage, enabling one to generate coalitions with desirable characteristics within seconds. This makes hypergraph use quite attractive for real-world, real-time scenarios.

We presented several coalition formation methods that employ hypergraphs for tackling the V2G problem, and evaluated their performance. Our proposed heuristic algorithm, in particular, was shown to be the most effective and efficient of our methods, as it is able to use a minimal number of EVs to provide the required capacity, discharge rate, and reliability to the Grid in a few milliseconds; while it exhibits exceptional scaling behaviour with respect to the number of EVs under consideration. Ours is the first approach that is able to deal with *large-scale* coalition formation for the V2G problem, while taking *multiple criteria* into account for creating the EV coalitions.

We are currently working on a *hybrid* method that combines the transversal and the heuristic approach. At the moment this algorithm yields similar results to the heuristic approach. Future work includes improving the clustering algorithm by equipping it with an alternative method for representing the vertices in the Euclidean space; and for identifying promising clusters.

References

1. Bistaffa, F., Farinelli, A., Cerquides, J., Rodríguez-Aguilar, J., Ramchurn, S.D.: Anytime coalition structure generation on synergy graphs. In: Proceedings of AAMAS 2014, pp. 13–20 (2014)
2. Chalkiadakis, G., Elkind, E., Wooldridge, M.: Computational aspects of cooperative game theory. Synth. Lect. Artif. Intell. Mach. Learn. **5**(6), 1–168 (2011)
3. Chalkiadakis, G., Greco, G., Markakis, E.: Characteristic function games with restricted agent interactions: core-stability and coalition structures. Artif. Intell. **232**, 76–113 (2016)
4. Chalkiadakis, G., Markakis, E., Jennings, N.R.: Coalitional stability in structured environments. In: Proceedings of AAMAS 2012, pp. 779–786 (2012)
5. Christianos, F., Chalkiadakis, G.: Employing hypergraphs for efficient coalition formation with application to the V2G problem. In: ECAI 2016–22nd European Conference on Artificial Intelligence, 29 August–2 September 2016, The Hague, The Netherlands, pp. 1604–1605 (2016)
6. Eiter, T., Gottlob, G.: Identifying the minimal transversals of a hypergraph and related problems. SIAM J. Comput. **24**(6), 1278–1304 (1995)
7. Hartigan, J.A., Wong, M.A.: Algorithm as 136: a k-means clustering algorithm. J. Roy. Stat. Soc.: Ser. C (Appl. Stat.) **28**(1), 100–108 (1979)
8. Jun, T., Kim, J.Y.: Hypergraph formation game. Hitotsubashi. J. Econ. **50**, 107–122 (2009)
9. Kamboj, S., Kempton, W., Decker, K.S.: Deploying power grid-integrated electric vehicles as a multi-agent system. In: Proceedings of AAMAS 2011, pp. 13–20 (2011)
10. Kamboj, S., Pearre, N., Kempton, W., Decker, K., Trnka, K., Kern, C.: Exploring the formation of electric vehicle coalitions for vehicle-to-grid power regulation. In: AAMAS Workshop on Agent Technologies for Energy Systems (ATES 2010) (2010)
11. de Oliveira Ramos, G., Burguillo, J.C., Bazzan, A.L.: Dynamic constrained coalition formation among electric vehicles. J. Braz. Comput. Soc. **20**(1), 1–15 (2014). http://dx.doi.org/10.1186/1678-4804-20-8
12. Rahwan, T., Ramchurn, S.D., Jennings, N.R., Giovannucci, A.: An anytime algorithm for optimal coalition structure generation. J. Artif. Intell. Res. (JAIR) **34**(1), 521–567 (2009)
13. Ramchurn, S.D., Vytelingum, P., Rogers, A., Jennings, N.R.: Putting the 'smarts' into the smart grid: a grand challenge for artificial intelligence. Commun. ACM **55**(4), 86–97 (2012)
14. Valogianni, K., Ketter, W., Collins, J., Zhdanov, D.: Effective management of electric vehicle storage using smart charging. In: Proceedings of 28th AAAI Conference on Artificial Intelligence, pp. 472–478 (2014)
15. Vinyals, M., Bistaffa, F., Farinelli, A., Rogers, A.: Stable coalition formation among energy consumers in the smart grid. In: Proceedings of AAMAS 2012 (2012)
16. Voice, T., Ramchurn, S.D., Jennings, N.R.: On coalition formation with sparse synergies. In: Proceedings of AAMAS 2012, pp. 223–230 (2012)

17. Zhou, D., Huang, J., Schölkopf, B.: Learning with hypergraphs: clustering, classification, and embedding. In: Advances in Neural Information Processing Systems, pp. 1601–1608 (2006)
18. Zick, Y., Chalkiadakis, G., Elkind, E.: Overlapping coalition formation games: charting the tractability frontier. In: Proceedings of AAMAS 2012, pp. 787–794 (2012)

Forming Stable Coalitions in Large Systems with Self-interested Agents

Pavel Janovsky[✉] and Scott A. DeLoach

Department of Computer Science, Kansas State University,
Manhattan, KS 66506, USA
{janovsky,sdeloach}@ksu.edu

Abstract. In coalition formation with self-interested agents both social welfare of the multi-agent system and stability of individual coalitions must be taken into account. However, in large-scale systems with thousands of agents, finding an optimal solution with respect to both metrics is infeasible.

In this paper we propose an approach for finding coalition structures with suboptimal social welfare and coalition stability in large-scale multi-agent systems. Our approach uses multi-agent simulation to model a dynamic coalition formation process. Agents increase coalition stability by deviating from unstable coalitions. Furthermore we present an approach for estimating coalition stability, which alleviates exponential complexity of coalition stability computation. This approach enables us to select a solution with high values of both social welfare and coalition stability.

We experimentally show that our approach causes a major increase in coalition stability compared to a baseline social welfare-maximizing algorithm, while maintaining a very small decrease in social welfare.

Keywords: Coalition formation · Coalition stability · Multi-agent simulation

1 Introduction

Coalition formation is a process of grouping of agents into *coalitions* in order to increase the agents' cooperation. Examples of coalition formation include task allocation or collective purchasing. A goal of coalition formation is often to increase social welfare of the multi-agent system. However, such a goal can generate unrealistic solutions if the agents prefer their own profit to the global social welfare. These self-interested agents would deviate from the computed social welfare-maximizing coalitions. Consider the following example[1]. Three agents x, y, and z, can form coalitions with the following distribution of profit: $\{x = 2, y = 2, z = 3\}, \{x = 3, y = 3\}, \{x = 1, z = 1\}, \{y = 1, z = 1\}, \{x = 0\}$,

---

[1] In this example we assume that social welfare is equal to sum of coalition values, which are in turn calculated by summing up agents' profits.

© Springer International Publishing AG 2017
N. Criado Pacheco et al. (Eds.): EUMAS 2016/AT 2016, LNAI 10207, pp. 109–123, 2017.
DOI: 10.1007/978-3-319-59294-7_10

$\{y = 0\}$, and $\{z = 0\}$. The first coalition yields the highest total social welfare of 7. However, agents x and y would jointly deviate from this coalition and form the second coalition in order to maximize their own profit.

In coalition formation with self-interested agents, *stability* of the coalitions, which measures the coalition's ability to de-incentivize any sub-coalition of agents from leaving the coalition, must be addressed as a concept that along with the social welfare influences the coalition formation algorithms and solutions. Coalition formation is usually split into three sub-problems [17]: coalition structure generation, solving the optimization problem in each coalition, and division of the coalition's profit among its agents. Coalition stability is relevant to the profit division sub-problem, and is addressed in literature mainly through the concept of a *core*, which is a set of allocations to the agents in a coalition, such that these allocations cannot be improved upon by allocations to a subset of these agents. While the *core* is a strong concept, its computation in a setting where coalition values are generated by general polynomial-time functions requires an evaluation of all $2^{|C|}$ possible sub-coalitions of each coalition C containing $|C|$ agents. In this setting checking whether a solution is in the *core* is *co-NP-complete* [7], and determining whether the *core* is non-empty is $\Delta_2^P - complete$ [7]. This complexity makes the use of the *core* in large-scale systems with thousands of agents infeasible. Therefore instead of the *core* we approach coalition stability using multi-agent simulation. Instead of looking for stable distribution of the coalition value to the agents, we specify an allocation scheme beforehand and let the agents utilize this information to choose more stable coalitions.

Specifically, the contributions of this paper are the following:

1. *An algorithm for large-scale coalition formation of thousands of agents that uses deviations of the agents in order to increase coalition stability.* Our approach uses multi-agent simulation, in which agents make decisions about joining, leaving, and deviating from coalitions. We show the approach in Sect. 3, and we discuss a deviation strategy in Sect. 3.1. Finally, we evaluate our algorithm experimentally in Sect. 4.
2. *An approach for selecting sub-optimal solutions based on their social welfare and coalition stability.* We discuss the ways to select a solution out of a pool of solutions for which stability is unknown and expensive to compute in Sect. 3.2.

To the best of our knowledge our approach is the first that uses multi-agent simulation to find suboptimal coalition structures with respect to social welfare and coalition stability in large-scale multi-agent systems, in which coalition values are computed using arbitrary polynomial-time functions.

2   Problem Statement

We study the coalition formation problem, in which agents $a_1, a_2, \ldots, a_n \in A$ form coalitions C_i such that each agent belongs to exactly one coalition. We assume that the agents have full information about each others' states.

A coalition structure CS is a set of all coalitions C_i that the agents formed. The task is to find a coalition structure that maximizes its social welfare as well as its stability.

In order to measure the social welfare of the formed coalition structure, we first define $v(C)$ as a value of coalition C, and $v(CS)$ as a value of the coalition structure as

$$v(CS) = \sum_{C \in CS} v(C), \tag{1}$$

where $v(C)$ is assigned to the coalition C by a polynomial-time function. The social welfare is represented by a gain metric, which was defined in [8] as $g(CS) = \frac{v(CS) - v(CS_0)}{n}$, where CS_0 denotes the coalition structure of singleton coalitions. The gain shows how much on average an agent benefits from coalition formation. We use gain to measure the social welfare of a coalition structure.

Self-interested agents maximize their own profit, which we define for agent a_j participating in coalition C_i as

$$p_{C_i}(a_j) = v(C_i \cup \{a_j\}) - v(C_i), \tag{2}$$

where the coalition values $v(C_i \cup \{a_j\})$ and $v(C_i)$ are computed right after and right before the agent entered the coalition respectively. The profit reflects marginal contributions of agents to the coalitions, [3] describes games that use this profit sharing scheme as Labor Union games. This definition of profit guarantees that the allocation to the agents granted at the point of entry to the coalition will not change later regardless of further additions of agents to the coalition. We discuss other profit sharing schemes in Sect. 5.

In order to measure stability of coalition structure CS we need to determine stability of all coalitions $C_i \in CS$. Determining the coalition stability is computationally expensive, because it requires evaluation of all $2^{|C|}$ sub-coalitions. We therefore introduce $stability_\alpha$ to approximate the stability of coalition structures. We say that a coalition C is α−stable if no sub-coalition D with $\langle 1, \alpha \rangle$ members can be formed in which some agents would benefit more and no agent would benefit less than in C. Formally,

C is α−stable iff $\nexists D \subset C, |D| \leq \alpha$:

$$\exists a_j \in D : p_D(a_j) > p_C(a_j) \land \forall a_j \in D : p_D(a_j) \geq p_C(a_j). \tag{3}$$

We denote S_α as the set of α−stable coalitions in CS, for which it holds that $\forall \alpha : S_{\alpha+1} \subseteq S_\alpha$. Finally we define $stability_\alpha$ of a coalition structure in terms of α as

$$stability_\alpha(CS) = \frac{|S_\alpha|}{|CS|} \tag{4}$$

where $|CS|$ denotes the number of coalitions in CS. It holds that

$$\lim_{\alpha \to max_{C_i \in CS}(|C_i|)} stability_\alpha(CS) = stability(CS), \tag{5}$$

where $stability(CS)$ is the true stability of CS, which we define as the ratio of stable coalitions in CS. Since $stability_\alpha$ is non-increasing with respect to α, it can serve as an upper estimate of the coalition structure stability.

Finally, we use the price of stability

$$PoS(CS_{sw}, CS_{sa}) = \frac{g(CS_{sw})}{g(CS_{sa})} \tag{6}$$

to show the ratio between the gain of social welfare maximizing solutions CS_{sw} and the gain of solutions reached by behavior of self-interested agents CS_{sa}.

3   Methodology

We find solutions to coalition formation using multi-agent simulation. We extend a multi-agent simulation framework for large-scale coalition formation proposed in [8], in which the agents maximize the social welfare. In that framework the agents use strategies to decide about leaving their coalitions and joining new coalitions. The coalitions are evaluated by a polynomial-time valuation function $f: C \rightarrow \mathbb{R}$. This process repeats in an iterative fashion, resulting in an agent-driven search of the state space of coalition structures. While [8] shows almost-optimal performance in small-scale scenarios and stable gain in large-scale scenarios, it does not consider stability of the solutions.

In order to increase stability of coalition structures we extend the algorithm from [8] by first allowing the agents to create more stable sub-coalitions within their coalition by the process of deviation, and second by selecting the best solution out of the pool of solutions generated by the simulation with respect to both social welfare and stability.

3.1   Deviation

Deviation allows agents to leave their current coalition along with other agents from the same coalition. We allow the agents to deviate from their coalitions in order to guide the search towards more stable coalition structures. There are two conditions that a sub-coalition of agents $D \subset C$ must satisfy in order to be able to deviate from a coalition C: (1) $\forall a_j \in D: p_D(a_j) \geq p_C(a_j)$, and (2) $\exists a_j \in D: p_D(a_j) > p_C(a_j)$. These conditions are satisfied by sub-coalitions in which no agent loses profit by deviation and at least one agent gains profit. If an agent finds a sub-coalition that satisfies these conditions, this sub-coalition will deviate from their current coalition C and form a new coalition, thus increasing the stability of the original coalition. Considering all $2^{|C|-1}$ possible sub-coalitions that an agent can be part of is infeasible, therefore agents use a heuristic to guide their search. Some possible heuristics are adding agents to the sub-coalition in order of increasing and decreasing profit, and in random order. Our experiments showed that most stable coalitions were found using the increasing profit heuristic. We therefore let the agents to form the sub-coalitions by adding other agents in order of increasing profit. An agent keeps adding other agents to the new sub-coalition as long as the above-mentioned conditions are met.

Deviation is performed in our model after the agents decide on leaving and joining coalitions. Each iteration of the simulation therefore consists of two steps: social welfare maximization by leaving and joining coalitions, and stability maximization by deviation. The agents deviate recursively i.e. they try to deviate from the new coalition created by their deviation.

3.2 Solution Selection

An inherent advantage of using multi-agent simulation for coalition formation is the fact that it creates a pool of solutions by storing all coalition structures encountered during the search. At the end of the simulation, [8] selects from this pool a solution that maximizes the gain. We propose to select a solution based on both gain and stability metrics. However, computing stability of a coalition structure is computationally expensive, therefore we use $stability_\alpha$ to estimate the true stability of the solutions.

We compute $stability_\alpha$ in an iterative fashion for increasing $\alpha \in \langle 1, \alpha_{max} \rangle$. We only have to determine whether a coalition is α-stable if it is $(\alpha - 1)$-stable. We mark a coalition C α-stable if in all permutations of all combinations of α agents from C some agents lose or no agent gains profit[2]. We then calculate $stability_\alpha$ using Eq. 4.

After $stability_\alpha$ of all coalition structures is computed, a multi-criteria optimization is used to select a best coalition structure based on its gain and $stability_\alpha$. Common approaches of multi criteria optimization are finding Pareto optimal solutions and designing a fitness function. In our experiments we used a simple fitness function that allows us to give preference to any of the criteria:

$$f(CS, \alpha) = w_g \cdot g_{norm}(CS) + w_s \cdot stability_\alpha(CS), \qquad (7)$$

where $g_{norm}(CS) \in \langle 0, 1 \rangle$ is a normalized gain of CS, $\alpha \in \langle 1, n \rangle$ is an input parameter that represents the trade-off between quality of solution stability estimate and computation time, and w_g and w_s are weights assigned to the two criteria[3]. Finally, the best coalition structure is returned, such that

$$CS_{best} = \underset{CS}{\mathrm{argmax}}\, f(CS, \alpha). \qquad (8)$$

Figure 1 shows the effect of deviation and solution selection. A combination of both of these approaches yields solutions with higher stability while only sacrificing a small fraction of the gain.

4 Experimental Analysis

We tested our algorithm in two coalition formation scenarios: collective energy purchasing and resource sharing.

---

[2] All permutations must be considered because the order in which agents join coalitions determines their profit.

[3] Given the values of $g_{norm}(CS)$ and $stability_\alpha(CS)$ for each CS, Pareto optimal solutions can also easily be found.

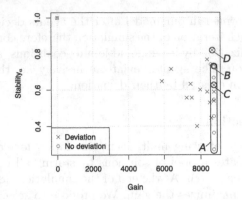

Fig. 1. Gain and *stability*$_\alpha$ of coalition structures generated by a single simulation with 100 agents, 15 iterations, and $\alpha = 4$. With no deviation and no solution selection, a coalition structure is selected randomly from A, since only the gain is maximized. Solution selection without deviation returns B. Deviation without solution selection returns C, and deviation used along with solution selection returns D.

The collective energy purchasing scenario, proposed in [20], models agents as households that buy electricity based on their requested daily energy profiles. Electricity can be bought at spot and forward markets. The spot market provides amounts of energy based on the current demand, while the forward market provides cheaper electricity which has to be bought ahead of time. Agents form coalitions in order to make their aggregate energy profiles more predictable so they could exploit the reduced prices of the forward market. The valuation function which represents the payment of a coalition was proposed in [20] as

$$v(C) = \sum_{t=1}^{T} q_S^t(C) \cdot p_S + T \cdot q_F(C) \cdot p_F + \kappa(C), \qquad (9)$$

where p_S and p_F represent unit prices at the spot and forward markets, respectively, $q_S^t(C)$ represents the amount of energy to be bought at the spot market at time t, and $T \cdot q_F(C)$ represents the total amount of energy to be bought at the forward market for time interval T (in our experiments, $T = 24$ represents a length of a daily energy profile). $\kappa(C) = -|C|^\gamma$ was proposed in [6] to represent the penalty for the coalition size. An algorithm given in [20] computes optimal energy amounts for a coalition given the coalition's aggregate energy profile. Using this algorithm, we obtain energy amounts $q_S^t(C)$ and $q_F(C)$ that we use to compute the coalition value $v(C)$. For this scenario we used a dataset of daily energy profiles of households in Portugal [11]. For each household we averaged daily energy profiles of all days in January 2014 into a single average daily energy profile. The unit prices were set to $p_S = -80$ and $p_F = -70$, as suggested in [20]. We use negative values because the coalition value $v(C)$ is maximized. Following [6] we set $\gamma = 1.1$.

The resource sharing scenario, proposed in [8], models a market in which cooperation is rewarded. Agents operate with resources, each agent can either have a surplus or shortage of each resource. Agents within coalitions are able to transfer their resource surpluses to agents with shortages. The coalition value depends on the amount of resources transferred. The valuation function was proposed in [8] for k resources as

$$v(C) = \sum_{l=1}^{k} min(b_C^+[l], b_C^-[l]) + \kappa(C), \qquad (10)$$

where $b_C^+[l]$ is the positive balance for resource l, which is the sum of surpluses of resource l over all agents in coalition C, and $b_C^-[l]$ is an absolute value of the negative balance computed with the shortages, respectively. $\kappa(C) = -|C|^\gamma$ [6] captures the penalty for the coalition size. We used an international trade dataset provided by the World Trade Organization [12], which stores import and export amounts in US dollars between 167 countries in 17 commodity types. The amount of each resource of each agent was computed as the difference between export and import amounts of the given country in the year 2014. Positive and negative values of the resulting resource amounts denote surplus and shortage respectively. Similarly as in [8], we set $\gamma = 2$ for the resource sharing scenario to prevent the grand coalition from being the trivial gain-maximizing solution.

Because the use of κ as a coalition size penalty causes agents to form small coalitions, we instead define κ as $\kappa = min(-|C|+\mu, 0)^\gamma$, which effectively allowed us to increase the average coalition size and thus make the problem harder to compute due to its exponential complexity. In our experiments we set $\mu = 10$.

Several agent strategies were studied in [8]. In our experiments we use the *local search* strategy [8], in which the agents perform a best response move to new coalitions i.e. the agents select coalitions which grant them maximal marginal profit. If the search reaches a local optimum for all agents, a random jump is applied by all agents in order to escape this optimum.

We used two values of α for evaluation of *stability*$_\alpha$. For the solution selection algorithm, we set $\alpha_{ss} = 3$ to allow the algorithm to quickly compute *stability*$_\alpha$ of multiple solutions, and for the final stability verification we set $\alpha = 4$ to obtain a better final stability estimate. In order to give equal preference to both gain and stability we set the weights $w_g = w_s = 1$.

In order to achieve reasonable run-times of our algorithm, we used the following number of iterations N in our experiments. For instances with number of agents $n < 100$ we set $N = 100$ and for instances with $n > 100$ we set $N = 10$.

We ran our Java implementation of the proposed algorithms on 2.7 GHz Intel Xeon E5 CPU with 2 GB of memory. We averaged our results over 10 random runs [4].

4.1   Experiment Results

We compared results of our algorithms with the baseline multi-agent simulation algorithm for coalition formation [8] using the *stability*$_\alpha$ and *price of stability* metrics. Average values of *stability*$_\alpha$ and *price of stability* are shown in

---

[4] Random runs are necessary because agents make decisions in random order.

Table 1. Trade-off between average stability and average price of stability achieved by our algorithms with $\alpha = 4$ and $n = \langle 20, 5000 \rangle$.

Algorithm		Results	
Deviation	Solution selection	Average $stability_\alpha$	Average PoS
No	No	0.3914	-
YES	No	0.6299	1.0308
No	YES	0.6665	1.0210
YES	YES	0.8185	1.0629

Table 1. The first row of Table 1 shows results of the baseline algorithm. The following rows show how the average $stability_\alpha$ increases when we plug in the proposed stability-increasing methods. As expected, the average *price of stability* is increasing with the increase in $stability_\alpha$, but the increase in *price of stability* is very low compared to the significant improvement in $stability_\alpha$. Table 1 therefore shows that our algorithms find solutions with much higher stability while only sacrificing a fraction of the social welfare.

Stability of our solutions is depicted in Fig. 2a in collective energy purchasing scenario and in Fig. 2c in resource sharing scenario. The use of solution selection algorithm never decreases the stability of the solutions, therefore the solutions generated by the solution selection algorithm always dominate the baseline algorithm with respect to stability. This dominance is not guaranteed by the deviation algorithm. However, in most instances the deviation algorithm achieves higher $stability_\alpha$ than the baseline algorithm. Finally, the highest increase in $stability_\alpha$ is achieved in majority of instances when the deviation and the solution selection algorithms are used together. As shown in Table 1, the average $stability_\alpha$ increases from 39% achieved by the baseline algorithm to 82% achieved by the combination of deviation and solution selection algorithms.

The solution selection algorithm evaluates $stability_\alpha$ of all coalition structures for given α_{ss}. Figure 2b shows $stability_\alpha$ and gain for varying values of α_{ss}, where $\alpha = 5$. As expected, the $stability_\alpha$ of the selected solution is increasing with increasing α_{ss}, since higher α_{ss} provides a better stability estimate. However, due to the inherent trade-off between coalition stability and social welfare, the gain decreases with increasing α_{ss}. Figure 2b only shows algorithms that include solution selection and are therefore affected by changing α_{ss}.

The number of iterations N affects the quality of the resulting coalition structure. We show $stability_\alpha$ and gain of our algorithm for varying numbers of iterations N in Fig. 2d. With the increasing number of iterations the agents have more opportunity to cooperate by creating coalitions, which leads to an increase in gain. However, higher social welfare might result in lower stability of the coalitions. This effect is most obvious in the results of the baseline algorithm, in which due to the increase in gain the $stability_\alpha$ drops significantly. However, when we plug in the stability-increasing approaches proposed in this paper, the decrease in $stability_\alpha$ is much slower.

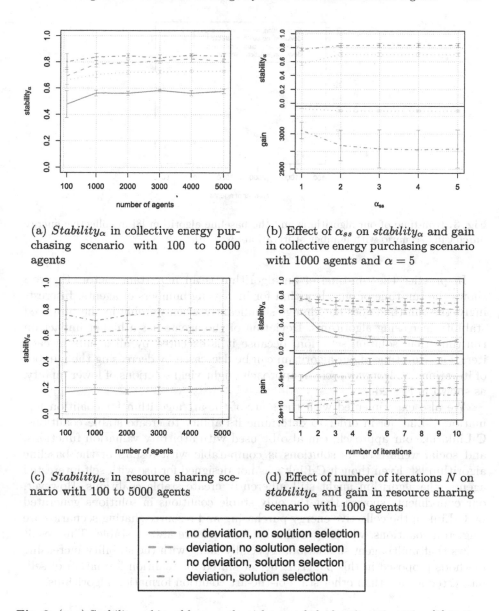

(a) *Stability*$_\alpha$ in collective energy purchasing scenario with 100 to 5000 agents

(b) Effect of α_{ss} on *stability*$_\alpha$ and gain in collective energy purchasing scenario with 1000 agents and $\alpha = 5$

(c) *Stability*$_\alpha$ in resource sharing scenario with 100 to 5000 agents

(d) Effect of number of iterations N on *stability*$_\alpha$ and gain in resource sharing scenario with 1000 agents

— no deviation, no solution selection
– – deviation, no solution selection
· · · · no deviation, solution selection
· – · deviation, solution selection

Fig. 2. (a, c) Stability achieved by our algorithms and the baseline algorithm [8] in the collective energy purchasing and resource sharing scenarios: combination of deviation and solution selection algorithms yields highest stability. (b) Effect of α_{ss} on *stability*$_\alpha$ and gain: higher α_{ss} yields better stability estimate and therefore increases stability of the selected solution. (d) Effect of number of iterations N on *stability*$_\alpha$ and gain: higher N yields higher gain because the agents have more opportunity to form coalitions, which naturally leads to a decrease in stability. Decrease in *stability*$_\alpha$ achieved by our algorithms is significantly lower than the decrease achieved by the baseline algorithm. Error bars show standard deviation of aggregated variables.

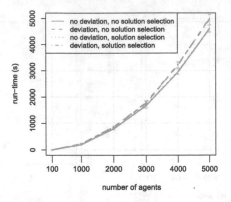

Fig. 3. Run-time of our algorithms and the baseline algorithm [8] in collective energy purchasing scenario with number of iterations $N = 10$.

In practice the run-time of an algorithm is an important factor. Figure 3 shows the run-time of our algorithm for increasing numbers of agents. Interestingly, the run-time does not change significantly when we plug in the proposed stability-increasing algorithms. Deviation of the agents has a higher impact on run-time than solution selection, because it is executed by all agents in each iteration. Run-time of our algorithm can be decreased by decreasing the number of iterations N, however such an approach might yield solutions of lower quality, as shown in Fig. 2d.

We also experimented with the state-of-the-art algorithm for coalition formation C-Link [6] in order to determine its ability to create stable coalitions. C-Link, like our approach, can also be used with arbitrary valuation functions, and social welfare of its solutions is comparable with results of the baseline algorithm [8]. Even though C-Link was not designed for use with self-interested agents, the algorithm might still inherently create stable coalitions. However, our experiments showed that the only stable coalitions in solutions generated by C-Link in the collective energy purchasing and resource sharing scenarios are singleton coalitions, which by definition in Eq. 3 are always stable. This result shows that multi-agent simulation, especially along with the stability-increasing methods proposed in this paper, is better suited for coalition formation of self-interested agents than other state-of-the-art coalition formation algorithms.

5   Discussion

We will now discuss some design choices that have to be made when designing a multi-agent system for coalition formation of self-interested agents. We will discuss various profit sharing schemes, definitions of stability, and behaviors of self-interested agents. Then we will analyze time complexity and convergence of our algorithms. Finally we will discuss practical usefulness of our approach.

Several profit sharing schemes have been proposed in the literature. Equal sharing [14] divides the coalition value equally among all its agents, fair value sharing [3] defines agents' payoff as marginal contribution to the coalition, labor union sharing [3], which we use in our experiments, defines agents' payoff as agents' marginal contribution to the coalition at the time of entry, and Shapley sharing [3] assigns payoffs based on agents' Shapley values. Among these sharing schemes, labor union is the only one in which consequent additions to the coalition do not affect agent's payoff assigned at the time of coalition entry. It is the only sharing scheme that models marginal contribution and at the same time is reasonably computationally efficient, which is why we used it in our experiments.

Several concepts have been used to describe coalition stability. Nash equilibrium describes a state in which no agent has an incentive to unilaterally deviate. A stronger concept is a core, which is a set of profit assignments to agents, such that no subset of agents in a coalition has an incentive to jointly deviate from the coalition. Our definition of stability in Eq. 3 is following the concept of the core. One might also consider a stricter version of the definition, in which all deviating agents must benefit by the deviation, i.e. $\forall a_j \in D \colon p_D(a_j) > p_C(a_j)$. However, this strict definition of stability yields high stability values for arbitrary coalitions, and therefore renders the problem less interesting.

Our algorithm searches the state space of coalition structures using three actions of the agents: leave a coalition, join a coalition, and deviate from a coalition. We designed these actions in order to search for coalition structures with high values of both social welfare and coalition stability. However, the space of possible agents' actions is not limited to actions used in this paper. For example, agents from multiple coalitions could jointly deviate, agents could decide whether to allow other agents to enter their coalition, agents could force other agents in their coalition to leave, etc. Adding new actions to the agents' action space will lead to new behavior of the multi-agent system. When designing agents' actions we must take into account the specific problem that is being solved, the effect of the actions on agents' behavior, and the computational complexity of the designed actions.

Searching the exponential state space of coalition structures can lead to exponential worst-case time complexity of the search algorithms. However, we show a polynomial time complexity of both deviation and solution selection algorithms with respect to number of agents n and a constant α_{ss} bound. Deviation of a single agent requires sorting the agents in the coalition by marginal profit. The agents can deviate recursively, therefore the complexity of deviation of a single agent is $O(\sum_{i=1}^{n}(i \cdot log(i)))$, for which an upper bound is $O(n^2 log(n))$. Solution selection searches through all permutations of all combinations of size $\langle 1, \alpha_{ss} \rangle$ of agents in a coalition. Evaluating a single coalition therefore requires $O(\sum_{i=1}^{\alpha_{ss}}(i! \cdot \binom{n}{i}))$ steps. For $\alpha_{ss} << n$ it holds that

$$\sum_{i=1}^{\alpha_{ss}} \left(i! \cdot \binom{n}{i} \right) \leq \alpha_{ss} \cdot \alpha_{ss}! \cdot \binom{n}{\alpha_{ss}} \leq \alpha_{ss} \cdot n^{\alpha_{ss}}, \qquad (11)$$

therefore the worst time complexity of finding $stability_\alpha$ for a single coalition with $\alpha = \alpha_{ss}$ is $O(n^{\alpha_{ss}})$. The worst-case time complexity of the solution selection algorithm is therefore $O(N \cdot n^{\alpha_{ss}+1})$, given the input of N coalition structures, each containing at most n coalitions. Worst-case time complexity of the baseline coalition formation algorithm is $O(N \cdot n^2)$, as was shown in [8].

Building on the complexity analysis above, Table 2 shows worst-case time complexity of our algorithms. Since we treat α_{ss} as a small constant, we get a polynomial complexity for all proposed algorithms. The analysis in Table 2 is very conservative, since we assume that each coalition structure contains n coalitions, each coalition is composed of n agents, and each sub-coalition deviating from coalition C is of size $|C| - 1$. The analysis does not include complexity of the valuation functions, as these are given as an input to the simulation. However, both collective energy purchasing and resource sharing valuation functions require constant time with respect to the number of agents n, and therefore do not affect the complexity analysis. Our algorithm is centralized, therefore we do not assume any additional cost of communication between agents, as would be the case with algorithms that distribute the computation among the agents.

Table 2. Worst-case time complexity of our algorithms and the baseline [8] as a function of number of iterations N, number of agents n, and a small constant α_{ss}. In our experiments we set $\alpha_{ss} = 3$.

Algorithm		Worst-case time complexity
Deviation	Solution selection	
No	No	$O(N \cdot n^2)$
Yes	No	$O(N \cdot n^3 \cdot log(n))$
No	Yes	$O(N \cdot n^{max(\alpha_{ss}+1,2)})$
Yes	Yes	$O(N \cdot n^{max(\alpha_{ss}+1,3)} \cdot log(n))$

An important aspect of an algorithm is its convergence behavior. The baseline algorithm converges if the random jump is not used [8]. Similarly, if the agents were only allowed to deviate, the simulation would converge from any initial state because each deviation splits coalitions and decreases the average coalition size. Therefore separate maximization of social welfare, as well as separate maximization of coalition stability, is guaranteed to converge. However, combining these steps in order to maximize both metrics does not guarantee convergence, because social welfare and coalition stability are somewhat contradictory goals.

Our algorithm can be used in real-world scenarios where coalition stability has to be considered. Solutions with high stability are more realistic, because they reflect decision making of self-interested agents. Such decision making might lower the social welfare of the solution, but as we showed in Table 1, the *price of stability* of our solutions only slightly increases with major increase in stability. Furthermore, the weights w_g and w_s in Eq. 7 can be adjusted to give preference to either the social welfare or stability.

6   Related Work

Many algorithms have been proposed that search for a coalition structure with optimal or sub-optimal social welfare without considering coalition stability. Among them we highlight dynamic programming approaches [5,15,22], hierarchical clustering for large numbers of agents [6], and approaches that use multi-agent simulation [8,10,13]. We refer the reader to a recent comprehensive survey on coalition structure generation in [16].

Theoretical properties of stability in coalition formation have been studied extensively. [18] provides an overview of social-welfare and stability in the coalition formation setting. [14] studies the existence of core stable coalition structures with respect to profit sharing rules and agents' preferences over coalitions.

Algorithms have been proposed to find stable coalitions in coalition formation games. [3] proposes algorithms to find Nash equilibria for various profit sharing schemes. Unlike [3], which assumes deviations of single agents only, we look for coalitions that are stable with respect to deviations of groups of agents. [1] computes profit sharing between agents that grants stability of the solutions for subadditive games only. Again, we do not require such restrictions on the valuation functions. An iterative approach for finding core-stable coalitions was proposed in [2]. While the approach in [2] is similar to ours, it can only be used in small scale scenarios due to its high complexity, as was shown in [4], where the algorithm from [2] was improved and empirically tested. An auction-based algorithm for creation of stable coalitions in large scale e-marketplaces is proposed in [21]. Coalition stability in a request for proposal domain is studied in [9], in which a negotiation protocol for coalition formation is introduced. There stability is demonstrated by showing that allowing agents to deviate from pure strategy profiles is not beneficial. It is unclear whether algorithms proposed in [21] and [9] can be modified for use with general polynomial-time valuation functions. Finally, [19] proposed algorithms that maximize social welfare and find stable payoff division among agents. However, the algorithms restrict the allowed size of coalitions, which renders the algorithms unusable in large-scale problem instances where large coalitions might occur.

7   Conclusion

Algorithms that find stable coalition structures are often proposed for settings that restrict the properties of the valuation functions. Practical aspects of the high complexity of finding stable coalitions for large-scale multi-agent systems are often not considered.

In this work we proposed an approach for increasing coalition stability in large-scale coalition formation with self-interested agents and arbitrary valuation functions. We modeled agent behavior using multi-agent simulation, in which we let agents to choose profitable coalitions and deviate from unstable coalitions. At the end of the simulation, we selected a solution out of a pool of generated coalition structures based on its social welfare and stability. We experimentally showed that our approach is able to increase the stability of the solutions in two real-world scenarios. We also showed that the necessary price for this increase in stability that our algorithm incurs to the social welfare is very low.

Some open questions and areas of further research, which we plan to investigate, include coalition formation of agents with limited information, distributed asynchronous simulation of coalition formation, and coalition formation with dynamically changing valuation functions.

Acknowledgements. This work was supported by the US National Science Foundation via Award No. CNS-1544705.

References

1. Anshelevich, E., Sekar, S.: Computing stable coalitions: approximation algorithms for reward sharing. In: Markakis, E., Schäfer, G. (eds.) WINE 2015. LNCS, vol. 9470, pp. 31–45. Springer, Heidelberg (2015). doi:10.1007/978-3-662-48995-6_3
2. Arnold, T., Schwalbe, U.: Dynamic coalition formation and the core. J. Econ. Behav. Organ. **49**, 363–380 (2002)
3. Augustine, J., Chen, N., Elkind, E., Fanelli, A., Gravin, N., Shiryaev, D.: Dynamics of profit-sharing games. In: 21st International Joint Conference on Artificial Intelligence, IJCAI 2011 (2011)
4. Bistaffa, F., Farinelli, A.: A fast approach to form core-stable coalitions based on a dynamic model. In: 2013 IEEE/WIC/ACM International Conference on Intelligent Agent Technology, IAT 2013 (2013)
5. Cruz-Mencía, F., Cerquides, J., Espinosa, A.: Optimizing performance for coalition structure generation problems' IDP algorithm. In: International Conference on Parallel and Distributed Processing Techniques and Applications (2013)
6. Farinelli, A., Bicego, M., Ramchurn, S., Zucchelli, M.: C-link: a hierarchical clustering approach to large-scale near-optimal coalition formation. In: 23rd International Joint Conference on Artificial Intelligence (2013)
7. Greco, G., Malizia, E., Palopoli, L., Scarcello, F.: On the complexity of the core over coalition structures. In: 22nd International Joint Conference on Artificial Intelligence (2011)
8. Janovsky, P., DeLoach, S.A.: Multi-agent simulation framework for large-scale coalition formation. In: 2016 IEEE/WIC/ACM International Conference on Web Intelligence (2016)
9. Kraus, S., Shehory, O., Taase, G.: Coalition formation with uncertain heterogeneous information. In: Proceedings of the 2nd International Joint Conference on Autonomous Agents and Multiagent Systems (2003)
10. Lerman, K., Shehory, O.: Coalition formation for large-scale electronic markets. In: 4th International Conference on MultiAgent Systems (2000)
11. Lichman, M.: UCI machine learning repository (2013). https://archive.ics.uci.edu/ml/datasets/ElectricityLoadDiagrams20112014
12. World Trade Organization (n.d.). http://stat.wto.org/StatisticalProgram/WSDBStatProgramSeries.aspx. Accessed 03 Mar 2016
13. Merida-Campos, C., Willmott, S.: Modelling coalition formation over time for iterative coalition games. In: 3rd International Joint Conference on Autonomous Agents and Multiagent Systems, AAMAS 2004 (2004)

14. Pycia, M.: Stability and preference alignment in matching and coalition formation. Econometrica **80**, 323–362 (2012)
15. Rahwan, T., Jennings, N.R.: An improved dynamic programming algorithm for coalition structure generation. In: 7th International Conference on Autonomous Agents and Multiagent Systems (2008)
16. Rahwan, T., Michalak, T.P., Wooldridge, M., Jennings, N.R.: Coalition structure generation: a survey. Artif. Intell. **229**, 139–174 (2015)
17. Sandholm, T., Larson, K., Andersson, M., Shehory, O., Tohmé, F.: Coalition structure generation with worst case guarantees. Artif. Intell. **111**, 209–238 (1999)
18. Sandholm, T.W., Lesser, V.R.: Coalitions among computationally bounded agents. Artif. Intell. **94**, 99–137 (1997)
19. Shehory, O., Kraus, S.: Feasible formation of coalitions among autonomous agents in nonsuperadditive environments. Comput. Intell. **15**, 218–251 (1999)
20. Vinyals, M., Bistaffa, F., Farinelli, A., Rogers, A.: Coalitional energy purchasing in the smart grid. In: 2012 IEEE International Energy Conference and Exhibition, ENERGYCON 2012 (2012)
21. Yamamoto, J., Sycara, K.: A stable and efficient buyer coalition formation scheme for e-marketplaces. In: Proceedings of the 5th International Conference on Autonomous Agents, AGENTS 2001 (2001)
22. Yun Yeh, D.: A dynamic programming approach to the complete set partitioning problem. BIT Numer. Math. **26**, 467–474 (1986)

Heuristic Methods for Optimal Coalition Structure Generation

Amir Hussin and Shaheen Fatima(⊠)

Department of Computer Science, Loughborough University,
Loughborough, UK
s.s.fatima@lboro.ac.uk

Abstract. The problem of finding the optimal coalition structure arises frequently in multiagent systems. Heuristic approaches for solving this problem are needed because of its computational complexity. This paper studies two such approaches: *tabu search* and *simulated annealing*. Through simulations we show that tabu search generates better quality solutions than simulated annealing for coalition games in *characteristic function form* and those in *partition function form*.

1 Introduction

In a multi-agent system, the agents work together and take cooperative actions to achieve complex tasks [18]. The effective formation of coalitions is therefore essential. Many situations require the formation of not just a single coalition but a coalition structure, i.e., an exhaustive partition of agents into non-overlapping coalititions. A primary challenge is to generate a coalition structure in which the entire system performance is maximised.

The optimal coalition structure generation problem is commonly modelled as a cooperative game in either *characteristic function form* or in *partition function form* [3]. The former are called characteristic function games (CFGs) and the latter partition function games (PFGs). In both CFGs and PFGs, the value of a coalition structure is given as the sum of the values of its coalitions. For CFGs, the value of a coalition is given in terms of its members. For PFGs, the value of a coalition depends not only on its members but also on how the external agents are organized. In other words, some *externalities* are inherent in PFGs.

For CFGs and more so for PFGs, finding an optimal coalition structure is computationally hard. A number of deterministic methods have been developed for PFGs [1,9,22] but they have exponential time complexity. This presents the need for developing effective heuristic methods for finding a good enough solution as quickly as possible, especially for games with a large number of agents. Such methods are important for example in mission critical systems where a group of agents representing emergency responders need to partition their resources so the emergency situation is handled optimally. In these systems the agents need to react quickly and time lost looking for the absolute optimal can severely impact on handling the emergency. A quick locally optimal solution would be better

N. Criado Pacheco et al. (Eds.): EUMAS 2016/AT 2016, LNAI 10207, pp. 124–139, 2017.
DOI: 10.1007/978-3-319-59294-7_11

than a delayed globally optimal one because the situation may have changed during the time.

In the existing literature on heuristic methods, various approaches such as simulated annealing, genetic programming, particle swarm and ant colony have been studied for optimal coalition structure generation for CFGs (see Sect. 6 for details). However, the use of tabu search has so far not been studied even for CFGs although tabu search was previously shown to work well for other search problems such as bin packing [7], power systems network partitioning [4], crew scheduling [6], quadratic assignment [16], and vehicle routing [2]. Moreover, the use of heuristics for PFGs has been little explored in the literature.

Given this, we aim to compare two heuristic methods: *tabu search* and *simulated annealing* for finding an optimal coalition structure for both CFGs and PFGs. A key difference between tabu search and simulated annealing is that the former has a memory for recording the moves made during the search while the latter is memory-less and relies only on a random selection of next move. Since the latter requires less resource it might be more useful especially when there is a large number of agents provided the quality of its solution is good enough. Our objective is to determine how its performance compares to that of tabu search.

For evaluating the performance of a method, we consider the *quality of solution* generated and also the *time* taken to generate it. Since performance depends on the type of input data, we empirically measure average performance over a range of inputs. For this, we consider ten different probability distributions (see Sect. 5 for details) from which the input data is drawn randomly and then calculate average performance. Simulation results indicate that tabu search performs better than simulated annealing for CFGs and PFGs; given the same amount of time, tabu search yields a solution that is closer to the exact optimum than the solution generated by simulated annealing. Both tabu search and simulated annealing methods we implemented have *anytime* property; the quality of solution generated improves with the running time.

The main contributions of this paper are: (i) it provides the first comparative evaluation of tabu search and simulated annealing for coalition structure generation, (ii) the evaluation is done for both CFGs and PFGs, and (iii) the evaluation is conducted extensively over a wide range of input data.

The paper is organised as follows. We begin in Sect. 2 by defining the problem. Section 3 is a description of tabu search and Sect. 4 of simulated annealing. Section 5 provides details of simulations set-up and a performance analysis of these two methods. Section 6 is about related literature and Sect. 7 draws conclusions.

2   Problem Specification

A coalitional game is a tuple $\langle A, v \rangle$ where $A = \{1, \ldots, n\}$ is a set of n agents and v is a *coalition value function*. The definition of v depends on the type of coalition game. There are two types of coalition games: CFGs and PFGs.

Definition 1. *A coalition structure is an exhaustive partition of A into non-overlapping coalitions.*

In accordance with convention, the coalitions in any coalition structure will be arranged in the increasing order of their smallest members with the agents in the coalition being arranged in alphabetical order.

For example, for $A = \{1,2,3\}$, the 5 possible coalition structures are: $\{\{1\}, \{2\}, \{3\}\}$, $\{\{1,2\}, \{3\}\}$, $\{\{1,3\}, \{2\}\}$, $\{\{1\}, \{2,3\}\}$, and $\{\{1,2,3\}\}$.

For n agents, there are $Bell(n) \sim \Theta(n^n)$ possible coalition structures, i.e., the number of coalition structures is exponential in n. Let Π^A denote the set of all possible coalition structures and $|\Pi^A|$ the cardinality of Π^A. We will first introduce CFGs and then PFGs.

CFGs: For these games, the value of a coalition depends solely on its members. v is a mapping of the form $v : 2^A \to \mathbb{R}$. It is a function that assigns a utility value to each subset, i.e., a *coalition* of A with $v(\phi) = 0$. All non-empty subsets of A are valid coalitions. A coalition is denoted by $C \subseteq A$ and the set of all possible coalitions as C^A. The cardinality of the this set is $|C^A| = 2^n - 1$.

Example 1: For $A = \{1,2,3\}$, v is defined as follows: $v(\{\phi\}) = 0$, $v(\{1\}) = 1$, $v(\{2\}) = 2$, $v(\{3\}) = 1$, $v(\{1,2\}) = 4$, $v(\{1,3\}) = 1$, $v(\{2,3\}) = 3$, $v(\{1,2,3\}) = 3$.

PFGs: For these games, the value of a coalition depends on its members and also on the coalition structure it is embedded in. v is a mapping of the form $v : 2^A \times \Pi^A \to \mathbb{R}$. It is a function that assigns a utility value to each pair comprised of (i) a subset $C \subseteq A$, i.e., a *coalition* and (ii) a partition in which C is embedded.

Example 2: For $A = \{1,2,3\}$, v is defined as follows: $v(\{1\}, \{\{1\}, \{2\}, \{3\}\}) = 1$, $v(\{1\}, \{\{1\}, \{2,3\}\}) = 2$, $v(\{2\}, \{\{1\}, \{2\}, \{3\}\}) = 1$, $v(\{2\}, \{\{1,3\}, \{2\}\}) = 4$, $v(\{3\}, \{\{1\}, \{2\}, \{3\}\}) = 2$, $v(\{3\}, \{\{1,2\}, \{3\}\}) = 1$, $v(\{1,2\}, \{\{1,2\}, \{3\}\}) = 7$, $v(\{1,3\}, \{\{1,3\}, \{2\}\}) = 5$, $v(\{2,3\}, \{\{1\}, \{2,3\}\}) = 4$, $v(\{1,2,3\}, \{\{1,2,3\}\}) = 3$.

The value of a structure CS is the sum of the values of its constituent coalitions. Thus we have:

$$v(CS) = \begin{cases} \sum_{C \in CS} v(C) & \text{for CFGs} \\ \sum_{C \in CS} v(C, CS) & \text{for PFGs} \end{cases}$$

Between all the $|\Pi^A|$ possible coalition structures, the problem is find one with the highest value, i.e., an *optimal coalition structure* which is defined as follows:

$$CS^* = \arg\max_{CS \in \Pi^A} v(CS) \tag{1}$$

Given the exponential number of possible structures, it is computationally infeasible to search the entire search space exhaustively. We therefore explore two heuristic search methods: *tabu search* and *simulated annealing*.

3   Heuristic Search Method 1: Tabu Search

We begin with a quick overview of tabu search and then describe the method we implemented for optimal coalition structure generation. Tabu search [10] is a general heuristic method that attempts to quickly find high quality solutions by using a *neighbourhood search* guided with *tabu memory*. The basic concept is to maintain a tabu list of points already visited in the search space and avoid re-visiting them and those points which are known to be inferior to ones in the tabu list. By avoiding solutions that are already visited, the method ensures that new parts of the search space are being investigated. This also helps to avoid local maxima and thus enables better solutions to be found as the search progresses.

Algorithm 1. TACOS: Tabu search algorithm for finding an optimal coalition structure

---

1: $tabuList \leftarrow [\ ]$ {Tabu list initially empty}
2: $CS \leftarrow$ randomly generated CS; {Generate a random start point}
3: $currentBest \leftarrow CS$
4: **for** $iterationCount \leftarrow 1, maxIterations$ **do** {see Table 2 for $maxIterations$}
5:     Generate a neighbourhood N of CS
6:     Find the $bestCS$ and the $worstCS$ in N
7:     **if** $worstCS$ not in $tabuList$ **then**
8:         Add $worstCS$ to $tabuList$
9:     **end if**
10:     **if** $v(bestCS) > v(currentBest)$ **then**
11:         $currentBest \leftarrow bestCS$
12:     **end if**
13:     **if** $bestCS$ not in $tabuList$ **then**
14:         add $bestCS$ to $tabuList$
15:         $CS \leftarrow bestCS$
16:     **else**
17:         $CS \leftarrow$ A randomly generated coalition structure that is not in $tabuList$
18:     **end if**
19: **end for**
20: Return $currentBest$

The tabu search method we implement is called TACOS (TAbu search for COalition Structure generation). The algorithm (see Algorithm 1) starts by constructing a random coalition structure as the initial starting point. The start point is the current best solution. This start point and its value are added as the first entry in the tabu list. The tabu list is an array that contains a list of coalition structures that is forbidden from being visited again as the search progresses. For the starting coalition structure, a neighbourhood is generated using *neighbourhood operators*. Four operators (explained in detail at the end of this section) were tested: *Split, Merge, Shift* and *Extract* to enable choosing the best combination. Between these four, the best combination was Shift and Extract.

Using Shift and Extract, a neighbourhood is generated and a *local maximum* and a *local minimum* are identified within it. The local minimum is added to the tabu list so that future iterations will rule out these candidates from being visited again (adding all the other solutions will result in a larger tabu list which will slow down the performance). If the local maximum is better than the current best, then the current best is updated.

During any iteration, if the local maximum is not in the tabu list, it is added to the list and search is continued from this point. On the other hand, if the local maximum is in the tabu list, it will not be explored as this point and its neighbourhood has already been visited. A random structure is then repeatedly generated until one that is not in the tabu list is found. This new structure becomes the continuation point for search.

The above process continues for a fixed number of iterations after which the current best solution is returned as the optimal one. It must be noted that the choice of neighbourhood operators (see Line 5 of Algorithm 1) is a key determinant of the performance of tabu search.

Neighbourhood Generation: Although tabu search is a general method, the neighbourhood operators are problem specific. They must be defined such that the search space is explored effectively and repeated generation of the same coalition structures is avoided. Well designed neighbourhood operators are crucial to the success of tabu search. We defined the following four neighbourhood operators:

Merge: The *immediate neighbour* $i_m(CS)$ of a coalition structure CS is the grand coalition if CS is the grand coalition. Otherwise, it is the structure obtained by merging the first two coalitions in CS. The neighbourhood N_m of CS is a set of coalition structures defined as follows:

$$N_m(CS) = i_m(CS) \cup i_m(i_m(CS)) \cup \ldots \cup i_m(GrandCoalition)$$

Extract: The neighbourhood N_e of a coalition structure CS is a the coalition structure obtained by making all the agents in the largest coalition of CS singletons.

Split: The *immediate neighbour* $i_s(CS)$ of a coalition structure CS is CS if CS is comprised of all singletons. Otherwise, it is the structure obtained by splitting the largest coalition in CS into two equal sized coalitions with split occuring in the middle. The neighbourhood N_s of CS is a set of coalition structures defined as follows:

$$N_s(CS) = i_s(CS) \cup i_s(i_s(CS)) \cup \ldots \cup i(AllSingletons)$$

Shift: The *immediate neighbour* $i_{sh}(CS)$ of a coalition structure CS is CS if CS is the grand coalition. Otherwise, it is the structure obtained by moving the first agent from the second coalition of CS into the first coalition. The neighbourhood N_{sh} of CS is a set of coalition structures defined as follows:

$$N_{sh}(CS) = i_{sh}(CS) \cup i_{sh}(i_{sh}(CS)) \cup \ldots \cup i(GrandCoaliiton)$$

In order to study the efficacy of the above four operators, Algorithm 1 was tested for various combinations of these operators on ten different types of input data (details of input data are in Sect. 5). Between these combinations, the Shift and Extract combination yielded the best quality solutions. Thus for comparing the performance of TACOS with SA, the Shift and Extract combination was used.

4 Heuristic Search Method 2: Simulated Annealing

Simulated annealing (SA) is a randomized local search method analogous to the metropolis algorithm [14]. It is based on the process of annealing in metallurgy [19]. As in gradient descent, this method iteratively generates random solutions. But in contrast to strict gradient descent, SA allows for a more extensive search for an optimal solution by accepting inferior solutions with some non-zero probability.

Algorithm 2. Simulated annealing algorithm for finding an optimal coalition structure

1: $CS \leftarrow$ randomly generated CS; {Generate a random start point}
2: $bestCS \leftarrow CS$
3: $InitialTemperature \leftarrow 1.0$ {Initialize temperature}
4: $\alpha \leftarrow 0.99$ {Initialize α used to update temperature}
5: **for** $iterationCount \leftarrow 1, maxIterations$ **do** {see Table 2 for $maxIterations$}
6:     Generate the neighbourhood N of CS using Shift and Extract
7:     $CS' \leftarrow$ A structure from N chosen uniformly at random
8:     **if** $v(CS') \geq v(CS)$ **then**
9:         $CS \leftarrow CS'$ {Update CS}
10:    **else**
11:        $Probability \leftarrow e^{\frac{v(CS')-v(CS)}{t}}$ {Set probability of accepting an inferior solution}
12:        $CS \leftarrow CS'$ {Update CS}
13:    **end if**
14:    **if** $v(CS) \geq v(bestCS)$ **then**
15:        $bestCS \leftarrow CS$ {Update $bestCS$}
16:    **end if**
17:    $t \leftarrow t \times \alpha$ {Update t}
18: **end for**
19: Return $bestCS$

The SA method we implemented is given in Algorithm 2. The method starts with a randomly chosen start point called CS. During each iteration, a random neighbour CS' of CS is generated. The structure CS' is a randomly chosen structure from the neighbourhood N of CS generated using the combination of Shift and Extract operators (because as with TACOS, the Shift and Extract combination was found to be the best for SA). If the value of CS' is better, then CS' becomes CS. Otherwise, with probability $e^{\frac{v(CS')-v(CS)}{t}}$ CS' becomes CS. The temperature is updated. The process is repeated for a fixed number of iterations and the best solution found is returned as the optimal solution.

5   Performance Evaluation

The TACOS and simulated annealing methods were implemented in Python and their performance was evaluated in terms of two criteria: *solution quality* and *time* to generate the solution. Let CS_{TACOS} be the coalition structure returned by TACOS, CS_{SA} that for simulated annealing, and CS_{OPT} be the *exact* optimal solution. The solution quality for TACOS (and analogously for SA) was measured as follows (Table 1):

$$\frac{v(CS_{TACOS})}{v(CS_{OPT})} \times 100 \tag{2}$$

For performance evaluation, the input data, i.e., the values of coalitions (see Eq. 1) is generated from a wide range of probability distributions taken from the literature [15, 24]:

1. **Uniform (Standard):** Python Mersenne twister pseudorandom number [13]: for all $C \in C^A$, the value $v(C) \sim U(0,1)$.
2. **Uniform (Sandholm):** For all $C \in C^A$, the value $v(C) \sim U(0,|C|)$.
3. **Normal (Rahwan):** For all $C \in C^A$, the value $v(C) \sim N(\mu,\sigma^2)$ where $\mu = 10 \times |C|$ and $\sigma = 1$.
4. **Exponential:** For all $C \in C^A$, the value $v(C) \sim |C| \times exp(\lambda)$, where $\lambda = 1$.
5. **Modified Uniform:** Each coalition's value is first drawn from $U(0, 10 \times |C|)$, the value is then increased by a random number $r \sim U(0, 50)$ with a probability of 0.2.

Table 1. A comparison of tabu search and simulated annealing.

Tabu search	Simulated annealing
Moves are random but recorded in tabu list to guide the search toward unexplored space	Moves are random and there is no record of moves
Advantage: Guided search and structured neighbourhood so only new solution space is explored avoiding repetition	Advantage: No neighbourhood structure, so search is quicker. Memory-less so requires less resource
Disadvantage: might cause a constrain on system resources	Disdvantage: Random selection could result in repeated moves and unguided jumps could leave the exploration stuck in worse parts of search space

6. **Modified Normal:** Each coalition's value is first drawn from $N(0, 10 \times |C|)$, the value is then increased by a random number $r \sim U(0, 50)$ with a probability of 0.2.

7. **NDCS:** For all $C \in C^A$, the value $v(C) \sim N(\mu, \sigma^2)$, where $\mu = |C|$ and $\sigma = \sqrt{|C|}$.

8. **Beta:** For all $C \in C^A$, the value $v(C) \sim |C| \times Beta(\alpha, \beta)$, where $\alpha = \beta = 0.5$.

9. **Gamma:** For all $C \in C^A$, the value $v(C) \sim |C| \times Gamma(k, \theta)$, where $k = \theta = 2$.

10. **Agent-based Uniform:** Each agent a in a coalition C is a given a random power drawn from $\rho_a \sim U(0, 10)$ to reflect its average contribution in all the coalitions it is a member of, then for every coalition C containing agent a, the actual power ρ_a^c of a in C is $\rho_a^c \sim U(0, 2\rho_a)$. The value of $C \in C^A$ is the sum of the powers of all member coalitions. For all $C \in C^A$, $v(C) = \sum_{a \in C} \rho_a^C$.

For the above distributions, the quality of solution for each method was evaluated for up to 25 agents for CFGs and 9 agents for PFGs. Note that, although the heuristic methods can run for larger games, finding the exact optimum (needed for calculating the solution quality given in Eq. 2) for them is computationally impractical. We present results for 25 agents for CFGs and 9 agents for PFGs. Both TACOS and the SA method we implemented are **oblivious to the type of probability distribution** from which the values of coalitions are drawn randomly. All simulations were run on a PC equipped with and Intel Xeon E5630 Processor running at 2.53 Ghz (2.8 Ghz Turbo) and 12 GB RAM.

The performance of both TACOS and SA depends on (i) the probability distribution from which the values of coalitions are drawn and (ii) the random start point. Some probability distributions require more iterations than others to reach the same quality of solution. The number of iterations for each distribution was fixed based on a preliminary evaluation of TACOS and SA. The number of iterations is listed in Table 2. For each probability distribution, average performance was measured as follows:

CFGs. The value of a coalition depends only on its members.

Step 1: For a probability distribution, generate a data set comprised of all possible coalition structures and their associated values. A data set is generated as follows. For each possible coalition, randomly draw a value from the probability distribution. The value of a coalition structure is the sum of the values of its coalitions as given in Eq. 1.

Step 2: For a probability distribution, generate ten different data sets by repeating Step 1.

Step 3: Repeat Step 2 for each of the ten probability distributions.

PFGs. The value of a coalition depends on the structure it is embedded in.

Step 1: For a probability distribution, generate a data set comprised of all possible coalition structures and their associated values. A data set is generated as follows. For each possible coalition structure, randomly draw a value from the probability distribution for each constituent coalition. The value of the structure is the sum of the values of its coalitions as given

Table 2. The number of iterations for each distribution. Time is in milliseconds (rounded to the next decimal).

Probability distribution	CFGs (for 25 agents)			PFGs (for 9 agents)		
	Number of iterations		Avg. time (ms)	Number of iterations		Avg. time (ms)
	TACOS	SA		TACOS	SA	
Uniform (Standard)	10000	20000	5500	25	75	9000
Uniform (Sandholm)	750	3000	400	250	375	90000
Normal (Rahwan)	50	150	30	10	20	3500
Exponential	200000	500000	120000	500	1000	180000
Modified uniform	100000	200000	55000	500	1500	180000
Modified normal	100000	200000	55000	500	1000	180000
NDCS	7500	30000	4000	500	1000	180000
Beta	600	2400	350	100	150	35000
Gamma	100000	350000	55000	100	250	35000
Agent-based uniform	200000	400000	120000	500	1500	180000

in Eq. 1. The difference between CFGs and PFGs is that, for the latter, a random value for a coalition is drawn for each structure it is embedded in. But for the former, the value of a coalition is drawn only once. Thus, for PFGs, depending on the random values drawn, externalities may be *positive* or *negative* [5].

Step 2: Repeat Step 2 for each of the ten probability distributions.

Since both TACOS and SA are sensitive to the start point which is random, these algorithms were run ten times for each data set. Average solution quality (with solution quality calculated as per Eq. 2) and average running time were then measured across the ten runs for each data set and across the ten data sets for each probability distribution.

TACOS versus Simulated Annealing: The average performance of TACOS was compared with the average performance for SA for each of the ten probability distributions. The results are as shown in Fig. 1 for CFGs and in Fig. 2 for PFGs.

Consider the results in Fig. 1 for CFGs. These results are for a system comprised of 25 agents. For each of the ten distributions, TACOS performed better than SA although the difference in performance varied form distribution to distribution. For the Normal (Rahwan) distribution, the performance of TACOS and SA was very close with the solution quality being 99.9% of the exact optimum. For the Beta and Uniform (Sandholm) distributions, TACOS achieved 99.9% and 98.7% respectively. The quality of solution was least for the Modified Normal and Modified Uniform distributions.

Consider the results in Fig. 2 for PFGs. These results are for a system comprised of 9 agents. While running the TACOS and SA algorithms for more than 9 agents is easy, computing the exact optimum is computationally demanding.

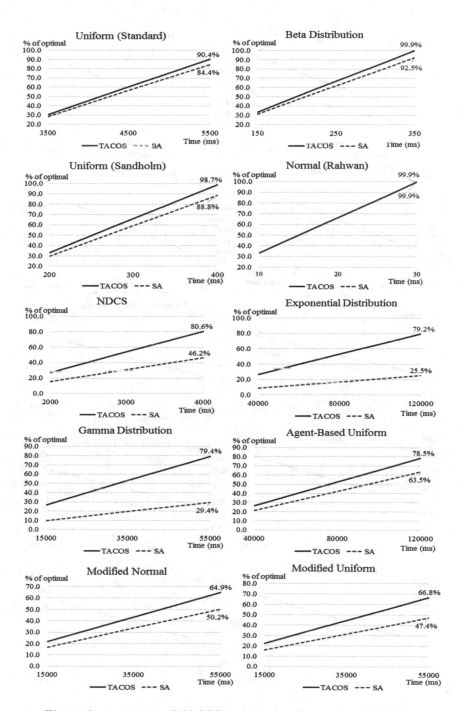

Fig. 1. A comparison of TACOS and simulated annealing for CFGs.

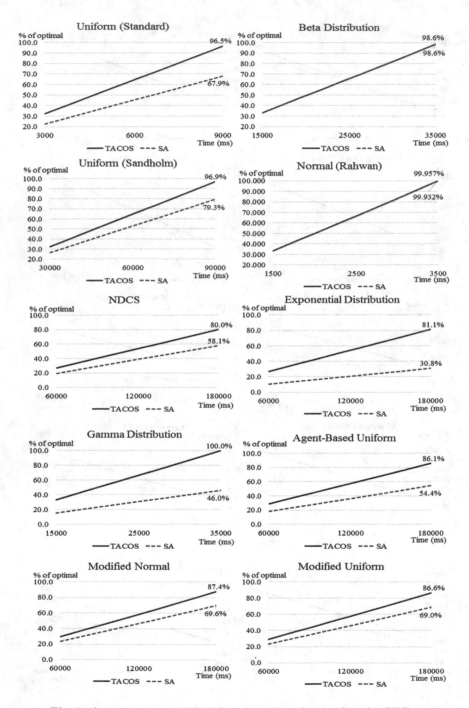

Fig. 2. A comparison of TACOS and simulated annealing for PFGs.

Although a 9 agent system is small, its analysis nevertheless helps in a comparative evaluation of TACOS and SA. For PFGs, TACOS generated better solutions than SA for each of the ten probability distributions. For the Gamma distribution, the heuristic solution for TACOS coincided with the exact optimum, for Normal (Rahwan) TACOS generated 99.96% of exact optimum while SA performed just fractionally below this level. For the Uniform (Standard), Beta, and Uniform (Sandholm) TACOS's solution was over 96% of the exact optimum. TACOS performed worst for the NDCS distribution achieving 80% of the exact.

Thus for both CFGs and PFGs, TACOS performed better than SA for each of the ten probability distributions. However, TACOS consumes more resource than SA in terms of its memory requirements.

Anytime Property: A key feature of both TACOS and SA is that their average performance improves with execution time; the more the time spent running them, the better the results for CFGs and PFGs. This anytime property is illustrated in Fig. 3 for TACOS for CFGs for each of the ten probability distributions.

6   Related Work

Existing methods for optimal coalition structure generation can be categorised into two types: *exact* and *approximate*. Exact algorithms return the absolute optimal solution by systematically exploring the space using methods such as dynamic programming to find an optimal one. Examples include [20, 23, 28]. Approximation methods that come with a guarantee on the quality of approximation include [1, 9, 22, 24, 26]. These methods in general have exponential running time (although polynomial time may be achieved by imposing restrictions on the coalitions that can form) which means that it is difficult for them to scale to large systems. Heuristic methods also generate approximate solutions but although they generally generate good solutions, there are no guarantees on the quality of solution. The advantage of these methods is that they typically have polynomial running time. The methods we explore in this paper belong to this class. In the remainder of this section, we will place our research in the context of existing heuristic methods that have previously been developed for coalition structure generation.

In their unpublished report Murillo et al. [17] used tabu search for set partitioning. The problem they addressed is to partition a set of objects so that similar items go into one class by assuming that the number of distinct classes is given (this is a special case of CFGs). They showed that tabu search performs better than simulated annealing and genetic algorithms. However, their simulations are limited to only five classes. There are two differences between their work and our paper. First, the problem we solve is much more general; we focus on determining the optimal coalition structure without knowing the number of partitions in the optimal structure. Thus, in their work, it is known that the optimal structure will contain, for example, five partitions. We find an optimal partition without knowing in advance how many coalitions that partition will contain. Second, they conducted simulations for a very restricted scenario in

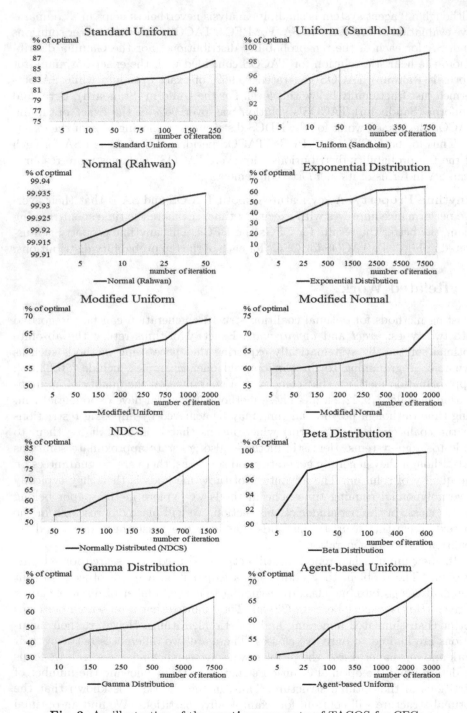

Fig. 3. An illustration of the **anytime** property of TACOS for CFGs.

which the optimal partition contains at most five classes (i.e., coalitions). We consider CFGs of up to 25 agents and determine the optimal structure without knowing the number of coalitions in it. Third, they only considered CFGs while we considered both CFGs and PFGs.

Sen and Dutta [25] used genetic algorithms to find optimal coalition structures. They showed empirically that a good enough solution can be achieved. This work is an exception to other existing literature in that the simulations are conducted for CFGs and PFGs. They considered a particular search space for simulations by imposing a strict regularity on it. In contrast to this work, we do not impose any regularity on the search space. The simulations we conducted are comprehensive; we evaluated the average performance over 10 different probability distributions for the values of coalitions.

Heuristic techniques such simulated annealing [12], greedy search [8], particle swarm [11], and ant colony optimisation [27] have previously been used for CFGs. Ant colony and particle swarm optimization are decentralized methods in that a group of entities simultaneously search for an optimal solution. In contrast, simulated annealing and tabu search are centralized methods. See [21] for a detailed survey of coalition structure generation methods.

In summary, our aim in this paper is to focus on centralized approaches. To date, tabu search has not been used for coalition structure generation. Given this, we studied the efficacy of tabu search which is a memory-based method relative to simulated annealing which is a memory-less method. Note that, although simulated annealing was used in [12], its evaluation was limited in that its performance was evaluated for only one specific probability distribution where the value of any coalition is a random number between 0 and 1 was used. In contrast, our evaluation is comprehensive in that we evaluated and compared tabu search and simulated annealing for the ten different types of probability distributions (listed in Sect. 5). Furthermore, unlike previous work on heuristic methods, we consider both CFGs and PFGs.

7   Conclusions

In this paper, we implemented two heuristic methods, tabu search (TACOS) and simulated annealing and compared their average performance over a range of input data. Each of the two methods implemented is *oblivious to the type of probability distribution*. For both CFGs and PFGs, TACOS performed better than SA for each of the ten probability distributions. The price to pay for better performance is the extra memory requirement for TACOS. Both TACOS and SA have anytime property.

This paper evaluated the performance of TACOS and SA for small PFGs. Further work is needed to extend the results to larger PFGs. In addition, this paper used the same neighbourhood operators for CFGs and PFGs. A redefinition of operators particularly suitable for PFGs could improve performance. This too needs further research.

References

1. Banerjee, B., Kraemer, L.: Coalition structure generation in multi-agent systems with mixed externalities. In: Proceedings of AAMAS, pp. 175–182 (2010)
2. Barbarosoglu, G., Ozgur, D.: A tabu search algorithm for the vehicle routing problem. Comput. Oper. Res. **26**, 255–270 (1999)
3. Chalkiadakis, G., Elkind, E., Wooldrdidge, M.: Computational Aspects of Cooperative Game Theory. Morgan and Claypool Publishers, San Rafael (2011)
4. Chang, C., Lu, L., Wen, F.: Power system network partitioning using tabu search. Electr. Power Syst. Res. **49**(1), 55–61 (1999)
5. Clippel, G.D., Serrano, R.: Margainal contributions and externalities in the value. Econometrica **76**(6), 1413–1436 (2008)
6. Combs, T., Moore, J.: A hybrid tabu search set partitioning approach to tanker crew scheduling. Mil. Oper. Res. **9**(1), 43–56 (2004)
7. Crainic, G., Perboli, G., Tadei, R.: Ts2pack: a two-level tabu search for the three-dimensional bin packing problem. Eur. J. Oper. Res. **195**, 744–760 (2004)
8. Di Mauro, N., Basile, T.M.A., Ferilli, S., Esposito, F.: Coalition structure generation with GRASP. In: Dicheva, D., Dochev, D. (eds.) AIMSA 2010. LNCS, vol. 6304, pp. 111–120. Springer, Heidelberg (2010). doi:10.1007/978-3-642-15431-7_12
9. Epstein, D., Bazzan, A.L.C.: Distributed coalition structure generation with positive and negative externalities. In: Correia, L., Reis, L.P., Cascalho, J. (eds.) EPIA 2013. LNCS, vol. 8154, pp. 408–419. Springer, Heidelberg (2013). doi:10.1007/978-3-642-40669-0_35
10. Glover, F., Laguna, M.: Tabu Search. Kluwer Academic Publishers, Dordrecht (1997)
11. Guo, B., Wang, D.: Optimal coalition structure based on particle swarm optimization algorithm in multi-agent system. In: Proceedings of the Sixth World Congress on Intelligent Control and Automation, pp. 2494–2497 (2006)
12. Keinänen, H.: Simulated annealing for multi-agent coalition formation. In: Håkansson, A., Nguyen, N.T., Hartung, R.L., Howlett, R.J., Jain, L.C. (eds.) KES-AMSTA 2009. LNCS, vol. 5559, pp. 30–39. Springer, Heidelberg (2009). doi:10.1007/978-3-642-01665-3_4
13. Matsumoto, M., Nishimura, T.: Mersenne twister: a 623-dimensionally equidistributed uniform pseudo-random number generator. ACM Trans. Model. Comput. Simul. **8**, 3–30 (1998)
14. Metropolis, N., Rosenbluth, A., Rosenbluth, M., Teller, A., Teller, E.: Equation of state calculations by fast computing machines. J. Chem. Phys. **21**, 1087–1092 (1953)
15. Michalak, T., Rahwan, T., Elkind, E., Wooldridge, M., Jennings, N.R.: A hybrid exact algorithm for complete set partitioning. Artif. Intell. **230**, 14–50 (2016)
16. Misevicius, A.: An implementation of the iterated tabu search algorithm for the quadratic assignment problem. OR Spectr. **34**, 665–690 (2012)
17. Murillo, A., Piza, E., Trejos, J.: A tabu search algorithm for partitioning. Technical report (1999)
18. Wooldridge, M.: An Introduction to Multiagent Systems. Wiley, Hoboken (2009)
19. Pham, D., Karaboga, D.: Intelligent optimisation techniques: Genetic Algorithms, Tabu Search, Simulated Annealing and Neural Networks. Springer, Heidelberg (2000)
20. Rahwan, T., Michalak, T., Jennings, N.R., Wooldridge, M., McBurney, P.: Coalition structure generation in multi-agent systems with positive and negative externalities. In: Proceedings of IJCAI, pp. 257–263 (2009)

21. Rahwan, T., Michalak, T.P., Wooldridge, M., Jennings, N.R.: Coalition structure generation: a survey. AI J. **229**, 139–174 (2015)
22. Rahwan, T., Michalak, M.W.T., Jennings, N.: Anytime coalition structure generation in multi-agent systems with positive or negative externalities. AI J. **186**, 95–122 (2012)
23. Rothkopf, M., Pekec, A., Harstad, R.: Computationally manageable combinational auctions. Manage. Sci. **229**, 1131–1147 (1998)
24. Sandholm, T., Larson, K., Andersson, M., Shehory, O., Tohme, F.: Anytime coalition structure generation with worst case guarantees. Artif. Intell. **111**(1–2), 209–238 (1999)
25. Sen, S., Dutta, P.: Searching for optimal coalition structures. In: Proceedings of AAMAS, pp. 287–292 (2000)
26. Shehory, O., Kraus, S.: Methods for task allocation via agent coalition formation. AI J. **101**(1–2), 165–200 (1998)
27. Sukstrienwong, A.: Searching optimal buyer coalition structure by ant colony optimization. Int. J. Math. Comput. Simul. **5**, 352–360 (2011)
28. Yeh, D.: A dynamic programming approach to the complete set partitioning problem. BIT Numer. Math. **26**(4), 467–474 (1986)

Increasing Use of Renewable Energy by Coalition Formation of Renewable Generators and Energy Stores

Pavel Janovsky$^{(\boxtimes)}$ and Scott A. DeLoach

Department of Computer Science, Kansas State University,
Manhattan, KS 66506, USA
{janovsky,sdeloach}@ksu.edu

Abstract. Renewable sources are not used to their full potential for electricity generation. Unpredictability of solar and wind power forces renewable generators to bid conservative generation amounts in a day-ahead market in order to avoid fees for failure to provide generation. In this paper we propose an approach to increase the use of renewable sources, which allows renewable generators to hedge against generation unpredictability by forming coalitions with energy stores. Inside these coalitions renewable generators purchase availability of energy stores to generate power when needed. Renewable generators use this availability to avoid fees for failure to provide committed generation whenever the current generation is lower than the committed value. We experimentally show that our approach allows renewable generators to commit to 100% of the predicted generation, thus increasing the use of renewable sources. We also show that our approach generates profit incentives for both renewable generators and energy stores to form coalitions.

Keywords: Renewable sources · Large-scale coalition formation · Multi-agent simulation

1 Introduction

Weather-related unpredictability of power generation by renewable resources forces renewable generators to produce conservative amounts of power. Electricity is traded ahead of time in a day-ahead energy market. In this market generators bid amounts of energy that they will be able to generate at given time slots. Since in the electricity market the supply must always match the demand, a failure to deliver the committed amount of energy can have major negative consequences, and it is therefore penalized. Consequently, the renewable generators, due to weather unpredictability, are forced to bid amounts that are lower than the predicted generation, thus decreasing the use of renewable resources [2].

In this paper we propose an approach that can be used to increase the use of renewable resources by forming coalitions between renewable generators and

© Springer International Publishing AG 2017
N. Criado Pacheco et al. (Eds.): EUMAS 2016/AT 2016, LNAI 10207, pp. 140–147, 2017.
DOI: 10.1007/978-3-319-59294-7_12

a high number of energy stores. We are not concerned with the type of energy stores, however we require them to be able to provide energy at a time that they commit to. This capability can be viewed as a commodity for which there is demand among the renewable generators. A renewable generator can buy coverage of some portion of the generation that it commits to. If the renewable generator is able to produce the entire amount of committed energy, it only pays the store owners for the coverage it ordered. On the other hand, if the renewable generator is not able to generate the committed energy, it can use part of the ordered coverage in order to avoid fees for failure to provide energy. A store owner is paid for the uncertainty coverage as well as for the amount of energy provided to the grid.

Specifically, this paper provides the following contributions:

1. An approach to increase use of renewable energy sources using coalition formation of renewable generators and energy store owners. We show our model of renewable sources and energy stores in Sect. 2, and we describe how to use multi-agent simulation for coalition formation of renewable generators and energy store owners in Sect. 3.
2. Experimental evaluation of the coalition formation process between renewable generators and energy store owners. We show that our approach increases use of renewable resources by increasing profit of renewable generators in Sect. 4.

2 Model

We model the renewable generators and energy store owners as agents in a multi-agent system. We describe all variables used in our model in Table 1. Renewable generators are modeled using a triplet $(g_c(t), g_r(t), u_r)$ for time t corresponding to the time slots. This triplet represents the generation committed and actually generated by the renewable generator, and a coverage uncertainty that the generator is willing to pay for. The energy store owners are modeled as a triplet (s_b, s_e, m) which represents the beginning and end of a time interval within which the store can provide power, and the maximum total amount of provided power.

2.1 Renewable Generators

In order to increase the use of renewable resources, an incentive has to be given to renewable generators to bid higher energy amounts in the day-ahead market. In this section we derive this incentive in a form of a profit function. We assume this profit function to be of the following form:

$$p_r = \sum_t p_r(t) = \sum_t (p_g \cdot \min(g_c(t), g_r(t)) - c_c(t) - c_f(t)), \qquad (1)$$

representing the fact that the renewable generator is paid for its generation, but has to pay for uncertainty coverage and failure to provide committed generation. This profit function assumes that $\forall t : g_c(t) = g_e(t)$, i.e. that the renewable generator will always commit to generate the estimated amount of energy.

Table 1. Description of model variables

$p_r(t)$	Profit of a renewable generator r that participates in coalition formation
$p_{ro}(t)$	Profit of a renewable generator r that does not participate in coalition formation
$g_c(t)$	Generation committed by a renewable generator
$g_e(t)$	Estimated generation of a renewable generator
$g_r(t)$	Real generation achievable by a renewable generator, not observable
$g_{sc}(t)$	Generation committed by an energy store
$g_{sr}(t)$	Real generation provided by an energy store
$u_r[\%]$	Percentage of g_c to be requested as coverage for uncertainty
$u(t)[\%]$	Percentage of $g_c(t)$ granted by energy stores as coverage for uncertainty
m	Maximum total amount of power to be distributed by an energy store
s_b, s_e	Energy store availability begin, end
p_g	Price for generation
p_c	Price for uncertainty coverage
p_f	Price for failure to provide committed generation
$c_c(t)$	Cost of uncertainty coverage
$c_f(t)$	Cost of failure to provide committed generation
$c_0[\%]$	Commitment of a renewable generator that does not participate in coalition formation
t	Time

The cost of uncertainty coverage $c_c(t)$ depends on the uncertainty coverage parameter $u(t)$ as follows: $c_c(t) = p_c \cdot u(t) \cdot g_c(t)$. The uncertainty cost is independent of the real generation $g_r(t)$, since the uncertainty coverage is paid for before the value of $g_r(t)$ is known. The uncertainty cost is calculated using the percentage of the coverage actually provided $u(t)$, for which it holds that $\forall t : u(t) \leq u_r$, since the store owners can commit less than the value requested by a renewable generator.

The cost of failure to provide committed generation $c_f(t)$ is determined using a difference between amounts of generation committed and actually provided as follows:

$$c_f(t) = p_f \cdot \max(g_c(t) - (g_r(t) + u(t) \cdot g_c(t)), 0). \tag{2}$$

Profit of a renewable generator in the coalition formation setting is therefore expressed as

$$p_r = \sum_t p_r(t) = \sum_t \Big(p_g \cdot \min(g_c(t), g_r(t)) - p_c \cdot u(t) \cdot g_c(t)$$
$$- p_f \cdot \max(g_c(t) - (g_r(t) + u(t) \cdot g_c(t)), 0) \Big). \tag{3}$$

Without coalition formation the renewable generator is forced to bid a lower amount to prevent paying the cost for failure to provide committed energy. On the other hand, the uncertainty coverage cost does not apply to this renewable generator. The profit of a renewable generator that does not participate in coalition formation with energy store owners is therefore

$$p_{r0} = \sum_t p_{r0}(t) = \sum_t \Big(p_g \cdot \min(c_0 \cdot g_e(t), g_r(t))$$

$$- p_f \cdot \max(c_0 \cdot g_e(t) - g_r(t), 0) \Big). \qquad (4)$$

2.2 Energy Stores

In order to simplify the problem we assume that energy stores are always able to sell their stored energy, either to renewable generators through the coalition formation process, or to some other party. We also assume that stores are always able to provide the committed amounts of energy. This assumption eliminates factors such as different types of stores, or whether stores buy the power from other subjects.

Following is the profit function of an energy store owner:

$$p = \sum_{t=s_b}^{s_e} (p_g \cdot g_{sr}(t) + p_c \cdot g_{sc}(t)). \qquad (5)$$

This profit function must satisfy the following constraints: $0 \le \sum_{t=s_b}^{s_e} g_{sc}(t) \le m$ and $\forall t : g_{sr}(t) \le g_{sc}(t)$, which limits the total amounts of energy committed and provided by the store. An energy store is incentivized to participate in coalition formation with renewable generators if $\sum_{t=s_b}^{s_e} p_c \cdot g_{sc}(t)$ is positive, which happens when a renewable generator purchases the uncertainty coverage from this store.

3 Coalition Formation Using Multi-agent Simulation

To simulate coalition formation of renewable generators and store owners we use the multi-agent simulation approach proposed in [4]. There a simulator is proposed in which agents leave and join coalitions in an iterative manner. This coalition formation process is used to search the state space of coalition structures, which are sets of coalitions, in order to find coalition structures with high social welfare. During the simulation agents use strategies to decide whether to leave their coalitions and which coalition to join. The strategy that achieves best results combines agent's best response, in which an agent searches for a coalition to which it can bring most benefit, with random jumps whenever a local optimum is reached. In this work we will therefore base the agents' strategy on that strategy. The coalitions are assigned values by a specified valuation function. Quality of solutions is represented in [4] by a social welfare, which is a sum of values of all coalitions in a coalition structure. The simulation generates a pool of coalition structures, from which a coalition structure with the highest social welfare is selected as the solution.

There are several differences between the approach in [4] and coalition formation of renewable generators with energy store owners. First, unlike in [4], coalition formation between renewable generators and energy store owners is not concerned with social welfare. Both renewable generators and energy store owners are self-interested agents, which seek only to maximize their own profit. This difference can be implemented by changing agents' strategies to find best fitting coalitions based on agents' profit instead of coalition value. Second, each coalition in our setting must always contain exactly one renewable generator. In terms of coalition formation we call these agents coalition leaders. Coalition leaders do not leave or join coalitions. On the other hand coalition leaders affect the profit of agents joining the coalitions, which consequently affects the behavior of the other agents. Finally, since the iterative coalition formation process yields pool of coalition structures, a single coalition structure must be selected as the solution. Unlike in [4], in which the solution is selected based on social welfare, in our setting we select a solution with the highest profit of renewable generators gained from participation in coalition formation.

Algorithm 1. Simulation of coalition formation between renewable generators and store owners

Input: number of energy stores, number of renewable generators, number of iterations N, number of time slots.
Output: coalition structure with highest profit of renewable generators.
1: initiate energy stores and renewable generators
2: create a coalition for each renewable generator
3: **for** iteration in $1 : N$ **do**
4:     **for all** energy stores in random order **do**
5:         **if** *energy_store*.strategy.leave **then**
6:             *energy_store*.coalition.recompute profit of energy stores after *energy_store*
7:             *energy_store*.coalition ← *energy_store*.strategy.pick_coalition
8:             calculate *energy_store*.profit
9:         **end if**
10:     **end for**
11:     save current coalition structure
12: **end for**
13: choose coalition structure with highest profit of renewable generators

The simulator for coalition formation of renewable generators and energy store owners is shown in Algorithm 1, and it works as follows. First, renewable generators are created and assigned estimated generation values for each time slot. Then energy stores are created and assigned the beginning and end of availability s_b and s_e, and maximum total amount of power m (line 1). Then we create coalitions, each containing one renewable generator (line 2). After this initialization step the simulation begins. In the simulation energy stores are deciding whether they should leave their coalitions and which coalitions they should join. When an energy store joins a coalition, its profit is increased, and the coalition is updated (lines 5–8). If an energy store leaves a coalition, profit of all stores that joined the coalition after this store is recalculated, since the distribution of their power might have changed after the removal (line 6). Finally, we select the coalition structure with highest profit of renewable generators (line 13).

4 Experimental Analysis

We experimentally evaluate the coalition formation algorithm in the renewable domain in order to show that our approach creates profit incentives for renewable generators to participate in coalition formation. We will also show that our coalition formation approach increases use of renewable resources.

The experiments were performed using the following setup. We tested our approach in scenarios with 50 renewable generators. Generation amounts for 24 time slots corresponding to one day were generated for each renewable generator at random from a uniform distribution $\mathcal{U}(0, 100)$, and the generators were given estimates of these amounts drawn from a normal distribution with standard deviation $\sigma = 20$. Parameters of the stores s_b, s_e, and m were generated randomly from uniform distributions $\mathcal{U}(0, 23)$ and $\mathcal{U}(0, 100)$ respectively. We set prices as follows: $p_g = 50$, $p_c = 10$, and $p_f = 100$. As a baseline we use a scenario in which renewable generators do not participate in coalition formation, in which case renewable generators only bid commitment percentage $c_0 = 80\%$ of predicted generation $g_e(t)$ to hedge against uncertainty. We let the simulation run for 10 iterations and then selected a coalition structure with highest sum of profit of renewable generators. All results were averaged over 10 random runs.

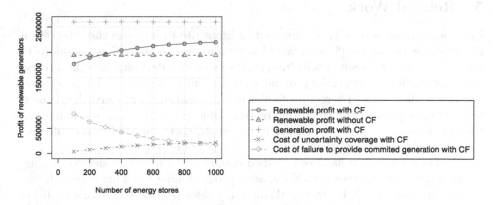

Fig. 1. Summarized profit of 50 renewable generators with 100 to 1000 energy stores

Figure 1 compares summarized profit of renewable generators that participate in coalition formation p_r with their profit in case they did not participate p_{r0}.

Generation profit is constant, since it is independent of the number of energy stores. On the other hand, with increasing number of energy stores the cost for failure to provide committed generation decreases and the cost of uncertainty coverage increases because the generators can cover more uncertainty. Since the decrease in the cost of failure to provide committed generation is larger than the increase in the cost of uncertainty coverage, the resulting profit is increasing. In scenarios with over 300 energy stores the profit of 50 renewable generators is greater if they participate in coalition formation.

Over all, the amount of renewable generation is increased because the generators are able to bid higher values. In Fig. 1 the generators not participating in coalition formation only bid 80% of the predicted generation $g_e(t)$, while generators utilizing coalition formation bid 100% of $g_e(t)$. Table 2 shows amounts of renewable generation with and without coalition formation as well as energy store use and total generation. Our approach yields a 13.5% increase in total renewable generation. Total generation of renewable generators and energy stores is increased by 30.4% due to coalition formation.

Table 2. Increase in renewable generation caused by coalition formation (CF) of 50 renewable generators and 1000 energy stores

Generation type	Generation amount	Increase in generation
Renewable generation without CF	45,837	–
Renewable generation with CF	52,012	**13.5%**
Energy store generation	7,780	–
Total generation with CF	59,792	**30.4%**

5 Related Work

Coalition formation has been proposed in literature to increase the integration of renewable resources. [8] uses law of large numbers to show that coalitions of renewable generators can benefit from their spacial distribution, since the adverse effects of prediction uncertainty are mitigated. Coalitions of renewable generators are also studied in [5]. There a profit sharing mechanism is proposed that is used to distribute profit after coalitions of renewable generators are formed. Even though the goals of [5,8] are similar to our goals, their approaches are different since they study homogeneous coalitions of renewable generators.

Coalition formation has been studied extensively. First approach for finding optimal coalition structures used dynamic programming [7]. This approach was further improved in [6]. Hierarchical clustering algorithm for large-scale coalition formation was proposed in [1]. Their algorithm finds high-quality sub-optimal coalition structures. The algorithm is however not suitable for coalition formation of self-interested agents, as was shown in [3]. Finally, [4] proposes a simulation framework for large-scale coalition formation. This framework is best suited for our scenario, since it is easily extensible to model self-interested agents, and it can be used to model renewable generators as well as energy stores.

6   Conclusion

In this paper we proposed an approach to increase use of renewable sources by allowing renewable generators to hedge against uncertainty by forming coalitions with energy stores. In these coalitions energy stores offer to cover generation that renewable generators committed to, but are unable to deliver due to prediction uncertainty. We model renewable generators and energy stores as self-interested agents, and we use multi-agent simulation to create coalition structures by allowing energy stores to leave and join coalitions based on their preference.

We experimentally show that our approach increases use of renewable resources. With the support of coalition formation with energy stores, renewable generators can afford to bid higher amounts of generation in the day-ahead market. In our experiments we show that renewable generators can bid 100% of the predicted generation and still gain profit, even when facing high fees for failure to provide committed generation. In our experimental setting our approach increased the use of renewable resources by 13.5%. We also show that forming coalitions with energy stores increases profit of renewable generators, which incentivizes them to increase renewable generation.

Acknowledgments. This work was supported by the US National Science Foundation via Award No. CNS-1544705.

References

1. Farinelli, A., Bicego, M., Ramchurn, S., Zucchelli, M.: C-link: a hierarchical clustering approach to large-scale near-optimal coalition formation. In: 23rd International Joint Conference on Artificial Intelligence (2013)
2. Holttinen, H., Meibom, P., Orths, A., Lange, B., Mark, O., Olav, J., Estanqueiro, A., Gomez, E., Sder, L., Strbac, G., Smith, J.C., van Hulle, F.: Impacts of large amounts of wind power on design and operation of power systems, results of IEA collaboration. In: 8th International Workshop on Large-Scale Integration of Wind Power into Power Systems as well as on Transmission Networks of Offshore Wind Farms (2009)
3. Janovsky, P., DeLoach, S.A.: Forming stable coalitions in large systems with self-interested agents. In: 14th European Conference on Multi-agent Systems EUMAS (2016)
4. Janovsky, P., DeLoach, S.A.: Multi-agent simulation framework for large-scale coalition formation. In: Proceedings of the 2016 IEEE/WIC/ACM International Conference on Web Intelligence (2016)
5. Nayyar, A., Poolla, K., Varaiya, P.: A statistically robust payment sharing mechanism for an aggregate of renewable energy producers. In: 2013 European Control Conference (ECC) (2013)
6. Rahwan, T., Jennings, N.R.: An improved dynamic programming algorithm for coalition structure generation. In: 7th International Conference on Autonomous Agents and Multiagent Systems (2008)
7. Yun Yeh, D.: A dynamic programming approach to the complete set partitioning problem. BIT Numer. Math. 26(4), 467–474 (1986)
8. Zhang, B., Johari, R., Rajagopal, R.: Competition and coalition formation of renewable power producers. IEEE Trans. Power Syst. 30(3), 1624–1632 (2015)

Proactive-DIEL in Evolving Referral Networks

Ashiqur R. KhudaBukhsh$^{(\boxtimes)}$, Jaime G. Carbonell, and Peter J. Jansen

Carnegie Mellon University, Pittsburgh, USA
{akhudabu,jgc,pjj}@cs.cmu.edu

Abstract. Distributed learning in expert referral networks is a new Active Learning paradigm where experts—humans or automated agents—solve problems if they can or refer said problems to others with more appropriate expertise. Recent work augmented the basic learning-to-refer method with proactive skill posting, where experts may report their top skills to their colleagues, and proposed a modified algorithm, proactive-DIEL (Distributed Interval Estimation Learning), that takes advantage of such one-time posting instead of using an uninformed prior. This work extends the method in three main directions: (1) Proactive-DIEL is shown to work on a referral network of automated agents, namely SAT solvers, (2) Proactive-DIEL's reward mechanism is extended to another referral-learning algorithm, ϵ-Greedy, with some appropriate modifications. (3) The method is shown robust with respect to evolving networks where experts join or drop off, requiring the learning method to recover referral expertise. In all cases the proposed method exhibits superiority to the state of the art.

Keywords: Active learning · Evolving referral network · Proactive skill posting

1 Introduction

Learning-to-refer in expert referral networks is a recently proposed active learning setting where an expert can refer problem instances to appropriate colleagues if she finds the task at hand difficult to solve [1]. Such a network draws inspiration from the real world examples of expert networks among physicians or within consultancy firms. The key problem is learning to direct the referrals based on the subject matter of the problem and on estimated expertise of colleagues. The state-of-the-art referral learning algorithm, DIEL (Distributed Interval Estimation Learning), has been further improved in an augmented learning setting where experts can advertise their top skills to colleagues upon joining the network [2]. The modified algorithm, dubbed proactive-DIEL, demonstrated superior performance even in the presence of noise in skill self-estimates and showed empirical evidence of being near-Bayesian-Nash Incentive Compatible, i.e., misreporting skills to receive more referrals provided little or no benefit.

Results presented in [2] were limited to synthetic data with well-behaved (e.g. Gaussian) distributions. In this work, we use a suite of 100 real SAT solvers as

© Springer International Publishing AG 2017
N. Criado Pacheco et al. (Eds.): EUMAS 2016/AT 2016, LNAI 10207, pp. 148–156, 2017.
DOI: 10.1007/978-3-319-59294-7_13

experts and SAT problem distributions as topics, and show that proactive-DIEL's superiority over DIEL also holds when the problem distributions and the behavior of the experts is not predictable in the aggregate, i.e., it is not following a known parameterizable distribution. Then we show that the reward-penalty mechanism and initialization proposed in proactive-DIEL translates well to another referral algorithm with some suitable modifications: proactive-ϵ-Greedy obtained superior performance than its corresponding non-proactive version. Finally, we relax a major assumption stated in both [1,2] by allowing dynamic addition and drop-off of experts, and demonstrate proactive-DIEL's strong resilience to such changes in network nodes and topologies even when substantial (e.g. multiple 20% changes).

After discussing related work, we review the DIEL model, describe skill posting and outline the distributed referral learning algorithms. Next, we describe our experimental set-up, and present our results and observations. We end with some general conclusions and some future research ideas.

2   Related Work

In terms of the learning setting and referral learning algorithm, our primary basis for this work was [1] which first proposed a novel learning setting in a context of Active Learning where experts are connected through a network and can refer instances to one another. The proposed algorithm (DIEL) built upon research on interval estimation learning, a reinforcement learning technique which strives to strike a balance between exploration and exploitation, first proposed in [3,4], and successfully applied to estimate the accuracy of multiple labelers in [5]. The referral framework drew inspiration from earlier work in referral chaining, first proposed in [6] and subsequently extended, for example, in [7–10]. In the current work, we have adopted the setting, along with some of the algorithms and assumptions for comparison.

This learning setting was further extended in [2], by allowing advertisement to colleagues (partially available priors), and the original DIEL algorithm modified, both for improved performance and to encourage incentive compatibility. There is a large body of literature where truthful mechanism design is the principal focus [11–14]. We have implemented and extended the same mechanism used in proactive-DIEL in our present work, without however proving incentive compatibility for our newly introduced algorithms, or taking any further steps to establish strategyproofness [15].

Finally, we used SATenstein [16], a highly parameterized Stochastic Local Search (SLS) SAT solver for experimental validation of proactive-DIEL on a real task of SAT solving. With a rich design space of 2.01×10^{14} candidate solvers drawing inspiration from most of the prominent SLS SAT solvers proposed in the literature, high-performance SATenstein solvers for specific SAT distributions can be obtained by using an automatic algorithm configurator. In our experiments, we used 100 such solvers obtained from the experiments in [17].

3   Referral Network

3.1   Preliminaries

Referral Network: Represented by a graph (V, E) of size k in which each vertex v_i corresponds to an expert e_i $(1 \leq k)$ and each bidirectional edge $\langle v_i, v_j \rangle$ indicates a *referral link* which implies e_i and e_j can refer problem instances to each other.

Subnetwork: The *subnetwork* of an expert e_i is the set of experts linked to e_i by a referral link.

Scenario: Set of m instances $(q_1, \ldots, q_m)$ belonging to n topics $(t_1, \ldots, t_n)$ that are to be addressed by the k experts $(e_1, \ldots, e_k)$.

Expertise: Expertise of an expert/question pair $\langle e_i, q_j \rangle$ is the probability with e_i can solve q_j.

Referral Mechanism: For a query budget $Q = 2$ (fixed across all our experiments), consists of the following steps.

1. A user issues q_j (*initial query*) to a randomly chosen expert e_i (*initial expert*).
2. Initial expert e_i examines the instance and solves it if possible. This depends on the *expertise* of e_i wrt. q_j.
3. If not, a *referral query* is issued by e_i to a *referred expert*, e_j, within her subnetwork. *Learning-to-refer* involves improving the estimate of who is most likely to solve the problem.
4. If the referred expert succeeds, she communicates the solution to the initial expert, who in turn, communicates it to the user.

Advertising Unit: A tuple $\langle e_i, e_j, t_k, \mu_{t_k} \rangle$, where e_i is the *target expert*, e_j is the *advertising expert*, t_k is the topic and μ_{t_k} is e_j's (advertised) topical expertise.

Advertising Budget: The number of advertising units available to an expert, following [2], set to twice the size of that expert's subnetwork. Effectively means that each expert reports her top two skills to everyone in her subnetwork.

Advertising Protocol: A one-time advertisement that happens right at the beginning of the simulation or when an expert joins the network. The advertising expert e_j reports to each target expert e_i in her subnetwork the two tuples $\langle e_i, e_j, t_{best}, \mu_{t_{best}} \rangle$ and $\langle e_i, e_j, t_{secondBest}, \mu_{t_{secondBest}} \rangle$, i.e., the top two topics in terms of the advertising expert's topic means.

   Further details regarding the assumptions involving expertise, network parameters, proactive skill posting mechanism and simulation details can be found in [1,2].

3.2   Referral Algorithms

From the point of view of a single expert, the decision to refer a problem is essentially an action selection problem where an action corresponds to picking one of a possible set of connected experts. Here, we give a short description of the action selection procedure of the referral algorithms we considered and cite relevant literature for further details.

DIEL: DIEL uses Interval Estimation Learning for action selection. The action a is chosen for which the upper-confidence interval $UI(a)$ is largest, where

$$UI(a) = m(a) + \frac{s(a)}{\sqrt{n}}$$

$m(a)$ is the mean observed reward, $s(a)$ is the standard deviation of the observed rewards and n is the number of observations so far. The intuition behind DIEL is to combine exploitation (via high mean) and exploration (via high variance) as needed. Following the earlier work [1,2], we initialize the mean reward, standard deviation and number of observations for all actions to 0.5, 0.7071 and 2 respectively for a smooth start (this is equivalent to an initialization with the two rewards of 0 and 1).

Proactive-DIEL: Proactive-DIEL differs from DIEL in two key ways [2]. First, the mean reward and standard deviation of the rewards are initialized differently. Standard deviation is initialized to 0 (to put more emphasis on the advertised priors). In presence of an advertisement unit, $\langle e_i, e_j, t_k, \mu_{t_k} \rangle$, the mean reward $reward_{mean}(e_i, t_k, e_k)$ is initialized to μ_{t_k}. In absence of such advertisement unit, (recall that the budget was assumed to suffice for advertising an expert's top two skills only) proactive-DIEL initializes the rewards as if the expert's skill was the same as on her second best topic, that is, with $\mu_{t_{secondBest}}$, effectively being an upper bound on the actual value. Second, in addition to binary rewards indicating success and failure, a failed task receives a probabilistic penalty to discourage willful misreporting.

ϵ-Greedy: Unlike DIEL, ϵ-Greedy's action selection choice is guided purely by the mean reward (it greedily picks the highest one) [18]. As a diversification step, with a small probability ϵ, a random action (in this case, selecting a connected expert at random) is chosen. There are several ways to choose an effective value for ϵ. In this work, we set ϵ to $\frac{\alpha * K}{N}$ (where K is the subnetwork size and N is the number of total observations). The value of the hyper-parameter α is set by a parameter sweep on a training set created with the same distributional parameters as the test set (for parameter description, see [1]).

4   Experimental Setup

The data set presented in [1] consisted of 1000 scenarios, each with 100 experts, 10 topics and a referral network. We use a random subset of 200 such scenarios in all our experiments. Our performance measure is the overall task accuracy of our multi-expert system.

The 100 SATenstein solvers we used are obtained by configuring SATenstein2.0 version (described in [17]) on six well-known SAT distributions.

Each of these solvers is configured on one of the six SAT distributions. We used the test sets of the SAT distributions as our pool of tasks. Detailed descriptions of the SAT distributions can be found in [16]. We carried out our experiments involving SAT solvers on a cluster of dual-core 2.4 GHz machines with 3 MB cache and 32 GB RAM running Linux 2.6.

5   Results

Before delving into the details, we first give a short description of our **key findings**:

- On an application where SAT solvers are experts, SAT distributions are topics and the task is to solve a SAT instance, our results show that here too proactive-DIEL beats DIEL in the early phase of learning.
- Proactive-ϵ-Greedy, the distributed referral learning version of ϵ-Greedy we proposed that uses proactive skill posting, beat the original version under the condition of truthful reporting of skills.
- While DIEL was well able to cope with small changes to the network, proactive-DIEL proved substantially more robust in the face of large and repeated changes, while consistently maintaining higher performance.

5.1   SATenstein SLS Solvers as Experts

All performance comparisons between DIEL and proactive-DIEL so far, have been on synthetic data [2]. We were curious to evaluate how that translates to a real task where, for instance, the noise on self-estimates does not follow a known parameterizable distribution. For this, we constructed a referral network of SAT solvers. Besides the importance of SAT solvers in industry and academia, what made this domain an attractive choice for us was our access to a large number of solvers with varying expertise on six well-known SAT distributions via SATenstein [16], and the fact that solutions can be verified trivially.

For our experiments, the budget C for solving each instance is set to 1 CPU second. A solver earns a reward of 1 if it finds a satisfying solution within C seconds, and 0 otherwise (on top of this, proactive-DIEL computes additional penalties depending on advertised skills). Expertise estimates for the SAT solvers are computed based on the number of correct solutions on a set of background data on the SAT distributions under consideration. Figure 1(a) gives an inkling how expertise levels between solvers may differ on two tasks. Figure 1(b) presents a comparison of the performance of proactive-DIEL with that of DIEL when applied to a referral network of SAT solvers (we considered 10 different referral networks randomly selected from our data set), with skill postings determined by these expertise self-estimates. We see that, while the eventual performance levels are very similar, proactive-DIEL ramps up significantly faster than its predecessor, in spite of the noise and uncertainty on the expertise self-estimates.

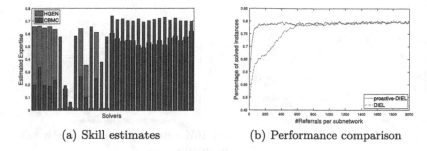

(a) Skill estimates   (b) Performance comparison

Fig. 1. Expertise estimates of a subset of solvers on background data of two SAT distributions and performance comparison with SATenstein solvers as experts.

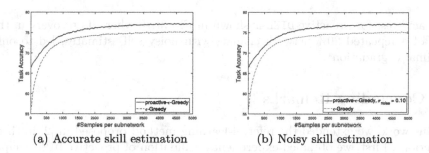

(a) Accurate skill estimation   (b) Noisy skill estimation

Fig. 2. Performance comparison of proactive-ε-Greedy and ε-Greedy.

5.2   Proactive-ε-Greedy

We extended the ε-Greedy algorithm with the reward-penalty mechanism used in proactive-DIEL in a straightforward way, with the exception that we do not impose a penalty during a diversification step even when the referred expert fails. Figure 2 shows that, with a similar initialization, the new algorithm (proactive-ε-Greedy) performs substantially better than the old. Figure 2(b) shows that this performance improvement holds even in the presence of noise in the self-estimates. Following [2], we considered $\hat{\mu} = \mu + \mathcal{N}(0, \sigma_{noise})$, where $\hat{\mu}$ is an expert's own estimate of her true topic-mean μ, and σ_{noise} is a small constant.

5.3   Evolving Networks

In practice, networks are not static – new experts join in and old experts leave – and robustness to such network changes is crucial for a referral algorithm's performance on real-world data. In these results, we explore a steady rate of network changes occurring at regular intervals (every 50 iterations, an iteration being 1000 initial queries). It is clear from Fig. 3 that proactive-DIEL is much more resilient to these network changes than DIEL (smaller dip, faster recovery).

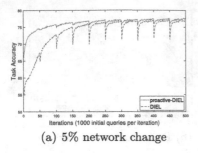 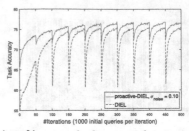

(a) 5% network change   (b) 20% network change and noisy self-estimates

Fig. 3. proactive-DIEL on dynamic networks.

The acid test for proactive-DIEL is shown in Fig. 3(b), where its recovery in the face of a repeated 20% network change, with noisy self-estimates, led to only minimal degradation[1].

6   Concluding Remarks

In this work, we extended the referral-learning method proposed in [2] in three directions. First, we obtained experimental validation of proactive-DIEL's superior performance over DIEL in learning to refer among actual agents (SAT solvers) without distributional assumptions. Next, we extended the initialization and reward-penalty technique proposed in proactive-DIEL to other methods and show an improved performance resilient to noisy self-estimates. Finally, we showed proactive-DIEL's robustness to evolving networks under severe network changes, an excellent property of proactive-DIEL hereto unexplored.

Possible future extensions to our work include:

- **Strategyproofness:** While willful skill misreporting was shown to be of little or no benefit when all other experts report truthfully in proactive-DIEL [2], we are yet to empirically evaluate the same for ϵ-Greedy. Also, a stronger degree of incentive compatibility, strategyproofness, would require truthfulness for optimal performance in all cases.
- **Expertise drift:** Whereas we explored experts joining and dropping off the referral network, the expertise of individual experts did not change with time. But in practice expertise may improve with practice or degrade due to fatigue or other factors. Devising algorithms to deal with time-varying expertise would be a meaningful research challenge.

---

[1] Note that the choice to use 50-iteration bursts is purely for visualization reasons and our results do not change qualitatively when we consider similar changes distributed across the entire course of the simulation. We also ran experiments with a large one-time network change from which both DIEL and proactive-DIEL recovered well.

- **Continuous rewards:** With the experiments with SAT solvers, it is very easy to conceive continuous rewards. If we treat (cutoff - run time) as reward, we would get 0 reward on a failure and higher rewards will imply faster solutions. Exploring reward mechanisms to handle continuous rewards could further improve network performance as an effective referral will maximize not only solution likelihood but also solution quality.

Acknowledgements. This research is partially funded by the National Science Foundation grant EAGER-1649225.

References

1. KhudaBukhsh, A.R., Jansen, P.J., Carbonell, J.G.: Distributed learning in expert referral networks. In: European Conference on Artificial Intelligence (ECAI), pp. 1620–1621 (2016)
2. KhudaBukhsh, A.R., Carbonell, J.G., Jansen, P.J.: Proactive skill posting in referral networks. In: Kang, B., Bai, Q. (eds.) AI 2016. LNCS, vol. 9992, pp. 585–596. Springer, Cham (2016). doi:10.1007/978-3-319-50127-7_52
3. Kaelbling, L.P.: Learning in Embedded Systems. MIT Press, Cambridge (1993)
4. Kaelbling, L.P., Littman, M.L., Moore, A.P.: Reinforcement learning: a survey. J. Artif. Intell. Res. **4**, 237–285 (1996)
5. Donmez, P., Carbonell, J.G., Schneider, J.: Efficiently learning the accuracy of labeling sources for selective sampling. In: Proceedings of KDD 2009, p. 259 (2009)
6. Kautz, H., Selman, B., Milewski, A.: Agent amplified communication, pp. 3–9 (1996)
7. Yolum, P., Singh, M.P.: Dynamic communities in referral networks. Web Intell. Agent Syst. **1**(2), 105–116 (2003)
8. Yu, B.: Emergence and evolution of agent-based referral networks. Ph.D. thesis, North Carolina State University (2002)
9. Yu, B., Venkatraman, M., Singh, M.P.: An adaptive social network for information access: theoretical and experimental results. Appl. Artif. Intell. **17**, 21–38 (2003)
10. Yu, B., Singh, M.P.: Searching social networks. In: Proceedings of AAMAS 2003 (2003)
11. Babaioff, M., Sharma, Y., Slivkins, A.: Characterizing truthful multi-armed bandit mechanisms. In: Proceedings of the 10th ACM Conference on Electronic Commerce, pp. 79–88. ACM (2009)
12. Biswas, A., Jain, S., Mandal, D., Narahari, Y.: A truthful budget feasible multi-armed bandit mechanism for crowdsourcing time critical tasks. In: Proceedings of the 2015 International Conference on Autonomous Agents and Multiagent Systems, International Foundation for Autonomous Agents and Multiagent Systems, pp. 1101–1109 (2015)
13. Tran-Thanh, L., Stein, S., Rogers, A., Jennings, N.R.: Efficient crowdsourcing of unknown experts using multi-armed bandits. In: European Conference on Artificial Intelligence, pp. 768–773 (2012)
14. Tran-Thanh, L., Chapman, A., Rogers, A., Jennings, N.R.: Knapsack based optimal policies for budget-limited multi-armed bandits. arXiv preprint arXiv:1204.1909 (2012)
15. Nisan, N., Roughgarden, T., Tardos, E., Vazirani, V.V.: Algorithmic Game Theory, vol. 1. Cambridge University Press, Cambridge (2007)

16. KhudaBukhsh, A.R., Xu, L., Hoos, H.H., Leyton-Brown, K.: Satenstein: automatically building local search sat solvers from components. In: IJCAI, vol. 9, pp. 517–524 (2009)
17. KhudaBukhsh, A.R., Xu, L., Hoos, H.H., Leyton-Brown, K.: Satenstein: automatically building local search sat solvers from components. Artif. Intell. **232**, 20–42 (2016)
18. Auer, P., Cesa-Bianchi, N., Fischer, P.: Finite-time analysis of the multiarmed bandit problem. Mach. Learn. **47**(2–3), 235–256 (2002)

Probabilistic Topic Modeling, Reinforcement Learning, and Crowdsourcing for Personalized Recommendations

Evangelos Tripolitakis and Georgios Chalkiadakis[(✉)]

School of Electrical and Computer Engineering,
Technical University of Crete, Chania, Greece
{vtripolitakis,gehalk}@intelligence.tuc.gr
http://www.ece.tuc.gr/

Abstract. We put forward an innovative use of probabilistic topic modeling (PTM) intertwined with reinforcement learning (RL), to provide personalized recommendations. Specifically, we model items under recommendation as *mixtures of latent topics* following a distribution with Dirichlet priors; this can be achieved via the exploitation of *crowdsourced information* for each item. Similarly, we model the *user herself* as an "evolving" document represented by its respective mixture of latent topics. The user's topic distribution is appropriately updated each time she consumes an item. Recommendations are subsequently based on the divergence between the topic distributions of the user and available items. However, to tackle the exploration versus exploitation dilemma, we apply RL to vary the user's topic distribution update rate. Our method is immune to the notorious "cold start" problem, and it can effectively cope with changing user preferences. Moreover, it is shown to be competitive against state-of-the-art algorithms, outperforming them in terms of sequential performance.

Keywords: Recommender systems · Applications of reinforcement learning · Graphical models · Crowdsourcing

1 Introduction

In this paper, we introduce a system that provides high quality, personalized recommendations, with minimal user interaction and without relying to others' ratings. We achieve that by *(a)* employing the key assumption that *users can be viewed as the amalgamation of items they consume* and *(b)* by exploiting, to the best extent possible, available *crowdsourced information* related to the items.

Our solution takes into account the *richness*, *complexity*, and *evolution* of user preferences by exploiting *latent* features, while at the same time identifying preference shifts, and adapting in a dynamic, transparent manner. Regarding the *cold-start* problem, we are able to perform high-quality suggestions. Further, the system presents computational efficiency, thus suitable to cope with large-scale

© Springer International Publishing AG 2017
N. Criado Pacheco et al. (Eds.): EUMAS 2016/AT 2016, LNAI 10207, pp. 157–171, 2017.
DOI: 10.1007/978-3-319-59294-7_14

data sets. Last, it designed to be domain-agnostic, hence minimizing the fine-tuning effort from the practitioner. Our work builds on the *"you are what you consume"* approach put forward by [3], but, crucially, employs *probabilistic topic modeling (PTM)* [17] and intertwines it with *reinforcement learning (RL)* [9] techniques.

Specifically, we model *both items* and *users* as distributions of topics with *Dirichlet priors* over *crowdsourced corpora* of documents, found in on-line communities producing peer-reviewed, unbiased information—here we use Wikipedia movie synopses. We thus replace *explicit* attributes (e.g. movie categories) by *latent* features in *both* user and item distributions. We adapt our recommendations policy using concepts from the RL literature. We inflict drastic changes to the user model *only* if there are strong indications of a decaying predictions performance. This is accomplished by the alteration of the system's *learning rate*: minimum changes are imposed if performance is strong when compared to its average within a past ratings window; on the other hand, we increase the learning rate significantly in order to move out of a series of low-rated recommendations. Moreover, we adopt an ϵ-greedy exploration strategy that occasionally selects random items to avoid "local maxima" in the recommendations space. Last but not least, we successfully tackle user preference shifts.

In summary, our approach *(i)* requires no clustering, does not predict ratings, and does not use hard-coded attributes (e.g. categories, genres, etc.); *(ii)* exploits crowdsourced information, which is widely available—and usually implies good quality, objective, peer-reviewed sources of information; *(iii)* requires minimal user interaction limited to user ratings; *(iv)* is unbiased and immune to external noise and "information poisoning", as it does not consider other users' behaviors: it just adheres to user's preferences; *(v)* it can cope with the "cold-start" problem (i.e. given limited or no background information about new users, we should be able to adjust the user interaction with the system in order to suggest proper items after a small number of iterations) since it does not require other users' ratings; *(vi)* it can cope with evolving user preferences, and even mood-changes; on the technical side, intertwining PTMs with RL methods is innovative and interesting; *(vii)* it provides intuition on the actual user interests, since these correspond to the PTM-inferred topics that relate to the particular user mostly (i.e., the most frequent ones in its associated topics distribution); *(viii)* allows for the easy online update and enrichment of items and user models and *(ix)* can scale-up by employing industry-proven algorithms; *(x)* it is not domain-specific, and could be used for cross-domain recommendations.

2   Related Work

Collaborative filtering (CF) techniques exploit ratings from similar users or items and try to predict the user's preference for each item, ignoring other background information [2, 4, 14, 16, 18]. CF algorithms received acclaim on the Netflix contest [10–12]. Nevertheless, CF suffers from the *cold-start* problem, requiring the a certain amount of ratings to operate. Similarly, newly-introduced items need a minimum number of ratings. The same issue applies to CF variations, where a considerable amount of transactions (e.g. purchases) needs to be available.

Content-based recommender systems have been proposed to work along with CF algorithms and form hybrid systems [6,13]. Melville et al. [5] proposed a content-based predictor to boost existing user data and exploit it for personalized recommendations using CF. Hoffman [15] introduced latent class variables in a mixture model setting, to search for user communities and profiles that present special interest.

[2] have also proposed the use of PTMs [1,19] for making recommendations for scientific articles; while [20] used topic modeling (via a generative model based on Latent Dirichlet Allocation) to exploit movie reviews and boost the performance of a CF system. These works, however, still rely on the ratings of multiple users (in the spirit of CF), and do not maintain an evolving user model, as we do in this paper—nor do they intertwine PTM with RL techniques.

We build on the work of [3] who, however represent users and items by *multivariate Gaussian distributions* over movie categories; our use of PTMs is a generic method providing immediate insights about user preferences, via the topics describing the user.

3 Theoretical Background

Here, we provide some background on PTMs and the key RL techniques used in this work. PTMs treat data as arising from a generative process that defines a joint probability distribution over observed and hidden variables corresponding to the underlying topic structure of a document, and then apply tractable Bayesian inference (e.g., sampling-based) methods to estimate the posterior distributions of the hidden variables.

In the *Latent Dirichlet allocation (LDA)* [1], all M documents are represented by mixtures of K topics with Dirichlet priors and N words in total. The parameters are the following: α is the parameter (a vector of positive reals) of the Dirichlet prior on the per-document topic distributions, β is the parameter (a vector of positive reals) of the Dirichlet prior on the per-topic word distribution, θ_i is the topic distribution for document i, ϕ_k is the word distribution for topic k, z_{ij} is the topic for the jth word in document i, and w_{ij} is the specific word. The LDA employs the following processes:

1. Select $\theta_i \sim Dir(\alpha)$, $Dir(\alpha)$: the Dirichlet distribution for α, for the document $i \in \{1 \dots M\}$
2. Select $\phi_k \sim Dir(\beta)$, $Dir(\beta)$: the Dirichlet distribution for β, for the word $k \in \{1 \dots N\}$
3. For each word $w_{ij} : i \in \{1 \dots M\}, j \in \{1 \dots N_i\}$, with N_i being the number of words of document i
   (a) Select $z_{ij} \sim Multinomial(\theta_i)$
   (b) Select $w_{ij} \sim Multinomial(\phi_{z_{ij}})$

In the MAS and RL literature several algorithms have been suggested for the variation of a *learning rate*, which governs the extent to which an agent's decisions are influenced by recent knowledge [9]. We focus on the WoLF ("Win or Learn Fast") principle adopting the concept of taking drastic measures when the agent is losing, and make small or no changes in case of a win streak [7, 8]. The decision is made considering the relation between the overall average performance and the performance within the k last steps. Hence, we introduce a δ_{win} and a δ_{lose} variation to the learning rate, for the cases the recommender predictions keep performing well, or worsen, respectively. Further, we adopt an ϵ-greedy strategy, to combat the "exploration vs. exploitation" dilemma [9], the recommender will suggest the most preferable item with probability $1 - \epsilon$; and chooses a random item otherwise.

4   Our Model

We offer personalized recommendations to a set of Z users $U = \{u_1, \ldots, u_Z\}$, taken from a set of M available items $Y = \{y_1, \ldots, y_M\}$. Users are first asked to select from a set at least one movie they like most. Upon this, the system returns a suggestion and asks users to rate it, in order to update their model. We use LDA to model both items and users as mixtures over topics with a *Dirichlet* prior. A set of assumptions are made for this model to apply: (a) There is descriptive information freely available for all items, (b) The descriptions are non-trivial. This means that we need at least a couple of paragraphs of text, (c) The descriptions are objective and do not contain other information than that which illustrates the characteristics/behavior/function of the item.

4.1   Item Modeling

Items $y_i \in Y, |Y| = M, 1 \leq i \leq M$ are represented by *documents* belonging to a corpus D, containing M documents. There are N words in total in the corpus *vocabulary*. We set the number of *topics* associated with the corpus to K. For each document, we choose:

1. $\theta_i \sim Dir_K(\boldsymbol{\alpha})$, where θ_i is the distribution of topics in document i, and $Dir_K(\boldsymbol{\alpha})$ is the Dirichlet distribution of parameter $\boldsymbol{\alpha}$.
2. $\phi_k \sim Dir_N(\boldsymbol{\beta})$, where ϕ_k is the word distribution for topic k, and $Dir_N(\boldsymbol{\beta})$ is the Dirichlet distribution of parameter $\boldsymbol{\beta}$.

$\boldsymbol{\alpha}$ and $\boldsymbol{\beta}$ are the Dirichlet parameters of topic distributions per document and word distributions per topic, respectively.

4.2   User Modeling

Similarly, each user u_j is modeled after a document represented by an evolving mixture of topics with Dirichlet prior. The distribution of topics mixture, follows, like items, a Dirichlet distribution. Hence: $\theta_j \sim Dir_K(\boldsymbol{\alpha})$, where θ_j is the distribution of topics in the single document that models the user, $Dir_K(\boldsymbol{\alpha})$ is the Dirichlet distribution of parameter $\boldsymbol{\alpha}$, and K the number of topics.

4.3   Item-Model and User-Model Updating

After the necessary preprocessing steps (i.e. stop word removal, stemming, and so on), the input corpus consisting of M crowdsourced documents is used to derive the final LDA model. This procedure is repeated for various number of topics K, until we reach a number that yields the lowest *perplexity* [21] score in a test set consisting of M_{test} documents. A simplified, tractable approach is viable via approximation methods utilizing sampling by [22]:

$$perplexity(D_{test}) = exp\{-\frac{\sum_{d=1}^{M_{test}} logp(\mathbf{w}_d)}{\sum_{d=1}^{M_{test}} N_d}\} \tag{1}$$

The number of words of document d belonging to the test set, is N_d. A decrease in perplexity is an indication of an increase in the predictive strength of the model.

Apart from the initial modeling of a set of available documents, new documents still need to be added to the corpus D. There are two alternatives: *(a)* model recalculation in batches; and *(b)* on-line LDA which is described by [23] and allows on-the-fly incorporation of new documents on the model. In our case, the corpus is fixed. In real-world environments, depending on the size and complexity of available documents, the practitioner is free to choose a suitable solution.

Then, in order to update the user-model, we need to incorporate three key factors: *(a)* The user's ratings of items that she consumes; *(b)* the possibility that she favors other types of items than those she used to, hence reflecting a mood shift; and *(c)* a potential exhaustion of preferable items.

Each time the user consumes an item, she provides a rating. This rating is used in the Bayesian updating of her topic mixture. As the topic distribution of the document that models the user is unknown, we utilize Bayes rule to take into account *observations* (user ratings), a *likelihood function* and a *marginal probability*, so as to derive a *posterior* distribution.

The likelihood function associates the prior with the observations, while preserving the form of the overall model. The posterior which is produced represents the updated belief for the prior, given the evidence. Using the posterior beliefs $f(\boldsymbol{\theta}|y)$, we are able to update our unknown model. In our case we use the *Dirichlet* and the *multinomial* distributions, which are conjugate. This is a useful property, which allows us to perform easy updates to the prior's *hyperparameters*, using a closed form equation, we will show below.

Given documents $\mathbf{y}$ and with topics mixtures $\boldsymbol{\theta}$, we have:

$$\boldsymbol{\theta} \sim Dir(\boldsymbol{\alpha} = \langle a_1, \ldots, a_K \rangle) \tag{2}$$

$$\mathbf{y} \sim Mult(\boldsymbol{\theta} = \langle \theta_1, \ldots, \theta_K \rangle) \tag{3}$$

In detail, the topic mixtures $\boldsymbol{\theta}$ are described by:

$$Dir(\boldsymbol{\theta}|a_1, \ldots, a_K) = \frac{\Gamma(a_1 + \ldots + a_K)}{\Gamma(a_1) \ldots \Gamma(a_K)} \prod_{i=1}^{K} \theta_i^{a_i - 1} \tag{4}$$

Given the evidence (document y) the posterior becomes:

$$f(\boldsymbol{\theta}|y) \propto f(\boldsymbol{\theta}, y) = f(\theta_1, \ldots, \theta_K | \alpha_1, \ldots, \alpha_K) f(y|\theta_1, \ldots, \theta_K)$$

$$\propto \prod_{j=1}^{K} \theta_j^{a_j-1} \prod_{j=1}^{K} \theta_j^{y^{(j)}} = \prod_{j=1}^{K} \theta_j^{a_j-1+(y^{(j)})} \quad (5)$$

The updated hyperparameters of the Dirichlet prior are:

$$a_j' = a_j + y^{(j)} \quad (6)$$

Therefore, we can update the user model by simply adding to each topic θ_k the respective topic counts from the document y that was just rated. Furthermore, we incorporate the user rating by repeating this step n times. For a user, depending on the t-th rating r of an item that was recommended, we update the user model by taking n samples, using:

$$n \propto \Delta_t^{\ r} - 1 \quad (7)$$

where: Δ_t is the variable learning rate (a real number) for the t-th recommended item and r is the actual rating.

Items that have been positively rated by the user, can be thought as having greater *influence* on the overall user preferences. Further, the intuition behind the Eq. 7 is that items rated by 0, 1 and 2 should have minimal or no influence on the evolution of the user's model. Contrary to that, items rated between 3 and 5 should contribute proportionally to their significance. We empirically found suitable values of Δ_t to lie between 1.0 and 4.0. Adjusting this variable learning rate allows us to move away from less promising areas of the search space (see *Algorithm* 1).

4.4   Recommendation Phase

The recommendation phase consists of two main functions: *(a)* the querying of the available low-dimensional representation of items to obtain the most appropriate, and *(b)* the monitoring of the system performance and adjustment of the learning rate. Once LDA has been run on the corpus and the initial user models have been built, the recommendation algorithm is displayed in the pseudocode of *Algorithm* 1.

Given the fact that both users and items are represented by the same distribution, we assess their similarity by employing the cosine distance D_{cosine} metric, which is a common measure in the information retrieval domain:

$$D_{cosine}(P, Q) = 1 - \frac{\sum_{i=1}^{n} P_i \times Q_i}{\sqrt{\sum_{i=1}^{n} P_i} \times \sqrt{\sum_{i=1}^{n} Q_i}} \quad (8)$$

where P, Q are distributions of the same type and same size.

Algorithm 1. Item recommendation

1: **procedure** RECOMMENDITEM
2:       with probability ϵ choose a random item, request a rating and go to **updateUser:**, with
             probability $1 - \epsilon$ continue
3:       **for** each item $y_i \in D$ **do**
4:             Calculate the cosine distance $D_{cosine}(y_i||u_j)$ between the item and the user u_j and
                 store it in an array
5:       **end for**
6:       Find the (non-recommended) item with the smallest cosine distance, ask user for a rating
7:       **updateUser:**
8:       Update the average of user ratings $\overline{r_{u_j}}$ and the average rating for the latest ξ recommenda-
             tions $\overline{r_{u_{j\xi}}}$
9:       **if** $\overline{r_{u_j}} > c \, \overline{r_{u_{j\xi}}}$ **then** % with $c \geq 1$
10:           $\Delta_{t+1} = \Delta_t + \delta_{lose}$
11:      **else**
12:           $\Delta_{t+1} = \Delta_t - \delta_{win}$
13:      **end if**
14:      Update user-model
15: **end procedure**

---

5   Experiments

We chose the *cinema movies* domain due its significance and popularity both scientifically-wise and business-wise. Instead of using domain-specific sites (e.g., IMDB), we chose Wikipedia as our source, which offers a large collection of lemmas with detailed plot summaries, actively checked for objectivity and clarity by a large number of contributors.

5.1   Information Collection, Pre-processing and Topic Model Selection

We developed a workflow, which operates on *any on-line source* with an API, for initial information collection. Further, we employed the MALLET [24] topic modeling toolkit which implements the LDA algorithm (plus necessary pre-processing tools - e.g., stop words removal). Regarding topic number optimization, we ran LDA on two sets of documents from Movielens 1M and 10M datasets, consisting of 3,137 and 8,721 text documents (containing movie synopses) respectively. We split our corpus, using a ratio of 80–20%, to yield training and test sets and calculated the perplexity for varying topic numbers according to Eq. 1. We found that the optimal number of topics is 280 and 240 respectively. We relaxed this to 75 topics as a trade-off between perplexity and computational cost.

Experimental Setup. Our algorithmic variants include: (a) one with a fixed learning rate Δ, set to 4.0 and no exploration and (b) one with variable $\Delta \in [1.0 \dots 4.0]$ and ϵ-greedy exploration set to 0.30. For both variants we update the user type taking n samples as in Eq. 7. Moreover, we optionally introduce "time-compensation" by multiplying (or not), the number of samples returned by Eq. 7 with an integer proportional (by a factor of 1.0 at our setup) to the current recommendation step number, hence favoring most recent ratings. We set $c = 1.1, \xi = 3, d_{win} = 0.05, d_{lose} = 0.3$. Last but not least, we validated the operation of our algorithm against a random setting, and investigated its adaptability to user mood shifts. For our experiments, we used 5 sets of 100 randomly-selected users from the Movielens 1M and 10M datasets[1], having 200 or more ratings each. We intentionally chose users with 200 or more ratings because we wanted to illustrate the non-trivial long-term learning behavior of our algorithm.

We compare our algorithm, *BYLI-LDA* with 2 existing methods: the "Bayes As You Like It (BYLI)", suggested Babas et al. (on the 1M dataset), and a sophisticated (with automatic retraining) implementation of the alternating least squares (ALS) algorithm for large, sparse matrix factorization (LSMF) by [16], on the Myrrix software. In detail, we check against a trained version of LSMF (using all database ratings for training, minus those of the 100 users in the set) and an untrained version of LSMF (as in [3]). Note that LSMF, being a CF method, has to first collect a small number of ratings in order to be able to return good recommendations, and thus cannot provide a meaningful recommendation at the first iteration.

The performance of recommendation algorithms is typically assessed by their Root Mean Square Error (RMSE); and RMSE calculation requires ratings predictions. Our algorithm, on the other hand, *does not* predict ratings, but simply suggests movies sequentially, based on its beliefs regarding the evolving user type. Actually, many algorithms do not explicitly calculate ratings, but just predict movie rankings. However, there is no standard way in the literature to transform a set of ranked results into predicted ratings, but these are typically calculated in a different way per algorithm (a fact that is justified by the suggestion of extra parameters such as user bias, item bias etc. [18]).

Regardless, we calculate RMSE by introducing a transformation function calculating the predicted rating of a recommendation: $r(i, j)_{predicted} \propto g(i, j)$. The transformation function $g(i, j)$ returns the predicted rating for an item i and a user j. We take a training set consisting of 80% of the movies each user has rated, and apply our algorithm. Next, we calculate the similarity vector of the movies in the training set and the user model, using our preferred similarity metric. Further, we calculate the distribution of ratings of each user and divide the similarity vector into parts whose lengths correspond to the frequency of each rating. For the test set (20% of users' ratings) we apply again our algorithm, get the *user-item distance* and calculate the predicted rating $r(i, j)_{predicted}$ and calculate the RMSE. The average RMSE is 1.14542, higher compared to errors reported on the literature for this dataset, typically from 0.8 to 1.0. Since we do not predict ratings, however, this result is not a cause of major concern: As we detail below, our algorithm performs very well when evaluated *wrt.: (a)* sequential performance, indicated by average per recommendation ratings across 200

---

[1] Datasets: *Movielens 1M*: *1M ratings, 6,040* users, *3,952* movies. *Movielens 10M*: *10M ratings, 71,567* users, *10,681* and movies. We found nontrivial data on Wikipedia for *3,137* movies on the 1M dataset and *8,721* movies on the 10M dataset.

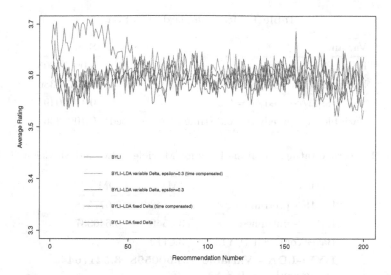

Fig. 1. BYLI-LDA vs BYLI; sequential recommendation performance on the 1M Movielens dataset

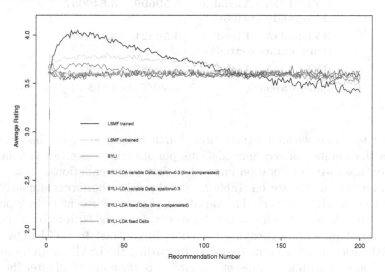

Fig. 2. BYLI-LDA vs BYLI and LSMF; sequential recommendation performance on the 1M Movielens dataset

recommendations over 10 runs; and *(b)* average ratings across all recommendations. All averages were taken across the 5 user sets.

Results and Evaluation on Movielens 1M. Our algorithm presents a stable behavior in all its variants, as it is clear from Fig. 1. This is also clear from the standard deviation that is displayed on Table 1 ranging from 0.0966 to 0.1019. Clearly, the results from the variants with exploration perform slightly better

Table 1. Mean standard deviation

Variant	Std
Fixed Δ	0.09657605
Fixed Δ (time compensated)	0.09774386
Variable Δ/ϵ-greedy $\epsilon = 0.3$	0.1019049
Variable Δ/ϵ-greedy $\epsilon = 0.3$ (time compensated)	0.1009336

Table 2. Average ratings of all methods for Movielens 1M and Movielens 10M.

Methods	1M	10M
LSMF - pretrained	3.6848	3.677518
LSMF - untrained	3.6540	3.646337
BayesYouLikeIt (BYLI)	3.6112	-
BYLI-LDA - Variable Δ/ϵ-greedy $\epsilon = 0.3$ (time compensated)	**3.600598**	**3.541764**
BYLI-LDA - Variable Δ/ϵ-greedy $\epsilon = 0.3$	**3.59699**	**3.540057**
BYLI-LDA - Fixed Δ (time compensated)	**3.59421**	**3.533575**
BYLI-LDA - Fixed Δ	**3.593851**	**3.53371**
Dataset average	3.581564	3.512422

compared to those without exploration. Furthermore, at closer inspection of Fig. 1 as the number of recommendations per user increases, all variants and especially those with exploration improve their recommendations.

Furthermore, as we see on Table 2, our algorithm performs similarly with BYLI, which is 0.18% better[2]. The variations that favor recent ratings perform slightly better than those who do not. Moreover, from the 60th recommendation onward, BYLI presents a decaying behavior, in contrast to BYLI-LDA whose sequential performance is far more stable. Regarding the LSMF, both its versions ("trained" and "untrained") present a decaying performance and after the 120th recommendation are outperformed by BYLI-LDA (Fig. 2).

Results and Evaluation on Movielens 10M. In this dataset, the average rating is 3.512422 instead of 3.581564 at the 1M dataset. Similar to the 1M experiments, our algorithm displays a stable behavior here too, as Fig. 3 shows.

The recommendations are better than the dataset average on all variations of our algorithm. Contrary to that, as we see on Fig. 4, the trained version of LSMF performs much better compared to the 1M dataset, due to increase of the training dataset by 10 times. On the other hand, it still exposes a decaying behavior

---

[2] BYLI had been evaluated on MovieLens 1M only.

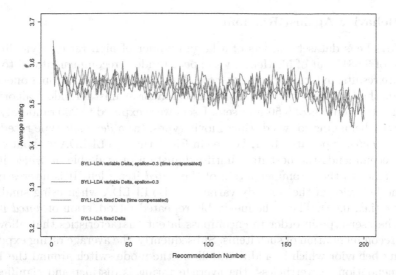

Fig. 3. BYLI-LDA Variants; performance on the 10M Movielens dataset

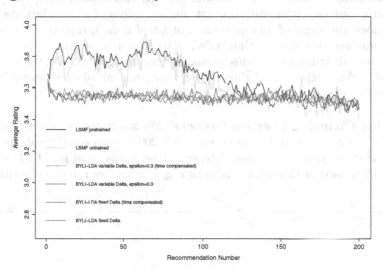

Fig. 4. BYLI-LDA vs LSMF; performance on the 10M Movielens dataset

starting around the 55th recommendation and converges to our algorithm. As in the case of the 1M dataset, the variants with variable learning rate exploration perform better compared to those with fixed learning rate and no exploration. Moreover, the favoring of newer ratings over older ones produces slightly better results on the variants with variable learning rate and exploration. The opposite happens (as in the case of 1M) to the fixed learning rate variants. The results are presented on Table 2 as well.

5.2   Behavior Against Random

The MovieLens dataset consists of a large number of high ratings (yielding an average of 3.5815 out of 5). Hence, we expect random recommendations to offer adequate results, in terms of average score. Thus, to validate the proper operation of our method, it is essential to display its behavior against a random algorithm.

Our setup consists of 5 50-user sets. Users were exposed to 200 randomly chosen movies belonging to two distinct movie types, (a) a *desirable* type rated by 5 and (b) a *hated* type rated by 1. We see in Fig. 5 that BYLI-LDA without exploration recommends the best item until exhaustion of available *desirable* items, and switches to the recommendation of the *hated* items left. It is interesting to note the behavior of the ϵ-greedy variants of BYLI-LDA when using small values for ϵ (i.e., 0.02), Then, the inevitable repeated introduction of *hated* items, alters the user-type in order to encompass latent characteristics that allow the future recommendation of such items. Subsequently, the average rating exposes a decaying behavior which in addition, follows the mode switch around the 100th recommendation. Nevertheless, the average rating is distinct and significantly higher compared to that of the random setting, hence confirming the proper operation of our algorithm. By contrast, higher values of ϵ (0.2) introduce significant noise (in terms of a large volume of *hated* items), rapidly deteriorating the performance of the algorithm. Obviously, in a real setting, this does not occur, as the distribution of *hated* items is totally different. On the contrary, as our Movielens experiments showed, exploration is absolutely desirable as it enhances the overall performance by avoiding local maxima.

Capturing Changing User Preferences. We simulated the occurrence of a preference (or a "mood shift") on a user with 200 ratings equally split between a *desirable* item type: b and a *hated* type: a. The behavior of BYLI-LDA (fixed Δ, no exploration) in this setting is as in Fig. 6. First, we ran our algorithm on

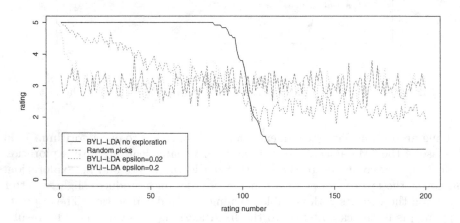

Fig. 5. BYLI-LDA variants vs random

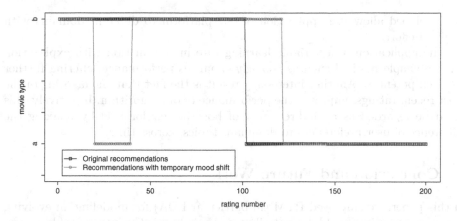

Fig. 6. Behavior when there is a mood shift (Color figure online)

a setting without mood shifts (black line with squares). The algorithm recommended first all available items of the *desirable* type, leaving for the end the *hated* items. On the other hand, we introduced from the 20th to the 40th recommendation (red line with diamonds), a temporary mood shift towards *hated* items. Our algorithm, instantly adapted and switched for 20 recommendations to type *a*. When the mood shift was over, BYLI-LDA switched again to the type *b* until the exhaustion of available items, hence recommending the remaining items of type *a*.

5.3   Discussion

All BYLI-LDA variants exhibit good sequential performance across all experimental settings. We note that our algorithm requires minimum tuning, and recommends items that consistently receive high actual ratings.

Table 3. Depiction of the first few most important topics and their respective words, for a specific user

Topic #	Words
46	Time virus future learns troop open search
71	Monster creature human giant fire body brain
70	Bank rob robbery work police crew kill thief

Our method, in contrast to LSMF (requiring an existing minimum number of recommendations), tackles the cold-start problem by providing personalized recommendations to a single user, in the absence of any other information. Furthermore, compared to both BYLI and LSMF, our algorithm provides insights about user preferences by providing the topics that describe the user through her item consumption history, as shown in Table 3. The algorithm and infrastructure we developed allow the application of our platform to different domains with minimal effort.

The application of a variable learning rate in conjunction with exploration using a simple method such as ϵ-*greedy* enhances performance, offering further research potential. Another interesting result is the fact that the favoring of the most recent ratings, improves the performance of our algorithm. Intuitively, this could be regarded as an indirect way of boosting exploration by relaxing the adherence of user preferences to dominant topics, across time.

6   Conclusion and Future Work

In this paper, we employed PTM (in particular LDA) for modeling an evolving user type as a mixture of latent attributes. As such, we offer interpretable recommendations and enhance the intuitions available on each recommendation step. Furthermore, we studied the effects of varying learning rate and a simple exploration approach, during user model updating, with minimal parameter tuning. Our approach is domain agnostic, and avoids the cold-start problem. Moreover, by using a peer-reviewed, objective corpus, along with its personalized user type updates, it cannot be easily "poisoned" by externally introduced bias. Though it does not surpass state-of-the-art approaches in this particular domain in terms of average recommendation ratings, it exhibits superior sequential performance. For all these reasons, it can be conceivably used as a complementary method to existing state-of-the-art approaches. Future work includes examining the impact of the number of topics K on algorithmic performance, employing more sophisticated RL algorithms, and applying our approach to different domains.

References

1. Blei, D.M., Ng, A.Y., Jordan, M.I.: Latent dirichlet allocation. J. Mach. Learn. Res. **3**, 993–1022 (2003)
2. Wang, C., Blei, D.M.: Collaborative topic modeling for recommending scientific articles. In: Proceedings of the 17th ACM SIGKDD International Conference on Knowledge Discovery and Data Mining, pp. 448–456. ACM (2011)
3. Babas, K., Chalkiadakis, G., Tripolitakis, E.: You are what you consume: a Bayesian method for personalized recommendations. In: Proceedings of the 7th ACM Conference on Recommender Systems, pp. 221–228. ACM (2013)
4. Koren, Y., Bell, R., Volinsky, C.: Matrix factorization techniques for recommender systems. Computer **42**(8), 30–37 (2009). IEEE
5. Melville, P., Mooney, R.J., Nagarajan, R.: Content-boosted collaborative filtering for improved recommendations. In: AAAI/IAAI, pp. 187–192 (2002)
6. Mooney, R.J., Roy, L.: Content-based book recommending using learning for text categorization. In: Proceedings of the Fifth ACM Conference on Digital Libraries, pp. 195–204. ACM (2000)
7. Bowling, M., Veloso, M.: Rational and convergent learning in stochastic games. In: Proceedings of the 17th International Joint Conference on Artificial Intelligence, vol. 2, pp. 1021–1026 (2001)

8. Bowling, M., Veloso, M.: Multiagent learning using a variable learning rate. Artif. Intell. **136**(2), 215–250 (2002). Elsevier

9. Sutton, R.S., Barto, A.G.: Introduction to Reinforcement Learning. MIT Press, Cambridge (1998)

10. Koren, Y.: The bellkor solution to the netflix grand prize. Netflix Prize Doc. **81**, 1–10 (2009)

11. Piotte, M., Chabbert, M.: The pragmatic theory solution to the netflix grand prize. Netflix Prize Doc. (2009). http://www.netflixprize.com/assets/GrandPrize2009_BPC_PragmaticTheory.pdf

12. Toscher, A., Jahrer, M., Bell, R.M.: The bigchaos solution to the netflix grand prize. Netflix Prize Doc. (2009). http://www.netflixprize.com/assets/GrandPrize2009_BPC_BigChaos.pdf

13. Langseth, H., Nielsen, T.D.: A latent model for collaborative filtering. Int. J. Approx. Reason. **53**(4), 447–466 (2012)

14. Bresler, G., Chen, G.H., Shah, D.: A latent source model for online collaborative filtering. In: Advances in Neural Information Processing Systems, pp. 3347–3355 (2014)

15. Hofmann, T.: Latent semantic models for collaborative filtering. ACM Trans. Inf. Syst. (TOIS) **22**(1), 89–115 (2004). ACM

16. Hu, Y., Koren, Y., Volinsky, C.: Collaborative filtering for implicit feedback datasets. In: Eighth IEEE International Conference on Data Mining, ICDM 2008, pp. 263–272. IEEE (2008)

17. Blei, D.M.: Probabilistic topic models. Commun. ACM **55**(4), 77–84 (2012). ACM

18. Koren, Y., Bell, R.: Advances in collaborative filtering. In: Ricci, F., Rokach, L., Shapira, B., Kantor, P.B. (eds.) Recommender Systems Handbook, pp. 145–186. Springer, Heidelberg (2011). doi:10.1007/978-0-387-85820-3_5

19. Agarwal, D., Chen, B.-C.: fLDA: matrix factorization through latent dirichlet allocation. In: Proceedings of the Third ACM International Conference on Web Search and Data Mining, pp. 91–100. ACM (2010)

20. Ling, G., Lyu, M.R., King, I.: Ratings meet reviews, a combined approach to recommend. In: Proceedings of the 8th ACM Conference on Recommender Systems, pp. 105–112. ACM (2014)

21. Kurimo, M.: Indexing audio documents by using latent semantic analysis and SOM. Elsevier (1999)

22. Wallach, H.M., Murray, I., Salakhutdinov, R., Mimno, D.: Evaluation methods for topic models. In: Proceedings of the 26th Annual International Conference on Machine Learning, pp. 1105–1112. ACM (2009)

23. Hoffman, M., Bach, F.R., Blei, D.M.: Online learning for latent dirichlet allocation. In: Advances in Neural Information Processing Systems, pp. 856–864 (2010)

24. McCallum, A.K.: MALLET: A Machine Learning for Language Toolkit (2002). http://mallet.cs.umass.edu

Proposal of an Action Selection Strategy with Expected Failure Probability and Its Evaluation in Multi-agent Reinforcement Learning

Kazuteru Miyazaki[1]([✉]), Koudai Furukawa[2], and Hiroaki Kobayashi[3]

[1] National Institution for Academic Degrees and Quality Enhancement of Higher Education, 1-29-1 Gakuennishimachi, Kodaira, Tokyo 185-8587, Japan
`teru@niad.ac.jp`
[2] IHI Transport Machinery Co., Ltd., 8-1 Akashi-cho, Chuo-ku, Tokyo 104-0044, Japan
[3] Meiji University, 1-1-1 Higashimita, Tama-ku, Kawasaki, Kanagawa 214-8571, Japan

Abstract. When multiple agents learn a task simultaneously in an environment, the learning results often become unstable. The problem is known as a concurrent learning problem and several methods have been proposed to resolve the problem so far. In this paper, we propose a new method that incorporates the expected failure probability (EFP) into the action selection strategy to give agents a kind of mutual adaptability. We confirm the effectiveness of the proposed method using Keepaway task.

1 Introduction

In the near future, a robot is expected to expand the work field into human living environment more deeply and widely. However, it is very difficult for a robot designer to take all relevant properties of the circumstances into account since they change depending on the target, learning method, available sensors, and so on. Therefore, it is desired for a robot to have the ability to adapt to the environment based on perceived information and experienced actions all by itself. Reinforcement learning (RL) [25] is one of such techniques.

Reinforcement Learning is a type of machine learning where the robot tries to solve a given task through trial-and-error searches using a valuation value called a reward or a penalty. In RL, due to the trial and error search, there is a possibility of finding a good solution that exceeds our expectation. Furthermore, the calm change in the environment is allowable. As RL, methods based on Temporal Difference (TD) learning, such as TD, Q-learning (QL), and Sarsa, are well known [25]. Their mathematical foundation is in dynamic programming. For QL, the optimality in a Markov decision process environment is guaranteed, but the rationality (the definition will be given later in 2.1) in a non-Markov environment is not guaranteed. Especially, multi-agent environment that is treated in this paper will be a non-Markov environment since multiple agents learn a task simultaneously in an environment.

© Springer International Publishing AG 2017
N. Criado Pacheco et al. (Eds.): EUMAS 2016/AT 2016, LNAI 10207, pp. 172–186, 2017.
DOI: 10.1007/978-3-319-59294-7_15

Despite important applications [3–6,16,19,21,22,24,26,27], it is difficult to apply RL to real-world problems because, first, learning requires too many trial-and-error searches. Second, no general guideline exists on how to design suitable reward and penalty signal values, though there are some works that deal with this problem [15,23]. While these are essentially neglected in theoretical researches, they become serious issues in real-world applications. Namely, unacceptable results may arise if inappropriate values were assigned to them [12,13].

In this paper, we are interested in approaches that treat reward and penalty signals independently and enhance successful experiences strongly to reduce the number of trial-and-error searches. They are known as exploitation-oriented learning (XoL) [14,15]. XoL has four features. (1) XoL learns more quickly by strongly tracing successful experiences. (2) XoL treats, rewards and penalties as independent signals, letting these signals be handled more intuitively and easily than the handling of concrete values. (3) XoL does not pursue optimality in itself, but it can be acquired with multi-start technique by resetting all memory to get a better policy. (4) XoL has its strength in the class that exceeds MDPs because it is a Bellman-free method.

One example of XoL learning methods with a type of a reward is Profit Sharing (PS) [7,8]. PS has a certain degree of rationality in a non-Markov environment. It has also validity in a multi-agent environment [9–11]. In addition, Rational Policy Making algorithm (PARP) [12,13] and Improved PARP (Imp-PARP) [26] can avoid penalties and ensure the rationality. Recently, as an improved type of ImpPARP, a method that uses Expected Failure Probability (EFP) [17,20] (with the probability of which the agent will receive penalty in the future, if the agent use the rule in the state) has been proposed.

We propose a new XoL, PSwithEFP, by incorporating EFP into the action selection strategy. PSwithEFP can learn a may-be-not-best but safer policy that avoids penalties in shorter time. The effectiveness of the proposed method is evaluated in a multi-agent environment using Keepaway task [24]. Under a multi-agent environment, there is a problem called *concurrent learning problem* [1,2] where learning performance degrades due to the discrepancy among learning agents since each agent cannot know policies learned by the other agents. We will apply PSwithEFP and other RL methods to Keepaway task and show the effectiveness of PSwithEFP.

2   Reinforcement Learning

2.1   Definition of Terms

A subject in RL is commonly called *an agent*. After receiving sensory inputs from the environment, the agent selects *an action* to perform. Sensory inputs and the selected action consist of a unit, called *a step*. The sensory inputs from the environment referred to as *a state*. A pair of a state and an action that is applicable in the state is referred to as *a rule*. If the agent selects the action a in the state s, the rule is described as *rule(s,a)* or simply, sa. A function that maps a state to an action is called *a policy*. A policy is *deterministic* if there is only one action for each state. A policy is *rational* if all of expected rewards per an action are positive.

In TD method, QL, Sarsa and, PS, parameters called *a weight* is given to each rule. The weight is a value-function, which represents an expected reward. The agent receives a reward or a penalty after applying $rule(s, a)$ when a certain condition is satisfied. A reward is given if the target was achieved and a penalty is given when the target became unachievable, though there are some works about an indirect reward (i.e. [9,10]). Typically, it is given to both of $rule(s, a)$ and the state s.

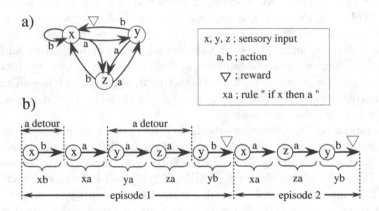

Fig. 1. (a) An environment of 3 sensory inputs and 2 actions. (b) An example of an episode and a detour

A sequence of steps that states from the initial state and ends with a reward or a penalty is called *an episode*. For example, when the agent selects xb, xa, ya, za, yb, xa, za, and yb in Fig. 1(a), there are two episodes $(xb \cdot xa \cdot ya \cdot za \cdot yb)$ and $(xa \cdot za \cdot yb)$, as shown in Fig. 1(b). If different rules are selected for the same state, that is, if the episode contains a loop, the loop is referred to as *a detour*. For example, an episode $(xb \cdot xa \cdot ya \cdot za \cdot yb)$ has two detours (xb) and $(ya \cdot za)$, as shown in Fig. 1(b). Rules that always exist in detours are referred to as *an ineffective rule*. If not so, it is called *an effective rule*. After obtaining the episode 1 of Fig. 1(b), rule xb, ya and za are ineffective rules and rule xa and yb are effective rules. When the episode 2 is experienced furthermore, rule za changes to a effective rule. A rule that has been directly given a penalty is called *a penalty rule*. If all rules for a state are penalty or irrational rules, the state is called *a penalty state*. If a destination after applying a rule is a penalty state, the rule is also classified as a penalty rule. If a rational policy does not receive any penalties, the policy is called *a penalty avoiding rational policy*.

2.2   Profit Sharing (PS)

PS learns a rational policy by propagating a reward backward along an episode when a reward is given. Assume that the action a_t was used in the state s_t at time t and let $Q(s_t, a_t)$ be a reward shared to $rule(s_t, a_t)$. In this paper, we use the following geometric decreasing function to propagate the reward backward;

$$Q(s_t, a_t) = S^{N-t} R, \quad t = 1, 2, \ldots, N, 0 < S < 1, \tag{1}$$

where R is the reward value, N is the episode length and S is the parameter called *the discount rate*.

2.3   Roulette Wheel Selection

The action selection method is one of the key elements of RL methods. In this paper, we use a roulette wheel selection. In the roulette selection, the probability of selecting $rule(s, a)$ is defined as follows;

$$p(a|s) = \frac{Q(s, a)}{\sum_{j=1}^{N_A} Q(s, a_j)}, \tag{2}$$

where $p(a|s)$ is the probability of selecting the action a in the state s. N_A is the number of available rules in the state.

2.4   XoL Methods to Avoid a Penalty

In RL, design of the reward is an important issue. If we use inappropriate values for a reward and a penalty, agents would not be able to receive any rewards [12,13]. XoL has been proposed to solve this problem by treating penalty separately from reward. For example, PARP improved the learning speed by avoiding penalty rules actively. In the following, we describe PARP and Imp-PARP briefly.

PARP and ImpPARP. PARP finds out penalty rules by searching the rule space that have been experienced until then. It therefore needs to store all experienced rules and the resulting states. It requires memory of the square order of the number of states. As the number of states increases, required memory for the learning becomes formidably large. ImpPARP has been proposed in order to solve this problem.

ImpPARP reduces the memory requirement by limiting the scope of the penalty rule exploration to the episode that just ended with a penalty. Therefore the order of the memory is reduced from the square order to the order of the number of states. On the other hand, the propagation speed of penalty rules becomes slower than PARP.

Expected Failure Probability. EFP was proposed in order to resolve the problem of delayed propagation of penalty in ImpPARP. EFP is defined for a rule and gives a probability that the episode will end with penalty after all if the rule is used. We can generally find out penalty rules faster than ImpPARP using EFP since EFP propagates swiftly like QL.

The theoretical expression of EFP of $rule(s,a)$ is given as follows;

$$p(E|rule(s,a)) = p(F|rule(s,a)) + \sum_{k=1}^{N_B} p(s_k|rule(s,a))p(E|s_k), \qquad (3)$$

where N_B is the number of states, $p(E|rule(s,a))$ is a probability that the trial will fail if $rule(s,a)$ is used, that is, our EFP, and $p(F|rule(s,a))$ is a probability that the trial will fail just after the rule is used, $p(s_k|rule(s,a))$ is a probability that the state will move to the state s_k after $rule(s,a)$ is used, and $p(E|s_k)$ is a probability that the trial will fail after it transits the state s_k.

The online calculation can be performed as follows;

– If the agent receives a penalty just after applying $rule(s,a)$,

$$p_t(E|rule(s,a)) = (1-\eta) \times p_{t-1}(E|rule(s,a)) + \eta. \qquad (4)$$

– If the state moves to the state s_k after applying $rule(s,a)$,

$$p_t(E|rule(s,a)) = (1-\eta) \times p_{t-1}(E|rule(s,a)) + \eta \times p(E|s_k), \qquad (5)$$

$$p(E|s_k) = \sum_{i}^{N_A} p(a_i|s_k)p(E|rule(s_k,a_i)), \qquad (6)$$

where $p_t(E|rule(s,a))$ is EFP of the $rule(s,a)$ at the iteration time t and the initial value is zero. η $(0 < \eta < 1)$ is *the failure probability propagation rate*.

Original EFP and Original EFP+. EFP was used as follows in papers [17, 20]; if $p_t(E|rule(s,a))$ exceeds γ, $rule(s,a)$ is labeled as a penalty rule and removed from selection candidates, where γ is the threshold value about a penalty rule. This method is referred to as **original EFP**.

In the original EFP, if all rules in a state became penalty rules, the agent cannot act any more. One solution of this dead end is to select a rule with the lowest EFP among them. In this paper, this method is referred to as **original EFP+**.

3   Calculation of the Failure Probability Propagation Rate

The failure probability propagation rate η is determined empirically in general. In this section, we propose how to determine η by $\hat{n}$, giving the number of times that the same rule can fail continuously, and γ, the EFP value p_n. It is possible to set η matched to the environment.

From Eq. (4), we can derive the following equation.

$$p_n = (1-\eta) \times p_{n-1} + \eta \qquad (7)$$

If we set $p_0 = 0$, we can get the following equation,

$$p_n = \sum_{k=1}^{n} \eta(1 - \eta)^{k-1} \tag{8}$$

that is,

$$p_n = \eta \frac{1 - (1 - \eta)^n}{1 - (1 - \eta)}. \tag{9}$$

Then,

$$p_n = 1 - (1 - \eta)^n \tag{10}$$

Since $p_{\hat{n}} \leq \gamma < p_{\hat{n}+1}$, we have

$$1 - \sqrt[\hat{n}+1]{1 - \gamma} > \eta > 1 - \sqrt[\hat{n}]{1 - \gamma} \tag{11}$$

p_n is the EFP value in the case of failure in n times continuously and n is the number of times that the failure continues. We can use Eq. (11) by setting the EFP value in the case of failure in n times continuously to the threshold value about a penalty rule named γ in original EFP and original EFP+. For example, if we set $\hat{n} = 3$ and $\gamma = 0.8$, η is 0.415. If we consider the case that the agent receives a penalty when it selected an action a in the state s, the value of $p(E|rule(s, a))$ at first is 0.415. If the agent receives a penalty continuously in the same condition, $p(E|rule(s, a))$ will be 0.658, and it reaches to 0.8 in the third times of the penalty acquisition. As a result, it has been achieved that the rule is regarded as a penalty rule after the agent received three penalties. It is consistent with the meaning of $\hat{n} = 3$.

4   Proposal of PSwithEFP

In original EFP and original EFP+, EFP is not utilized sufficiently, since EFP never affects to the action selection probability until EFP exceeds the threshold γ. In this paper, we incorporate EFP to the action selection method Eq. (2) as follows;

$$pe(a|s) = \frac{(1 - p(E|rule(s, a)))Q(s, a)}{\sum_{j=1}^{N_A}(1 - p(E|rule(s, a_j)))Q(s, a_j)}, \tag{12}$$

where $pe(a|s)$ is a probability of action selection. Furthermore, since the selection probability of the action is also used in the calculation of EFP, Eq. (6) becomes as follows;

$$p(E|s_k) = \sum_{i}^{N_A} pe(a_i|s_k)p(E|rule(s_k, a_i)). \tag{13}$$

By this modification, EFP can affect the action selection directly and immediately and no rule is excluded as a penalty rule. This means that more successful rules are selected with larger probability and that it never occurs that an important rule is excluded as a penalty rule. The method is referred to as **PSwithEFP**.

5   Application to the Keepaway Task

5.1   Keepaway Task

The proposed method, PSwithEFP, is applied to Keepaway Task [24] in order to show the effectiveness in a multi-agent environment. Keepaway task is a Robocup soccer sub-task and it aims that the keeper team keeps the ball in a limited area without being deprived of the ball by the taker team as long as possible. We use 3 keepers (keeper 1, keeper 2 and keeper 3) and two takers (taker 1 and taker 2). This 3-vs-2 keepaway task occupies a 290 [cm] × 240 [cm] playing field. These agents are initially located as shown in Fig. 2 where pink agents are keepers, yellow agents are takers. The red circle is the ball. Therefore keeper 1 is the ball-holding agent. In this paper, the purpose of learning is to keep the ball in the area and make passes among keepers as many times as possible without being stolen by takers. A reward is given when they made a pass successfully. It is important for keepers to learn cooperative behaviors such as making a pass to the other taker agent or moving to an open space to catch the ball.

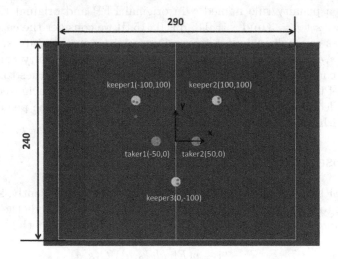

Fig. 2. Environment for keepaway task (Color figure online)

Three keepers perform learning independently for a common weight table and two takers do not perform learning. In a multi-agent learning environment, concurrent learning problem often occurs. That is, even if a keeper selects an effective rule to pass a ball, if the other keeper does not select an appropriate rule corresponding to it and loses the ball as a result, then both keepers will equally receive a penalty. As a result, the rule, pass a ball, may be labeled as a penalty rule. Then the learning performance of original EFP and EFP+ may be significantly lowered by concurrent learning problem, since actions are not selected from penalty rules. We will show that PSwithEFP can solve this problem.

5.2 Simulation Setting

Basic Setting. When the ball is deprived by a taker or goes out of the field, one trial ends. Then, each agent is relocated to the initial positions as shown in Fig. 2 and another trial starts. When a keeper passes a ball to the other keeper successfully, both keepers will receive a reward. A keeper that had the ball will receive a penalty, if the ball is stolen by a taker or goes out of the field. One experiment contains 30,000 trials and 30 experiments were done with different random seeds where η of EFP is 0.415 that is derived from Eq. (11), reward and initial value of Q are 10 and 100, respectively, discount rate of a reward is 0.8 that is also used in PS and EFP, learning rate and discount rate of Sarsa and QL are 0.8 and 0.2, respectively, and λ of Sarsa(λ) is 0.8. These values were determined by preliminary experiments.

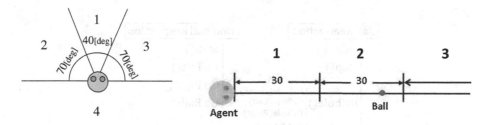

Fig. 3. Angular relationships   **Fig. 4.** Distance index

State Variables. The state variables are mainly composed by three types of sensory inputs. One group contains angular relationships between keeper 1 and the other agents or the ball as shown in Fig. 3. For example, if there is taker 2 in the position of the front right 70° of keeper 1, we have received the flag "3" as the sensory input about the angular relationship between keeper 1 and taker 2. Another is a distance index between keeper 1 and the ball as shown in Fig. 4. The others are six distance labels among keeper 1 and the other agents as shown in Fig. 5 where TAKER is the closest taker agent to keeper 1. In Fig. 5, the number 1, 2, and 3 are assigned in the order closer to keeper 1. For example, the flag "A" means that keeper 2 is the closest to keeper 1, and the taker that is closest to keeper 1 is the farthest. Therefore we have $18,432$ states.

Actions. We prepare the following six macro actions;

- **Stop()**: stay at the current location,
- **Dribble(α)**: dribble in the direction α,
- **Kick(α)**: kick in the direction α,
- **Go Ball()**: turn to the ball and moves one step,
- **Go Left()**: turn by 45° to the left and move one step,
- **Go Right()**: turn by 45° to the right and move one step,

flag	keeper 2	keeper 3	TAKER
A	1	2	3
B	1	3	2
C	2	1	3
D	3	1	2
E	2	3	1
F	3	2	1

Fig. 5. Distance label

where α is selected from the set $\{ahead, left, right\}$, "ahead" means the front direction and "left" or "right" is $45°$ to the left or right. Dribble() and Kick() are achieved by pushing the ball forward, but the pushing strength of Dribble() is one third of Kick().

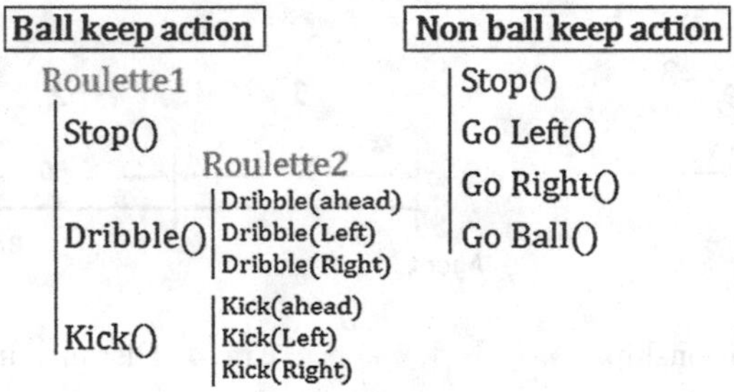

Ball keep action	**Non ball keep action**
Roulette1	Stop()
Stop()	Go Left()
Roulette2	Go Right()
Dribble(ahead)	
Dribble() Dribble(Left)	Go Ball()
Dribble(Right)	
Kick(ahead)	
Kick() Kick(Left)	
Kick(Right)	

Fig. 6. Action selection

Keeper 1, the ball keeper, selects an action by two stages as shown in Fig. 6. Fist, keeper 1 selects an action from the set {Stop(), Dribble(), Kick()} using roulette 1 where the maximum weights of {Dribble(ahead), Dribble(Left), Dribble(Right)} and {Kick(ahead), Kick(Left), Kick(Right)} are assigned to the weights of Dribble() and Kick(), respectively. Second, if the selected action is one of Dribble() or Kick(), the direction α is selected with another roulette (Roulette 2). Keeper 2 and keeper 3 select an action from the set {Stop(), Go Ball(), Go Left(), GoRight()}. Taker agents always use "Go Ball()." Each agent selects an action in the order of keeper 1, keeper 2, keeper 3, taker 1 and taker 2. If one action has been completed, the next agent selects and executes an action. Furthermore, Sarsa and QL could not learn successfully, since this task is non-Markovian environment.

5.3 Results and Discussion

Figure 7 shows the results of the number of successful passes for original EFP+, PS, PSwithEFP, Sarsa, Sarsa(λ) and QL. 30 experiments were carried out changing random seeds. The horizontal axis is the number of trials, and the vertical

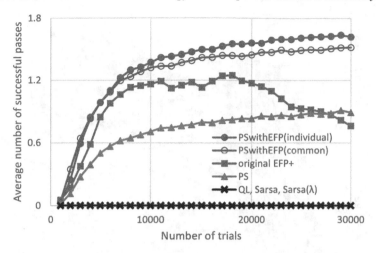

Fig. 7. Average pass success times

axis represents the average number of successful passes every 30 experiments. It is plotted each 1000 trials.

From Fig. 7, we can confirm that Sarsa, Sarsa(λ) and QL were not able to learn anything because they are strongly affected by the concurrent learning problem and they require many trial and error searches even if there is no concurrent learning problem.

In the case of original EFP+, the average number of successful passes increased up to about 1.2 until around 15000 trials. Then, it lowered finally down to about 0.8 at 30000 trials. This is due to the concurrent learning problem. In contrast, in the case of PSwithEFP, it does not seem to be affected by any concurrent learning problem. Even if EFP value of a rule increased by other keeper's failure, the rule is not excluded from action candidates but the selection probability of the rule decreases. This allows the other keepers to learn more, and, if the rule is truly useful, it will be used in the better situation and the EFP will decrease. However, in the case of PS, keepers learn the skill successfully, but PSwithEFP is more speedy in learning and more successful in the number of passes than PS. There are two results of PSwithEFP in Fig. 7. Three keeper agents use an individual weight table in PSwithEFP(individual) though they use a common weight table in PSwithEFP(common). PSwithEFP(individual) is better than PSwithEFP(common). Therefore, the best keeper's strategies will not similar among them. We use PSwithEFP(individual) in the next section.

All of 30 experimental results for PSwithEFP shown in Fig. 8. This figure shows that the learning efficiency depends on the random seed but the learning itself is still successful.

It shows the effectiveness of PSwithEFP in this experiment. Furthermore, it also shows the robustness to the concurrent learning problem.

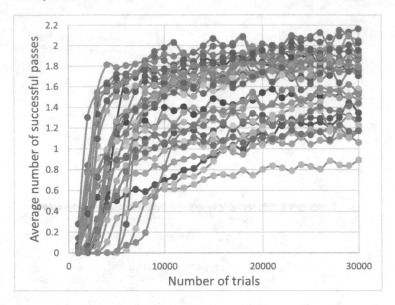

Fig. 8. 30 results of PSwithEFP.

6 Proposal of How to Use PSwithEFP

6.1 Basic Concept

Though we showed the effectiveness of PSwithEFP in multiagent learning called Keepaway task, rather large variation was observed in the final numbers of successful passes. This is due to the exploitation-oriented aspect of PS. As well known, the initial PS learning often has a large impact upon the final result. Therefore we propose how to use PSwithEFP in order to reduce the problem.

6.2 How to Use PSwithEFP

Our proposal is as follows;

First, we run multiple times PS from the initial state like multi-start method. Next, we select non-convergence performance one among them. Then, we start the learning with our PSwithEFP after setting the learned results to the initial parameters.

If we follow this procedure, we can reduce the influence of exploitation-oriented aspects of PS as shown in the next subsection. Note that we use PS in the first stage to save the computational power.

6.3 Simulation Results and Discuccsion

First, we show some results where agents learned with PS during the initial 5000 trials and PSwithEFP was simply used for the rest of 25000 trials without any

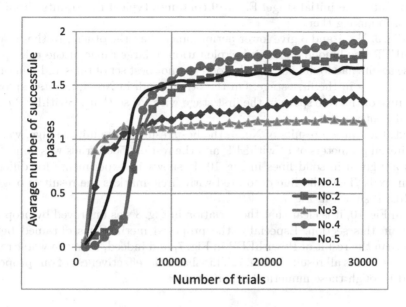

Fig. 9. 5 trials of PSwithEFP

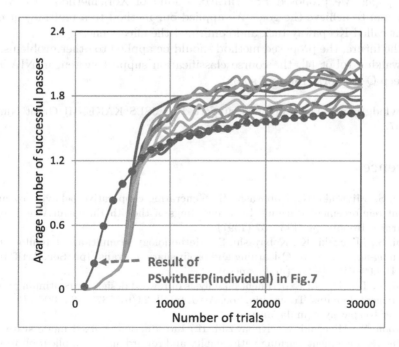

Fig. 10. Best result of PSwithEFP

selection after the initial stage. Figure 9 containes typical five results (from No. 1 to No. 5) among them.

In Fig. 9, No. 1 and 3 give lower performance than the others. In these cases, PSwithEFP was hindered effective exploitation of large range of the rule space, because agents had found out a fairly good but not best set of rules and reinforced them intensely in the first stage. On the other hand, in No. 4, agents exploited large range of the rule space in the first stage with PS so that PSwithEFP could learn efficiently.

Next, the learned results of No. 4, the best result in the initial stage, was set to the initial prameters of PSwithEFP and the rest of 25000 trials was done. The results are given in solid lines in Fig. 10. It shows 10 experiments for different random seeds. The solid line decorated with circle mark is the result of original PSwithEFP shown in Fig. 7.

From Fig. 10, it is clear that the variation in Fig. 8 was improved by proposed method in this section. Especially, the proposed method has obtained better results than the result of PSwithEFP in Fig. 7, and indeed, even the worst result in Fig. 10 exceeds all results in Fig. 7. This shows the effectiveness of our proposed method through these numerical experiments.

7 Conclusions

In this paper, we proposed PSwithEFP, a kind of XoL methods, to avoid a penalty and to achieve the goal. We applied our method to a multi-agent environment called Keepaway task and confirmed the effectiveness.

In the future, the proposed method should be applied to other problems, e.g. biped walking robot [4], the course classification support system in NIAD-UE [16], Deep-Q network [18], and so on.

Acknowledgment. This work was supported by JSPS KAKENHI Grant Number 26330267.

References

1. Arai, S., Miyazaki, K., Kobayashi, S.: Generating cooperative behavior by multi-agent reinforcement learning. In: Proceedings of the 6th European Workshop on Learning Robots, pp. 143–157 (1997)
2. Arai, S., Miyazaki, K., Kobayashi, S.: Methodology in multi-agent reinforcement learning-approaches by Q-learning and profit sharing. Trans. Jpn. Soc. Artif. Intell. **13**(4), 609–618 (1998). (in Japanese)
3. Arai, S., Tanaka, N.: Experimental analysis of reward design for continuing task in multiagent domains. Trans. Jpn. Soc. Artif. Intell. **21**(6), 537–546 (2006). RoboCup Soccer Keepaway - (in Japanese)
4. Kuroda, S., Miyazaki, K., Kobayashi, H.: Introduction of fixed mode states into online reinforcement learning with penalty and reward and its application to waist trajectory generation of biped robot. J. Adv. Comput. Intell. Intell. Inform. **16**(6), 758–768 (2013)

5. Matsui, T., Goto, T., Izumi, K.: Acquiring a government bond trading strategy using reinforcement learning. J. Adv. Comput. Intell. Intell. Inform. **13**(6), 691–696 (2009)

6. Merrick, K., Maher, M.L.: Motivated reinforcement learning for adaptive characters in open-ended simulation games. In: Proceedings of the International Conference on Advanced in Computer Entertainment Technology, pp. 127–134 (2007)

7. Miyazaki, K., Yamamura, M., Kobayashi, S.: On the rationality of profit sharing in reinforcement learning. In: Proceedings of the 3rd International Conference on Fuzzy Logic, Neural Nets and Soft Computing, pp. 285–288 (1994)

8. Miyazaki, K., Yamamura, M., Kobayashi, H.: A theory of profit sharing in reinforcement learning. Trans. Jpn. Soc. Artif. Intell. **9**(4), 580–587 (1994). (in Japanese)

9. Miyazaki, K., Kobayashi, S.: Rationality of reward sharing in multi-agent reinforcement learning. New Gener. Comput. **19**(2), 157–172 (2001)

10. Miyazaki, K., Arai, S., Kobayashi, S.: A theory of profit sharing in multi-agent reinforcement. Learning **14**(6), 1156–1164 (1999). (in Japanese)

11. Miyazaki, K., Kobayashi, S.: An extension of profit sharing to partially observable Markov decision processes: proposition of PS-r* and its evaluation. J. Jpn. Soc. Artif. Intell. **18**(5), 285–296 (2003). (in Japanese)

12. Miyazaki, K., Kobayashi, S.: Reinforcement learning for penalty avoiding policy making. In: Proceedings of the 2000 IEEE International Conference on Systems, Man and Cybernetics, pp. 206–211 (2000)

13. Miyazaki, K., Tsuboi, S., Kobayashi, S.: Reinforcement learning for penalty avoiding rational policy making. Trans. Jpn. Soc. Artif. Intell. **16**(2), 185–192 (2001). (in Japanese)

14. Miyazaki, K., Kobayashi, S.: Exploitation-oriented learning PS-r#. J. Adv. Comput. Intell. Intell. Inform. **13**(6), 624–630 (2009)

15. Miyazaki, K.: Proposal of an exploitation-oriented learning method on multiple rewards and penalties environments and the design guideline. J. Comput. **8**(7), 1683–1690 (2013)

16. Miyazaki, K., Ida, M.: Proposal and evaluation of the active course classification support system with exploitation-oriented learning. In: Sanner, S., Hutter, M. (eds.) EWRL 2011. LNCS, vol. 7188, pp. 333–344. Springer, Heidelberg (2012). doi:10.1007/978-3-642-29946-9_32

17. Miyazaki, K., Muraoka, H., Kobayashi, H.: Proposal of a propagation algorithm of the expected failure probability and the effectiveness on multi-agent environments. In: SICE Annual Conference 2013, pp. 1067–1072 (2013)

18. Miyazaki, K.: Exploitation-oriented Learning XoL with deep learning - comparison with a deep Q-network. The Papers of Technical Meeting on "Systems", IEE Japan, pp. 7–12 (2016). (in Japanese)

19. Mnih, V., Kavukcuoglu, K., Silver, D., Graves, A., Antonoglou, I., Wierstra, D., Riedmiller, M.: Playing atari with deep reinforcement learning. In: NIPS Deep Learning Workshop 2013 (2013)

20. Muraoka, H., Miyazaki, K., Kobayashi, H.: Proposal of a propagation algorithm of the expected failure probability and the effectiveness on multi-agent environments. Trans. Inst. Electr. Eng. Jpn. C **136**(3), 273–281 (2016). (in Japanese)

21. Randløv, J., Alstrøm, P.: Learning to drive a bicycle using reinforcement learning and shaping. In: Proceedings of the 15th International Conference on Machine Learning, pp. 463–471 (1998)

22. Silver, D., Huang, A., Maddison, C.J., Guez, A., Sifre, L., Driessche, G., Schrittwieser, J., Antonoglou, I., Panneershelvam, V., Lanctot, M., Dieleman, S., Grewe, D., Nham, J., Kalchbrenner, N., Sutskever, I., Lillicrap, T., Leach, M., Kavukcuoglu, K., Graepel, T., Hassabis, D.: Mastering the game of Go with deep neural networks and tree search. Nature **529**, 484–489 (2016)
23. Singh, S., Lewis, R.L., Barto, A.G., Sorg, J.: Intrinsically motivated reinforcement learning: an evolutionary perspective. IEEE Trans. Auton. Ment. Dev. **2**(2), 70–82 (2010)
24. Stone, P., Sutton, R.S., Kuhlamann, G.: Reinforcement learning toward robocup soccer keepaway. Adapt. Behav. **13**(3), 165–188 (2005)
25. Sutton, R.S., Barto, A.G.: Reinforcement Learning: An Introduction, A Bradford Book. MIT Press, Cambridge (1998)
26. Watanabe, T., Miyazaki, K., Kobayashi, H.: A new improved penalty avoiding rational policy making algorithm for keepaway with continuous state spaces. J. Adv. Comput. Intell. Intell. Inform. **13**(6), 678–682 (2009)
27. Yoshimoto, J., Nishimura, M., Tokita, Y., Ishii, S.: Acrobot control by learning the switching of multiple controllers. J. Artif. Life Robot. **9**(2), 67–71 (2005)

Resource Re-allocation for Data Inter-dependent Continuous Tasks in Grids

Valeriia Haberland[1][(⊠)], Simon Miles[2], and Michael Luck[2]

[1] Tungsten Centre for Intelligent Data Analytics,
Goldsmiths, University of London, London, UK
v.haberland@gold.ac.uk
[2] Department of Informatics, King's College London, London, UK
{simon.miles,michael.luck}@kcl.ac.uk

Abstract. Many researchers focus on resource intensive tasks which have to be run continuously over long periods. A Grid may offer resources for these tasks, but they are contested by multiple client agents. Hence, a Grid might be unwilling to allocate its resources for long terms, leading to tasks' interruptions. This issue becomes more substantial when tasks are data inter-dependent, where one interrupted task may cause an interruption of a bundle of other tasks. In this paper, we discuss a new resource re-allocation strategy for a client, in which resources are re-allocated between the client tasks in order to avoid prolonged interruptions. Those re-allocations are decided by a client agent, but they should be agreed with a Grid and can be performed only by a Grid. Our strategy has been tested within different Grid environments and noticeably improves client utilities in almost all cases.

Keywords: Continuous inter-dependent tasks · Resource re-allocation · Client's decision-making mechanism

1 Introduction

Recently much research has focused on smart systems which, for example, monitor the level of pollution in the environment [5]. These systems have to acquire and process data continuously to be able to produce up-to-date results, and the tasks which process these data have to be run continuously and for long periods of time [7,8]. It is desirable for these tasks to run without interruption, but short interruptions whose duration depends on the nature of a task, may not affect significantly the controlled parameters e.g., temperature. These tasks also have to be executed for so long periods of time that a Grid is unable or unwilling to allocate them for the whole period at once. This means that a task will be interrupted after some agreed period of time and it has to obtain new resources [8]. A task might also be interrupted unexpectedly due to a resource failure. Here, we assume that the resource availability changes near-periodically over time [1,9,11], allowing its peaks to be approximately overseen in the future [8].

These tasks can also depend on each others' data, i.e. one task might require data from other tasks in order to run. For example, two data streams which

© Springer International Publishing AG 2017
N. Criado Pacheco et al. (Eds.): EUMAS 2016/AT 2016, LNAI 10207, pp. 187–201, 2017.
DOI: 10.1007/978-3-319-59294-7_16

monitor temperature and humidity are linked as the weather observation in the airport [12]. Other use cases include traffic monitoring (control) on a road [19], where the vehicles' speed and location are streamed in order to identify traffic congestion. These scenarios show continuous tasks linked in terms of data and it would be realistic for these tasks to run simultaneously.

Some research e.g., [10,13], focuses on execution of inter-dependent tasks, but it is generally lacking decision making mechanisms for a client in respect of allocation and execution of such tasks. The dependence among tasks is often depicted in terms of the data exchange and has an explicit connection between sender and recipient tasks. In our model, the tasks do not have just an explicit dependence, but also an implicit one which means that a failure of the recipient-task affects the execution of the corresponding sender-task as much as the sender-tasks affect the execution of their recipients. We also take into account that tasks are not executed just once, but have to be executed continually over the long term, where any failed tasks might affect a controlled parameter.

Hence, if data is not received in time by a recipient-task, then the client's system will produce erroneous results to some degree, i.e. the longer this delay, the larger the probability that the last received data from a sender-task is significantly different from the current data that would be received. As time passes, the recipient-task has to stop eventually, avoiding to produce substantially deviated results. In comparison, other work generally does not focus on how a client agent can avoid or shorten these delays in the case of highly contested Grid resources and how those delays may affect its system.

We propose a new resource re-allocation strategy, *SimTask*, for a client which allows a client agent to exchange the allocated resources among its own tasks by negotiating with the *Grid Resource Allocator* (GRA). The aim of this exchange is to avoid long interruptions which cause a significant change in the parameter controlled by the interrupted task e.g., a significant drop in temperature. This strategy incorporates a decision-making mechanism for a client agent (referred further as a client) to initiate resource re-allocation and choose the most appropriate task for donating resources. The agents' abilities [21] as to decide autonomously and respond actively to any changes are crucial for this mechanism, considering the large number of negotiating agents at the same time.

The paper is structured as follows.[1] Section 2 discusses related work in respect of the inter-dependent tasks. Then, Sect. 3 describes the formal model, while Sect. 4 presents our SimTask re-allocation strategy. The evaluation results are discussed in Sect. 5, and Sect. 6 concludes the paper.

2   Related Work

In this paper, we focus on the tasks which run near-continuously [7,8] over time, and also depend on each other's data. In other words, each task sends a data point to another task, while processing new input data. Hence, these tasks have to be

---

[1] The authors thank King's College London for sponsoring this work as a part of Ph.D. research [6].

run simultaneously in terms of processing each input data point as soon as it has arrived, and repeat this processing over time. Much research e.g., [10,13,15,23], considers processing of inter-dependent tasks in Grid systems where dependencies are presented as a *directed acyclic graph*. In particular, Meriem and Belabbas [15] dynamically allocate tasks to resources, which arrive as a continuous stream over time. Dynamic allocation is meant to respond to any resource availability changes in a Grid, and resolve the problem of load-balancing at run-time. Although all this work considers task dependencies in resource allocation, tasks are not considered to be repeated continuously in real-time. Nevertheless, this research describes relevant concepts which can be applicable to continuous tasks such as *spare time* [23], which defines the maximal time of task execution before it affects the schedule of dependent tasks. Other work considers a *cyclic task graph* [17,18,22], where tasks are executed repeatedly over time and each task in a cycle obtains and sends data. Here, the cycles of task dependencies are represented in terms of data, instructions, etc.

There are other examples of inter-dependent tasks that were discussed in the literature. For example, the work [14] focuses on accomplishing a high-level task by completing a number of *time-constrained possibly inter-dependent other tasks* e.g., gathering information from the Web in order to offer appropriate products to the customers. Motwani et al. [16] focus on *continuous queries* (e.g. continuous tasks), which process stream data from multiple sources. A continuous query is the type of query which is issued once for a particular data-type and then runs continuously, updating a client with new results without being issued repeatedly [3,20]. In the work [16], one query may consist of a number of sub-queries (operators), where the outputs of these sub-queries might be shared with other queries or sub-queries. Although this work discusses the techniques to approximate the query outputs in the case of scarce resources, it does not focus on how data delays or failed sub-queries might affect the results from other sub-query or query, or whether the latter query can even be performed.

Different platforms (engines) e.g., *Apache Storm* [2], attempt to solve the problems of scalability, performance and memory usage in terms of execution of data streams. However, the problem of tasks' inter-dependencies as discussed above and how they can be run without some input data is not the focus of these engines. Note that in an open and dynamic computational environment such as a Grid, where other clients also require resources, it might be difficult to re-allocate a task without affecting other clients' interests.

3   Formal Model

In this work, we consider that tasks have inter-dependencies, where some tasks, *sender-tasks*, send data to other tasks, *recipient-tasks*. The dependencies among tasks are presented as a *rooted tree* Tr, where data streams flow from the bottom to the top of this tree (i.e. from leaf to root). Each node of this tree denotes a task i and each edge indicates a data inter-dependence between sender-task $i \in N$ and recipient-task $j \in N$ with a weight $\alpha_{i,j} \in [0,1]$. The weight denotes the *level of importance* of the data from a particular sender-task for the corresponding recipient-task, i.e. each edge has a direction from the lower-layer tasks (senders) towards the upper-layer tasks (recipients) of the tree. In this way, some tasks in the middle of the tree are also senders and recipients at the same time. We assume that each sender-task has only one corresponding recipient-task, but every recipient-task might have one or more sender-task(s). We also assume that the sum of weights for all sender-tasks which are connected directly to the same recipient-task is equal to 1.0, and the smaller this weight $\alpha_{i,j}$, the less impact sender-task, i, has on the work of recipient-task, j. This model of task inter-dependencies can follow, for example, a scenario of data aggregation from multiple sources by counting, adding, etc. the data instances over some time [4]. We also consider a *sub-tree* $sTr_k \in Tr$ with the root task $k \in \mathbb{N}$.

Here, we define an abstract *parameter* P which is estimated by client tasks. This parameter $P_{i,S_i}(t) \in \mathbb{R}$ for task $i \in \mathbb{N}$ with the corresponding set of direct sender-tasks $S_i = \{m, ..., k\}$ at time t is a real-life characteristic (e.g. temperature), which is continuous or can be presented as continuous over time $t \in \mathbb{R}$, considering $|(P_{i,S_i}(t + \Delta t) - P_{i,S_i}(t))/P_{i,S_i}(t)| \ll 1$ where $\Delta t \in \mathbb{R}$ is an arbitrary small time step. The parameter $P_{i,S_i}(t)$ is estimated directly by task i, if this task belongs to the lowest layer of a tree, i.e. $S_i \in \emptyset$. If task i belongs to any upper layer of a tree, i.e. $S_i \neq \emptyset$, then $P_{i,S_i}(t)$ is estimated as a linear combination of all parameters $P_{j\neq i,S_j}(t)$ sent by its sender-task(s)[2]

$$P_{i,S_i}(t) = \sum_{j \in S_i} \alpha_{j,i} \times P_{j\neq i,S_j}(t), \ S_i \neq \emptyset, \ i,j \in \mathbb{N},$$ where S_j can be empty set.

3.1 Status and Layer

In our model, each task i has its *status* $Status_i(t)$ of execution at time t, which can be: *'interrupted'* means a task is not running and does not possess resources; *'stopped'* denotes a task is not running (i.e. its recipient-task is interrupted or it has produced inaccurate results for too long), but it possesses resources; *'inaccurate'* means a task is running, but at least one of its sender-task(s) either does not send any data or sends inaccurate data; *'accurate'* means a task is running and all its sender-tasks send accurate data. A task produces inaccurate data when at least one of its sender-tasks has status other than 'accurate'.

We also consider that each task i belongs to a specific layer $Layer_i$ in a tree, and sends its data, except the root task, to the corresponding recipient-task j which belongs to the nearest upper layer, i.e. $Layer_j = Layer_i + 1$. Note that the lower layer tasks are stopped when a recipient-task on the top of a sub-tree or the whole tree is stopped or interrupted. This means that if sender-tasks have no tasks to send their data to, they are stopped. This dependence shows the continuous and real time nature of the tasks.

3.2 Damping and Delay Time

As we discussed a notion of short interruption, we define a *damping time* which determines for how long a task can be interrupted or stopped without substantial

---
[2] A linear combination is chosen for a greater clarity of evaluation of SimTask.

negative consequences for parameter estimation e.g., a significant rise in temperature. If any task has been interrupted or stopped, then it does not estimate this parameter any more. In this way, a parameter changes in a way which is not under control of a client. Hence, the longer this task is not running, the higher probability that the change of this parameter might have a substantial negative effect for a client. We consider that this effect occurs when the damping time $\tau_i^{dam}(t_d)$, starting at time $t_d \in \mathbb{R}$, has passed for task i. That is, the absolute difference $\Delta P_{i,S_i}(t)$ between the last produced value of parameter $P_{i,S_i}(t_d)$ by task i before interruption and the linearly extrapolated value of this parameter $P_{i,S_i}^{ex}(t)$ at time t becomes larger than the predefined threshold $\eta_i^{dam} \in \mathbb{R}$. This threshold is determined by the nature of this parameter.

A *delay time* determines for how long a task can be running when it has to use inaccurate data for its calculations and it stops after this time. A delay time $\tau_i^{del}(t_{dl}, t)$, starting at time $t_{dl} \in \mathbb{R}$, for recipient-task $i \in \mathbb{N}$ is the duration of time when this task can still run, but it has to use inaccurate input data for its calculations due to the interruption of some (at least one) sender-task(s) from its sub-tree sTr_i. This time ends when the absolute difference $\Delta P_{i,S_i}(t) = \sum_{j \in S_i} \alpha_{j,i} \Delta P_{j \neq i, S_j}(t)$, $S_i \neq \emptyset$ at time t becomes larger than the predefined threshold $\eta_i^{del} \in \mathbb{R}$, where $\eta_i^{del} < \eta_i^{dam}$. Note that the difference $\Delta P_{i,S_i}(t)$ is a linear combination of such differences for the lower layer tasks which belong to a sub-tree sTr_i and have the statuses of execution as 'inaccurate', 'stopped' or 'interrupted'. As for the lowest layer tasks, i.e. $S_j = \emptyset$, these differences at time t are calculated as $\Delta P_{j,S_j}(t) = P_{j,S_j}(t_{dl}) - P_{j,S_j}^{ex}(t)$, where $P_{j,S_j}(t_{dl})$ is the last value of parameter produced by task j before its interruption at time t_{dl}. The difference $\Delta P_{i,S_i}(t)$ may change dramatically if some sender-tasks switch to other statuses of execution. The delay time for recipient-task i becomes longer (i.e. $\Delta P_{i,S_i}(t)$ becomes smaller), if at least one of its sender-task(s) switches to the 'accurate' status, and shorter if this switch is opposite.

3.3 Client Utility

In our model, each task is *near-continuous* [7,8], and hence each task i has periods of interruption $\tau_{i,l}^{int} \in \mathbb{R}$ and execution $\tau_{i,l}^{exe} \in \mathbb{R}$, and the pairs of consecutive interruption and execution periods $\left(\tau_i^{int}, \tau_i^{exe}\right)_l$ have a counter $l \in \mathbb{N}$ within a total duration of task execution $\tau^{tot} \in \mathbb{R}$. Each $\tau_{i,l}^{int}$ starts at $t_{i,l-1}^{end}$ and ends at $t_{i,l}^{str}$, while each $\tau_{i,l}^{exe}$ starts at $t_{i,l}^{str}$ and ends at $t_{i,l}^{end}$. τ^{tot} starts at t_{tot}^{str}, when a client has submitted initial resource requests for all its tasks, and ends at t_{tot}^{end} for all tasks. The start and end times for τ^{tot} are the same for all tasks as they are expected to be run simultaneously. If one task is interrupted, this starts affecting negatively the lower layer tasks from the same sub-tree and all upper layer tasks from the same branch at once. We also consider a *cumulative duration of interruption* $\tau_{i,l}^{cum} = \sum_{k=1}^{l} \tau_{i,k}^{int}$ for each task i which reflects on the overall success of task execution.

In addition to single and cumulative interruptions [7,8], our model of interdependent tasks also considers inaccurate processing of data as a factor which negatively affects client utility. That is, the longer the task is running with inaccurate input data (not running), the more substantial becomes a negative impact on client utility. The impact of any negative factor (interruption or inaccurate data processing) is designed as the corresponding damping function $SI\left(\tau_{i,l}^{int}\right)$ for a single interruption, $CI\left(\tau_{i,l}^{cum}\right)$ for a cumulative interruption and $IP\left(\hat{\tau}_i^{del}\left(t_{dl},t\right)\right)$ for a duration of inaccurate data processing $\hat{\tau}_i^{del}\left(t_{dl},t\right)$, starting at t_{dl}. The duration $\hat{\tau}_i^{del}\left(t_{dl},t\right)$ denotes a part of delay time $\tau_i^{del}\left(t_{dl},t\right)$ which has passed till time t. Each damping function produces values from the interval $]0,1]$, where 1 denotes no impact. These functions comply with our assumption that the client's estimation of the parameter becomes gradually rather than immediately unrealistic after the task's failure, which also echoes the notion of short interruption. Only execution periods contribute positively to client utility, and the amount of such contribution is affected negatively by these damping functions:

$$SI\left(\tau_{i,l}^{int}\right) = \frac{1}{e^{\left(\tau_{i,l}^{int}-\tau_{int[i]}^{max}(t_d)\right)/\epsilon_{int[i]}(t_d)}+1},$$

$$CI\left(\tau_{i,l}^{cum}\right) = \frac{1}{e^{\left(\tau_{i,l}^{cum}-\tau_{cum[i]}^{max}(t_d)\right)/\epsilon_{cum[i]}(t_d)}+1}, \tag{1}$$

$$IP\left(\hat{\tau}_i^{del}\left(t_{dl},t\right)\right) = \frac{1}{e^{\left(\hat{\tau}_i^{del}(t_{dl},t)-\tau_{del[i]}^{max}(t_{dl},t)\right)/\epsilon_{del[i]}(t_{dl},t)}+1},$$

where $\tau_{int[i]}^{max}(t_d)$, $\tau_{cum[i]}^{max}(t_d)$ and $\tau_{del[i]}^{max}(t_{dl},t)$ are inflection points, which denote the durations of time after which client utility is noticeably affected by the corresponding factor, and $\epsilon_{int[i]}(t_d)$, $\epsilon_{cum[i]}(t_d)$ and $\epsilon_{del[i]}(t_{dl},t)$ determine the speed of decrease of the corresponding damping functions around the inflection points. As $SI\left(\tau_{i,l}^{int}\right)$ and $CI\left(\tau_{i,l}^{cum}\right)$ show the impact of interruptions on client utility, their inflection points can be calculated in proportion to the damping time $\tau_i^{dam}(t_d)$. In this work, $\tau_{int[i]}^{max}(t_d) = \tau_i^{dam}(t_d)$ as the damping time shows how fast task's interruption substantially affects client utility in terms of the unobserved changes in the estimated parameter. Considering $IP\left(\hat{\tau}_i^{del}\left(t_{dl},t\right)\right)$ shows the impact of inaccurate data processing on client utility, its inflection point is equal to the delay time $\tau_i^{del}\left(t_{dl},t\right)$. The values of $\epsilon_{int[i]}(t_d)$, $\epsilon_{cum[i]}(t_d)$ and $\epsilon_{del[i]}(t_{dl},t)$ are calculated in proportion to their respective inflection points.

In our work, the *effectiveness function* $E\left(t\right)$ [7,8] demonstrates the success of task execution over time t. This function changes only during execution periods, and it can be reduced, multiplying by the values of damping functions. First, an estimate $Es\left(t, E\left(t_{i,l-1}^{end}\right)\right)$ is linearly increasing during an execution period:

$$Es\left(t, E\left(t_{i,l-1}^{end}\right)\right) = \frac{\left(1 - E\left(t_{i,l-1}^{end}\right)\right)t + E\left(t_{i,l-1}^{end}\right)t_{tot}^{end} - t_{i,l}^{str}}{t_{tot}^{end} - t_{i,l}^{str}}. \tag{2}$$

This estimate $Es\left(\cdot\right)$ starts increasing from the value of effectiveness function $E\left(t_{i,l-1}^{end}\right)$ at the end of previous execution period $\tau_{i,l-1}^{exe}$ towards the desirable end of execution at time t_{tot}^{end} when the value of effectiveness function is equal to 1. The full effectiveness function is presented below:

$$E\left(t\right) = \begin{cases} Es\left(t, E\left(t_{i,l-1}^{end}\right)\right) SI\left(\tau_{i,l}^{int}\right) CI\left(\tau_{i,l}^{cum}\right) IP\left(\hat{\tau}_i^{del}\left(t_{dl},t\right)\right), \\ \qquad if\ \tau_{i,l}^{exe} \neq 0\ and\ \tau_i^{del}\left(t_{dl},t\right) \neq 0, \\ Es\left(t, E\left(t_{i,l-1}^{end}\right)\right) SI\left(\tau_{i,l}^{int}\right) CI\left(\tau_{i,l}^{cum}\right), \\ \qquad if\ \tau_{i,l}^{exe} \neq 0\ and\ \tau_i^{del}\left(t_{dl},t\right) = 0, \\ E\left(t_{i,l-1}^{end}\right), \qquad\qquad\qquad if\ \tau_{i,l}^{exe} = 0. \end{cases} \quad (3)$$

Note that the values of $SI\left(\tau_{i,l}^{int}\right)$ and $CI\left(\tau_{i,l}^{cum}\right)$ are constants within an execution period $\tau_{i,l}^{exe}$ (i.e. $\tau_{i,l}^{exe} \neq 0$), while the values of $IP\left(\hat{\tau}_i^{del}\left(t_{dl},t\right)\right)$ decrease within this period. $IP\left(\hat{\tau}_i^{del}\left(t_{dl},t\right)\right)$ affects the effectiveness of task execution only when task i is using inaccurate input data (i.e. $\tau_i^{del}\left(t_{dl},t\right) \neq 0$) from its sender-task(s). The utility U_i for each task i is calculated as the square under the broken curve of $E\left(t\right)$, i.e.

$$U_i = 1/S_{max} \sum_{l=1}^{L_i} \int_{t_{i,l}^{str}}^{t_{i,l}^{end}} E\left(t\right) dt. \quad (4)$$

$S_{max} = \tau^{tot}/2$ is the largest possible square under $E\left(t\right)$ if task i has no failures till t_{tot}^{end} and L_i is the number of execution periods within $\left[t_{tot}^{str}, t_{tot}^{end}\right]$.

The total client utility U_{total} is calculated as a sum of all U_i with the respective coefficients ϖ_i which denote the task's level of relevance for the client.

$$U_{total} = \sum_{i=1}^{N} \varpi_i \times U_i, \quad (5)$$

where N denotes the total number of client tasks. The sum of ϖ_i over all client tasks is equal to 1.0, where the total sum of all ϖ_i from the same tree layer is equal for each layer. In this way, the upper layer tasks have a more substantial impact on the client's utility, according to our model.

4   Re-allocation Strategy

In this paper, a novel re-allocation strategy *SimTask* for a client is proposed which allows a client to exchange the allocated resources among its own tasks by negotiating such exchange with the GRA. The tasks which lost resources can resume their execution instead of other tasks, and the tasks which have donated their resources to other tasks are called *donor-tasks*. Note that a client is only allowed to ask the GRA to re-allocate resources among its own tasks, but it cannot ask the GRA to re-allocate resources from another client's tasks. The aim of this internal resource re-allocation is to avoid too long interruptions which might lead to substantial utility loss. As long as the length of time is only considered as a resource allocated by the GRA, then a task cannot share this resource with the other task, but it can donate this resource to the other task. Note that the scalability of this approach can potentially be increased if tasks are clustered into relatively data-independent groups with their respective trees and client agents, which is the focus of our future research.

A problem following from resource re-allocation is not only which task to stop in order to launch the interrupted one with a smaller loss in the client utility, but also to which extent the GRA is willing to make an exchange of the allocated resources between client tasks. Hence, the GRA is assumed to allow such re-allocations, but only with a penalty due to its own resource cost, i.e. a task might be allocated a much shorter donor's remainder of execution period.

4.1   Condition to Use the Strategy

A client decides whether an interrupted task has not been running for too long and, therefore, it needs to be donated resource from another client's task. The resource re-allocation from one task to another one might not be beneficial for a client, because another task has to be interrupted instead of the current one and the re-allocated remainder of execution period can be shortened by the GRA. However, if any task is interrupted for so long that its damping time $\tau_i^{dam}(t_d)$ is passed, then the client's utility will be substantially decreased. Hence, we argue that the interrupted task has to receive resources before its damping time is exceeded. Then, the condition for resource re-allocation is:

$$\hat{\tau}_{i,l}^{int}(t) > k_i^{dam} * \tau_i^{dam}(t_d),\qquad(6)$$

where $\hat{\tau}_{i,l}^{int}(t)$ is the current duration of interruption and $k_i^{dam} \in [0,1]$ determines a portion of $\tau_i^{dam}(t_d)$ which becomes critical for a client's task. That is, if the duration of interruption becomes longer than a specified part of the damping time, a client starts negotiation with the GRA in respect of resource re-allocation from a chosen donor-task to this task i.

4.2   Criteria to Choose a Donor-Task

When a client decides that the interrupted task should be donated a resource from another task, then it has to choose a donor-task whose remainder (or a part of it due to the GRA's penalty) of the execution period might be re-allocated to this interrupted task. Here, a client aims to choose a donor-task which will have the least impact on the client's utility, if it loses its resources. We distinguish two criteria to choose the best donor-task, where the first one shows the duration of time which can be allocated for the interrupted task and the second one considers the dependencies between a donor candidate and other tasks.

The Execution Period's Remainder. Generally, a client prefers to allocate a longer execution period for the interrupted task, and this execution period should preferably end at the maximum of resource availability [7,8]. In the context of this paper, it is only important to note that our previously developed negotiation strategy, ConTask, was intended for a client to start the next interruption period in the proximity of a peak of resource availability. Hence, it is desirable for the donor's remainder of execution period to have at least one maximum of resource availability. A client also considers that the re-allocated remainder $\tau_{j,l}^{rem}(t)$ can substantially be shortened by the GRA.

Hence, a client is designed to find donor-task j with a remainder $\tau_{j,l}^{rem}(t)$ of execution period which is closer to an arithmetical average $\tau_{av}^{rem}(t)$ between the minimum acceptable $\tau_{min}^{rem}(t)$ and the maximum available $\tau_{max}^{rem}(t)$ remainders among all client tasks which possess resources at time t. The maximum available remainder $\tau_{max}^{rem}(t)$ is the longest remainder available among the client tasks. The minimum acceptable donor-task's remainder $\tau_{min}^{rem}(t)$ of execution period should ideally end around the next maximum of resource availability from the current point in time. However, if all available remainders have no peaks of resource availability, the minimum acceptable remainder $\tau_{min}^{rem}(t)$ is calculated as $\tau_{min}^{rem}(t) = k^{rem} \times \tau_{max}^{rem}(t)$, where $k^{rem} \in [0,1]$ is a chosen coefficient.

Assume $Rem_{j,l}(t)$ is the first criterion for a client to choose the best donor-task. This criterion is a function which formally reflects the client's preference in respect of the duration of the execution period's remainder as discussed above and its values are from 0 to 1, i.e. from the worst to the best donor-task. If the execution remainder is shorter than the minimum acceptable one, this function will return a negative number, which is then algorithmically substituted by 0. Although those tasks are not excluded as possible donors, they are unlikely to be chosen. This function is presented below for the donor candidate j at time t.

$$Rem_{j,l}(t) = \frac{\left(\tau_{j,l}^{rem}(t) - \tau_{min}^{rem}(t)\right) \times \left(\tau_{max}^{rem}(t) - \tau_{j,l}^{rem}(t)\right)}{(\tau_{av}^{rem}(t) - \tau_{min}^{rem}(t)) \times (\tau_{max}^{rem}(t) - \tau_{av}^{rem}(t))}. \tag{7}$$

The Donor-Task's Dependencies. A client aims to minimise the negative impact on its utility when a donor task loses its resource. Assume that a client has a list of donor candidates and each of them has some remaining execution time. However, the data from these candidates have different levels of importance in respect of their corresponding recipient-task(s). If the recipient-task of the donor candidate is running, then a client has to estimate when this task will be stopped due to inaccurate input data, considering the corresponding donor candidate is interrupted. If the data from this donor candidate is of less importance for its corresponding recipient-task, then the delay time for this recipient-task will be longer. The longer delay time means the longer task is able to run with inaccurate data, contributing into the client utility. In the case when the recipient-task i of the donor candidate has already been 'stopped' or 'interrupted', the desirable donor candidate j for a client should still be of less importance to this recipient-task as defined by the weight $\alpha_{j,i}$.

Consequently, a client prefers more as a donor that task j at time t which has the smallest level of importance for its recipient-task. This condition means that the most preferable donor candidate should ideally have the longest remaining delay time $\check{\tau}_i^{del}(t_{dl}, t) = \tau_i^{del}(t_{dl}, t) - \hat{\tau}_i^{del}(t_{dl}, t)$ for its recipient-task i in the case it is chosen as a donor if its recipient-task is running, or the smallest level of importance $\alpha_{j,i}$ if its recipient-task is not running among all donor candidates. Hence, a variable $Con_j^i(t_{dl}, t)$ is determined at time t for each donor candidate j, which value varies from the least 0 to most 1 preferable donor candidate (this applies to other variables below).

$$Con_j^i(t_{dl}, t) = \begin{cases} \dfrac{\check{\tau}_i^{del}(t_{dl}, t) - \check{\tau}_{min}^{del}(t)}{\check{\tau}_{max}^{del}(t) - \check{\tau}_{min}^{del}(t)}, & when\ task\ i\ is\ running, \\[2mm] \dfrac{\alpha_{max} - \alpha_{j,i}}{\alpha_{max} - \alpha_{min}}, & when\ task\ i\ is\ not\ running. \end{cases} \tag{8}$$

where $\check{\tau}_{max}^{del}(t)$ and $\check{\tau}_{min}^{del}(t)$ would be the longest and shortest remaining delay times at time t among all running recipient-tasks of donor candidates as if those candidates were chosen as donors, while α_{max} and α_{min} are the largest and smallest levels of importance among all client tasks (not only donor candidates).

The donor candidates from the lower layers of a tree are considered to be more preferable for a client as compared to the donor candidates from the upper layers, because interruption of an upper layer task will decrease the client utility more significantly than interruption of a lower layer task. The root task indicates the highest layer $N_{lay} - 1$, while the lowest layer of a tree is identified as a zero layer. Hence, a variable

$$Lay_j = 1 - (Layer_j/(N_{lay} - 1)), \quad Lay_j \in [0, 1]. \tag{9}$$

is defined, which value varies between 0, i.e. the least, and 1, i.e. the most preferable donor candidate.

A client also considers a status of execution $Status_j(t)$ (see Sect. 3.1) of a donor candidate j at time t. A client does not consider tasks with the status 'interrupted' as possible donor candidates. The 'stopped' donor candidates are considered to be the most preferable for a client in terms of the least negative impact on the client utility. However, if a donor candidate has the status 'inaccurate' or 'accurate' and it is interrupted, then this will affect negatively all other dependent tasks which are running without or smaller error. That is, the statuses 'inaccurate' and 'accurate' are regarded as equally non-preferable statuses. Finally, we introduce a variable $Stat_j(t)$ for a donor candidate j as:

$$Stat_j(t) = \begin{cases} 0, & if\ Status_j(t) = \text{'interrupted'}, \\ \lambda, & if\ Status_j(t) = \text{'inaccurate'} \vee \text{'accurate'}, \\ 1, & if\ Status_j(t) = \text{'stopped'}, \end{cases} \tag{10}$$

where $\lambda \in\ ]0, 1[$. The second criterion for a client to choose the best donor-task is a function $Dep_j^i(t_{dl}, t)$, $j \in S_i$, $j \neq i$, which determines the client's decision in terms of the values from 0 to 1, considering client preferences mentioned above.

$$Dep_j^i(t_{dl}, t) = Con_j^i(t_{dl}, t) \times Lay_j \times Stat_j(t). \tag{11}$$

A function $Don_{j,l}^i (t_{dl}, t)$, which produces a value from 0 to 1 for each donor candidate j, combines both client criteria, $Rem_{j,l}(t)$ and $Dep_j^i (t_{dl}, t)$, as:

$$Don_{j,l}^i (t_{dl}, t) = W_{rem} \times Rem_{j,l}(t) + W_{dep} \times Dep_j^i (t_{dl}, t), \qquad (12)$$

where the weights W_{rem} and $W_{dep} \in [0, 1]$ and their sum is equal to 1. In other words, a client might prioritise the execution period's remainder of a donor task over the impact of this task's interruption on a task tree, and vice verse. A client chooses a donor candidate j for which $Don_{j,l}^i (t_{dl}, t)$ is the largest at time t.

5   Evaluation

We evaluate the SimTask re-allocation strategy in terms of the client utility, compared to the case when this strategy is not used, in various Grid environments with different weights in respect of criteria to choose a donor-task. The different environments are modelled by varying the probability of unexpected task interruption and an accuracy of the client's estimation of the resource availability maximum as this accuracy shows the level of periodic determinism in resource availability fluctuations. The probability of unexpected task interruption denotes the reliability of the Grid system in terms of resource failure and/or withdrawal.

The more accurate a client is able to identify the maximum of resource availability, the more favourable conditions are for negotiation during the tasks' expected interruptions. The different priorities (see Eq. (12)) over criteria to choose the best donor-task denote whether the most suitable remaining execution period $\tau_{j,l}^{rem}(t)$ or the least relevant donor candidate in respect of other tasks' execution affects the client decision to the larger extent.

In our evaluation, a client has 40 tasks which are connected hierarchically as a four-layer tree, where each task has three sender-tasks (if applicable) respectively. The values of $\alpha_{i,j}$ are generated randomly for each test, where all tasks have to be run continuously and simultaneously for $\tau_{dl}^{exec} = 300000$ virtual seconds. The period of change in resource availability is equal to 3000 virtual seconds. The average client utility is then calculated over 200 runs. Note that k_i^{dam} (see Eq. (6)) and λ (see Eq. (10)) are set to 0.5 and 0.6 for all tasks.

A possibility for a task to obtain a longer duration of an execution period is simulated, following a periodicity of resource availability, where these durations fluctuate periodically over time. The probability of successful negotiation also increases when resources are more available. We also assume that in the resource re-allocation negotiation the GRA is less greedy than in the ordinary negotiation, because it re-allocates resources which are granted to a client. Hence, the re-allocation negotiation has a high probability of succeeding. The change of an estimated parameter $P_{i,S_i}(t)$ can be modelled with any functional dependence which satisfies the condition stated in Sect. 3.2. For transparency, it is modelled as a periodic function over time, considering that this parameter should not change abruptly (e.g. temperature).

5.1 Grid Environments

In this section, we evaluate the change in the client's utility for the different
probabilities of unexpected task interruption and levels of accuracy with which
a client estimates the maximum of resource availability. These different settings
simulate more or less favourable Grid environments for negotiation. The probabilities of unexpected task interruption are considered in the interval between
$1.E-02$ and $1.E-06$. The probabilities larger than $1.E-02$ are considered to
be non-realistic, because all tasks would be interrupted almost every virtual
second. Figure 1 supports this assumption as it shows that the client utility
changes insignificantly above the probability $5.E-04$ and it generally tends to
zero towards the larger probabilities. This occurs due to the fewer number of
unexpected task interruptions which is approximately the same for such small
probabilities and any possible difference averages over multiple runs.

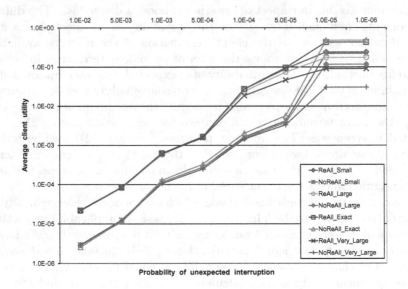

Fig. 1. The changes in the client utility in the different Grid environments

The different level of accuracy with which a client is able to estimate the
maximum of resource availability mean that a task might stop running farther
from the maximum of resource availability due to the client's inability to estimate
this maximum accurately. Then, it will be more challenging for a client to obtain
an acceptable execution period through an ordinary negotiation with the GRA.
In this case, a client is more likely to use the SimTask re-allocation strategy in
order to run the interrupted tasks. We consider four different levels of accuracy in
the estimation of the maximum resource availability by a client, where a precise
estimation is indicated as 'Exact', while an inaccurate estimation with a small
deviation is indicated as 'Small', with a large deviation as 'Large', and with a

very large deviation as 'Very_Large' in Fig. 1. Here, a small deviation (positive or negative) from the maximum resource availability is considered to be up to 1% of the duration of a period (one virtual day) of resource availability fluctuation. Large and very large deviations denote up to 2% and 4% of the duration of this period respectively. Finally, we compare the cases when a client uses the SimTask re-allocation strategy (i.e. 'ReAll') and when it does not use this strategy (i.e. 'NoReAll'). In the cases 'ReAll', the weights which are used to choose the best donor-task are $W_{rem} = 0.3$ and $W_{dep} = 0.7$ (see Eq. (12)), and these weights is the most successful combination among all considered combinations as discussed in the following section.

Figure 1 shows the average client utilities for the different probabilities of unexpected task interruption in a logarithmic scale. Note that the SimTask re-allocation strategy improves the client utility in almost all presented cases, except for the two smallest probabilities when the maximum resource availability can be estimated precisely. An effectiveness of the re-allocation strategy decreases when the number of unexpected interruptions drastically drops and negotiation conditions are favourable in terms of resource availability. However, in the cases of small, large or very large estimation deviations, the SimTask re-allocation strategy shows a noticeable improvement (especially, for the larger deviations) in the client's utility over the cases when this strategy is not used.

5.2   Client Priorities

We evaluate how the priorities for the two criteria which are used to choose the best donor-task, might affect the client's utility for the different probabilities of unexpected task interruption. Here, we consider the different values of W_{rem} and W_{dep} for the SimTask re-allocation strategy 'ReAll', which is compared to the cases when this strategy is not used, i.e. 'NoReAll' and 'NoReAll_NoMax'. The case 'NoReAll_NoMax' also considers that a client cannot estimate the maximum resource availability, while all other cases assume that a client can estimate it with high precision. Figure 2 shows the average client utilities for the different weights over various Grid environments, where W_{rem} and W_{dep} are indicated on the labels 'ReAll' e.g., 'ReAll_0.0_1.0' denotes $W_{rem} = 0.0$ and $W_{dep} = 1.0$.

Generally, the utilities for the case $W_{rem} = 0.3$ and $W_{dep} = 0.7$ are larger than for all other combinations of the weight coefficients. Note that a strict prioritisation of one of the criteria, i.e. 'ReAll_1.0_0.0' or 'ReAll_0.0_1.0', generally show the smallest utilities among all weights' combinations. However, 'ReAll_0.0_1.0' demonstrates the larger utilities for the smaller probabilities (below 5.E−04). Hence, it is more beneficial for a client to prioritise the criterion $Dep_j^i(t_{dl}, t)$ a bit more over the criterion $Rem_{j,l}(t)$, i.e. 'ReAll_0.3_0.7'. Note that the difference in utilities is not large for the cases where the weights are more balanced such as 'ReAll_0.3_0.7', 'ReAll_0.7_0.3' and 'ReAll_0.5_0.5', while 'ReAll_0.3_0.7' usually shows the better utilities. However, the best choice of those weights might depend on a use case. Finally, the SimTask re-allocation strategy with any weights' combination outperforms almost all cases 'NoReAll_'.

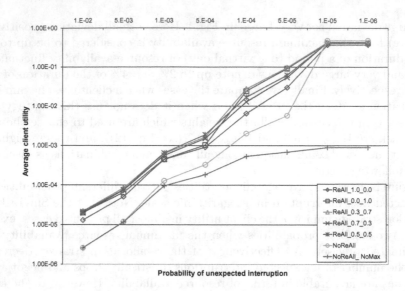

Fig. 2. The changes in the client utility with the different preferences criteria

6 Conclusions and Future Work

This paper presents a formal model for inter-dependent continuous tasks, where some tasks depend on data from other tasks. This model takes into account not only a direct data dependence between a sender and recipient-tasks, but also a reverse dependence when a sender-task is stopped due to the interruption (stopping) of its recipient-task. If a recipient-task does not receive data from some (all) of its corresponding sender-tasks for some time, it stops due to a substantial increase in its parameter estimation's error. If one task is interrupted, it affects its whole sub-tree and all corresponding recipients up to the root.

Here, a new re-allocation strategy, SimTask, has been introduced which allows a client agent to re-allocate resources among its own tasks through negotiation with the GRA, if ordinary resource negotiation becomes too long as resources are contested by other clients. This strategy includes a decision mechanism with two criteria to choose a donor-task if necessary. These criteria consider the execution period's remainder of each candidate and its importance for other tasks in a tree. As evaluated, SimTask increases the client utility for almost all probabilities of unexpected task interruption with the different estimation accuracy of the maximum resource availability.

References

1. Andrzejak, A., et al.: Characterizing and predicting resource demand by periodicity mining. Netw. Syst. Manag. **13**(2), 175–196 (2005)
2. Apache: Storm - distributed and fault-tolerant realtime computation. http://storm.incubator.apache.org/. Accessed June 2014

3. Babu, S., et al.: Continuous queries over data streams. SIGMOD Rec. **30**(3), 109–120 (2001)
4. Barbieri, D.F., et al.: C-SPARQL: SPARQL for continuous querying. In: The 18th International Conference on World Wide Web, pp. 1061–1062. ACM, New York (2009)
5. Ghanem, M., et al.: Sensor grids for air pollution monitoring. In: The 3rd UK e-Science All Hands Meeting (2004)
6. Haberland, V.: Strategies for the execution of long-term continuous and simultaneous tasks in grids. Ph.D. thesis, NMS, King's College London, UK (2015)
7. Haberland, V., et al.: Negotiation to execute continuous long-term tasks. In: Schaub, T., et al. (ed.) The 21st European Conference on Artificial Intelligence. Frontiers in Artificial Intelligence and Applications, vol. 263, pp. 1019–1020 (2014)
8. Haberland, V., et al.: Negotiation strategy for continuous long-term tasks in a grid environment. Auton. Agents Multi-agent Syst. **31**(1), 130–150 (2017)
9. Iosup, A., et al.: The grid workloads archive. Future Gener. Comput. Syst. **24**(7), 672–686 (2008)
10. Jin, H., et al.: A run-time scheduling policy for dependent tasks in grid computing systems. In: The 6th International Conference on Parallel and Distributed Computing, Applications and Technologies, pp. 521–523 (2005)
11. Kondo, D., et al.: Characterizing and evaluating desktop grids: an empirical study. In: The 18th International Parallel and Distributed Processing Symposium (2004)
12. Le-Phuoc, D., et al.: A middleware framework for scalable management of linked streams. Web Semant.: Sci. Serv. Agents World Wide Web **16**, 42–51 (2012)
13. Lee, L.T., et al.: A non-critical path earliest-finish algorithm for inter-dependent tasks in heterogeneous computing environments. In: The 11th IEEE International High Performance Computing and Communications, pp. 603–608 (2009)
14. Lesser, V., et al.: Evolution of the GPGP/TAEMS domain-independent coordination framework. Auton. Agents Multi-agent Syst. **9**(1–2), 87–143 (2004)
15. Meriem, M., Belabbas, Y.: Dynamic dependent tasks assignment for grid computing. In: Hsu, C.-H., Yang, L.T., Park, J.H., Yeo, S.-S. (eds.) ICA3PP 2010. LNCS, vol. 6082, pp. 112–120. Springer, Heidelberg (2010). doi:10.1007/978-3-642-13136-3_11
16. Motwani, R., et al.: Query processing, resource management, and approximation in a data stream management system. In: The 1st Biennial Conference on Innovative Data Systems Research, pp. 245–256 (2003)
17. Sandnes, F.E., Sinnen, O.: Stochastic DFS for multiprocessor scheduling of cyclic taskgraphs. In: Liew, K.-M., Shen, H., See, S., Cai, W., Fan, P., Horiguchi, S. (eds.) PDCAT 2004. LNCS, vol. 3320, pp. 354–362. Springer, Heidelberg (2004). doi:10.1007/978-3-540-30501-9_75
18. Sardinha, A., et al.: Scheduling cyclic task graphs with SCC-Map. In: The 3rd Workshop on Applications for Multi-Core Architectures, pp. 54–59 (2012)
19. Sequeda, J.F., et al.: Linked stream data: a position paper. In: The 2nd International Workshop on Semantic Sensor Networks, vol. 522, pp. 148–157 (2009)
20. Terry, D., et al.: Continuous queries over append-only databases. SIGMOD Rec. **21**(2), 321–330 (1992)
21. Wooldridge, M., Jennings, N.R.: Intelligent agents: theory and practice. Knowl. Eng. Rev. **10**, 115–152 (1995)
22. Yang, T., et al.: Heuristic algorithms for scheduling iterative task computations on distributed memory machines. IEEE Trans. Parallel Distrib. Syst. **8**(6), 608–622 (1997)
23. Zhao, H., et al.: A low-cost rescheduling policy for dependent tasks on grid computing systems. In: The European Across Grids Conference, pp. 21–31 (2004)

Self-adaptive Distribution System State Estimation

Alexandre Perles[✉], Guy Camilleri, and Marie-Pierre Gleizes

Institut de Recherche en Informatique de Toulouse,
Université Fédérale de Toulouse, Toulouse, France
{alexandre.perles,guy.camilleri,marie-pierre.gleizes}@irit.fr

Abstract. Electricity plays an increasingly important role in our society. Indeed, we are moving toward the era of "everything electric". The needs evolving, it is mandatory to rethink the way electricity is produced and distributed. This then introduces the concept of an autonomous and intelligent power system called the Smart Grid.

One characteristic of the Smart Grid is its ability to control itself. To do this, papers in literature suggest that the state of the controlled network should be estimated.

This paper proposes an agent-based architecture to enable the transition to the Smart Grid, a design and an implementation of agent behaviors aiming at solving the State Estimation problem. Based on the Adaptive Multi-Agent System theory, the developed system allows from local interactions between agents to estimate in a reasonable time and computational complexity the state of a distribution system.

1 Introduction

Nowadays, electrical networks in the world are made of a set of nodes connected with unidirectional links. This approach is used to facilitate the transport of electricity. The electricity is generated at one point by the producer, and is provided to consumers through the lines. Thus, the only control point is located at the source and if a fault occurs on a network, it is easier to locate and to isolate it. Although it has been used for decades, this approach is expected to evolve with the concept of Smart Grid [1,3,6,20].

From the papers [3,6,20], the concept of Smart Grid can be defined as follow: *the Smart Grid is an autonomous electrical network able to adapt itself to client's needs in a secured, ecological and economical way. It enables bidirectional exchanges of electricity and information through lines.*

Roche [18] presents some motivations to move from classical electrical networks toward the Smart Grid: the increase of energy demand, the global warming, the increase of distributed and renewable generation and the depletion of resources currently used for energy generation.

The demand in energy is growing fast. The worldwide energy demand is expected to rise by over 150% from 2010 to 2050 under the Energy Technology Perspectives 2010 (ETP 2010) Baseline Scenario and over 115% between 2007

N. Criado Pacheco et al. (Eds.): EUMAS 2016/AT 2016, LNAI 10207, pp. 202–216, 2017.
DOI: 10.1007/978-3-319-59294-7_17

and 2050 under the Blue Map Scenario [10]. Moreover, since the 1960's, the temperatures of air and water are more and more away from normal conditions. This is called the global warming. Given this situation, some governments have decided to promote new technologies and the usage of renewable energy. Besides the global warming, we are going to run out of currently used resources. For the previously mentioned reasons, the number of distributed and renewable generators is going to increase quickly resulting in as many additional control points which will obviously result in the increase of complexity to ensure voltage range and more generally a good quality of service. It is therefore necessary to find a solution to control this new network type.

One solution to control an electrical network is to firstly determine its state. This is referred to as System State Estimation. Indeed, knowing the state of an electrical network allows for example to detect faults in a network and also to prevent or to remove them. Although efficient methods are known to solve the State Estimation problem on transmission networks (such as in the paper of Monticelli [15]), the Distribution System State Estimation is not trivial. This is mainly due to the radial structure of such systems and the low amount of sensors.

To handle the previously expressed problems, works have been realized in order to reduce the computation complexity. In works such as [5,8,14,23,24], problems are distributed between multiple agents and then aggregated to a "Control Agent" (or an "Aggregator Agent") able to interact with these smaller entities. We notably can find, in the paper of Ghazvini et al. [9], a division of an electrical network into multiple zones considered to be enough small to minimize the complexity of computations made on it while maintaining their efficiencies. This method reduces the complexity however the cutting into zones is not trivial and the synchronization of these estimations brings other problems.

This paper presents an innovative approach based on Multi-Agent System to allow the transition to the Smart Grid and notably the State Estimation by exploiting the Newton-Raphson numerical method (see [17]) locally to each bus.

In the first part of this paper, the State Estimation problem and its potential role in the Smart Grid is detailed. Secondly, the Adaptive Multi-Agent System approach is described as an alternative to traditional methods. And finally, the design and evaluation of the developed system is presented.

2   Problem Description

An electrical system is composed of various entities. Buses are nodes of the network to which can be connected lines, producers, consumers, ... These buses can be equipped with voltage magnitude sensors or power sensors. All these sensors give informations (voltage magnitude, injected power, ...) about the state of a network. However, networks can't be fully equipped because this is too much expensive and sensors are not 100% accurate. So the problem is to estimate the voltage of each bus in the network without having sensors at each bus. Moreover, the amount of power consumed at consumer sites is generally not known which increases the difficulty of the problem.

The State Estimation problem can be defined as follow: *finding the most likely state of the system based on quantities that are measured and the model of this system and filtering the errors of the sensors thanks to their redundancy.* Solving the State Estimation problem is the process of estimating the voltage of each bus of a network. To do so, the topology of the network as well as the values returned by sensors and an estimation of power injection at load buses are known.

It exists three types of measurements. **Real measurements** are the one provided by physical sensors, **Pseudo-Measurements** are rough estimations of the power injected at consumer sites and **Virtual Measurements** are the power injected at zero-injection buses (buses to which no generator nor load are connected).

Let z be the set of measurements (real measurements, pseudo-measurements and virtual measurements) at a given time t. These measurements can be expressed as the sum of the real observed value and an error due to the imprecision of sensors:

$$z = h(x) + e \qquad (1)$$

With:

- x: the state vector of the network,
- h: the model of the network,
- e: the error vector of measurements.

In a State Estimation problem, the function h is known as well as the set of measurements z.

For this multi-agent study, we consider consumers and producers connected to the bus as an abstract and unique entity which is an integral part of the bus. Consequently, the reader must have in mind that the sum of productions and consumptions on a bus is referred to as "bus injection".

The State Estimation problem can be solved by using the statistic method of maximum likelihood estimation. By assuming the interdependence of measurements and their Gaussian distribution, determining the state of a network can be expressed as solving an optimization problem where the objective function is formulated as a sum of Weighted Least Squares in which the weighted squares are the differences between the model values and the measures weighted by the precision of the corresponding measurement type.

The corresponding objective function to minimize is:

$$\sum_{s \in \text{Sensors}} \left(\frac{z_s - h_s(x)}{\sigma_s} \right)^2 \qquad (2)$$

With z_s the measure, $h_s(x)$ the value calculated with the model and σ_s the variance of the distribution of the sensor s.

A lot of works have been done on transmission system state estimation. However, classic optimization approaches applied to distribution systems have a high computational complexity [11]. Also, few studies have been made to propose a multi-agent approach to solve the state estimation problem by applying a decomposition of the problem in smaller problems easier to solve, followed by an aggregation of these solutions [13, 16, 22].

The most part of these studies have formulated the problem as a Weighted Least Square Minimization problem and solved it globally with global numeric methods. It consists in minimizing the weighted square of errors between the model and measured values.

Examples of the application of such method to distribution networks can be found in the literature [4, 12, 19]. The main drawback of this kind of approach is that it requires to work with the whole set of equations with large matrices resulting in a resolution with a non-negligible complexity. In addition to state estimation, some works have been done to improve the estimation made for pseudo-measurements.

Most of these approaches are based on the Newton-Raphson numerical method [17]. The Newton-Raphson method is a mathematical method to find an approximation of the roots of a function. The resolution is iterative and requires that the starting point is close to the solution.

In this study, we propose to evaluate the relevance of using an Adaptive Multi-Agent System based on a local application of the Newton-Raphson method for solving the State Estimation problem in distribution networks.

3   Adaptive Multi-agent Systems

To solve this problem, the Adaptive Multi-Agent Systems approach seems to be particularly suitable and provides, thanks to its design process, an openness allowing to add future features which is a mandatory for a system aiming at controlling the Smart Grid. Moreover, the dynamic and distributed aspects of these new networks confirm the relevance of such an approach.

An Adaptive Multi-Agent System is a Multi-Agent System in which the emergence process is used to provide a global answer adapted to the problem from local cooperative interactions between agents [21].

3.1   Cooperation

The cooperation in an Adaptive Multi-Agent System is the process of mutual support between agents of this system. It is a question of finding the right equilibrium between acting to reach its own goal and helping other agents to reach their own without having a global knowledge of the system. In order to identify the agent which is struggling the most, agents have the ability to assess their criticalities.

3.2   Criticality

The criticality of an agent represents the state of dissatisfaction of it regarding its local goal [7]. The criticality of an agent is a value assessing the difficulty an agent has to reach its goal at a given situation. This value evolves and is expected to be minimal for all agents when the problem is solved.

4   An Adaptive Multi-agent System for the Distribution of Intelligence in Power Systems

In this section, we present the developed multi-agent system aiming at solving the State Estimation problem. This system was designed in accordance with the Adaptive Multi-Agent System theory and following the ADELFE (Atelier de Développement de Logiciels à Fonctionnalité Émergente) methodology (see [2]). The developed system aims at estimating the state of an electrical system. To achieve this, agents act locally to estimate the state of the bus they are associated to. The State Estimation problem also consists in benefiting of sensors redundancy to filter errors. The agents also have to cooperate to distribute the errors among the voltage sensors. From the collective resolution, it emerges the State Estimation of the global system.

This part presents the agentification of the entities composing an electrical network, the interactions between these entities and the cooperative behaviors of these agents.

4.1   Cooperative Agents

In order to allow a certain flexibility in the future evolutions of the developed system, we have made the decision to agentify the buses as well as voltage sensors as they are major actors in the State Estimation and are expected to evolve during the solving process. Agents are autonomous in their decision-making and act locally. Moreover, this fine granularity allows to reduce the impact a change can have in the controlling system.

In our system, we have defined two types of agents: Bus Agents and Voltage Magnitude Sensor Agents. For each bus, it's possible to have two associated agents: a Bus Agent and a Voltage Magnitude Sensor Agent. However, a Voltage Magnitude Sensor Agent is present on the bus only if a voltage magnitude sensor is attached to that bus.

- The goal of a bus agent is to determine a consistent voltage magnitude and phase angle (according to the network) of the bus it is associated to.
- The goal of a Voltage Magnitude Sensor Agent is to determine the voltage magnitude at the bus it is associated to thanks to the values returned by the voltage sensor and the bus agent associated to the bus.

The Fig. 1 represents an example of a piece of power system as well as all the used types of agent and their interactions.

4.2   Interactions Between the Entities

To give the ability to the agents to cooperate and reach their goal, they need to be able to interact with other agents.

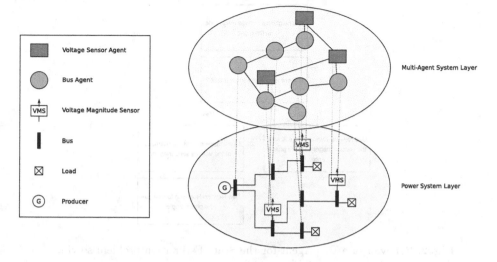

Fig. 1. Multi-agent system coupled with a piece of power system

The different interaction types are the following:

Interactions Between the Bus Agents. The goal of Bus Agents is to determine the voltage magnitude and phase angle at the bus they are associated to. To do that, they need to be aware of, at each step for each agent in its neighborhood, the current estimation of voltage (magnitude and phase angle). The only interaction between the Bus Agents is about the current value of their respective voltage estimations.

Interactions Between the Voltage Magnitude Sensor Agents and the Bus Agents. The Bus Agents need to know the value estimated by the Voltage Magnitude Sensor Agent associated to the bus if any. Moreover, the Voltage Magnitude Sensor Agents need to know the difference between their estimated voltage magnitude and the one estimated by the Bus Agent associated to the same bus.

Interactions Between the Voltage Magnitude Sensor Agents. The Voltage Magnitude Sensor Agents try to distribute the sensors errors among them. Therefore, they need to communicate in order to cooperate.

4.3 Cooperative Behavior of Bus Agents

The behavior of a Bus Agent depends on the presence of a Voltage Magnitude Sensor Agent on the bus.

- In the presence of a Voltage Magnitude Sensor Agent, the bus agent can get the current estimated voltage magnitude of the Voltage Magnitude Sensor Agent and uses it as its voltage magnitude estimation. Then, the bus agent applies the Newton-Raphson method to estimate the phase angle value.

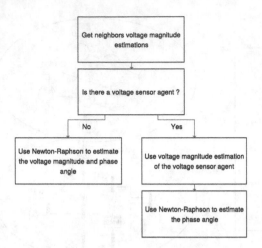

Fig. 2. Behavior of a Bus Agent for the State Estimation problem solving

– In the absence of a Voltage Magnitude Sensor Agent, the bus agent applies the Newton-Raphson method to estimate both the voltage magnitude and the phase angle.

The Fig. 2 presents the behavior of a Bus Agent. This algorithm is mainly based on the function *NewtonRaphson.Compute*. This function takes in parameters the current estimated voltage (magnitude and phase) of the agent as well as the current estimated voltage of its neighbors. From this information, the function computes an iteration of the Newton-Raphson method and returns a new voltage value.

In the decision phase, the bus agent calculates the voltage (complex number) with the Newton-Raphson method. In the case in which it is not associated to a Voltage Magnitude Sensor Agent, the bus agent uses the voltage value obtained with the Newton-Raphson method. In the other case, the bus agent uses the voltage magnitude estimated by the associated Voltage Magnitude Sensor Agent and the voltage phase angle calculated with the Newton-Raphson method.

4.4 Cooperative Behavior of Voltage Magnitude Sensor Agents

Roughly, Bus Agents are expected to find the voltage which locally satisfies the Kirchhoff's Current Law (the sum of currents flowing into a bus must be equal to the sum of currents flowing out of that bus). Voltage Magnitude Sensor Agents are here to correct the value provided by voltage magnitude sensor by cooperating with others Voltage Magnitude Sensor Agents to help Bus Agents to reach their goal (which is satisfying the Kirchhoff's Current Law on their bus).

The goal of a Voltage Magnitude Sensor Agent is to determine the real voltage magnitude thanks to the value given by the voltage sensor it is associated to and the voltage magnitude estimation made by the bus agent associated to its bus. To do it, a Voltage Magnitude Sensor Agent knows at least one other Voltage Magnitude Sensor Agent. It allows each Voltage Magnitude Sensor Agent to cooperate with the others. Moreover, contrarily to Bus Agents, Voltage Magnitude Sensor Agents can exchange messages.

Supposing the errors of voltage sensors are equitably distributed, each Voltage Magnitude Sensor Agent negotiates with its neighbors to determine its correct value.

In order to understand the cooperative behavior of a Voltage Magnitude Sensor Agent, it is necessary to define some terms that will be used in the following parts:

- *The **Estimated Voltage Magnitude Value** is the supposed value of the voltage magnitude at the associated bus by the Voltage Magnitude Sensor Agent.*
- *The **Offset of a Voltage Magnitude Sensor Agent** is the signed difference between its Estimated Voltage Magnitude Value and the value returned by the voltage magnitude sensor.*

In order to minimize the objective function (see the formula (2)), Voltage Magnitude Sensor Agents start with the voltage magnitude given by the physical sensor. This obviously corresponds to the smallest squared value. It then changes its value to match with the constraints imposed by the Kirchhoff's Current Law. If a Voltage Magnitude Sensor Agent has to increment its estimated value to solve a constraint, it must be sure that another agent will decrease its own by the same factor and vice-versa. Thus, it allows agents to change their estimated value as long as it doesn't increase the Weighted Squares sum without calculating it. As the agents are cooperative, they will try to help each other by compensating the offset a Voltage Magnitude Sensor Agent needs to do as long as this latter is more critical.

The Fig. 3 details the three phases of a cycle of a Voltage Magnitude Sensor Agent.

Criticality of a Voltage Magnitude Sensor Agent. The criticality of a Voltage Magnitude Sensor Agent is the difference between its Estimated Voltage Magnitude Value and the voltage magnitude calculated by the associated bus agent with the Newton-Raphson method. In other words, a Voltage Magnitude Sensor Agent is satisfied when the value it has found is equal to the one found by the associated bus agent.

$$|estimatedVoltageMagnitude(self) - estimatedVoltageMagnitude(busAgent)|$$
$$(3)$$

Perception. The perception phase consists in acquiring all the informations the agent needs to take a cooperative decision. During the perception phase, a Voltage Magnitude Sensor Agent perceives:

- the criticality of each of its neighbors,

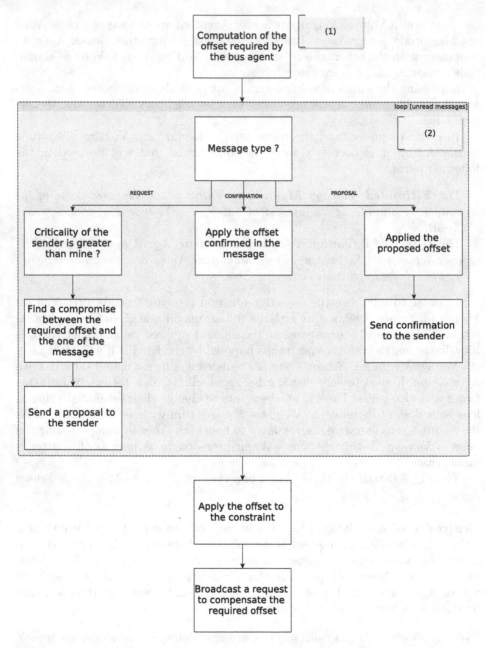

Fig. 3. Behavior of a voltage magnitude sensor agent for the State Estimation problem solving

- the messages previously sent by its neighbors,
- the last voltage magnitude sensed by the voltage sensor it is associated to,
- the voltage magnitude calculated by the bus agent of the bus it belongs to.

Decision. The first part (1) of the decision process is to compare the value estimated by the bus agent with the Newton-Raphson method and compare it to the value currently estimated by the Voltage Magnitude Sensor Agent. This gives the required offset. Then, the agent has to consider messages received from its neighbors (2). As mentioned previously, only Voltage Magnitude Sensor Agents can exchange messages. It exists three kinds of message: an offset request (REQUEST), a proposal (PROPOSAL) and an offset confirmation (CONFIRM).

Offset Request. This type of message is intended to ask a neighbor to modify its Estimated Voltage Magnitude Value in order to compensate the modification the sender wants to do on its own Estimated Voltage Magnitude Value.

Proposal. Once an agent receives an offset request, it can answer with a Proposal message to propose a modification of its own offset.

Offset Request Confirmation. The agent which has sent the first message (Offset Request) may have received a proposal. If it still fits its needs, the agent can confirm this operation.

In the case in which an agent receives an Offset Request, it has to decide if it must help the sender. To do that, it observes the criticality of the sender. If this latter is greater than its own, it answers with a proposal to inform it that it can compensate the requested offset.

In the case in which an agent receives a proposal, it has to confirm the offset it wants to be compensated.

Finally, in the case in which an agent receives an Offset Confirmation, it has to fulfill its engagement because it is cooperative and change its value.

The following table summarizes these rules:

Condition	Action
Received an offset request and the emitter is more critical	Send a proposal
Received a proposal	Send a confirmation for absorbing the offset
Received a confirmation	Absorb the offset

This cooperative behavior is intended to guarantee that if an agent moves its estimated voltage magnitude from the one of its sensor, another agent will do the same in the other direction. This behavior allows to distribute the voltage magnitude sensors errors among the sensors.

Action. In the case where its Estimated Voltage Magnitude Value is different than the voltage magnitude calculated by the bus agent, it means that the Voltage Magnitude Sensor Agent is not yet satisfied. Therefore, the agent has to broadcast an Offset Request to its neighborhood. Finally, the agent updates its criticality value with the formula 3.

This cooperative behavior is aimed at distributing the sensors errors among these latter. The following part presents the results of evaluations made on this system.

5   Evaluation

Multiple evaluations have been made with the proposed system. In each case, at least 1,000 resolutions have been made. This part presents the results of these evaluations: Performance over the amount of voltage sensors, filtering quality, computation time and self-adaptation.

In order to determine the quality of a solution to the State Estimation problem, it is, first and foremost, necessary to define a criteria of quality. A solution to the State Estimation problem is considered as acceptable if the maximal relative voltage magnitude estimation error is lower than 1%.

The relative voltage magnitude estimation error of a bus is expressed as a percent of error and is calculated with the following formula:

$$\frac{\text{Real Value} - \text{Estimated Value}}{\text{Real Value}} \cdot 100 \tag{4}$$

5.1   Performance over the Amount of Voltage Sensors

The Fig. 4 presents performance results on the application of the developed system to solve the State Estimation problem on a 111-bus distribution system. On this network, we have defined 6 configurations of voltage sensors. The first configuration contains only one voltage sensor. The second one contains two voltage sensors and so on.

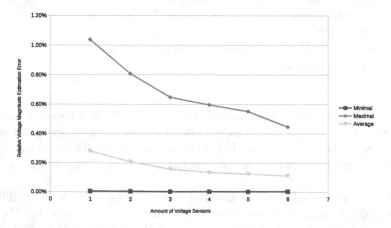

Fig. 4. Performance evaluation on a 111-bus distribution system

For each configuration, 1,000 resolutions have been made. For each of these resolutions, a random noise has been added to the voltage magnitude sensors values to simulate the imprecision of sensors.

On these 1,000 resolutions, we have measured the maximal voltage magnitude estimation errors. Finally, for each configuration, we have calculated the minimal, maximal and average of these maximal values.

We can observe on the Fig. 4 that with only two sensors, the system is able to estimate the state of the network with a maximal relative voltage magnitude estimation error lower than 1%. Moreover, this highlights the fact that redundancy of sensors improves the accuracy of the State Estimation. The errors of sensors being 1%, the results show that the system is able to improve the accuracy of the estimation thanks to the redundancy of sensors.

5.2 Filtering Quality

For a given voltage magnitude sensor and its associated bus, we have observed over 10,000 resolutions the values returned by the voltage sensor and the values found by the system. This allows to determine whether or not the system is able to provide better voltage magnitude estimation than the one provided by sensors. The Fig. 5 presents the distribution of obtained value. It can be observed that the Gaussian of the estimation is twice thinner than the one of the sensor. The parameters of the Gaussian are presented in the Table 1. This results show that the voltage magnitude estimations of the system are twice less wrong than the values returned by the sensors.

σ is the standard deviation of the voltage sensor present at this bus. τ is the standard deviation of the results obtained thanks to the system.

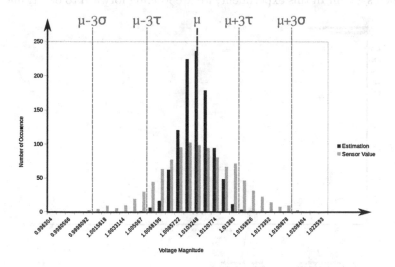

Fig. 5. Gaussian distribution of a voltage sensor and the State Estimation for a bus

Table 1. Standard deviations and mean value of the bus observed

Real value (μ)	1.014676
Estimation standard deviation (τ)	0.0014324118
Estimation mean value	1.014665402
Sensor standard deviation (σ)	0.0033071471
Sensor mean value	1.014882942

5.3   Computation Time

For a given 111-bus network and a given configuration, good performances have
been observed. Generally, the system requires less than one second to provide an
accurate result. However, in some cases, the system needs up to 244 ms to provide
an accurate solution. This may be due to the imprecision of measurements and
special situations in which agents can be.

The following values have been measured:

	Minimum	Maximum	Average
Time (in seconds)	0.104	0.244	0.13191
Number of cycles	303	714	381.591

5.4   Self-adaptation

Finally, an experimentation have been realized to determine the robustness of the
developed system. In this experiment, we are looking forward to determine if the

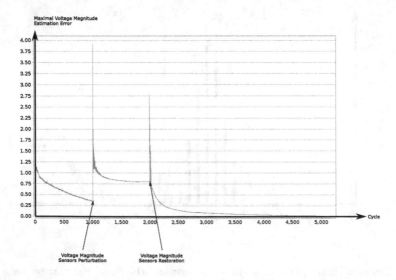

Fig. 6. Impact of the addition of a perturbation during the resolution process

system is able to resist to perturbations. We have launched a State Estimation solving on the 111-bus network. Then, at the cycle 1,000, we have introduced a supplementary random noise to each voltage sensor values to observe the reaction of the system. These noises have then been removed at the cycle 2,000.

As expected, the Fig. 6 shows that the system is able to adapt itself to perturbations and that it tries to find the most likely solution despite the noise added to sensors values.

6   Conclusion and Perspectives

In this paper, we have highlighted the fact that moving from current electrical network to the concept of Smart Grid requires a reconsideration of the way electrical network problem are treated. After a brief introduction, the State Estimation problem is presented as a Weighted Least Square optimization problem. Then, the Adaptive Multi-Agent System theory is presented. After that, an innovative approach, based on it, is proposed to solve the State Estimation problem. The cooperative behaviors of the two types of agents of this system allows them to locally estimate the state of the bus they are associated to and to filter the sensor errors. The results of the evaluations made on the system show the relevance of using an Adaptive Multi-Agent System for the Smart Grid in terms of performance and self-adaptation. Research will be continued to improve the error filtering. Also, an interesting perspective could be to evaluate the adaptation capability over configuration changes. Moreover, in real situations, communication can be suddenly interrupted. It is therefore necessary to handle this case. Finally, connecting the multi-agent system to a good quality network simulator would allow to evaluate the robustness of the system against perturbations (load evolutions, fault on lines, ...).

References

1. Ahat, M.: Smart grid and optimization. Am. J. Oper. Res. **03**(01), 196–206 (2013)
2. Bonjean, N., Mefteh, W., Gleizes, M.P., Maurel, C., Migeon, F.: ADELFE 2.0. In: Cossentino, Massimo, Hilaire, Vincent, Molesini, Ambra, Seidita, Valeria (eds.) Handbook on Agent-Oriented Design Processes, pp. 19–63. Springer, Heidelberg (2014). doi:10.1007/978-3-642-39975-6_3
3. Canadian Electricity Association: The smart grid : a pragmatic approach (2010)
4. Chilard, O., Grenard, S., Devaux, O., de Alvaro Garcia, L.: Distribution state estimation based on voltage state variables: assessment of results and limitations. In: 20th International Conference and Exhibition on Electricity Distribution - Part 1, CIRED 2009 (0524), pp. 1–4 (2009)
5. de Oliveira Saraiva, F., Asada, E.N.: Multi-agent systems applied to topological reconfiguration of smart power distribution systems. In: 2014 International Joint Conference on Neural Networks (IJCNN), pp. 2812–2819, July 2014
6. Department of Energy: Communications requirements of smart grid technologies (2010)

7. Di Marzo Serugendo, G., Gleizes, M.P., Karageorgos, A.: Self-organising Software: From Natural to Artificial Adaptation. Springer, Heidelberg (2011)
8. Eriksson, M., Armendariz, M., Vasilenko, O., Saleem, A., Nordstrom, L.: Multi-agent based distribution automation solution for self-healing grids. IEEE Trans. Ind. Electron. **0046**(c), 1 (2015)
9. Ghazvini, M., Abedini, R., Pinto, T., Vale, Z.: Multiagent system architecture for short-term operation of integrated microgrids. IFAC Proc. **47**(3), 6355–6360 (2014)
10. International Energy Agency: Technology Roadmap, Smart Grid (2011)
11. Likith Kumar, M., Maruthi Prasanna, H., Ananthapadmanabha, T.: A literature review on distribution system state estimation. Procedia Technol. **21**, 423–429 (2015)
12. Lu, C., Teng, J., Liu, W.H.: Distribution system state estimation. IEEE Trans. Power Syst. **10**(I), 229–240 (1995)
13. Lu, Z.G., Zhang, J., Feng, T., Cheng, H.L.: Distributed agent-based state estimation considering controlled coordination layer. Int. J. Electr. Power Energy Syst. **54**, 569–575 (2014)
14. Lukovic, S., Kovac, E.B.: Adapting multi-agent systems approach for integration of prosumers in smart grids, pp. 1485–1491, July 2013
15. Monticelli, A.: Electric power system state estimation. Proc. IEEE **88**(2), 262–282 (2000)
16. Nguyen, P.H., Kling, W.L.: Distributed state estimation for multi-agent based active distribution networks (2010)
17. Powell, L.: Power System Load Flow Analysis (Professional Engineering). McGraw-Hill, New York (2004)
18. Roche, R.: Algorithmes et architectures multi-agents pour la gestion de l'énergie dans les réseaux électriques intelligents (2012)
19. Roytelman, I., Shahidehpour, S.M.: State estimation for electric power distribution systems in quasi real-time conditions. IEEE Trans. Power Deliv. **8**(4), 2009–2015 (1993)
20. Singer, J.: Enabling Tomorrow's Electricity System: Report of the Ontario Smart Grid Forum (2010)
21. Videau, S.: Contrôle de processus dynamiques par systèmes multi-agents adaptatifs: application au contrôle de bioprocédés. Ph.D. thesis, July 2011
22. Voropai, N.I., Kolosok, I.N., Massel, L.V., Fartyshev, D.A., Paltsev, A.S., Panasetsky, D.A.: A multi-agent approach to electric power systems. In: Alkhateeb, F. (ed.) Multi-Agent Systems - Modeling, Interactions, Simulations and Case Studies. InTech (2011). doi:10.5772/15708. https://www.intechopen.com/books/multi-agent-systems-modeling-interactions-simulations-and-case-studies/a-multi-agent-approach-to-electric-power-systems
23. Yan, X.W., Shi, L.B., Yao, L.Z., Ni, Y.X., Bazargan, M.: A multi-agent based autonomous decentralized framework for power system restoration. In: 2014 International Conference on Power System Technology (POWERCON), pp. 871–876, October 2014
24. Zoka, Y., Yorino, N., Watanabe, M., Kurushima, T.: An optimal decentralized control for voltage control devices by means of a multi-agent system. In: 2014 Power Systems Computation Conference, Wroclaw, pp. 1–8 (2014). doi:10.1109/PSCC.2014.7038469. http://ieeexplore.ieee.org/stamp/stamp.jsp?tp=&arnumber=7038469&isnumber=7038098

Spatial Real-Time Price Competition in the Dynamic Spectrum Access Markets

Marcel Vološin[1]($\boxtimes$), Juraj Gazda[1], Peter Drotár[1], Gabriel Bugár[2], and Vladimír Gazda[3]

[1] Department of Computers and Informatics, Technical University of Kosice, Košice, Slovakia
marcel.volosin@student.tuke.sk, {juraj.gazda,peter.drotar}@tuke.sk
[2] Department of Electronics and Multimedia Communications, Technical University of Kosice, Košice, Slovakia
gabriel.bugar@tuke.sk
[3] Department of Finance, Technical University of Kosice, Košice, Slovakia
vladimir.gazda@tuke.sk

Abstract. We present the agent-based model of the real-time spectrum trading market. Real-time means that the frequency spectrum is allocated to the operators in real-time and thus, the capacities of the operators are dynamically varying. The agent-based model consists of the two levels. The first level (the wholesale market) deals with the spectrum distribution towards the operators, where the operators compete for the spectrum resources. The second level (the retail market) presents the place where the operators compete with each-other to provide their services to the end-users. In our model, the operators are assumed to be heterogeneous in terms of the quality of service (QoS) perception. The heterogeneity of the operators exists due to the different placement of their base-stations (BTSs) in the investigated region. The BTS in the middle of the region is naturally favored, because of the unique spectral efficiency it provides to the end-users. We numerically analyze the volumes of the frequency spectra purchased by the operators, average revenue and the retail price of the operators under the consideration of three different pricing mechanisms.

Keywords: Agent-based modelling · Dynamic spectrum access · Retail market · Spatial competition · Wholesale market

1 Introduction

The mobile Internet market shows strong evidence of the rapid traffic growth due to the increased demand from the side of the legacy and emerging network services. This is actually the fundamental motivation of the recent technological and legislative movement towards the application of the *dynamic spectrum access* (DSA) technique. The standard regulatory entities have the strong intention to

© Springer International Publishing AG 2017
N. Criado Pacheco et al. (Eds.): EUMAS 2016/AT 2016, LNAI 10207, pp. 217–229, 2017.
DOI: 10.1007/978-3-319-59294-7_18

support the roll-out of this mechanisms in order to intensify the growth and the efficiency of the mobile spectrum market [1].

Within DSA scope, two types of spectrum market model can be recognized, i.e. primary and secondary market [2]. In the former case, the spectrum usage is licensed mainly in the long-term (months, years), while in the latter case, the available spectrum can be distributed in an extremely short time scale (minutes, hours) in order to accommodate the end-users' demand. With the increased granularity of the Internet traffic, specially the secondary markets raises its importance. There exist many research [3–5] suggesting the adaptive and flexible dynamically varying secondary spectrum market regimes that are aligned with the prerequisites of the regulators to guide the evolution of the market mechanism.

Existing models of wireless access markets can be classified into two general categories, the bottom-up and top-down models, respectively [6]. The bottom-up approaches model each entity, and its interactions with other participating entities at a granular level of detail. Moreover the entities are characterized by the bounded rationality when dealing with their decisions [7]. The emergence of macroscopic observable properties, i.e. global consequences of the microscopic behavior and interactions are frequently studied withing the Agent-Based modelling systems. This class of the models designed to the analysis of the spectrum markets efficiency were implemented successfully in various cases, i.e. the enhancement of the spectrum utilization by allowing the incumbent users to further lease the spectrum to the other entities) [8], the price dynamics in a competitive spectrum market [9], the efficiency of the brokerage mechanism, auction based approach and direct trading [10], determination of the network utilization load whereby the economic impacts significantly affect the market economy [11] and economic efficiency together with the level of the tax distortion [12].

There exist multiple agent-based papers dealing with the techno-economic analysis of the markets. For instance, the cited smart grid market has received attention lately from the agent community [13,14]. This paper presents the agent-based spectrum trading model, which studies the competition of five secondary operators competing to serve a common pool of end-users. The operators dynamically lease the spectrum from the spectrum owner (e.g. state) on the wholesale market, and then compete to sell the frequency resource on the retail market to maximize their individual revenues. The operator's choice regarding the amount of the frequency spectrum is governed by the application of the reinforcement comparison. On the retail market, we examine the application of the three previously reviewed pricing strategies (trial-and-error [15], successful-ratio strategy [11] and linear-reward strategy [9]). We consider the 2-stage agent-based model with incomplete information (i.e. rationally bounded agents) to study the operators' investment and pricing decisions as well as the interactions between the operators and the end-users. In the model, we follow Hotelling principle [16], which is usually used to model the distribution of consumers in the linear region. Here, the mass of the end-users is uniformly located within the coverage of each operators' base-station (BTS). Each end-user inelastically demands one unit of frequency spectra and purchases from the operator that charges the lowest price for the given Quality-of-Service (QoS).

So far, little attention has been paid to the role of the economy and pricing in spatial competition among the operators with variable spectrum bandwidth providing the wireless services to the stochastic number of the end-users. In this paper, we focus on the investigation on the impact of the various pricing strategies on the spectrum market efficiency (in terms of the operator's average profit). We also examine the role of the competition among the operators, where exists the operator with the most feasible BTS coverage region, while those located at the edge of the linear region are characterized by the effective-coverage penalty.

2   System Model

The system diagram and corresponding interacting entities are shown in Fig. 1. In the model we consider the spectrum owner, which is commonly represented by the state, 5 operators dynamically leasing the frequency spectrum on the wholesale market and set of the end-users that are placed in the linear region following the Hotelling spatial distribution. Note that there is no interference between overlapping effective regions of the operators' network since they are operated on different spectra, i.e., the interweave heterogeneous networks architecture [17]. The spectrum leasing price, denoted by p, is set by the spectrum owner (e.g. state). Within the simulation scope, we pose rather relaxing assumption regarding the fixed price for the frequency unit on the wholesale market. In real scenario, the price can vary based on the instantaneous demand for the spectrum occurring on the retail market. However, in order to focus on the competition of the operators on the retail market, we keep the wholesale price as fixed. Thus, there are two distinct markets, the wholesale market, in which spectrum owner offers network resources to service providers, and a retail market, in which service providers offer mobile communications to end-users.

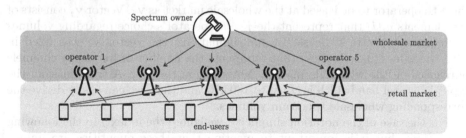

Fig. 1. Real-time secondary spectrum market network and the corresponding entities

2.1   Wholesale Spectrum Market

At time slot t, the operator leases the frequency spectrum from the owner, which corresponds to the expected total amount of frequency spectrum utilized by the end-users in the retail market. Here we can see some analogy with restructured electricity markets. By contrast, existing mobile communications markets create an oligopoly structure in which a few mobile network operators offer mobile communications directly to users. This structure, much like the monopoly utility structure of old, limits competition among service providers.

In order to create the vital wholesale spectrum market, we decided to look for the inspiration in the smart grid electricity systems. The authors in [18] used reinforcement learning allowing the service providers to learn the behavior of the electricity network and the change of retail-price to make an optimal pricing decision in the retail market. However it should be noted when dealing with the wholesale spectrum trading model there are certain differences that should be emphasized: (1) spectrum goods have a nonstorable character; (2) postponing its consumption is impossible (consumption runs in real time). These facts makes the situation with the wholesale spectrum trading more simplified compared to the traditional wholesale electricity market. The traditional Markov decision problem (MDP) could be successfully reduced to one state (under the assumption that the spectrum consumption can not be postponed), which resemblances typical multi-armed bandit problem. In our model the particular arms of the bandit are represented by the volumes of the frequency spectra purchased on the wholesale market by the operator.

There exist several heuristics methods capturing distinct ideas on handling the exploration/exploitation trade-off in solving typical multi-armed bandit problem. In this paper we decided to use reinforcement comparison [19] method that maintains a distribution over actions which is not computed directly from the empirical means. These methods also maintain an average expected reward $\bar{r}(t)$. The probability of selecting an arm (frequency spectrum chunk) is computed by comparing its empirical mean with $\bar{r}(t)$. The probability will be increased if it is above average, and decreased otherwise.

The spectrum owner offers N frequency channels at the wholesale market. Now, let us define the k-size vector of the available frequency spectrum chunks of the j-th operator to be leased at the wholesale market as $\mathbf{v}_j$. Vector $\mathbf{v}_j$ consists of the elements $v_j(i)$ that represent the $j-th$ operator's choice regarding volumes of frequency spectra to lease. In our simulations, the vector $\mathbf{v}_j$ was filled in with the values $[0, 2, \ldots, \frac{1}{2}N]$ that represents the number of frequency channels purchased on the wholesale market. Note that in the LTE-A transmission, the typical channel bandwidth is equal to 180 kHz and thus, we can easily derive the corresponding wholesale spectrum volumes.

For the sake of the notation simplicity, we ignore the index j in the following expressions, but it is important to mention that these quantities are unique for each operator. The algorithm maintains a set of preferences, $\pi_i(t)$, for each possible choice of the operator (i.e. for $v(i)$). At each turn $t = 1, 2, \ldots$, the probability $p_i(t)$ is computed using a Boltzmann distribution based on these preferences:

$$p_i(t) = \frac{\exp^{\pi_i(t)}}{\sum_{j=1}^{k} \exp^{\pi_j(t)}}. \tag{1}$$

If $v(i)(t)$ is played at turn t, and reward $r(t)$ is received, the preference is updated as:

$$\pi_{i(t)}(t+1) = \pi_{i(t)}(t) + \beta(r(t) - \bar{r}(t)). \tag{2}$$

Also at every turn, the mean of the rewards is updated as:

$$\bar{r}(t+1) = (1-\alpha)\bar{r}(t) + \alpha r(t). \tag{3}$$

Here, α is the step-size parameter that controls the weight of the mean reference update.

Without going into details of supply dynamics, the reward $r(t)$ is equal to the gross profit of the operator's total revenue minus the cost of goods sold. In our model, the cost of goods are represented by the total expenses spent on the wholesale market (which is directly related to the amount of the leased frequency spectrum) and the total revenue is the profit achieved in the retail market due to providing of the services to the end-users.

2.2   Retail Spectrum Market

We consider a limited geographical region in which the distribution of the end-users follow Hotelling distribution. Five operators provide services to the users within specified region. Each operator has just one BTS throughout the region, however each has different effective coverage region, according to its placement. We assume that the available bandwidth of the operators is finite and that all sessions established between the users and the operators are of variable duration.

The model presented here is developed from the concept of utility function that has been widely used in the recent literature. The idea is to employ this concept derived from micro-economics [8] to mathematically depict the QoS degree perceived by the users. We assume that a utility function U maps some quality related-parameter r, $0 \le r \le \infty$ onto an interval of real numbers. Here, we assume that QoS is given by the spectrum efficiency of the end-user-operator pair, thus this parameter should be included in the end-user utility function (higher spectrum efficiency of end-user-operator pair results in higher utility).

Let us define the spectrum efficiency of the transmission between ith end-user with respect to jth operator as:

$$r_{i,j} = \log_2\left[1 + \frac{P_s}{N_0}\left(\frac{d_{i,j}}{L/4}\right)^{-2}\right], \tag{4}$$

where P_s is the signal power, N_0 is the additive white Gaussian noise (AWGN) variance, $d_{i,k}$ is the distance between the i-th end-user and k-th base station and L is the total length of the linear region ($L = 1000\,\text{m}$ in our simulation setup). We set $P_s = 2N_0$, which guarantees the end-user a Signal-to-Noise ratio (SNR), $SNR = 3\,\text{dB}$ at the distance of $L/4 = 250\,\text{m}$ from the operator's BTS.

The utility of ith end-user with respect to jth operator is defined then as the mapping $U_{i,j} : \mathbb{R}_0^+ \rightarrow \langle 0, 1 \rangle$:s

$$U_{i,j} = e^{-\alpha\left(\frac{1}{r_{i,j}}\right)^{\beta}}. \tag{5}$$

In our model, the main focus is paid to the capacity of the network. The operators purchase the limited (and variable) number of the available frequency channels on the wholesale market and then, aim to maximize his total revenue by selling the frequency resources on the retail market. Thus, it seems necessary to measure the utility of the end-users jointly with the role of pricing from the operators perspective. Here, the perception of the service for the end-users is remarkably different if the price is increased (reduced). In practice, end-users are satisfied with the service if both quality and price paid are considered as acceptable [20].

From the above given discussion it seems reasonable to assign to each end-user an acceptance probability $\mathcal{A}_{i,j}$, for which we emphasize the dependence on QoS (through the utility U) and the paid price p. Thus, the acceptance probability of the i-th end-user to accept the offer of the j-th operator is a function of price p and utility U variables, defined as a mapping $\mathcal{A}_{i,j} : \langle 0, 1 \rangle^2 \to \langle 0, 1 \rangle$, which can be expressed as:

$$\mathcal{A}_{i,j}(U_{i,j}, p_{i,j}) = 1 - e^{-cU_{i,j}^{\delta}(1-p_{i,j})^{\gamma}}, \tag{6}$$

where $\delta, \gamma \geq 0$ are the parameters of sensitivity of the end-user to both, the utility and the price, respectively.

2.3   Price Adaptation Process

The pricing strategy is the fundamental component of the gross operator's total revenue. In our model, we distinguish among three different strategies (trial-and-error, successful-ratio and linear-reward strategy), which description is given in this section.

Trial-and-Error Strategy. When the spectrum demand functions are unknown and varying over time, possible solution to maximize the revenue of the operator is to continuously adjust the spectrum price based on the observed cumulative profit. Simple method to achieve this is the trial-and-error procedure as proposed in [21]. In the trial-and-error approach, the prices are generated stochastically and tried out for a given period of time. If profit of the operator is improved after the adoption of a new price, that price is taken. Otherwise the operator reverts back to the previous price and the whole process continues.

Successful-Ratio Strategy. The formula was recently proposed in [12]. Here, the price of i-th operator is dynamically adjusted in each time period. The price p_i is adaptively accommodated as follows:

$$p_i = p_{i,-1} + (\Psi_{i,-1} - 0.5) \cdot \mu, \tag{7}$$

where p_i is the channel price of the ith operator in a current period and $\Psi_{i,-1}$ is the acceptance ratio of the ith operator price in the previous period, ($\Psi_{i,-1} \in [0,1]$). Parameter μ is the price change shaping parameter. In the price adaptation process, price evolution is dependent on the average acceptance of the offered price by the end-users as follows:

$$\Psi_i = \begin{cases} 1/2 & (BW_{avail,i} = 0) \wedge (S_i = 0) \\ 0 & (BW_{avail,i} > 0) \wedge (S_i = 0) \\ \dfrac{S_i^{idle->conn}}{S_i} & (BW_{avail,i} > 0) \wedge (S_i > 0), \end{cases} \qquad (8)$$

where S_i represents the number of the end-users that maximize their acceptance probability $\mathcal{A}_i$ presuming to connect to ith operator. $BW_{avail,i}$ is the number of unoccupied frequency channels of ith operator and $S_i^{idle->conn}$ is the number of end-users accepting the offer by connecting to i-th operator. Note that the agent's acceptance decision has a probabilistic character determined by the end-user's acceptance probability and thus, $S_i^{idle->conn} \leq S_i$. The pricing definition formulated in (7) ensures that the operators establish the price in the given time frame based on their previous experience with the end-user price acceptance and simultaneously, formula offers smooth price evolution.

Linear-Reward Strategy. This strategy was introduced in [9] for the application in the dynamic spectrum agile markets. We have modified it to be used in the 2-level game, taking into account the cumulative profit resulting from the interaction on both, the retail and wholesale market, respectively.

The operators have a finite price level. Let $p_{i,j}, j \in [0, m_i]$ be the m_i price candidate for the i-th operator. Then the strategy for seller i is defined to be a probability vector $\mathbf{p}_i = [p_{i,1}, \ldots, p_{i,m_i}]^T$, where the operator i chooses action $a_{i,j}$ with probability $p_{i,j}$. The algorithm of the gradual price adaptation can be described as follows:

- Define the initial probability vector $\mathbf{p}_i(0)$ for each operator
- At every time instant t, the operator chooses the action $a_{i,j}$ related to the probability vector $\mathbf{p}_i$ stochastically.
- The operator receives the profit, which is interpreted in our model as the difference between the revenue achieved in the retail market and the total expenses spent for the spectrum resources in the wholesale market.
- Each operator updates the action probability vector according to the rule:

$$p_{i,j}(k+1) = p_{i,j}(k) - \eta u_i(k) p_{i,j}(k) \qquad a(k) \neq p_{i,j}, \qquad (9)$$

$$p_{i,j}(k+1) = p_{i,j}(k) + \eta u_i(k) \sum_{s \neq j} p_{i,s}(k) \qquad a(k) = p_{i,j}, \qquad (10)$$

$$i = 1, \ldots, N, j = 1, \ldots, m_i, \qquad (11)$$

where η is the step size parameter and u_i is normalized profit of the ith operator.
- The algorithm stops, when there are no incremental changes of the probability vector $\mathbf{p}_i$ between the iterations.

3   Agent-Based Implementation of the Model

The pseudo-codes of the retail-activities of the end-users and operators are described in this section. Note that the wholesale market consists solely of distributing the available frequency resources across all operators according to reinforcement comparison (see Eq. 1) and thus is for the sake of clarity omitted here and the focus is paid on the retail-market activities.

Operator. The behavior of the agent representing the operator consists of two main operations: request processing and price adaptation. Request processing is carried out via a request queue, in which all incoming requests from the end-users are stored until they are processed by the operator in the order in which they arrived. The operator receives three types of requests from the end-users: $PRICE$ requests, $CONNECTION$ requests and $REMOVAL$ requests. A $PRICE$ request is handled by sending an actual price for a frequency channel to the sender of the request, but only if the available bandwidth BW_{AVAIL} is non-zero (otherwise the BTS is not capable of accepting more end-users). Provided the end-user accepts the price offer, it sends the CONNECTION request to the operator. When the connection is finished and end-user has no willingness to use the operator's services, it sends the REMOVAL request to the operator. The detailed operator's actions are described in the following pseudo-code Algorithm 1.

Algorithm 1. The operator request processing (performed continuously)

1: **for all** Operators **do**
2:     **while** request queue is not empty **do**
3:         take the oldest request
4:         identify the *sender*
5:         identify the *request_type*
6:         **if** *request_type* $==$ $PRICE$ **then**
7:             **if** $BW_{avail} > 0$ **then**
8:                 Send *price* to *sender*
9:             **else**
10:                 Send N/A to *sender*
11:             **end if**
12:         **else if** *request_type* $==$ $CONNECTION$ **then**
13:             allocate a free channel to *sender*
14:             $BW_{avail} \leftarrow BW_{avail} - 1$
15:             ACK to *sender*
16:         **else if** *request_type* $==$ $REMOVAL$ **then**
17:             free the channel allocated to *sender*
18:             $BW_{avail} \leftarrow BW_{avail} + 1$
19:             ACK to *sender*
20:         **end if**
21:     **end while**
22: **end for**

End-User. The agent of the end-user can take one of three internal states – *IDLE*, *ACTIVE* or *CONNECTED*. In the *IDLE* state, the agent is inactive and transmits/receives no signal. In each time step, the end-user can be randomly switched to the *ACTIVE* state with a probability P_{act} and it starts the spectrum trading process by sending a request to each operator. Based on the price offered by each operator and the corresponding utility, the end-user decides whether to connect to one of the operators (and switch to the *CONNECTED* state) or return to the *IDLE* state to repeat the same process in the next time step. Moreover, when the operator is in the *CONNECTED* state in a particular time step, the operator disconnects (switches to the *IDLE* state) with the probability P_{disc} or remains in the *CONNECTED* state with the probability $1 - P_{disc}$. Again, the detailed pseudo-code of the end-user interactions is given in Algorithm 2.

Algorithm 2. Decision process of the end-user repeated in each time step

---

1: **for all** end-users **do**
2:    **if** *state* $==$ *CONNECTED* **then**
3:       **if** $uniform(0, 1) < P_{disc}$ **then**
4:          End-user disconnects
5:          *state* $\leftarrow$ *IDLE*
6:       **else**
7:          End-user remains *CONNECTED*
8:       **end if**
9:    **else**
10:       **if** $uniform(0, 1) < P_{act}$ **then**
11:          *state* $\leftarrow$ *ACTIVE*
12:          **for all** Operators **do**
13:             End-user sends price request to j operator
14:             End-user calculates U_j
15:             End-user calculates $A_j(U_j, p_j)$
16:          **end for**
17:          $j^* \leftarrow \underset{j}{arg\ max}(A_j)$ (j^* is the index of the operator providing maximum A)
18:          **if** $uniform(0, 1) < AP_{j^*}$ **then**
19:             End-user connects to operator$_{j^*}$
20:          **else**
21:             *state* $\leftarrow$ *IDLE*
22:          **end if**
23:       **else**
24:          *state* $\leftarrow$ *IDLE*
25:       **end if**
26:    **end if**
27: **end for**

---

4   Results

The agent-based simulations were conducted in Netlogo [22]. Moreover, the RNetLogo package delivers an interface to embed the agent-based modeling platform NetLogo into R environment and thus, all statistics were exported and evaluated in R. The parameters of the agent-based simulation are summarized in Table 1. The simulation framework consisted of 100000 simulation periods for each spectrum pricing method. Within one simulation session, we eliminated the first 15 000 periods to ignore the non-stationary development (transient state of the model) of the performance characteristics caused by initial parameter setting.

In the Fig. 2a we can see the average volumes of the frequency channels traded on the wholesale market. Our assumptions were confirmed, since the operator with central BTS purchases the highest volumes of the channels. The operators located at the edge of the investigated region are naturally penalized and their volumes are significantly lower. Applying the linear-reward on the retail market results in the highest volumes of the purchased channels on the wholesale market, followed by the successful-ratio and trial-end-error strategies. Figure 2b illustrates the revenue of the owner of the frequency spectrum when different pricing strategies are applied on the retail market. As we can see, the spectrum owner's revenue reaches the maximum, when the linear-reward strategy is applied on the retail market.

Table 1. Table of parameters

Parameter	Value	Description
L	$L = 1000\,m$	Length of the investigated region
$N_{operators}$	5	Number of the operators
N_{end_users}	250	Number of the end users
P_{act}	0.35	Probability of activation
P_{disc}	0.2	Probability of disconnection
α	0.2	Price shaping parameter
β	2	Price shaping parameter
γ	0.0001	Price sensitivity of the end-user
δ	2	Utility sensitivity of the end-user
c	4	Coefficient of the acceptance probability
μ	0.2	Price-learning parameter (successful-ratio strategy)
η	0.001	Price-learning parameter (linear-reward strategy)
N	100	Number of the frequency channels to be leased on the wholesale market
p	0.3	Wholesale price
α	0.1	Parameter of the reinforcement comparison algorithm
β	0.1	Parameter of the reinforcement comparison algorithm

Figure 2c investigates the average prices occurring on the retail market. Here, we need to pay our attention to the case, when the linear-reward strategy is used. Interestingly, the prices are significant higher compared to the other pricing strategies and moreover, we do not see any relevant differences among the prices of the central and boardening operators. This is not confirmed when applying remaining pricing strategies, where the central operator applies significantly higher prices compared to the other, less favorable situated operators. The situation with the linear-reward function suggests that the price increase is the result of the spontaneously formed oligopoly situation of the operators. This is perceived here as an emergent phenomenon identifiable via the price effects. An oligopoly is a market form in which a market or industry is dominated by a small number of sellers (oligopolists). Oligopolies can result from various forms of collusion which reduce competition and lead to higher prices for consumers [23].

Due to the formation of the oligopoly market, the profits of the operators are also increased. This fact is confirmed in the Fig. 2d, where we can observe that the operators' profit dominates in the scenario, when the linear-reward pricing strategy is applied. In this case, the successful-ratio strategy performs the worst and we can observe significant gaps in the operator's revenue when comparing it with other pricing strategies.

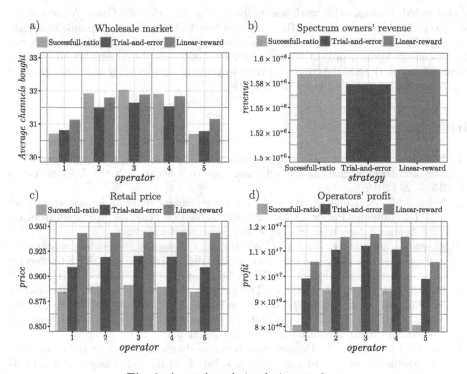

Fig. 2. Agent-based simulation results

5 Conclusions

In this paper, we implemented the 2-level agent-based model of DSA market, where we distinguished between the wholesale and retail market. On the wholesale market, the operators compete to get the demanded frequency spectrum channel that maximize their long-term revenue. In this case, we formulated the competition on the wholesale market as the typical multi-armed bandit problem, where we applied conventional reinforcement comparison technique. On the other hand, the operators on the retail market compete with their services to attract the end-user demand. Three different pricing mechanisms were implemented in order to shed the light on the mutual interactions of the agents (operators) on both, the wholesale and retail market, respectively. The operator localized in the center of the investigated region is capable of attracting the largest mass of the end-users and to generate the highest revenue. It should be noted though that we observed the emergence phenomena resulting from the agents interaction, which is the formulation of the oligopoly market when the linear-reward pricing strategy is applied. Further discussion regarding the oligopoly practices in DSA needs detailed investigation, which will be the subject of the study in our follow-up work.

Acknowledgments. This work was supported by the Scientific Grant Agency of the Ministry of Education, Science, Research and Sport of the Slovak Republic under the contract No. 1/0766/14. This work was also supported by the Slovak Research and Development Agency, project number APVV-15-0055 and by European intergovernmental framework COST Action CA15140: Improving Applicability of Nature-Inspired Optimisation by Joining Theory and Practice.

References

1. Wallsten, S.: Is there really a spectrum crisis? Disentangling the regulatory, physical, and technological factors affecting spectrum license value. Inf. Econ. Policy **35**, 7–29 (2016)
2. Peha, J.M., Panichpapiboon, S.: Real-time secondary markets for spectrum trading. Telecommun. Policy **28**(78), 603–618 (2004). A selection of papers from the 31st Annual Telecommunications Policy Research Conference
3. Zheng, L., Joe-Wong, C., Tan, C.W., Ha, S., Chiang, M.: Secondary markets for mobile data: feasibility and benefits of traded data plans. In: 2015 IEEE Conference on Computer Communications (INFOCOM), pp. 1580–1588. IEEE (2015)
4. Pan, M., Li, M., Li, P., Fang, Y.: The network architecture for spectrum trading. In: Pan, M., et al. (eds.) Spectrum Trading in Multi-Hop Cognitive Radio Networks. SpringerBriefs in Electrical and Computer Engineering, pp. 1–9. Springer, Heidelberg (2015). doi:10.1007/978-3-319-25631-3_1
5. Shi, G., Liu, Y., Mu, X.: Cooperative spectrum sharing in cognitive radio networks: a centralized contracted-based approach. Int. J. Multimed. Ubiquit. Eng. **11**(3), 351–360 (2016)
6. Fortetsanakis, G., Papadopouli, M.: On multi-layer modeling and analysis of wireless access markets. IEEE Trans. Mob. Comput. **14**(1), 113–125 (2015)
7. Conlisk, J.: Why bounded rationality? J. Econ. Lit. **34**(2), 669–700 (1996)
8. Tonmukayakul, A., Weiss, M.B.: A study of secondary spectrum use using agent-based computational economics. NETNOMICS Econ. Res. Electron. Netw. **9**(2), 125–151 (2008)
9. Xing, Y., Chandramouli, R., Cordeiro, C.: Price dynamics in competitive agile spectrum access markets. IEEE J. Sel. Areas Commun. **25**(3), 613–621 (2007)

10. Yoon, H., Hwang, J., Weiss, M.B.: An analytic research on secondary-spectrum trading mechanisms based on technical and market changes. Comput. Netw. **56**(1), 3–19 (2012)
11. Pastirčák, J., Friga, L., Kováč, V., Gazda, J., Gazda, V.: An agent-based economy model of real-time secondary market for the cognitive radio networks. J. Netw. Syst. Manag. **24**(2), 427–443 (2015)
12. Gazda, J., Kováč, V., Tóth, P., Drotár, P., Gazda, V.: Tax optimization in an agent-based model of real-time spectrum secondary market. Telecommun. Syst. **64**, 1–16 (2016)
13. Karnouskos, S., De Holanda, T.N.: Simulation of a smart grid city with software agents. In: Third UKSim European Symposium on Computer Modeling and Simulation, EMS 2009, pp. 424–429. IEEE (2009)
14. Gomez-Sanz, J.J., Garcia-Rodriguez, S., Cuartero-Soler, N., Hernandez-Callejo, L.: Reviewing microgrids from a multi-agent systems perspective. Energies **7**(5), 3355–3382 (2014)
15. Sairamesh, J., Kephart, J.O.: Price dynamics and quality in information markets. Decis. Support Syst. **28**(1), 35–47 (2000)
16. Grønnevet, G.A., Hansen, B., Reme, B.-A.: Spectrum policy and competition in mobile data. Inf. Econ. Policy **37**, 34–41 (2016)
17. Sharma, S.K., Chatzinotas, S., Ottersten, B.: Interference alignment for spectral coexistence of heterogeneous networks. EURASIP J. Wirel. Commun. Netw. **2013**(1), 1–14 (2013)
18. Kim, B.-G., Zhang, Y., van der Schaar, M., Lee, J.-W.: Dynamic pricing for smart grid with reinforcement learning. In: 2014 IEEE Conference on Computer Communications Workshops (INFOCOM WKSHPS), pp. 640–645. IEEE (2014)
19. Kaelbling, L.P., Littman, M.L., Moore, A.W.: Reinforcement learning: a survey. J. Artif. Intell. Res. **4**, 237–285 (1996)
20. Georgilakis, P.S., Orfanos, G.A., Hatziargyriou, N.D.: Computer-assisted interactive learning for teaching transmission pricing methodologies. IEEE Trans. Power Syst. **29**(4), 1972–1980 (2014)
21. Yang, H., Meng, Q., Lee, D.-H.: Trial-and-error implementation of marginal-cost pricing on networks in the absence of demand functions. Transp. Res. Part B: Methodol. **38**(6), 477–493 (2004)
22. Tisue, S., Wilensky, U.: NetLogo: a simple environment for modeling complexity. In: International Conference on Complex Systems, Boston, MA, vol. 21, pp. 16–21 (2004)
23. Frank, R.H., Glass, A.J.: Microeconomics and Behavior. McGraw-Hill, New York (1991)

Using Automated Approximate Satisfaction in Parameter Search for Dynamic Agent Models

Jan Treur[(✉)]

Behavioural Informatics Group, Vrije Universiteit Amsterdam,
Amsterdam, The Netherlands
j.treur@vu.nl

Abstract. Numerical agent models often include a number of parameters. The values of such parameters are usually determined by using some numerical parameter tuning method based on numerical empirical data. However, in many cases no numerical empirical data are available, but properties for dynamic patterns are known that should be fulfilled, as requirements. Classical numerical parameter tuning methods normally cannot work with such dynamic properties, as they can only be true or false. To remedy this, in this paper the notion of approximate satisfaction of dynamic properties is introduced. It adds a numerical measure to the logical notion of satisfaction. By doing this, numerical optimization methods for parameter estimation become applicable to support the design of dynamic agent models for which dynamic properties have been specified as requirements.

1 Introduction

To model cognitive or social processes, often dynamic agent models are used, for example, expressed by numerical relations such as difference or differential equations; e.g., [13, 17]. A model description usually is based on (assumed) local mechanisms for a process which describe how specific states within a process interact. As an example, a mechanism can be modelled for the process that activation of a sensory representation state for some stimulus s makes that as a response a preparation state for some action a is activated. From a number of such local mechanisms the dynamic patterns of the overall process or behavior emerge, for example, showing that the action a is performed after sensing stimulus s.

A modeler may work from different viewpoints. One viewpoint is that the local mechanisms are known and incorporated in the model, but the types of patterns that may emerge from them are not known. Then by simulation experiments for different characteristics, as represented by settings for initial values, parameter values, and input from the environment, such emergent patterns can be explored. For example, the agent shows action a after sensing stimulus s. Subsequently it can be investigated whether such patterns are realistic in the sense that they also occur in the real world. If they actually do occur, this contributes to validation of the model.

N. Criado Pacheco et al. (Eds.): EUMAS 2016/AT 2016, LNAI 10207, pp. 230–247, 2017.
DOI: 10.1007/978-3-319-59294-7_19

Another viewpoint is that not only knowledge on the local mechanisms is available at forehand and incorporated in the model, but also at least some behavioural patterns are known at forehand, for which it is assumed that they occur in the real world. For example, it is known that the occurrence of stimulus s always leads to a response a. In this case dynamic properties describing such patterns can serve as a kind of requirements for the model. The model will not be considered satisfactory when it cannot generate these patterns for at least some of the characteristics (settings for initial values, parameter values, and input from the environment). In an informal sense often requirements play a role in a modeling process: what behavior is the model expected to show? However, in modeling such requirements usually are kept rather informal. Such dynamic properties can play a role in a modelling process similar to the role of requirements in a more general context within a software engineering process, as a way of focusing the design process on what the system being developed is expected to provide. In the example, the focus can be on mechanisms realizing a causal path from stimulus s to action a: a mechanism for internally representing a sensed stimulus, a mechanism for triggering action preparation from stimulus representations, and a mechanism for action execution from an action preparation state.

For specification of such (required) dynamic properties in a more formal manner, temporal logical languages have been developed, in which also numbers can be incorporated; e.g., [8, 10–12, 18]. When the model does generate the patterns described by the requirements for certain settings, this can be considered *verification* of the model with respect to the requirements. When these requirements themselves are known to correspond to patterns observed in the real world (validation of the requirements) and when the model in turn was found to satisfy the requirements, via them validation of the model is obtained.

Models usually have to take into account a number of characteristics of the situation that is modelled. Such characteristics can involve, for example, specific quantities describing the mental or neurological structures of a person (for example, the strength of the association between sensory representation of s and preparation for a), or the structure of a social network, or contextual elements of the external world. Usually in a computational model parameters are used to represent such characteristics. The advantage of having such parameters in a model is that they enable to use and tune the model for different situations: for example, for persons with different mental or neurological structures, for different social networks, or for different contextual elements in the external world. In fact, the model represents a large space of possibilities indicated by all combinations of values of the parameters, in addition to the initial values and input from the environment over time.

For one given specific situation at hand the parameters have to be assigned values that represent that situation: by finding such values, knowledge of the specific characteristics of the situation is acquired. However, such a tuning to specific characteristics is not always easy, as often a situation that is modelled does not simply show these characteristics. They have to be acquired or estimated. To support this, numerical parameter estimation methods are available; e.g., [2, 16]. They assume that empirical numerical values for state variables of the model are given and they optimise parameter values of the model by minimising a numerical error measure for the deviation of the state variables of the model from these empirical values. These empirical values serve as a specific type of requirements for the model. However, such measurable empirical values are not always easy to obtain. The existing parameter estimation methods cannot handle other types of requirements, as usually no numerical error measures are known for them.

The approach introduced in this paper opens the possibility to use parameter estimation methods for any types of requirements by providing an error measure for the extent to which a requirement is (dis)satisfied. This error measure is based on the notion of approximate satisfaction introduced in this paper. This notion provides a bridge between two worlds or communities: between numerical methods (e.g., parameter estimation methods for dynamical models) and logical methods (e.g., satisfaction and verification of properties). Using approximate satisfaction enables to integrate logical methods and numerical methods.

In this paper, in Sect. 2 dynamic properties in conceptual and in numerical-logical representations are briefly introduced; more details can be found in Appendix A [20]. In Sects. 3 and 4 the notions of satisfaction and approximate satisfaction are introduced. In Sect. 5 it is discussed how this can be used in heuristic parameter search for a dynamic model.

2 Dynamic Properties

Dynamic properties can be expressed in different manners and types of representation, from conceptual representations to more formal representations. In Appendix A [20] a more detailed description of dynamic properties is presented. Here only a brief summary is included. A numerical dynamical model for which dynamic properties are considered is assumed to describe a number of states X over time by state variables for these states; for example, in such a model $X(t)$ is used to denote the value of state X at time t, and $X(t + \Delta t) = X(t) + (...) \Delta t$ denotes a difference equation for state X, where $(...)$ is an expression in terms of one or a number of state values $Y(t)$. *Conceptual representations* of dynamic properties make use of (structured) natural language expressions. These expressions refer to a number of aspects: states (also called state variables), time points, relations between states and time points, state relations or state properties, temporal order relations between time points such as 'before' and 'after', 'later', logical relations such as 'when.., ..', 'and', 'or', 'not', 'eventually', 'always', 'never', 'during', 'for some time point', or 'for all time points'. An example of a conceptual representation of a dynamic property is:

> At any point in time t,
> when at t the sensory representation state for stimulus s has level ≥ 0.8,
> at some point in time $t' > t$ the preparation state for action a has level ≥ 0.7.

Formal *numerical-logical representations* of dynamic properties are expressed in a hybrid numerical-logical manner using a sorted temporal predicate logic in which sorts and expressions for numbers and (order and equality) relations between them are incorporated. Sorts are assumed to be finite and to only contain elements named by constants, which are denoted by nonitalic symbols. For real numbers, for example, this means that representations are assumed within some given finite interval and in a fixed number of digits. A sort TIME is used for time points (real numbers), a sort VALUE for values (real numbers), STATE and TRACE, each with the variable notations shown below and with standard equality relation =. Sorts TIME and VALUE are also equipped with an ordering relation < :

sort	TIME	VALUE	STATE	TRACE
variable	$t, t', t_1, t_2, \ldots$	$V, V_1, V_2, \ldots$	$X, Y, \ldots$	$tr, \ldots$

There are different, alternative ways to refer to values (see Table 2); two main categories are *functional* and *relational value indicators*. Two *functional* value indicators are: $X(t)$ for any constant for a state X, and any time expression t, and $V(tr, X, t)$, for any constant or variable for state X, trace tr, and any time expression t. Here for each state X, a unary function symbol $X(..)$ from TIME to VALUE is assumed, and one ternary function symbol $V(.., .., ..)$ from TRACExSTATExTIME to VALUE. Alternatively, relational value indicators can be used: has_value(X, t, V) for any constant or variable for a state X, time t and value V, or has_value_at(tr, X, t, V) for any constant or variable for a state X, trace tr, time expression t, and value V. Here has_value(..) is a relation on STATExTIMExVALUE and has_value_at(..) is a relation on TRACEx-STATExTIMExVALUE. Sometimes the expressions with explicit references to traces tr are called *reified*, in this case trace-reified. In Table 1 an overview is shown of some different types of value indicators.

Table 1. Value indicators

	Functional	Relational
plain	$X(t)$	has_value(X, t, V)
reified	$V(tr, X, t)$	has_value_at(tr, X, t, V) *or* holds (state(tr, t), has_value(X, V), true)

Here the relational representation holds (state(tr, t), has_value(X, V), true) (or the same with false) is one that may be considered for languages such as TTL (see also Sect. 5), situation calculus or event calculus. Note that in this expression has_value(X, V) is a term expression, not to be confused with the relational expression has_value(X, t, V). For reasons of transparency for a given dynamic property it is recommended to make a choice for one and the same type of value indicators. The advantage of using $X(t)$ is that it is most intuitive, as the same notation is often used to describe numerical dynamical models, for example, in the form of difference or differential equations. However, not all logical languages allow functions. Moreover, no variables over states or traces are possible using this representation, which limits the expressive power of the format. Two example formalizations of the earlier mentioned dynamic property by functional and relational value indicators, respectively, are:

$$\forall t_1 [\text{srs}_s(t_1) \geq 0.8 \rightarrow \exists t_2 [t_2 > t_1 \wedge \text{ps}_a(t_2) \geq 0.7]]$$
$$\forall t_1 [[\exists V_1 \text{has\_value\_at}(\underline{tr}, \text{srs}_s, t_1, V_1) \wedge V_1 \geq 0.8] \rightarrow$$
$$\exists t_2 [t_2 > t_1 \wedge [\exists V_2 \text{has\_value\_at}(\underline{tr}, \text{ps}_a, t_2, V_2) \wedge V_2 \geq 0.7]]]$$

Here srs$_s$ is the formalization of the sensory representation state of s and ps$_a$ of the preparation state for a. *Traces* are also expressed by numerical-logical representations. For example, assume that in trace $\underline{tr}$ the states srs$_s$ and ps$_a$ have the values at different time points shown in Table 2. Note that underlined nonitalic symbols are used for constants.

Table 2. Simple example trace

State\time	0	1	2	3	4	5	6
srs$_s$	0.1	0.3	0.6	0.75	0.84	0.85	0.85
ps$_a$	0	0.1	0.3	0.5	0.6	0.64	0.66

To represent a given trace, the 4-ary relation **trace**(.., .., .., ..) on TRACEx-STATExTIMExVALUE is used. Examples of information shown in Table 2 are formally represented as **trace**($\underline{tr}$, srs$_s$, 2, 0.6) **or trace**($\underline{tr}$, ps$_a$, 2, 0.3). A *trace* with name constant $\underline{tr}$ is represented as a set of instances (by name constants) of **trace**($\underline{tr}$, X, t, V) with the same first argument $\underline{tr}$. A *set of traces* $\mathcal{Tr}$ is represented as a set of instances of **trace**(tr, X, t, V).

3 Satisfaction of Dynamic Properties

For dynamic properties it can be checked whether they are satisfied in a given trace or set of traces; see Table 3. Such a checking method basically follows the notion of satisfaction relation in logic, or interpretation of a statement in an algebraic and/or relational structure (e.g., [7]). It can be described for dynamic properties using any type of value indicator. For the sake of simplicity and space limitation here it is shown only for the reified relational type of value indicator. In that case numerical expressions are generic numerical expressions such as $V_1 - V_2 \geq V_3$; once the variables have been instantiated, they can be evaluated in a generic manner simply by calculation of arithmetical relationships. Let $\mathcal{Tr}$ be a given set of traces represented by a set of instances of **trace**(tr, X, t, V). The canonical structure $\mathcal{S}(\mathcal{Tr})$ for $\mathcal{Tr}$ in which a closed (i.e., without free variables) dynamic property A is interpreted consists of a number of finite domains corresponding to sorts such as TRACE, TIME, STATE, VALUE, in which each element has a name constant; for example for the sort VALUE all real number representations in a fixed number of digits and between some lower and upper bound (for example, the interval [0, 1] in two digits) can be chosen, and similarly for the sort TIME. In addition, in this structure $\mathcal{S}(\mathcal{Tr})$ for these domains relations and functions are defined for the (symbols for) relations and functions in the language, such as has_value_at(...), and the ordering and arithmetical relations and functions used. Here the relation corresponding to has_value_at(...) is defined in $\mathcal{S}(\mathcal{Tr})$ to describe the information as given in the set of traces $\mathcal{Tr}$: an instance of the relation has_value_at(m, X, t, V) holds in $\mathcal{S}(\mathcal{Tr})$ iff the corresponding instance of **trace**(m, X, t, V) is included in the set of traces $\mathcal{Tr}$, or shortly:

has_value_at(tr, X, t, V) in $\mathcal{S}(\mathcal{Tr})$ iff **trace**(tr, X, t, V) $\in \mathcal{Tr}$

Table 3. Description of a checking method

Evaluation of formula		Evaluation of subformulae
1.	**eval**($A \wedge B$, true)	iff	**eval**(A, true) and **eval**(B, true)
2.	**eval**($A \vee B$, true)	iff	**eval**(A, true) or **eval**(B, true)
3.	**eval**($A \rightarrow B$, true)	iff	**eval**(A, false) or **eval**(B, true)
4.	**eval**($\neg A$, true)	iff	**eval**(A, false)
5.	**eval**($\forall V\, A$, true)	iff	**eval**(A, true) for all instances of V
6.	**eval**($\exists\, V\, A$, true)	iff	**eval**(A, true) for at least one instance of V
7.	**eval**($A \wedge B$, false)	iff	**eval**(A, false) or **eval**(B, false)
8.	**eval**($A \vee B$, false)	iff	both **eval**(A, false) and **eval**(B, false)
9.	**eval**($A \rightarrow B$, false)	iff	**eval**(A, true) and **eval**(B, false)
10.	**eval**($\neg A$, false)	iff	**eval**(A, true)
11.	**eval**($\forall V\, A$, false)	iff	**eval**(A, true) for at least one instance of V
12.	**eval**($\exists V\, A$, false)	iff	**eval**(A, false) for all instances of V
13.	**eval**(has_value_at(tr, X, t, V) true)	iff	**trace**(tr, X, t, V) $\in \mathcal{S}(\mathcal{T}\!\ast)$
14.	**eval**(has_value_at(tr, X, t, V), false)	iff	**trace**(tr, X, t, V) $\notin \mathcal{T}\!\ast$
15.	**eval**(gne, true)	iff	expression gne evaluates to true
16.	**eval**(gne, false)	iff	expression gne evaluates to false

The idea of checking a property A (represented as a logical formula) in this canonical structure $\mathcal{S}(\mathcal{T}\!\ast)$ is that the evaluation of whether A is true or false in $\mathcal{T}\!\ast$ (indicated by **eval**(A, true) or **eval**(A, false)) is reduced in a compositional manner to evaluating the truth of parts of the property (its sub-formulae) in the structure $\mathcal{T}\!\ast$. This can be done according to the scheme shown in Table 4 where A and B denote dynamic properties or parts thereof. Here V can indicate any variable tr, X, t, V, and gne denotes any generic numerical expression.

In an algorithmic sense a dynamic property can be checked by processing the scheme in a top down-manner, where each line is interpreted as a definition of a routine or procedure or method (with head or name in the left column) specified by calling one or two of the others (indicated in the right column), and returning a value true or false based on the outcomes of them. Note that all formulae involved are closed: they do not have free variables; when a quantifier is eliminated for the variable instances are substituted. Within the software environment of TTL [1, 15], such a checking method has been implemented.

Note that a slightly adapted variant of this algorithm is applicable as well for partial traces. In that case it may happen that neither **eval**(A, true) nor **eval**(A, false) can be found true, as in the set of traces basic information to decide this is lacking. So in that case three types of outcomes are possible:

eval(A, true)   is found true: A is true for $\mathcal{T}\!\ast$
eval(A, false)   is found true: A is false for $\mathcal{T}\!\ast$
neither **eval**(A, true) nor **eval**(A, false)   is found true: A is unknown for $\mathcal{T}\!\ast$

4 Approximate Satisfaction

Sometimes a dynamic property is not fulfilled in a trace or set of traces $\mathcal{T}\mathfrak{r}$, but in some sense it is not so far from a property that is fulfilled. In such a case the dynamic property may be considered to be approximately satisfied, and it can be useful if some measure can be determined expressing how far the property is from full fulfilment. A notion of approximate satisfaction can play an important role in heuristic methods to determine suitable values for parameters, as will be illustrated in Sect. 5.

The notion of approximate satisfaction can be defined in a precise manner as shown in this section. The idea is to find values for deviations for values of states at the time points relevant for the dynamic property so that this dynamic property is fulfilled if the values of the states at these relevant time points are changed by adding these deviation values to them. Before explaining the generic approach, as an example, consider dynamic property A:

$$\forall t_1 < 6[\exists V_1 \text{has\_value\_at}(\underline{tr}, \text{srs}_s, t_1, V_1) \land V_1 \land 0.8 \rightarrow$$
$$\exists t_2[t_2 > t_1 \exists[\exists V_2 \text{has\_value\_at}(\underline{tr}, \text{ps}_a, t_2, V_2) \land V_2 \geq 0.7]]]$$

In this dynamic property there are two state relations which can make it fail on a given trace $\underline{tr}$. For example, assume that trace $\underline{tr}$ is specified by Table 2 above (and the specifications shown under this table). Until time point 3, the implication holds in a trivial manner as the antecedent

$$\exists V_1 \text{has\_value\_at}(\underline{tr}, \text{srs}_s, t_1, V_1) \land V_1 \geq 0.8$$

is not fulfilled. However, from time point 4 on the antecedent holds, and therefore the consequent

$$\exists t_2[t_2 > t_1 \land [\exists V_2 \text{has\_value\_at}(\underline{tr}, \text{ps}_a, t_2, V_2) \land V_2 \geq 0.7]]$$

should also hold to have the property satisfied. But the consequent never holds, as the value of state ps_a becomes at most 0.66. Nevertheless, as 0.66 is only 0.04 under the required 0.7, in a sense the property almost holds: it holds approximately. How can such a notion of *approximate satisfaction* be defined for this case?

The Idea of Approximate Satisfaction
The idea is to allow for some deviations, by adding (small) *deviation values* D_1 and D_2 to the value variables V_1 and V_2 in numerical expressions (but not in the has_value(..) or has_value_at(..) atoms), and then check again. So property A is rewritten by the following substitutions within numerical expressions:

$$V_1 \implies V_1 + D_1$$

$$V_2 \implies V_2 + D_2$$

By this substitution the following dynamic property $A(D_1, D_2)$ with free deviation variables D_1 and D_2 of sort VALUE is obtained:

$$\forall t_1 < 6[\exists V_1 \text{has\_value\_at}(\underline{\text{tr}}, srs_s, t_1, V_1) \wedge V_1 + D_1 \geq 0.8 \rightarrow$$
$$\exists t_2 [t_2 > t_1 \wedge [\exists V_2 \text{has\_value\_at}(\underline{\text{tr}}, ps_a, t_2, V_2) \wedge V_2 + D_2 \geq 0.7]]]$$

By assuming that the absolute values of both D_1 and D_2 are at most equal to some (small) nonnegative value D indicating *maximal deviation*, from this property $A(D_1, D_2)$ the following property $A_{md}(D)$ can be obtained:

$$\exists D_1, D_2 [A(D_1, D_2) \wedge |D_1| \leq D \wedge |D_2| \leq D]$$

For the example trace $\underline{\text{tr}}$ shown in Table 1 this property $A_{md}(D)$ holds when D is chosen 0.04 (or higher).

A more general setup for this notion of approximate satisfaction is as follows. For each dynamic property A, it will be explained how a number of deviation variables $D_1,.., D_k$ of sort VALUE can be added, obtaining dynamic property $A(D_1,.., D_k)$. First, the idea of requiring the absolute deviations $|D_i|$ to be at most D is generalized by requiring some *aggregation* $c(D_1,.., D_k)$ of the deviations $D_1,.., D_k$ to be at most D. Here $c(D_1,.., D_k)$ is a *combination function* which aggregates the values of an arbitrary number k of deviations $D_1,.., D_k$ (which themselves can be positive, 0, or negative) into a nonnegative value.

Properties of Combination Functions

Nonnegative	$c(D_1, .., D_k) \geq 0$ for all $D_1, .., D_k$
Values 0 for all D_i iff the aggregation is 0	$D_i = 0$ for all $i \Leftrightarrow c(D_1, .., D_k) = 0$
Symmetric in its arguments	$c(D_1, .., D_k) = c(E_1, .., E_k)$ when $E_1, .., E_k$ is a permutation of $D_1, .., D_k$
Monotonic for the $|D_i|$	$c(D_1, .., D_k) \leq c(E_1, .., E_k)$ when for all i it holds $|D_i| \leq |E_i|$
Monotonic for extension of arguments	$c(D_1, .., D_k) \leq c(D_1, .., D_m)$ for $k \leq m$
Indifferent for deviation values 0	$c(D_1, .., D_k) = c(D_1, .., D_k, 0, ..., 0)$

Examples of such combination functions are:

- Maximal absolute deviation $c_{md}(D_1, .., D_k) = \max(|D_1|, ..., |D_k|)$
- Sum of absolute deviations $c_{sad}(D_1, .., D_k) = |D_1| ...+ |D_k|$
- Sum of squares of deviations $c_{ssd}(D_1, .., D_k) = D_1^2 + ...+ D_k^2$

To obtain values within the [0, 1] interval these functions can be combined with a monotonic function mapping the real numbers ≥ 0 into the [0, 1] interval, for example, by rigorously mapping all values D above 1 to 1, or, more smoothly, for example, by the logistic function defined by

$$\text{algoistic}_{\sigma,\tau}(D) = [\frac{1}{1 + e^{-\sigma(D-\tau)}} - \frac{1}{1 + e^{\sigma\tau}}](1 + e^{-\sigma\tau})$$

with steepness σ and threshold τ, or by a negative exponential function $1-e^{-\sigma D}$, or by a broken, rational function $\sigma D/(1 + \sigma D)$.

Defining a Formula for the Minimal Aggregated Deviation from Satisfaction
Given a dynamic property, expressed as a closed formula A (no free variables), to define a formula $A(D_1,.., D_k)$ with added deviation variables $D_1,.., D_k$, first as indicated in Sect. 2 in a standard manner functional value indicators $X(t)$ or $V(tr, X, t)$ are replaced by reified relational value indicators involving numerical variables V_i for the indicated values, and relational has_value_at(..) atoms for these values, thereby taking care of different variable names. Then for each variable V_i occurrence in a numerical expression in A, a deviation variable D_i of sort VALUE is introduced in A by a substitution

$$V_i = \; > \; > V_i + D_i$$

Thus a formula $A(D_1,.., D_k)$ with free variables $D_1,.., D_k$ is obtained. Next, for a chosen combination function $c(..)$ define

$$A_c(D) = D \geq 0 \wedge \exists D_1, .., D_k[c(D_1, .., D_k) \leq D \wedge A(D_1, .., D_k) \wedge Q(D_1, .., D_k)]$$

Here $Q(D_1,.., D_k)$ is a formula that takes care that deviation values for the same states at the same time points are kept equal:

$$Q(D_1, .., D_k) = \wedge_{(X_1,t_1),(X_2,t_2)\in I_A}[X_1 = X_2 \wedge t_1 = t_2 \rightarrow D_{X_1,t_1} = D_{X_2,t_2}]$$

This formula $A_c(D)$ with free variable D has monotonicity properties such as

$$A_c(D) \wedge D' \geq D \Rightarrow A_c(D')$$
$$\neg A_c(D') \wedge D \leq D' \Rightarrow \neg A_c(D)$$

Moreover, define

$$A_c * (D) = A_c(D) \wedge \forall D'[A_c(D') \rightarrow D \leq D']$$

This formula defines at most one value D, as it holds

$$A_c * (D) \wedge A_c * (D') \Rightarrow D = D'$$

This value D defined by $A_c*(D)$ is the minimal aggregated deviation possible satisfying the formula $A_c(D)$ for a given trace or set of traces $\mathcal{T}r$. The formula $\exists D \, A_c*(D)$ is satisfied for a given set of traces $\mathcal{T}r$ if and only if such a D exists, and if it is satisfied, this provides a unique instance for D. Based on this $A_c{}^*(D)$ the degrees of dissatisfaction and satisfaction can be defined.

Definition (Degrees of Dissatisfaction and Satisfaction)
For a given set of traces $\mathcal{T}$, for a closed dynamic property A the following is defined. Here $c(..)$ is a combination function.

Degree of dissatisfaction of dynamic property A

$$\text{ddiss}_c(A) = D \quad \text{if } A_c * (D) \text{ holds for some } D \le 1$$
$$\qquad\qquad\quad 1 \quad \text{otherwise}$$

Degree of satisfaction of dynamic property A

$$\text{ds}_c(A) = 1 - \text{ddiss}_c(A)$$

If needed, the given set of traces $\mathcal{T}$ is added as an argument or subscript to the notations $\text{ddiss}_c(A)$ and $\text{ds}_c(A)$. So, in this way the formula $A_c{}^*(D)$ or $\exists D\, A_c{}^*(D)$ defines the degree of dissatisfaction (and satisfaction) of property A. Checking this $\exists D\, A_c{}^*(D)$ for a set of traces $\mathcal{T}$ successfully will provide an instance for D which is the value of the degree of dissatisfaction for A with respect to $\mathcal{T}$. This will be discussed in more detail in Sect. 5. Note that for equivalent formulae $A \equiv B$ it follows that $A_c(D) \equiv B_c(D)$ from which it follows $A_c{}^*(D) \equiv B_c{}^*(D)$. Therefore

$$A \equiv B \Rightarrow \text{ddiss}_c(A) = \text{ddiss}_c(B) \wedge \text{ds}_c(A) = \text{ds}_c(B)$$

Moreover, note that for $A_c{}^*(D)$ also alternative but equivalent variants are possible, such as

$$\exists D_1, .., D_k [c(D_1, .., D_k) = D \wedge A(D_1, .., D_k) \wedge Q(D_1, .., D_k)] \wedge$$
$$\neg \exists E_1, .., E_k [c(E_1, .., E_k) < D \wedge A(E_1, .., E_k) \wedge Q(E_1, .., E_k)]$$

or

$$\exists D_1, .., D_k [A(D_1, .., D_k) \wedge Q(D_1, .., D_k) \wedge$$
$$\neg \exists E_1, .., E_k [c(E_1, .., E_k) < c(D_1, .., D_k) \wedge A(E_1, .., E_k) \wedge Q(E_1, .., E_k)]]$$

The efficiency of checking may differ for different variants.

Composition Laws for Approximate Dissatisfaction and Satisfaction
A number of composition laws can be derived for the degrees of dissatisfaction and satisfaction; see Table 4. For proofs, see Appendix B [20].

Table 4. Composition laws

$ddiss_c(T) = 0$ $ddiss_c(\bot) = 1$	$ds_c(T) = 1$ $ds_c(\bot) = 0$
$ddiss_c(A \lor B) = \min(ddiss_c(A), ddiss_c(B))$	$ds_c(A \lor B) = \max(ds_c(A), ds_c(B))$
$ddiss_c(A \land B) \geq \max(ddiss_c(A), ddiss_c(B))$	$ds_c(A \land B) \leq \min(ds_c(A), ds_c(B))$
$ddiss_c(A \land B) = \max(ddiss_c(A), ddiss_c(B))$	$ds_c(A \land B) = \min(ds_c(A), ds_c(B))$
for $c(..) = $ max absolute deviation	for $c(..) = $ max absolute deviation
$ddiss_c(A \rightarrow B) \leq \min(1\text{-}ddiss_c(A), ddiss_c(B))$	$ds_c(A \rightarrow B) \geq \max(1\text{-}ds_c(A), ds_c(B))$
$ddiss_c(\exists X\, A(X)) = \min_{\underline{c}\ for\ X}(ddiss_c(A(\underline{c})))$	$ds_c(\exists X\, A(X)) = \max_{\underline{c}\ for\ X}(ds_c(A(\underline{c})))$
$ddiss_c(\forall X\, A(X)) \geq \max_{\underline{c}\ for\ X}(ddiss_c(A(\underline{c})))$	$ds_c(\forall X\, A(X)) \leq \min_{\underline{c}\ for\ X}(ds_c(A(\underline{c})))$
$ddiss_c(\neg A) + ddiss_c(A) \leq 1$	$ds_c(\neg A) + ds_c(A) \geq 1$
$ddiss_c(\neg A) \leq 1 - ddiss_c(A)$	$ds_c(\neg A) \geq 1 - ds_c(A)$

These composition laws have similarities to those considered for logics for reasoning with uncertainty or vagueness; e.g., [5, 6, 9, 19].

5   Application in Parameter Search

As discussed in the introduction, a main motivation to define some approximate satisfaction measure for a dynamic property for a set of traces was to obtain the possibility to apply numerical heuristic approximation methods involving such dynamic properties. Suppose requirements for a model have been identified in the form of dynamic properties, and there is confidence that they indeed describe the behavior that is expected. Then a number of values of parameters can be tried until values are found such that the model shows the behavior fulfilling the requirements. Usually this is already done intuitively by a modeler. However, for models with many parameters the question how to find proper values for the parameters poses a nontrivial search problem. To be able to apply a standard heuristic search method, a measure is needed to indicate how far from fulfillment the requirement is: an error measure. An error measure usually aggregates the individual deviations for different states and time points. For dynamic properties such an error measure was not available. As approximate satisfaction as introduced in this paper provides such an error measure for dynamic properties, these heuristic methods can now be applied to requirements expressed by dynamic properties.

Roughly spoken, for a given model and set of requirements written as one closed conjunctive formula A, the formula $\exists D\ A_c^*(D)$ defined in Sect. 4 is considered and the proposed heuristic method follows a cyclic pattern using four processes that each can be performed in an automated manner:

- Select values for the model parameters.
- Run a simulation to generate a trace for the chosen parameters.
- Check $\exists D\ A_c^*(D)$ for the generated trace, thereby determining the degree of dissatisfaction D.
- Evaluate the chosen parameter values based on the degree of dissatisfaction found, and propose improved parameter values.

Here, depending on the heuristic method used, the process in the last bullet may involve additional cycles to compare different options before proposing improved parameter values. The third and fourth bullet will be discussed in more detail.

The language TTL [1, 15] (with its automated checker) is an example of a reified temporal predicate logic language. This means in particular that states X and state properties P can be represented as individuals which can also be indicated by variables over which quantifiers can be used, and the same holds for traces tr. Here state properties P are specific properties of an overall state such as has_value(X, V) expressing that state X has value V, or

$$\text{has\_value}(X_1, V_1) \wedge \text{has\_value}(X_2, V_2) \wedge V_1 < V_2$$

expressing that state X_1 has value V_1 and state X_2 has value V_2 and $V_1 < V_2$. Within TTL the predicate holds(S, P, TV) relates an overall state S to a state property P in such a manner that truth value TV is true indicates that P holds in overall state S and TV is false indicates that it does not hold in overall state S. Moreover, for a given trace tr to indicate the overall state in a trace tr at some time point t the expression state (tr, t) is used. So, for example,

$$\text{holds}(\text{state}(tr, t), P, \text{ false})$$

indicates that within the overall state of trace tr at time t state property P is false. To obtain an expression in TTL for a dynamic property A the following types of substitutions can be done, for example, from reified functional value indicators:

$$\text{V}(tr, X, t_1) < \text{V}(tr, X, t_2):$$
$$\exists V_1, V_2[\ \text{holds}(\text{state}(tr, t_1), \text{has\_value}(X, V_1),\ \text{true})\ \&$$
$$\text{holds}(\text{state}(tr, t_2), \text{has\_value}(Y, V_2),\ \text{true})\ \& V_1 < V_2]$$

This has been done within the TTL editor for the example property A considered to obtain property $\exists D\ A_c{}^*(D)$ as shown in the screen shot in Fig. 1.; here c(..) is the combination function based on maximal absolute deviation. The checker in the TTL software environment generates as output not only a conclusion on whether or not a dynamic property is satisfied, but in case of an existential formula that is satisfied also the instance found for the existential quantifier that makes the property satisfied. Therefore it provides the value for the degree of dissatisfaction, as this is defined by an existential quantifier in the formula $\exists D\ A_c{}^*(D)$. So, suppose after having chosen initial values $(W_1, \ldots, W_k)$ for the parameters $(P_1, \ldots, P_k)$, a simulation trace $\underline{tr}(W_1, \ldots, W_k)$ for these parameter values was generated, using the model with given initial values and environmental input. Then by the approach described above the degree of dissatisfaction for the requirement A for this trace

$$\text{ddiss}(A(\text{tr}(W_1, \ldots, W_k)))$$

is found by the automated checking process. A heuristic method can be used to propose improved values for the parameters; e.g. [2, 16]. For example, a stochastic method may make a jump to another point in the environment of the current point of parameter values, generate a trace for these new values, check property A for it, and if the degree of dissatisfaction is lower, propose these values as new values for the parameters, and if not, try again. Various heuristic methods are available, only requiring an error measure. They all can be applied by using the introduced degree of dissatisfaction as error measure. For this section, just the steepest descent method (also called hill climbing) has been chosen to illustrate the process in more detail.

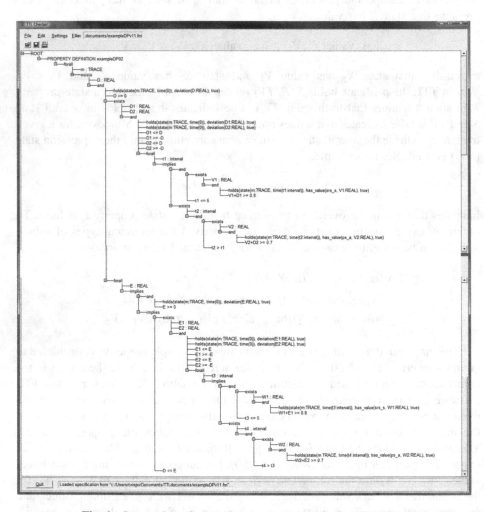

Fig. 1. Screen shot of example property $A_c*(D)$ in the TTL editor

For the steepest descent search method in each iteration the sensitivities S_{Pi} of ddis $(A(\underline{tr}(W_1, \ldots, W_k)))$ for the parameter values $W_1, \ldots, W_k$ are determined. Mathematically, these sensitivities can be defined as partial derivatives:

$$S_{Pi} = \partial ddis(A(\underline{tr}(W_1, \ldots, W_k))) / \partial W_i$$

These sensitivities cannot be calculated in a symbolic manner, but they are approximated by generating k additional simulation traces for the parameter values $W_1, \ldots, W_i + \varepsilon, \ldots, W_k$ based a small change $\Delta W_i = \varepsilon$ each time to just one of these parameter values, and then by checking these traces for property $\exists D\ A_c^*(D)$ and determining the approximated sensitivity S_{Pi} by

$$\Delta ddis(A(\underline{tr}(W_1, \ldots, W_k)))/DW_i =$$
$$[ddis(A(\underline{tr}(W_1, \ldots, W_i + \Delta W_i, \ldots, W_k))) - ddis(A(tr(W_1, \ldots, W_k)))]/\Delta W_1$$

After the k sensitivities have been found for the k parameters $P_1, \ldots, P_k$, new values for these parameters P_i are determined by adding an amount proportional to their sensitivity:

$$\text{new } W_i = W_i + \eta S_{Pi}$$

where η is a speed factor of the process.

In more detail the general overall process using the steepest decent method is shown in Box 1. The whole process is illustrated for an example model to which the

Box 1. Overview of the parameter search process

1. Choose initial values $(W_1, \ldots, W_k)$ for the parameters $(P_1, \ldots, P_k)$
2. Generate a simulation trace $\underline{tr}(W_1, \ldots, W_k)$ for these parameter values, using the model with given initial values and environmental input
3. Determine the degree of dissatisfaction for A for this trace
   $$ddiss(A(\underline{tr}(W_1, \ldots, W_k)))$$
   by the checking process for $\exists D\ A_c^*(D)$
4. If $ddiss(A(\underline{tr}(W_1, \ldots, W_k))) = 0$ terminate, as then the parameters found fully satisfy the requirement: $ds(A(\underline{tr}(W_1, \ldots, W_k))) = 1$. Else continue with 5.
5. For each parameter P_i do:
   a. Change its value W_i by adding a small number ε
   b. Generate a simulation trace $\underline{tr}(W_1, \ldots, W_i+\varepsilon, \ldots, W_k)$ for the modified value $W_i+\varepsilon$ of P_i, while the parameters P_j for $j \neq i$ keep their values W_j
6. Determine the degree of dissatisfaction
   $$ddiss(A(\underline{tr}(W_1, \ldots, W_i + \varepsilon, \ldots, W_k)))$$
   for all these traces by the checking process for $\exists D\ A_c^*(D)$
7. Determine the current sensitivities S_{Pi} of the degree of dissatisfaction for parameter P_i based on the difference in degrees of dissatisfaction between the generated traces:
   $$S_{Pi} = (ddiss(A(\underline{tr}(W_1, \ldots, W_i + \varepsilon, \ldots, W_k))) - ddiss(A(\underline{tr}(W_1, \ldots, W_k)))) / \varepsilon$$
8. Determine new values for the parameters P_i by adding an amount proportional to their sensitivity:
   $$\text{new } W_i = W_i + \eta\ S_{Pi}$$
   Here η is a speed factor of the process.
9. Continue with 2.

approach has been applied. For the sake of simplicity of the presentation a model of only two states is considered: a sensory representation state srs_s for stimulus s and a preparation state ps_a for action a. Two parameters are considered: speed factor η_a and connection weight ω_a. The impact of state srs_s on state ps_a is modeled in a nonlinear way by a logistic function:

$$ps_a(t+\Delta t) = ps_a(t) + \eta_a[\mathbf{alogistic}_{\sigma,\tau}(\omega_a srs_s(t)) - ps_a(t)]\,\Delta t$$
$$\text{where } \mathbf{alogistic}_{\sigma,\tau}(X) = [(1/(1+e^{-\sigma(X-\tau)})) - (1/(1+e^{\sigma\tau}))]\,(1+e^{-\sigma\tau})$$

The state srs_s is considered input for the process. The search space is the set of pairs of values (W_1, W_2) for the speed factor and connection weight parameter, respectively. At each iteration such a pair of values is determined and the model is used to generate a simulation trace $\underline{tr}(W_1, W_2)$ for these values. By the checking process for this trace for $\exists D\ A_c{}^*(D)$, the degree of dissatisfaction $ddis(A(\underline{tr}(W_1, W_2)))$ for the chosen requirement A:

$$\forall t_1 [\exists V_1 has\_value\_at(\underline{tr}, srs_s, t_1, V_1) \wedge V_1 \geq 0.8 \rightarrow$$
$$\exists t_2 [t_2 > t_1 \wedge [\exists V_2 has\_value\_at(\underline{tr}, ps_a, t_2, V_2) \wedge V_2 \geq 0.7]]]$$

As long as this is not 0, a next iteration can be performed, based on values determined according to the steepest descent method described in Sect. 5.

In the example process, $\varepsilon = 0.01$, and $\eta = 0.05$ were chosen. The combination function to aggregate deviations was the max function.

In Fig. 2 the patterns for the degree of satisfaction and dissatisfaction are shown. Initially, starting with speed factor 0.1 and connection weight 0.4, there was only satisfaction up to about 0.3. The steepest decent method was able to increase the satisfaction to 1 in 5 steps, which goes hand in hand with the deviation expressed as dissatisfaction decreasing to 0.

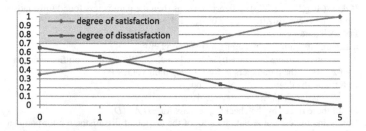

Fig. 2. Degree of satisfaction and dissatisfaction over the iterations

The evolution of the two parameter values is shown in Fig. 3. It can be seen that first the speed factor is changed most, but from point 2 on the connection weight is changed more. The parameter values found at point 5 are speed factor 0.33831 and connection weight 0.72038; these are the first pair of values encountered that realise full satisfaction of the chosen requirement: deviations 0 and ds(A(tr(0.33832, 0.72038))) = 1. In Fig. 4 it is shown how the sensitivities develop during the process. It can be seen that initially the speed factor had the highest sensitivity, but from point 1 on the connection weight had the highest sensitivity. Accordingly after point 1 the connection weight is changed more as is seen in Fig. 3. Note that the end point of the process provides a minimum, as the deviation has become 0, which is the lowest value globally, so it is a global minimum. However, more values may exist with the same deviation 0. For example, the graphs suggest that parameter values a bit above the values found will also have deviation 0, which indeed is the case.

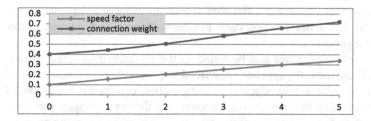

Fig. 3. Parameter values over the iterations

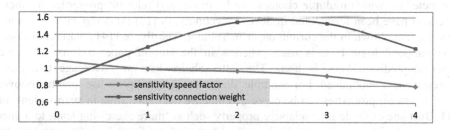

Fig. 4. Sensitivities over the iterations

6 Discussion

In this paper a notion of approximate satisfaction of dynamic properties of dynamic agent models was introduced. It adds a numerical measure to the logical notion of satisfaction. By doing this, numerical optimization methods for parameter estimation become applicable to support the design of dynamical agent models for which dynamic properties have been specified as requirements. This extends numerical methods by the possibility to involve logical notions within them. Conversely, it makes it possible to add numerical optimization methods to logical methods.

Note that this approach also covers the more traditional approaches to parameter estimation based on a given empirical data set. In these approaches an error function takes the differences between simulated values and empirical values for all given data points (state, time, value) as a point of departure. Suppose the empirical data are given as a set of triples $(\underline{X}_i, \underline{t}_j, \underline{V}_{i,j})$, $i = 1, 2, ..., j = 1, 2$. where $\underline{X}_i, \underline{t}_j$ refer to specific states and time points, and $\underline{V}_{i,j}$ to the available empirical values for these states and time points. Moreover, suppose the simulated values for a specific simulation trace $\underline{tr}$ for the same states and time points are indicated by $V(\underline{tr}, \underline{X}_i, \underline{t}_j)$. Then the relevant differences are $V(\underline{tr}, \underline{X}_i, \underline{t}_j) - \underline{V}_{i,j}$. Then the strict way of expressing a requirement is:

$$A = \wedge_{i,j} V(\underline{tr}, \underline{X}_i, \underline{t}_j) = \underline{V}_{i,j}$$

When for this requirement A the degree of dissatisfaction is determined by checking $\exists D\ A_c*(D)$ for a given trace $\underline{tr}$, based on a combination function defined by the sum of squares of the deviations, then the method introduced here does exactly what a traditional parameter estimation would do using the sum of squares as error function. In that sense the approach put forward here is a generalization of these traditional approaches.

Only a few approaches can be found in the literature that relate to the proposed approach. From them the approach described in [14] probably is most close. Also there a form of approximate satisfaction is used (called continuous valuation). However, there are some clear differences to the approach in the current paper. First of all, in [14] a fixed function for aggregation of the deviations is used based on the square root of the sum of squares of deviations, and a broken function mapping the resulting values to the [0, 1] interval. In the current paper, this combination function for aggregation is a parameter for which multiple choices can be made, and relevant properties for these functions have been formulated in Sect. 4. Secondly, in [14] no composition laws are presented, as shown in the current paper in Table 4. Thirdly, in [14] a variant of linear time temporal logic LTL is used, whereas in the current paper a form of reified temporal predicate logic is used. The latter choice has the advantage that more expressiveness is obtained. For example, due to the possibility to use quantifiers over states or traces, properties can be expressed that are not expressible in such variants of LTL. Just one example is an adaptive property such as 'more exercising leads to higher skill', which can be expressed in the reified temporal predicate logic chosen here by using two quantifiers over traces tr_1 and tr_2 and comparing the two traces tr_1 and tr_2 with respect to 'exercising' and 'skill'; for example, 'if in tr_2 exercising has a higher value than in tr_1, then also skill has a higher value in tr_2 than in tr_1'.

The introduced approach can also be seen as a generalization of certain approaches to flexible constraint satisfaction; e.g., [3, 4]. For future research this relation will be analyzed in more depth. Moreover, for future research the aim is to develop an integrated environment in which the cycle of processes described in Sect. 5 happens automatically, whereas for now only an implementation for each sub-process is available but the output-input connections between the sub-processes have to be done manually.

References

1. Bosse, T., Jonker, C.M., van der Meij, L., Sharpanskykh, A., Treur, J.: Specification and verification of dynamics in agent models. Int. J. Coop. Inf. Syst. **18**, 167–193 (2009)
2. Chong, E.K.P., Zak, S.H.: An Introduction to Optimization. Wiley, Hoboken (2013)

3. Dubois, D., Fargier, H., Prade, H.: Propagation and satisfaction of flexible constraints. In: Yager, R.R., Zadeh, L.A. (eds.) Fuzzy Sets, Neural Networks, and Soft Computing, pp. 166–187. Van Nostrand Reinhold, New York (1994)
4. Dubois, D., Fargier, H., Prade, H.: The calculus of fuzzy restrictions as a basis for flexible constraint satisfaction. In: Proceedings of 2nd IEEE International Conference on Fuzzy Systems, San Francisco, CA, pp. 1131–1136 (1993)
5. Dubois, D., Lang, J., Prade, H.: Fuzzy sets in approximate reasoning, Part 2: logical approaches. Fuzzy Sets Syst. **40**, 203–244 (1991)
6. Dubois, D., Prade, H.: Possibility theory, probability theory and multiple-valued logics: a clarification. Ann. Math. Artif. Intell. **32**, 35–66 (2002)
7. van Dalen, D.: Logic and Structure, 3rd edn. Springer Verlag, New York (1994)
8. Ferber, J., Gutknecht, O., Jonker, C.M., Müller, J.P., J.P., and J. Treur: Organization Models and Behavioural Requirements Specification for Multi-Agent Systems. In: Y. Demazeau, F. Garijo (eds.) Multi-Agent System Organisations. Proceedings of the 10th European Workshop on Modelling Autonomous Agents in a Multi-Agent World, MAAMAW 2001 (2001)
9. Giangiacomo, G.: Fuzzy logic: Mathematical Tools for Approximate Reasoning. Kluwer Academic Publishers, Dordrecht (2001)
10. Herlea, D.E., Jonker, C.M., Treur, J., Wijngaards, N.J.E.: Specification of bahavioural requirements within compositional multi-agent system design. In: Garijo, F.J., Boman, M., (eds.) MAAMAW 1999. LNCS, vol. 1647, pp. 8–27. Springer, Heidelberg (1999). doi:10.1007/3-540-48437-X_2
11. Damian, D.E., Jonker, C.M., Treur, J., Wijngaards, N.J.: Integration of behavioural requirements specification within compositional knowledge engineering. Knowl.-Based Syst. **18**, 353–365 (2005)
12. Pohl, K., Rupp, C.: Requirements Engineering Fundamentals. Rocky Nook, Santa Barbara (2011)
13. Port, R.F., van Gelder, T.: Mind as Motion: Explorations in the Dynamics of Cognition. MIT Press, Cambridge (1995)
14. Rizk, A., Batt, G., Fages, F., Soliman, S.: Continuous valuations of temporal logic specifications with applications to parameter optimization and robustness measures. Theor. Comput. Sci. **412**, 2827–2839 (2011)
15. Sharpanskykh, A., Treur, J.: A temporal trace language for formal modelling and analysis of agent systems. In: Dastani, M., Hindriks, K.V., Meyer, J.J.C. (eds.) Specification and Verification of Multi-Agent Systems, pp. 317–352. Springer, Heidelberg (2010)
16. Strejc, V.: Least squares parameter estimation. Automatica **16**, 535–550 (1980)
17. Treur, J.: Network-Oriented Modeling: Addressing Complexity of Cognitive, Affective and Social Interactions. Series in Understanding Complex Systems. Springer, Heidelberg (2016)
18. Van Lamsweerde, A.: Requirements Engineering: From System Goals to UML Models to Software Specifications. Wiley, Chichester (2009)
19. Zadeh, L.: Fuzzy sets as the basis for a theory of possibility. Fuzzy Sets Syst. **1**, 3–28 (1978). Reprinted in Fuzzy Sets Syst. **100**(Suppl.), 9–34 (1999)
20. URL Appendix. http://few.vu.nl/~treur/EUMAS16appsatAppendix.pdf

EUMAS 2016: Applications

A Cognitive Agent Model for Desire Regulation Applied to Food Desires

Altaf Hussain Abro and Jan Treur[(✉)]

Behavioural Informatics Group, Vrije Universiteit Amsterdam,
De Boelelaan 1081, 1081 HV Amsterdam, The Netherlands
{a.h.abro,j.treur}@vu.nl

Abstract. In this paper a neurologically inspired cognitive agent model for desire regulation is presented that describes the desire generation process and a number of desire regulation strategies. This work addresses antecedent-focused desire regulation strategies. These strategies include reinterpretation, attention deployment and situation modification. The model has been used to perform a number of simulation experiments concerning food desire and eating behaviour.

Keywords: Desire · Regulation strategies · Cognitive agent model · Food

1 Introduction

In recent years obesity and overweight have received much attention from researchers to find causes and develop interventions to avoid obesity, particularly in the field of neuroscience [1]. Neurological evidence suggests that there are several brain regions involved in food rewarding mechanisms and in the desire for unhealthy food and its regulation [1, 2]. Persons often make use of various regulation strategies to regulate their desire of food and this helps them to make food choices [3]. To change the eating behaviour or lifestyle of persons there is a need to develop intelligent systems which can help persons to adopt healthy eating behaviour or change their lifestyle. There is much work going on the computational modelling of human behaviour [4, 5] that can provide basis for the development of such human-aware systems. Giuliani and Berkman [6] have taken the emotion regulation process model of Gross [7, 8] thereby assuming that food craving is also an affective state so that its regulation involves the emotion regulation strategies to regulate the desire-associated emotions:

> 'Food craving can be defined as the subjective sense of wanting a certain food, and features both food-related affective/motivational components (e.g., wanting to eat the food, being motivated to approach it) and cognitions (e.g., intrusive thoughts about the food).... If craving is an affective state, then the Process Model may be a useful framework to better understand the various ways that craving may be regulated. Here, we apply this model to craving, and review select evidence that different food craving regulation strategies fit within this model.' [6], p. 48.

In the current paper a different perspective is chosen, independent of the question in how far desires are affective states or are associated to emotions. In the process of desire generation the causal chain leading to a desire is considered and regulation strategies addressing one of the steps in this chain are considered as antecedent-focused

© Springer International Publishing AG 2017
N. Criado Pacheco et al. (Eds.): EUMAS 2016/AT 2016, LNAI 10207, pp. 251–260, 2017.
DOI: 10.1007/978-3-319-59294-7_20

strategies; this notion generalises the similar notion for emotions. Just following this causal chain three possibilities for regulation can be identified: (1) modifying beliefs that interpret the world (also called reinterpretation), (2) modifying the own sensing of the world, for example by changing the gaze direction (also called attention deployment) and (3) modifying the world itself (situation modification). This work extends the model of desire generation and making of choices for actions in [5] by introducing desire regulation mechanisms. The neuroscientific literature suggests that the food craving can be downregulated using cognitive regulation strategies [9–12]. The neurological underpinnings of such regulation processes have been studied through fMRI techniques. Studies [3, 13] shows that the ventrolateral PFC and posterior parietal cortex seem more active for the duration of both upregulation and downregulation, and were functionally coupled with vmPFC and dlPFC during cognitive regulation. For example, the cognitive reinterpretation strategy is used to reinterpret or change the thoughts about palatable food, and it works more effectively to inhibit the mesocorticolimbic activity and associated food craving. On the other hand during desire suppression there was more activity in the prefrontal cortex [11]. Other studies about attention deployment [11], explained that it works to change the attention away from the particular food cues. Furthermore studies [14, 15] suggest that interaction between areas between prefrontal PFC and sensory areas occurs in the sense that PFC has a major control role for directing attention to a location, a feature, or an object.

2 A Cognitive Agent Model for Desire Regulation

This section describes the proposed computational cognitive agent model for desire regulation in detail. The model (see Fig. 1 and Table 1) shows how a desire (illustrated for a food desire or food craving) is generated and then how the desire regulation strategies work to regulate the desire. Furthermore, it describes how both bodily factors or unbalances (e.g., low blood sugar level, being hungry) and environmental factors (e.g., palatable food) can generate the desire, and how cognitive regulation strategies are integrated in the desire generation process.

2.1 Desire Generation and Making of Choices for Actions

The proposed model extends the model of desire generation and making of choices [5], which is visible in the lower part of Fig. 1 (that part is indicated with solid arrows and states without filling any colour and the extended part includes all doted arrows and states filled with green colour). It is assumed that a desire can be generated either from below the neck (a bodily unbalance such as being hungry) or above the neck (being attracted to cues in the environment; e.g., palatable food). In this model both perspectives have been integrated.

In the conceptual model the *body state of unbalance* bs_{ub} is assumed to be generated by *metabolic activity* m_{ub}. Through the *sensor state* ss_{ub} and *sensory representation state* srs_{ub} the body unbalance leads to a desire ds_{ub} (e.g. for eating), so the person may undertake actions (e.g., eat) and reduce the body unbalance. On the other hand the environment can also affect the generation of a desire (e.g., attractive food).

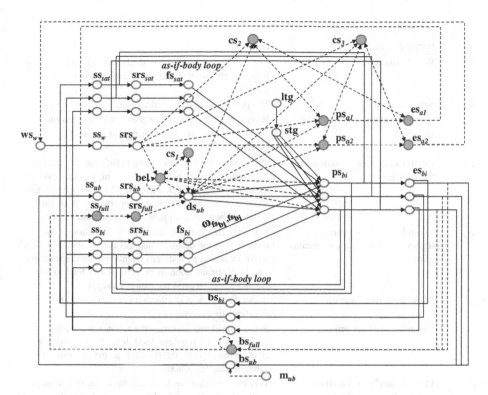

Fig. 1. Conceptual representation of the computational model of desire regulation (Color figure online)

To model this, the environment situation is represented by *world state* ws_w and the person senses it through the *sensor state* ss_w and represents it by the *sensory representation state* srs_w. Based on these representations the person forms beliefs to interpret the world state (the food). If positive beliefs are stronger then the desire will be stronger. Alternatively, if a person has more negative beliefs (e.g., this food is not healthy) then he may have a less strong desire.

After desire generation persons often look around for various options of actions (for eating), which may depend on availability and opportunities as well. In this case three action options have been modeled so the person may make decisions regarding these actions (food choices for the eating). Making food choices also involves long term and short term goals, for example: if a person has the long term goal to reduce body weight, he or she may start to achieve that by generating more specific short term goals, in this scenario to eat healthy food (low calories food) instead of fast food (high calories food). Long term goals and short term goals are represented in the model by ltg and stg, respectively.

In making of food choices for eating, some other factors are also considered such as how much that particular food option expected satisfaction feelings, this has been done through the internal predictive loop known as *as-if-body loop* [16]. It uses the information of the options for which a person is prepared to eat, these *preparation states* are

Table 1. Overview of the states of the proposed model (see also Fig. 1)

Name	Informal name	Description
ws_w	World state w	This models the current world situation which the person is facing, the stimulus, in this example w is a food stimulus
ss_w	Sensor state for w	The person senses the world through the sensor state
srs_w	Sensory representation state for w	Internal representation of sensory world information on w
bel_i	Beliefs	These represents the interpretation of the world information
cs_1	Control state 1 for reinterpretation of the stimulus	This control state is monitoring beliefs and the desire, to determine whether (beliefs lead to a high desire level. If so, by becoming activated the control state suppresses this positive belief, which gives the opportunity for alternative beliefs to become dominant. (first regulation strategy)
cs_2	Control state 2 for attention deployment reducing the stimulus effect	This state monitors the sensory representation of the stimulus and the desire. When this control state becomes active by action a_1 it diverts attention from the stimulus, e.g., to divert attention from high calories food to low calories food. (second regulation strategy)
ps_{a_1}	Preparation for action a_1	Preparation to deploy attention (e.g., change gaze direction) by an action a_1
es_{a_1}	Execution state for action a_1	In the considered scenarios the action a is attention deployment that regulates food desire by focusing the attention away from the stimulus, so the intensity of stimulus can be reduced
cs_3	Control state 3 for situation modification to avoid eating	This state monitors feelings and the sensor representation of the world situation, to determine whether a situation is unwanted. If so, the control state activates the preparation and execution of action a_2 to change this situation (third regulation strategy)
ps_{a_2}	Preparation for action a_2	Preparation to modify the world situation ws_w by an action a_2
es_{a_1}	Execution state for action a_2	In the considered scenarios the action a_2 is changing the situation by decreasing the level of world state w
m_{ub}	Metabolism for ub	This represents the metabolic energy level affecting unbalance state ub: low while being inactive and high while being active
bs_{ub}	Body state of ub	This represents a bodily unbalance ub. For example, underlying being hungry; if a person is becoming hungry, the body unbalance ub increases, and after eating there will be lower or no unbalance
ss_{ub}	Sensor state for body unbalance ub	The person senses bodily unbalance state ub, providing sensory input
srs_{ub}	Sensory representation of ub	Internal sensory representation of body unbalance ub
bs_{full}	Fulness body state of $full$	A bodily state that represents fulness
ss_{full}	Sensor state for bodily state $full$	The person senses body state $full$, providing sensory input
srs_{full}	Sensory representation of $full$	Internal sensory representation of bodily state $full$
ds_{ub}	Desire for unbalance ub	Generating a desire to compensate for body unbalance ub (e.g., desire to eat to get rid of a state of being hungry)

(continued)

Table 1. (*continued*)

Name	Informal name	Description
ps_{b_i}	Preparation for an action b_i	Preparation for an action b_i to fulfil the desire. In this example the b_i represent the associated available food choices
fs_{b_i}	Feeling b_i	For example, a feeling state fs_{b_i} for the eating action b_i
srs_{b_i}	Sensory representation of b_i	Internal sensory representation of body state for b_i in the brain
ss_{b_i}	Sensor state for b_i	The person senses the body states through the sensor state
ss_{sat}	Sensor state for satisfaction *sat*	The person senses the external body states providing sensory input to the feelings of satisfaction
srs_{sat}	Sensory representation of *sat*	Internal representation of the body aspects of feelings of satisfaction *sat*
fs_{sat}	Feeling for satisfaction *sat*	Feeling of satisfaction; these are the feelings about the considered food choice, how much satisfactory it is
es_{b_i}	Execution state for action b_i	In the scenarios action b_i is to eat food of a particular choice for, to reduce the body unbalance *ub*
bs_{b_i}	Body state for b_i	This is the body state related to eating that particular food
ltg	Long term goal	This represents the long term goal, to lose weight, for example
stg	Short term goal	Short term goal refers to smaller incremental way of achieving long term goals for example start to eat healthy avoid from fast food etc.
$\omega_{fs_{b_i},ps_{b_i}}$	Learnt connections	These connections are learnt by Hebbian learning This models how the generated feeling affect the preparation for response b_i

represented by ps_{b_i}. Based on these preparation states through the representation states srs_{b_i} and feelings fs_{b_i} he or she may choose from the available options. The weights $\omega_{fs_{b_i}ps_{b_i}}$, of the connections from feeling states fs_{b_i} to preparation states ps_{b_i} are used as learnt connections over time, through experiences [17]. The person can go for one or more than one available food options as well. The *execution state* es_{b_i} represents performing (eating) actions; when a person starts such an (eating) action then on one hand it will reduce the body *unbalance* bs_{ub} (reduce the hunger). On the other hand it provides the information about the selected food choices that is another aspect which can affect the making of food choices is the expected *feelings of satisfaction* fs_{sat} from the available food options and person sense this through the *sensory state* ss_{sat} and *sensory representation state* srs_{sat}. So the in decision making of food choices involves various factors.

As mentioned above, this model extends the model of desire generation and making of action choices, so due to the lack of space, refer to the original article [5] for more details of this part of the model.

2.2 Cognitive Regulation Strategies for Food Desire

Antecedent-focused regulation strategies can be used in different phases of the causal paths in the desire generation process. These cognitive regulation strategies for the causal path from world state to sensing and representing it to beliefs interpreting it, include cognitive reinterpretation (modifying the beliefs on the world situation), attention deployment (modifying the sensing of the situation), and situation modification (modifying the situation itself). The first regulation strategy discussed is cognitive reinterpretation, it is one of the commonly used regulation strategies. As discussed in Sect. 2 reinterpretation works by altering the meaning of a stimulus (thinking about the food in different way) which can effectively reduce the food craving. For example, by thinking about the negative consequences of such food [10, 13, 18].

To model reinterpretation two types of belief states bel_i (positive bel_1 and negative bel_2) have been taken into account, both belief states bel_i are alternative interpretations and suppress each other via an inhibition connection; if a person has stronger positive beliefs towards craved food then it strengthens desire ds_{ub} and then person may go for an (eating) action. On the other hand a person may start reinterpreting that food in a different way (e.g., food is spoiled) in that case the control state cs_1 (used for reinterpretation) become active and suppress the positive beliefs so the alternative negative belief gets more strength and the desire becomes less, so that the person may not eat, or he or she may change his or her choice, based on the alternative interpretation about the environmental stimulus.

The second regulation strategy considered in this model is attention deployment. It is used to regulate the food craving by focusing attention away from the sensed cue, for example food, so that the person may get a lower desire level. For example, being in a situation where a variety of food is available, a person may be more attracted towards fast food (high calories food) in the sense that it leads to a high level of desire, so to regulate such desire he or she may change or divert attention to other types of food such as more healthy food instead of fast food, so in this way the attention deployment strategy works to downregulate the food craving desire.

To model the attention deployment strategy *control state* cs_2 is used, for example when a person has positive beliefs about sensed food which lead to the desire, but by using this control mechanism a person can prepare and undertake action a_1 through ps_{a_1} and es_{a_1} to turn the gaze away to focus attention on something less craving thus decreasing the stimulus influence on the sensory state ss_w, so then the environmental influence becomes low which may lead to less desire or even no more desire.

The third desire regulation strategy is situation modification. It refers to change or leave such kind of craving environment, which leads to the desire. For example: being in a palatable environment a person may not control himself/herself from eating that craving food, so he/she may modify or change the situation by moving away from such palatable environment. In this model the *control state* cs_3 is used for situation modification, this control state receives the impact from *desire* ds_{ub} and the stimulus through sensory representation of the world srs_w and then prepare ps_{a_2} and undertake es_{a_2} action a_2 of changing the environment ws_w or situation, so in this way the situation is modified reducing the level of ws_w.

2.3 Numerical Representation of the Cognitive Agent Model

The proposed cognitive agent model presented above (Fig. 1) with further description given above in (Table 1) represents a network of (cognitive and affective) mental states in a conceptual manner, in this case as a graph. To generate a numerical representation of the model out of a conceptual representation the states Y get activation values indicated by $Y(t)$: real numbers (often between 0 and 1) over time points t, where the time variable t ranges over the real numbers. Using these labels the numerical representation has the form of the following difference or differential equation for detailed description see [19]:

$$Y(t + \Delta t) = Y(t) + \eta_Y [c_Y(\omega_{X_1,Y}X_1(t), \ldots, \omega_{X_k,Y}X_k(t)) - Y(t)] \Delta t$$
$$dY(t)/dt = \eta_Y [c_Y(\omega_{X_1,Y}X_1(t), \ldots, \omega_{X_k,Y}X_k(t)) - Y(t)]$$

The numerical representation chosen for Hebbian learning is (similar to [32]):

$$\omega_{fs_{b_i},ps_{b_i}}(t + \Delta t) = \omega_{fs_{b_i},ps_{b_i}}(t) + [\eta \, fs_{b_i}(t) \, ps_{b_i}(t) \, (1 - \omega_{fs_{b_i},ps_{b_i}}(t)) - \zeta \, \omega_{fs_{b_i},ps_{b_i}}(t)] \Delta t$$

3 Simulation Results

In this section the simulation results of the cognitive agent model discussed above are described; the various simulation experiments have been performed by taking different scenarios into account using the Matlab environment. The simulation was executed for 180 time points; the time step $\Delta t = 0.1$ and all update speeds were $\eta = 0.1$. Due to lack of space the rest of the parameter values of weights for connections between the states and the values for parameters threshold τ and steepness σ are provided as an internet appendix [20] in Tables 2 and 3 respectively. These parameters values have been obtained by taking into consideration the patterns that are known from literature and searching for the ranges of parameter values that provide such patterns. The initial values for all states were set to zero. Before discussing the simulation results, a real world scenario provides an insight how a person may use desire regulation strategies in his daily routine.

> Peter is present in an attractive food environment and he is already overweight and moving to an obesity problem. He wants to reduce his weight to avoid obesity, so he wants to control himself from eating high calories food (e.g., fast food), so being in such situation he may apply the different regulation strategies to control himself. He may reinterpret the food by taking its consequences (food is not good for health) in his mind. Or he can move or turn his attention away from that palatable food to any other, more healthy food. Or he may change the situation, for example by leaving the environment.

3.1 Desire Regulation by the Situation Modification Strategy

In this simulation experiment it is shown how the situation modification strategy works. Figure 2(a) shows that if a person is present in palatable food environment, and he has positive beliefs about the food, and then the desire to eat that food increases, and he starts to prepare to eat, as can be seen in Fig. 3(b). But he still has the option to leave the situation. Situation modification (Fig. 2(c)) is applied to change the situation. So when the control state cs_3 becomes active it prepares to take action of situation modification to change world state ws_w. When the influence of the world state or stimulus starts to decrease the desire to eat that craved food also fades away, and all other states will go down as well because there is no more stimulus there.

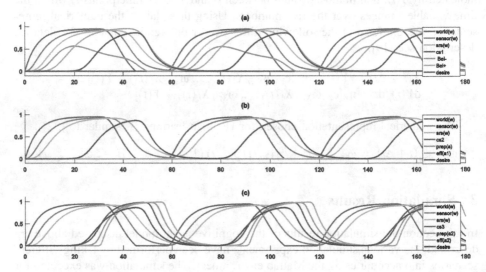

Fig. 2. Three regulation strategies (a) reinterpretation (b) attention deployment (c) situation modification. Only situation modification is active in this scenario

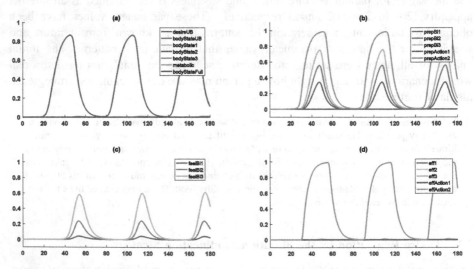

Fig. 3. The lower part of the model relates to (a) desire generation (b) eating options (preparations) (c) feelings and (d) execution states (actions)

4 Conclusion

The cognitive agent model for desire regulation presented in this paper has been used to conduct simulation experiments with various scenarios based on real life examples showing how a palatable food environment leads to food desire generation and how desire regulation strategies can play their role to downregulate the desire. In this paper antecedent focused regulation strategies have been addressed, covering cognitive reinterpretation, attention deployment and situation modification.

Some recent research [2] describes food craving as an affective state and it can be regulated cognitively. According to Giuliani and Berkman [6] the neural bases of craving regulation are similar to those underlying the regulation of negative emotions; he mapped the food craving regulation strategies into an emotion regulation framework, so that this framework (described by Gross [7, 21, 22]) could be applied in a straightforward manner. To map the emotion regulation model onto food desire and craving regulation processes, [6] describes various ways that food craving may be regulated as emotion regulation. For example, in situation selection a person may avoid purchasing of craved food or to avoid from going to such places where craved food is available. In situation modification a person can change his situation if a desire to eat craved food becomes too high then he or she may move away from that environment to modify/change his situation. Attention deployment is a form of regulation in which a person may deploy attention away from palatable food; e.g., he or she may change his attention from that craved food to light food for eating. Reinterpretation or cognitive change works by reinterpreting the stimulus, in this case the palatable food; e.g., if a person reinterprets that craved food is not good for health, in this way the desire to eat craved food may decrease. The response modulation strategy works by suppression of the desire [6].

This cognitive agent model may provide a basis to develop intelligent systems that support persons to avoid overweight and obesity. The simulation experiments show by real life examples that by applying desire regulation strategies persons can avoid certain types of food and can keep themselves healthy.

References

1. Berridge, K.C., Ho, C.-Y., Richard, J.M., DiFeliceantonio, A.G.: The tempted brain eats: pleasure and desire circuits in obesity and eating disorders. Brain Res. **1350**, 43–64 (2010)
2. Giuliani, N.R., Mann, T., Tomiyama, A.J., Berkman, E.T.: Neural systems underlying the reappraisal of personally-craved foods. J. Cogn. Neurosci. **26**(7), 1390–1402 (2014). http://dx.doi.org/10.1162/jocn_a_00563
3. Hutcherson, C.A., Plassmann, H., Gross, J.J., Rangel, A.: Cognitive regulation during decision making shifts behavioral control between ventromedial and dorsolateral prefrontal value systems. J. Neurosci. **32**(39), 13543–13554 (2012)
4. Bosse, T., Hoogendoorn, M., Memon, Z.A., Treur, J., Umair, M.: A computational model for dynamics of desiring and feeling. Cogn. Syst. Res. **19–20**, 39–61 (2012)

5. Abro, A.H., Treur, J.: Doubting what to eat : a computational model for food choice using different valuing perspectives. In: Proceedings of the 23rd International Conference on Neural Information Processing, ICONIP 2016 (2016)
6. Giuliani, N.R., Berkman, E.T.: Craving is an affective state and its regulation can be understood in terms of the extended process model of emotion regulation. Psychol. Inq. **26**(1), 48–53 (2015)
7. Gross, J.J.: The emerging field of emotion regulation: an integrative review. Rev. Gen. Psychol. **2**(3), 271–299 (1998)
8. Gross, J.J.: Handbook of Emotion Regulation. Guilford Press, New York City (2007)
9. Hollmann, M., Hellrung, L., Pleger, B., Schlögl, H., Kabisch, S., Stumvoll, M., Villringer, A., Horstmann, A.: Neural correlates of the volitional regulation of the desire for food. Int. J. Obes. **36**(5), 648–655 (2012)
10. Giuliani, N.R., Calcott, R.D., Berkman, E.T.: Piece of cake. Cognitive reappraisal of food craving. Appetite **64**, 56–61 (2013)
11. Siep, N., Roefs, A., Roebroeck, A., Havermans, R., Bonte, M., Jansen, A.: Fighting food temptations: The modulating effects of short-term cognitive reappraisal, suppression and up-regulation on mesocorticolimbic activity related to appetitive motivation. Neuroimage **60** (1), 213–220 (2012)
12. Volkow, N.D., Wang, G.J., Fowler, J.S., Tomasi, D., Baler, R.: Food and Drug Reward: Overlapping Circuits in Human Obesity and Addiction, pp. 1–24. Springer, Heidelberg (2011)
13. Kober, H., Mende-Siedlecki, P., Kross, E.F., Weber, J., Mischel, W., Hart, C.L., Ochsner, K. N.: Prefrontal-striatal pathway underlies cognitive regulation of craving. Proc. Natl. Acad. Sci. **107**(33), 14811–14816 (2010)
14. Ferri, J., Hajcak, G.: Neural mechanisms associated with reappraisal and attentional deployment. Curr. Opin. Psychol. **3**, 17–21 (2015)
15. Esghaei, M., Xue, C.: Does correlated firing underlie attention deployment in frontal cortex? J. Neurosci. **36**(6), 1791–1793 (2016)
16. Damasio, A.R.: The Feeling of What Happens: Body and Emotion in the Making of Consciousness. Harcourt, Brisbane (2000)
17. Hebb, D.O.: The Organization of Behavior. A Neuropsychological Theory, p. 335. Wiley, New York (2002)
18. Volkow, N.D., Wang, G.-J., Baler, R.D.: Reward, dopamine and the control of food intake: implications for obesity. Trends Cogn. Sci. **15**(1), 37–46 (2011)
19. Treur, J.: Dynamic modeling based on a temporal–causal network modeling approach. Biol. Inspired Cogn. Archit. **16**(16), 131–168 (2016)
20. Abro, A.H., Treur, J.: Appendix: A Cognitive Agent Model for Desire Regulation Applied to Food Desires. Appendix, November 2016
21. Gross, J.J.: Emotion regulation in adulthood: timing is everything. Curr. Dir. Psychol. Sci. **10**(6), 214–219 (2001)
22. Gross, J.J., Thompson, R.A.: Emotion regulation: conceptual foundations (2007)

A Topological Categorization of Agents for the Definition of Attack States in Multi-agent Systems

Katia Santacà[1]([⊠]), Matteo Cristani[1], Marco Rocchetto[2], and Luca Viganò[3]

[1] Dipartimento di Informatica, Università di Verona, Verona, Italy
katia.santaca@univr.it
[2] SnT, University of Luxembourg, Luxembourg City, Luxembourg
[3] Department of Informatics, King's College London, London, UK

Abstract. We propose a topological categorization of agents that makes use of the multiple-channel logic (MCL) framework, a recently developed model of reasoning about agents. We firstly introduce a complete formalization of prejudices on agents' attitudes and propose an extension of the rules of the MCL framework. We then use RCC5 (the Region Connection Calculus) to categorize different agents in Multi-Agent Systems (MAS) based on the collaboration, competence, and honesty of agents. We discuss the possibility of using RCC3 and RCC8 and generalize our results to define an upper bound on the number of different types of agents in MAS. Finally, we apply our topological categorization to a specific MAS that describes a Cyber-Physical System, for which we define, categorize and discuss the resulting attack states.

1 Introduction

Much effort has been devoted to the characterization of different agents in *Multi-Agent Systems (MAS)*, ranging from works that employ Dynamic Epistemic Logic and Public Announcement Logics (PAL) [13] to more recent approaches such as [1]. These works have studied an agent's beliefs and announcements, typically under the assumption that agents are always truthful and sincere. However, as discussed in, e.g., [2], this assumption is an oversimplification since most MAS contain a number of agents that are clearly neither sincere nor truthful. This is, for instance, the case in the systems that are typically considered in the security research community, where dishonest (and thus neither sincere nor truthful) agents are used to formalize attacks to the systems under consideration. As a result, a number of research paper have focused their attention to spotting unintended or even malicious behavior in MAS. We specifically focus on *Cyber-Physical Systems (CPS)* as examples of such problems as reported widely in [6,11] and in [7], where an agent-based model of CPS is considered.

M. Rocchetto—This work was carried out while Marco was with iTrust at Singapore University of Technology and Design.

N. Criado Pacheco et al. (Eds.): EUMAS 2016/AT 2016, LNAI 10207, pp. 261–276, 2017.
DOI: 10.1007/978-3-319-59294-7_21

Distinguishing between the different types of agents in a MAS is a difficult task. This is witnessed by the fact that although a characterization of agents would obviously play a crucial role in the understanding of different aspects and facets in MAS, a proper definition is still missing. General problems with agency and norms, namely social regulations, are presented in [3], where many open problems are discussed. Further investigations, including those in *Public Announcement Logic* [1], have devised a pathway to follow, with many problems in the definitions still open. A step in this direction has been carried out in [2], which introduced a general logical framework called *Multiple Channel Logic Framework (MCL)*. However, the focus of [2] is on the definition of the framework and little attention is payed to the definition of a general categorization of all the possible agents that could be defined using MCL.

The overall goal of this paper is the definition of a general categorization of agents, based on MCL. We focus, in particular, on the application of MAS for reasoning about security systems, such as CPS. More specifically, our contributions are three-fold:

1. We define a topological categorization of agents in MAS, obtaining 50 new rules in the MCL framework.
2. We identify a theoretical limit to the maximum number of different types of agents in a MAS (defined using MCL).
3. As an example of a concrete application, we apply our topological categorization to define attack states for a MAS that describes a general CPS. Our case study ultimately allows us to show that our categorization of agents can be used to reason about the security of CPS and, more generally, MAS.

We proceed as follows. In Sect. 2, we provide background on the MCL framework that we have employed as a basis of our categorization of agents. In Sect. 3, we define agents and summarize the Region Connection Calculus. In Sect. 4, we propose a categorization of agents for MAS by extending the MCL framework. In Sect. 5, we define an upper bound on the number of different types of agents. In Sect. 6, we apply our categorization to the security of CPS. In Sect. 7, we draw some conclusions.

2   Background: The MCL Framework

In this section, we summarize the main features of the Multiple Channel Logic Framework MCL of [2], which provides the basis for our work in this paper.

2.1   Announcements, Beliefs and Facts

MCL is a logical framework that is able to relate announcements, agents' beliefs, and true statements on multiple communication channels, where the channels of MCL are logical spaces in which agents make *public* announcements (private channels are out of the scope of MCL). More specifically, MCL is a three-layered, labeled, modal logic framework:

- The first layer is a propositional calculus that is used to express what agents share, i.e., the logical representation of an assertion.
- The second layer is a multi-modal calculus with three different modalities: B (*belief*), which allows one to assert that an agent believes in a proposition, and $T_\square$ and $T_\lozenge$ to state that a given proposition is *asserted* by an agent respectively in every channel or at least one channel.
- The third layer is for *agent tagging*, which defines prejudice about communicative attitudes of agents (see Sect. 2.3 for more details).

Propositional formulae in the first layer of MCL are of the form

$$\varphi := A \mid \neg\varphi \mid \varphi \wedge \varphi \mid \varphi \vee \varphi,$$

where A denotes a propositional letter, and $\neg$, $\wedge$ and $\vee$ are the standard connectives for negation, conjunction and disjunction, respectively.

Modal formulae in the second layer of MCL are of the form

$$\mu := B[\lambda : \varphi] \mid T_\square[\lambda : \varphi] \mid T_\lozenge[\lambda : \varphi] \mid \sim\mu$$

where φ denotes a propositional formula, λ an agent and $\sim$ a negation.

$B[\lambda : \varphi]$ intuitively means that the agent λ believes in the formula φ; note that, as is standard, an agent might believe a false formula.

$T_\square[\lambda : \varphi]$ intuitively means that the agent λ announces φ in every channel. More formally, when λ announces φ in a channel C, then he announces φ in any channel C' that is accessible from C. $T_\lozenge[\lambda : \varphi]$ denotes that the agent λ announces φ at least in one channel. In fact, the semantics of MCL relates the notion of accessibility to the notion of *observation*: a channel C' is accessible from a channel C when the observer of C also observes C'. We won't however go into the details of the Kripke-style semantics of MCL, which is given in [2] along with a proof of the soundness and completeness of MCL.

We can then define the following three sets with respect to an agent λ:

- *Announcements* $\mathbb{A}_\lambda = \{\varphi.T_\lozenge[\lambda : \varphi]\}$ is the set of formulae announced by λ in one or more channels.
- *Beliefs* $\mathbb{B}_\lambda = \{\varphi.B[\lambda : \varphi]\}$ is the set of the formulae believed to be true by λ.
- *Facts* $\mathbb{F}$ is the set of *axiomatic* formulae.

2.2 Assumptions on the Agents in MCL

MCL imposes the following assumptions on the agents:

- *Atemporal channels*: announcements are made in a channel and hold forever.
- *Belief revision*: if an agent makes two opposite announcements in the same channel, then the agent has changed his point of view.
- *Coherent agents*: an agent makes coherent announcements in a single channel, although he might make opposite announcements in a different channel.
- *Consistent agents*: an agent either believes in the truthfulness of a statement or in the truthfulness of the opposite statement, but not in both at once.
- *No beliefs*: if an agent does not assert something, this doesn't imply that the agent believes the opposite.
- *Provable facts*: there exist provable facts that are not matter of opinions.

Table 1. Description of different agent types in MCL.

Agent type	Notation	Description
Weakly collaborative	$+(W_{Cl})\lambda$	λ announces his beliefs in at least one channel
Strongly collaborative	$+(S_{Cl})\lambda$	λ announces his beliefs in every channel
Sincere	$+(S)\lambda$	λ believes every announcement he makes
Competent	$+(Co)\lambda$	Everything believed by λ is true
Omniscient	$+(O)\lambda$	λ believes every true formula

2.3 Different Types of Agents in MCL

In MCL, a number of different tags, called *prejudices*, are associated to different types of agents. A tag is defined as $\alpha ::= +(X)\lambda \mid -(X)\lambda$, where X is the name of a prejudice associated to an agent λ. A prejudice is the assumption of a direct dependency between two of three types of logical tokens assertions, beliefs, and facts in the system for one particular agent. For instance, when we say that an agent is sincere, we mean that when he makes an assertion, then he has the belief of that assertion. We introduce the list of the possible combinations in Sect. 4. We then have the five agent types given in Table 1. The adjective *weak* and *strong* are only applied to the collaborative prejudice (in MCL) and differentiate between an agent who asserts what he believes on *at least one* (i.e., $T_\diamond[\lambda : \varphi]$) or *all* (i.e., $T_\square[\lambda : \varphi]$) the channels, respectively.

Figure 1 shows the introduction ($[I.]$) and elimination ($[E.]$) rules for prejudice given in [2]. Note that only negative tags can be derived, i.e., positive tags only appear in the premises of a rule. This is because the intended meaning of a positive prejudice can easily be defined in second-order logic quantifying on the formula asserted or believed by an agent. Hence, a positive tag cannot be introduced after one assertion or belief of an agent, e.g., an agent has to know any topic discussed to be tagged as competent $+(Co)$. On the other hand, the existential quantifier characterizing the negative tags allows for the introduction

$$\text{R.32} \quad \frac{\varphi \quad +(O)\lambda}{B[\lambda : \varphi]} \quad [\text{E.} +(O)] \qquad \text{R.33} \quad \frac{B[\lambda : \varphi] \quad +(Co)\lambda}{\varphi} \quad [\text{E.} +(Co)]$$

$$\text{R.34} \quad \frac{B[\lambda : \varphi] \quad +(W_{Cl})\lambda}{T_\diamond[\lambda : \varphi]} \quad [\text{E.} +(W_{Cl})] \qquad \text{R.35} \quad \frac{B[\lambda : \varphi] \quad +(S_{Cl})\lambda}{T_\square[\lambda : \varphi]} \quad [\text{E.} +(S_{Cl})]$$

$$\text{R.36} \quad \frac{T_\diamond[\lambda : \varphi] \quad +(S)\lambda}{B[\lambda : \varphi]} \quad [\text{E.} +(S)] \qquad \text{R.37} \quad \frac{\sim B[\lambda : \varphi] \quad \varphi}{-(O)\lambda} \quad [\text{I.} -(O)]$$

$$\text{R.38} \quad \frac{B[\lambda : \varphi] \quad \neg\varphi}{-(Co)\lambda} \quad [\text{I.} -(Co)] \qquad \text{R.39} \quad \frac{B[\lambda : \varphi] \quad \sim T_\diamond[\lambda : \varphi]}{-(W_{Cl})\lambda} \quad [\text{I.} -(W_{Cl})]$$

$$\text{R.40} \quad \frac{B[\lambda : \varphi] \quad \sim T_\square[\lambda : \varphi]}{-(S_{Cl})\lambda} \quad [\text{I.} -(S_{Cl})] \qquad \text{R.41} \quad \frac{T_\diamond[\lambda : \varphi] \quad \sim B[\lambda : \varphi]}{-(S)\lambda} \quad [\text{I.} -(S)]$$

Fig. 1. The rules for prejudice in MCL

of negative tags, e.g., if an agent does not know a single topic, he is tagged as incompetent $-(Co)$. This is not explicitly formalized in [2] and we introduce a fully-fledged formalization of tags in Sect. 3. Furthermore, in [2], the weak and strong adjective are used only for a collaborative agent and, e.g., the rules for the sincere agent (rules R.36 and R.41 in Fig. 1) only consider assertions in at least one channel. In our formalization, we consider weak and strong prejudice for each assertion used in a rule.

3   Agents in MAS

In MCL, agents are defined by using the three main components of the framework: the sets $\mathbb{A}_\lambda, \mathbb{B}_\lambda$ and $\mathbb{F}$ of announcements, beliefs and facts. A natural step is to define how many different types of agents can be defined out of these three sets. To do that, we first extend the results of [2] by considering the relations between these three sets and then use these relations to define agents in MCL.

Intuitively, we can define the following three relations:

- *Collaboration* $(\mathbb{A}_\lambda, \mathbb{B}_\lambda)$ is the relation between beliefs and announcements of an agent λ. This relation defines the level of collaboration of λ as the *quantity* of data an agent announces with respect to the data he believes. For example, if an agent asserts everything he believes, he is collaborative (recall that belief can be false, in which case the agent might not be competent).
- *Competence* $(\mathbb{B}_\lambda, \mathbb{F})$ is the relation between beliefs of an agent λ and true facts. This relation defines the level of competence of λ and is related to the *quality* of data an agent produces. For example, if everything an agent believes is also true, he is competent (note that this is not the definition of knowledge since an agent could believe in false formulae).
- *Honesty* $(\mathbb{A}_\lambda, \mathbb{F})$ is the relation between announcements made by an agent λ and true facts. This relation defines the level of honesty of λ. For example, if everything an agent shares on a channel is also true, then he is honest.[1]

Given that these three relations are over sets, they express *mereological* relations. We use the *Region Connection Calculus* (RCC) to reason on the different "levels" of collaboration/competence/honesty and to identify which are the different possible relations between the three sets $\mathbb{A}_\lambda$, $\mathbb{B}_\lambda$ and $\mathbb{F}$. This ultimately defines how many different types of agents we can theoretically consider.

RCC, as defined in [4,8], is an axiomatization of certain spatial concepts and relations in first-order logic. In its broader definition, the RCC theory is composed by eight axioms, and is known as RCC8, but here we restrict to RCC5 by not considering tangential connections between spatial regions. We discuss the choice of RCC5 in more detail in Sect. 5.

We define *parthood* as the primitive binary inclusion relation $\subseteq$, which is reflexive, antisymmetric and transitive. In Table 2, we define the relations of

---

[1] Note that honesty is not necessary related to correctness. In fact, we define an agent as honest if he asserts the truth even if he does not believe in what he asserts.

Table 2. RCC3, RCC5, and RCC8 relations between spatial regions X, Y and Z

			Name	Notation	Definition
			Connects with	$C(X,Y)$	$X \subseteq Y$
			Disconnected from	$\neg C(X,Y)$	$X \nsubseteq Y$
			Part of	$P(X,Y)$	$\forall Z\ C(Z,X) \rightarrow C(Z,Y)$
			Overlaps	$O(X,Y)$	$\exists Z\ P(Z,X) \wedge P(Z,Y)$
●			Overlaps Not Equal	$ONE(X,Y)$	$O(X,Y) \wedge \neg EQ(X,Y)$
●	●	●	Equal to	$EQ(X,Y)$	$P(X,Y) \wedge P(Y,X)$
●	●	●	DiscRete from	$DR(X,Y)$	$\neg O(X,Y)$
	●	●	Partial-Overlap	$PO(X,Y)$	$O(X,Y) \wedge \neg P(X,Y) \wedge \neg P(Y,X)$
	●		Proper-part-of	$PP(X,Y)$	$P(X,Y) \wedge \neg P(Y,X)$
	●		Proper-part-of-inverse	$PPi(X,Y)$	$P(Y,X) \wedge \neg P(X,Y)$
		●	Externally Connected	$EC(X,Y)$	$C(X,Y) \wedge \neg O(X,Y)$
		●	Tangential PP	$TPP(X,Y)$	$PP(X,Y) \wedge \exists Z\ [EC(Z,X), EC(Z,Y)]$
		●	Tangential PPi	$TPPi(X,Y)$	$TPP(Y,X)$
		●	Non-tangential PP	$NTPP(X,Y)$	$PP(X,Y) \wedge \neg \exists Z\ [EC(Z,X), EC(Z,Y)]$
		●	Non-tangential PPi	$NTPPi(X,Y)$	$NTPP(Y,X)$

RCC3, RCC5 and RCC8, where X, Y and Z are sets (spatial regions) of formulae and *Connects with* expresses the parthood relation. By applying these relations to the pairs $(\mathbb{A}_\lambda, \mathbb{B}_\lambda), (\mathbb{B}_\lambda, \mathbb{F})$ and $(\mathbb{A}_\lambda, \mathbb{F})$, we can distinguish between different levels of collaboration, competence and honesty. Every tuple representing the combination of the three relations defines a different type of agent.

$$Agent = \langle RCC5_1(\mathbb{A}_\lambda, \mathbb{B}_\lambda),\ RCC5_2(\mathbb{B}_\lambda, \mathbb{F}),\ RCC5_3(\mathbb{A}_\lambda, \mathbb{F}) \rangle$$

where $RCC5_1, RCC5_2$ and $RCC5_3$ are relations in RCC-5. As we discuss in Sect. 5, some combinations of $RCC5_1, RCC5_2$ and $RCC5_3$ are topologically incorrect.

4   Categorization of Agents

We now consider the details of every RCC5 relation between each pair of $\mathbb{A}_\lambda$, $\mathbb{B}_\lambda$ and $\mathbb{F}$ and we define 15 different prejudices. Our list is complete with respect to RCC5, i.e., no other relations can be considered. We will use overline numbers to identify the new rules we introduce, whereas the decimals for the rules were already defined in [2].

4.1   Collaboration

Sincere $PP(\mathbb{A}_\lambda, \mathbb{B}_\lambda)$. A sincere agent λ is defined by the proper part of his announcements with respect to his beliefs. More formally, for any propositional formula φ,

$$\text{if } T_*[\lambda : \varphi] \text{ then } B[\lambda : \varphi],$$

where $*$ identifies one of the two modalities in MCL, i.e., $* \in \{\Box, \Diamond\}$.

This type of agent announces *only* what he believes ($\Rightarrow$) but does not announce everything he believes ($\nLeftarrow$). As already defined in [2], we can negate the formula of a sincere agent and provide deduction rules to define when an agent is *not* sincere as follows. For a non-sincere agent λ^2, there exists a propositional formula φ such that

$$T_*[\lambda : \varphi] \text{ and } \sim B[\lambda : \varphi].$$

We can then define rules that formalize that if an agent asserts, even only once, something that he does not believe in, then he is non-sincere:

$$R.41 \quad \frac{T_\diamond[\lambda : \varphi] \quad \sim B[\lambda : \varphi]}{-(W_S)\lambda} \quad [I.-(W_S)] \qquad R.\bar{1} \quad \frac{T_\square[\lambda : \varphi] \quad \sim B[\lambda : \varphi]}{-(S_S)\lambda} \quad [I.-(S_S)]$$

As we discussed in Sect. 2.3, the notion of weak and strong is only applied to the notion of collaborative agent in MCL. We avoid this asymmetry and we introduce the notion of weak and strong for all the prejudices involving a relation with announcements. This explains why we have now used W_S in R.41 instead of S of MCL (as in Fig. 1). We extend the elimination rules accordingly:

$$R.\bar{2} \quad \frac{\sim B[\lambda : \varphi] \quad + (W_S)\lambda}{\sim T_\diamond[\lambda : \varphi]} \quad [E.+(W_S)] \qquad R.\bar{3} \quad \frac{\sim B[\lambda : \varphi] \quad + (S_S)\lambda}{\sim T_\square[\lambda : \varphi]} \quad [E.+(S_S)]$$

$$R.36 \quad \frac{T_\diamond[\lambda : \varphi] \quad + (W_S)\lambda}{B[\lambda : \varphi]} \quad [E.+(W_S)] \qquad R.\bar{4} \quad \frac{T_\square[\lambda : \varphi] \quad + (S_S)\lambda}{B[\lambda : \varphi]} \quad [E.+(S_S)]$$

Collaborative $PPi(\mathbb{A}_\lambda, \mathbb{B}_\lambda)$. Symmetrically to a sincere agent, a collaborative agent λ is defined by the proper part of his beliefs with respect to his announcements: for any propositional formula φ,

$$\text{if } B[\lambda : \varphi] \text{ then } T_*[\lambda : \varphi].$$

This type of agent announces everything he believes ($\Rightarrow$) but what he says is *not only* what he believes ($\not\Leftarrow$). Hence, some of the announcements are intentionally against his beliefs (these announcements might be accidentally true facts but we will discuss this case later in this section). If we negate the definition of collaborative, we obtain that if an λ's belief has not been announced (i.e., there exists φ such that $B[\lambda : \varphi]$ and $\sim T_*[\varphi : \lambda]$), then λ is *not* collaborative. As for the sincere agent, we define strong and weak prejudice with $\square$ and $\diamond$, respectively:

$$R.39 \quad \frac{B[\lambda : \varphi] \quad \sim T_\diamond[\lambda : \varphi]}{-(W_{Cl})\lambda} \quad [I.-(W_{Cl})] \qquad R.40 \quad \frac{B[\lambda : \varphi] \quad \sim T_\square[\lambda : \varphi]}{-(S_{Cl})\lambda} \quad [I.-(S_{Cl})]$$

$$R.34 \quad \frac{B[\lambda : \varphi] \quad + (W_{Cl})\lambda}{T_\diamond[\lambda : \varphi]} \quad [E.+(W_{Cl})] \qquad R.35 \quad \frac{B[\lambda : \varphi] \quad + (S_{Cl})\lambda}{T_\square[\lambda : \varphi]} \quad [E.+(S_{Cl})]$$

$$R.\bar{5} \quad \frac{\sim T_\diamond[\lambda : \varphi] \quad + (W_{Cl})\lambda}{\sim B[\lambda : \varphi]} \quad [E.+(W_{Cl})] \qquad R.\bar{6} \quad \frac{\sim T_\square[\lambda : \varphi] \quad + (S_{Cl})\lambda}{\sim B[\lambda : \varphi]} \quad [E.+(S_{Cl})]$$

---

[2] Slightly abusing notation, we are using λ for both a sincere and non-sincere agent.

Fair $EQ(\mathbb{A}_\lambda, \mathbb{B}_\lambda)$. A fair agent λ is defined by the equality between the sets of his announcements and beliefs: for any propositional formula φ,

$$T_*[\lambda : \varphi] \text{ if and only if } B[\lambda : \varphi].$$

Hence, a fair agent is an agent who believes in *everything* he announces ($\Rightarrow$) and who announces *only* what he believes ($\Leftarrow$). As before, in order to give the rules for MCL, we first negate the definition of the fair agent. For a non-fair agent λ, there exists a propositional formula φ such that

$$(\sim T_*[\lambda : \varphi] \text{ and } B[\lambda : \varphi]) \text{ or } (\sim B[\lambda : \varphi] \text{ and } T_*[\lambda : \varphi]).$$

The left and right disjuncts are exactly the definitions of *PPi* and *PP*, respectively. Hence, the introduction and elimination rules have been already considered in the previous two cases.

Saboteur $PO(\mathbb{A}_\lambda, \mathbb{B}_\lambda)$. A saboteur agent λ is defined by the partial overlap of his announcements with respect to his beliefs: for any propositional formula φ,

$$B[\lambda : \varphi] \text{ or } T_*[\lambda : \varphi].$$

This type of agent may announce something that he believes but also that he does not believe, or does not announce something he believes.

$$\text{R.7} \ \frac{\sim B[\lambda : \varphi] \quad \sim T_\diamond[\lambda : \varphi]}{-(W_I)\lambda} \quad [\text{I.}-(W_I)] \qquad \text{R.8} \ \frac{\sim B[\lambda : \varphi] \quad \sim T_\square[\lambda : \varphi]}{-(S_I)\lambda} \quad [\text{I.}-(S_I)]$$

$$\text{R.9} \ \frac{\sim T_\diamond[\lambda : \varphi] \quad +(S_I)\lambda}{B[\lambda : \varphi]} \quad [\text{E.}+(S_I)] \qquad \text{R.}\overline{10} \ \frac{\sim T_\square[\lambda : \varphi] \quad +(S_I)\lambda}{B[\lambda : \varphi]} \quad [\text{E.}+(S_I)]$$

$$\text{R.}\overline{11} \ \frac{\sim B[\lambda : \varphi] \quad +(W_I)\lambda}{T_\diamond[\lambda : \varphi]} \quad [\text{E.}+(W_I)] \qquad \text{R.}\overline{12} \ \frac{\sim B[\lambda : \varphi] \quad +(W_I)\lambda}{T_\square[\lambda : \varphi]} \quad [\text{E.}+(W_I)]$$

Braggart $DR(\mathbb{A}_\lambda, \mathbb{B}_\lambda)$. A braggart agent λ is defined by the discrete-from relation between his announcements and beliefs: for any propositional formula φ,

$$\sim T_*[\lambda : \varphi] \text{ or } \sim B[\lambda : \varphi].$$

This agent *only* announces what he does not believe and he does not announce what he believes. Reasoning on the negated definition (i.e., on a non-braggart agent λ for which there exists a propositional formula φ such that $T_*[\lambda : \varphi]$ and $B[\lambda : \varphi]$), we can define that if (at least once) the agent states something he believes in, then he is non-braggart.

$$\text{R.}\overline{13} \ \frac{T_\diamond[\lambda : \varphi] \quad B[\lambda : \varphi]}{-(W_B)\lambda} \quad [\text{I.}-(W_B)] \qquad \text{R.}\overline{14} \ \frac{T_\square[\lambda : \varphi] \quad B[\lambda : \varphi]}{-(S_B)\lambda} \quad [\text{I.}-(S_B)]$$

$$\text{R.}\overline{15} \ \frac{T_\diamond[\lambda : \varphi] \quad +(S_B)\lambda}{\sim B[\lambda : \varphi]} \quad [\text{E.}+(S_B)] \qquad \text{R.}\overline{16} \ \frac{T_\square[\lambda : \varphi] \quad +(S_B)\lambda}{\sim B[\lambda : \varphi]} \quad [\text{E.}+(S_B)]$$

$$\text{R.}\overline{17} \ \frac{B[\lambda : \varphi] \quad +(W_B)\lambda}{\sim T_\diamond[\lambda : \varphi]} \quad [\text{E.}+(W_B)] \qquad \text{R.}\overline{18} \ \frac{B[\lambda : \varphi] \quad +(W_B)\lambda}{\sim T_\square[\lambda : \varphi]} \quad [\text{E.}+(W_B)]$$

4.2   Competence

Competent $PP(\mathbb{B}_\lambda, \mathbb{F})$. An agent's beliefs are a subset of the true formulae. Hence, all the agent's beliefs are facts but there may be true formulae "out" of his beliefs. An agent λ is competent if, for every propositional formula φ, if $B[\lambda : \varphi]$ then $\varphi \in \mathbb{F}$.

R.38 $\dfrac{B[\lambda : \varphi] \quad \neg\varphi}{-(Co)\lambda}$ [I. $-(Co)$]

R.33 $\dfrac{B[\lambda : \varphi] \quad +(Co)\lambda}{\varphi}$ [E. $+(Co)$]   R.$\overline{19}$ $\dfrac{\sim B[\lambda : \varphi] \quad +(Co)\lambda}{\neg\varphi}$ [E. $+(Co)$]

Omniscient $PPi(\mathbb{B}_\lambda, \mathbb{F})$. An agent λ is omniscient if the set of formulae he believes is a superset of the actually true formulae: for any propositional formula φ, if $\varphi \in \mathbb{F}$ then $B[\lambda : \varphi]$.

R.37 $\dfrac{\sim B[\lambda : \varphi] \quad \varphi}{-(O)\lambda}$ [I. $-(O)$]

R.32 $\dfrac{\varphi \quad +(O)\lambda}{B[\lambda : \varphi]}$ [E. $+(O)$]   R.$\overline{20}$ $\dfrac{\sim B[\lambda : \varphi] \quad +(O)\lambda}{\neg\varphi}$ [E. $+(O)$]

Wise $EQ(\mathbb{B}_\lambda, \mathbb{F})$. A wise agent λ is defined by the equality between the sets of his beliefs and facts, i.e., he *only* believes in true formulae and knows *all* the true facts: for any propositional formula φ, $\varphi \in \mathbb{F}$ if and only if $B[\lambda : \varphi]$. The rules generated are exactly the rules of PP_i and PP.

Incompetent $PO(\mathbb{B}_\lambda, \mathbb{F})$. An incompetent agent λ is defined by the partial overlap of his beliefs with the true facts, therefore part of his belief are not facts, and this makes the agent incompetent: for any propositional formula φ, $\varphi \in \mathbb{F}$ or $B[\lambda : \varphi]$. This type of agent believes in true and false formulae, and there exist facts that he does not believe in, but he won't believe a false formula φ.

R.$\overline{21}$ $\dfrac{\neg\varphi \quad \sim B[\lambda : \varphi]}{-(In)\lambda}$ [I. $-(In)$]

R.$\overline{22}$ $\dfrac{\neg\varphi \quad +(In)\lambda}{B[\lambda : \varphi]}$ [E.$+(In)$]   R.$\overline{23}$ $\dfrac{\sim B[\lambda : \varphi] \quad +(In)\lambda}{\varphi}$ [E.$+(In)$]

Ignorant $DR(\mathbb{B}_\lambda, \mathbb{F})$. An ignorant agent λ is defined by the discrete-from relation between true formulae and beliefs: for any propositional formula φ, $\neg\varphi \in \mathbb{F}$ or $\sim B[\lambda : \varphi]$. Therefore, this agent *only* believes in false formulae.

R.$\overline{24}$ $\dfrac{\varphi \quad B[\lambda : \varphi]}{-(Ig)\lambda}$ [I. $-(Ig)$]

R.$\overline{25}$ $\dfrac{\varphi \quad +(Ig)\lambda}{\sim B[\lambda : \varphi]}$ [E.$+(Ig)$]   R.$\overline{26}$ $\dfrac{B[\lambda : \varphi] \quad +(Ig)\lambda}{\neg\varphi}$ [E.$+(Ig)$]

4.3   Honesty

Honest $PP(\mathbb{A}_\lambda, \mathbb{F})$. An agent is honest if every formula he asserts is a fact, and the agent's assertion are a subset of the true formulae: for any propositional formula φ, if φ then $\mathrm{T}_*[\lambda : \varphi]$.

$$\text{R.}\overline{27}\ \frac{\varphi \quad \sim \mathrm{T}_\diamond[\lambda : \varphi]}{\text{-}(W_H)\lambda}\ \ [\text{I. -}(W_H)] \qquad \text{R.}\overline{28}\ \frac{\varphi \quad \sim \mathrm{T}_\square[\lambda : \varphi]}{\text{-}(S_H)\lambda}\ \ [\text{I.-}(S_H)]$$

$$\text{R.}\overline{29}\ \frac{\varphi \quad +(W_H)\lambda}{\mathrm{T}_\diamond[\lambda : \varphi]}\ \ [\text{E.+}(W_H)] \qquad \text{R.}\overline{30}\ \frac{\varphi \quad +(S_H)\lambda}{\mathrm{T}_\square[\lambda : \varphi]}\ \ [\text{E.+}(S_H)]$$

$$\text{R.}\overline{31}\ \frac{\sim \mathrm{T}_\diamond[\lambda : \varphi] \quad +(W_H)\lambda}{\neg\varphi}\ \ [\text{E.+}(W_H)] \quad \text{R.}\overline{32}\ \frac{\sim \mathrm{T}_\square[\lambda : \varphi] \quad +(S_H)\lambda}{\neg\varphi}\ \ [\text{E.+}(S_H)]$$

Oracle $PPi(\mathbb{A}_\lambda, \mathbb{F})$. An agent λ is an oracle if, for any propositional formula φ, if $\mathrm{T}_*[\lambda : \varphi]$ then $\varphi \in \mathbb{F}$.

$$\text{R.}\overline{33}\ \frac{\mathrm{T}_\diamond[\lambda : \varphi] \quad \neg\varphi}{\text{-}(W_{Or})\lambda}\ \ [\text{I. -}(W_{Or})\,] \qquad \text{R.}\overline{34}\ \frac{\mathrm{T}_\square[\lambda : \varphi] \quad \neg\varphi}{\text{-}(S_{Or})\lambda}\ \ [\text{I.-}(S_{Or})\,]$$

$$\text{R.}\overline{35}\ \frac{\mathrm{T}_\diamond[\lambda : \varphi] \quad +(W_{Or})\lambda}{\varphi}\ \ [\text{E.+}(W_{Or})] \quad \text{R.}\overline{36}\ \frac{\mathrm{T}_\square[\lambda : \varphi] \quad +(S_{Or})\lambda}{\varphi}\ \ [\text{E.+}(S_{Or})]$$

$$\text{R.}\overline{37}\ \frac{\neg\varphi \quad +(W_{Or})\lambda}{\sim \mathrm{T}_\diamond[\lambda : \varphi]}\ \ [\text{E.+}(W_{Or})] \qquad \text{R.}\overline{38}\ \frac{\neg\varphi \quad +(S_{Or})\lambda}{\sim \mathrm{T}_\square[\lambda : \varphi]}\ \ [\text{E.+}(S_{Or})]$$

Right $EQ(\mathbb{A}_\lambda, \mathbb{F})$. An agent λ is right if, for any propositional formula $\varphi, \varphi \in \mathbb{F}$ if and only if $\mathrm{T}_*[\lambda : \varphi]$. We omit the rules since they are the same as for PP and PP_i.

Incorrect $PO(\mathbb{A}_\lambda, \mathbb{F})$. An agent λ is incorrect if, for any propositional formula $\varphi, \varphi \in \mathbb{F}$ or $\mathrm{T}_*[\lambda : \varphi]$. The announcements of this type of agent might be true or false, and he only announces part of the facts (i.e., a subset of the facts will never be announced by him).

$$\text{R.}\overline{39}\ \frac{\neg\varphi \quad \sim \mathrm{T}_\diamond[\lambda : \varphi]}{-(W_{Ir})\lambda}\ \ [\text{I. -}(W_{Ir})\,] \qquad \text{R.}\overline{40}\ \frac{\neg\varphi \quad \sim \mathrm{T}_\square[\lambda : \varphi]}{-(S_{Ir})\lambda}\ \ [\text{I.-}(S_{Ir})\,]$$

$$\text{R.}\overline{41}\ \frac{\neg\varphi \quad +(W_{Ir})\lambda}{\mathrm{T}_\diamond[\lambda : \varphi]}\ \ [\text{E.+}(W_{Ir})] \qquad \text{R.}\overline{42}\ \frac{\neg\varphi \quad +(S_{Ir})\lambda}{\mathrm{T}_\square[\lambda : \varphi]}\ \ [\text{E.+}(S_{Ir})]$$

$$\text{R.}\overline{43}\ \frac{\sim \mathrm{T}_\diamond[\lambda : \varphi] \quad +(W_{Ir})\lambda}{\varphi}\ \ [\text{E.+}(W_{Ir})] \quad \text{R.}\overline{44}\ \frac{\sim \mathrm{T}_\square[\lambda : \varphi] \quad +(S_{Ir})\lambda}{\varphi}\ [\text{E.+}(S_{Ir})]$$

False $DR(\mathbb{A}_\lambda, \mathbb{F})$. A false agent λ is defined by the discrete-form relation between true formulae and his assertions, i.e., for any propositional formula φ, $\neg\varphi \in \mathbb{F}$ or $\sim \mathrm{T}_*[\lambda : \varphi]$. In other words, everything he announces is false.

$$\text{R.}\overline{45}\ \frac{\varphi\ \ \mathrm{T}_\diamond[\lambda:\varphi]}{-(W_F)\lambda}\quad [\mathrm{I.}{-}(W_F)] \qquad\qquad \text{R.}\overline{46}\ \frac{\varphi\ \ \mathrm{T}_\square[\lambda:\varphi]}{-(S_F)\lambda}\quad [\mathrm{I.}{-}(S_F)]$$

$$\text{R.}\overline{47}\ \frac{\varphi\ +(W_F)\lambda}{\sim \mathrm{T}_\diamond[\lambda:\varphi]}\quad [\mathrm{E.}{+}(W_F)] \qquad\qquad \text{R.}\overline{48}\ \frac{\varphi\ +(S_F)\lambda}{\sim \mathrm{T}_\square[\lambda:\varphi]}\quad [\mathrm{E.}{+}(S_F)]$$

$$\text{R.}\overline{49}\ \frac{\mathrm{T}_\diamond[\lambda:\varphi]\ +(W_F)\lambda}{\neg\varphi}\quad [\mathrm{E.}{+}(W_F)] \qquad \text{R.}\overline{50}\ \frac{\mathrm{T}_\square[\lambda:\varphi]\ +(S_F)\lambda}{\neg\varphi}\quad [\mathrm{E.}{+}(S_F)]$$

5 On the Topology of MAS

In this section, we justify the use of RCC5 instead of RCC3 or RCC8, and discuss the relation between the topology we consider and the agent types.

5.1 RCC3, RCC5, and RCC8

As already mentioned in Sect. 3, there exist three different types of RCC, based on the number of topological relations considered: RCC3, RCC5, and RCC8. RCC3 considers the three different topological relations listed in Table 2: *ONE*, *EQ*, and *DR*. The topological relations *EQ* and *DR* are the same as in RCC5 (see Table 2), whereas *ONE* defines the overlap relation between two regions with the additional constraint that the regions cannot be fully overlapping (i.e., they cannot be two exact copies of the same region).

The relation *ONE* in RCC3 is detailed in RCC5 with the relations *PP*, *PPi*, and *PO*. Hence, considering RCC5 instead of RCC3 results in a more accurate and expressive categorization of agents. However, the same reasoning cannot be applied to RCC8. In fact, even if RCC8 is more detailed than RCC5 as it considers more topological relations, the additional topological relations considered by RCC8 cannot be applied for the categorization of agents in MCL. As showed in Table 2, RCC8 considers tangential connections, where, informally, two tangential regions are near enough so that no other region can fit between the two (without overlapping them), but are not overlapping at any point. This is formalized by the *EC* relation. In addition, in RCC8, each of the two relations *PP* and *PPi* is detailed into tangential and non-tangential.

In our work, the elements of the three sets $\mathbb{A}$, $\mathbb{B}$ and $\mathbb{F}$ are not ordered. In other words, we are not considering the distance between those elements (or between regions containing those elements). Hence, given any pair of (sub-)sets between $\mathbb{A}$, $\mathbb{B}$ and $\mathbb{F}$, regardless of the sets being near or far apart between each other, we consider them as disjoint (i.e., *DR*).

5.2 An Upper Bound on the Number of Different Types of Agents

Applying RCC over a finite number of sets, we obtain a definite number of resulting combinations. Hence, applying RCC over $\mathbb{A}_\lambda, \mathbb{B}_\lambda, \mathbb{F}$, we obtain a definite number of different types of agents. In this section, we show the general upper bound on the number of different agents with respect to the type of RCC (RCC5, RCC3 or RCC8) considered.

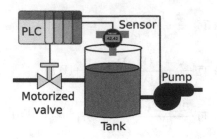

Fig. 2. Representation of the test case

Table 3. Number of agents with respect to different RCC

	Theoretical	Correct
RCC3	$3^3 = 27$	15
RCC5	$5^3 = 125$	54
RCC8	$8^3 = 512$	193

The general formula to calculate the number of different types of agents is $r^{\binom{n}{k}}$, where r is the number of relations with arity k, between n different sets, where r^e is the number of permutation of r relations over e elements with repetitions, with e being the number of k-ary combinations of n sets, $\binom{n}{k}$. In our case, $\binom{n}{k} = 3$ since we consider 3 sets ($\mathbb{A}, \mathbb{B}, \mathbb{F}$), and all the relations considered in the RCC are binary. Hence, using RCC5 (with five different spatial relations) over three sets, we can theoretically define up to 125 different type of agents. However, only 54 of the 125 (as showed in [4] and derived by the composition table of RCC5) combinations are topologically correct with respect to the definition of the relations of RCC5. Generalizing to all the RCCs, in Table 3 we calculate the number of different agents with respect to all the variations of RCC (i.e., with 3, 5 or 8 spatial relations). Due to space limits, we omit the composition table for RCC3, RCC5 and RCC8. Hence, even if considering a different number of sets than the three $\mathbb{A}, \mathbb{B}$ and $\mathbb{F}$ exponentially affects the number of theoretical agents, the application of RCC downscales that number of a factor that ranges from 1.8 to 2.5. In addition, using RCC5 we consider 3.6 times more (different) types of agents than RCC3, but using RCC8 would allow us to consider 3.5 times more different agents.

6 Use Case

In this section, we show that both the framework and the categorization of agents that we have given can be applied to reason about the security of CPS.

6.1 Cyber-Physical Systems

We use the term CPS to refer to systems that consist of networked embedded systems, which are used to sense, actuate, and control physical processes. Examples of CPS include industrial water treatment facilities and power plants. CPS have seen a rapid increase in automation and connectivity, which threatens to increase their vulnerability to malicious attacks. Let us now use our approach to address the problem of defining security-related attack states for CPS.

Description of the Case Study. Similarly to [5,9], we consider a CPS (depicted in Fig. 2) to be composed by five agents:

- A *tank* containing water.
- A *controller* (e.g., a PLC) that controls the water level so that the tank does not (underflow or) overflow.
- A *water level indicator* (e.g., a Sensor) that communicates the readings of the level of the water inside the tank to the PLC.
- A *motorized valve* and a *pump* that (controlled by the PLC) regulate the inflow and outflow of water respectively.

Mapping $\mathbb{A}, \mathbb{B}$, and $\mathbb{F}$ to CPS. It is possible that the three sets $\mathbb{A}, \mathbb{B}$ and $\mathbb{F}$ contain at the same time different formulae that contain each element of the topological space φ. Hence, every assertion and belief must be objective (since it can be part of $\mathbb{F}$). This implies that formulae like $\varphi := highLevel(tank, water)$ cannot be considered in our reasoning since "high" is considered to be subjective. In contrast, we can use objective formulae such as $\varphi := level(tank, 20\ L)$.

When considering a CPS (and security systems in general, e.g., security protocols) as a MAS, the message exchange between different agents can be formalized by means of *assertions*. In addition, redundant channels are often employed to reduce security treats (or assertions are required over multiple channels as, e.g., in two-factor authentication) and then it is fair to assume that assertions can be done over single or multiple channels. Finally, the inspection of the memory of any software/hardware of the CPS (supposing a white-box analysis) reveals the actual *beliefs*, while the *facts* in a CPS are defined by the physical laws of the physics. We can summarize our mapping as follows:

- $\mathbb{A}_\lambda$ defines the values communicated by the agent λ.
- $\mathbb{B}_\lambda$ defines the computational results of the agent λ.
- $\mathbb{F}$ defines the environmental values, i.e., the real values of the system.

6.2 Single-Channel Attack States

We are now in a position to show that we can directly apply our topological categorization to any agent in our CPS. For simplicity, we first use only the RCC5 relations EQ and DR, and then extend our results to all RCC5 relations.

Optimal System Status. Suppose that the tank contains $20\ L$ of water, e.g., $level(tank, 20\ L) \in \mathbb{F}$, where $level$ is a predicate, and $tank$ and $20\ L$ are propositional constants. For the sake of simplicity, we also suppose that the system is in idle (both the motorized valve and the pump are off). When the system is *not* compromised, the sensor correctly computes the level of the water in the tank (e.g., $level(tank, 20\ L) \in \mathbb{B}_{sensor}$) and correctly communicates to the PLC the computed value of water in the tank (e.g., $level(tank, 20\ L) \in \mathbb{A}_{sensor}$). We can then define the optimal status of the sensor as the triple $\langle EQ(\mathbb{A}_{sensor}, \mathbb{B}_{sensor}), EQ(\mathbb{B}_{sensor}, \mathbb{F}), EQ(\mathbb{A}_{sensor}, \mathbb{F}) \rangle$.

System Under Attack. Suppose that the sensor is communicating wrong values to the PLC (i.e., $DR(\mathbb{A}_{sensor}, \mathbb{F})$). As showed in Table 4, we have three mutually exclusive cases:

Table 4. Example of attack states for the water level sensor

State of the sensor	$(\mathbb{A}, \mathbb{B})$	$(\mathbb{B}, \mathbb{F})$	$(\mathbb{A}, \mathbb{F})$
Optimal	EQ	EQ	EQ
Sensor compromised	EQ	DR	DR
Communication compromised	DR	EQ	DR
Fully compromised	DR	DR	DR

1. The sensor is working properly $EQ(\mathbb{B}_{sensor}, \mathbb{F})$, therefore (topologically) the communication between the sensor and the PLC has been compromised, i.e., $DR(\mathbb{A}_{sensor}, \mathbb{B}_{sensor})$.
2. The communication between the sensor and the PLC has not been compromised $EQ(\mathbb{A}_{sensor}, \mathbb{B}_{sensor})$, therefore the sensor is *not* sending what it computes $DR(\mathbb{B}_{sensor}, \mathbb{F})$.
3. Both the communication and the sensor have been compromised.

As a consequence of the discussion in Sect. 5.2, between the optimal and the fully compromised status of the sensor there must be 52 other different statuses. Due to lack of space, we cannot go into the details of each status, but we can generalize the attack states into three main categories, as follows:

- RCC5$(\mathbb{A}, \mathbb{B})$ expresses the relation between the values communicated and the ones computed by an agent.
- RCC5$(\mathbb{B}, \mathbb{F})$ expresses the relation between the values computed and the true environmental values.
- RCC5$(\mathbb{A}, \mathbb{F})$ expresses the relation between the values communicated and the true environmental values.

Defense mechanisms that check sudden changes in physical readings (see [12] for an example of how this is defined in MAS with logical systems) are often adopted in CPS. To bypass the security mechanisms, during an attack, the optimal status will likely pass through most of the 52 intermediate statuses.

6.3 Multiple-Channel Attack States

A countermeasure often applied in CPS (but not limited to CPS) is the implementation of redundant channels. As proposed in [10], in our case study one could implement a dedicated system that interprets the readings of the sensor and directly closes the motorized valve if an upper threshold is reached. We can leverage the modal operators to define such communications and to define even more sophisticated attack states. For example, given a state $\mathbb{A}_{sensor}, \mathbb{B}_{sensor}, \mathbb{F}$ in MCL, we can check if one or all the channels that the sensor uses to communicate with the PLC have been compromised, as defined in (1) and (2) respectively:

$$\{\mathbb{A}_{sensor}, \mathbb{B}_{sensor}, \mathbb{F}\} \vdash -(S_{Fair})_{sensor} \qquad (1)$$

$$\{\mathbb{A}_{sensor}, \mathbb{B}_{sensor}, \mathbb{F}\} \vdash -(W_{Fair})_{sensor} \qquad (2)$$

Based on the approach we have proposed in this paper, we can formalize the optimal/attack states of a CPS, reason on the properties of the CPS by means of prejudices in MCL, and obtain therefore a control upon the concept of redundancy as expressed above. Our approach is not specific to CPS but can potentially be applied to any MAS (as long as the elements of the topological space are objective).

7   Conclusion

We proposed a topological categorization of agents for MCL using RCC5. We defined an upper bound on the number of different agents in a MAS and we applied our results to the security of CPS. We showed that our results can be used to address the problem of defining attack states for CPS. We are currently working on an implementation of our framework. We have also been extending MCL to capture the intents of agents, which will ultimately allow us to consider human agents in the formalization of MAS.

References

1. Balbiani, P., Seban, P.: Reasoning about permitted announcements. J. Philos. Logic **40**(4), 445–472 (2011)
2. Cristani, M., Olivieri, F., Santaca, K.: A logical model of communication channels. In: Lavangnananda, K., Phon-Amnuaisuk, S., Engchuan, W., Chan, J. (eds.) Intelligent and Evolutionary Systems. Springer, Cham (2016)
3. Grossi, D., Royakkers, L., Dignum, F.: Organizational structure and responsibility: an analysis in a dynamic logic of organized collective agency. Artif. Intell. Law **15**(3), 223–249 (2007)
4. Grütter, R., Scharrenbach, T., Bauer-Messmer, B.: Improving an RCC-derived geospatial approximation by OWL axioms. In: Sheth, A., Staab, S., Dean, M., Paolucci, M., Maynard, D., Finin, T., Thirunarayan, K. (eds.) ISWC 2008. LNCS, vol. 5318, pp. 293–306. Springer, Heidelberg (2008). doi:10.1007/978-3-540-88564-1_19
5. Kang, E., Adepu, S., Jackson, D., Mathur, A.P.: Model-based security analysis of a water treatment system. In: SEsCPS (2016)
6. Khaitan, S., McCalley, J.: Design techniques and applications of cyberphysical systems: a survey. IEEE Syst. J. **9**(2), 350–365 (2015)
7. Lin, J., Sedigh, S., Miller, A.: Modeling cyber-physical systems with semantic agents. In: COMPSACW (2010)
8. Lin, T.Y., Liu, Q., Yao, Y.Y.: Logics systems for approximate reasoning: approximation via rough sets and topological spaces. In: ISMIS (1994)
9. Rocchetto, M., Tippenhauer, N.O.: CPDY: extending the Dolev-Yao attacker with physical-layer interactions. In: Ogata, K., Lawford, M., Liu, S. (eds.) ICFEM 2016. LNCS, vol. 10009, pp. 175–192. Springer, Cham (2016). doi:10.1007/978-3-319-47846-3_12
10. Sabaliauskaite, G., Mathur, A.P.: Intelligent checkers to improve attack detection in cyber physical systems. In: CyberC (2013)

11. Sanislav, T., Miclea, L.: Cyber-physical systems - concept, challenges and research areas. Control Eng. Appl. Inform. **14**(2), 28–33 (2012)
12. Urbina, D., Giraldo, J., Cardenas, A.A., Tippenhauer, N.O., Valente, J., Faisal, M., Ruths, J., Candell, R., Sandberg, H.: Limiting the impact of stealthy attacks on industrial control systems. In: CCS (2016)
13. Van Benthem, J., Van Eijck, J., Kooi, B.: Logics of communication and change. Inf. Comput. **204**(11), 1620–1662 (2006)

Agents and Dementia — Smart Risk Assessment

Steve Williams and Berndt Müller[✉]

Faculty of Computing, Engineering and Science,
University of South Wales, Pontypridd, UK
{steve.williams1,bertie.muller}@southwales.ac.uk

Abstract. This paper describes applied research in the development
of mobile, wearable and other smart technology to assist people with
mild to moderate symptoms of dementia. With safety and security paramount, the primary objective is to prolong independence of the person
with symptoms and provide an element of relief to families from what can
become a full-time burden of care. Intelligent agents recognise activity in
its context, assess risk and subsequently act to recover persons who wander or become lost. Results indicate that constant activity monitoring
without ethically controversial tracking is possible without the necessity
of invading privacy.

1 Introduction

'Dementia' describes a collection of symptoms that result from damage to the
brain due to a number of conditions, the most common of these is Alzheimer's
disease. Only 43% of persons with dementia (PwD) are diagnosed[1], but the
number of people affected was recently estimated as 850,000 in the UK and over
46.8 million globally. This is predicted to double every 20 years.[2]

With an immense impact on the PwD and their family common symptoms
include memory loss, difficulty remembering routes and becoming confused in
unfamiliar places. Wandering and getting lost can happen during any stage of
the disease, with it being reported that 40% get lost at some point and about
5% get lost repeatedly [1]. 1% of PwD die while lost and half of those who are
missing for more than 24 h die or are seriously injured [2]. The resultant 'burden
of care' for a family member can be overwhelming.

With the emergence of connected smart-devices a unique opportunity to provide individualised care in the community arises. Although not well suited to the
whole spectrum of symptoms or to all stages of the disease, Assistive Technology
(AT), in the right circumstances, has the potential to improve the quality of life
for PwD and their families [3,4]. Smart-phones, wearable technology and devices

---

[1] http://www.healthcare-today.co.uk/doclibrary/documents/pdf/826_Mapping_the_
dementia_gap.pdf.

[2] https://www.alz.co.uk/research/world-report-2015.

© Springer International Publishing AG 2017
N. Criado Pacheco et al. (Eds.): EUMAS 2016/AT 2016, LNAI 10207, pp. 277–284, 2017.
DOI: 10.1007/978-3-319-59294-7_22

may, when made bespoke form the basis of a solution useful to PwD with mild to moderate and perhaps particularly early onset symptoms.

The hypothesis is that smart technology for monitoring PwD may be used to preserve independence, allow a reduction of carer burden and thus increase the time that they may be cared for in the community. This, it is thought will provide benefits for the PwD, their family unit and the healthcare provider. PwD should be supported to remain independent in their communities for as long as possible[3]. The cost of full time care is significant and this can lead to ad-hoc measures being put in place, the burden of care sometimes leads to ill health and a poor outcome for the carer (see footnote 3) [5]. Particular AT solutions have shown to prolong the ability of PwD to continue living at home by an average of 8 months [6]. We have established a test-bed to develop agents on multiple platforms that seek to address issues in what is now a mature ethical and privacy debate.

2   Ethics and Barriers to the Use of AT

Ethics. Monitoring those considered to be vulnerable has been debated for decades [7]. Benefits include safety, independence and peace of mind [8,9], but there is some concern that monitoring or recording an individual's location present ethical and privacy issues [3,10]. When Police in the UK used GPS tracking to recover lost PwD in 2013, this resulted in an outcry in the media. In relation to dementia, one dilemma discussed is this: where is the greater breach of rights? Is it a locked door resulting in the loss of liberty or monitored autonomous movement using AT leading to loss of privacy? [8–10]. [8] analyses the opinions of cognitively intact older people, finding that they favoured the use of AT, in a small participatory study PwD disliked remote monitoring and surveillance, while carers pragmatically prioritised safety [11]. With smart-phones, the risk of broadcasting a user's location is known. Advocates of digital privacy see an opportunity for surveillance to a level which is similar to that predicted by Orwell in his famous novel '1984'.

Barriers. In 2013 a randomised controlled trial commenced in the UK assessing whether AT will significantly extend the time PwD continue to live independently and safely in their own homes [12,13] suggests investment in technology to manage the overall cost of dementia, but mentions barriers, such as underdeveloped technologies, a weak evidence base, cost, staff skills and AT awareness. There is no clear verdict on acceptance of AT by health professionals and users are often making their own decisions. Lack of evidence [13,14], patient-led learning; the 'DIY' approach and a lack of a single point of access or an authority giving advice and support are key problems [3,14].

For PwD, human relationships are the most important thing and AT should only be seen as an aid [3,6]. While it may ease the burden of care and enable independence, a solution should encompass moral and ethical concerns, we do this through participatory user-centred design, model validation and intelligent agents.

---

[3] https://www.alz.co.uk/adi/pdf/dfc-principles.pdf.

3 Bespoke Prototype Development

Adopting the principles of beneficence and non-maleficence a debate is necessary, but it is currently thought that if the PwD gets into a situation that is not safe, ethical arguments change. A morally acceptable solution is being researched where human rights of privacy and autonomy are pre-eminent, but safety and security are paramount. In the simplest use case, if a PwD is walking outside at midnight and it's $-3\,°C$, the risk of exposure is high. The computing capacity of mobile devices and a home-base 'hub' will be used to assess risk of the circumstance in which activity is taking place, activity patterns will be compared those that have been 'learnt' or are otherwise known to be acceptable. Data is gathered and processed directly, initially on a phone, but the mechanisms developed in this research will be applicable in future miniaturised wearable devices. Multiple agents on the mobile device(s) and hub interact, private information will only be shared externally if a clear instance of recovery necessitates this.

Invasive tracking of movement by another person is not advocated, but in recovery GPS and Wi-Fi locations may be made visible, sensors will also be used while indoors to contextualise activity. All data such as activity patterns and location are kept private. Minimal data propagation and encryption will be used to reduce the risk of interception or abuse.

4 Ubiquitous Assistive Technology

Technical systems that support elderly people and people with special needs in activities of daily living (ADL) are available across Europe [16]. Technology, as discussed in studies of Ambient Assisted Living (AAL) and Ambient Intelligence discuss health, safety, security, peace of mind, independence, mobility and social contact. Capabilities, strengths and weaknesses of cognitive aids and sensors have been reviewed concluding that evaluation of these should be evidence based and be carried out in real world settings [15]. To achieve trust in a technological solution, failure or false alerts are not acceptable. Likewise, if a system is intrusive or unacceptable in use it will not be adopted.

Mark Weiser, often referred to as the father of ubiquitous computing said: "The most profound technologies are those that disappear. They weave themselves into the fabric of everyday life until they are indistinguishable from it" [17]. It may be argued that mobile and wearable technology is already part of everyday life and it is their unobtrusiveness that may assist in adoption of such a system.

5 Activity Recognition (AR)

The developing field of activity recognition has recently brought about many commercial attempts at wearable devices. These products are used to inspire and motivate users to live a healthier lifestyle. We have evaluated the potential worth to PwD of smart-phones, wearables and suitable in-home products.

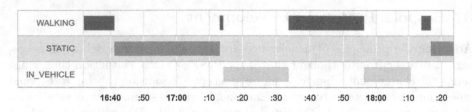

Fig. 1. AR timeline using data from a smart-phone

AR on a Smart-Phone. In our experiments, we evaluated the Android AR API. An agent is able to analyse summary data in the form of activities from sensors on the phone in real time. On return to the LAN data is uploaded to a trusted hub where learning of 'normal' activities takes place. A library of activity is again analysed using server based scripting languages such as PHP and Node.js. Figure 1 visualises results purely for the purposes of explanation and to assist in the study. A period of walking, then sitting is followed by a short walk to a car, then driving and finally a return trip back home. A sequence of events can be recognised and – when compounded with map data – if the context of the walking (between 17:34 and 17:56) is a shop, the whole sequence may be recognised as an instance of 'going shopping'. Since this is not an event that requires intervention (the user successfully did the shopping and returned home), there is no need for invasion of privacy. Extended walking at the shop or not driving home would of course elevate a measure of current risk and actions based on that.

AR Using Wearable Technology. Commercially available wearable devices allow monitoring of activity and vital signs. Many of the devices come with an open API that may be used for bespoke software development. A fitness monitor wristband and a smart-watch were used to evaluate our methodology. The sensors in these devices are used to recognise activity. Comparing different devices showed significant quantitative discrepancies of, e.g., heart rate and step count. Despite this inaccuracy, the fundamental activity was reliably detected on all devices.

Human stress monitoring may be done with a wearable patch [18]. Agitation is linked with heart rate [19], this and anxiety are the second and third most common behavioural abnormalities in persons with Alzheimer's disease [20] and accelerate the potential of transition to full time care [21]. Actively monitored heart rate will be used as a measurement of risk.

Sleep disturbances are a common behavioural symptom associated with Alzheimer's Disease [22]. Increased walking at night corresponds with disruption of diurnal rhythm and is disruptive to ADL [23], it is a major reason for nursing home admission [24]. Over 6 months of activity was collected using a Fitbit and just about 11 weeks' information was gathered using a Jawbone Up3. The recorded sleep activity from both was an accurate representation of actual behaviour. Data including quality of sleep can be accessed programmatically through the manufacturer's API using oAuth 2.0 and for example Python scripting. Trends in sleep activity may be useful in assessing the risk of night time wandering. Both devices use Bluetooth Low Energy (BLE) for data transfer

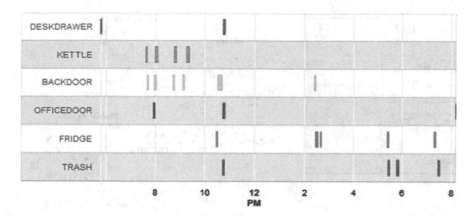

Fig. 2. In-home activity recognition

between the device and a tethered phone, Fitbit provide encryption. Sleep activity in the previous week will be used as a predictor of the risk of night-time wandering, again a key measure of underlying risk.

A fully programmable Android smart-watch, was selected for its sensors and the possibility of bespoke software development. It is possible to trigger alerts or reminders, e.g., if the wearer is out of range of a phone, alerts may be vibration or audible reminders. The watch can be used to find the phone, it can respond to voice commands and can display graphics, photos, or text.

AR in the Home. 'Nearables'[4] are small and portable BLE devices built on beacon technology. Nearables and beacons were evaluated with very good results when placing them on everyday items (see Fig. 2). Quantitative measurement of proximity, location and movement may be captured inside and outside the house. Temperature of a kettle, fridge and cooker may be measured through their thermal sensor, as well as the movement of doors or other objects using the built-in accelerometer. In our approach, sensor data is combined to make compound assertions about the context the person is currently acting in. E.g., if the front door moves, a person goes out of range of a hub and the phone is static, it is likely that the person is outside without the phone. Beacons can be placed outdoors or in shops, and can store longitude and latitude. For the purpose of in-house monitoring, a home hub was developed running Node.js on a low cost single board computer. Approximate distance from beacons to the hub may be calculated from the signal strength. The used beacons are powered by batteries with an advertised battery life of up to 60 months. They are unobtrusive, require no installation apart from placement and are low cost.

Long term data is being collected to enable learning of individual activity patterns that can be used to assess the risk factor of actions in real time. Categorisation of risks are determined in discussions with user groups, including PwD, carers, health professionals and an ethics panel.

---

[4] http://developer.estimote.com/nearables/.

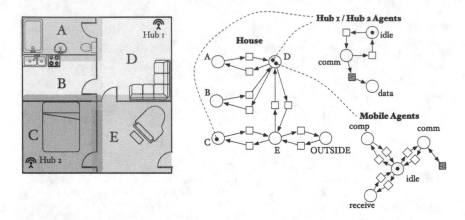

Fig. 3. Agent-based design for a home comprising five zones

6 An Agent-Based Architecture

Activity recognition and assessment described above are implemented as a multi-agent system. Depending on the size of the home, there will be a number of hubs, each with its own hub agent. All agents communicate securely on the LAN or via BLE. Mobile agents are currently implemented on smart-phones. They communicate directly with the hubs when they are within reach of the respective Wi-Fi signal. All agents contextualise sensor data and run algorithms to assess the current risk potential of the person being monitored. At a later stage, there will be agents on wearables such as smart watches and wristbands.

A schematic architecture of our system is given in Fig. 3. This shows zones in the home, some sensors, hubs and mobile devices. We have modelled this using the nets-within-nets paradigm [25]. Hub agents and agents on mobile devices are modelled by nets that reside in the Petri net representing the environment, i.e., the respective zone in the home or the current outdoor location. The agents' decision-making components are also modelled as nets within the agent net and data can be transmitted from all agents to the hub agents through channels that become available when they are within reach of a hub.

7 Conclusion

Initial results suggest that it is possible to monitor activity with socially accepted and widely available devices in an unobtrusive way. Furthermore, activity monitoring without invasive tracking is possible without invading privacy. Another key to success is the reliability of agents and their implementation on low energy devices. The former is addressed by formal models for validation of processes involving the agents (such as Petri nets), while the latter is achieved by optimisation of algorithms with respect to the frequency of sensor polling. The user acceptance of any device will heavily rely on the success of these considerations.

Though the current prototype requires the individual to carry a smart-phone, the advancement in sensors and battery technology will make a final product even more wearable and unobtrusive. Future work will focus on clarification of user requirements and moral acceptability; algorithms for agents are to determine risk situations from comparison with expected activity; dealing with dynamic changes to normal activity due to the progression of the disease; addressing key viability issues such as reliability, battery life, and user acceptance.

Acknowledgements. This work is supported by Knowledge Economy Skills Scholarships (KESS-2), a pan-Wales higher level skills initiative part funded by the Welsh Government's European Social Fund (ESF) and is partly sponsored by SymlConnect Limited.

References

1. McShane, R., et al.: Getting lost in dementia: a longitudinal study of a behavioral symptom. Int. Psychogeriatr. **10**(3), 253–260 (1998)
2. Rowe, M.A.: A look at deaths occurring in persons with dementia lost in the community. Am. J. Alzheimer's Dis. Other Dement. **18**(6), 343–348 (2003)
3. Alzheimer's Society: Alzheimer's Society Position Statement - Assistive technology (2013). https://www.alzheimers.org.uk/site/scripts/documents_info.php?documentID=552 Accessed 6 Sep 2016
4. Egan, K.J., Pot, A.M.: Encouraging innovation for assistive health technologies in dementia: barriers, enablers and next steps to be taken. J. Am. Med. Dir. Assoc. **17**(4), 357–363 (2016)
5. Brodaty, H., Donkin, M.: Family caregivers of people with dementia. Dialogues Clin. Neurosci. **11**, 217–228 (2009)
6. Riikonen, M., Mäkelä, K., Perälä, S.: Safety and monitoring technologies for the homes of people with dementia. Gerontechnology **9**(1), 32–45 (2010)
7. Zwijsen, S., Niemeijer, A., Hertogh, C.M.: Ethics of using assistive technology in the care for community-dwelling elderly people: an overview of the literature. Aging Mental Health **15**(4), 419–427 (2011)
8. Landau, R., et al.: What do cognitively intact older people think about the use of electronic tracking devices for people with dementia? a preliminary analysis. Int. Psychogeriatr. **22**(08), 1301–1309 (2010)
9. McShane, R.: Should patients with dementia who wander be electronically tagged? Yes. BMJ **346**, 3603 (2013)
10. Welsh, S., et al.: Big brother is watching you - the ethical implications of electronic surveillance measures in the elderly with dementia and in adults with learning difficulties. Aging Ment. Health **7**(5), 372–375 (2003)
11. Godwin, B.: The ethical evaluation of assistive technology for practitioners: a checklist arising from a participatory study with people with dementia, family and professionals. J. Assist. Technol. **6**(2), 123–135 (2007)
12. Leroi, I., et al.: Does telecare prolong community living in dementia? a study protocol for a pragmatic, randomised controlled trial. Trials **14**(1), 349 (2013). Accessed 6 Sep 2016
13. Knapp, M., et al.: The case for investment in technology to manage the global costs of dementia (2016). http://www.piru.ac.uk/projects/current-projects/supporting-people-with-dementia-using-technology.html Accessed 6 Sep 2016

14. Newton, L., Dickinson, C., Gibson, G., Brittain, K., Robinson, L.: Exploring the views of GPs, people with dementia and their carers on assistive technology: a qualitative study. BMJ Open **6**(5), e011132 (2016)
15. Bharucha, A.J., Anand, V., Forlizzi, J., Dew, M.A., Reynolds, C.F., Stevens, S., Wactlar, H.: Intelligent assistive technology applications to dementia care: current capabilities, limitations, and future challenges. Am. J. Geriatr. Psychiatry **17**(2), 88–104 (2009)
16. Gaßner, K., Conrad, M.: ICT enabled independent living for elderly: a status-quo analysis on products and the research landscape in the field of ambient assisted living (AAL) in EU-27. Technical report. Institute for Innovation and Technology, Berlin (2010). ISBN 978-3-89750-160-7
17. Weiser, M.: The computer for the 21st century. Sci. Am. **265**(3), 66–75 (1991)
18. Yoon, S., Sim, J.K., Cho, Y.H.: A flexible and wearable human stress monitoring patch. Sci. Rep. **6**, 23468 (2016)
19. Sakr, G.E., Elhajj, I.H., Huijer, H.A.S., Riley-Doucet, C., Debnath, D.: Subject independent agitation detection. In: IEEE/ASME International Conference on Advanced Intelligent Mechatronics. IEEE (2008)
20. M.S., M., J.L., C., Fiorello, T., Gornbein, J.: The spectrum of behavioral changes in Alzheimer's disease. Neurology **46**(1), 130–135 (1996)
21. Gibbons, L.E., Teri, L., Logsdon, R., McCurry, S.M., Kukull, W., Bowen, J., McCormick, W., Larson, E.: Anxiety symptoms as predictors of nursing home placement in patients with Alzheimer's disease. J. Clin. Geropsychol. **8**(4), 335–342 (2002)
22. McCurry, S., Gibbons, L., Logsdon, R., Teri, L.: Anxiety and nighttime behavioral disturbances. Awakenings in patients with Alzheimer's disease. J. Gerentological Nursing **30**(1), 12–20 (2004)
23. Hope, T., Tilling, K.M., Gedling, K., Keene, J.M., Cooper, S.D., Fairburn, C.G.: The structure of wandering in dementia. Int. J. Geriatr. Psychiatry **9**(2), 149–155 (1994)
24. Cipriani, G., Lucetti, C., Nuti, A., Danti, S.: Wandering and dementia. Psychogeriatrics **14**(2), 135–142 (2014)
25. Valk, R.: Object petri nets. In: Desel, J., Reisig, W., Rozenberg, G. (eds.) ACPN 2003. LNCS, vol. 3098, pp. 819–848. Springer, Heidelberg (2004). doi:10.1007/978-3-540-27755-2_23

Coordination of Sensors Deployed on Airborne Platform: A Scheduling Approach

Ludovic Grivault[1,2]([✉]), Amal El Fallah-Seghrouchni[1],
and Raphaël Girard-Claudon[2]

[1] Laboratoire d'Informatique de Paris 6 - LIP6, Paris, France
{ludovic.grivault,amal.elfallah}@lip6.fr
[2] Thales Airborne Systems, Elancourt, France
raphael.girard-claudon@fr.thalesgroup.com

Abstract. Remote Piloted Air Vehicle are operating in highly critical contexts. These platforms carry a wide collection of instruments, mostly a set of sensors aiming to collect data from the environment called the *theater*. This set of sensors offers a large panel of functions to the platform's manager during the flight. Today, the needs transformation as well as the numerous environment and industrial constraints turn the design of the multi-sensor system's architecture into a complex task. In this article, we will quickly present the multi-sensor agent-based architecture we elaborated and then detail the scheduling mechanisms we developed within this architecture.

1 Introduction

In this article, we will study the management of resources on Remote Piloted Air Vehicle (RPAS). Our approach aims to design a suitable architecture to deal with resources, i.e. various sensors in our target application. We adopt multi-agent paradigm by using an agent-based architecture for multi-sensor and multi-function system [1]. We will show in this article how the sensors coordination can by ensured by temporal scheduling within this architecture.

Today, the evolution of battlefields due to many factors, including new technologies and conflicts' transformation, leads to emerging needs [2]. These needs directly impact the development of airborne platforms and thus of Multi-Sensor System (MSS). On the one hand, new operating conditions imply the use of autonomous platforms with advanced flexibility and multirole capabilities [3]. On the other hand, the technologies' fast evolution together with the cost reduction objective entail industries to develop more reliable and durable systems [4]. Sensors carried by RPAS are now able to perform a large panel of functions such as image acquisition, spectrum analysis, and object tracking [5]. All these sensors play a major role in operation and their optimization became essential.

From a MSS point of view, both of the orthogonal constraints cited earlier lead to a new architecture which is able to enhance the MSS' autonomy and resilience on the one hand and to optimize the sensors' usage on the other

© Springer International Publishing AG 2017
N. Criado Pacheco et al. (Eds.): EUMAS 2016/AT 2016, LNAI 10207, pp. 285–292, 2017.
DOI: 10.1007/978-3-319-59294-7_23

hand [1]. The sensors' coordination is supported by scheduling mechanisms developed to satisfy the platform requirements as well as the architecture constraints.

2 System's Requirements

Nowadays, airborne platforms are used worldwide as a strategic asset during different kinds of operations including conflicts, surveillance and rescue. These operations occur in highly dynamic environments with a low predictability under scenarios combining up to a thousand entities. Theater's entities all have their own behaviors, speeds and trajectories. In this context, onboard instruments (i.e. sensors) allow the platform, hence the mission manager, to collect knowledge from the field.

Throughout years, sensors became complex systems, able to share data, communicate and, since recently, collaborate. Sensors are all specific to different physical dimensions (electromagnetics at different wavelengths, optics, infrared, etc.) and different scopes (few meters to hundreds of kilometers, shallow to wide angles, etc.). Because of this variety of sensors, collaboration between sensors allows us to deduce new data concerning the environment by overlapping outputs coming from many sensors. This operation is called track merging (a track being a set of data received from an object on the field).

- The sensors' scopes and ranges are not limitless, the functions' set is expanding, and with a maximum of entities on the field of about one thousand, the global sensors' capacity is the main limit for the enhancement of the MSS.
- As a result of sensor limits in term of range and scopes, the platform's localization is one of the main requisites to the sensors efficiency. This requirement implies that the MSS has to be fully aware of the platform trajectory and speed.
- Because of the criticality of the context and the mission's objectives, operators are expecting a certain determinism from the decisions proposed by the MSS. The MSS will be following clearly defined rules specifying sensors' actions and which tasks will be accepted by the scheduler.

3 Related Work

Agent-based online architectures are currently used within many Airports' Air Traffic Controller (ATC) [6,7]. These agent ATC architectures demonstrated the advantages brought by agents in term of autonomy. Objectives of ATC are about controlling traffic in geographical areas [8]. This task is usually done by a human operator who can be potentially overburdened depending on area frequentation [9]. In this context, agents can be used to follow the location of aircraft in a geographical area and assist/alert the operator along different situations.

In ATC, agents are mainly used as secondary operators assisting the main system's user with automatic treatment, discharging the operator from a certain workload. ATCs have many constraints in common with a MSS, especially complex field's visualization, data overloads, high criticality and low delays.

Driving sensors through a multi-agent system was studied before in the context of sensor-mission assignment [10]. Sensors were agentified and sharing missions given by a mission manager in order to improve the sensors loads and consumptions. In our system, the SMS is also generating mission goals by analyzing the data coming from the field and making sensors plans in consequence. This feature leads the MSS to support low-level sensors' requirements as well as high-level autonomy goals simultaneously.

4   Temporal Scheduling of Resources

4.1   Agent-Based Architecture for MSS

Figure 1 show the studied architecture. At first sight, the MSS acts as an interface between the Mission Manager and the sensors' apertures set. In this context the agent has a double role: creating high-level sensors' objectives and generating accurate sensors' resources allocation plans.

The scheduler receives all the plans from the agents in order to schedule them accurately on sensors' timelines. Because of the number of objects present on the field (i.e. a large number of agents within the architecture), the scheduling is one of the most essential processes in our system.

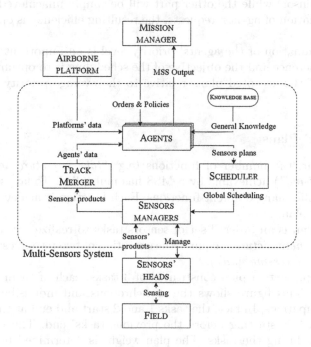

Fig. 1. The agent-based MSS architecture.

4.2   Sensor-Suite's Efficiency

The efficiency of the sensor suite relies on the consistency of realized tasks according to many parameters such as weather, the platform's attitude, the MSS state, field objects' behaviors and operators requests.

The highest efficiency is reached if the sensor suite collected the maximum volume of significant information (from the operational point of view) about the field regarding all the previous parameters.

To answer these requirements, one solution is to attribute a priority level to each agent. This agent's priority reflects the potential interest of the field object and hence allows a proportional access to sensors. The priority level is defined by operational rules.

The great number of objects (i.e. up to 500) on the field implies a big number of sensors' plans created by the agents. Many of these plans can be insignificant from an operational point of view. As an example, we can imagine a scenario in which the platform tracks an important object on the field through the radar sensor, the importance of the object implies a high level of priority.

If the platform is approaching a highway used by 300 vehicles with low operational interest, the matching agents will all send sensors plans corresponding to an identification procedure. After sorting by priority order, all the requests will not be achievable by the same sensor. A part would be realized by another one (e.g. camera sensor) while the other part will be simply unachieved. In spite of a partial realization of agents' requests, the resulting efficiency is optimal in the given situation.

The determination of the agents' priority level is an important point of the scheduling coherence and the objective of the scheduling is to optimize the average priority of the accepted plans relative to the average priority of the total tasks set.

4.3   Sensors' Plans

Year after year, the number of functions (e.g. *"take a picture"* or *"listen to signals on M-band"*) achievable by a MSS has multiplied. Today, sensors allow the pilot to fulfill many different functions. Each function is achieved through a specific sensor plan.

A sensor plan is an ordered set of sensors tasks to realize a sensor function (e.g. *"take a camera picture"* requires the execution of two resources: a *"camera"* and an *"optic processing unit"*).

Figure 2 represents a plan constituted of 3 tasks, each of them needs a distinct resource. This figure shows the asynchronous and indivisible features of resources' occupations. In fact, the tasks 1 and 2 start and end at the same time while the task 3 is starting before the previous tasks' end. The resources are fully allocated during the tasks. The plan weight is determined by agents and reflect the importance of executing the plan at an operational level.

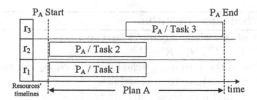

Fig. 2. A sensor plan P_A on 3 resources.

4.4 Scheduling of Plans and Tasks

The scheduler takes into account plans issued by agents and the scheduled plans on the timelines. Their different priorities lead to a global plan for all resources depending on each sensors plan's weight. The resulting global plan is divided into two distinct parts. The first part is a compact scheduling leading to a dense occupation and optimization of resources by interleaving tasks. This scheduling is done until a short-term limit. The second scheduling is fulfilled for the remaining period, beginning at the short-term limit and finishing at a later time limit. This scheduling is less optimized and allows agents to know the progression of the acceptance of their plans. A resulting scheduling example is shown in Fig. 3. If a plan is not accepted in the short-term or long-term schedule, the agent is advised about the refusal of the plan and is able to submit a new plan on a different resource. The scheduling algorithm is described by the Algorithm 1.

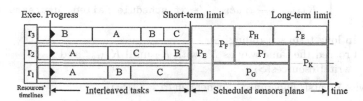

Fig. 3. Plans scheduling.

5 Simulation

Since testing in real situations is complex and very expensive to be achieved with this kind of platform and MSS, we implemented this architecture in simulation. Hence, we developed a special test scenario, able to show the main decisions an operator takes during a mission. This scenario gathers up to 10 steps where the platform is deployed in different contexts with different criticality and have been validated by operationals. Thanks to this scenario we can now compare decisions taken by our MSS architecture with the behavior of traditional ones.

Figure 4 is the visualization of the main window of the simulation engine.

The downer frame represents functions and resources available in the MSS. Framed resources and functions are currently working. The links between

---

Algorithm 1. Scheduling Algorithm

Input: $\mathcal{P}$ the set of the whole Agents' Plans such as
$\quad\quad \forall\, P_k \in \mathcal{P}, k = [1 \ldots K], K \in \mathbb{N}$
Output: $\mathcal{S}$ the set of the resources' schedules and $\mathcal{S}_1, \mathcal{S}_2$ the two subsets of the
$\quad\quad$ short term and long term schedules
Data: T_1, T_2: short and long term time limits, $T_1 < T_2$
K_{1Max}, K_{2Max}: booleans, true if the number of scheduled tasks is the highest for
the periods $[0 \ldots T_1[\ and\ [T_1 \ldots T_2[$

```
 1  begin
 2  │   K₁,K₂;      /* number of plans achievable in [0...T₁[ and [T₁...T₂[ */
 3  │   K₁ₘₐₓ,K₂ₘₐₓ ⟵ false;
 4  │   P ⟵ sortPlansByPriority(P);
 5  │   begin short term scheduling
 6  │   │   K₁ ⟵ approximateK₁(P);
 7  │   │   while ¬K₁ₘₐₓ do
 8  │   │   │   P₁ ⟵ selectFirstPriorityPlans(P,0...K₁);
 9  │   │   │   S₁ ⟵ schedule(P₁);
10  │   │   │   if scheduleSuccess then
11  │   │   │   │   if K₁ₘₐₓ then
12  │   │   │   │   │   writeResources(S₁);
13  │   │   │   │   else
14  │   │   │   │   │   increase(K₁); /* write scheduling results on resources
                        timelines */
15  │   │   │   else
16  │   │   │   │   decrease(K₁);
17  │   │   │   │   K₁ₘₐₓ ⟵ true;      /* if schedule failed, decrease K₁ */
18  │   begin long term scheduling
19  │   │   Proceed the same way as K₁ with K₂ until K₂ₘₐₓ and
            writeResources(S₂);
20  │   adviseAgents("unplanned",ownersOf(P_{K₂}...P_N));
```

---

functions depict the functions' dependencies of sensors. One feature of the simulation is to force a sensor breakdown by selecting the checkbox down under the resource. This feature shows the ability of the architecture to redirect plans on available resources.

At this step of the scenario, an objective is given to the platform: search the object A in a particular area. After 2 min and many sensors tasks the Obj. A was found as expected without human control on the MSS' sensors. The vigil mode of the RPAS, which was turned on at the startup of the MSS, planned and executed the use of an electromagnetic detector to watch the platform's environment. It detected the presence of a emitter (e.g. radar, Obj on the figure) and identified it. In reality, the MSS is not making the platform turn but the Mission manager is deciding to go toward the object after the MSS shared data received and proposed an identification procedure on a particular point

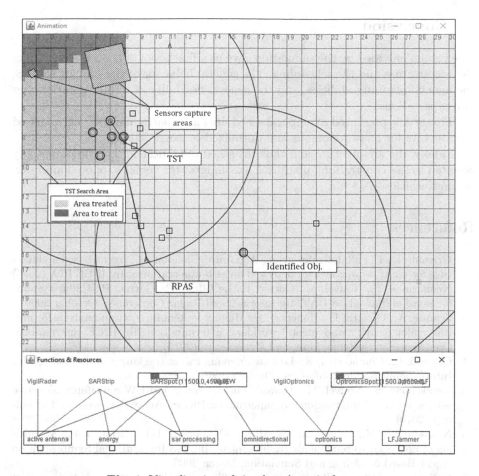

Fig. 4. Visualization of simulator's main frames.

of interest (proposition emitted by the corresponding agent). The detection of objects led to the activation of different other sensors and effectors (such as emitters).

Some functions were implemented to enhance the robustness of the MSS including agent death and replication for avoiding blocking agents situations. The MSS' global behavior matched our expectations during simulations and sensors' tasks were scheduled in time with coherence regarding the simulated field. Work should be done to refine choice models concerning agents' plans, sensors' behaviors, and objects' behaviors.

The scheduling is converging thanks to a time limit set in the scheduler. This process' time limit allows the scheduler to take fast decisions by constraining the number of exchanges between the agents. This feature guarantees to find a solution to the scheduling problem in a given time when increasing the number of field's objects despite a non-optimal global schedule. The selection of the K_1 first priority plans guarantee the maximum average priority in the time limit.

6   Conclusion

The results provided by the simulation gave us a first proof of concept concerning the architecture and the scheduling. The general behavior of the simulated MSS, the agents' planning abilities, and the general flexibility of implementation met our expectations.

This article presented a temporal scheduling for a particular MSS agent-based architecture for an autonomous and optimized sensors' driving.

Finally, the architecture and thus the scheduling method may be potentially adapted to less constraining platforms like underwater vehicles, piloted aircrafts, or land vehicles.

References

1. Grivault, L., El Fallah-Seghrouchni, A., Girard-Claudon, R.: Agent-based architecture for multi-sensors system deployed on airborne platform. In: IEEE ICA (2016)
2. Kemkemian, S., Nouvel, M., Cornic, P., Le Bihan, P., Garrec, P.: Radar systems for sense and avoid on UAV. In: International Radar Conference, October 2009
3. Schulte, A., Donath, D., Honecker, F.: Human-system interaction analysis for military pilot activity and mental workload determination. In: IEEE International Conference on Systems, Man, and Cybernetics (2015)
4. Chabod, L., Chamouard, E.: Low cost moving target tracking and fire control. In: International Radar Conference, October 2009
5. Kemkemian, S., Nouvel, M.: Toward common radar and EW multifunction active arrays. In: IEEE International Symposium on Phased Array Systems and Technology (2010)
6. Nguyen-Duc, M., Guessoum, Z., Marin, O., Perrot, J.-F., Briot, J.-P.: A multi-agent approach to reliable air traffic control. In: 2nd International Symposium on Agent Based Modeling and Simulation, March 2008
7. Callantine, T.J.: CATS-based air traffic controller agents. NASA report NASA/CR-2002-211856 (2002)
8. Tumer, K., Agogino, A.: Distributed agent-based air traffic flow management. In: The Sixth International Joint Conference on Autonomous Agents and Multi-Agent Systems - AAMAS (2007)
9. Ibrahim, Y., Higgins, P., Bruce, P.: Evaluation of a collision avoidance display to support pilots' mental workload in a free flight environment. In: IEEE International Conference on Industrial Engineering and Engineering Management (2013)
10. Le, T., Norman, T.J., Vasconcelos, W.: Agent-based sensor-mission assignment for tasks sharing assets. In: IFAAMA (2009)

Experimental Evaluation of Agent-Based Localization of Smart Appliances

Stefania Monica$^{(\boxtimes)}$ and Federico Bergenti

Dipartimento di Matematica e Informatica, Università degli Studi di Parma,
Parco Area delle Scienze 53/A, 43124 Parma, Italy
{stefania.monica,federico.bergenti}@unipr.it

Abstract. This paper presents an experimental evaluation of the performance of a novel add-on module for JADE intended to provide agents with estimates of their positions in known indoor environments with no need of dedicated infrastructures or specific onboard devices. First, the paper motivates the work and it details relevant assumptions regarding the applicability of the proposed module. The framework that the module provides to host localization algorithms is outlined, and the specific nomenclature is introduced. Then, the algorithm which ships with the module is briefly presented. Finally, the experimental campaign used to assess the performance of localization is detailed. Experimental results show that the accuracy of stationary localization is sufficient for envisaged application scenarios.

1 Introduction

Agent technology has been advocated as the ultimate solution for most of the inherent issues of software for mobile devices since the end of the nineties. The group of companies that initially teamed to establish the *Foundation for Intelligent Physical Agents* (*FIPA*), now IEEE FIPA Standards Committee (www. fipa.org), was composed of telecommunication operators and manufacturers of mobile appliances. *JADE* (*Java Agent and DEvelopment framework*) [1], the tool that was eventually chosen as a reference implementation of FIPA specifications, was conceived under direct funding of a telecommunication operator. Four of the major manufacturers of mobile appliances of the time started a joint research initiative in 1998 to bring agent technology to what we used to call *Java-enabled phones* [2,3], which eventually became the base of JADE for Android [4]. Finally, a geolocalized chat application for Android developed using JADE by members of the JADE team predates Whatsapp by months [5]. We used to call them *nomadic agents* at the time—to make a clear distinction with the then popular mobile agents—and nomadic agents were considered one of the most promising applications of agent technology.

The evolution that we recently witnessed from mobile devices to smart appliances has tightened the link which connects agent technology with the world of software for the smart appliances of today and of tomorrow. The adjective *embodied* is traditionally attached to agents, and the adjective *physical* was chosen too

N. Criado Pacheco et al. (Eds.): EUMAS 2016/AT 2016, LNAI 10207, pp. 293–304, 2017.
DOI: 10.1007/978-3-319-59294-7_24

in the acronym FIPA, because agents have all the features needed to fruitfully use the sensors and the actuators that were added to mobile devices to make them smart appliances. Notably, the smart appliances of today—and even more those of tomorrow—offer much more resources than in the past and the major challenge of agents for smart appliances is no longer about managing the lack of resources; rather it is about providing agents with the possibility of effectively interfacing with the physical world they live in.

Examples of the significant opportunities that the synergic combination of agents and smart appliances offer has been already explored with a major evolution of JADE which has been introduced to address a specific, yet very important, application area, where agents have already shown their benefits [6]. *AMUSE (Agent-based Multi-User Social Environment)* [7] is an open-source platform built on top of JADE to tackle specific issues of online social games, and it has been already used to experiment mixed-reality games [8,9]. Actually, one of the most interesting characteristics of online social games specifically intended for mobile users is that the physical world of the user can be embedded in the game as an effective game element.

One of the weaknesses that we observe in available smart appliances is that they do not yet offer support for accurate indoor localization. While accurate outdoor localization is effectively achieved using various assisted technologies, accurate indoor localization is still an open problem. This paper reports recent results that show how a novel JADE add-on module can be used to effectively provide agents with accurate localization capabilities in indoor scenarios using only off-the-shelf WiFi technology available in all smart appliances. In detail, the prototyped module can be used to develop JADE and AMUSE agents capable of sensing their location with respect to a fixed reference frame by measuring the distances between the appliance where the agent is running and the access points of the WiFi network. The measured distances are then fed to a localization algorithm that provides the agent with an estimate of its location and that allows using such an estimate as a major game element for location-aware games. Examples of such games include social games in large indoor areas with high concentrations of potential users, like the halls of shopping malls, the waiting areas of airports, and the covered markets often found in historic cities. Such areas typically offer dedicated WiFi coverage by means of access points whose position is known with a good accuracy. The knowledge of the positions of access points together with the possibility of estimating the distance between each access point and the user's appliance allow providing agents on smart appliances with good estimates of their location with no need of a dedicated infrastructure.

A localization accuracy of less than 2 m is needed to discriminate, e.g., the shop window in front of which the user is located, and in this paper we show, through illustrative examples, that such an accuracy can be achieved by using the presented techniques. It is worth noting that the implemented prototype does not assume that the appliance is connected to one of the WiFi networks of the area; rather it only assumes that the WiFi receiver is enabled on the appliance.

The paper mainly focuses on presenting one of the localization algorithms available in the JADE add-on module, and a detailed description of the architecture of the module and of its API is left for a future paper. In Sect. 2, the localization framework is introduced and the chosen algorithm is briefly summarized. In Sect. 3, a few illustrative experimental results are shown. Finally, Sect. 4 concludes the paper.

2   Location-Aware Agents on Smart Appliances

In order to provide information on the position of the appliance that hosts an agent, ranging and localization capabilities have been integrated in JADE by means of a dedicated add-on module. The module already provides an algorithm to perform localization, but it is open, allowing other algorithms to be used, provided that they implement specific interfaces [10]. Such interfaces are meant to support a localization approach which involves two steps. First, the agent uses the module to acquire range estimates between the smart appliance where it is running and the *Access Points* (*APs*) of the network. Then, the module transparently feeds such range estimates to a localization algorithm which computes an estimate of the position of the appliance, which is normally called *Target Node* (*TN*) using the accepted nomenclature of localization algorithms. Finally, the agent is informed of its current position.

2.1   Acquisition of Range Estimates

Concerning the range acquisition phase, let us observe that each communication between the TN and any of the AP in range allows obtaining an estimate of the distance between them, and other valuable information, such as the *BSSID* (*Basic Service Set IDentification*) of the responding AP. Assuming that the position of each AP is known, each mapped BSSID can be associated with the coordinates of the corresponding AP and, hence, each distance estimate can be also related to the coordinates of the corresponding AP. The possibility of associating the physical position of an AP with each distance estimate between a TN and that AP is a fundamental condition to apply the localization algorithm, as shown in the following. The implemented localization algorithm relies on the distance estimates between some APs with known positions and the TN. Such range estimates are derived from the received power of the WiFi signal using the Friis formula, according to which the average received power $\bar{P}(\rho)$ at distance ρ can be expressed as [11]

$$\bar{P}(\rho) = P_0 - 10\beta \log_{10} \frac{\rho}{\rho_0} \tag{1}$$

where P_0 is the known power at the reference distance ρ_0. An estimate of the average received power $\bar{P}(\rho)$ yields the value of the distance ρ by inverting (1).

In the considered localization framework, we rely on the range estimates from three APs to estimate the position of the smart appliance. This means that, even if more than three APs are available, the position of the TN is estimated only relying on the range estimates from three of them. More complex localization algorithms, relying on a larger number of range estimates, could also be implemented, even though they would have a higher computational cost. Let us introduce some notation. The coordinates of the APs are denoted as

$$\underline{s}_i = [x_i, y_i, z_i]^T \qquad i \in \{1, 2, 3\} \tag{2}$$

where T represents the transpose symbol. We remark that we assume that the coordinates of the APs are known to the agent in charge of the localization. The (unknown) position of the TN is denoted as

$$\underline{u} = [\bar{x}, \bar{y}, \bar{z}]^T \tag{3}$$

so that the exact distance between the TN and the i-th AP can be written as

$$\rho_i \triangleq \|\underline{u} - \underline{s}_i\| \qquad i \in \{1, 2, 3\}. \tag{4}$$

From now on, we make an additional assumption which allows simplifying the localization algorithm, i.e., we assume that the height $\bar{z}$ of the considered TN is known. Defining as

$$h_i = |\bar{z} - z_i| \qquad i \in \{1, 2, 3\} \tag{5}$$

the difference between the height $\bar{z}$ of the TN and the height z_i of the i-th AP, it is possible to evaluate the projections of the distances $\{\rho_i\}_{i=1}^3$ on the plane $z = \bar{z}$ where the TN lies. According to the Pythagoras theorem, they can be written as

$$r_i = \sqrt{\rho_i^2 - h_i^2} \qquad i \in \{1, 2, 3\}. \tag{6}$$

We recognize that this may seem a strong assumption. However, even if the true height is not accurately known, in the considered scenarios, in which people are holding smart appliances in their hands, it can be reasonably approximated to, e.g., $\bar{z} = 1$ m. Errors in the order of a few cm on the value of $\bar{z}$ would not impact much on the performance of the proposed localization framework. Instead, this assumption has the advantage of simplifying the localization algorithm as if the considered scenario was a bidimensional one (i.e., as if the coordinates of the i-th AP were $[x_i, y_i, \bar{z}]$, for $i \in \{1, 2, 3\}$).

Using this notation, the true position of the TN can be found by intersecting the three circumferences lying on the plane $\{z = \bar{z}\}$, centered in $\{[x_i, y_i]\}_{i=1}^3$, and with radii $\{r_i\}_{i=1}^3$. Unfortunately, the true distances $\{\rho_i\}_{i=1}^3$ between each AP and the TN are not known and, hence, the values of $\{r_i\}_{i=1}^3$ cannot be evaluated. Instead, one needs to rely on the WiFi-based range estimates obtained according to (1), which are denoted as $\{\hat{\rho}_i\}_{i=1}^3$. Given such estimates and the values of $\{h_i\}_{i=1}^3$, it is possible to evaluate the projections of the estimated distances on the plane $z = \bar{z}$ where the TN lies. Analogously to (6), they can be expressed as

$$\hat{r}_i = \sqrt{\hat{\rho}_i^2 - h_i^2} \qquad i \in \{1, 2, 3\}. \tag{7}$$

The values of $\{\hat{r}_i\}_{i=1}^3$ can finally be used to feed the considered localization algorithm.

2.2   The Implemented Localization Algorithm

Various range-based localization algorithms have been proposed in the literature [12] and any of them could be implemented in the JADE add-on module.
Notably, the module ships with an implemented algorithm commonly called *CI*
(*Circumference Intersection*) algorithm [13]. The algorithm is simple and intuitive and, in order to shortly describe it, let us introduce some notation. The
starting point of this algorithm is the following system of equations

$$\begin{cases} \hat{C}_1 : (\hat{x} - x_1)^2 + (\hat{y} - y_1)^2 = \hat{r}_1^2 \\ \hat{C}_2 : (\hat{x} - x_2)^2 + (\hat{y} - y_2)^2 = \hat{r}_2^2 \\ \hat{C}_3 : (\hat{x} - x_3)^2 + (\hat{y} - y_3)^2 = \hat{r}_3^2 \end{cases} \tag{8}$$

which represents the three circumferences lying on the plane $\{z = \bar{z}\}$, centered
in $\{[x_i, y_i]\}_{i=1}^3$, and with radii $\{\hat{r}_i\}_{i=1}^3$. Since the radii are affected by errors,
the three circumferences in (8) do not intersect in a single point, as it would
happen if the actual values of $\{r_i\}_{i=1}^3$ were known. To overcome this problem,
we intersect pairs of them, i.e., we define the following three sets obtained by
intersecting the three different pairs of circumferences

$$I_1 = \hat{C}_1 \cap \hat{C}_2 \qquad I_2 = \hat{C}_1 \cap \hat{C}_3 \qquad I_3 = \hat{C}_2 \cap \hat{C}_3. \tag{9}$$

Each of the three sets $\{I_i\}_{i=1}^3$ may contain two (possibly coincident) points, if
the considered circumferences intersect, or it can be empty, if the considered
circumferences do not intersect.

Assuming that the three sets $\{I_i\}_{i=1}^3$ are not empty, we choose a point from
each of them in order to guarantee that the three selected points are the nearest
ones to each other. More precisely, we choose $\underline{p}_1 \in I_1$, $\underline{p}_2 \in I_2$, and $\underline{p}_3 \in I_3$ so
that the following conditions are satisfied

$$\|\underline{p}_1 - \underline{p}_2\| = \min_{\underline{p} \in I_1, \underline{q} \in I_2} \|\underline{p} - \underline{q}\| \tag{10}$$

$$\|\underline{p}_1 - \underline{p}_3\| = \min_{\underline{q} \in I_3} \|\underline{p}_1 - \underline{q}\|. \tag{11}$$

Given these three points, the TN position estimate is chosen as their baricenter.

If two circumferences do not intersect, the corresponding set defined in (9)
would be empty. For instance, if $\hat{C}_1$ and $\hat{C}_2$ do not intersect, then I_1 in (9) is
empty. In this case, the estimate of the TN position is based on the remaining
intersections, whenever possible. More precisely, the TN position estimate would
be the baricenter of the two nearest points of I_2 and I_3.

In Sect. 3, experimental results obtained using the CI algorithm are shown.
The performance of the proposed framework is evaluated in correspondence of
four different TN positions, for each of which 100 localization estimates are
performed and they are denoted as

$$\hat{\underline{u}}^{(j)} = [\hat{x}^{(j)}, \hat{y}^{(j)}] \qquad j \in \{1, \dots, 100\}. \tag{12}$$

We remark that the third coordinate is omitted in (12), since is assumed to be
known and equal to $\bar{z}$.

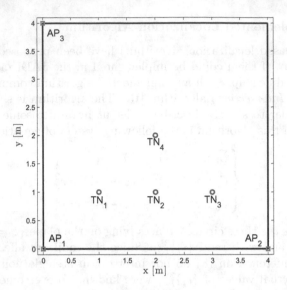

Fig. 1. The projections on the plane $z = 1\,\mathrm{m}$ of the positions of the three considered APs (magenta squares) and four different TN positions (blue circles) are shown. (Color figure online)

3   Experimental Results

In order to test the applicability of the agent-based localization algorithm previously described, we performed tests in an illustrative indoor scenario, namely a room whose sides are $4\,\mathrm{m}$ long. Three APs, denoted as $\{AP_i\}_{i=1}^3$, were positioned in the room and a proper coordinate system is defined, according to which the coordinates of the APs, expressed in meters, are

$$\underline{s}_1 = [0, 0, 3]^T \qquad \underline{s}_2 = [4, 0, 3]^T \qquad \underline{s}_3 = [0, 4, 3]^T. \tag{13}$$

With this configuration of APs, four different positions for the smart appliance are subsequently considered inside the room. The coordinates of such positions, expressed in meters, are

$$\begin{aligned}
\underline{u}_1 &= [1, 1, 1]^T & \underline{u}_2 &= [2, 1, 1]^T \\
\underline{u}_3 &= [3, 1, 1]^T & \underline{u}_4 &= [2, 2, 1]^T.
\end{aligned} \tag{14}$$

Figure 1 shows the projections on the plane $z = 1\,\mathrm{m}$ (where the TNs are assumed to lie) of positions of the three fixed APs (magenta squares) and the four different positions of the TN (blue circles), denoted as $\{TN_i\}_{i=1}^4$. Let us remark that in the considered scenario all APs are placed at the same height, namely $3\,\mathrm{m}$. The same holds for the TN positions, for which the height is $1\,\mathrm{m}$. However, the proposed localization approach is general and it does not require that the APs share the same height. Moreover, different heights for the TNs could also be considered. The only important point in order to apply the proposed localization

Table 1. Values of the minimum distance d_{min} (first row), the maximum distance d_{max} (second row), and the average distance d_{avg} (third row), relative to the position estimates of: TN_1 (first column); TN_2 (second column); TN_3 (third column); and TN_4 (fourth column).

	TN_1	TN_2	TN_3	TN_4
d_{min} [m]	$9 \cdot 10^{-3}$	$1 \cdot 10^{-2}$	$2 \cdot 10^{-2}$	$7 \cdot 10^{-2}$
d_{max} [m]	1.23	1.14	1.21	1.02
d_{avg} [m]	0.34	0.38	0.63	0.58

framework, is that the heights of all the APs and of the TN must be known, so that the projections $\{\hat{r}\}_{i=1}^{3}$ of the range estimates can be determined, as shown in (7).

In order to evaluate the performance of the proposed localization algorithm, let us define

$$d^{(j)} = ||\hat{\underline{u}}^{(j)} - [\bar{x}, \bar{y}]|| \qquad j \in \{1, \dots, 100\} \qquad (15)$$

where $[\bar{x}, \bar{y}]$ represents the vector containing the abscissa and the ordinate of the true TN position. Observe that (15) represents the distance error between the projection of the true TN position and the projection of the TN position estimate in the j-th iteration on the plane $z = \bar{z}$. The definition of the distance error (15) allows introducing

$$d_{min} = \min_{i \in \{1,\dots,100\}} d^{(j)} \qquad d_{max} = \max_{i \in \{1,\dots,100\}} d^{(j)} \qquad (16)$$

which represent the minimum and the maximum values of the distance errors and

$$d_{avg} = \frac{1}{100} \sum_{i \in \{1,\dots,100\}} d^{(j)} \qquad (17)$$

which represents the average value of the distance error.

Table 1 shows above-mentioned metrics, for each of the TN positions in (14). From Table 1 it can be observed that the values of the minimum distance error d_{min} are in the order of a few cm, while the values of the maximum distance error d_{max} vary from 1.02 m, corresponding to TN_4, to 1.23 m, corresponding to TN_1. Hence, it can be concluded that the values of d_{min} relative to the four different TN positions are similar to each other and the same holds for d_{max}. The values of the average distance error d_{avg} vary from 0.34 m, corresponding to TN_1, to 0.63 m, corresponding to TN_3. Such values guarantee that the performance is adequate for the considered localization purpose.

In the remaining part of this section, the details relative of the distance errors $\{d^{(j)}\}_{j=1}^{100}$ are shown for each of the four considered TN positions.

3.1 First Scenario

First, the TN is positioned in the point with coordinates $\underline{u}_1$ defined in (14). Such a point is denoted as TN_1 in Fig. 1. In this case, the true distances $\{\rho_i\}_{i=1}^{3}$

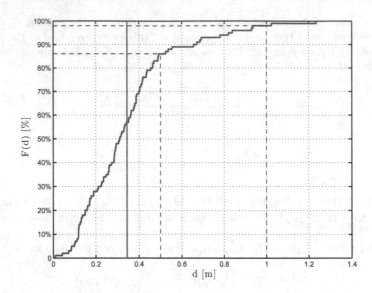

Fig. 2. The CDF of the distance errors $\{d^{(j)}\}_{j=1}^{100}$ (blue line) and the value of the average distance error d_{avg} relative to the position estimates of TN_1 are shown. (Color figure online)

between the i-th AP and the TN, expressed in meters, are

$$\rho_1 \simeq 2.45 \text{ m} \qquad \rho_2 \simeq 3.74 \text{ m} \qquad \rho_3 \simeq 3.74 \text{ m}.$$

Recalling that the difference between the height of the APs and that of TN_1 is 2 m, it is then possible to evaluate the projections of the range estimates on the plane $z = 1$ m. They can be obtained, according to the Pythagoras theorem, as

$$r_1 \simeq 1.41 \text{ m} \qquad r_2 \simeq 3.16 \text{ m} \qquad r_3 \simeq 3.16 \text{ m}.$$

Range estimates from each of the three APs are acquired and used to estimate the position of TN_1, according to the CI algorithm described in Sect. 2. This procedure is iterated 100 times, thus obtaining 100 position estimates $\{\hat{\underline{u}}^{(j)}\}_{j=1}^{100}$ for TN_1, from which the values of the distance errors $\{d^{(j)}\}_{j=1}^{100}$ defined in (15) can be evaluated.

Figure 2 shows the *Cumulative Distribution Function (CDF)* (blue line) of the distance errors $\{d^{(j)}\}_{j=1}^{100}$ obtained in correspondence of TN_1. The average value of the distance error d_{avg} is 0.34 m and it is shown in Fig. 2 (red line). From Fig. 2 it can be observed that the distance error is smaller than 0.5 m in 86% of the cases and it is smaller than 1 m in 98% of the cases.

3.2   Second Scenario

Let us now consider the results relative to the TN positioned in the point denoted as TN_2 in Fig. 1, whose coordinates are denoted as $\underline{u}_2$ in (14). The true distances

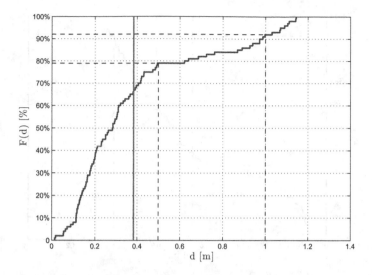

Fig. 3. The CDF of the distance errors $\{d^{(j)}\}_{j=1}^{100}$ (blue line) and the value of the average distance error d_{avg} relative to the position estimates of TN$_2$ are shown. (Color figure online)

$\{\rho_i\}_{i=1}^3$ between the i-th AP and the TN, expressed in meters, are

$$\rho_1 \simeq 3 \text{ m} \qquad \rho_2 \simeq 3 \text{ m} \qquad \rho_3 \simeq 4.12 \text{ m}.$$

As when considering TN$_1$, the projections of the range estimates on the plane $z = 1$ m on which the TN lies can be evaluated, according to the Pythagoras theorem, as

$$r_1 \simeq 2.23 \text{ m} \qquad r_2 \simeq 2.23 \text{ m} \qquad r_3 \simeq 3.60 \text{ m}.$$

To estimate the position of TN$_2$, 100 range estimates from each of the three APs are acquired and used to feed the CI algorithm, thus leading to 100 position estimates $\{\hat{\underline{u}}^{(j)}\}_{j=1}^{100}$ for TN$_2$.

Figure 3 shows the CDF (blue line) of the distance errors $\{d^{(j)}\}_{j=1}^{100}$ obtained when considering TN$_2$. The average value of the distance error d_{avg} is also shown (red line) and it corresponds to 0.38 m. Observe that it is similar to that relative to TN$_1$. From Fig. 3 it can be observed that the distance error is smaller than 0.5 m in 79% of the cases and it is smaller than 1 m in 92% of the cases. These percentages are slightly smaller than those relative to TN$_1$.

3.3   Third Scenario

Let us now consider the TN denoted as TN$_3$ in Fig. 1. In this case, the true distances $\{\rho_i\}_{i=1}^3$ between the i-th AP and the TN, expressed in meters, are

$$\rho_1 \simeq 3.74 \text{ m} \qquad \rho_2 \simeq 2.45 \text{ m} \qquad \rho_3 \simeq 4.69 \text{ m}$$

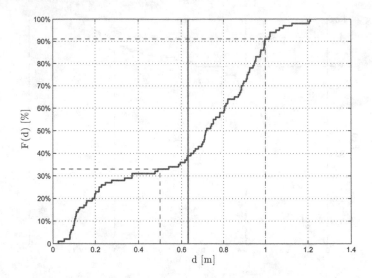

Fig. 4. The CDF of the distance errors $\{d^{(j)}\}_{j=1}^{100}$ (blue line) and the value of the average distance error d_{avg} relative to the position estimates of TN_3 are shown. (Color figure online)

and their projections on the plane $z = 1\,\mathrm{m}$ can be computed as

$$r_1 \simeq 3.16\,\mathrm{m} \qquad r_2 \simeq 1.41\,\mathrm{m} \qquad r_3 \simeq 4.24\,\mathrm{m}.$$

The acquisition of 100 range estimates from each AP allows the derivation of 100 position estimates $\{\underline{\hat{u}}^{(j)}\}_{j=1}^{100}$, relying on the CI algorithm.

Figure 4 shows the CDF (blue line) of the distance errors $\{d^{(j)}\}_{j=1}^{100}$ relative to the position estimates of TN_3. The average value of the distance error d_{avg} is also shown (red line) and it equals 0.63 m. From Fig. 4 it can be observed that the distance error is smaller than 0.5 m in 33% of the cases and it is smaller than 1 m in 91% of the cases. It can be concluded that the localization of TN_3 is slightly less accurate than that of TN_1 and TN_2. This may be due to the fact that TN_3 is quite far from two of the three APs (namely, AP_1 and AP_3), and, hence, the range estimates that it receives from these APs are affected by larger errors, due to signal propagation, resulting in less accurate position estimates.

3.4   Fourth Scenario

Finally, let us now consider the TN denoted as TN_4 in Fig. 1. This corresponds to considering the TN in the middle of the room. In this case, the true distances $\{\rho_i\}_{i=1}^3$ between the i-th AP and the TN, expressed in meters, are

$$\rho_1 = \rho_2 = \rho_3 =\simeq 4.36\,\mathrm{m}.$$

According to the Pythagoras theorem, the projections of the distances on the plane $z = 1\,\mathrm{m}$ can be computed as

$$r_1 = r_2 = r_3 \simeq 2.83\,\mathrm{m}$$

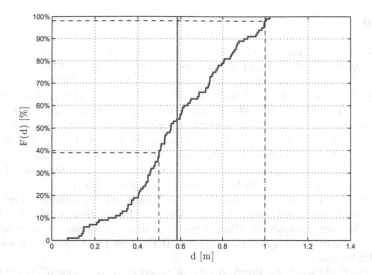

Fig. 5. The CDF of the distance errors $\{d^{(j)}\}_{j=1}^{100}$ (blue line) and the value of the average distance error d_{avg} relative to the position estimates of TN$_4$ are shown. (Color figure online)

As in the previous scenarios, 100 range estimates from each of the three APs are acquired and used to derive 100 estimates $\{\underline{\ddot{u}}^{(j)}\}_{j=1}^{100}$ for the position of TN$_4$.

Figure 5 shows the CDF (blue line) of the distance errors $\{d^{(j)}\}_{j=1}^{100}$ obtained in correspondence of TN$_4$. The average value of the distance error d_{avg}, corresponding to 0.58 m, is also shown (red line). Figure 5 shows that the distance error is smaller than 0.5 m in 39% of the cases and it is smaller than 1m in 98% of the cases.

4   Conclusion

This paper presented an experimental evaluation of the performance of indoor localization that we can currently expect from JADE agents using a novel add-on module. The module offers agents the possibility of having accurate estimates of their location in known indoor environments with no need of a dedicated infrastructure or specific onboard sensors. The obtained results show that agents can reasonably assume an accuracy of 2 m in stationary localizations, which meets the requirements of targeted applicative scenarios. In particular, such an accuracy is sufficient, for example, to use the position of the user as a specific game element of social games in large indoor areas like the halls of shopping malls, the waiting areas of airports, and the covered markets of historic cities. In detail, the analysed algorithm allows a JADE agent to acquire range estimates from the access points of the WiFi infrastructure, which are assumed to be in known positions, and to use such estimates to have real-time information on the position of the smart appliance which hosts the agent.

References

1. Bellifemine, F., Caire, G., Greenwood, D.: Developing Multi-agent Systems With JADE. Wiley Series in Agent Technology. Wiley, Hoboken (2007)
2. Adorni, G., Bergenti, F., Poggi, A., Rimassa, G.: Enabling FIPA agents on small devices. In: Klusch, M., Zambonelli, F. (eds.) CIA 2001. LNCS (LNAI), vol. 2182, pp. 248–257. Springer, Heidelberg (2001). doi:10.1007/3-540-44799-7_28
3. Bergenti, F., Poggi, A.: LEAP: a FIPA platform for handheld and mobile devices. In: Meyer, J.-J.C., Tambe, M. (eds.) ATAL 2001. LNCS (LNAI), vol. 2333, pp. 436–446. Springer, Heidelberg (2002). doi:10.1007/3-540-45448-9_33
4. Bergenti, F., Caire, G., Gotta, D.: Agents on the move: JADE for android devices. In: Proceedings of Workshop From Objects to Agents (2014)
5. Ughetti, M., Trucco, T., Gotta, D.: Development of agent-based, peer-to-peer mobile applications on Android with JADE. In: Proceedings of the 2nd International Conference on Mobile Ubiquitous Computing, Systems, Services and Technologies. UBICOMM 2008, pp. 287–294. IEEE Computer Society, Washington, DC, USA (2008)
6. Bergenti, F., Franchi, E., Poggi, A.: Agent-based interpretations of classic network models. Comput. Math. Organ. Theory **19**, 105–127 (2013)
7. Bergenti, F., Caire, G., Gotta, D.: Agent-based social gaming with AMUSE. In: Proceedings of 5th International Conference on Ambient Systems, Networks and Technologies (ANT 2014) and 4th International Conference on Sustainable Energy Information Technology (SEIT 2014). Procedia Computer Science, vol. 32, pp. 914–919 (2014)
8. Monica, S., Bergenti, F.: Location-aware JADE agents in indoor scenarios. In: Proceedings of 16th Workshop "Dagli Oggetti agli Agenti" (WOA 2015), Napoli, Italy, June 2015
9. Bergenti, F., Monica, S.: Location-aware social gaming with AMUSE. In: Demazeau, Y., Ito, T., Bajo, J., Escalona, M.J. (eds.) PAAMS 2016. LNCS (LNAI), vol. 9662, pp. 36–47. Springer, Cham (2016). doi:10.1007/978-3-319-39324-7_4
10. Monica, S., Bergenti, F.: A comparison of accurate indoor localization of static targets via WiFi and UWB ranging. In: de la Prieta, F., et al. (eds.) PAAMS 2016. AISC, pp. 111–123. Springer, Cham (2016). doi:10.1007/978-3-319-40159-1_9. ISSN: 21945357. ISBN: 978-331940158-4
11. Gezici, S., Poor, H.V.: Position estimation via ultra-wide-band signals. Proc. IEEE **97**(2), 386–403 (2009)
12. Monica, S., Ferrari, G.: Accurate indoor localization with UWB wireless sensor networks. In: Proceedings of the 23rd IEEE International Conference on Enabling Technologies: Infrastructure for Collaborative Enterprises (WETICE 2014), Parma, Italy, pp. 287–289, June 2014
13. Monica, S., Ferrari, G.: An experimental model for UWB distance measurements and its application to localization problems. In: Proceedings of the IEEE International Conference on Ultra Wide Band (ICUWB 2014), pp. 297–302 (2014)

Exploring Feature-Level Duplications on Imbalanced Data Using Stochastic Diffusion Search

Haya Abdullah Alhakbani$^{(\boxtimes)}$ and Mohammad Majid al-Rifaie

Department of Computing, Goldsmiths, University of London, London, UK
{h.alhakbani,m.majid}@gold.ac.uk

Abstract. One of the computer algorithms inspired by swarm intelligence is stochastic diffusion search (SDS). SDS uses some of the processes and techniques found in swarm to solve search and optimisation problems. In this paper, a hybrid approach is proposed to deal with real-world imbalanced data. The proposed model involves oversampling the minority class, undersampling the majority class as well as optimising the parameters of the classifier, Support Vector Machine (SVM). The proposed model uses Synthetic Minority Over-sampling Technique (SMOTE) to perform the oversampling and the agents of a swarm intelligence technique, SDS, to perform an 'informed' undersampling on the majority classes. In addition to comparing the agents-led undersampling with random undersampling, the results are contrasted against other best known techniques on nine real-world datasets. Moreover, the behaviour of SDS agents in this context is also analysed.

Keywords: Swarm intelligence · Agents · Class imbalance · Stochastic diffusion search · SVM

Class imbalance – a major problem in machine learning – occurs when the number of instances in the majority class is significantly higher than the number of instances in the minority class. It is present in a number of real-world classification applications, like oil spill detection from satellite images, detection of fraudulent online credit card and diagnosis of rare diseases [6,10,14]. The issue has been receiving some attention in the literature (e.g. [6,14]) mostly due to the fact that data mining models tend to be influenced with the skewed data distribution, therefore the minority class is usually misclassified leading to bad performance.

Several solutions have been suggested in the literature to address this issue, amongst which are data-level techniques, algorithmic-level techniques and a combination of both. At the data level, solution is achieved by applying sampling on the dataset until it is balanced. However, this issue faces the challenges of the loss of important information and over fitting to balance the data. Despite these challenges researches are still implementing techniques to overcome this issue; one approach is to generate new synthetic instances from the minority class. The approach, SMOTE, takes a subset of the minority class samples

© Springer International Publishing AG 2017
N. Criado Pacheco et al. (Eds.): EUMAS 2016/AT 2016, LNAI 10207, pp. 305–313, 2017.
DOI: 10.1007/978-3-319-59294-7_25

(two or more) and creates a synthetic example using k-Nearest Neighbour algorithm (k-NN) [5]. At the algorithmic level, solutions can be applied by adjusting the cost parameter to improve the model's performance on imbalanced datasets. This approach is shown to perform well when dealing with imbalanced dataset [12].

Stochastic diffusion search (SDS) that is one of the established swarm intelligence (SI) techniques which has been applied to various areas of optimisation, medical diagnosis, data clustering, and many more [1]. It is originally attributed to Bishop in 1989 [3], as a population based matching algorithm that uses direct communication patterns such as cooperative transport found among social insects to perform evaluation of search space. In SDS, the agents population have 'hypotheses' about the possible solutions; these hypotheses are partially evaluated in order to provide feedback that ensure the agents convergence on promising solutions. Using SDS, agents communication and the 'partial' evaluation of hypotheses play the critical role in the performance of the agents and the emergence of "intelligence" [1].

In this work, SDS is applied to the problem of class imbalance in machine learning. Primarily, SDS, in this context, is tasked with the undersampling of the majority class and Synthetic Minority Over-sampling Technique (SMOTE) is tasked with the oversampling of the minority class. Moreover, to solve the problem at the algorithmic level Support Vector Machine (SVM) values; C and gamma are optimised using a grid search and 5 cross validations to train and test the classifier. Key research questions raised in the paper are:

- What is the impact of the duplication at dataset's feature-level (the role of duplications on each individual feature) on the undersampling process?
- How could SDS provide a way to address the feature-level duplications?
- Does proposed model in the paper, which uses SDS for undersampling, provides any outperformance compared to random undersampling as well as other techniques?
- Is it possible to make a recommendation on when to use the method proposed in this paper? In other words, which types of datasets are more responsive to the proposed technique?

1   Experiment

Some previous work (e.g. [4]) have shown that a combination of data level and algorithmic level solutions can improve the model performance on imbalanced datasets. In the experiments conducted for this work, the first task is the application of SDS to undersample the majority class where the aim is to reduce the size of majority class (SDS's search space). The proposed model uses SDS to undersample the majority class to around fifty percent; in cases where the minority class instances need to be oversampled (to reach a comparable size with undersampled majority class) SMOTE is applied, with the following configurations: class is set to zero to detect the minority class automatically; nearest neighbours is set to 5 as this will create synthetic instances from the five nearest

Table 1. Summary of datasets used in this experiment

Dataset	No. of instances	Missing values	Minority class	Majority class	Distribution	Continuous Features	Discrete Features	SMOTE
Oil spills	937	No	41	896	0.04:0.96	49	0	Yes
Yeast	483	No	20	463	0.04:0.96	8	0	Yes
Abalone	731	No	42	689	0.06:0.94	7	1	Yes
Vehicle	846	No	199	647	0.23:0.77	18	0	Yes
Breast cancer	699	Yes	241	458	0.34:0.66	9	0	No
Bank marketing	4119	No	451	3668	0.11:0.89	10	10	Yes
Thoracic surgery	470	No	70	400	0.15:0.85	3	13	Yes
Ionosphere	351	No	126	225	0.35:0.65	34	0	No
Hepatitis	155	Yes	32	132	0.21:0.79	6	13	Yes

neighbours; the percentage of instances to create depends on the majority class size; and the number of seeds used for the sampling is set to 0.

At the algorithmic level, the model uses SVM algorithm, where parameters like C (misclassification cost) and gamma for the radial kernel are optimised using a grid search, which is a simple search through a range of parameters. The range for C has been defined as $[2^{-5}, 2^{15}]$ and the range of gamma as $[2^{-15}, 2^{3}]$ [8]. The search is performed using 5 cross validation and multi-threading to run multiple process at a time. The hybrid approach is then contrasted against random undersampling (along with SVM optimisation). To evaluate the proposed model, nine imbalanced datasets are used in this work. The datasets are available from the University of California, Irvine (UCI) Machine Learning Repository, plus the Oil Spills dataset [9]. The datasets, all collected from real-world cases, vary greatly in their class distributions, sizes and features characteristics (continuous and discrete features). The full list of dataset used are shown in Table 1.

Applying SDS to Undersample the Majority Class Instances: In this experiment, the number of SDS agents is empirically set to be half of the search spaces (half the number of instances); quarter of the SDS population size is set for the number of iterations to undersample the majority class. Initially a model (an instance from the majority class) is randomly selected from the search space (the entire majority class instances) and the agents are set to find the closest match (an instance) from the remaining items of the search space. Once a match or the most similar item is found, it is removed from the majority class with the aim of removing redundant data. Given that this process aims at undersampling the majority class without removing useful information, removing the closest match to a randomly selected model prevents the deletion of useful information from the search space. The initialisation, test and diffusion phases of SDS are expanded with more details to shed more light as to how SDS is adapted for the purpose of undersampling. In the initialisation phase each agent is assigned to a hypothesis from the search space (i.e. a random instance number from the majority class). Subsequently, in the *test phase*, a randomly selected micro-feature (*one of the attributes of the instance*) is compared against the corresponding micro-feature of the model (i.e. the corresponding attribute of the model); if the randomly selected micro-feature of the hypothesis is within the threshold of the model's micro-feature, the agent is set to active, otherwise inactive (threshold vector calculation is described in Sect. 1.1). This process is repeated for all the agents, after which all agents are either active or inactive. Once the status of all the agents are determined in the test phase, the next phase starts. In the *diffusion phase*, each inactive agent randomly picks another agent; if the randomly selected agent is active, its hypothesis (i.e. instance number) is shared with the inactive agent, otherwise the selecting agent picks a random hypothesis (a random instance number) from the search space. The cycle of test-diffusion phases are repeated equal to the number of iterations allowed. Then the instance which has attracted the largest number of agents is labelled as the '*closest match*' and thus removed from the search space. The model is then transferred to another list 'models list'. In the next step, another model is randomly chosen from the remaining instances, its closest match is found and removed from the search space and the new model is then added to the 'models list'. Once the sum of the size of the models list and the remaining search space reaches the number of interest (i.e. when the majority class is downsized), the undersampling process is terminated.

1.1 Feature Dependent Threshold Vector

There are two types of features or attributes in the datasets (i.e. continuous and discrete). Depending on their types, feature's threshold is calculated accordingly and separately (for each feature). For continuous features, the thresholds are found by calculating the median values (excluding the zeros) of the difference between the values of the features. Following the same analogy, for the discrete features, the threshold is calculated using $\tau_i = \frac{1}{n-1}$, where τ_i is the threshold of feature i, and n is the number of discrete values. Therefore, τ returns the value of the 'gap' between each neighbouring discrete value.

Using the method described for calculating the threshold vector, τ, the algorithm can perform an evaluation as to whether any two selected values from the same feature can be considered 'adjacent' values. Therefore, using τ during the test phase for each agent, the proximity of the instances can be partially evaluated (though each individual feature comparison). SDS has shown in many other applications, that after several iterations, it is capable of finding the closest match, which can then be removed as part of the undersampling process. This process guarantees that while the most similar item is removed from the search space, the model, which represents the deleted item is kept and used later during the classification process. This process is repeated until the dataset is completely undersampled to the desired size.

2   Results

The summary of the results are shown in Table 2 where the results of SVM classifying after random undersampling (RND-SVM) and SDS undersampling (SDS-SVM) are reported and contrasted against other methods from the existing

Table 2. Results for the datasets

		G-mean	AUC	F-measure	Accuracy	Sensitivity	Specificity
Oil spills	RND-SVM	35.27%	0.648	69.61%	56.27%	**100.00%**	12.44%
	SDS-SVM	**98.74%**	**0.999**	**98.74%**	**98.74%**	99.58%	97.92%
	DataBoost-IM [7]	67.70%	NA	55.0%	96.60%	46.30%	**98.90%**
	PNN [15]	NA	0.847	NA	NA	NA	NA
Yeast	RND-SVM	**91.43%**	**0.969**	**90.86%**	91.26%	**94.00%**	88.94%
	SDS-SVM	90.33%	0.965	89.74%	90.11%	94.00%	86.81%
	DataBoost-IM [7]	66.9%	NA	58.0%	**97.3%**	45.00%	**99.90%**
	GSVM-RU [11]	NA	0.845	68.8%	NA	NA	NA
Abalone	RND-SVM	88.69%	0.951	89.29%	88.62%	**91.43%**	88.00%
	SDS-SVM	**89.83%**	**0.957**	**89.39%**	**89.77%**	91.11%	88.57%
	GSVM-RU [11]	86.5%	NA	60.4%	NA	NA	NA
	DataBoost-IM [7]	61.1%	NA	45.0%	94.6%	38.0%	**98.1%**
Vehicle	RND-SVM	**98.45%**	0.995	**98.46%**	**98.45%**	99.06%	97.85%
	SDS-SVM	**98.45%**	**0.999**	**98.46%**	**98.45%**	**99.37%**	97.54%
	DataBoost-IM [7]	95.7%	NA	93.7%	97.0%	93.4%	**98.1%**
	PNN [15]	NA	0.983	NA	NA	NA	NA
Breast cancer	RND-SVM	**97.70%**	**0.996**	**97.71%**	**97.70%**	**98.33%**	97.08%
	SDS-SVM	95.81%	0.972	95.77%	95.83%	97.07%	94.58%
	DataBoost-IM [7]	96.40%	NA	95.2%	96.70%	95.40%	**97.3%**
Bank marketing	RND-SVM	**92.91%**	0.972	**93.43%**	93.06%	97.05%	88.95%
	SDS-SVM	90.96%	0.966	91.46%	91.07%	94.04%	88.00%
	HybridDA [2]	NA	**0.98**	NA	**96.73%**	**97.93%**	**94.82%**
Thoracic surgery	RND-SVM	71.69%	0.755	70.51%	71.82%	68.88%	74.63%
	SDS-SVM	**73.51%**	**0.767**	**72.78%**	**73.59%**	**71.94%**	**75.12%**
	Boosted SVM [10]	65.7%	NA	NA	NA	60.00%	72.00%
Ionosphere	RND-SVM	94.01%	0.979	93.77%	94.15%	**97.69%**	90.48%
	SDS-SVM	**95.32%**	**0.986**	**95.27%**	**95.31%**	96.03	94.62%
	CSB2 [13]	93.00%	NA	89.7%	82.90%	96.5%	89.7%
	DataBoost-IM [7]	92.3%	NA	91.2%	94.0%	87.3%	**97.7%**
Hepatitis	RND-SVM	91.02%	0.960	90.62%	91.21%	**93.55%**	88.57%
	SDS-SVM	**91.98%**	**0.963**	**91.47%**	**92.42%**	87.10%	**97.14%**
	CSB2 [13]	80.9%	NA	63.4%	80.6%	81.3%	80.5%
	DataBoost-IM [7]	76.2%	NA	62.6%	83.8%	65.6%	88.6%

literature. Table 1 shows in which of the datasets SMOTE is used to oversample the minority class as with RND-SVM and SDS-SVM. The results in Table 2 shows that in most cases SDS-SVM is outperforming RND-SVM. In order to investigate the reason behind this difference of performance, the redundancy at instance and feature levels will be discussed below.

Analysing Instance and Feature Levels Redundancy: It is intuitive that having a dataset with a high level of duplication would mean that picking a randomly selected instance and removing it as part of the undersampling process is less likely to cause the removal of important information. This hypothesis is clearly demonstrated with two of the datasets used (i.e. Yeast, and Breast Cancer) where there are duplications at instance level making all the features of some samples identical with some others. Table 3 (No. of Duplicates) shows the duplications (percentage of duplicate instances) for both of these datasets.

Table 3. Instance and feature duplication rates

	Instance level figures	Features level figures			Best model
Datasets	No. of duplicates	Median	Average	Standard deviation	
Oil spills	0	81.47%	68.65%	32.61	**SDS-SVM**
Yeast	25 (5.39%)	91.25%	92.54%	4.61	RND-SVM
Abalone	0	61.62%	58.01%	33.57	**SDS-SVM**
Vehicle	0	94.12%	88.46%	13.43	**SDS-SVM**
Breast cancer	231 (50.43%)	95.19%	95.26%	0.2	RND-SVM
Bank marketing	0	99.72%	98.48%	4.18	RND-SVM
Thoracic surgery	0	99.50%	94.90%	10.63	**SDS-SVM**
Ionosphere	0	4.88%	7.67%	6.3	**SDS-SVM**
Hepatitis	0	97.01%	81.30%	26.15	**SDS-SVM**

While this justifies the outperformance of RND-SVM over SDS-SVM, this neither justifies the outperformance of RND-SVM in Bank Marketing nor offers a strong reason for the outperformance of SDS-SVM in all the remaining datasets. For this purpose the redundancy at the feature level is explored as shown in Table 3 where the number of repetition in each feature is calculated and then the median, mean and standard deviation of all the feature repetitions are taken into account. Considering these figures, a link can be established between a high level of similarity (duplications) between the features (e.g. combination of median (or average) and standard deviation) and the performance of SDS-SVM. For instance in the case of the Oil Spills dataset, the median repetition of 81.47% and the standard deviation of 32.61% indicate a varying level of duplications across various features, which leads to the the outperformance of SDS-SVM which partially evaluates the instances. In terms of the Bank Marketing where there is no duplication of instances, there is a high level of duplication at feature level with median of 99.72% and standard deviation of only 4.14% which justifies the good performance of RND-SVM. In all other cases (Oil Spills, Abalone, Vehicle, Thoracic Surgery, Ionosphere and Hepatitis), where feature-level duplication is not high, and there are no large standard deviations (causing a larger level of oscillations), SDS-SVM is a recommended method to use. As can be seen, feature-level duplication analysis also cater for the instance-level duplication analysis, thus providing a better insight on which of the two algorithms to use.

Investigating Agents Behaviour: SDS algorithm adopted for the purpose of undersampling is responsive towards feature-level duplications and when there are many duplications at feature level, the number of active agents is higher; this is illustrated in the graphs of Fig. 1, where the Bank dataset with the high feature-level duplications is shown (on the left) as opposed to the Ionosphere dataset (on the right) where the feature-level duplication is much lower (with the median of 4.88% and the standard deviation of 6.3). The oscillating behaviour of the population's activity is attributed to the micro-feature evaluation of each of the agents. In other words, if an agent picks a certain micro-feature and becomes

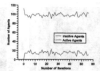

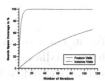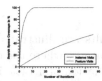

Fig. 1. Convergence of agents over the iterations allowed for the Bank datasets (left) and the Ionosphere datasets (Right)

Fig. 2. Search space coverage for the Oil Spills dataset (left) and the Ionosphere dataset (right)

active, it is likely that other agents are attracted towards the hypothesis of that agent, thus adopting the same hypothesis (but a randomly selected and likely different micro-feature); if the newly selected micro-feature is not within the threshold, this would lead to the agent inactivity for the next cycle. This mechanism assists the agents to only maintain their activities when a hypothesis is (in most of its micro-feature selections) within the calculated threshold.

One interesting feature of the algorithm is that high activity level of the population does not always correspond to convergence to a single instance. While this in itself is a useful feature for identifying more (than one) similar instances, this characteristic is yet to be experimented in the future work. Also it would be worthwhile to explore whether each trial (i.e. removal of one similar instance from the search space) could be terminated depending on the activity level of the populations.

Search Space Coverage: In case of the SDS algorithm and its partial function evaluation, while SDS might visit each instance 'briefly' (i.e. checking one of few features), it does not run a greedy comparison on all of the instance's features. Therefore, the agent aims to 'form an idea' before spending further computational time (by itself or by attracting other agents). This behaviour of the agents can be summarised in two sets of experiments: the first would be to explore the percentage of the instances visited by the SDS agents, and the second is to calculate the percentage of all features visited from the whole of the dataset (i.e. all the features of all the instances). The results of these two experiments are shown in the graphs of Fig. 2. It is shown that while the empirically chosen values for the number of agents and the iterations suffice in visiting the instances at least once, not all the features are (or need to be) visited.

In another experiment, the frequency of agents visiting each feature is explored, investigating the distribution of agents' exploration capability in the search space with the ultimate goal of finding the closest match. For this purpose, three datasets with varying degrees of feature-level duplication are chosen

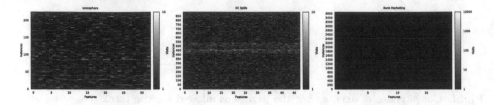

Fig. 3. Frequency of visiting individual features in three datasets.

and the results are illustrated in Fig. 3. For instance, in the case of the Bank Marketing dataset where the duplication is very high the median of 99.72% and standard deviation of 4.14%, it is shown the agents are converged to the closest matches (showing themselves as stripe of white lines) while in the case of the Oil Spills and Ionosphere, the agents presence is distributed in the search space. Also in terms of the Oil Spills dataset, instances in position 450 to 550 are attracting more agent visits which is attributable their similarity to the model which is located at position 471.

3   Conclusion and Future Work

This paper proposes a model which uses a SI algorithm (SDS) which is assigned to perform the undersampling of the majority classes in imbalanced datasets. This work presents an analysis of both instance and feature levels redundancies and establishes a link between the feature-level duplications and the role of feature-level undersampling mechanism. This analysis is accompanied by an investigation of the behaviour of the agents through their activity level during the undersampling process. It is shown that the agents activity is directly proportional to the level of redundancy in the datasets (not only at the instance level, but more importantly, the feature level). Another investigation carried out in this work is the ability of the algorithm to comprehensively explore the search space without having to greedily investigate all the features of all the instances in the dataset. As part of the future research, various coverage percentages could be explored and thus associating the coverage percentage with the termination criteria. This might shed light on the 'bare essential' coverage needed before removing an instance. Another ongoing study is being conducted on the link between the agents activity level and the termination criteria as well as the possibility of removing more than one instance from the dataset where the agents share a 'similar interest' in multiple instances.

References

1. Al-Rifaie, M.M., Bishop, J.M.: Stochastic diffusion search review. J. Behav. Robot. **3**, 155–173 (2013)

2. Al-Rifaie, M.M., Alhakbani, H.A.: Handling class imbalance in direct marketing dataset using a hybrid data and algorithmic level solutions. In: 2016 SAI Computing Conference (SAI), pp. 446–451 (2016). doi:10.1109/SAI.2016. 7556019. http://ieeexplore.ieee.org/stamp/stamp.jsp?tp=&arnumber=7556019& isnumber=7555953
3. Bishop, J.: Stochastic searching networks. In: Proceedings of 1st IEE Conference on Artificial Neural Networks, pp. 329–331, London, UK (1989)
4. Burez, J., Van den Poel, D.: Handling class imbalance in customer churn prediction. Expert Syst. Appl. **36**(3), 4626–4636 (2009)
5. Chawla, N.V.: Data mining for imbalanced datasets: an overview. In: Maimon, O., Rokach, L. (eds.) Data Mining and Knowledge Discovery Handbook, pp. 853–867. Springer, Heidelberg (2005). doi:10.1007/0-387-25465-X_40
6. Chawla, N.V.: Data mining for imbalanced datasets: an Overview. In: Maimon, O., Rokach, L. (eds.) Data Mining and Knowledge Discovery Handbook, pp. 875–886. Springer, Heidelberg (2009). doi:10.1007/978-0-387-09823-4_45
7. Guo, H., Viktor, H.L.: Learning from imbalanced data sets with boosting and data generation: the databoost-im approach. ACM SIGKDD Explor. Newslett. **6**(1), 30–39 (2004)
8. Hsu, C.-W., Chang, C.-C., Lin, C.-J.: A practical guide to support vector classification. Technical report, Department of Computer Science, National Taiwan University (2003). http://www.csie.ntu.edu.tw/~cjlin/papers/guide/guide.pdf
9. Kubat, M., Holte, R.C., Matwin, S.: Machine learning for the detection of oil spills in satellite radar images. Mach. Learn. **30**(2–3), 195–215 (1998)
10. Lesperance, Y., Wagnerg, G., Birmingham, W., r Bollacke, K., Nareyek, A., Walser, J.P., Aha, D., Finin, T., Grosof, B., Japkowicz, N., et al.: Aaai 2000 workshop reports. AI Mag. **22**(1), 127 (2001)
11. Tang, Y., Zhang, Y.Q., Chawla, N.V., Krasser, S.: Svms modeling for highly imbalanced classification. IEEE Trans. Syst. Man Cybern. Part B (Cybern.) **39**(1), 281–288 (2009)
12. Thai-Nghe, N., Gantner, Z., Schmidt-Thieme, L.: Cost-sensitive learning methods for imbalanced data. In: The 2010 International Joint Conference on Neural Networks (IJCNN), pp. 1–8. IEEE (2010)
13. Ting, K.M.: A comparative study of cost-sensitive boosting algorithms. In: Proceedings of the 17th International Conference on Machine Learning. Citeseer (2000)
14. Weiss, G.M.: Mining with rarity: a unifying framework. ACM SIGKDD Explor. Newslett. **6**(1), 7–19 (2004)
15. Zhang, X., Li, Y.: A positive-biased nearest neighbour algorithm for imbalanced classification. In: Pei, J., Tseng, V.S., Cao, L., Motoda, H., Xu, G. (eds.) PAKDD 2013. LNCS, vol. 7819, pp. 293–304. Springer, Heidelberg (2013). doi:10.1007/ 978-3-642-37456-2_25
16. Zieba, M., Tomczak, J.M., Lubicz, M., Swiatek, J.: Boosted svm for extracting rules from imbalanced data in application to prediction of the post-operative life expectancy in the lung cancer patients. Appl. Soft Comput. **14**, 99–108 (2014)

Normative Industrial Symbiotic Networks: A Position Paper

Vahid Yazdanpanah$^{(\boxtimes)}$, Devrim Murat Yazan, and W. Henk M. Zijm

University of Twente, Enschede, The Netherlands
{v.yazdanpanah,d.m.yazan,w.h.m.zijm}@utwente.nl

Abstract. In this paper, we introduce a normative, multi-agent perspective on the field of industrial symbiosis research and propose normative institutions as a key technology for operating Industrial Symbiotic Networks (ISNs), both as a framework to represent and reason about dynamic behaviour of ISNs and as a platform for design and maintenance of such networks. We discuss the requirements of normative agent-based frameworks for ISNs with respect to agent interactions, joint commitments, and the organisation to monitor interactions in ISNs.

1 Introduction

As a key concept in facilitated industrial practices, *industrial symbiosis* "engages traditionally separate industries in a collective approach to competitive advantage involving physical exchange of material, energy, water, and byproducts" [7]. Among various approaches that aim at providing a framework for representing and reasoning about industrial symbiosis, we encounter proposals with different perspectives. In [5], the interactions amongst industrial firms are seen as processes, the study of [17] has a statistical point of view which merely focuses on the case of the National Industrial Symbiosis Programme (NISP) in the UK [14], and [23] is focused on organizational perspectives. One point of agreement among these studies is the dynamic nature of industrial symbiosis. In other words, an Industrial Symbiotic Network (ISN) is not a fixed and static institution but a dynamic and evolving one. In this respect, one significant contribution that clearly goes beyond the traditional definition of industrial symbiosis by Chertow [7], is the study of [16]. In the latter, the main attempt is to provide a more relaxed and dynamic definition for industrial symbiosis which is not limited to geographical proximity and is broader than the focus on waste-resource exchanges only. We see that this definition is successful in describing the behaviour of ISNs that are based on sharing both tangible and intangible assets. However, more work needs to be done in tailoring it for specifying the dynamics of the complex behaviour of ISNs, regarding temporal aspects. For instance, an ISN that is operating now might face different economic circumstances (e.g., market price) as well as structural settings (e.g., entrance of new ISN members) in a later stage. These possible changes can influence the efficiency and stability of ISNs over time. Roughly speaking, is an ISN today still

© Springer International Publishing AG 2017
N. Criado Pacheco et al. (Eds.): EUMAS 2016/AT 2016, LNAI 10207, pp. 314–321, 2017.
DOI: 10.1007/978-3-319-59294-7_26

an ISN tomorrow or the next quarter? We claim that answering such a question, necessitates modelling approaches that incorporate the long-term behaviour and subtleties of temporal behaviour of ISNs.

Presence of multiple decision makers and heterogeneity of industrial firms with respect to their interests and preferences make multi-agent systems a natural modelling paradigm for formal specification and verification of the properties of such networks. Moreover, ISNs are not aiming to merge industrial firms but to establish a loose bounding and control. Hence, we believe that applying formal modelling approaches in the mature field of normative multi-agent systems and norm-based coordination mechanisms can result in frameworks that are expressive enough to represent and reason about multi-dimensional behaviour of ISNs. To our knowledge, although some studies on industrial symbiosis, e.g. [1,3], consider the agent-based paradigm, they merely focus on agent-based simulation and scenario analysis. As part of the European Union's *Horizon 2020* research and innovation programme, the *SHAREBOX* project focuses, among other things, on the analysis, modelling, design and maintenance of ISNs and on decision-support tools that enable secure operation of such networks. In this position statement, we (1) see ISNs as instances of normative multi-agent systems [4], (2) discuss the requirements that need to be taken into account to formalize normative ISNs, and (3) introduce norm-aware institutions as a coordination mechanism for ISNs. Normative agent-based approaches has been successfully used for specification and verification of multi-agent organizations [6,8,21]. We now build on such well-established frameworks and propose a similar approach to specify, analyse and manage ISNs, both as platforms for designing new instances and as logical platforms to analyse and reason about the behaviour of existing ISNs.

The remainder of this paper is organized as follows. In Sect. 2, we provide a general analysis of our normative conception of industrial symbiosis. In Sects. 3 and 4, we discuss agent interactions in ISNs, explain modelling requirements to express joint agreements, and introduce regulatory institutions to coordinate ISNs. Finally, we note some challenging issues in modelling the complex behaviour of ISNs in Sect. 5 and conclude in Sect. 6.

2   Normative Industrial Symbiosis: Conceptual Analysis

Imagine a realistic scenario[1] in which five industrial firms, represented by agents[2] i, j, k, l, and m, are located and active in an industrial region where i and j are metal industries, k is a recycling plant, and both l and m are chemical industries (Fig. 1). The two metal industries have *zinc waste* as their main waste that was traditionally disposed at high cost. Moreover, the two chemical industries l and m have regular demand for *zinc powder* as their main primary input. On the other hand, both l and m have excess *steam waste* that is traditionally disposed to the

---

[1] This scenario is adapted from an ISN located at Ulsan, South Korea [18].

[2] In this paper, we simplify industrial firms and represent any industry as a single industrial agent. I.e., we dismiss the decision-making processes within each firm and focus on the interactions amongst industries.

environment while i and j are using turbines that require high amounts of steam. In this case, a reasonable solution that is both economically and environmentally beneficial for all the involved industries is to establish an industrial symbiotic relation that involves: a long-term collaboration for exchanging resources, an agreement in which the rules of collaboration are stated, and a secure mechanism that guarantees the maintenance and security of such a collaboration.

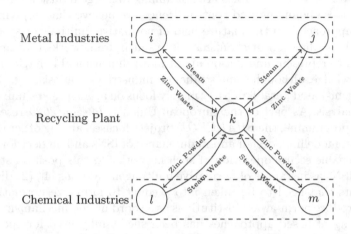

Fig. 1. Industrial symbiosis scenario

Communication is Essential and Distinguishable: Let us assume that the involved agents in this symbiosis scenario have become conscious of the benefits of a long-term collaboration and are willing to make commitments to each other. For instance, m offers that it can deliver a specific amount of steam per month to j if j delivers a specific amount of zinc waste per month to k. We highlight that such an offer does not affect the industrial environment. In other words, the offer of m to deliver an amount is distinguishable from the act of delivering. However, it is not rational that m just delivers such an amount before first offering it and getting the confirmation that j accepts the offer. We say that for long-term collaboration (and not a spontaneous industrial interaction) the communication actions between the involved agents are necessary. As framed by Grosz [13], "collaboration requires communication". Thus, we make distinction between industrial actions that affect the state of environment and communication actions. Such a distinction is in-line with Searle's fundamental approach to define institutions and his distinction between *physical* and *institutional* actions [19].

Collaboration Agreements: In order to enable the regulation of the collaborative relations among the involved industries in a multi-agent ISN, a formalism to represent the mutual agreements is required. We argue that due to the dynamicity of the industrial context and the possible strategic behaviour of industrial agents, static contracts and regiment-based approaches that impose pre-determined restrictions on the actions of industries may not be effective. We follow [9,22] in their argument that, in order to stabilize the collaboration (as a desired situation), it is not efficient to impose constraints on unwanted behaviour. But an apt solution would be: to define norms that reflect the goals of the industrial symbiosis, to detect violations, and to react to violations. For example, if j accepts the above-mentioned offer from m, agent m is expected to follow the norm (to collaborate) and to deliver the promised resource as stated in its offer. More general, collaborative agreement of an industrial symbiosis can be expressed as a set of formal propositions that denote the joint commitments of industrial agents.

Normative Institution: In the industrial context in which a set of hetero-geneous agents may become involved in an ISN, agent's deviations from the desired behaviours may occur due to various reasons, e.g., strategic behaviour of involved industries. Hence, in order to maintain industrial symbiosis and to incentivize external industries to join such a platform, mechanisms to system-atize and secure the set of desired behaviours are essential. For such a purpose a *normative institution* is widely proposed as a solution concept for coordination and regulation of agent behaviour [2,4,22]. In such an institution, a set of norms (that could be specified as normative rules) aims to enforce the goals of the institution. On the other hand, individual agents update the state of the envi-ronment (mainly) by means of performing industrial acts or update the state of the institution (mainly) by means of performing institutional acts. For example, after the above-mentioned offer (from m), agent j may confirm that it accepts the offer. Such a confirmation by j in combination with the former offer by m can be *counted as* the establishment of a joint commitment between m and j. Such a set of rules, e.g., the rule that the combination of a well-defined offer and a related confirmation *counts as* the establishment of a joint commitment, forms the first regulating component of our proposed representation of industrial symbiosis as a normative institution. Now, imagine that m (despite the joint commitment) violates the norm and refuses to deliver the resources. In such cases (of norm violation) the institution can react by applying sanction rules [6]. E.g., refusing to bring about the situations that are mentioned in a joint commitment can result in being disqualified for industrial trade for a given amount of time. The set of sanction rules forms the second regulatory component of our normative industrial symbiosis framework.

3   Industry Interactions and Joint Commitments

Possible actions that industrial agents can perform in an ISN to influence their environment or to interact with each other consist of two exclusive sets of actions: *communication actions*, e.g., offering another firm that a specific amount of resources can be delivered by a specific deadline, and *industrial actions*, e.g., delivering a specific amount of resources to another firm subject to specified conditions. Roughly speaking, industrial actions influence the actual state of the shared industrial environment amongst industrial firms (involved in an ISN) while communication actions do not influence the state of the industrial environment. For modeling the agent interactions in an ISN, we assume a set of involved agents in the ISN, a set of propositional variables that reflect the possible states in the industrial environment, and a domain-specific set of legal communication phrases. Accordingly, a communication action can be seen as the apprising of a legal communication phrase by one of the agents in the ISN towards another member of ISN while an industrial action by an agent (in the ISN) would be to bring about a propositional variable. E.g., in our ISN scenario, the communication act of agent m, *offering* the monthly delivery (mon) of steam waste (sw) to the recycling plant k, can be represented by the communication phrase $offer(m, k, mon, sw)$. Our approach to limit communication phrases to a set of sufficiently expressive phrases follows the approach of [8]. Moreover, our action categorization correlate with classification of *institutional* and *physical* acts in the sense of [19].

One aspect that we consider crucial as a distinction between ISN practices and traditional business-to-business relations is the duration that such practices last. In our view, an industry-industry relation should not be called industrial symbiosis if it basically occurs in reaction to a spontaneous industrial need (for a primary input) but has no concern for a long-term relationship between the involved industries. In order to specify and maintain the long-term relationships amongst agents, *commitment-based* approaches [11] propose a deontic perspective in which agents commit to other agents that they bring about a specific proposition before a given due or/and with respect to the occurrence of some other conditions. The fundamental work of Telang and Singh [21] tailors this commitment-based approach for cross-organizational business models. In a general form, they say that a debtor agent commits to a creditor agent that if the creditor brings about a given proposition p by a specific due, the debtor will bring about a given proposition q by a specific due. We follow their method in modelling joint commitments in ISNs and assume a set of involved agents in the ISN, a set of propositional variables that reflect the possible states in the industrial environment, and a set of integer deadlines. Accordingly, a given joint commitment between two agents in an ISN specifies that the debtor agent is committed to bring about a given propositional variable p before deadline d_1 if the creditor agent brings about a given propositional variable q before deadline d_2.

4   Industrial Symbiosis Institution

Following our proposal to model ISNs using commitment-based agreement technologies, we see the necessity to securely manage and maintain the well-being and (as defined by [7]) the "[...] competitive advantages involving physical exchange of materials, energy, water and by-products [...]" in ISNs. Hence, we need mechanisms to coordinate the behaviour of involved agents in ISNs and to enforce desired behaviours, e.g., the compliance of agents to joint commitments. There exists several multi-agent frameworks (see [10,12,20]) proposing normative institutions as a solution concept for enforcing desired behaviours in electronic/trading institutions. We follow this line of research and propose a normative institution, specified by *facts*, *norms*, and *sanctions*, as a concept that enables the self-organization of ISNs.

In brief, the *fact* component, which consists of institutional and industrial facts, reflects the state of the institution, e.g., the set of already established commitments. In the *norm* component, the set of normative rules that relate industrial/institutional acts to (updated) industrial/institutional facts will be specified. This component reflects the desired behaviours and in a sense the way that an ISN designer expects that her ISN will work. Finally, *sanction* rules in the third component specify the sanctions to be introduced in case of norm violation by the involved agents in an ISN. In our ISN scenario, one norm instance could be that if an agent i accepts an offer of j, agent j should bring about the offer, e.g., should deliver the offered resource before a specific deadline. In this case, acting otherwise will be considered as a norm-violating behaviour (by j) and triggers the sanction rule (against j). The fact component can be programmed using propositional variables while both the norm and sanction rules can be expressed as Searle's *count-as* rules [19]. Our goal is to provide a full description of such ISN-tailored normative notions (formal specification, dynamics and desired properties) in future work.

5   Discussion: Modelling the Complex Behaviour of ISNs

As noted earlier, the design and management of ISNs must consider various issues such as the behaviour over time of this industrial multi-agent system (temporal aspects) as well as mechanisms to monitor (and ensure) the commitment of involved industries to organizational objectives of the industrial symbiosis (coordination and control mechanisms). Fulfilling such necessities asks for comprehensive modelling frameworks, reasoning languages, and operational semantics to represent ISNs and to analyse their behaviour. In the following, we discuss some of the dimensions that we believe a formal model of ISNs should take into account. We view industrial firms that are involved in an ISN as agents with a high level of autonomy regarding their decision-making. In such a system, regulations provided by industrial symbiosis cannot intervene but can exogenously monitor the behaviour of agents and can only impose coordination policies, e.g., sanctions, in case of observing a violation. Accordingly, we see formal normative concepts (e.g., compliance and violation), suitable notions to formulate needed operational semantics for ISNs. Moreover, normative platforms such as proposed in [21] and [8] provide notions that need to be tailored: (1) for reasoning about the temporal properties of ISNs and (2) to formulate a logical characterization of the discussed concepts in this paper.

Due to the involvement of multiple agents in ISNs and their possible conflict of preferences, analysing the coalitional capacities of the possible sub-groups would be helpful for implementing a collusion-proof mechanism to supervise and maintain ISNs. For example, in our industrial symbiosis scenario, imagine a case in which the two zinc waste providers attempt to refuse to deliver for a specific period. Such (undesired) group decisions can strongly influence the efficiency of ISNs. Then the challenge for the industrial symbiosis designer will be to evaluate the effectiveness of the sanction rules to avoid such an undesired possibility. Therefore, sanction rules must be designed with respect to coalitional capacities of the involved agents. Otherwise, the ISN will be vulnerable to collusional actions. Moreover, considering coalitional capacities and strategy proofness of an ISN incentivizes newcomers to join and benefit from the collaboration in a secure fashion.

A final key aspect concerns the relation of a given ISN member with industries that are not involved in the ISN. It is essential to design communication protocols to efficiently communicate and interact with agents that are not (yet) a member of an ISN. This approach relates our work to the line of research on the concept of *Industrial Ecology (IE)* [15]. In this sense, we see any ISN as a loosely coupled subset of IE that agrees to collaborate (internally) based on a specific *agreement technology*; however, it is able to relate to exogenous industrial agents that are active in the IE as its (external) industrial environment.

6   Conclusion

We have proposed a normative perspective and discussed requirements to be taken into account for formal representation and design of ISNs as institutions. Our proposal distinguishes between industrial and communication actions of the involved agents, follows a dynamic formalism by which the joint commitments of industrial agents can be expressed, and uses norm and sanction rules to regulate agent interactions and to avoid commitment violations. Although we discussed ISNs in the institutional level, the decision-making process of each industrial agent remains unresolved. This is how an industrial agent decides to offer to another agent or accept one. One alternative to deal with such decisions should be a rank of industries, with respect to the preferences of the ranker, which allows agents to choose the best ones to make an agreement with. For future work, we aim to apply methods from normative multi-agent systems to industrial symbiosis research and focus on formalizing operational semantics and designing a platform for analyzing the temporal behaviour of ISNs in strategic settings.

Acknowledgement. This research is funded by European Union's *Horizon 2020* programme under grant agreement No. 680843.

References

1. Albino, V., Fraccascia, L., Giannoccaro, I.: Exploring the role of contracts to support the emergence of self-organized industrial symbiosis networks: an agent-based simulation study. J. Clean. Prod. **112**, 4353–4366 (2016)
2. Andrighetto, G., Governatori, G., Noriega, P., van der Torre, L.W.: Normative Multi-agent Systems, vol. 4. Schloss Dagstuhl-Leibniz-Zentrum fuer Informatik, Wadern (2013)

3. Batten, D.F.: Fostering industrial symbiosis with agent-based simulation and participatory modeling. J. Ind. Ecol. **13**(2), 197–213 (2009)
4. Boella, G., Van Der Torre, L., Verhagen, H.: Introduction to normative multiagent systems. Comput. Math. Organ. Theory **12**(2–3), 71–79 (2006)
5. Boons, F., Spekkink, W., Jiao, W.: A process perspective on industrial symbiosis. J. Ind. Ecol. **18**(3), 341–355 (2014)
6. Bulling, N., Dastani, M.: Verifying normative behaviour via normative mechanism design. IJCAI **11**, 103–108 (2011)
7. Chertow, M.R.: Industrial symbiosis: literature and taxonomy. Annu. Rev. Energy Environ. **25**(1), 313–337 (2000)
8. Dastani, M., van der Torre, L., Yorke-Smith, N.: Commitments and interaction norms in organisations. Auton. Agents Multi-agent Syst. **31**, 1–43 (2015)
9. Dignum, V., Dignum, F.: Modelling agent societies: co-ordination frameworks and institutions. In: Brazdil, P., Jorge, A. (eds.) EPIA 2001. LNCS, vol. 2258, pp. 191–204. Springer, Heidelbreg (2001). doi:10.1007/3-540-45329-6_21
10. Dignum, V., Vázquez-Salceda, J., Dignum, F.: OMNI: introducing social structure, norms and ontologies into agent organizations. In: Bordini, R.H., Dastani, M., Dix, J., El Fallah Seghrouchni, A. (eds.) ProMAS 2004. LNCS, vol. 3346, pp. 181–198. Springer, Heidelberg (2004). doi:10.1007/978-3-540-32260-3_10
11. Fornara, N., Colombetti, M.: A commitment-based approach to agent communication. Appl. Artif. Intell. **18**(9–10), 853–866 (2004)
12. García-Camino, A., Noriega, P., Rodríguez-Aguilar, J.A.: Implementing norms in electronic institutions. In: Proceedings of the Fourth International Joint Conference on Autonomous Agents and Multiagent Systems, pp. 667–673. ACM (2005)
13. Grosz, B.J.: The contexts of collaboration. In: Korta, K., Sosa, E., Arrazola, X. (eds.) Cognition, Agency and Rationality, vol. 79, pp. 175–187. Springer, Netherlands (1999). doi:10.1007/978-94-017-1070-1_11
14. Laybourn, P., Clark, W.: National industrial symbiosis programme: a year of achievement. NISP (National Industrial Symbiosis Programme) (2004)
15. Lifset, R., Graedel, T.E.: Industrial ecology: goals and definitions. In: A handbook of industrial ecology, pp. 3–15 (2002)
16. Lombardi, D.R., Laybourn, P.: Redefining industrial symbiosis. J. Ind. Ecol. **16**(1), 28–37 (2012)
17. Paquin, R.L., Howard-Grenville, J.: The evolution of facilitated industrial symbiosis. J. Ind. Ecol. **16**(1), 83–93 (2012)
18. Park, H.S., Behera, S.K.: Methodological aspects of applying eco-efficiency indicators to industrial symbiosis networks. J. Clean. Prod. **64**, 478–485 (2014)
19. Searle, J.R.: The Construction of Social Reality. Simon and Schuster, New York (1995)
20. Sierra, C., Rodriguez-Aguilar, J.A., Noriega, P., Esteva, M., Arcos, J.L.: Engineering multi-agent systems as electronic institutions. Eur. J. Inform. Prof. **4**(4), 33–39 (2004)
21. Telang, P.R., Singh, M.P.: Specifying and verifying cross-organizational business models: an agent-oriented approach. IEEE Trans. Serv. Comput. **5**(3), 305–318 (2012)
22. Vázquez-Salceda, J., Aldewereld, H., Dignum, F.: Implementing norms in multi-agent systems. In: Lindemann, G., Denzinger, J., Timm, I.J., Unland, R. (eds.) MATES 2004. LNCS, vol. 3187, pp. 313–327. Springer, Heidelberg (2004). doi:10.1007/978-3-540-30082-3_23
23. Walls, J.L., Paquin, R.L.: Organizational perspectives of industrial symbiosis: a review and synthesis. Organ. Environ. **28**(1), 32–53 (2015)

Novel Multi-agent Protocols for Islamic Banking Commodity Trading

Amer Alzaidi[1(✉)] and Dimitar Kazakov[2]

[1] Information System Department,
Faculty of Computing & Information Technology,
University of Jeddah, Jeddah, Saudi Arabia
aalzaidi@uj.edu.sa
[2] Computer Science Department, University of York, York, UK
dimitar.kazakov@york.ac.uk

Abstract. Multi-agent systems can play a critical role in Islamic banking development by creating or reforming existing financial products that improve final output and solving a number of legal issues related to Islamic Sharia law. This paper introduces novel multi-agent protocols for a commodity-trading platform to be used for Islamic banking. This work focuses on the most popular (and debated) Islamic banking product, a personal financing product that involves commodity trading rather than direct lending. The protocols in question handle communication in a heterogeneous multi-agent platform to assist three types of actors: banks, retailers and individuals in need of cash.

1 Introduction

While electronic markets have traditionally been used only for trading company shares, a large proportion of commodities new are traded via online or electronic markets. This paper describes part of a research project to develop a multi-agent platform for Islamic banking commodities trading. The new electronic market proposes to solve issues related to the most popular Islamic banking product, Tawarruq. This product is based on buying and selling commodities under certain rules, which requires an efficient system and compliance with Sharia (Islamic law).

The paper introduces protocols for the multi-agent platform. It starts with a description of Islamic banking and how sales are conducted under Sharia to illustrate the main rules of Tawarruq. Then, it describes the difference between how personal Tawarruq should be and the current practice by banks as well as gives an example of the current commodity market used for Tawarruq. The second part of the paper shows the proposed market design and protocols governing the market.

2 Islamic Banking

Risk and equity sharing are a prominent feature of Islamic banking. A vital aspect of Islamic banking is the prohibition of interest (riba). Islamic banks do not charge or pay interest in the usual manner, in which the interest amount is predetermined and is taken

© Springer International Publishing AG 2017
N. Criado Pacheco et al. (Eds.): EUMAS 2016/AT 2016, LNAI 10207, pp. 322–330, 2017.
DOI: 10.1007/978-3-319-59294-7_27

as a present price of the principle credit. Sharia accepts a capital reward for loan providers, solely on a profit-loss-sharing basis [8]. This means that the profit or loss margin will depend on how well or badly the investment project has performed. Another vital feature of Islamic banking is its entrepreneurial aspect. The system focuses not only on financial growth but also on the physical growth of economic production.

2.1 Sales in Islam

Below are some of the fundamental rules in the Islamic Sharia law that must be fulfilled before a sale can take place between the parties involved:

1. The product of the sale should exist at the time of the sale. This means that anything that is non-existent at the time of the sale or that will exist in the future cannot be sold [4]. An example would be selling a car that has not yet been manufactured but is expected to be manufactured at some point in the future.
2. The seller should own the product being sold at the time of the sale. This means that if the owner is trying to sell something that he or she has bought on credit without transferring the ownership or which is not completely in his or her possession, it cannot be sold [4].
3. The product to be sold must be in the physical or constructive possession of the seller at the time of the sale. "Constructive possession" is a situation in which the seller does not physically possess the product but owns all of the rights to the product and incurs any liabilities, including the risks involved in damage to the product, at the time of the sale [4].

2.2 Tawarruq

Tawarruq literally means to "ask for silver", as silver was the original form of currency. It can be interpreted as "asking for money" [2].

Generally speaking, Tawarruq means a person having a commodity or an asset, which is either bought to keep or bought with the intention of trading (i.e., selling to obtain cash).

From an economic view, Tawarruq can be defined as "a particular sale for acquiring liquidity" [2]. The acquired liquidity can be used to pay back a debt, which is not deferrable, or it may be used for personal expenses. It might result in the seller getting instant cash, through Tawarruq being exercised as a plan by the mutawarriq (the owner), to acquire liquidity [12]. Subsequently, the customer will be in charge of selling the commodity or another asset he or she owns, either for trade or for possession, in order to obtain cash that the seller can use for any lawful investment or for personal use [2].

Tawarruq can be classified into two different types: personal Tawarruq and organised Tawarruq.

2.3   Personal Tawarruq

Personal Tawarruq involves a person buying something on credit and selling it to obtain cash. A customer buys a commodity from a seller on deferred payments that add up to more than the actual cash price of the commodity. The customer then has all the rights to sell the commodity to another buyer for cash; this is the fundamental concept of Tawarruq [10]. Tawarruq means to support trading and fair transactions with a chance of winning or losing, whereas conventional lending is a 100% losing scenario in which somebody takes an amount of cash from a bank and repays it with interest.

Based on Sharia, the following principles direct the legitimacy of the Tawarruq process:

The seller must own the product.

The product cannot be resold back to the original seller. If this happens, the entire transaction will be considered void. It is considered cheating on the regulation and misses the main objective of Tawarruq, which is to support trading and moving commodities in the market rather than money for money.

The three most common scenarios for personal Tawarruq are the following:

1. A person is in need of cash but is unable to find anyone to give him or her an interest-free loan. The person therefore buys a commodity from a seller on deferred payments and sells it to a third party, who cannot be the original seller of the commodity. In this type of Tawarruq situation, the original seller is unaware of the intention of the customer, i.e., to obtain cash.
2. A person is denied an interest-free loan but is offered credit to buy a commodity on deferred payments. However, the price of the commodity is the actual market price. This allows the market to obtain more commodities.
3. The same as the previous scenario, but the seller adds a profit margin onto the basic price of the commodity since the commodity is being sold on credit.

Most Sharia scholars agree on scenarios (1) and (2) because they are basic, normal commodity trading, but some scholars are doubtful about (3), adding a profit margin onto the actual commodity price, which is a kind of interest on the amount lent and takes advantage of the customer who needs cash by adding more unjustified costs onto the commodity market price.

2.4   Organised Tawarruq

Organised Tawarruq is different from personal Tawarruq in the sense that the seller (the bank) is in full control of the transaction and decides on how the customer will get the cash once the transaction is completed [11].

Organised Tawarruq alters the usual steps because the commodity moves from the seller to a buyer theoretically and not physically. The rationale behind this is to reduce the cost of the Tawarruq in storing, delivering and marketing the commodity. These cost-saving tactics have forced the banks to devise new business models in order to secure customer benefits. Tawarruq customers are interested in the cash that they will have after the commodity has been sold and not in the commodity itself. Therefore,

Table 1. Differences between organised and personal Tawarruq

	Organised Tawarruq	Personal Tawarruq
Who finds the final buyer?	The bank can prearrange with the final buyer to purchase the commodity even before the bank sells it to the customer, to avoid price changes	There is no link between the bank and the final buyer
Who resells the product?	The bank	The customer
Who collects the money?	The bank collects and then deposits the money into the customer's account	The customer

customers have nothing to do with the storage, delivery or marketing of the commodity [6]. In the interest of the customer, the banks set up different models, under which they sell the commodity to the customer on deferred payments and then receive the customer's authorisation to sell the commodity to a third party, depositing the cash in the customer's bank account (Table 1).

The most recent Sharia scholars' opinion issued by the Organisation of the Islamic Conference Fiqh Academy in 2009 announced organised Tawarruq was forbidden [5].

Organised Tawarruq takes the process fully away from the customer's hands and uses the customer's need for cash as motivation to increase the bank's profit in selling the commodity to the customer, with a huge profit percentage on top of the commodity market price, which forces the customer to resell in a guaranteed losing transaction. This process is against human logical thinking—why would customers buy commodities when they know for sure that they will lose money in the reselling?

2.5   Islamic Commodity Market

An example of the current Islamic commodity market is the Bahrain Financial Exchange (Bait Al Bursa). The Bahrain Financial Exchange (BFX) is an inter-border and multi-asset exchange in the Middle East and North African region. Bait Al Bursa is BFX's Islamic financial division, which offers an exclusive Sharia-abiding financial instrument for electronic trade. Bait Al Bursa symbolises the "Home of Exchanges" and represents BFX's idea of offering a single location for all of the exchange-traded business in the Islamic finance sector. Bait Al Bursa is devoted to introducing novel and inventive solutions that fulfil the requirements of the present Islamic financial market. It is the first committed platform in the area to provide exchange-traded solutions to the Islamic finance market. Bait Al Bursa focuses on forming a new standard in Islamic finance by bringing in new, Sharia-abiding exchange-traded financial products [5].

3   Platform for Smart Tawarruq

Five types of agents interact in our platform for Tawarruq:

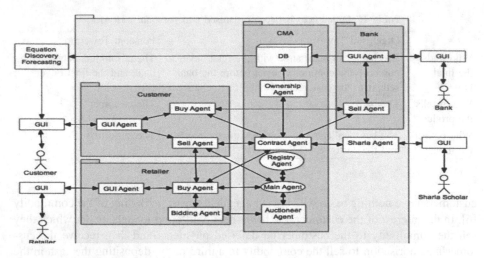

Fig. 1. Proposed architecture for smart Tawarruq multi-agent platform

1. The bank, a commodity provider for the customer to buy from.
2. The customer, who has access to a forecasting tool [1] to obtain a view of next-day price movements, request to buy the commodity from the bank and then resell it to retailers.
3. The retailer, as the final buyer of the commodity from the customer by auctions or direct offers.
4. The Sharia agent: Tawarruq must be supervised by an external independent department that includes a number of Sharia scholars to ensure that commodities are not traded more than once in the market and to make sure that the customer does not resell the commodity to the original owner. This agent is purely for supervision.
5. The capital market authority (CMA) is a facilitator between the system's stakeholders. It is a facilitator and has nothing to do with the rules; see Fig. 1.

3.1 Customer Order Tawarruq Protocol

A customer ordering a Tawarruq from the bank interacts with the customer graphical user interface (GUI) agent by adding buying preferences. The GUI agent sends the buying preferences to the customer's buying agent to prepare an official offer request from the bank's selling agent, who has already received the bank's selling preferences from the bank GUI. The bank's selling agent checks the customer request and evaluates it based on the customer's selling preferences. If the customer passes, then the bank's selling agent calculates an offer based on the bank's equation and sends the final offer to the customer's buying agent. The customer's buying agent checks the offer and accepts it if it matches the customer's buying preferences. Both the customer's buying agent and the bank's selling agent enter into a contract protocol and pass the output to their own GUI.

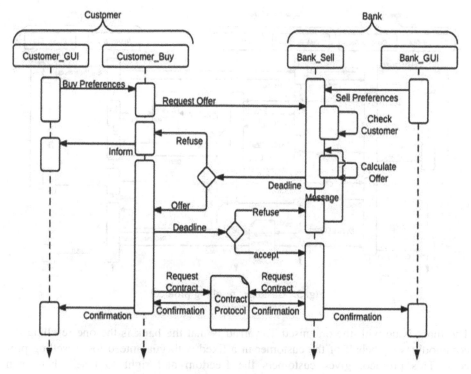

Fig. 2. Customer order Tawarruq protocol

To simplify the protocol, UML diagrams are used to represent the protocol sequence; see Fig. 2. In this protocol, the customer chooses what commodity to buy, as compared to the current process of the organised Tawarruq, where it is imposed by the bank.

3.2 Customer Resell Protocol

The customer GUI receives a message from the customer's buying agent, confirming that the customer owns the product now. The GUI sends the selling preferences to the customer's selling agent, who will first register with the CMA registry agent and then request an offer from the CMA main agent and choose a selling strategy. Retailers register with the CMA registry and send their buying preferences to the CMA main agent. Now, the CMA main agent will know the customer's product and the selling strategy. If the customer chooses to sell to the highest bidder, then the CMA main agent (the inquiry registry agent) gets a list of the retailers interested in this commodity from the registry agent. The agent then sends the product details to all of them and requests an offer. Every retailer that receives the request calculates an offer and then sends it back to the CMA main agent, who will compare all of the offers and then send the highest offer along with the retailer's details to the customer's selling agent. The customer's selling agent and retailer's buying agent enter into a contract protocol. On the other hand, if the customer chooses to sell at auction, then the CMA main agent will create an auction and enter into an auction protocol with the retailers; see Fig. 3.

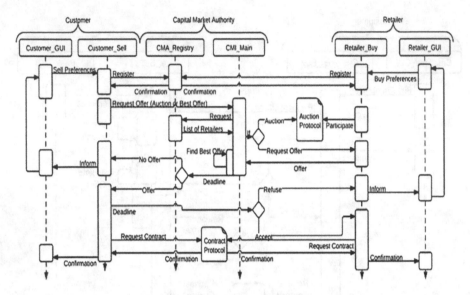

Fig. 3. Customer reselling protocol

The main issue with the organised Tawarruq is that the bank is the one reselling the commodities on behalf of the customer in a fixed with guaranteed loss reselling process. This protocol gives customers the freedom and right to resell their own commodities.

3.3 Auction Protocol

The CMA main agent can find the highest offer if the customer chooses the highest-offer selling strategy, but if the customer chooses to sell at auction, there are a number of auction strategies, such as English and Dutch auctions. This protocol proposes a new auction strategy to maximise the customer return: a three-round auction. The customer sends the product details and reserve price. The CMA main agent gets a list of all the retailers that want to buy products from the auction from the registry agent retailers. The CMA main agent creates an auctioneer for each auction. The auctioneer announces the product, sends the starting bid price and requests the first-round bid. The retailers first check whether the start price is higher than their maximum; if so, they drop out of the auction and notify the auctioneer. If not, the retailers calculate their bids based on how long they can stay in the market and how many products they have to buy to hit their own targets (as set by the retailers). The auctioneer receives the first-round bids, then announces the winner of the first round and uses the bid as the minimum price for the second round of bidding. Some retailers will drop out, but others will submit their bid for the second round. In the third and final round, retailers will submit their bids, and the auctioneer will send the winning bid and the retailer's details to the CMA main agent and then to the customer's selling agent. Both the customer's selling agent and the retailer's buying agent will enter into a contract protocol to finalise the deal; see Fig. 4.

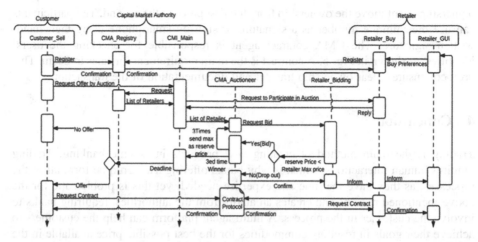

Fig. 4. Auction protocol

3.4 Contract Protocol

Each deal, whether ordering or reselling Tawarruq, ends by using a contract protocol. The protocol legally sanctions the deal between the two participants by signing and registering the contract. The CMA contract agent starts to create a contract once the agent receives a contract request from both contract parties. After creating the contract, which includes the product type, name, quantity, method of payment, date of payment etc., the CMA agent sends the contract to the Sharia agent for authorisation. The Sharia agent checks the history of both participants and the product movement history to stop products from going in and out of the market more than once. The Sharia agent checks the contract and ensures that it is Sharia compliant. Once the Sharia agent authorises the contract, the contract agent will send the contract to the participants to sign. The CMA contract agent will receive the signed contracts and then request that the CMA

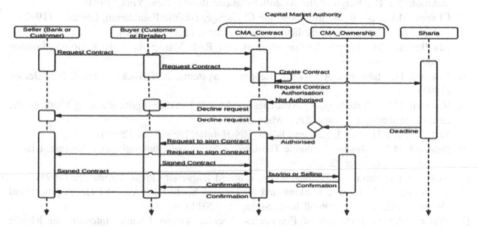

Fig. 5. Contract protocol

ownership agent move the ownership from the first party to the second. The participants can use their unique number as a signature or sign by smartphone using their hand-written signature. The CMA contract agent is responsible for checking the users' identities, as shown in Fig. 5. A contract is the main requirement for sales in Islam. This protocol ensures clear ownership transfer and documentation of the transaction.

4   Conclusion

Trading is the main method of creating new products in Islamic banking. Trading requires human interactions, which is why banks offering Tawarruq perform all of the processes, as they have the time and expertise needed, yet this is problematic for the above-mentioned reasons and creates an alarm from the authorities, requiring banks to involve the customer in the process. A multi-agent platform can help the customers to achieve their goals in reselling commodities for the best possible price available in the market by putting them in the middle of the process and allowing them to resell their commodities by themselves in an open market governed by supply and demand, with the chance of generating profit when demand is high and the chance of losing money if demand is low. The protocols in this paper are proposed to control the market movement and agent communication. The product ownership flow handling commodities going from the bank to the customer and then to the retailer requires our protocols to be compliant with Islamic Sharia law. A multi-agent platform can represent participants and act on their behalf. Islamic banking products require independent supervision, which multi-agents can strongly support.

References

1. Alzaidi, A., Kazakov, D.: Equation discovery for financial forecasting in the context of Islamic banking. In: Artificial Intelligence and Applications, IASTED, Innsbruck (2011)
2. Bakhash, S.: The Reign of the Ayatollahs. Basic Books, New York (1984)
3. Chapra, M.U.: Islam and the Economic Challenge. Islamic Foundation, Leicester (1992)
4. Labib, S.Y.: Capitalism in medieval Islam. J. Econ. Hist. **29** (1966)
5. Mahlknecht, M.: Islamic Capital Markets and Risk Management. Risk Books, London (2009)
6. Nomani, F., Rahnema, A.: Islamic Economic Systems. Zed Books Limited, New Jersey (1994)
7. Rammal, H.G., Zurbruegg, R.: Awareness of Islamic banking products among Muslims: the case of Australia. J. Financ. Serv. Mark. (2006)
8. Sait, S., Lim, H.: Land, Law and Islam. UN-Habitat, New York (2006)
9. Siddiqui, M.N.: Muslim Economic Thinking: A Survey of Contemporary Literature. Islamic Foundation, Leicester (2007)
10. Roy, O.: The Failure of Political Islam. Harvard University Press, Cambridge (1994)
11. Venardos, A.M.: Islamic Banking and Finance in South-East Asia: Its Development and Future. World Scientific Publishing, Singapore (2011)
12. Waleed, A.: Methodology of Economics: Secular Versus Islamic. International Islamic University, Kuala Lumpur (2008)

EUMAS 2016: Simulations

Agent-Based Simulation for Software Development Processes

Tobias Ahlbrecht[1][(✉)], Jürgen Dix[1], Niklas Fiekas[1], Jens Grabowski[2], Verena Herbold[2], Daniel Honsel[2], Stephan Waack[2], and Marlon Welter[2]

[1] Department of Informatics, Clausthal University of Technology,
Julius-Albert-Str. 4, 38678 Clausthal-Zellerfeld, Germany
{tobias.ahlbrecht,dix,niklas.fiekas}@tu-clausthal.de
[2] Institute of Computer Science, Georg-August-Universität Göttingen,
Goldschmidtstrasse 7, 37077 Göttingen, Germany
{grabowski,dhonsel,waack,mwelter}@informatik.uni-goettingen.de,
verena.herbold@cs.uni-goettingen.de

Abstract. Software development is a costly process and requires serious quality control on the management level: Managing a project with more than 10 programmers over several years is a highly nontrivial task. We are building tools for helping the manager to predict the future development of the project based on certain adjustable parameters.

The main idea is to view the software process as *agent-based simulation* in a multiagent system (MAS). This approach requires combining three different areas: (1) mining patterns from past projects, (2) modeling the software development process in a multiagent environment, and (3) running the simulation on a scalable multiagent platform.

Keywords: Agents · Simulation · Software/management processes · Software evolution · Mining software repositories · Conditional random fields

1 Introduction

We introduce the *SimSe* project[1] ("Agent-based simulation models in support of monitoring the quality of software projects") funded by the *Simulationswissenschaftliches Zentrum (SWZ)*, a joint institution of the University of Göttingen and Clausthal University of Technology.

The project manager of a software project is interested in *minimizing* the number of bugs, as well as the overall costs and at the same time *maximizing* the quality of maintenance. In order to do so, she needs answers to questions like: Where are *error-prone* parts in the code? This leads to the following rough idea: *Simulate alternative evolutions of the project by modifying certain parameters.*

---

[1] https://www.simzentrum.de/en/research-projects/agent-based-simulation-models-in-support-of-monitoring-the-quality-of-software-projects/.

© Springer International Publishing AG 2017
N. Criado Pacheco et al. (Eds.): EUMAS 2016/AT 2016, LNAI 10207, pp. 333–340, 2017.
DOI: 10.1007/978-3-319-59294-7_28

The results can be used to find out suitable parameter settings. This results in a feedback loop for software project managers. The problem is of course to *(1) choose the right parameters*, and, *(2) make the simulation as realistic as possible*.

The idea of this Agent-based simulation of software evolution is quite simple: we view *software artifacts* as *passive* agents, and *developers* as *active* agents. Active agents *generate, extend, correct and refactor* software artifacts through *commit* actions. A detailed description of this model can be found in [7].

In our simulation model, elaborated in Sect. 4, we are simulating several parameters, which are obtained by mining *based on commits* stored in the repository, e.g., changes to the source code: the *effect and costs of refactoring*, the (change in the) *behavior* of developers, *communication* between developers, and *goal-orientedness* and *improved experience* of developers.

The paper is structured like following: We present related work in Sect. 2. and investigate mining methods for parameter estimation in Sect. 3. The main part of this paper is Sect. 4, where we introduce the necessary software engineering constructs that we model in the simulation. Our platform and the assessment of simulation results are presented in Sect. 5. Finally, we conclude with Sect. 6.

2 Related Work

Only few approaches exist in the area of monitoring software quality with simulation methods. An agent-based simulation model for software evolution was presented by Smith and Ramil [14]. They can reproduce different facets of software evolution, e.g., the number of complex entities, the number of touches, and distinct patterns for system growth, but almost all of them need different parameter sets. Our model we proposed in [7], differs from Smith et al. in so far that it is not grid-based and agents do not perform a random walk. In our work, all instantiated agents live in one environment and relationships are represented as graphs. Furthermore, our simulation model requires only parameters for effort and size to simulate projects that have similar growth trends.

For the prediction of software quality in general there are many approaches in the literature. [3] analyze the impact of software graphs on defect-proneness and maintainability. In particular, they consider source-code based graphs and developer collaboration graphs. In our work, we also describe relations between software entities and between developers. Bhattacharya et al. [3] include more graphs concerning the structure of the software, e.g., call graphs, which we also plan to do.

3 Parameter Mining for the Simulation Model

In this section we describe how to extract necessary information from open source repositories using data mining methods. In [8,9], we presented mining methods to obtain parameters for various simulation models. These models cover different aspects of software evolution, such as the growth of a project, bug introducing rates, or the lifespan of bugs.

With the model presented in [7] we are able to simulate the quality trend of software projects. However, the structure of the simulated *ChangeCoupling* graph is not close enough to the mined one. Thus, we have to extend the simulation model (Sect. 4) which leads to additional mining effort. For this extension we require more knowledge about the developer behavior and certain source-code patterns: Both are described below.

3.1 Specialized Developer Behavior

To estimate the effort of developers, it is of great importance to understand their driving factors and the evolution of their work. Since developers are humans, driving factors and workload depend on several factors: motivation, interests, dedication to the project, or time constraints. For the simulation of quality assurance, a deeper understanding of different types of developers is needed. The team constellation represents a simulation parameter, which has an impact on the overall project quality. For example, less active contributors may introduce more bugs.

Developers' actions are not solely visible in their commit behavior. Given the whole history of a project, it can be hard to derive a complete picture of the behavior of developers. Also their role is an important factor for the involvement in the project. For the developer role definition, we distinguish between core developers, major developers, and minor developers. We look at the evolution of four metrics describing the contribution: commits, bugfixes, mailing list posts, and bug comments. We use Hidden Markov Models (HMMs) for describing this evolution in a dynamic way. HMMs are stochastic models flexible for examining discrete time observations. We describe and validate this approach in our recent work [10] using six open source projects with 106 developers. There we compare individual models and general models for the different developer types. For all individual HMMs that could be trained, we found out that contribution behavior can be well described with individual models. Using general models performs about 5% worse, but can be applied even though the individual calculation is not possible, e.g., because of a small input space.

3.2 Source-Code Change Patterns

To recognize different change patterns, commits of open source projects will be analyzed. We are currently implementing a mining framework that processes commits in order identify refactorings. For this, we mine and compare the abstract syntax trees (ASTs) of different versions of the software.

Our aim is to find a large number of change patterns with detailed information about what happens when one of them applies. This includes dependency changes as well as changes of software metrics like the size or the complexity of classes or methods.

4   Modeling the Software Process

As stated in [7], we propose a simulation model of software processes that predicts the quality trend of software projects. In this section, we briefly describe this model as well as its limitations and pave the way for improvements.

In the model, we consider software entities and bugs as passive agents and developers as active ones. The developer's commit behavior is responsible for the evolutionary process of the software development under simulation. Therefore, we focus on modeling the create, update, delete, and bugfix functionality of developers.

To model dependencies between entities we have chosen to use networks. This provides us with more sophisticated modeling possibilities than the grid based approach proposed by Smith and Ramil [14]. One to he most important networks is the *ChangeCouplingNetwork*: This network represents dependencies between software entities that are changed together several times. It serves as input for the automated assessment.

For modeling and simulation purposes we used *Repast Simphony* [12], an open source framework for agent-based simulation. This tool was well suited for modeling small to medium projects. It is not appropriate for the large number of agents that we intend to simulate in future studies.

The resulting simulation model reveals issues concerning the structure of the simulated change coupling graph and the bug fix probabilities of developers. Plans addressed to this issues will be considered in Subsects. 4.1 and 4.2.

4.1   Modeling Developer Goals and Plans

One of the challenges is to model the entity selection of a commit. Without knowledge about the intention of the developer, software entities are selected mainly randomly as mentioned in [7]. This results in significant differences between a simulated and a mined, i.e., real change coupling graph.

To reduce the coincidence, we plan to use the prominent BDI [16] approach for future simulation models. In such a model, developers formulate goals based on their beliefs and build plans to reach them. One example, how the decision process of a developer leads to an action, is depicted in Fig. 1.

Beliefs are the current state of the project, represented as software metrics, as well as a parameter that can be set by the manager each time the simulation runs. Thus, we can easily compare differently configured simulation runs with each other. Goals are, for example, add new features, fix bugs, improve the maintainability, or reduce the complexity of the project. A developer agent selects the goal based on its beliefs. From time to time the beliefs have to be revised.

Plans are patterns that should, when applied to the software graph, achieve a goal. They can also be concatenated to reach a goal.

To get a realistic model we need patterns for different source code changes like refactorings, bug fixes, or additional functionality. The formulation of them requires preliminary work in terms of mining open source repositories (described in Sect. 3.2). Valuable information about one pattern are how software metrics

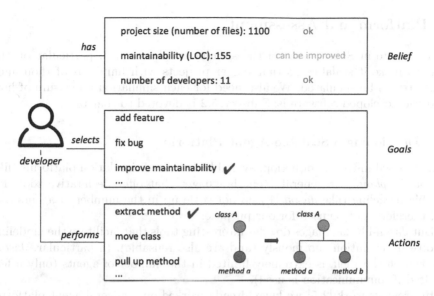

Fig. 1. Example for developer's goals and plans. The developer works on a method that is hard to maintain because it has too many lines of code. To improve maintainability the developer applies the refactoring extract method that splits the method.

like the complexity or the lines of code change, how many files will be touched and how the touched files are connected.

To apply the above introduced patterns we need a more detailed software dependency graph. It should be detailed enough to deal with plans and goals of developers: dependencies of classes, methods, and variables need to be modeled to deal with metrics, but more abstract than the concrete syntax-tree of the project. Its size is expected to be 10 times more than the change coupling graph.

We believe that this model improves the structure of the simulated change coupling graph significantly, but it also adds additional requirements on the simulation platform. Therefore, we are developing our own scalable agent platform as described in Sect. 5.1.

4.2 Modeling Communication Between Developers

The experience of a developer, which is an important factor of the probability to fix a bug, is closely related to the communication between the developers. In software projects communication occurs in mailing lists or issue tracking systems. The platform proposed in Sect. 5.1 provides cooperation skills which allows us to model interactions between the developers. For modeling, however, not just the occurrence and the extent of communication activities, but also the intentions behind are important. It is of special interest for us how the communication relates to actions which can be retraced later in the repository. We are currently working on the analysis of this and the impact on decisions during the project.

5   Platform and Assessment

We elaborate in Subsect. 5.1 on the simulation platform, in particular on the ideas to make it scalable, so that bigger projects with hundreds of thousands of agents can be simulated. We also need for each simulation a measure of how good the developed software is: Subsect. 5.2 is devoted to that task.

5.1   Developing a Scalable Agent Platform

As mentioned in the introduction, available dedicated simulation platforms (like *Repast Simphony*) or general agent languages that offer declarative tools for suitable modeling (like *Jason* [4]) do not scale up in the number of agents and can, therefore, not be used for our purpose.

But *Jason*-like languages do offer interesting tools that facilitate the modeling of software evolution enormously (and are also reusable). In particular, *Jason*, as taken off the shelf, is extremely limited in the number of agents (only a few hundred if communication is used).

In previous work [2,5] we have already worked on a general agent platform, *MASeRaTi*, to deploy huge numbers of agents (in the area of traffic simulation). Many techniques and design decisions will be reused. Instead of reimplementing *Jason* from scratch, we focus on a new approach, based on *MapReduce*.

The main idea of *MapReduce* is to distinguish between synchronized and non-synchronized objects and then to identify parts of the simulation that are completely independent from each other and can thus be processed in parallel. Agents that are working on the same part of the world or are communicating with each other need to be synchronized among them: groups doing independent work need not.

The main step in our approach is to find an efficient translation from *Jason* to *MapReduce*: see [1] for a detailed discussion including the benchmark of our approach.

Previous approaches were either limited in the use of agent models [13] or in the expressibility of the underlying language [15]. Our platform, in contrast, supports full *Jason*-style *AgentSpeak*. Using *MapReduce* allows us to get a linear scale-up in the number of agents.

5.2   Automated Assessment

The simulated change coupling graph of the software project under study forms the graphical basis of automated assessment. Every node (software entity) of this graph is augmented with the preliminary label *problematic* or with the preliminary label *acceptable* both calculated on grounds of software metrics.

The change coupling graph and its preliminary label sequence are the input of automated assessment, which in turn is aimed at replacing the preliminary assessment labels by final ones denoted by *acceptable* or by *problematic* as well. This is motivated by the fact that the overall judgment of a software entity is strongly influenced by those entities that are dependent on it.

Taking a pattern from the Ising model of statistical mechanics [11], we created a conditional random field-based model to determine the final entity labeling. In line with the Ising model, we introduced conformity weights rewarding that preliminary labels and final labels coincide, and a coupling parameter rewarding that final labels of adjacent nodes are equal. To determine the final software entity assessment label sequence, we make a *maximum posterior probability* prediction. Since this problem is NP-hard, we adopted to this end a Viterbi heuristics devised by Dong *et al.* in [6].

Here are the future challenges of automated assessment:

1. Devise an algorithm to determine the conformity weights and the coupling parameter automatically.
2. Adapt the Viterbi heuristics devised in [6] to very large software graphs.
3. Adapt known sampling algorithms using Markov Chain Monte Carlo Methods to be able to replace final labels by its posterior probabilities.
4. Check the applicability of the assessment approach by analyzing and simulating open source projects.

6 Conclusions and Outlook

The project reported in this paper is a continuation of two previous projects (https://simzentrum.de/en/education/softwarequalitaetssicherung-mit-hilfe-vo n-simulationsverfahren/ and https://simzentrum.de/en/research-projects/ desim/) and is scheduled for three years. We can therefore build on solid foundations and experiences. In order to make more precise predictions of the behavior of the developers, we need to model their plans and intentions. Therefore we have chosen *Jason* which provides language constructs for suitable modeling.

Our aim in the future is fourfold: (1) We have to find out which other constructs we need for suitable modeling, (2) how to integrate them in a *scalable* simulation platform, (3) how to mine appropriate information from open source repositories, and (4) develop an overall simulation model (as an extension of the current one) that takes all these tasks into account.

Acknowledgment. The authors thank the SWZ Clausthal-Göttingen (https://www. simzentrum.de/en/) that partially funded our work (both the former projects "Simulation-based Quality Assurance for Software Systems" and "DeSim", and the recent project "SimSe").

References

1. Ahlbrecht, T., Dix, J., Fiekas, N.: Scalable multi-agent simulation based on mapreduce (forthcoming). Technical report IfI-16-03, TU Clausthal (2016). http://www. in.tu-clausthal.de/fileadmin/homes/techreports/ifi1603ahlbrecht.pdf
2. Ahlbrecht, T., Dix, J., Fiekas, N., Kraus, P., Müller, J.P.: An architecture for scalable simulation of systems of cognitive agents. Int. J. Agent-Oriented Softw. Eng. **5**, 232–265 (2016)

3. Bhattacharya, P., Iliofotou, M., Neamtiu, I., Faloutsos, M.: Graph-based analysis and prediction for software evolution. In: Proceedings of the 34th International Conference on Software Engineering (ICSE). IEEE (2012). ISBN 978-1-4673-1067-3
4. Bordini, R.H., Hübner, J.F., Wooldridge, M.: Programming Multi-Agent Systems in AgentSpeak Using Jason. Wiley, Hoboken (2007). http://eu.wiley.com/Wiley CDA/WileyTitle/productCd-0470029005.html. ISBN 9780470057476
5. Dalpiaz, F., Dix, J., van Riemsdijk, M.B. (eds.): EMAS 2014. LNCS. Springer, Cham (2014). doi:10.1007/978-3-319-14484-9. ISBN 978-3-319-14483-2
6. Dong, Z., Wang, K., Dang, T.K.L., Gültas, M., Welter, M., Wierschin, T., Stanke, M., Waack, S.: CRF-based models of protein surfaces improve protein-protein interaction site predictions. BMC Bioinform. **15**(1), 1–14 (2014). doi:10.1186/1471-2105-15-277. http://dx.doi.org/10.1186/1471-2105-15-277. ISSN 1471-2105
7. Honsel, D., Honsel, V., Welter, M., Grabowski, J., Waack, S.: Monitoring software quality by means of simulation methods. In: 10th International Symposium on Empirical Software Engineering and Measurement (ESEM) (2016)
8. Honsel, V., Honsel, D., Grabowski, J.: Software process simulation based on mining software repositories. In: ICDM Workshop (2014)
9. Honsel, V., Honsel, D., Herbold, S., Grabowski, J., Waack, S.: Mining software dependency networks for agent-based simulation of software evolution. In: ASE Workshop (2015)
10. Honsel, V., Herbold, S., Grabowski, J.: Hidden Markov models for the prediction of developer involvement dynamics and workload. In: 12th International Conference on Predictive Models and Data Analytics in Software Engineering (PROMISE) (2016)
11. Ising, E.: Beitrag zur Theorie des Ferromagnetismus. Zeitschrift für Physik A Hadrons and Nuclei (1925). ISSN 0044–3328
12. North, M.J., Collier, N.T., Ozik, J., Tatara, E.R., Macal, C.M., Bragen, M., Sydelko, P.: Complex adaptive systems modeling with repast simphony. Complex Adapt. Syst. Model. **1**, 3 (2013)
13. Radenski, A.: Using mapreduce streaming for distributed life simulation on the cloud. In: ECAL, pp. 284–291 (2013)
14. Smith, N., Ramil, J.F.: Agent-based simulation of open source evolution. In: Software Process Improvement and Practice (2006)
15. Wang, G., Vaz Salles, M., Sowell, B., Wang, X., Cao, T., Demers, A.J., Gehrke, J., White, W.M.: Behavioral simulations in mapreduce. CoRR, abs/1005.3773 (2010). http://arxiv.org/abs/1005.3773
16. Weiss, G.: Multiagent Systems. MIT Press, Cambridge (2013). ISBN 9780262018890

An Applicability of ABC Method to Inverse Simulation and Application to Triage Simulation

Atsushi Kobayashi$^{(\boxtimes)}$, Koji Suginuma, and Masakazu Furuichi

Graduate School of Industrial Technology, Nihon University,
Narashino, Chiba, Japan
ciat15001@g.nihon-u.ac.jp,
{suginuma.koji,furuichi.masakazu}@nihon-u.ac.jp

Abstract. We proposed TRISim, a multi-agent simulation tool, to study hospital triage operation methods. By inputting various combinations of model parameters, we can obtain the results to explore the correlation between parameters. We can derive an optimum set of parameters by exploring many parameters manually, but this is a time-consuming task. Herein, we propose Inverse TRISim, a method to automate the task of finding an optimal combination of parameters using the artificial bee colony (ABC) algorithm.

Keywords: Triage · Multi-agent simulation · MAS · ABC

1 Introduction

When a large-scale disaster occurs, patients with different emergency needs visit the same hospitals for treatment and diagnosis; hence, emergency control of medical operations is very important. When the number of patients exceeds hospital capacity, it is impossible to rescue all patients via a normal medical response. Therefore, medical organizations require management criteria for such situations; they should follow national standards of triage systems, such as the Japan Triage Acuity Scale (JTAS) [1] or Emergency Severity Index (ESI) [2]. These standards are defined for use in emergency situations to assign treatment priority based on the severity of each patient's condition, so that the best medical treatment can be provided to the maximum number of injured patients under the constraints of the medical environment.

Triage operation methods are evaluated in each hospital based on local triage standards; it is important to consider the characteristics of each hospital by evaluating previous triage results, which depend on triage method and urgency levels; many studies have analyzed waiting times and nursing quality using real-world data [3]. Simulation-based approaches are also possible. In this study, we examine emergency patient waiting time with queueing simulation [4]. Other studies, using multi-agent simulations to perform post hoc evaluation of triage results [5], have shown that more precise simulation methods are needed.

Using TRISim [6], hospital managers can analyze the triage protocol for their hospital plan renovations and new hospital development. To use TRISim for such

N. Criado Pacheco et al. (Eds.): EUMAS 2016/AT 2016, LNAI 10207, pp. 341–349, 2017.
DOI: 10.1007/978-3-319-59294-7_29

planning, a variety of parameters—numbers of rooms, equipment, doctors, nurses, etc. —must be explored. However, it is difficult to find the optimal parameters manually. In this study, we propose and develop Inverse TRISim to automate the discovery of these values.

2 Proposed System

2.1 TRISim

TRISim is designed to support hospital managers by simulating the overall triage operation method; the system concept and model are shown in Fig. 1.

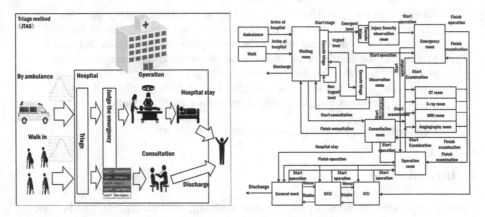

Fig. 1. Overview and system model of TRISim

A patient visits an emergency department by walk-in or ambulance. A doctor or triage nurse examines the patient based on emergency level. The patient is admitted to the hospital after an operation, given emergency medical treatment, or simply examined by a doctor. Finally, the patient is discharged from the hospital. TRISim systemizes these processes in an emergency department.

Waiting room model: Patients arriving at an emergency department by walk-in or ambulance are examined by a doctor or triage nurse. After arrival, a triage nurse or doctor decides on the urgency level of each patient. After a patient is assigned an urgency level, the patient is moved to an observation room, a consultation room, or an emergency room, depending on the required treatment.

Injury severity observation room model: Nurse agents assigned to this room periodically triage entering patients. Patients are moved to emergency rooms as the rooms become vacant, but are required to wait in this room until then.

Emergency room model: Doctor agents assigned to this room examine and operate on entering patients. Patients are moved to the intensive care unit (ICU) after an operation. If the ICU is not vacant, the patient is moved to the high care unit (HCU).

ICU model: Patients entering this room gradually recover from trauma. The healing methods used for recovery are chosen based on statistical data with geometric series to decrease the length of hospital stay. They are moved to the HCU when trauma status is subthreshold and wait in the ICU when the HCU is not available.

HCU model: Patients entering this room have gradually recovered from trauma by being treated in the ICU or are waiting in the HCU for an ICU vacancy. Patients are moved to a general ward when their trauma is subthreshold.

General ward model: By receiving treatment in the ICU and HCU, trauma patients gradually recover. They are moved to the HCU when their trauma status exceeds a threshold and wait in the HCU when the ICU has no vacancies. They are discharged when their trauma status is subthreshold.

Consultation room model: A doctor diagnoses patients entering this room; patients are moved to the emergency room depending on their urgency levels. They are moved to an operation, examination, or waiting room as a result of the doctor's consultation.

Operation room model: Doctors operate on patients entering this room and patients recover from trauma depending on the type of operation and the body part affected. Patients move to the ICU, HCU, or general ward depending on the severity of their conditions after operation.

Examination room model: A clinical engineer assigned to this room examines the severity of trauma of patients entering this room on requests from doctors. Patients are moved to the return room after examination. In this study, we consider x-ray, CT, MRI, and angiography rooms as our examination rooms.

Each room is composed of doctor, nurse, and clinical engineer agents. Each agent behaves per the processes and parameters of publicly available information or data. Patients are processed based on trauma severity and survival rate [6]. TRISim simulates these processes by simulating all entities through multi-agent simulation.

2.2 Inverse TRISim

To study triage operation methods, hospital managers can run a simulation with TRISim; to study combinations of parameters, hospital managers can run the simulation repeatedly. However, it is very difficult to find a globally optimized solution because the possible combination of parameters is enormous. In order to solve this problem, an inverse simulation method is considered effective [7].

This study proposes Inverse TRISim, which introduces inverse simulation based on TRISim as a tool to optimize triage operation methods in hospitals. Figure 2 shows an overview of the Inverse TRISim conceptual and operation models.

The Inverse TRISim operation system model is composed of forward and inverse simulation components. In the forward simulation, the input parameters are the number of rooms, doctor agents, nurse agents and clinical engineer agents, along with any other specific hospital model data. When a forward simulation begins, TRISim takes these parameters, and then simulates and outputs the results.

In the inverse simulation, an inverse simulation controller (ISC) creates a first generation of hospital model parameters to be given to Inverse TRISim, from which simulation results are derived. Then, the ISC calculates an evaluation index using these results.

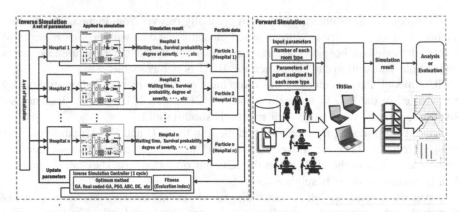

Fig. 2. Overview of the Inverse TRISim conceptual model

Next, the ISC generates a second generation of hospital parameters using a heuristic method. This cycle continues until the results converge to the optimum parameter set.

The inverse simulation method estimates model parameters to optimize the evaluation value (based on the evaluation index). To estimate the model parameters appearing in the simulation, inverse simulation controls the optimization based on the evaluation index. To control the inverse simulation, metaheuristic methods, such as genetic algorithms (GAs), are used.

In previous studies of inverse simulation, bit-string GA [7, 8], which does not always converge to the global optimum [9], has been used. Recently, real-coded GAs have been proposed [9], and are expected to be applicable for global optimization. Furthermore, metaheuristics, such as particle swarm optimization (PSO) [10] and the artificial bee colony (ABC) [11, 12] algorithm, efficiently converge on globally optimal solutions even for high-dimensional feature vectors. In our study, we use the ABC algorithm for this reason.

The ABC algorithm optimizes many search points stochastically, inspired by the action of bees and swarm intelligence. In the ABC algorithm, element component models are composed of the food sources and three kinds of bees—employed bees, onlooker bees, and scout bees—which have three difference search methods. The employed bees are attached to one of the food sources.

(1) Employed bee search: Employed bees search for the highest evaluated food source in the neighborhood of its own attached food sources.
(2) Onlooker bee search: The onlooker bee searches in the neighborhood of highly evaluated food sources resulting from the employed bees' search.
(3) Scout bee search: In (1) and (2), when food sources do not update for more than a certain search count threshold, the bees attached to the food sources temporarily become scout bees. These bees can drastically change the location of attached food sources.

3 Experiment

In our previous study, we preliminarily validated TRISim for forward simulation. In this study, we have performed preliminary evaluation of Inverse TRISim by applying the general hospital model used in our previous study.

3.1 Scenario

In our evaluation, we assume that a standard or large number of patients are visiting a large medical center [13] and simulate changes over one day. In this hospital model, both the emergency and critical care centers are composed of ICUs, HCUs, general wards, consultation rooms, emergency rooms, waiting rooms, operation rooms, CT rooms, MRI rooms, and angiography rooms. In this scenario, the agents are doctors, nurses, clinical engineers, and patients. Doctors, nurses, and clinical engineer agents are assigned to the ICUs and HCUs. Clinical engineer agents are assigned to x-ray, CT, MRI, and angiography rooms. Doctor and nurse agents are assigned to consultation, emergency, and operation rooms. Nurse agents are also assigned to observation, severity injury observation, and waiting rooms.

3.2 Condition

The conditions in this experiment were set based on patient arrival density data from Seirei Hamamatsu Hospital [14]. Figure 3 shows the patient arrival density over a 24-hour period beginning at 8:30 AM. These graphs approximate real patient arrival density data by logistic density of walk-in and ambulance patients.

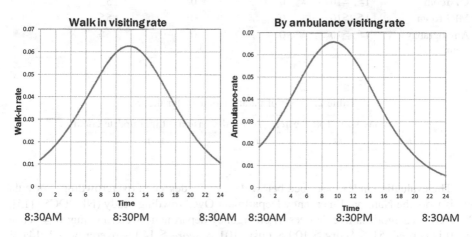

Fig. 3. Patient arrival density

Table 1 shows the constraint conditions: the number of each room type and the number of doctors, nurses, and clinical engineers assigned to each room in the hospital.

Simulations were performed for one day with a 10-s time step. Table 2 shows the parameters used for controlling the inverse simulation (used for the ABC algorithm, which were determined based on previous study [12]). Initial parameters were set randomly to small numbers of each room type and agent to measure whether the optimization method is effective.

Table 1. Constraint condition parameters for hospital model

	Range of number of rooms	Range of number of doctors	Range of number of nurses	Range of number of clinical engineers
Exploring room	$1\leqq, \leqq20$	$1\leqq, \leqq3$	$1\leqq, \leqq4$	0
Operation room	$1\leqq, \leqq20$	$1\leqq, \leqq3$	$1\leqq, \leqq10$	0
Emergency room	$1\leqq, \leqq20$	$1\leqq, \leqq3$	$1\leqq, \leqq10$	0
Observation room	$0\leqq$	$1\leqq, \leqq3$	$2\leqq$	0
Injury severity observation room	$0\leqq$	$1\leqq, \leqq3$	$2\leqq$	0
ICU	$1\leqq, \leqq30$	$2\leqq$	$7\leqq$	0
HCU	$1\leqq, \leqq30$	$2\leqq$	$7\leqq$	0
Waiting room	1	0	$7\leqq$	0
General ward	$1\leqq$	$2\leqq$	$7\leqq$	0
X-ray room	$1\leqq, \leqq10$	0	0	$5\leqq$
CT room	$1\leqq, \leqq10$	0	0	$5\leqq$
MRI room	$1\leqq, \leqq10$	0	0	$5\leqq$
Angiography room	$1\leqq, \leqq10$	0	0	$5\leqq$

Table 2. A set of parameters used for the ISC

	Colony size	Total search	Vector dimensions	Limit update count
#	30	15	46	180

The evaluation index described below defines the degree of overcrowding. Formula (1) is from the National Emergency Department Overcrowding Study (NEDOCS) [15]. NEDOCS categorizes five degrees of emergency department overcrowding: $0 \leqq Score \leqq 50$ is normal, $51 \leqq Score \leqq 100$ is busy, $101 \leqq Score \leqq 140$ is overcrowded, $141 \leqq Score \leqq 180$ is severe, and $180 \leqq Score$ is a disaster.

$$NEDOCS = -20 + 85.8 \times \left(\frac{Total\,patients}{ED\,Beds}\right) + 600 \times \left(\frac{Admits}{Hospital\,beds}\right) + 13.4$$
$$\times (Ventilators) + 0.93 \times (Longest\,admit) + 5.64 \times (Last\,bed\,time) \quad (1)$$

Formula (1) is composed of seven parameters. *Total patients* is the total number of patients in the emergency room. *ED Beds* is the total number of emergency department beds. *Admits* is the total number of admitted patients in the emergency room. *Hospital beds* is the total number of hospital beds. *Ventilators* is the number of patients who are equipped with ventilators or respirations in the emergency room. *Longest admit* means the longest patient boarding time (in hours). *Last bed time* means the time from arrival to a bed for the patient most recently assigned one.

3.3 Result

We performed a preliminary inverse simulation experiment, and our NEDOCS optimization values are shown in Fig. 4. In the initial state, on the leftmost graph, the NEDOCS value is 171.3 because the number of rooms is too small; this value indicates severe overcrowding. The NEDOCS value decreases as the generations advance, and finally, the NEDOCS value falls to 16.8 after 1000 generations, a value indicative of the best overcrowding status in the NEDOCS evaluation index. On the right side of Fig. 4, the graph illustrates the estimation result of the number of consultation rooms when TRISim optimizes the NEDOCS value with inverse simulation.

We can determine that it is possible to estimate initial parameters that optimize the evaluation index with inverse simulation. In the future, we will study constraint conditions for each parameter to obtain appropriate values. In addition, we will analyze the inverse simulation results with formulas from other evaluation indexes.

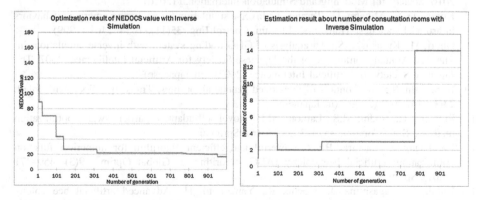

Fig. 4. Optimization result of NEDOCS values with Inverse TRISim (1000 generations)

4 Conclusion

We proposed and developed Inverse TRISim as a tool for hospital managers to study optimal triage operation methods and hospital organization for multiple hospitals. Inverse TRISim uses the inverse simulation method and enables automatic estimation of the model parameters that optimize the set evaluation index. In contrast to the previous study, which uses a bit-string genetic algorithm, this study uses the ABC method. As our preliminary experiment result shows, one aspect of our method is shown. In our future study, we will demonstrate the performance differences between our method and previous methods.

References

1. Japanese Association for Acute Medicine and Journal of Japanese Association for Emergency Nursing: Urgency Decision Support System JTAS 2012 Guidebook, Herusu Shuppan (2012). (in Japanese)
2. Agency for Healthcare Research and Quality: Emergency Severity Index (ESI) A Triage Tool for Emergency Department Care Version 4, Implementation Handbook 2012 edn. (2011)
3. Ueno, Y.: Evaluation of the quality of triage system by nurses at the emergency services. Jpn. Assoc. Acute Med. **20**(3), 116–125 (2009). (in Japanese)
4. Lin, D., Patrick, J., Labeau, F.: Estimating the waiting time of multi-priority emergency patients with downstream blocking. Health Care Manag. Sci. **17**, 88–99 (2014). Springer
5. Centeno, A.P., Martin, R., Sweeney, R.: REDSim: a spatial agent-based simulation for studying emergency departments. In: Proceedings of the 2013 Winter Simulation Conference, pp. 1431–1442. IEEE Press (2013)
6. Kobayashi, A., Masakazu, F.: TRISim: TRIage simulation of a simulation system to exploit and assess triage operation for hospital managers. In: Spring Simulation Multi-Conference 2016. Society for Modeling and Simulation International (2016)
7. Kurahashi, S., Minami, U., Terano, T.: Inverse simulation for analyzing emergent behaviors in artificial societies. Trans. Soc. Instrum. Control Eng. **35**(11), 1454–1461 (1999)
8. Ohori, M., Kurahashi, S.: An analysis of GHG trading system with inverse simulation. In: The 21st Annual Conference of the Japanese Society for Artificial Intelligence, 2007. The Japanese Society for Artificial Intelligence (2007). (in Japanese)
9. Kobayashi, S.: The frontiers of real-coded genetic algorithms. Trans. Jpn. Soc. Artif. Intell. **24**(1), 147–162 (2009). (in Japanese)
10. Pronsing, C., Sodhi, M.S., Lamond, B.F.: Novel self-adaptive particle swarm optimization methods. Soft. Comput. 3579–3593 (2016). Springer
11. Karaboga, D., Basturk, B.: A powerful and efficient algorithm for numerical function optimization: artificial bee colony (ABC) algorithm. J. Global Optim. **39**(3), 459–471 (2007). Springer
12. Utani, A., Nagashima, J., Gocho, R., Yamamoto, H.: Advanced artificial bee colony (ABC) algorithm for large-scale optimization problems. Inst. Electron. Inf. Commun. Eng. **94**(2), 425–438 (2011). (in Japanese)
13. Nihon University Hospital. (in Japanese). http://www.nihon-u.ac.jp/hospital/outline/. Accessed 31 Oct 2016

14. Seirei Hamamatsu Hospital: Clinical Indicator 2014. (in Japanese) http://www.seirei.or.jp/hamamatsu/hama/clinical_indicator/PDF/10.pdf. Accessed 31 Oct 2016
15. Weiss, S.L., Richards, J., Fernandez, M., Schwab, R., Stair, T.O., Vicellio, P., Levy, D., Brautigan, M., Johnson, A., Nick, T.G.: Estimating the degree of emergency department. J. Soc. Acad. Emerg. Med. **11**(1), 38–50 (2004)

Monitoring the Impact of Negative Events and Deciding About Emotion Regulation Strategies

Adnan Manzoor$^{(\boxtimes)}$, Altaf Hussain Abro, and Jan Treur

Behavioural Informatics Group, Vrije Universiteit Amsterdam,
De Boelelaan 1081, 1081 HV Amsterdam, The Netherlands
{a.manzoorrajper,a.h.abro,j.treur}@vu.nl

Abstract. Humans have a number of emotion regulation strategies at their disposal, from which in a particular situation one or more can be chosen. The focus of this paper is on the processes behind the choice of these regulation strategies. The paper presents a neurologically inspired cognitive computational model of a monitoring and decision mechanism for emotion regulation incorporating different strategies (expressive suppression, reappraisal or reinterpretation, and situation modification). It can be tuned to specific characteristics of persons and events.

Keywords: Cognitive modeling · Emotion · Regulation

1 Introduction

Emotions play a vital role for a person to function responsibly in society. Proper handling of negative emotions such as stress and anxiety help us to perform our daily life activities in an efficient manner, and not become vulnerable to stress-related disorders such as depression or PTDS. It has been found that individuals can apply different emotion regulation strategies [1]. Several types of emotion regulation strategies exist which can be effective in particular circumstances. Two of them which have received much interest of researchers over the years are reappraisal and emotion suppression [2]. An important but often neglected part of the emotion regulation process is a decision making process determining under which circumstances different strategies are selected [3]. Which strategy is applied depends on a number of factors, such as a person's context, an internal monitoring and assessment concerning her feeling intensity, and her individual characteristics or preferences. Empirical studies such as [4] show that individual differences exist when it comes to prefer one strategy over another and also these differences exist when some individual applies a combination of emotion regulation strategies.

In this paper the role of monitoring and assessment, and control mechanisms to recognize a type of negative emotion and to choose for one or more strategies are explored computationally. The first process acts as an identification stage as described in [3, 5, 6] which recognizes and assesses the negative feelings and their intensity.

© Springer International Publishing AG 2017
N. Criado Pacheco et al. (Eds.): EUMAS 2016/AT 2016, LNAI 10207, pp. 350–363, 2017.
DOI: 10.1007/978-3-319-59294-7_30

Based on this assessment one or more control states are activated for specific emotion regulation strategies. For example, if the intensity of an emotion is very high, then multiple regulation strategies might be employed at the same time (which also depends on the personality traits). On the other hand if the intensity is very low, then only emotion suppression could be enough to be applied or if it is of a moderate level, then it could be the case that only appraisal and emotion suppression are chosen. Several simulation experiments that have been realized show how the model can take into account different kinds of personalities and varying levels of negative stimuli and feelings.

2 Neurological Background

When emotional responses compete with important goals or with socially more appropriate responses, often regulation of them takes place [7, 8]. Emotion regulation can make use of a variety of specific strategies to affect the emotion response levels [9]. Emotion regulation uses control functions in order to activate one or more of the different strategies to generate, maintain and adjust the emotional responses [10]. By such emotion regulation mechanisms, persons have the ability to suppress negative influences from the environment and maintain a form of emotional homeostasis [11, 12]. Emotions can be regulated in different stages of the emotion generation process [11–13] distinguish antecedent-focused strategies (those that address processes before an emotion has an effect on the behavior) from response-focused strategies (those that are used when the emotional response is already coming as expression or behavior). Note that the different types of emotion regulation share a common effect on the level of emotion, but may differ much in the path followed to achieve this effect. Moreover, multiple strategies can be used at the same time, so that multiple paths are followed in parallel with a combined effect on the emotion level.

The current paper focuses on the monitoring and control for three different emotion regulation strategies: (1) situation modification (2) reinterpretation, and (3) expressive suppression [12, 14]. Here the first two are antecedent-focused strategies and the third is a response-focused strategy. Situation modification [12] addresses the very first part of the causal chain from trigger to emotion, namely the external trigger itself by performing actions that change the external situation in such so that the trigger becomes more harmless. Reinterpretation works by changing the assigned meaning or interpretation of an emotional stimulus in a way that changes its emotional impact [15]. Expressive suppression is a form of response modulation that involves inhibiting ongoing emotion-expressive behavior [12].

The model presented here was inspired by a number of neurological theories relating to fMRI experiments. Much emphasis has been put in the literature on the role that is played by a bidirectional interaction between the amygdala and the prefrontal cortex (PFC). In experiments often fMRI measurements have been made focusing on activity in these brain areas, and anatomically their connections have been analysed. For both, correlations have been found with (the extent of success in) actual emotion regulation; e.g., [16–18]. For example, it has been found that less interaction or weak connections between amygdala and prefrontal cortex lead to less adequate emotion regulation [8]. The general idea is that upward interaction from amygdala to PFC can have the function of monitoring, in order to get an internal representation of the level of emotion within the prefrontal cortex, which is used to achieve a form of assessment of this level of emotion within the prefrontal cortex, whereas the downward interaction from PFC to amygdala makes it possible to control and modify amygdala activation. In the process of monitoring and assessing the level of emotion, leading to PFC activity, interaction with some areas other than the amygdala may occur as well, as these areas can also play an important role in developing emotions and feelings.

So, upward interactions can be considered from multiple areas. Also in relation to the control function of the PFC and connections from there to other areas some differentiation is needed. For different regulation strategies different brain areas need to be affected. For a response-focused strategy such as expressive suppression, maybe a main effect can be to suppress amygdala activation in a more direct manner, but maybe also other areas involved in actual expression of the emotion have to be suppressed. Furthermore, for an antecedent-focused strategy such as reinterpretation it is quite plausible that the control from the PFC has to affect the interpretation, and not the amygdala in a more direct manner. For example, in this case the PFC may affect (working) memory in order to achieve the reinterpretation. After this reinterpretation has been accomplished, in turn the renewed emotion generation process (based on the new interpretation) will affect the emotion level, including amygdala activity. In such a case a more direct suppression of amygdala activation might still take place as well, but then that effect may have to be attributed to a different regulation strategy which occurs in parallel, for example, expressive suppression.

After all, it is also a matter of clear definition to distinguish the different strategies. For example, it may be tempting to define the reinterpretation strategy in such a manner that it also includes the expressive suppression strategy, given empirical data that may have difficulty to distinguish the two. However, from a conceptual perspective it is more useful to define the two strategies as exclusive so that different paths can be attributed to different strategies, even if they occur in the same experiment. The latter choice is made in this paper. To control different pathways in order to achieve emotion regulation according to different strategies the PFC has to involve different areas within the brain. In some recent studies such as [16, 19] attempts are made to relate different regulation strategies to activity in different brain areas. See, for example, [16] which describes that expressive suppression relates to an increase of brain activation in a right prefronto-parietal regulation network, and reinterpretation engages a different control network comprising left ventrolateral prefrontal cortex and orbitofrontal cortex.

3   The Cognitive Model

The computational model was designed as a temporal-causal network model; see [20]. An overview of the states and causal relations of the proposed model is depicted in Fig. 1. A description of each state is available in Table 1. The states of this model can be classified in six groups: the environment, emotion generation, emotion regulation selection strategy 1, 2 and 3, and, last but not least, an internal monitoring and selection mechanism for the decision making. The monitoring process is modelled by the connections from the feeling state fs_b to a number of monitoring states ms_i (which can be any number but in the simulations has been chosen as 3), and the selection process is modelled by the connections of the monitoring states to the control states. The upward connections model the connections from amygdala to PFC that are used for monitoring the lower level processes in the brain (see Sect. 2). If the feeling intensity reaches at a certain threshold (which may differ for different kinds of persons), the monitoring system reflects this by activating some of the monitoring states. In addition, by some inhibiting connections between them the monitoring states are made mutually exclusive and recognize specific types of stressful situations: monitoring state ms_1 recognizes low intensity feeling, ms_2 recognizes moderate level feeling and ms_3 high intensity negative feeling. This inhibition-based process between the monitoring states can be considered as a form of assessment, leading to one unique indication of the situation concerning the stress level.

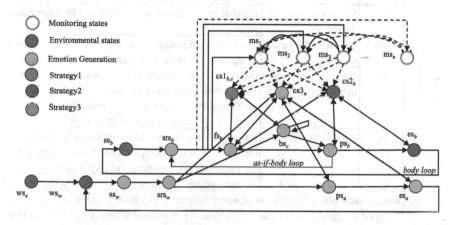

Fig. 1. Conceptual representation of the computational model

This single monitoring state obtained is the basis for a form of decision, by activating one or more control states for specific regulation strategies. A person's characteristics for these monitoring and decision processes are represented by the weights of the connections to the monitoring states and from the monitoring states to the control states, respectively. The selection process involves the three emotion regulation strategies covered here. Depending on the situation and personality of an individual, one, two or all of these regulation strategies are selected. For example, if the feeling is intense then situation modification may be chosen by the person, depending on her characteristics.

The main states representing the environment are ws_w and ws_e. Here ws_w indicates the person's environment state and ws_e covers external events which may affect the environment of the person. The state of the world is sensed by the person via sensor state ss_w and represented by state srs_w.

This sensory information can be interpreted by both a positive belief bs_{c1} and a negative belief bs_{c2}, which represent two different interpretations of the same world condition. These conflicting beliefs compete with each other by mutual inhibiting connections. In the considered scenario, the negative belief bs_{c1} has an effect on the state of preparation for negative emotional response ps_b which leads to sensory body representation srs_b and to the negative feeling fs_b. Subsequently, fs_b has an impact on

Table 1. Overview of the states of the proposed model (see also Fig. 1)

Domain	Formal	Informal name	Description
Environment	ws_w	World state w	This characterizes the current world situation which the person is facing
	ws_e	World event e	Circumstances in the world affecting the world situation in a stress-inducing way
Emotion Generation	ss_w	Sensor state for w	The person senses the world through the sensor state, providing sensory input
	srs_w	Sensory representation of w	Internal representation of sensory world information on w
	srs_b	Sensory representation of b	The person maintains a body representation srs_b for b in the brain. Here b is embodying the associated emotion, in the considered scenarios a negative emotion. Before performing an action, a feeling state fs_b for the action is generated by a predictive as-if body loop, via the sensory representation state srs_b.
	fs_b	Feeling associated to body state b	
	bs_c	Belief state for c	Interpretation of the world information; in the case of different, exclusive interpretations for the same world information, they may suppress each other
	ps_b	Preparation for b	Preparation for a response involving body state b
Emotion Regulation Strategy 1	**Reappraisal** Re-interpretation of world information by belief change: changing the assigned meaning to a stimulus with negative emotional effects (e.g., by believing that a noisy restaurant will become more quiet soon).		
	$cs1_{b,c}$	Control state for reappraisal of belief c to avoid feeling b	By becoming activated this control state suppresses the belief for c, which gives the opportunity for alternative beliefs to become dominant.
Emotion Regulation Strategy 2	**Suppression of emotion-expressive behaviour** Inhibition of the expression, for example, hide one's true feelings from another person (e.g., hiding one's fear when standing up to a bully).		
	$cs2_b$	Control state for expressive suppression to avoid feeling b	By becoming activated this control state suppresses the execution state for b.
	ss_b	Sensing body state b	To maintain the body representation srs_b for b, the person senses the body state b.
	es_b	Execution state for b	Body expression of b, for example a fear expression

Emotion Regulation Strategy 3		**Situation modification** For this strategy the person performs an action in the external world to change a situation which triggers negative emotions into a better one (e.g., leaving a noisy restaurant and enter a quiet place).	
		$cs3_{b,a}$	Control state for situation modification a to avoid feeling b	By becoming activated this control state activates the preparation and execution of action a to change the situation.
		ps_a	Preparation for action a	Preparation to modify the situation by action a
		es_a	Execution state for action a	The action a is changing the situation (decreasing the level of world state w)
Monitoring and Selection processes		ms_1	Recognizes low feeling level	The monitoring states are involved in two processes, one which is responsible for monitoring of the feeling (connections to the monitoring states) and reaching a form of assessment (by some inhibiting links between them), and the second process is concerned with the selection of the appropriate regulation strategies (connections from the monitoring states to the control states).
		ms_2	Recognizes moderate feeling level	
		ms_3	Recognizes high feeling level	

the preparation state ps_b, which in turn has an impact on feeling state, fs_b, through srs_b which makes the process recursive; this is often called an as-if body loop in the literature (e.g. [21]). Other states, depicted in Fig. 1, are control states related to three emotion regulation strategies described below.

As described in Sect. 2, emotions can be controlled in different phases of the process during which emotions are generated [12]. The first strategy discussed focuses on reinterpretation of the world information by changing bad beliefs about the situation into more positive ones; this is done as follows. Suppose two beliefs bs_{c1} and bs_{c2} are two different, exclusive interpretations of the world state, where bs_{c2} associates to bad feelings fs_b. The exclusiveness is modelled by mutual inhibiting connections. Suppose the person has generated belief state bs_{c2} as dominant, and by her monitoring and decision mechanism she decides for activation of control state $cs1_{b,c}$. Consequently this control state weakens the belief bs_{c2} and due to this, the positive belief bs_{c1} can become dominant, which provides an alternative, more positive interpretation of the world. Also expressive suppression can be used to decrease negative emotions. In the model, when it is decided to activate control state $cs2_b$ for this second strategy, this suppresses the expression of the emotional response es_b. This es_b is sensed by the person him or herself through the body loop, and through that it has a decreasing effect on the emotion level. The third emotion regulation strategy considered is situation modification. Leaving an annoying place or person is an example of this strategy. In the model the control state for this kind of emotion regulation is $cs3_{b,a}$. A decision to activate this control state leads to preparing and performing an action a (i.e., states ps_a and es_a) which can change the situation (characterized by ws_w), for example walking away from a noisy place to a quiet place.

The conceptual representation of the model is represented as a number of states and connections between them, shown in Fig. 1 and verbally in Table 1, with in addition:

- For each connection from state X to state Y a *weight* $\omega_{X,Y}$ (a number between -1 and 1), for the strength of the impact through this connection; a negative weight is used for suppression
- For each state Y a *speed factor* η_Y (a positive value) and (a reference to) a standard *combination function* $c_Y(...)$ used to aggregate multiple impacts from different states on one state Y.

For a numerical representation of the model the states Y get activation values indicated by $Y(t)$: real numbers between 0 and 1 over time points t, where the time variable t ranges over the real numbers. More specifically, the conceptual representation of the model (as shown graphically in Fig. 1 and verbally in Table 1) can be transformed in a systematic or even automated manner into a numerical representation as follows [20]:

- At each time point t each state X connected to state Y has an *impact* on Y defined as $\textbf{impact}_{X,Y}(t) = \omega_{X,Y} X(t)$ where $\omega_{X,Y}$ is the weight of the connection from X to Y
- The *aggregated impact* of multiple states X_i on Y at t is determined using a *combination function* $c_Y(..)$:

$$
\begin{aligned}
\textbf{aggimpact}_Y(t) &= c_Y(\textbf{impact}_{X_1,Y}(t), \ldots, \textbf{impact}_{X_k,Y}(t)) \\
&= c_Y(\omega_{X_1,Y}X_1(t), \ldots, \omega_{X_k,Y}X_k(t))
\end{aligned}
\tag{1}
$$

where X_i are the states with connections to state Y.

- The effect of $\textbf{aggimpact}_Y(t)$ on Y is exerted over time gradually, depending on *speed factor* η_Y:

$$
\begin{aligned}
& Y(t+\Delta t) = Y(t) + \eta_Y[\textbf{aggimpact}_Y(t) - Y(t)]\Delta t \\
\text{or} \quad & dY(t)/dt = \eta_Y[\textbf{aggimpact}_Y(t) - Y(t)]
\end{aligned}
\tag{2}
$$

- Thus the following *difference* and *differential equation* for Y are obtained:

$$
\begin{aligned}
& Y(t+\Delta t) = Y(t) + \eta_Y[c_Y(\omega_{X_1,Y}X_1(t), \ldots, \omega_{X_k,Y}X_k(t)) - Y(t)]\Delta t \\
\text{or} \quad & dY(t)/dt = \eta_Y[c_Y(\omega_{X_1,Y}X_1(t), \ldots, w_{X_k,Y}X_k(t)) - Y(t)]
\end{aligned}
\tag{3}
$$

For all states for the standard combination function either the *identity function* $\textbf{id}(.)$ or the *advanced logistic sum combination function* $\textbf{alogistic}_{\sigma,\tau}(...)$ is used [20]:

$$
c_Y(V) = \textbf{id}(V) = V
$$

$$
c_Y(V_1, \ldots V_k) = \textbf{alogistic}_{\sigma,\tau}(V_1, \ldots, V_k) = \left(\frac{1}{1+e^{-\sigma(V_1+\ldots+v_k-\tau)}} - \frac{1}{1+e^{\sigma\tau}}\right)(1+e^{-\sigma\tau})
\tag{4}
$$

Here σ is a steepness parameter and τ a threshold parameter. The advanced logistic sum combination function has the property that activation levels 0 are mapped to 0 and it keeps values below 1. The identity function id(..) is used for the states with a single impact: ssw, ssb. For all other states the advanced logistic sum combination function is used. For example, for the feeling state fs_b the model is numerically represented in difference equation form as

$$\mathbf{aggimpact}_{fs_b}(t) = \mathbf{alogistic}_{\sigma,\tau}(\omega_{srs_b,fs_b} srs_b(t), \omega_{cs1_{b,c},fs_b} cs1_{b,c}(t),$$

$$\omega_{cs2_b,fs_b} cs2_b(t)\omega_{cs3_{b,a},fs_b} cs3_{b,a}(t))$$

$$fs_b(t+\Delta t) = fs_b(t) + \eta_{fs_b}[\mathbf{aggimpact}_{fs_b}(t) - fs_b(t)]\Delta t \qquad (5)$$

In this way the model represented conceptually in Fig. 1 is transformed into a numerical representation of the model in terms of difference or differential equations. The simulations are performed by applying a computational simulation method to this numerical model representation, in a dedicated software environment. All the simulations were performed within the MATLAB™ environment.

4 Scenarios and Simulation Results

The computational model presented above has been used to perform number of simulation experiments addressing the selection of emotion regulation strategies. This has been done for different scenarios describing different cases with different levels of stimulus and negative feeling, and varying from selection of just one of the regulation strategies to selecting multiple regulation strategies at the same time. Scenarios also vary on certain characteristics of the person, such as: sensitivity of a person for negative stimuli, and a person's preferences for regulation strategies.

For example, some persons may have a higher preference for the situation modification strategy (e.g., they tend to try to escape from a disturbing situation), maybe in combination with a high sensitivity for disturbing stimuli, whereas other types of persons may prefer the other regulation strategies while staying in the same situation. More specifically, some persons are good in suppression of their negative feelings related to a stimulus and keep the same interpretation and stay in the same situation, whereas other persons may prefer to try to reinterpret (reappraise) the situation in a more positive way by changing the negative beliefs about the situation into positive beliefs, in oreder to reduce the level of negative feelings. Another category of persons may be quite sensitive to the stimulus and initially try to reduce their level of negative feelings by suppression and may use the reinterpretation strategy to make their positive beliefs more stronger against the negative beliefs, and if they fail to do so they still may try to escape from the bad situation or try to modify the situation in another way.

The simulation experiments demonstrate the role of the monitoring, assesment and decision making with an important role for the monitoring states, which are used as a basis to select one or more of the three available regulation strategies. The selection process starts when a monitoring state reflects that a certain type (level) of negative feeling arises. In a very first stage just a low level of negative feeling fs_b triggers monitoring state ms_1 (indicating a low level of feeling), which in turn may lead to a decision to activate one or more regulation strategies preferred by the person for such a low level of negative feeling (recall that these preferences are represented by the weights of the connections from the monitoring state to the three control states). Then there are two possibilities: these strategies are adequate and limit the feeling level, or the feeling level still increases so that monitoring state ms_2 (indicating a mediate level of feeling) is triggered. In the latter case this monitoring state ms_2 in turn may lead to a decision to activate another selection of regulation strategies. Again there are two possibilities: these strategies may limit the feeling level, or the feeling level still increases to the situation that monitoring state ms_3 (indicating a high level of feeling) is triggered. In the latter case again another selection of regulation strategies can be decided for. A specific case of such a scenario is shown in Table 2. In the scenario indicated in this table the first regulation strategy used (after ms_1 is triggered) is suppression of the negative feeling.

Table 2. Regulation selection choices for an example scenario

Feeling level	Triggered monitoring state	Selected regulation strategies
Low	ms_1	Suppression
Median	ms_2	Reappraisal
High	ms_3	Situation modification

This means that based on ms_1 it is decided to activate control state $cs2_b$ in order to suppress the negative feeling. In a second stage, when the level of negative feeling increases further, due to the development of negative beliefs about the situation, this triggers the next monitoring state ms_2, and based on that it is decided to activate control state $cs1_{b,c}$ for the second regulation strategy: reappraisal (reinterpretation). This starts to down-regulate the negative feelings in a different way by changing (reinterpreting) the meaning of the stimulus (switching of a negative belief to a positive belief). The control state $cs1_{b,c}$ is usually slower compared to $cs2_b$, because humans often take much time to change their beliefs about the environment (stimulus), so it takes some more time to change beliefs. The third and last monitoring state ms_3 triggers when the level of feeling becomes high; then based on this it is decided to activate the third control state $cs3_{b,a}$ which initiates situation modification by performing the (physical) action needed to achieve that. As this situation modification strategy involves movement, it is slower and takes some more time compared to two other regulation strategies mentioned above which involve mental processes instead of physical action.

Note that in Table 2 for each monitoring state exactly one regulation strategy is selected. However, it is also possible that the strategies selected for a lower level of the feeling are still selected as well for higher levels of the feeling. The more specific simulation results discussed here are based on the following scenario. The person is in a restaurant which has become rather noisy, and this triggers negative feelings. First she suppresses these negative feelings. Moreover, she tries to suppress her negative belief about being in a noisy restaurant the whole evening to give space for a positive belief (it will soon become more quiet). However still some negative feeling remains. Therefore she decides to leave the restaurant. The simulation executes for 120 time points with $\Delta t = 0.1$. Details of the values for parameters used in the simulation are given in Table 3 (threshold τ, steepness σ, and update speed η) and in Table 4 (connection weights between all states).

Table 3. Values of threshhold, steepness and update speed

State	τ	σ	η	State	τ	σ	η
ms_1	0.08	50	6	es_b	0.5	4	6
ms_2	0.32	50	6	$cs2_b$	2	5	6
ms_3	0.6	50	6	ss_b	0.5	4	6
ps_b	0.4	4	6	ws_w	0.1	5	0.4
fs_b	0.1	4	6	ss_w	0.2	4	6
bs_{c1}	0.1	8	6	srs_w	0.2	4	6
bs_{c2}	0.36	15	6	ps_a	0.4	5	6
$cs1_{b,c}$	1.5	15	0.5	es_a	0.5	100	6
srs_b	0.2	3	6	$cs3_{b,a}$	1.2	5	0.1

Table 4. Values of parameters used: connection weights

Weight		Weight		Weight		Weight	
$\omega_{esa,wsw}$	-1	$\omega_{srsb,fsb}$	0.9	$\omega_{cs1b,c,fsb}$	-0.1	$\omega_{psb,cs2b}$	0.8
$\omega_{wsw,ssw}$	0.5	$\omega_{esb,cs2b}$	0.8	$\omega_{cs2b,fsb}$	-0.2	$\omega_{cs3b,a,esa}$	0.8
$\omega_{ssw,srsw}$	0.9	$\omega_{srsw,psa}$	0.1	$\omega_{cs3b,a,fsb}$	-0.3	$\omega_{psa,esa}$	0.7
$\omega_{srsw,bsc1}$	0.3	$\omega_{cs3b,a,psa}$	1	$\omega_{bsc2,psb}$	0.7	$\omega_{srsw,cs3b,a}$	0.8
$\omega_{cs1b,c,bsc1}$	0.0	$\omega_{fsb,cs3b,a}$	0.3	$\omega_{fsb,psb}$	0.7	$\omega_{ms1,cs1b,c}$	1
$\omega_{bsc1,bsc2}$	-0.2	$\omega_{fsb,ms1}$	0.9	$\omega_{cs2b,psb}$	-0.2	$\omega_{ms1,cs2b}$	1
$\omega_{srsw,bsc2}$	0.9	$\omega_{fsb,ms2}$	0.9	$\omega_{psb,srsb}$	0.6	$\omega_{ms1,cs3b,a}$	1
$\omega_{cs1b,c,bsc2}$	-0.25	$\omega_{fsb,ms2}$	0.9	$\omega_{ssb,srsb}$	0.8	$\omega_{ms2,cs1b,c}$	1
$\omega_{bsc1,bsc2}$	-0.2	$\omega_{ms2,ms1}$	-1	$\omega_{psb,esb}$	0.7	$\omega_{ms2,cs2b}$	1
$\omega_{fsb,cs1b,c}$	3	$\omega_{ms3,ms1}$	-1	$\omega_{cs2b,esb}$	-0.1	$\omega_{ms2,cs3b,a}$	1
$\omega_{bsc2,cs1b,c}$	1	$\omega_{ms3,ms2}$	-1	$\omega_{esb,ssb}$	0.7	$\omega_{ms3,cs1b,c}$	1
$\omega_{bsc1,cs1b,c}$	0.0	$\omega_{ms3,cs3b,a}$	1	$\omega_{fsb,cs2b}$	0.1	$\omega_{ms3,cs2b}$	1

Table 5. Personality variation for sensitivity

Person	$\omega_{srsb,fsb}$	Personality type
Person_ 1	0.3	Less sensitive to the stimulus
Person _2	0.6	More sensitive to the stimulus
Person _3	0.9	Most sensitive to the stimulus

The personality type concerning sensitivity to a stimulus has been taken into account by varying the connection strength of the weights $\omega_{srsb,fsb}$ between the sensory representation of the b and the feeling state fs_b. Table 5 shows the variation in personality type from less sensitive to most sensitive. The model has been executed a large number of times with such scenarios; in Fig. 2 one of them is depicted, the person has high sensitivity to the stimulus.

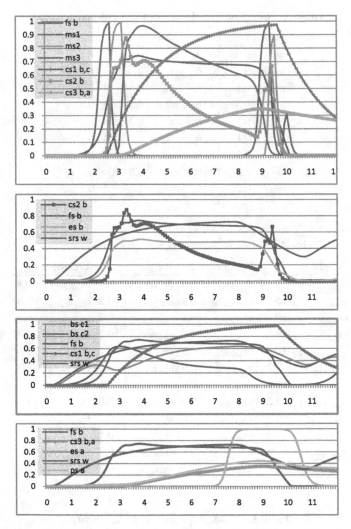

Fig. 2. Simulation results of scenario 3 for person_3 (most sensitive to the stimulus). Upper graph: monitoring and decision process. Three lower graphs: the 3 controlled regulation strategies

As the upper graph shows, when the simulation starts, first ms_1 becomes active, after a while ms_2, and in the last phase ms_3. The graph also shows the control states; first based on ms_1 it is decided to activate the emotion suppression control state $cs2_b$. It suppresses the negative feeling (shown in the second graph) but as the negative feeling still increases, ms_2 is triggered, and based on this it is decided to activate control state $cs1_{b,c}$ for the reappraisal strategy. This alters the beliefs by suppressing the negative belief, resulting in strengthening of positive belief and at the same time the negative feeling decreases (shown in the third graph). After applying two strategies, the level of negative feeling still is increasing, which triggers ms_3, and based on this it is decided to activate control state $cs3_{b,a}$ for situation modification. Due to this the person moves away (change of situation) from the stimulus and gets rid of the negative feelings (shown in the last graph).

5   Discussion

In this paper, a neurologically inspired cognitive computational model for internal monitoring and decision making about the selection of emotion regulation strategies has been presented. The model covers three emotion regulation strategies (expressive suppression, reappraisal or reinterpretation, and situation modification), adopted from [22] which lacks an internal monitoring and decision model as addressed in the current paper. A number of simulation experiments have been performed according to different scenarios, thereby considering different personality characteristics and intensities of stimuli. The decision process to select one or more particular regulation strategies primarily takes the assessed current feeling state into account, but can easily be extended to involve other elements as well.

The obtained human-like model can be used in different ways. As a first application it can be a basis for virtual characters showing emotions and applying emotion regulation strategies in a flexible way depending on the situation. Secondly, the model can be used as an ingredient to develop human-aware or socially aware computing applications; e.g., [23–25]. More specifically, in [25, 26] it is shown how such applications can be designed with knowledge of human processes as a main ingredient, represented by a computational model of these processes which is embedded within the application. Such computational models can have the form, for example, of qualitative causal models, or of dynamical numerical models. The computational model for decision making about emotion regulation proposed here can be used in such a way to design a human-aware software application to support persons with stress-related problems and professionals supporting them.

In the literature a number of computational emotion regulation models have been proposed over the years, one of which was presented in [27]. Here a theory of appraisal was modeled. The presented model is based on the idea that emotions are generated based on an individual's interpretation of the situation. In this approach the model is based on symbolic and numeric representations and appraisal operates on them, whereas our approach uses a dynamical systems representation. Different coping strategies are proposed in that paper, e.g., "belief-related coping" which can be related to reappraisal in the model proposed here. A difference is that the model presented in the current paper focuses on modeling the decision making process in an explicit manner, and that the modeling approach here is based on temporal-causal networks as described in [20, 28].

References

1. Samson, A.C., Hardan, A.Y., Podell, R.W., Phillips, J.M., Gross, J.J.: Emotion regulation in children and adolescents with autism spectrum disorder. Autism Res. **8**, 9–18 (2015)
2. Balzarotti, S., John, O.P., Gross, J.J.: An Italian adaptation of the emotion regulation questionnaire. Eur. J. Psychol. Assess. **26**, 61–67 (2010)
3. Gross, J.J.: Emotion regulation: current status and future prospects. Psychol. Inq. **26**, 1–26 (2015)
4. Marsella, S., Gratch, J., Wang, N., Stankovic, B.: Assessing the validity of a computational model of emotional coping. In: 2009 3rd International Conference on Affective Computing and Intelligent Interaction and Workshops, pp. 1–8. IEEE (2009)
5. Webb, T.L., Gallo, I.S., Miles, E., Gollwitzer, P.M., Sheeran, P.: Effective regulation of affect: an action control perspective on emotion regulation. Eur. Rev. Soc. Psychol. **23**(2012), 143–186 (2012)
6. Bonanno, G.A., Burton, C.L.: Regulatory flexibility an individual differences perspective on coping and emotion regulation. Perspect. Psychol. Sci. **8**, 591–612 (2013)
7. Côté, S., Gyurak, A., Levenson, R.W.: The ability to regulate emotion is associated with greater well-being, income, and socioeconomic status. Emotion **10**, 923–933 (2010)
8. Van Dillen, L.F., Heslenfeld, D.J., Koole, S.L.: Tuning down the emotional brain: an fMRI study of the effects of cognitive load on the processing of affective images. Neuroimage **45**, 1212–1219 (2009)
9. Cuijpers, P., Van Straten, A., Warmerdam, L.: Behavioral activation treatments of depression: a meta-analysis. Clin. Psychol. Rev. **27**, 318–326 (2007)
10. Christopher, S., Trittschuh, E.H., Monti, J.M., Mesulam, M.-M., Egner, T.: Neural repetition suppression reflects fulfilled perceptual expectations. Nat. Neurosci. **11**, 1004–1006 (2008)
11. Gross, J.J.: Emotion regulation in adulthood: timing is everything. Curr. Dir. Psychol. Sci. **10**, 214–219 (2001)
12. Gross, J.J.: The Emerging field of emotion regulation: an integrative review. Rev. Gen. Psychol. **2**, 271–299 (1998)
13. Gross, J.J., Thompson, R.A.: Emotion regulation: conceptual foundations. In: Gross, J. J. (ed.) Handbook of Emotion Regulation, pp. 3–24. Guilford Press, New York (2007)
14. Gross, J.J.: Emotion regulation: affective, cognitive, and social consequences. Psychophysiology **39**, 281–291 (2002)
15. Lazarus, R.S., Alfert, E.: Short-Circuiting of Threat by Experimentally Altering Cognitive Appraisal. The Journal of Abnormal and Social Psychology **69**, 195–205 (1964)
16. Dörfel, D., Lamke, J.-P., Hummel, F., Wagner, U., Erk, S., Walter, H.: Common and differential neural networks of emotion regulation by detachment, reinterpretation, distraction, and expressive suppression: a comparative fMRI investigation. Neuroimage **101**, 298–309 (2014)
17. Kim, M.J., Loucks, R.A., Palmer, A.L., Brown, A.C., Solomon, K.M., Marchante, A.N., Whalen, P.J.: The structural and functional connectivity of the amygdala: from normal emotion to pathological anxiety. Behav. Brain Res. **223**, 403–410 (2011)

18. Phelps, E.A., Delgado, M.R., Nearing, K.I., LeDoux, J.E.: Extinction learning in humans: role of the amygdala and vmPFC. Neuron **43**, 897–905 (2004)
19. Ochsner, K.N., Gross, J.J.: The neural bases of emotion and emotion regulation: a valuation perspective. In: Gross, J.J. (ed.) Handbook of Emotional Regulation, 2nd edn. Guilford, New York, pp. 23–41 (2014)
20. Treur, J.: Dynamic modeling based on a temporal-causal network modeling approach. Biol. Inspired Cogn. Archit. (2016, to appear). https://www.researchgate.net/publication/289193241_Dynamic_Modeling_Based_on_a_Temporal-Causal_Network_Modeling_Approach
21. Damasio, A.: The Feeling of What Happens: Body Emotion and the Making of Consciousness. Vintage, London (1999)
22. Abro, A.H., Manzoor, A., Tabatabaei, S.A., Treur, J.: A computational cognitive model integrating different emotion regulation strategies. Proced. Comput. Sci. **71**, 157–168 (2015). Proc. BICA 2015
23. Pentland, A.: Socially aware computation and communication. IEEE Comput. **38**, 33–40 (2005)
24. Pantic, M., Pentland, A., Nijholt, A., Huang, T.S.: Human computing and machine understanding of human behavior: a survey. In: Proceedings of the International Conference on Multimodal Interfaces, pp. 239–248 (2006)
25. Treur, J.: On human aspects in ambient intelligence. In: Mühlhäuser, M., Ferscha, A., Aitenbichler, E. (eds.) AmI 2007. CCIS, vol. 11, pp. 262–267. Springer, Heidelberg (2008). doi:10.1007/978-3-540-85379-4_33
26. Bosse, T., Hoogendoorn, M., Klein, M.C.A., Treur, J.: A generic agent architecture for human-aware ambient computing. In: Mangina, E., et al. (eds.) Agent-Based Ubiquitous Computing, pp. 35–62. World Scientific Publishers, Atlantis Press, Singapore, Paris (2009)
27. Marsella, S.C., Gratch, J.: EMA: a process model of appraisal dynamics. Cogn. Syst. Res. **10**, 70–90 (2009)
28. Treur, J.: Network-Oriented Modeling: Addressing Complexity of Cognitive, Affective and Social Interactions. Series on Understanding Complex Systems, p. 503. Springer International Publishing, Switzerland (2016)

Scalable Multi-agent Simulation
Based on **MapReduce**

Tobias Ahlbrecht$^{(\boxtimes)}$, Jürgen Dix, and Niklas Fiekas

Department of Informatics, Clausthal University of Technology,
Julius-Albert-Str. 4, 38678 Clausthal-Zellerfeld, Germany
{tobias.ahlbrecht,dix,niklas.fiekas}@tu-clausthal.de

Abstract. Jason is perhaps the most advanced multi-agent programming language based on *AgentSpeak*. Unfortunately, its current Java-
based implementation does not scale up and is seriously limited for simulating systems of hundreds of thousands of agents.

We are presenting a scalable simulation platform for running huge
numbers of agents in a Jason style simulation framework. Our idea is
(1) to identify independent parts of the simulation in order to parallelize
as much as possible, and (2) to use and apply existing technology for
parallel processing of large datasets (e.g. MapReduce).

We evaluate our approach on an early benchmark and show that it
scales up linearly (in the number of agents).

1   Introduction

The work reported in this paper is part of a bigger project on using agent-
based simulation for quality control of software development processes [1]. In
this project we need a platform that is able to simulate a huge number of agents,
(hundreds of thousands or even more).

Current approaches implemented in Java often do not scale up (see [2] for
a detailed discussion). Similarly, declarative approaches (e.g. those based on
AgentSpeak) are well suited for modeling simulations, but do not support efficient implementation.

Here we focus on a new approach for implementing scalable multi-agent simulation platforms with MapReduce. The main idea is to identify parts of the
simulated environment that are completely independent from each other and
can thus be processed in parallel. This is particularly useful in scenarios based
on large existing datasets, but can also be applied to multi-agent simulation in
general.

In the following we give a very brief introduction to Jason and MapReduce and
comment on related work. The main part is Sect. 2, where we show how Jason
can be interpreted in a way that is compatible with MapReduce. While previous
approaches have used limited agent models [8] or restricted languages [11] our
approach supports full Jason-style *AgentSpeak*. We believe that similar agent
languages can be translated accordingly.

© Springer International Publishing AG 2017
N. Criado Pacheco et al. (Eds.): EUMAS 2016/AT 2016, LNAI 10207, pp. 364–371, 2017.
DOI: 10.1007/978-3-319-59294-7_31

Key points of any simulation are (1) modeling and (2) implementing the environment: we elaborate on both in Sect. 3. Finally we evaluate our approach in Sect. 4 using a benchmark for our early proof of concept implementation[1] and conclude with Sect. 5.

1.1 Jason

Jason is a Java based platform for multi-agent simulation with an extended version of *AgentSpeak* [4]. *AgentSpeak* is a language to describe BDI agents that mixes a declarative approach to reasoning (Prolog) and an imperative way of stating plans [9]. Jason extends the language with useful functionality such as agent communication. Jason is widely used [3] but does not scale well when the simulation size is increased beyond thousands of agents, even when the agents are very simple.

1.2 MapReduce

MapReduce is a programming paradigm designed to simplify the parallel processing of large datasets [5] by abstracting away low level architecture (single thread, multi-core computer, grid of commodity computers), synchronization, error recovery, locking and distribution of work among the nodes of a cluster. The algorithm is defined in terms of *map* and *reduce* functions that operate on key value pairs. Map functions operate independently on key value pairs $\langle k, v \rangle$. After a shuffling step that groups items by their keys, *reduce* functions operate on sequences of values in each group:

$$\text{Map} : (K, V) \rightarrow (K, V)^*; \quad \text{Reduce} : (K, V^*) \rightarrow (K, V)^*$$

Algorithms in terms of these functions can be executed using a MapReduce framework like Spark, Hadoop, MR4C, MapReduce-MPI or Disco, which automatically partition the dataset for parallel execution.

1.3 Related Work

There are several design patterns for MapReduce that have been used outside of agent simulation. Lin and Schatz [7] describe algorithms that allow communication along the edges of graphs. Zhang et al. [14] provide a technique for parallelizing spatial joins. These have then been used in agent system simulation with agent models that have been restricted accordingly: Radenski [8] uses graph algorithms to simulate cellular automatons. Wang et al. [11] use spatial joins for behavioral simulations, where agent actions are restricted to associative operations on the environment.

---

[1] Source code available at https://github.com/niklasf/pyson.

2   Translating **Jason** to **MapReduce**

When agents deliberate but do not communicate or execute actions in the environment they can be executed independently in Map steps. In this section we discuss key requirements for a Jason interpreter that allows doing that. The key point is to represent the state of agents and the state of the environment in *key value pairs* such that *actions that advance the simulation can be performed efficiently with Map and Reduce steps.*

Most MapReduce platforms commit datasets to disk after each MapReduce step. However this overhead can be avoided for multi-agent simulation: In case of data loss computation steps can simply be repeated. We therefore choose Apache Spark as our underlying platform. Spark features the concept of *Resilient Distributed Datasets* with configurable levels or persistence. Additionally, Spark uses the scripting language Python as one of the primary supported languages. This allows us to use Python as a single language for the platform as well as for scripting the simulated environment and available actions. There are three key requirements for the Jason interpreter:

- **Serializability:** The state of agents must be serializable at any given time to allow Spark to serialize and transmit them to other nodes of the cluster.
- **Ability to pause and resume individual agents:** In distributed computing local operations are near-instant while network operations take orders of magnitudes more time. An agent waiting for data from the network needs to be paused in order not to block the execution of other agents.
- **Memory efficiency:** The interpreter must have a low memory footprint so that hundreds of thousands of agents can fit into main memory.

For memory efficiency we embed native Python data types directly into Jason (`bool`, `int` and `long` and `float` for numerics, `tuple` for lists). Variables and belief literals are defined as classes in Python (`Var()` and `Literal(functor, args)`). All other Python objects are treated as atoms. To avoid making copies of objects, all substitutions (mappings of variables to terms) are kept in a separate dictionary. Additionally, agents have a stack of substitutions and choice points that allows them to undo failed partial unifications.[2]

To allow pausing and resuming individual agents (even while they are executing a Prolog query) we use Python generators to iterate over alternatives, with a technique similar to YieldProlog[3]. Finally the Python implementation PyPy guarantees serializability of Python objects including functions, closures and generators.

For AgentSpeak(L) the control flow in a plan is linear. Jason defines additional control structures such as branches and loops. To capture both we represent plans as a control flow graph where nodes are high level instructions. Each node has at most two outgoing edges labeled `success` or `failure` that are followed depending on the result of the current instruction. If a node does not have the corresponding edge this is interpreted as plan achievement or plan failure respectively (Fig. 1).

---

[2] This technique is well known in Prolog interpreters [12,13].
[3] http://yieldprolog.sourceforge.net/.

```
+!assign_bugs <-
    for (bug(N)) {
        .send(developer ,
            tell , bug(N));
    }.
```

+!assign_bugs : TrueQuery	
manager	push_query(TermQuery(bug(N)))
manager	next_or_fail
developer	add_belief(bug(N))
manager	noop

success

failure

(a) Jason source code   (b) The constructed control flow graph

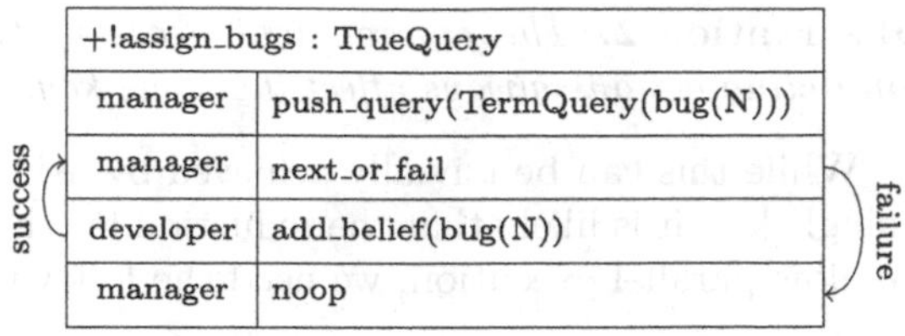

Fig. 1. Example: a `manager` agent sends bug details to a `developer` agent

Intentions in *AgentSpeak* are defined as a stack of partially instantiated plans [9]. To avoid copying plans for each instantiation we use a separate intention data structure instead. The data structure contains (i) the instantiated plan head from the point of view of the caller, (ii) a pointer to the current instruction in the control flow graph, (iii) the current substitution `scope` (mapping of variables to terms), (iv) stacks to undo unifications and continue with a different choice (`stack`, `query_stack`, `choicepoint_stack`). The corresponding set of instructions is given in the appendix.

Observation 1 (Correct-, and Completeness). *The described interpreter satisfies the hard requirements outlined above. In addition, all Jason programs can be transformed to programs in our instruction set.*

3   Handling the Environment

To simulate the environment, a number of different object types have to be modeled. Possible *actions* and *percepts* make up a major part, as they imply the environment's behavior and thus determine the computational effort. Environments need a notion for each "thing" that is not an agent: we call it *artifact*.

The entire state of the simulation is stored in key value pairs. It comprises the agents $\langle uuid, agent \rangle$ and artifacts from the environment. A cycle of the simulation starts with a map step where each agent state is mapped to the next. Messages to other agents are emitted as key value pairs using a Jason-style belief annotation for the sender: $\langle recipientUuid, message[source(senderUuid)] \rangle$. Actions selected by the agent emit additional key values pairs (usually of the form $\langle affectedArtifactUuid, action \rangle$).

The actual effects of the actions are computed in a reduce phase where key value pairs are grouped by recipient or affected artifact. Reduce operations in Spark must be associative. Additionally commutativity is a reasonable requirement to achieve deterministic results even when the order of the values is nondeterministic. Actions that return results must include the UUID of the agent so that results can be emitted as a key value pair $\langle uuid, resultMessage \rangle$.

Values for distinct keys are reduced in parallel. This leads directly to the following observation.

Observation 2. *The environment needs to be designed such that potentially conflicting actions always affect the same key.*

While this can be trivially achieved by using a monolithic environment with a single key, it is likely that the reduction for that key will be a bottleneck. Thus, to allow parallel execution, we need the following complementary goal.

Observation 3. *Independent actions must affect distinct keys.*

For many scenarios there is a natural way to decompose the environment into key value pairs. For example Wang et al. [11] partition a spatial environment into overlapping areas to simulate social force. Since areas overlap, the same action (effects) may be sent to multiple keys. Summation is used as an associative and commutative reduce operation. However, as not all simulations decompose spatially (see the *Simulating Software Evolution* scenario) we propose the following additions:

- Instead of hardcoding the concept of spatial location we introduce groups that agents can subscribe to and send multicast messages to. This mechanism will also be exploited for percept generation and distribution.
- Deterministic reservoir sampling [10] as an associative and commutative operation to fairly select one of multiple conflicting actions. This works for arbitrary actions since they no longer have to be associative and/or commutative themselves.

Currently, the whole environment has to be hand-coded as a Python script. The next step is to provide a thin wrapper around Spark to abstract away from its concrete functionality so as not to burden the user with having to learn everything about MapReduce in order to use the platform. In a later step, the final environment metamodel will be combined with our already existing Jason metamodel to provide the user with schematic modeling facilities (i.e. diagramming) to enable kick-starting new projects.

3.1   Application: Simulating Software Evolution

As mentioned before, the platform is part of a bigger project on simulating software development processes using agent-based technology to gain insights on (specific) software evolution. In this scenario, agents can perform abstract modifications on the software project, i.e. "fix bugs" or "refactor methods". Representing the developers with simple agents already proved a viable solution [6]. However, to get more detailed results, it is necessary to equip agents with better reasoning and planning capabilities. This will enable them to adopt goal-oriented behavior, e.g. based on code change patterns. Furthermore, beliefs will be crucial to simulate how the agents gain experience in the process (see [1]).

Exploiting MapReduce will also greatly benefit the simulations' running time, enabling those of large software projects with many (behaviorally) complex developers and even those where multiple projects form an ecosystem exchanging resources and information.

4 Evaluation

Ahlbrecht et al. [2] have developed a simple benchmark to compare several platforms based on different implementations. It models the throughput of the interpreter on a single node (it relates to the implementation described in Sect. 2).
We compare the performance of our platform running on different Python interpreters (Python 2, Python 3, PyPy) with the performance of other platforms
(Jason, *Maserati*)[4] (Fig. 2).

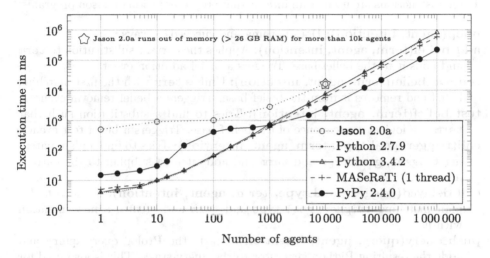

Fig. 2. Execution times of the counting scenario for increasing numbers of agents

Jason 2.0a runs out of memory for 50 000 agents, but could potentially complete the simulation on a machine with even more RAM. The other platforms
scale roughly linearly as expected for this simple scenario. We achieve the best
performance with PyPy which uses *Just-In-Time compilation* and *hotspot optimization* (see the disproportional speedup for a medium number of agents).

5 Conclusion

We have presented a scalable Jason interpreter that is part of a bigger project on
quality control of software development processes (see [1]). However, we believe
our approach is rather general and can be applied to similar agent languages
based roughly on *AgentSpeak* (which allows us to use the built-in modelling
constructs). All that needs to be done is to find a suitable translation of this
language into MapReduce (as described in Sect. 2). An advantage of our approach
is the possibility to use off-the-shelf professional tools to deal with MapReduce.

---

[4] The test environment is a pristine Debian Jessie using an Intel Xeon CPU @
4 × 2.30 GHz and 26 GB RAM.

Our evaluation shows linear scalability (in the number of agents) in a simple benchmark, even for a reimplementation of Jason. It remains to test other benchmarks and to tailor our system for the application in the planned project. But we are planning to apply our approach also to other areas, where parallelization in the simulation of an environment pays off.

A   Set of Instructions

These instructions are used as an intermediate representation of Jason programs:

noop(agent, intention): Does nothing and succeeds always.
add_belief(term, agent, intention): Applies the current substitution to `term` and adds it to the belief base. Triggers a belief addition event.
remove_belief(term, agent, intention): Unifies `term` with the first matching belief and removes it from the belief base. Triggers a belief removal event.
test_belief(term, agent, intention): Tries to find a substitution such that `term` is a logical consequence of the belief base. Triggers a belief test event.
call(trigger, goal_type, term, agent, intention): Tries to find a plan matching `trigger`, `goal_type` and `term` and adds it as a subplan to the current intention.
call_delayed(trigger, goal_type, term, agent, intention): Tries to find a plan matching `trigger`, `goal_type` and `term` and creates a new intention with it.
push_query(query, agent, intention): Starts the Prolog query `query` and adds the resulting Python generator to the query stack. This is also used for actions that can yield multiple results.
next_or_fail(agent, intention): Tries to advance the topmost generator.
pop_query(agent, intention): Removes the topmost generator from the stack.

References

1. Ahlbrecht, T., Dix, J., Fiekas, N., Grabowski, J., Herbold, V., Honsel, D., Waack, S., Welter, M.: Agent-based simulation for software development processes. Technical report IfI-16-02, TU Clausthal, September 2016 (to appear). http://www.in.tu-clausthal.de/fileadmin/homes/techreports/ifi1602ahlbrecht.pdf
2. Ahlbrecht, T., Dix, J., Fiekas, N., Kraus, P., Müller, J.P.: An architecture for scalable simulation of systems of cognitive agents. Int. J. Agent-Orient. Softw. Eng. **5**, 232–265 (2016)
3. Bordini, R., Dix, J.: Chapter 13: Programming multi-agent systems. In: Weiss, G. (ed.) Multiagent Systems, pp. 587–639. MIT-Press, Cambridge (2013)
4. Bordini, R.H., Hübner, J.F., Wooldridge, M.: Programming Multi-agent Systems in AgentSpeak Using Jason (Wiley Series in Agent Technology). Wiley, Hoboken (2007). ISBN 0470029005
5. Dean, J., Ghemawat, S.: MapReduce: simplified data processing on large clusters. Commun. ACM **51**(1), 107–113 (2008). ISSN 0001-0782, doi:10.1145/1327452.1327492. http://doi.acm.org/10.1145/1327452.1327492

6. Honsel, V., Honsel, D., Herbold, S., Grabowski, J., Waack, S.: Mining software dependency networks for agent-based simulation of software evolution. In: 2015 30th IEEE/ACM International Conference on Automated Software Engineering Workshop (ASEW), pp. 102–108. IEEE (2015)
7. Lin, J., Schatz, M.: Design patterns for efficient graph algorithms in MapReduce. In: Proceedings of 8th Workshop on Mining and Learning with Graphs, MLG 2010, pp. 78–85. ACM, New York (2010). ISBN 978-1-4503-0214-2, doi:10.1145/1830252. 1830263. http://doi.acm.org/10.1145/1830252.1830263
8. Radenski, A.: Using MapReduce streaming for distributed life simulation on the cloud. ECAL **2013**, 284–291 (2013)
9. Rao, A.S.: AgentSpeak(L): BDI agents speak out in a logical computable language. In: Velde, W., Perram, J.W. (eds.) MAAMAW 1996. LNCS, vol. 1038, pp. 42–55. Springer, Heidelberg (1996). doi:10.1007/BFb0031845
10. Vitter, J.S.: Random sampling with a reservoir. ACM Trans. Math. Softw. (TOMS) **11**(1), 37–57 (1985)
11. Wang, G., Salles, M.A.V., Sowell, B., Wang, X., Cao, T., Demers, A.J., Gehrke, J., White, W.M.: Behavioral simulations in MapReduce. CoRR, abs/1005.3773 (2010). http://arxiv.org/abs/1005.3773
12. Wielemaker, J., Schrijvers, T., Triska, M., Lager, T.: SWI-Prolog. Theory Pract. Log. Prog. **12**(1–2), 67–96 (2012)
13. Winikoff, M.: W-Prolog (1996). http://waitaki.otago.ac.nz/michael/wp/index. html
14. Zhang, S., Han, J., Liu, Z., Wang, K., Xu, Z.: SJMR: parallelizing spatial join with MapReduce on clusters. In: Proceedings of 2009 IEEE International Conference on Cluster Computing, 31 August – 4 September 2009, New Orleans, Louisiana, USA, pp. 1–8 (2009). doi:10.1109/CLUSTR.2009.5289178. http://dx.doi.org/10. 1109/CLUSTR.2009.5289178

EUMAS 2016: Theoretical Studies

Expansion and Equivalence Relations on Argumentation Frameworks Based on Logic Programs

Juan Carlos Nieves[(✉)]

Department of Computing Science, Umeå University,
901 87 Umeå, Sweden
jcnieves@cs.umu.se

Abstract. Expansion and equivalence relations have been explored in the settings of abstract argumentation. However, in terms of structured arguments, expansion and equivalence relations have not been explored in the settings of structured arguments based on logic programs. In this paper, we draw connections between resulting argumentation frameworks from logic programs considering expansion and equivalence relations. We show that by considering different methods for constructing arguments and defining attack relations, one can define different expansion and equivalence relations between the resulting argumentation frameworks from logic programs. Moreover, we extended results from abstract argumentation into structured arguments based on logic programs.

1 Introduction

Argumentation has been regarded as a non-monotonic reasoning approach since it was suggested as an inference reasoning approach [22]. Dung showed that argumentation inference can be regarded as a logic programming inference with *negation as failure* [10]. Indeed logic programming with negation as failure has been playing an important role in the developments of argumentation. For instance, it has been shown that well-accepted argumentation semantics can be characterized in terms of the inference of logic programming semantics[1]. Moreover, some of the well-performed argumentation solvers are based on logic programming solvers [8]. We can observe that most of these developments have been done in the settings of *abstract argumentation*. This means that these developments consider arguments without an internal structure. Hence the use of these developments in applications which require arguments with an internal structure is not straightforward.

We can argue that depending of the specification language of a knowledge base and the purpose of the arguments, one can define different internal structures of an argument [1,2,10,12,17]. In the settings of logic programming with negation as failure, one can find different approaches for constructing *structured*

---

[1] A summary of these characterizations can be found in Sect. 4 of [20].

© Springer International Publishing AG 2017
N. Criado Pacheco et al. (Eds.): EUMAS 2016/AT 2016, LNAI 10207, pp. 375–389, 2017.
DOI: 10.1007/978-3-319-59294-7_32

arguments [5,10,16,24]. Structured arguments based on logic programs are usually characterized by a tuple of the form $\langle S, C \rangle$ where S is called the *support* of the argument and c is called the *conclusion* of the argument. S is a subset of a logic program, which *derives* the conclusion c. The main differences between the different approaches for constructing arguments rely on the conditions which have to satisfy S. There are approaches which only ask for syntactic constraints on S [24] and other approaches ask for semantic-based inference conditions on S [16]. Hence, depending on the approach for constructing arguments, one can construct different sets of arguments from the same knowledge base. For instance, let P be the following simple program: Moreover, these sets of arguments constructed from a knowledge base will affect both the inferred information from a given knowledge base and the quality of the inferred information[2].

Against this background, we draw connections between resulting argumentation frameworks from logic programs considering expansion and equivalence relations [1,4,9,19]. Given the dynamics of argumentation processes, *e.g.*, dialogues between rational agents [18], equivalence and expansion relations in argumentation have emerged as a relevant research thread in order to compare and relate different argumentation frameworks. In this paper, we focus our attention to a quite common syntactic-based approach for constructing arguments [21,24] and a semantic-based approach for constructing arguments [16]. We will show that considering the different sets of arguments which can be constructed following these approaches, one can define expansions between argumentation frameworks resulting from a logic program. We will also observe that the way of defining attack relations between arguments has consequences in the structure of the resulting argumentation frameworks. We introduce the property of *sub-argument transitive attack property* which is not fulfilled by the syntactic-based approach for defining attacks between arguments. On the other hand, this property is fulfilled by the semantic-based approach for defining attacks between arguments. In the last part of the paper, we identify a class of logic programs which suggests equivalences in terms of the outputs of the resulting argumentation frameworks.

Let us observe that to the best of our knowledge, the results presented in this paper are the first results which connect structured-based argumentation based on logic programming and expansion relations. It worth mentioning that, in the literature of formal argumentation, expansion and equivalence relations have been explored mainly in the settings of abstract argumentation.

The rest of the paper is split as follows: In Sect. 2, a basic background about logic programming and argumentation theory is introduced. In Sect. 3, we identify relevant differences of the resulting argumentation frameworks from a logic programming by considering different approaches for constructing arguments. In Sect. 4, we show properties of the argumentation frameworks resulting from a logic program *w.r.t.* expansion relations and equivalence relations in terms of outputs. In the last section, we outline our conclusions and future work.

---

[2] By quality of the inferred information, we mean the satisfaction of conditions such as *consistency* [7].

2   Background

In this section, a basic background on logic programming and argumentation theory is presented. In terms of logic programming, the class of extended logic programs and the stable model semantics are defined. Regarding argumentation theory, basic definitions on argumentation semantics and relations of expansion and equivalence between argumentation frameworks (based on arguments without an internal structure) are presented.

We are assuming that the reader has a basic knowledge on classical logic and logic programming with negation as failure. Indeed, by space limitation, concepts such as interpretation, model, minimal model, stratified logic programs are not defined. For an introduction of these concepts, we encourage the reader to see [3].

2.1   Extended Logic Programs

Let us introduce the language of a propositional logic, which is constituted by propositional symbols: $p_0, p_1, \ldots$; connectives: $\wedge, \leftarrow, \neg, \ not, \top$; and auxiliary symbols: $(,)$, in which $\wedge, \leftarrow$ are 2-place connectives, $\neg, \ not$ are 1-place connectives and $\top$ is a 0-place connective. The propositional symbols, the 0-place connective $\top$ and the propositional symbols of the form $\neg p_i$ $(i \geq 0)$ stand for the indecomposable propositions, which we call *atoms*, or *atomic propositions*. The atoms of the form $\neg a$ are also called *extended atoms* in the literature. In order to simplify the presentation, we call them atoms as well. The negation symbol $\neg$ is regarded as the so-called *strong negation* in the Answer Set Programming literature [3], and the negation symbol *not* as *negation as failure*. A literal is an atom, a (called a positive literal), or the negation of an atom *not* a (called a negative literal). A (propositional) extended normal clause, C, is denoted:

$$a \leftarrow b_1 \wedge \cdots \wedge b_j \wedge not\ b_{j+1} \wedge \cdots \wedge not\ b_{j+n} \qquad (1)$$

in which $j + n \geq 0$, a is an atom, and each b_i $(1 \leq i \leq j+n)$ is an atom. We use the term *rule* as a synonym of *clause* indistinctly. When $j+n = 0$, the clause is an abbreviation of $a \leftarrow \top$ (a *fact*), such that $\top$ is the propositional atom that always evaluates to true. In a slight abuse of notation, we sometimes write the clause (1) as $a \leftarrow \mathcal{B}^+ \wedge not \mathcal{B}^-$, in which $\mathcal{B}^+ := \{b_1, \ldots, b_j\}$ and $\mathcal{B}^- := \{b_{j+1}, \ldots, b_{j+n}\}$. An extended logic program P is a finite set of extended normal clauses. When $n = 0$, the clause is called an *extended definite clause*. By $\mathcal{L}_P$, we denote the set of atoms which appear in P. The handling of strong negation in our logic programs will be done as it is usually done in Answer Set Programming literature [3]. Essentially, each atom of the form $\neg a$ is replaced by a new atom symbol a' that does not appear in the language of the program. A program without extended atoms will be called a *normal logic program*. Therefore, we can induce a normal logic program from an extended normal logic program by replacing each extended atom with a new symbol. For instance, let P be the program: $a \leftarrow q; \neg q \leftarrow r$, then, by replacing each extended atom with a new atom symbol, we will have: $a \leftarrow q; q' \leftarrow r$.

In the literature, different logic programming semantics have been proposed for capturing extended logic programs [13,14]. In this paper, the stable model semantics is considered in order to build arguments. Stable model semantics is one of the most influential logic programming semantics in the non-monotonic reasoning community and is defined as follows:

Definition 1 [14]. *Let* P *be a normal logic program. For any set* $S \subseteq \mathcal{L}_P$, *let* P^S *be the definite logic program obtained from* P *by deleting*

(i) *each rule that has a formula not l in its body with* $l \in S$, *and then*
(ii) *all formulæ of the form not l in the bodies of the remaining rules.*

Hence S *is a stable model of* P *iff* S *is a minimal model of* P^S. *STABLE*(P) *denotes the set of stable models of* P.

2.2 Argumentation Theory

In this section, we introduce basic concepts on abstract argumentation. To this end, the so called *argumentation frameworks* are introduced. Considering argumentation frameworks, argumentation-based inferences have been defined in terms of *argumentation semantics* [10]. Hence, some well-acceptable argumentation semantics will be defined. In the last part of this section, some definitions about expansion and equivalence relations between argumentation frameworls are defined.

Argumentation Semantics: We start by defining the basic structure of an argumentation framework (AF).

Definition 2 [10]. *An argumentation framework is a pair* $AF := \langle AR, attacks \rangle$, *where* AR *is a finite set of arguments, and* attacks *is a binary relation on* AR, *i.e.* attacks $\subseteq AR \times AR$.

We say that *a attacks b* (or *b is attacked by a*) if $attacks(a, b)$ holds. Similarly, we say that a set S of arguments attacks b (or b is attacked by S) if b is attacked by an argument in S. We say that c *defends* a if b attacks a and c attacks b.

Let us observe that an AF is a simple structure which captures the conflicts of a given set of arguments. In order to select *coherent points of view* from a set of conflicts of arguments, Dung introduced the so-called *argumentation semantics*. These argumentation semantics are based on the concept of an *admissible set*:

Definition 3 [10]

– *A set S of arguments is said to be conflict-free if there are no arguments a, b in S such that a attacks b.*
– *An argument* $a \in AR$ *is acceptable with respect to a set S of arguments if and only if for each argument* $b \in AR$: *If b attacks a then b is attacked by S.*
– *A conflict-free set of arguments S is* admissible *if and only if each argument in S is acceptable w.r.t. S.*

Let us introduce some notation in order to define some argumentation semantics. Let $AF := \langle AR, attacks \rangle$ and $S \subseteq AR$. $S^+ = \{b | a \in S$ and $(a, b) \in attacks\}$.

From a general point of view, an argumentation semantics σ is a function which assigns to an argumentation framework AF a set of sets of arguments denoted by $\mathcal{E}_\sigma(AF)$. Each set of $\mathcal{E}_\sigma(AF)$ is called σ-extension.

Definition 4 [6,10,11]. *Let $AF := \langle AR, attacks \rangle$ be an argumentation framework. An admissible set of argument $S \subseteq AR$ is:*

- *a* stable *extension of AF ($S \in \mathcal{E}_{stb}(AF)$) if S attacks each argument which does not belong to S.*
- *a* preferred *extension of AF ($S \in \mathcal{E}_{pr}(AF)$) if S is a maximal (w.r.t. set inclusion) admissible set of AF.*
- *a* complete *extension of AF ($S \in \mathcal{E}_{co}(AF)$) if each argument, which is acceptable with respect to S, belongs to S.*
- *a* grounded *extension of AF ($S \in \mathcal{E}_{gr}(AF)$) if S is a minimal (w.r.t. set inclusion) complete extension.*
- *a* semi-stable *extension of AF ($S \in \mathcal{E}_{ss}(AF)$) if S is a complete extension such that $S \cup S^+$ is maximal w.r.t. set inclusion.*
- *an* ideal *extension of AF ($S \in \mathcal{E}_{id}(AF)$) if S is contained in every preferred extension of AF.*

In addition to the argumentation semantics based on admissible sets, there are other approaches for defining argumentation semantics. One of these approaches is the approach based on *conflict-free sets*, e.g., [23]. Considering conflict-free sets, Verheij introduced the so-called *stage semantics*:

Definition 5 *Let $AF := \langle AR, attacks \rangle$ be an argumentation framework. E is a stage extension of AF ($E \in \mathcal{E}_{stg}(AF)$) if E is a conflict free set and $E \cup E^+$ is maximal w.r.t. set inclusion.*

One can observe that given an argumentation semantics σ and an argumentation framework AF, $\mathcal{E}_\sigma(AF)$ can have more than one σ-extension. Hence, one can define different status of an given argument *w.r.t.* σ.

Definition 6 (Status of arguments) [1]. *Let $AF := \langle AR, attacks \rangle$ be an argumentation framework, $a \in AR$ and σ be an argumentation semantics.*

- *a is sceptically accepted w.r.t. σ iff $a \in \bigcap_{E \in \mathcal{E}_\sigma(AF)} E$.*
- *a is credulously accepted w.r.t. σ iff $a \in \bigcup_{E \in \mathcal{E}_\sigma(AF)} E$.*
- *a is rejected accepted w.r.t. σ iff $a \notin \bigcup_{E \in \mathcal{E}_\sigma(AF)} E$.*

Expansion and Corresponding Equivalence Notions: The evaluation of equivalence between argumentation frameworks considering different argumentation semantics have been explored by the argumentation community [4,19]. The following definition introduces some relations of equivalence which have been explored in the settings of abstract argumentation without considering a particular argumentation semantics:

Definition 7 [4]. *Let AF and AF' be two argumentation frameworks. AF' is an expansion of $AF = \langle AR, attacks \rangle$ (denoted by $AF \preceq_E AF'$) iff $AF' = \langle AR \cup AR', attacks \cup attacks' \rangle$ where $AR \cap AR' = attacks \cap attacks' = \emptyset$. An expansion is called*

1. *normal ($AF \preceq_N AF'$) iff $\forall a, b$ if $(a, b) \in attacks'$ then $a \in AR'$ or $b \in AR'$.*
2. *strong ($AF \preceq_S AF'$) iff $AF \preceq_N AF'$ and $\forall a, b$ if $(a, b) \in attacks'$ then it does not hold that $a \in AR$ and $b \in AR'$.*
3. *local ($AF \preceq_L AF'$) iff $AR' = \emptyset$.*

Informally speaking, an expansion of an argumentation framework suggests the introduction of new attack relations. These new attack relations can consider new arguments or not. Essentially, a normal expansion introduces new attack relations such that each new attack relation considers new arguments. A strong expansion considers only attacks of new arguments such that the new arguments are not attacked by the original arguments. A local expansion considers new attacks; but, these new attacks are identified considering only the original arguments.

Now let us consider the ideas of equivalence between argumentation frameworks. The following definition introduces different relations of equivalence considering the concepts of expansions and argumentation semantics:

Definition 8 [4]. *Give an argumentation semantics σ. Two argumentation frameworks AF and AF' are*

1. *standard equivalence w.r.t. σ ($AF \equiv^\sigma AF'$) iff AF and AF' possess the same extensions under σ, i.e. $\mathcal{E}_\sigma(AF) = \mathcal{E}_\sigma(AF')$.*
2. *expansion equivalence w.r.t. σ ($AF \equiv^\sigma_E AF'$) iff for each argumentation framework AF^*, $AF \cup AF^* \equiv^\sigma AF' \cup AF^*$ holds,*
3. *normal expansion equivalence w.r.t. σ ($AF \equiv^\sigma_N AF'$) iff for each argumentation framework AF^*, such that $AF \preceq_N AF \cup AF^*$ and $AF' \preceq_N AF' \cup AF^*$, $AF \cup AF^* \equiv^\sigma AF' \cup AF^*$ holds,*
4. *strong expansion equivalence w.r.t. σ ($AF \equiv^\sigma_S AF'$) iff for each argumentation framework AF^*, such that $AF \preceq_S AF \cup AF^*$ and $AF' \preceq_S AF' \cup AF^*$, $AF \cup AF^* \equiv^\sigma AF' \cup AF^*$ holds,*
5. *local expansion equivalence w.r.t. σ ($AF \equiv^\sigma_L AF'$) iff for each argumentation framework AF^*, such that $AF \preceq_L AF \cup AF^*$ and $AF' \preceq_L AF' \cup AF^*$, $AF \cup AF^* \equiv^\sigma AF' \cup AF^*$ holds,*

Unlike expansion relations which are only concern on understanding the new information which added to an argumentation framework, equivalence relations also consider restrictions on how to keep the inferred information from argumentation frameworks considering argumentation semantics.

Let us observe that all the concepts introduced until now are based on abstract arguments. This means that arguments have no a internal structure. In the following section, structured arguments are explored. These structured arguments are constructed from knowledge bases which are expressed in terms of extended normal logic programs.

3   Structured Arguments

In this section, we explore two approaches for constructing arguments from logic programs. One approach suggests syntactic-based constrains for defining the supports of the suggested arguments [24]. On the other hand, the other approach suggests semantic-based constrains for the supports of the suggested arguments [16]. As we have observed in Definition 7, attack relations are quite critical for defining expansions of argumentation frameworks. Hence, we introduce an attack relation property which is mainly oriented to structured arguments since this property is based on the idea of sub-arguments. The introduced property is called sub-argument transitive attack property. We will observe that the syntactic-based approach suggested by [24] does not fulfill the so called *sub-argument transitive attack property* (see Proposition 1).

Let us start with the syntactic based approach. The following definition introduces a syntactic-based approach for constructing arguments. As the authors claim in [24], this definition of structured arguments is close related to the suggested definitions by other authors [21].

Definition 9 [24]. *Let P be a normal logic program. An argument A based on P is a finite tree of rules from P such that:*

1. *each node (of the form $c \leftarrow a_1 \wedge \cdots \wedge a_n \wedge not\, b_1 \wedge \cdots \wedge not\, b_m$ with $n \geq 0$ and $m \geq 0$) has exactly n children, each having a different head $a_i \subset \{a_1, \ldots, a_n\}$ $(1 \leq i \leq n)$ and*
2. *no rule occurs more than once in any root-originated branch of the tree.*

An argument A will be denoted by a tuple of the form $\langle S, c \rangle$ such that S is the set of rules that appear in the tree of A and c is the head of the rule which appears in the root of the tree of A. Arg_P^1 denotes the set of all the arguments built from P according to Definition 9.

Relationships between arguments are defined by the concept of *attack*. Intuitively, an attack between arguments emerges whenever there is a *disagreement* between arguments. Considering the arguments constructed according to Definition 9, the following definition of attack has been defined:

Definition 10 [24]. *Let P be a normal logic program and $A, B \in Arg_P^1$ such that $A = \langle S_A, c_A \rangle$ and $B = \langle S_B, c_B \rangle$. We say that A attacks B if not c_A appears in S_B. $At^1(Arg_P^1)$ denotes the set of all the attack relationships between the arguments belonging to the set of arguments Arg_P^1.*

Definition 9 follows a syntactic-based approach for constructing the support of arguments. Another option for constructing supports of arguments is to follow a semantic-based approach. In the following definition, the stable model semantic is considered for defining the restrictions of the support of an argument:

Definition 11 [16]. *Given an extended logic program P and $S \subseteq P$. $Arg_P = \langle S, a \rangle$ is an argument under the stable model semantics, if the following conditions hold:*

1. *S is a stratified logic program,*
2. *$a \in M$ such that $M \in STABLE(S)$,*
3. *S is minimal w.r.t. the set inclusion satisfying 2,*
4. *$\nexists c \in \mathcal{L}_P$ such that $\{c, \neg c\} \subseteq M$ and $M \in STABLE(S)$.*

By Arg_P^2, we denote the set of all the arguments built from P according to Definition 11. Let us observe that if $\langle S, a \rangle \in Arg_P^2$, then $STABLE(S)$ has exactly one stable model. Moreover, unlike Definition 9 which considers normal logic programs, Definition 11 is considering extended logic programs. It is worth mentioning that Arg_P^2 can be constructed considering Well-Founded-Semantics [13].

From here on, Arg_P will refer to either Arg_P^1 or Arg_P^2.

One can consider also a semantic-based approach for defining attack relations between arguments.

Definition 12 (Attack relationship between arguments). *Let P be an extended logic program. Let $A, B \in Arg_P$ such that $A = \langle S_A, c_A \rangle$ and $B = \langle S_B, c_B \rangle$. Let $E_A = \bigcap_{M \in STABLE(S_A)} M$ and $E_B = \bigcap_{M \in STABLE(S_B)} M$, we say that A attacks B if one of the following conditions holds:*

1. *$a \in E_A$ and $\neg a \in E_B$.*
2. *$a \in E_A$ and $a \in \mathcal{L}_{S_B} \setminus E_B$.*

$At^2(Arg_P)$ *denotes the set of all the attack relationships between the arguments belonging to the set of arguments Arg_P.*

Definition 12 identifies attacks between arguments by considering the inferred atoms of each support of the arguments. If there are inconsistencies between the inferred atoms from the supports, attacks between the arguments are defined. The first condition looks for inconsistencies considering strong negation. The second condition looks for inconsistencies considering the semantic interpretation of the atoms.

From here on, $At(Arg_P)$ will refer to either $At^1(Arg_P^1)$ or $At^2(Arg_P)$. As we can observe, Definition 9 and Definition 11 suggest different approaches for constructing arguments. In order to understand the differences between these two approaches for constructing arguments, let us consider the class of normal logic programs which is the class of logic programs in common between the arguments constructed according to Definition 9 and the arguments constructed according to Definition 11.

Proposition 1. *Let P be a normal logic program. The following condition holds:*

1. *$Arg_P^2 \subseteq Arg_P^1$.*

Proof. There are two cases to show:

(a) If $A \in Arg_P^2$, then $A \in Arg_P^1$: If $A \in Arg_P^2$ and $A = \langle S, a \rangle$, then S is a stratified logic program. Since S is minimal (*w.r.t.* set inclusion), then each rule which belongs to S appears only once in S. It is direct to see that one can build a three T from S considering Condition 1 of Definition 9. Moreover the root of T is a rule of the form $a \leftarrow \mathcal{B}^+ \wedge not\ \mathcal{B}^-$. Hence, $A \in Arg_P^1$.

(b) $\exists A \in Arg_P^1$ such that $A \notin Arg_P^2$: Let us suppose that $a \leftarrow not\ a \in P$. Then, $\langle \{a \leftarrow not\ a\}, a \rangle \in Arg_P^1$. However, since $STABLE(\{a \leftarrow not\ a\}) = \{\}$, $A \notin Arg_P^2$.

Let us observe that it can be the case that for a given normal logic program P, $Arg_P^2 = Arg_P^1$ can be true; however, $At^2(Arg_P^2) \subseteq At^1(Arg_P^1)$ does not hold for any normal logic program P. In order to illustrate this situation, let us consider the following example:

Example 1. Let P be a normal logic program with the following set of clauses:

$$n \leftarrow a \qquad p \leftarrow c$$
$$a \leftarrow not\ c \qquad c \leftarrow \top$$

We can see that $Arg_P^1 = Arg_P^2 = \{Arg_1, Arg_2, Arg_3, Arg_4\}$ where the arguments are defined as follows:

$$Arg_1 = \langle \{n \leftarrow a, a \leftarrow not\ c\}, n \rangle$$
$$Arg_2 = \langle \{a \leftarrow not\ c\}, a \rangle$$
$$Arg_3 = \langle \{p \leftarrow c, c \leftarrow \top\}, p \rangle$$
$$Arg_4 = \langle \{c \leftarrow \top\}, c \rangle$$

Considering the attack relations suggested by Definition 10, $At^1(Arg_P^1) = \{(Arg_4, Arg_1), (Arg_4, Arg_2)\}$. On the other hand considering the attack relations suggested by Definition 12, $At^2(Arg_P^2) = \{(Arg_4, Arg_1), (Arg_4, Arg_2), (Arg_3, Arg_1), (Arg_3, Arg_2)\}$.

In order to understand why $At^2(Arg_P^2)$ and $At^1(Arg_P^1)$ are different even that Arg_P^2 and Arg_P^1 can be the same set of arguments, let us introduce the binary relation of *sub-argument*.

Definition 13 (Sub-argument). *Let $A = \langle S_A, g_A \rangle$, $B = \langle S_B, g_B \rangle$ be two arguments. A is a sub-argument of B if and only if $S_A \subset S_B$.*

Considering the idea of sub-arguments, the *sub-argument transitive attack property* is defined as follows:

Definition 14 (Sub-argument transitive attack). *Let P be a normal logic program and $A, B, C \in At(Arg_P)$ such that B is a sub-argument of A. $At(Arg_P)$ fulfill sub-argument transitive attack property if the following conditions hold:*

1. *if B attacks C, then A attacks C.*
2. *if C attacks B, then C attacks A.*

Considering the arguments introduced by Example 1, we can see that $At^1(Arg_P^1)$ contains the attack rations in order to satisfy Condition 2 of Definition 14; however, $At^1(Arg_P^1)$ does not contain the attack relations in order to satisfy Condition 1 of Definition 14. On the other hand, $At^2(Arg_P^2)$ contains all the attack relations in order to satisfy the property of sub-argument transitive attack. These observations can be expressed in the following proposition:

Proposition 2. *Let P be a normal logic program. The following statements hold:*

(a) $At^1(Arg_P^1)$ does not fulfill the property of sub-argument transitive attack.
(b) $At^2(Arg_P^2)$ fulfills the property of sub-argument transitive attack.

Proof

(a) The proof is direct by Example 1 which introduces a contra-example.
(b) Direct by Proposition 5 from [16].

Now that we have defined the concepts of arguments and attacks, let us define the concept of argumentation framework with respect to a logic program as follows:

Definition 15. *Let P be a logic program. The resulting argumentation framework w.r.t. P is the tuple: $AF_P = \langle Arg_P, At(Arg_P) \rangle$.*

4   Expansion Relations and Equivalence Criteria

In this section, we show properties of the argumentation frameworks resulting from a logic program *w.r.t.* expansion and equivalence relations in terms of outputs.

Let us start observing that given a normal logic program P, $AF_P^1 = \langle Arg_P^1, At^1(Arg_P^1) \rangle$ and $AF_P^2 = \langle Arg_P^2, At^2(Arg_P^2) \rangle$, $AF_P^2 \preceq_E AF_P^1$ is false. As we observed in Example 1, $At^2(Arg_P^2)$ could contain more attack relations than $At^1(Arg_P^1)$, even though $Arg_P^2 \subseteq Arg_P^1$ holds. Hence, given that $Arg_P^2 \subseteq Arg_P^1$ holds, an interesting question can be: can we define an expansion for AF_P^2 considering Arg_P^1? The answer is yes.

Proposition 3. *Let P be a normal logic program, $AF_P^1 = \langle Arg_P^1, At^1(Arg_P^1) \rangle$, $AF_P^2 = \langle Arg_P^2, At^2(Arg_P^2) \rangle$ and $AF_P^3 = \langle Arg_P^1, At^1(Arg_P^1) \cup At^2(Arg_P^1) \rangle$. The following relations hold:*

(a) $AF_P^1 \preceq_L AF_P^3$
(b) $AF_P^2 \preceq_N AF_P^3$

Proof

(a) The proof is direct by the fact that $At^1(Arg_P^1) \subseteq At^1(Arg_P^1) \cup At^2(Arg_P^1)$.
(b) We start introducing the following notation: $Arg = Arg_P^1 \setminus Arg_P^2$ and $At = (At^1(Arg_P^1) \cup At^2(Arg_P^1)) \setminus At^2(Arg_P^2)$.

Not let us introduce the following observations:

Ob-1: If $Arg_P^2 \subseteq Arg_P^1$, then $At^2(Arg_P^2) \subseteq At^1(Arg_P^1) \cup At^2(Arg_P^1)$.

Ob-2: If $\langle S, c \rangle \in Arg$ then either S is not a stratified logic program or S is a stratified logic program but $c \notin \bigcap_{M \in STABLE(S)} M$.

By Proposition 1 and Ob-1, it is direct to see that $AF_P^2 \preceq_E AF_P^3$ is true. By Ob-2, if $A \in Arg$, then the attack relations *w.r.t.* A appear in $At^1(Arg_P^1)$; hence, if $\exists C \in Arg_P^1$ such that C attacks A or A attacks C, these attack relations belong to At. Therefore, $AF_P^2 \preceq_N AF_P^3$.

Let us observe that considering AF_P^2 and AF_P^3, as they were defined in Proposition 3, it does not hold $AF_P^2 \preceq_S AF_P^3$. In order to illustrate this observation, let us consider the following example:

Example 2. Let P be the following logic program:

$$a \leftarrow not\ a$$
$$a \leftarrow not\ b$$
$$b \leftarrow not\ a$$

We can see that $Arg_P^1 = \{Arg_1, Arg_2, Arg_3\}$ and $Arg_P^2 = \{Arg_2, Arg_3\}$ such that:
$Arg_1 = \langle \{a \leftarrow not\ a\}, a \rangle$
$Arg_2 = \langle \{a \leftarrow not\ b\}, a \rangle$
$Arg_3 = \langle \{b \leftarrow not\ a\}, b \rangle$

Moreover, $At^1(Arg_P^1) = \{(Arg1, Arg1), (Arg2, Arg1), (Arg2, Arg3), (Arg3, Arg2)\}$ and $At^2(Arg_P^2) = \{(Arg2, Arg3), (Arg3, Arg2)\}$. Considering $AF_P^3 = \langle Arg_P^1, At^1(Arg_P^1) \cup At^2(Arg_P^1) \rangle$ as an expansion of $AF_P^2 = \langle Arg_P^2, At^2(Arg_P^2) \rangle$. We can see that an argument from Arg_P^2 attacks the new argument introduced by Arg_P^1, *i.e.* Arg_2 attacks Arg_1; hence, AF_P^3 cannot be considered as a strong expansion of Arg_P^2. However, AF_P^3 is a normal expansion of AF_P^2.

Self-loop attacks have been observed as an important condition in the exploration of equivalence [4]. By self-loop attacks, we mean binary relation of the form: an argument A is self-loop attacked if $(A, A) \in attacks$. In [16], it was shown that the resulting argumentation frameworks following a semantics-based approach avoid to contain self-loop attacked arguments. Considering these results, we can show the following relevant theorem:

Proposition 4. *Let P, G be two extended logic programs and $AF_P = \langle Arg_P^2, At^2(Arg_P^2) \rangle$ and $AF_G = \langle Arg_G^2, At^2(Arg_G^2) \rangle$. For any $\Phi \in \{E, N, S\}$ and any argumentation semantics $\sigma \in \{stg, stb, ss, pr, id, gr, co\}$:*

$$AF_P = AF_G \text{ iff } AF_P \equiv_\Phi^\sigma AF_G$$

Moreover, for $\sigma \in \{stg, ss, pr, id\}$:

$$AF_P = AF_G \text{ iff } AF_P \equiv_L^\sigma AF_G$$

Proof. Proposition 7 from [16] has shown that given an extended logic program P, the resulting argumentation framework $AF_P = \langle Arg_P^2, At^2(Arg_P^2) \rangle$ has no arguments which are self-loop attacked. Hence, the proof is direct by Proposition 4.2 from [4].

4.1 Equivalence Criteria

Amgoud *et al.* [1] have studied equivalence between argumentation systems with structured arguments in terms of *outputs*. In this section, we present results in the study of equivalence regarding outputs. In particular, we identify a class of logic programs which suggests equivalences in terms of outputs. To this end, we extend some concepts introduced by Amgoud *et al.* in order to capture argumentation frameworks constructed from logic programs.

Given a set of arguments E, $Base(E) = \bigcup_{\langle S,g \rangle \in E} S$.

Definition 16 (Outputs). *Let $AF_P = \langle Arg_P, At(Arg_P) \rangle$ be the resulting argumentation from the extended logic program P and σ be an argumentation semantics.*

- $Sc_\sigma(AF_P) = \{A | A \in Arg_P$ *is sceptical accepted w.r.t.* $\sigma\}$.
- $Cr_\sigma(AF_P) = \{A | A \in Arg_P$ *is credulously accepted w.r.t.* $\sigma\}$.
- $Output_\sigma^{sc}(AF_P) = \{g_A | A \in Arg_P$ *such that $A = \langle S_A, g_A \rangle$ and A is sceptical accepted w.r.t.* $\sigma\}$.
- $Output_\sigma^{cr}(AF_P) = \{g_A | A \in Arg_P$ *such that $A = \langle S_A, g_A \rangle$ and A is credulously accepted w.r.t.* $\sigma\}$.
- $Bases_\sigma(AF_P) = \{Base(E) | E \in \mathcal{E}_\sigma(AF_P)\}$.

We introduce our own version of a subset of equivalence criteria introduce by [1].

Definition 17. *Let $AF_P = \langle Arg_P, At(Arg_P) \rangle$ and $AF_G = \langle Arg_G, At(Arg_G) \rangle$ be the resulting argumentation frameworks from the logic programs P and G, respectively. Given an argumentation semantics σ, AF_P and AF_G are equivalent EQ_i $(AF_P \equiv_{EQ_i}^\sigma AF_G)$ iff EQ_i holds where $i \in 1, \ldots, 6$ and*

EQ.1 $\mathcal{E}_\sigma(AF_P) = \mathcal{E}_\sigma(AF_G)$,
EQ.2 $Sc_\sigma(AF_P) = Sc_\sigma(AF_G)$,
EQ.3 $Cr_\sigma(AF_P) = Cr_\sigma(AF_G)$,
EQ.4 $Output_\sigma^{sc}(AF_P) = Output_\sigma^{sc}(AF_G)$,
EQ.5 $Output_\sigma^{cr}(AF_P) = Output_\sigma^{cs}(AF_G)$,
EQ.6 $Bases_\sigma(AF_P) = Bases_\sigma(AF_G)$.

Considering the equivalence criteria introduced by Definition 17, syntactic-based arguments and semantics-based arguments, an interesting question is:

Is there a class of logic programs which suggests argumentation frameworks which are equivalent in terms of outputs?

The following proposition identifies a class of logic programs which is an initial answer for the aforementioned question.

Proposition 5. *Let P be a stratified normal logic program such that if $a \leftarrow \mathcal{B}^+ \wedge$ not $\mathcal{B}^- \in P$ then $a \notin \mathcal{B}^+$ and $\mathcal{B}^+ \cap \mathcal{B}^- = \emptyset$, $AF_P^3 = \langle Arg_P^1, At^2(Arg_P^1) \rangle$, $AF_P^2 = \langle Arg_P^2, At^2(Arg_P^2) \rangle$. The following conditions hold:*

$$AF_P^1 \equiv_{EQ_i}^\sigma AF_G^3$$

where $i \in 1, \ldots, 6$ and $\sigma \in \{stb, pr, co, gr, ss, id, stg\}$.

Proof (Sketch). Let us start observing that if P is a stratified normal logic program such that if $a \leftarrow \mathcal{B}^+ \wedge$ not $\mathcal{B}^- \in P$ then $a \notin \mathcal{B}^+$ and $\mathcal{B}^+ \cap \mathcal{B}^- = \emptyset$, then $Arg_P^1 = Arg_P^2$. Hence, the proof is direct by the fact that $At^2(Arg_P^1) = At^2(Arg_P^2)$.

Let us observe that in Proposition 5, both AF_P^3 and AF_P^2 are considering attack relations which are identified following a semantic-based approach. Moreover, the class of programs which is suggested by Proposition 5 avoids clauses which are tautologies. In this regards, let us observe that the syntactic-based approach for constructing arguments can suggest arguments which their supports contain clauses which are tautologies. On the other hand, the semantic-based approach for constructing arguments does not suggest arguments which their supports contain tautologies.

5   Conclusions and Future Work

Currently there is an intensive research which is mainly oriented to abstract argumentation. However, whenever we consider structured arguments there are different factors which can affect the structure of the resulting argumentation frameworks from a knowledge base.

It is direct to observe that constructing arguments from a logic program considering different (syntactic and semantic) constrains of the supports of these arguments will give place to different argumentation frameworks (Proposition 1 and Proposition 2). Hence to consider different constructions of arguments is not redundant since the resulting argumentation frameworks can infer different information from a given logic program. Moreover, these differences can give place to different strategies for expanding argumentation frameworks (Proposition 3). Let us observe that in a given sequence of *assert moves* in an agent-based dialogue, we are basically expanding argumentation frameworks [18].

It seems that by considering syntactic and semantic restrictions for identifying attack relations, different sets of attack relations can be defined (Proposition 2). We have shown that some properties of structured arguments can help to extend results of abstract argumentation into structured argument as it is the case of self-loop attacks and equivalence relations (Proposition 4). Considering equivalence in terms outputs, we identified a class of logic programs which suggests equivalences in terms of outputs of the resulting argumentation frameworks (Proposition 5).

In the future work, we aim to extend our study considering structured arguments suggested by Dung [10] and the structured arguments suggested by Assumption-Based argumentation ABA [5]. As we have observed with the results of this paper, the way of identifying attack relations affects the final structure of the resulting argumentation frameworks. Moreover, considering different sets of attack relations can define different kind of expansions of the resulting argumentation frameworks from logic programs. Hence, the identification of proper definitions of attack relation is also a goal of our research. It is worth mentioning that in the settings of structured arguments based on classical logic, one can also identify different classes of attacks [15]. However, the definition of these classes of attacks cannot be applied directly in the settings of structured arguments based on logic programming because the inconsistency is defined in other terms *e.g.*, the lack of model.

The identification of classes of logic programs in which different structured argumentation approaches coincide seems to be a relevant issues since these classes of logic programs can define different algorithms for getting the same outcomes. Hence, this issue is also part of our future work.

References

1. Amgoud, L., Besnard, P., Vesic, S.: Equivalence in logic-based argumentation. J. Appl. Non-Class. Log. **24**(3), 181–208 (2014)
2. Amgoud, L., Prade, H.: Using arguments for making and explaining decisions. Artif. Intell. **173**, 413–436 (2009)
3. Baral, C.: Knowledge Representation, Reasoning and Declarative Problem Solving. Cambridge University Press, Cambridge (2003)
4. Baumann, R., Woltran, S.: The role of self-attacking arguments in characterizations of equivalence notions. J. Log. Comput. **26**(4), 1293–1313 (2016). doi:10.1093/logcom/exu010
5. Bondarenko, A., Dung, P.M., Kowalski, R.A., Toni, F.: An abstract, argumentation-theoretic approach to default reasoning. Artif. Intell. **93**, 63–101 (1997)
6. Caminada, M.: Semi-stable semantics. In: Dunne, P.E., Bench-Capon, T.J. (eds.) Proceedings of COMMA, vol. 144, pp. 121–130. IOS Press, Amsterdam (2006)
7. Caminada, M., Amgoud, L.: On the evaluation of argumentation formalisms. Artif. Intell. **171**, 286–310 (2007)
8. Charwat, G., Dvořák, W., Gaggl, S.A., Wallner, J.P., Woltran, S.: Methods for solving reasoning problems in abstract argumentation - a survey. Artif. Intell. **220**, 28–63 (2015)
9. Chesñevar, C.I., Simari, G.R., Godo, L., Alsinet, T.: Expansion operators for modelling agent reasoning in possibilistic defeasible logic programming. In: EUMAS 2005 - Proceedings of the Third European Workshop on Multi-Agent Systems, Brussels, Belgium, December 7–8, 2005, pp. 474–475 (2005)
10. Dung, P.M.: On the acceptability of arguments and its fundamental role in non-monotonic reasoning, logic programming and n-person games. Artif. Intell. **77**(2), 321–358 (1995)

11. Dung, P.M., Mancarella, P., Toni, F.: Computing ideal sceptical argumentation. Artif. Intell. **171**(10–15), 642–674 (2007)
12. Elvang-Gøransson, M., Krause, P., Fox, J.: Acceptability of arguments as 'logical uncertainty'. In: ECSQARU, pp. 85–90 (1993)
13. Gelder, A.V., Ross, K.A., Schlipf, J.S.: The well-founded semantics for general logic programs. J. ACM **38**(3), 620–650 (1991)
14. Gelfond, M., Lifschitz, V.: The stable model semantics for logic programming. In: Kowalski, R., Bowen, K. (eds.) 5th Conference on Logic Programming, pp. 1070–1080. MIT Press, Cambridge (1988)
15. Gorogiannis, N., Hunter, A.: Instantiating abstract argumentation with classical logic arguments: postulates and properties. Artif. Intell. **175**(9–10), 1479–1497 (2011)
16. Guerrero, E., Nieves, J.C., Lindgren, H.: Semantic-based construction of arguments: an answer set programming approach. Int. J. Approx. Reason. **64**, 54–74 (2015)
17. Modgil, S., Prakken, H.: The ASPIC$^+$ framework for structured argumentation: a tutorial. Argum. Comput. **5**(1), 31–62 (2014)
18. Nieves, J.C., Lindgren, H.: Deliberative argumentation for service provision in smart environments. In: Bulling, N. (ed.) Multi-Agent Systems. LNCS, vol. 8953, pp. 388–394. Springer, Cham (2015)
19. Oikarinen, E., Woltran, S.: Characterizing strong equivalence for argumentation frameworks. Artif. Intell. **175**(14–15), 1985–2009 (2011)
20. Osorio, M., Nieves, J.C.: Range-based argumentation semantics as two-valued models. Theor. Pract. Log. Program. **17**(1), 75–90 (2017)
21. Prakken, H., Sartor, G.: Argument-based extended logic programming with defeasible priorities. J. Appl. Non-Class. Log. **7**(1), 25–75 (1997)
22. Prakken, H., Vreeswijk, G.A.W.: Logics for defeasible argumentation. In: Gabbay, D., Günthner, F. (eds.) Handbook of Philosophical Logic, vol. 4, 2nd edn, pp. 219–318. Kluwer Academic Publishers, Dordrecht (2002)
23. Verheij, B.: Two approaches to dialectical argumentation: admissible sets and argumentation stages. In: Proceedings of the Eighth Dutch Conference on Artificial Intelligence (NAIC 1996) (1996)
24. Wu, Y., Caminada, M., Gabbay, D.M.: Complete extensions in argumentation coincide with 3-valued stable models in logic programming. Stud. Log. **93**(2–3), 383–403 (2009)

On a Formal Treatment of Deception
in Argumentative Dialogues

Kazuko Takahashi$^{(\boxtimes)}$ and Shizuka Yokohama

School of Science and Technology, Kwansei Gakuin University,
2-1, Gakuen, Sanda 669-1337, Japan
ktaka@kwansei.ac.jp, rec2016yoko@gmail.com

Abstract. This paper formalizes a dialogue that includes dishonest arguments in persuasion. We propose a dialogue model that uses a predicted opponent model and define a protocol using this prediction with an abstract argumentation framework. We focus on deception as dishonesty; that is, the case in which an agent hides her knowledge. We define the concepts of dishonest argument and suspicious argument by means of the acceptance of arguments in this model. We show how a dialogue including dishonest arguments proceeds according to the protocol and discuss a condition for a dishonest argument to be accepted without being revealed.

Keywords: Argumentation · Dialogue · Persuasion · Dishonesty · Opponent model

1 Introduction

Persuasion is a popular form of dialogue that can help in reaching an agreement between agents. It is considered to be a process of solving inconsistency between agents' beliefs. Dialogue systems based on argumentation frameworks have been studied because argumentation is an efficient technique for handling inconsistency [1–3,9,11]. Several strategies are used to succeed in persuasion, and agents may sometimes lie or hide information that is disadvantageous to them to succeed in persuasion. However, few studies have examined dialogue that includes such dishonest arguments.

Dishonesty in argumentation frameworks was studied by Caminada. He classified dishonesty in dialogues into three types [6]: giving the negation of her belief (lie), generating an argument of which she does not know the truth (which he calls "bullshit"), and hiding an argument that she knows (deception). Sakama formalized the former two types using argumentation frameworks [14,15]. This formalization was made from the viewpoint of the agent who offers a dishonest argument, and not from that of the agent receiving it. That is, the dialogue proceeds without the receiver knowing what is going on, and she does not suspect

---

Shizuka Yokohama—Currently, NEC Co., Ltd.

N. Criado Pacheco et al. (Eds.): EUMAS 2016/AT 2016, LNAI 10207, pp. 390–404, 2017.
DOI: 10.1007/978-3-319-59294-7_33

her opponent's argument or reveal its dishonesty. Basically, to suspect the opponent's argument or reveal its dishonesty, especially to point out a deception, an agent should know, or at least predict, the opponent's belief.

Consider the following situation in which students are selecting a research laboratory.

Alice tries to persuade Bob to apply to the same laboratory. Alice knows that Professor Charlie is strict, as well as generous. Alice, who prefers strict professors, wants to apply to Charlie's laboratory. However, Bob wants to work for a generous professor, but not for a strict professor, and Alice knows his intention.

Alice probably says, "Let's apply to Charlie's laboratory, because he is generous," hiding the fact that Charlie is strict, to persuade Bob. If Bob does not know of Charlie's reputation, he does not suspect Alice and accepts her argument.

However, assume that Bob knows both that (i) Charlie is strict and about Alice's knowledge (ii) Alice not only knows that Charlie is strict but also that Bob does not like strict professors. If Alice says, "Let's apply to Charlie's laboratory because he is generous," then he suspects its truth, and may say, "You know that Charlie is strict, and you also know that I do not like strict professors. Don't try to persuade me by hiding that fact." Alice deceives Bob, and it is based on the fact that Bob knows about Alice's knowledge whether he suspects her argument and points out her deception.

In the previous work [17], we formalized a persuasion dialogue using a predicted opponent model. We proposed a strategy and discussed what should be in a predicted opponent model so that persuasion does not fail. However, dishonest arguments were not discussed there.

In this paper, we modified our protocol to admit dishonest arguments of deception and formalize the mechanism used for giving a dishonest argument, suspecting an argument, pointing out a deception, and making an excuse.

In our dialogue model, each agent has two argumentation frameworks: her own and the prediction of her opponent's. A dialogue protocol is defined based on these frameworks. A dishonest argument and a suspicious argument are defined using the labelling semantics. The argumentation frameworks are updated as a dialogue proceeds. Accepted arguments in the current argumentation framework are considered to be her current beliefs. When her opponent gives an argument that is not accepted in her prediction of the opponent's argumentation framework, then she can point out the fact that the argument is suspicious. When an agent points out a suspicious argument, the opponent will make an excuse, if possible. An excuse may be accepted or suspected again. Also, if an excuse cannot be given, the suspect of the argument is not cleared. An agent sometimes succeeds in persuasion by accumulating dishonest arguments, and sometimes fails with the revelation of those dishonest arguments.

We illustrate how the defined protocol works and show that an excuse can be finally accepted after repetitive excuses if the agent always gives honest arguments. Furthermore, we discuss conditions on the agents' argumentation frameworks so that an agent succeeds in persuasion using dishonest arguments.

The rest of the paper is organized as follows. Section 2 describes the argumentation framework on which our model is based. Section 3 formalizes our dialogue protocol and concepts regarding dishonesty. Section 4 shows how this protocol works. Section 5 discusses the properties of the model. Section 6 compares our approach with other approaches. Finally, Sect. 7 presents our conclusions.

2   Argumentation Framework

Dung's abstract argumentation framework is defined as the pair of a set and a binary relationship on the set [7].

Definition 1 (argumentation framework). An argumentation framework *is defined as a pair* $\langle AR, AT \rangle$ *where AR is the set of arguments and AT is a binary relationship on AR, called* an attack. *If* $(A, A') \in AT$, *we say that A attacks A'.*

We define inclusions between argumentation frameworks.

Definition 2 (sub-AF). *Let* $\mathcal{AF}_1 = \langle AR_1, AT_1 \rangle$ *and* $\mathcal{AF}_2 = \langle AR_2, AT_2 \rangle$ *be argumentation frameworks. If* $AR_1 \subseteq AR_2$ *and* $AT_1 = AT_2 \cap (AR_1 \times AR_1)$, *then it is said that* $\mathcal{AF}_1$ *is* a sub-argumentation framework (sub-AF, in short) *of* $\mathcal{AF}_2$ *and denoted by* $\mathcal{AF}_1 \subseteq \mathcal{AF}_2$.

For a given argumentation framework, we give its semantics based on labelling [4].

Definition 3 (labelling). *Let* $\mathcal{AF} = \langle AR, AT \rangle$ *be an argumentation framework. A labelling is a total function* $\mathcal{L}^{\mathcal{AF}}$: *from AR to* $\{in, out, undec\}$.

The idea underlying the labelling is to give each argument a label. Specifically, the label *in* means that the argument is accepted in the argumentation framework, the label *out* means that the argument is rejected, and the label *undec* means one abstains from an opinion as to whether the argument is accepted or rejected.

Definition 4 (complete labelling). *Let* $\mathcal{AF} = \langle AR, AT \rangle$ *be an argumentation framework and* $\mathcal{L}^{\mathcal{AF}}$ *its labelling. If the following condition holds for each $A \in AR$, then* $\mathcal{L}^{\mathcal{AF}}$ *is said to be* a complete labelling *on* $\mathcal{AF}$.

1. $\mathcal{L}^{\mathcal{AF}}(A) = in$ *iff* $\forall A' \in AR$ ($(A', A) \in AT \Rightarrow \mathcal{L}^{\mathcal{AF}}(A') = out$).
2. $\mathcal{L}^{\mathcal{AF}}(A) = out$ *iff* $\exists A' \in AR$ ($(A', A) \in AT \wedge \mathcal{L}^{\mathcal{AF}}(A') = in$).
3. $\mathcal{L}^{\mathcal{AF}}(A) = undec$ *iff* $\mathcal{L}^{\mathcal{AF}}(A) \neq in \wedge \mathcal{L}^{\mathcal{AF}}(A) \neq out$.

Note that if an argument A is attacked by no arguments, then $\mathcal{L}^{\mathcal{AF}}(A) = in$.

Definition 5 (grounded labelling). *Let* $\mathcal{AF}$ *be an argumentation framework. The* grounded labelling *of* $\mathcal{AF}$ *is a complete labelling* $\mathcal{L}^{\mathcal{AF}}$ *where a set of arguments that are labelled 'in' is minimal with respect to set inclusion.*

A unique grounded labelling exists for any argumentation framework. For argumentation framework $\mathcal{AF}$ and its complete/grounded labelling $\mathcal{L}^{\mathcal{AF}}$, the set of arguments labelled *in* coincides with a complete/grounded extension of $\mathcal{AF}$ in extension-based semantics [4]. There are various semantics based on labelling, but here, we use the term "labelling" to mean grounded labelling.

Additionally, we define several other concepts used in Sect. 5 where we discuss the properties of this model.

Definition 6 (argumentation framework on an argument). *Let* $\mathcal{AF} = \langle AR, AT \rangle$ *be an argumentation framework, and* $A \in AR$ *be an argument. A sub-AF* $\mathcal{AF}' = \langle AR', AT' \rangle$ *that satisfies the following conditions is called an argumentation framework of* $\mathcal{AF}$ *on* A:

- $A \in AR'$
- *If* $B \in AR'$ *and* $(C, B) \in AT$, *then* $C \in AR'$ *and* $(C, B) \in AT'$

If an argumentation framework is a tree, it is said to be an *argumentation tree*. In an argumentation tree, the depth of the root node is 0, and a node at which the depth is even/odd is called an *even/odd node*.

Definition 7 (strong argumentation framework). *Let* $\mathcal{TAF}_1$ *and* $\mathcal{TAF}_2$ *be argumentation trees of which the root nodes correspond to the same argument, and* $\mathcal{TAF}_1 \subseteq \mathcal{TAF}_2$. *For any argument* A *of a leaf that is an odd node in* $\mathcal{TAF}_1$, *there exists an argument* A' *that attacks* A *in* $\mathcal{TAF}_2$. *Then it is said that* $\mathcal{TAF}_2$ *is stronger than* $\mathcal{TAF}_1$.

We can divide argumentation tree into a finite number of strategic argumentation trees.

Definition 8 (strategic argumentation tree). *For an argumentation tree, its* strategic argumentation tree *is its sub-AF containing all the child nodes of each even node and exactly one child node of each odd node.*

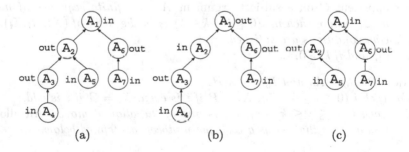

Fig. 1. Argumentation tree and its strategic argumentation trees with their labels

For example, Fig. 1(a) shows an argumentation tree and Fig. 1(b), (c) show its strategic argumentation trees.

3 Argumentative Dialogue Model

An argumentative dialogue is a sequence of arguments provided by agents following the protocol. Each agent has her own argumentation framework, as well as her prediction of the opponent's argumentation framework, and makes a move in a dialogue using them. When an argument is given, then these argumentation frameworks are updated.

Consider a dialogue between agents X and Y. We assume a *universal argumentation framework* $\mathcal{UAF}$ that contains every argument that can be constructed from all the available information in the universe [14]. We naturally assume that $\mathcal{UAF}$ does not contain an argument that attacks itself. Let $\mathcal{AF}_X$ and $\mathcal{AF}_Y$ be argumentation frameworks of X and Y, respectively, where $\mathcal{AF}_X$, $\mathcal{AF}_Y \subseteq \mathcal{UAF}$; let $\mathcal{PAF}_Y$ and $\mathcal{PAF}_X$ be X's prediction of Y's argumentation framework and Y's prediction of X's argumentation framework respectively. That is, X has two argumentation frameworks, $\mathcal{AF}_X$ and $\mathcal{PAF}_Y$, and Y has $\mathcal{AF}_Y$ and $\mathcal{PAF}_X$. We assume several inclusion relationships among these argumentation frameworks. First, we assume $\mathcal{PAF}_X \subseteq \mathcal{AF}_X$ and $\mathcal{PAF}_Y \subseteq \mathcal{AF}_Y$, because common sense or widely prevalent facts are known to all agents, while there may be some facts that only the opponent knows and other facts that the agent is not sure whether the opponent knows. Additionally, we assume that $\mathcal{PAF}_Y \subseteq \mathcal{AF}_X$, $\mathcal{PAF}_X \subseteq \mathcal{AF}_Y$, because a prediction is made using an agent's own knowledge.

We introduce acts in a persuasion dialogue. The act *assert* is asserting an argument, *suspect* is pointing out a suspicious argument, and *excuse* is giving an excuse for it.

Definition 9 (act). *An act is assert, suspect, or excuse.*

Definition 10 (move). A move *is a triple* (X, R, T), *where X is an agent, R is an argument, and T is an act.*

Definition 11 (dialogue). A dialogue d_k $(k \geq 0)$ between a persuader P and her opponent C on a subject argument A_0 *is a finite sequence of moves* $[m_0, \ldots, m_{k-1}]$ *where each m_i $(0 \leq i \leq k - 1)$ is in the form of (X_i, R_i, T_i) and the following conditions are satisfied:*
   $d_0 = [\,]$; and if $k > 0$,

   (i) $X_0 = P$, $R_0 = A_0$ and $T_0 =$ assert.
   (ii) For each i $(0 \leq i \leq k - 1)$, $X_i = P$ if i is even, $X_i = C$ if i is odd.
   (iii) For each i $(0 \leq i \leq k - 1)$, m_i is one of the allowed moves. An allowed move *is a move that obeys a dialogue protocol, as defined below.*

For a dialogue $d_k = [m_0, \ldots, m_{k-1}]$, an argumentation framework of agent X for d_k is denoted by $\mathcal{AF}_X^{d_k}$. An agent X's prediction of Y's argumentation framework for d_k is denoted by $\mathcal{PAF}_Y^{d_k}$. $\mathcal{AF}_X^{d_0}$ and $\mathcal{PAF}_Y^{d_0}$ are X's argumentation framework and her prediction of Y's argumentation framework given at an initial state.

A dialogue protocol is a set of rules for each act. An agent can give an argument contained in her argumentation framework at an instant. The preconditions of each act of agent X for d_k are formalized as follows. Hereafter, the symbol "_" in a move stands for anonymous.

Definition 12 (allowed move). Let X, Y be agents, and $d_k = [m_0, \ldots, m_{k-1}]$ be a dialogue. Let $\mathcal{AF}_X^{d_k} = \langle AR_X^{d_k}, AT_X^{d_k} \rangle$ and $\mathcal{PAF}_Y^{d_k} = \langle PAR_Y^{d_k}, PAT_Y^{d_k} \rangle$ be X's argumentation framework and X's prediction of Y's argumentation framework for d_k, respectively. If a move m_k satisfies the precondition, then m_k is said to be an allowed move for d_k.

When $k = 0$, $(X, A_0, assert)$ is an allowed move where A_0 is a subject argument.

When $k > 0$, the precondition of each move is defined as follows.

- $(X, A, assert)$:
  - $m_k \neq m_i$ for $\forall i$ $(0 \leq i < k)$
    (It is not allowed more than once throughout the dialogue.)
  - $m_{k-1} \neq (Y, \_, suspect)$
    (The act immediately before the move is not suspect.)
  - $\exists j$ $(0 \leq j < k)$; $m_j = (Y, A', \_)$ and $(A, A') \in AT_X^{d_k}$
    (It is a counterargument to an argument previously given.)
- $(X, A, suspect)$:
  - $m_{k-1} \neq (Y, \_, suspect)$
    (The act immediately before the move is not suspect.)
  - $\exists j$ $(0 \leq j < k)$; $m_j = (Y, A', \_)$ and $(A, A') \in PAT_Y^{d_k}$
    (It is a counterargument to an argument previously given in her prediction.)
  - $\mathcal{L}^{\mathcal{PAF}_Y^{d_k}}(A) \neq out$
    (The label is not out in her prediction.)
- $(X, A, excuse)$:
  - $m_{k-1} = (Y, A', suspect)$ and $(A, A') \in AT_X^{d_k}$ and $(\ \neg\exists(A_0, A_1, \ldots, A_n)$, $(n > 1)$ where $A_0 = A_n = A$, $A_1 = A'$ and $(A_{i-1}, A_i) \in AT_X^{d_k}$ $(1 \leq \forall i \leq n)\ )$
    (The act immediately before the move is suspect, and a counterargument to the argument immediately preceding this one, and there is no cycle of attacks including (A, A').)

Basically, an agent can give either a move of $(X, \_, assert)$ or $(X, \_, suspect)$ when both are allowed. However, we give priority to the move of *suspect* because here we are interested in dishonest arguments and it is not suitable to leave a suspicious argument.

A move of type *suspect* is to point out: "I suspect that you used argument A' while hiding another argument A." Y then has to demonstrate that they are not being deceptive by immediately giving a counterargument. This is an excuse. Intuitively, when X thinks that Y is deceiving them, X is suspicious; then Y immediately asserts that they believe what they are saying.

At each move, an argument in each agent's argumentation framework is disclosed. This may cause new arguments and new attacks to be put forward.

A move of type *suspect* represents a suspicion on the previous argument, and leads to no new arguments. This leads us to the following definition of an update of an argumentation framework with respect to a particular argument.

Definition 13 (update of argumentation framework). *Let* $\mathcal{UAF} = \langle UAR, UAT \rangle$ *be a universal argumentation framework. Let* $\mathcal{AF} = \langle AR, AT \rangle$ *be an argumentation framework,* $A \in UAR$*, and* S *be a set of arguments caused to be generated by* A*, where the condition "if* $A \in AR$ *then* $S \subseteq AR$*" holds. Then,* $\mathcal{AF}' = \langle AR \cup AR', AT \cup AT' \rangle$ *is said to be* an argumentation framework of $\mathcal{AF}$ *updated by* A*, where* $AR' = \{A\} \cup S$ *and* $AT' = \{(B,C) | (B,C) \in UAT, (B \in AR', C \in AR) \vee (B \in AR, C \in AR') \vee (B \in AR', C \in AR')\}$ [1].

After the move $m_k = (X, R, T)$, the following updates are performed: d_{k+1} is obtained from d_k by adding m_k to its end; $\mathcal{AF}_Y^{d_{k+1}}$, $\mathcal{PAF}_X^{d_{k+1}}$ and $\mathcal{PAF}_Y^{d_{k+1}}$ are argumentation frameworks of $\mathcal{AF}_Y^{d_k}$, $\mathcal{PAF}_X^{d_k}$ and $\mathcal{PAF}_Y^{d_k}$ updated by R, respectively; $\mathcal{AF}_X^{d_k}$ remains unchanged.

Deception is giving an argument while hiding an argument that attacks it, and "dishonesty" in this paper means deception.

Definition 14 (honest/dishonest move). *For a dialogue* $d_k = [m_0, \ldots, m_{k-1}]$ *where* $m_k = (X, R, T)$*, if* $\mathcal{L}^{\mathcal{AF}_X^{d_k}}(R) = in$*, then* m_k *is said to be* X*'s* honest move *and* R *is said to be* an honest argument; *otherwise,* m_k *is said to be* X*'s* dishonest move *and* R *is said to be* a dishonest argument.

Definition 15 (suspicious move). *For a dialogue* $d_k = [m_0, \ldots, m_{k-1}]$ *where* $m_{k-1} = (X, R, assert)$ *or* $m_{k-1} = (X, R, excuse)$*, if* $\mathcal{L}^{\mathcal{PAF}_X^{d_k}}(R) \neq in$*, then* m_{k-1} *is said to be* a suspicious move *for* Y*, and* R *is said to be* a suspicious argument.

Definition 16 (cleared suspicious argument). *If* $m_{k-1} = (X, R, T)$ *is a* suspicious move *for* Y*, and there exists* h*;* $k < h$ *and* $\mathcal{L}^{\mathcal{PAF}_X^{d_h}}(R) = in$*, then* R *is said to be a* cleared suspicious argument *for* Y *at* d_h*, and it is said that a* suspicious argument R for Y is cleared *at* d_h.

Note that "honest" is a concept for the persuader, whereas "suspicious" is that for her opponent. Hence, a dishonest argument is not always a suspicious argument and a suspicious argument is not always a dishonest argument.

If neither agent has an allowed move, then the dialogue terminates. There are two types of termination. The first case is the one in which an agent cannot make an excuse when her opponent points out her deception. In this case, she is regarded as dishonest because she cannot make an excuse, regardless of whether she actually made a dishonest move. The second case is the one in which there exists d_k such that neither agent can make an *assert* or *suspect* move. In this case, it is said that *persuasion of* X *by a subject argument* A_0 *succeeds* if $\mathcal{L}^{\mathcal{AF}_Y^{d_k}}(A_0) = in$ holds; *persuasion by a subject argument fails,* otherwise.

---

[1] $\mathcal{AF}'$ can be calculated without assuming $\mathcal{UAF}$ and S, if we handle an argumentation framework instantiated with logical formulas. In this case, we construct an argumentation framework by logical deduction from a given set of formulas [1,17].

4   Examples of Dishonest Dialogues

We consider three scenarios in which suspicious moves occur. In these scenarios, persuader X gives dishonest arguments so that she tries to make the opponent Y to believe a subject argument. The opponent Y may suspect X's argument and point out the deception, X tries to give an excuse against Y's pointing out. These scenarios show how the opponent Y reveals X's dishonest arguments using her prediction.

Let $\mathcal{AF}_X^{d_0}$ and $\mathcal{PAF}_X^{d_0}$ be X's argumentation framework and Y's prediction of X's argumentation framework given at an initial state. For simplicity, we assume in these scenarios that no new arguments can be derived from the argument put forward at each move.

Scenario 1:

(X, A, assert): "Let's apply to Charlie's laboratory, because he is generous."
(Y, B, suspect): "You know that Charlie is strict, and you also know that I do not like strict professors. Don't try to persuade me by hiding this fact."
(X, C, excuse): "No, he is not strict, because I got an excellent grade last year, although my report was not very good."
(Y, D, suspect): "I don't think so, because I heard that some students failed. Don't try to persuade me by hiding this fact."

Assume that $\mathcal{AF}_X^{d_0}$ and $\mathcal{PAF}_X^{d_0}$ are shown in Fig. 2(a) and (b), respectively. In this case, $\mathcal{AF}_X^{d_0}$ is unchanged and $\mathcal{PAF}_X^{d_0}$ is changed after the move m_2 (Fig. 2(c)).

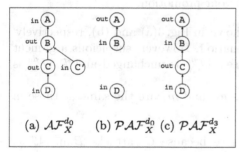

(a) $\mathcal{AF}_X^{d_0}$ (b) $\mathcal{PAF}_X^{d_0}$ (c) $\mathcal{PAF}_X^{d_3}$ (a) $\mathcal{AF}_X^{d_0}$ (b) $\mathcal{PAF}_X^{d_0}$ (c) $\mathcal{PAF}_X^{d_3}$

Fig. 2. Argumentation frameworks in Scenario 1

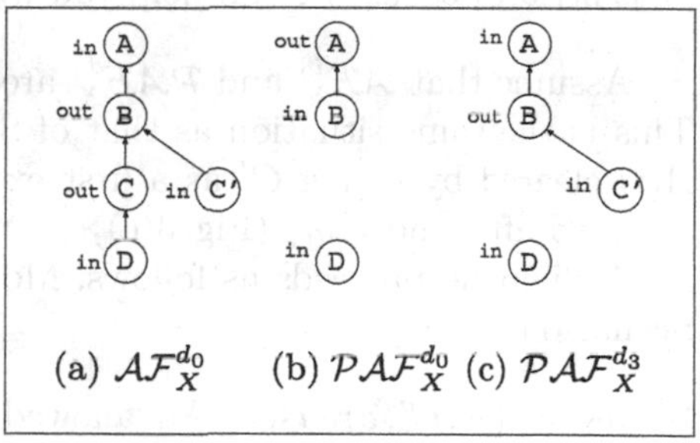

Fig. 3. Argumentation frameworks in Scenario 2

A dialogue proceeds as follows.

1. $m_0 = (X, A, assert)$: The first move. It is a suspicious move for Y because $\mathcal{L}^{\mathcal{PAF}_X^{d_1}}(A) \neq in$.

2. $m_1 = (Y, B, suspect)$: An allowed move because $\mathcal{L}^{\mathcal{PAF}_X^{d_1}}(B) \neq out$ and B attacks A in $\mathcal{PAF}_X^{d_1}$.

3. $m_2 = (X, C, excuse)$: An allowed move because C attacks B in $\mathcal{AF}_X^{d_2}$. An attack (D, C) is an attack of $\mathcal{UAF}$, because $\mathcal{AF}_X^{d_0} \subseteq \mathcal{UAF}$. Therefore, $\mathcal{PAF}_X^{d_2}$ is updated by C to get $\mathcal{PAF}_X^{d_3}$. It is also a suspicious move for Y because $\mathcal{L}^{\mathcal{PAF}_X^{d_3}}(C) \neq in$ (Fig. 2(c)).

4. $m_3 = (Y, D, suspect)$: An allowed move because $\mathcal{L}^{\mathcal{PAF}_X^{d_3}}(D) \neq out$ and D attacks C in $\mathcal{PAF}_X^{d_3}$.

5. X cannot give an *excuse* and the dialogue terminates at d_4.

When C is given by X, it causes Y to create a new opportunity for an attack against X. Note that X has C' as a counterargument to B. However, the move containing C' is not allowed as m_4, because X should make an excuse for D in m_3 immediately.

In X's viewpoint, she gave two arguments, A and C. A is an honest argument, because $\mathcal{L}^{\mathcal{AF}_X^{d_0}}(A) = in$ and C is a dishonest argument, because $\mathcal{L}^{\mathcal{AF}_X^{d_2}}(C) \neq in$. In Y's viewpoint, both arguments are suspicious arguments for Y, and neither is cleared at d_4, because $\mathcal{L}^{\mathcal{PAF}_Y^{d_4}}(A) \neq in$ and $\mathcal{L}^{\mathcal{PAF}_Y^{d_4}}(C) \neq in$.

This scenario shows that X deceives her opponent, and that the deception is revealed.

Scenario 2:
The third argument in Scenario 1 is replaced by the following argument.

(X, C', excuse): "You should apply to Charlie's lab., despite the fact that he is strict, because he can help you with your promotion."

Assume that $\mathcal{AF}_X^{d_0}$ and $\mathcal{PAF}_X^{d_0}$ are shown in Fig. 3(a) and (b), respectively. This is the same situation as that of Scenario 1. However, suspicious argument A is cleared by giving C' as a first excuse. $\mathcal{AF}_X^{d_0}$ is unchanged and $\mathcal{PAF}_X^{d_0}$ is changed after move m_2 (Fig. 3(c)).

A dialogue proceeds as follows. Moves m_0 and m_1 are the same as those in Scenario 1.

3. $m_2 = (X, C', excuse)$: An allowed move because C' attacks B in $\mathcal{AF}_X^{d_2}$, $\mathcal{PAF}_X^{d_2}$ is updated by C' to get $\mathcal{PAF}_X^{d_3}$, and as a result, m_2 is not a suspicious move for Y because $\mathcal{L}^{\mathcal{PAF}_X^{d_3}}(C') = in$ (Fig. 3(c)).

4. Y cannot give *suspect* any more.

From X's viewpoint, she gave two arguments A and C', both of which were honest because $\mathcal{L}^{\mathcal{AF}_X^{d_0}}(A) = in$ and $\mathcal{L}^{\mathcal{AF}_X^{d_2}}(C') = in$. From Y's viewpoint, A is a suspicious argument for Y but finally cleared at d_3. C' is not a suspicious argument intrinsically. Agent Y may have more arguments, because $\mathcal{PAF}_X^{d_3} \subseteq \mathcal{AF}_Y^{d_3}$. Therefore, if Y has an allowed move for d_3, then the dialogue continues by enabling a move of type *assert*; otherwise, it terminates, and X succeeds in persuading Y, because $\mathcal{L}^{\mathcal{A}\mathcal{F}_Y^{d_3}}(A) = in$.

This scenario shows that X is always honest and even if her moves are suspicious, they are finally cleared.

Scenario 3:
The following argument is added to the end of the dialogue in Scenario 1.

(X, E, excuse): "It's just a rumour. I read the publication board and found out that all the students passed the exam."

Assume that $\mathcal{A}\mathcal{F}_X^{d_0}$ and $\mathcal{P}\mathcal{A}\mathcal{F}_X^{d_0}$ are shown in Fig. 4(a) and (b), respectively. It is a modified version of Scenario 1. The difference is that $\mathcal{A}\mathcal{F}_X^{d_0}$ has more arguments E and F. After moves m_2 and m_4, respectively, $\mathcal{A}\mathcal{F}_X^{d_0}$ is unchanged and $\mathcal{P}\mathcal{A}\mathcal{F}_X^{d_0}$ is changed (Fig. 3(c), (d)).

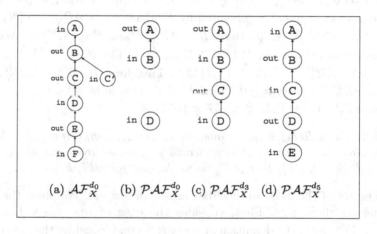

$$\text{(a) } \mathcal{A}\mathcal{F}_X^{d_0} \quad \text{(b) } \mathcal{P}\mathcal{A}\mathcal{F}_X^{d_0} \quad \text{(c) } \mathcal{P}\mathcal{A}\mathcal{F}_X^{d_3} \quad \text{(d) } \mathcal{P}\mathcal{A}\mathcal{F}_X^{d_5}$$

Fig. 4. Argumentation frameworks in Scenario 3

A dialogue proceeds as follows. Moves from m_0 to m_3 are the same as those in Scenario 1.

5. $m_4 = (X, E, excuse)$: An allowed move because E attacks D in $\mathcal{A}\mathcal{F}_X^{d_4}$, $\mathcal{P}\mathcal{A}\mathcal{F}_X^{d_4}$ is updated by E, and as a result, m_4 is not a suspicious move for Y because $\mathcal{L}^{\mathcal{P}\mathcal{A}\mathcal{F}_X^{d_5}}(E) = in$ (Fig. 4(d)).
6. Y cannot give *suspect* any more.

From X's viewpoint, she gave three arguments A, C and E. A is an honest argument, because $\mathcal{L}^{\mathcal{A}\mathcal{F}_X^{d_0}}(A) = in$ whereas C and E are dishonest arguments, because $\mathcal{L}^{\mathcal{A}\mathcal{F}_X^{d_2}}(C) \neq in$ and $\mathcal{L}^{\mathcal{A}\mathcal{F}_X^{d_4}}(E) \neq in$. From Y's viewpoint, A and C

are suspicious arguments for Y and cleared at d_5 because $\mathcal{L}^{\mathcal{PAF}_X^{d_5}}(A) = in$ and $\mathcal{L}^{\mathcal{PAF}_X^{d_5}}(C) = in$. E is not a suspicious argument intrinsically. Similar to the case in Scenario 2, X succeeds in persuasion depending on $\mathcal{AF}_Y^{d_5}$.

This scenario shows that X deceives repetitively, and that it is not revealed.

5   Properties of the Model

We discuss two properties that hold in our dialogue model. The first one implies that an excuse can be finally accepted after repetitive excuses if the agent always gives honest arguments. The second one shows a condition in which a suspicious argument is finally cleared.

Lemma 1. *For a dialogue d_k, $\mathcal{PAF}_X^{d_k} \subseteq \mathcal{AF}_X^{d_k}$ holds.*

Proof. We prove this by induction. Let $\mathcal{AF}_X^{d_k} = \langle AR_X^{d_k}, AT_X^{d_k} \rangle$ and $\mathcal{PAF}_X^{d_k} = \langle PAR_X^{d_k}, PAT_X^{d_k} \rangle$. $\mathcal{PAF}_X^{d_0} \subseteq \mathcal{AF}_X^{d_0}$ holds. For $k > 0$, let $m_{k-1} = (X_{k-1}, R, T)$ and S be a set of arguments generated by R. $PAR_X^{d_k} = PAR_X^{d_{k-1}} \cup \{R\} \cup S$. If $X_{k-1} = X$, $AR_X^{d_{k-1}} = AR_X^{d_k}$. Here, $R \in AR_X^{d_{k-1}}$ and $S \subseteq AR_X^{d_{k-1}}$. According to the induction hypothesis, $PAR_X^{d_{k-1}} \subseteq AR_X^{d_{k-1}}$. Therefore, $PAR_X^{d_k} \subseteq AR_X^{d_k}$. If $X_{k-1} = Y$, $AR_X^{d_k} = AR_X^{d_{k-1}} \cup \{R\} \cup S$. Therefore, $PAR_X^{d_k} \subseteq AR_X^{d_k}$. Thus, $PAR_X^{d_k} \subseteq AR_X^{d_k}$ for every $k \geq 0$. From the definition of attacks, it is trivial that $PAT_X^{d_k} \subseteq AT_X^{d_k}$. Thus, $\mathcal{PAF}_X^{d_k} \subseteq \mathcal{AF}_X^{d_k}$ holds.   □

Lemma 2. *For a dialogue $d_{h+1} = [m_0, m_1, \ldots, m_k, \ldots, m_h]$, if $m_{k-1} = (X, R, T)$ is a suspicious move for Y, R is a cleared suspicious argument at d_h but not cleared at d_i ($k \leq i < h$), then $\mathcal{AF}_X^{d_i}$ is unchanged for all i; $k \leq i < h$.*

Proof. The act of the move m_i is either *excuse* or *suspect*. We prove the lemma depending on these acts. First, consider the case of $m_i = (X, B, excuse)$. $\mathcal{AF}_X^{d_{i+1}} = \mathcal{AF}_X^{d_i}$ from the definition of update. Second, consider the case of $m_i = (Y, B, suspect)$. Let $\mathcal{AF}_X^{d_i} = \langle AR_X^{d_i}, AT_X^{d_i} \rangle$ and $\mathcal{PAF}_X^{d_i} = \langle PAR_X^{d_i}, PAT_X^{d_i} \rangle$. Here, $B \in PAR_X^{d_i}$, and $PAR_X^{d_i} \subseteq AR_X^{d_i}$ from Lemma 1. $AR_X^{d_{i+1}} = AR_X^{d_i} \cup \{B\}$ holds, since B does not cause new arguments to be generated. Thus, $AR_X^{d_{i+1}} \subseteq AR_X^{d_i}$ holds. Similarly, $AT_X^{d_{i+1}} \subseteq AT_X^{d_i}$ holds. Thus, $\mathcal{AF}_X^{d_{i+1}} \subseteq \mathcal{AF}_X^{d_i}$ holds. On the other hand, $\mathcal{AF}_X^{d_i} \subseteq \mathcal{AF}_X^{d_{i+1}}$ holds from the definition of update. Hence, $\mathcal{AF}_X^{d_{i+1}} = \mathcal{AF}_X^{d_i}$ holds.   □

Proposition 1. *For a dialogue $d_{k+1} = [m_0, \ldots, m_{k-1}, m_k]$, let $m_{k-1} = (X, A, T)$ and $m_k = (Y, B, suspect)$. If $m_{k-1} = (X, A, T)$ is an honest move, then X can give an honest move $m_{k+1} = (X, C, excuse)$.*

Proof. Let $\mathcal{AF}_X^{d_k} = \langle AR_X^{d_k}, AT_X^{d_k} \rangle$ and $\mathcal{PAF}_X^{d_k} = \langle PAR_X^{d_k}, PAT_X^{d_k} \rangle$. Since m_{k-1} is an honest move and X's argumentation framework does not change after giving m_{k-1}, $\mathcal{L}^{\mathcal{AF}_X^{d_k}}(A) = in \cdots$ (1). On the other hand, since $m_k = (Y, B, suspect)$,

$\mathcal{L}^{\mathcal{PAF}_X^{d_k}}(B) \neq out$ and $(B, A) \in PAT_X^{d_k}$. Here, $(B, A) \in AT_X^{d_k}$, because $\mathcal{PAF}_X^{d_k} \subseteq \mathcal{AF}_X^{d_k}$ from Lemma 1. From (1), $\mathcal{L}^{\mathcal{AF}_X^{d_k}}(B) = out$, which means that there exists an argument C such that $(C, B) \in AT_X^{d_k}$ and $\mathcal{L}^{\mathcal{AF}_X^{d_k}}(C) = in$. $\mathcal{L}^{\mathcal{AF}_X^{d_{k+1}}}(C) = in$, because $\mathcal{AF}_X^{d_k} = \mathcal{AF}_X^{d_{k+1}}$ from Lemma 2. Thus, $(C, B) \in AT_X^{d_{k+1}}$ and $\mathcal{L}^{\mathcal{AF}_X^{d_{k+1}}}(C) = in$. Thus, $m_{k+1} = (X, C, excuse)$ is X's allowed move and an excuse for m_k.   □

Next, we consider the condition on which a suspicious argument is finally cleared.

We do not have to survey all possible dialogues to decide it, but just check the argumentation frameworks at the state in which the suspicious argument occurs. We use strategic argumentation trees of the argumentation tree on a subject argument. Intuitively, for the argumentation tree on a subject argument, each strategic argumentation tree represents a set of possible dialogues based on a persuader's specific moves.

The condition should be that the opponent has no attack to the persuader's argument in the final move of type *excuse*, according to her prediction. Since the opponent's prediction is a subset of the persuader's argumentation framework, all leaf nodes in the persuader's argumentation framework are labelled *in*. This condition is rather strict and can be loosened so that: first, the labels of the leaf nodes are not necessarily *in*, and second, it is enough to consider only one strategic argumentation tree.

Before describing the condition, we introduce the concept of a complemented argumentation framework (compl-AF). When an agent is given a new argument by her opponent, a new attack may be generated from the existing arguments to the new argument by the update process. The complemented argumentation framework contains the possible results of the succeeding updates.

Definition 17 (compl-AF). *Let $\mathcal{AF} = \langle AR, AT \rangle$ be an argumentation framework and $\mathcal{TAF}$ be an argumentation tree, such that $\mathcal{AF} \subseteq \mathcal{TAF}$. If there exists a branch $(A_1, \ldots, A_{n-1}, A', A_n)$ in $\mathcal{TAF}$ such that $A_1, \ldots, A_{n-1}, A_n \in AR$ and $A' \notin AR$, then set $AR' = AR \cup \{A'\}$, $AT'' = AT \cup \{(A_n, A'), (A', A_{n-1})\}$. An argumentation framework $\langle AR', AT' \rangle$ obtained by doing this update for all such arguments A' is said to be a complemented argumentation framework (compl-AF, in short) of $\mathcal{AF}$ wrt $\mathcal{TAF}$.*

Compl-AF is an argumentation tree. Figure 5 shows its example.

Proposition 2. *For a dialogue d_k ($k > 0$), assume that $m_{k-1} = (X, A, \_)$ and $m_k = (Y, B, suspect)$ are given. Let $\mathcal{TAF}_X^{d_k}$ be an argumentation framework of $\mathcal{AF}_X^{d_k}$ on a subject argument. (i) If $\mathcal{TAF}_X^{d_k}$ is an argumentation tree, and (ii) if there exist a strategic argumentation tree SS_X of $\mathcal{TAF}_X^{d_k}$ and a strategic argumentation tree SS_Y of the compl-AF of $\mathcal{PAF}_X^{d_k}$ wrt $\mathcal{TAF}_X^{d_k}$, such that SS_X is stronger than SS_Y, then there exists h such that $k < h$, $\mathcal{L}^{\mathcal{PAF}_X^{d_h}}(A) = in$.*

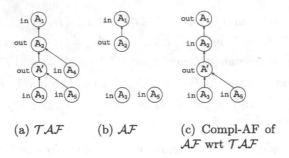

(a) $\mathcal{TAF}$ (b) $\mathcal{AF}$ (c) Compl-AF of
                                                        $\mathcal{AF}$ wrt $\mathcal{TAF}$

Fig. 5. Complemented argumentation framework

Sketch of Proof.

SS_X is a sub-AF of $\mathcal{AF}_X^{d_k}$ and it is an argumentation tree. The idea of the proof is: first showing that X can proceed in a dialogue along a branch of SS_X and give *excuse* whenever Y gives *suspect*; and then relating this to the labelling of $\mathcal{PAF}_X^{d_h}$.

First, we show that X can give *excuse* whenever Y gives *suspect*. For each k', such that $k \leq k'$, X can give a move $m_{k'+1} = (X, D, excuse)$ against a move $m_{k'} = (Y, C, suspect)$ as follows.

- If there is an attack (D, C) in $\mathcal{PAF}_X^{d'_k}$, then it is also an attack in $\mathcal{AF}_X^{d'_k}$, and so $m_{k'+1}$ is an allowed move.
- Else if there is an attack (D, C) in SS_Y, it is also an attack in SS_X, and so $m_{k'+1}$ is an allowed move.
- Otherwise, there exists an attack (D, C) in SS_X, where C is an argument of an odd node of SS_Y, because SS_X is stronger than SS_Y, and so $m_{k'+1}$ is an allowed move.

Next, we relate this to the labelling of $\mathcal{PAF}_X^{d_h}$. There exists d_h for which there is no allowed move. In the third case, argument D that is not included in SS_Y appears in the move. Assume that SS'_Y is obtained by adding all such arguments that appear in $m_{k+1}, \ldots, m_h$, to the odd nodes of SS_Y. Then, all of the leaves of SS'_Y are even nodes, and $\mathcal{L}^{SS'_Y}(A) = in$ and $\mathcal{L}^{SS'_Y}(B) = out$. Thus, there exists an argument E that attacks B such that $\mathcal{L}^{SS'_Y}(E) = in$. Considering $\mathcal{PAF}_X^{d'_k}$ is updated in the above second and third cases, $SS'_Y \subseteq \mathcal{PAF}_X^{d_h}$ holds. Since SS'_Y is an update of a strategic argumentation tree SS_Y, the argument E attacks B is also in $\mathcal{PAF}_X^{d_h}$, and $\mathcal{L}^{\mathcal{PAF}_X^{d_h}}(E) = in$. Thus, $\mathcal{L}^{\mathcal{PAF}_X^{d_h}}(B) = out$, and finally we get $\mathcal{L}^{\mathcal{PAF}_X^{d_h}}(A) = in$. □

This proposition shows a condition for which a suspicious argument is cleared if the agent selects a proper move under the specified condition. For example, suspicious arguments are cleared in Scenario 2, but not cleared in Scenario 1.

From this property, when a persuader has enough arguments in her argumentation framework that can attack whatever argument her opponent gives, she may succeed in persuasion without her dishonesty being revealed.

6 Related Works

There have been a few works on dishonest argumentation. Caminada proposed a classification of dishonesty occurring in multi-agent systems as well as human society, and described the relationship with argumentation [6]. Sakama formalized an untrusted argumentation including a lie and bullshit [14,15]. His formalization is from the viewpoint of the agent who gives a dishonest argument, and not from the agent that receives it. He did not define a protocol for pointing out a lie or one for making an excuse. On the other hand, we consider the situation from the viewpoints of both agents, and define protocols for pointing out a deception and making excuses. Additionally, his model is simpler in which only one argument is added at each move, while we consider the case where more arguments are caused to be generated. Rahwan et al. discussed hiding and lying in argumentation using game-theory techniques [12]. The most significant difference between our work and these other works is the usage of a predicted argumentation framework.

It is essential to consider an opponent's beliefs, especially when handling a strategic dialogue. Several works have examined this issue. Thimm et al. studied a strategy that reflected an opponent's belief [16], but they did not relate the belief to an acceptance of an argumentation framework. Rienstra et al. presented a strategy for selecting the best move from multiple opponent models with probability [13], and Hadjinikolis el al. showed an approach for augmenting opponent models from accumulated dialogues with an agent's likelihood [8]. They evaluated their approaches experimentally, whereas we focused on the theoretical aspects of our protocols. Black et al. investigated the usage and maintenance of opponent models formally, illustrating a simple persuasion dialogue with different types of persuader [5]. These works also did not discuss dishonesty.

Prakken et al. studied the "burden of proof" in legal persuasion dialogues [10]. They focused on the case where an agent has to prove a subject or an argument by following protocols. An agent who is subjected to a move of type *excuse* is considered to have the burden of proof in our persuasion dialogue model. In contrast to our model, they discussed dialogues at the protocol level without considering argumentation frameworks.

7 Conclusions

We have formalized a dialogue that includes dishonest arguments in persuasion. Deception is a technique often used in real society, which is not regarded as dishonest at first glance. We formalized an argumentative dialogue that includes this situation. To this end, we proposed a dialogue model that uses a prediction of the opponent's argumentation framework. This is the first attempt at formalizing deception in this manner in the treatment of argumentative dialogues. Extension of this model should be considered so that it can handle other types of dishonest arguments, such as lies and bullshit.

404   K. Takahashi and S. Yokohama

We have also discussed the conditions required for an agent to successfully, dishonestly, persuade her opponent without revealing her dishonesty. We will generalize these conditions in future work.

Furthermore, in this paper we assume that a predicted argumentation framework is included within an actual one. The properties of models without this assumption should also be investigated.

References

1. Amgoud, L., Maudet, N., Parsons, S.: Modeling dialogues using argumentation. In: ICMAS2000, pp. 31–38 (2000)
2. Amgoud, L., de Saint-Cyr, F.D.: An axiomatic approach for persuasion dialogs. In: ICTAI 2013, pp. 618–625 (2013)
3. Bench-Capon, T.: Persuasion in practice argument using value-based argumentation frameworks. J. Log. Comput. **13**(3), 429–448 (2003)
4. Baroni, P., Caminada, M., Giacomin, G.: An introduction to argumentation semantics. Knowl. Eng. Rev. **26**(4), 365–410 (2011)
5. Black, E., Hunter, A.: Reasons and options for updating an opponent model in persuasion dialogues. In: Black, E., Modgil, S., Oren, N. (eds.) TAFA 2015. LNCS (LNAI), vol. 9524, pp. 21–39. Springer, Cham (2015). doi:10.1007/978-3-319-28460-6_2
6. Caminada, M.: Truth, Lies and Bullshit; distinguishing classes of dishonesty. IJCAI Workshop on Social, Simulation, pp. 39–50 (2009)
7. Dung, P.M.: On the acceptability of arguments and its fundamental role in non-monotonic reasoning, logic programming and n-person games. Artif. Intell. **77**, 321–357 (1995)
8. Hadjinikolis, C., Siantos, Y., Modgil, S., Black, E., McBurney, P.: Opponent modelling in persuasion dialogues. In: IJCAI 2013, pp. 164–170 (2013)
9. Prakken, H.: Formal systems for persuasion dialogue. Knowl. Eng. Rev. **21**(2), 163–188 (2006)
10. Prakken, H., Reed, C., Walton, D.: Dialogues about the burden of proof. In: ICAIL 2005, pp. 115–124 (2005)
11. Rahwan, I., Simari, G. (eds.): Argumentation in Artificial Intelligence. Springer, Heidelberg (2009)
12. Rahwan, I., Lason, K., Tohmé, F.: A characterization of strategy-proofness for grounded argumentation semantics. In: IJCAI 2009, pp. 251–256 (2009)
13. Rienstra, T., Thimm, M., Oren, N.: Opponent models with uncertainty for strategic argumentation. In: IJCAI 2013, pp. 332–338 (2013)
14. Sakama, C.: Dishonest arguments in debate games. COMMA 2012, pp. 177–184 (2012)
15. Sakama, C., Caminada, M., Herzig, A.: A formal account of dishonesty. Log. J. IGPL **23**(2), 259–294 (2015)
16. Thimm, M., García, A.J.: On strategic argument selection in structured argumentation systems. In: McBurney, P., Rahwan, I., Parsons, S. (eds.) ArgMAS 2010. LNCS (LNAI), vol. 6614, pp. 286–305. Springer, Heidelberg (2011). doi:10.1007/978-3-642-21940-5_17
17. Yokohama, S., Takahashi, K.: What should an agent know not to fail in persuasion? In: Rovatsos, M., Vouros, G., Julian, V. (eds.) EUMAS/AT -2015. LNCS (LNAI), vol. 9571, pp. 219–233. Springer, Cham (2016). doi:10.1007/978-3-319-33509-4_18

Propositional Belief Merging with T-conorms

Henrique Viana[(⊠)] and João Alcântara

Department of Computer Science, Federal University of Ceará, Fortaleza, Brazil
henrique.viana@ifce.edu.br, jnando@lia.ufc.br

Abstract. We analyze in this paper the impact of introducing fuzzy T-conorm operators in the area of belief merging. There are mainly two subclasses of merging operators: the utilitarian and the egalitarian ones. We prove that a T-conorm merging operator can be included in the subtype of egalitarian operators. We also study how the different T-conorm operators behave with respect to their logical properties and how this affects their rationality.

1 Introduction

When we face conflicting information coming from several sources, it is natural to try to reach a coherent piece of information from this contradiction. To tackle this problem, several merging operators have been defined and characterized in a logical way. Among them, the well-known model-based merging operators obtain a result by resorting to both a distance measure on interpretations and an aggregation function [14].

Considering the area of propositional belief merging, which studies the aggregation of independent and equally reliable sources of beliefs expressed in propositional logic, we need to consider some aspects of rationality. Indeed, there are two classes of belief merging operators: the utilitarian and egalitarian operators [8,14].

Utilitarianism sustains the idea that the best choice for a group is that which maximizes utility of the group. Utility can be measured in several ways, but is usually related to the well-being of the agents, e.g., the distance measure on interpretations for the model-based belief merging. The *sum* merging operator [14] is an example of utilitarian operator. Egalitarianism, on the other hand, tries to reach equality for all agents. The *max* [16] and *leximax* [14] merging operators are some examples of egalitarian operators. Intuitively, they seek to promote equality of the group by favoring the agents with the least well-being.

This work aims at exploring further egalitarian operators. The idea is to relax the *max* operator and employ fuzzy connectives. As it is known, T-conorms are functions stronger than the *max* operator, which can be commonly used to capture the worst cases in some group decision problems. The motivation for this paper is to offer a new view about different merging operators with good logical

This research is supported by CNPq and CAPES.

N. Criado Pacheco et al. (Eds.): EUMAS 2016/AT 2016, LNAI 10207, pp. 405–420, 2017.
DOI: 10.1007/978-3-319-59294-7_34

properties and rationality. Then we will prove that extensions of *max* operator can still preserve some logical properties and additionally earn new specific properties. Besides the original logical properties presented in literature, we will consider three other egalitarian conditions: the Hammond Equity Condition [8], Pigou-Dalton Principle [6,8] and the Harm Principle [2,4,17]. We will prove that in some cases, restricted versions of these axioms may be satisfied by some T-conorms. Lastly, we will make a connection between T-conorm operators and the *leximax* operator.

The paper is structured as follows. In Sects. 2 and 3, we will present some basic notions of propositional belief merging and T-conorms, respectively. In Sect. 4, we will find the main contributions of this work, where we will introduce different T-conorm operators and will explore their respective logical properties. In Sect. 5, we will investigate the connection between T-conorm operators and the egalitarian reasoning of the Leximax Principle. Finally, in Sect. 6 we will conclude the paper. Due to lack of space, the proofs have been omitted and can be found in [25].

2   Propositional Belief Merging

2.1   Preliminaries

We will consider a propositional language $\mathcal{L}$ over a finite alphabet $\mathcal{P}$ of propositional variables. An interpretation ω is a function from $\mathcal{P}$ to $\{0,1\}$. The set of all interpretations is denoted by Ω. An interpretation ω is a model of a formula φ ($\omega \models \varphi$) if and only if it makes it true in the usual classical truth functional way. Let φ be a formula, $mod(\varphi)$ denotes the set of models of φ, i.e., $mod(\varphi) = \{\omega \in \Omega \mid \omega \models \varphi\}$.

A belief base K can be seen as a propositional formula φ representing the beliefs of an agent. Let $K_1, \ldots, K_n$ be n belief bases (not necessarily different). We call belief set the multi-set E consisting of those n belief bases: $E = \{K_1, \ldots, K_n\}$. We denote $\bigwedge E$ the conjunction of the belief bases of E, i.e., $\bigwedge E = K_1 \wedge \cdots \wedge K_n$. The union of multi-sets will be denoted by $\sqcup$.

A pre-order $\leq$ over Ω is a reflexive and transitive relation on Ω. A pre-order is total if $\forall \omega_i, \omega_j \in \Omega$, $\omega_i \leq \omega_j$ or $\omega_j \leq \omega_i$. Let $\leq$ be a pre-order over Ω, we define $<$ as follows: $\omega_i < \omega_j$ iff $\omega_i \leq \omega_j$ and $\omega_j \not\leq \omega_i$, and $\approx$ as $\omega_i \approx \omega_j$ iff $\omega_i \leq \omega_j$ and $\omega_j \leq \omega_i$. We say $\omega_i \in min(mod(\varphi), \leq)$ iff $\omega_i \models \varphi$ and $\forall \omega_j \in mod(\varphi)$ $\omega_i \leq \omega_j$. Let E_1, E_2 be two belief sets. E_1 and E_2 are equivalent, noted $E_1 \equiv E_2$, iff there is a bijection f from $E_1 = \{K_{11}, \ldots, K_{n1}\}$ to $E_2 = \{K_{12}, \ldots, K_{n2}\}$ such that $\models f(K_{i1}) \leftrightarrow K_{i2}$.

2.2   Logical Properties

We employ a logical definition for merging in the presence of Integrity Constraints (IC), that is, we give a set of properties an operator has to satisfy to have a rational behavior concerning the merging. Additionally, the result of the merging has to obey a set of integrity constraints represented by a propositional formula μ. We will consider merging operators Δ mapping a belief set E and an integrity constraint μ to a set of interpretations that represents the merging of E according to μ.

Definition 1 (IC merging operators [14]**).** *Let* $E, E_1,\ E_2$ *be belief sets;* K_1, K_2 *be belief bases; and* μ, μ_1, μ_2 *be propositional formulas.* Δ_μ *is an IC merging operator if and only if it satisfies the following postulates:*

(IC0) $\Delta_\mu(E) \models \mu$.
(IC1) If μ *is consistent, then* $\Delta_\mu(E)$ *is consistent.*
(IC2) If $\bigwedge E$ *is consistent with* μ, *then* $\Delta_\mu(E) \equiv \bigwedge E \wedge \mu$.
(IC3) If $E_1 \equiv E_2$ *and* $\mu_1 \leftrightarrow \mu_2$, *then* $\Delta_{\mu_1}(E_1) \equiv \Delta_{\mu_2}(E_2)$.
(IC4) If $K_1 \models \mu$ *and* $K_2 \models \mu$, *then* $\Delta_\mu(\{K_1, K_2\}) \wedge K_1$ *is consistent if and only if* $\Delta_\mu(\{K_1, K_2\}) \wedge K_2$ *is consistent.*
(IC5) $\Delta_\mu(E_1) \wedge \Delta_\mu(E_2) \models \Delta_\mu(E_1 \sqcup E_2)$.
(IC6) If $\Delta_\mu(E_1) \wedge \Delta_\mu(E_2)$ *is consistent, then* $\Delta_\mu(E_1 \sqcup E_2) \models \Delta_\mu(E_1) \wedge \Delta_\mu(E_2)$.
(IC7) $\Delta_{\mu_1}(E) \wedge \mu_2 \models \Delta_{\mu_1 \wedge \mu_2}(E)$.
(IC8) If $\Delta_{\mu_1}(E) \wedge \mu_2$ *is consistent, then* $\Delta_{\mu_1 \wedge \mu_2}(E) \models \Delta_{\mu_1}(E)$.

See [14] for explanations of these properties. Besides these logical postulates, two main sub-classes of IC merging operators have been defined. They are the subclass of IC majority operators, which have been tailored to resolve conflicts by adhering to the majority wishes (utilitarianism), and the subclass of IC arbitration operators, which have been conceived to resolve conflicts by looking for a more consensual behavior (egalitarianism).

Definition 2 (IC majority and arbitration operators [14]**).** *An IC merging operator is a majority operator if it satisfies* **(Maj)** $\exists n \Delta_\mu(E_1 \sqcup \underbrace{E_2 \sqcup \cdots \sqcup E_2}_{n}) \models$
$\Delta_\mu(E_2)$. *An IC merging operator is an arbitration operator if it satisfies* **(Arb)** *If* $\Delta_{\mu_1}(\{K_1\}) \equiv \Delta_{\mu_2}(\{K_2\}), \Delta_{\mu_1 \leftrightarrow \neg\mu_2}(\{K_1, K_2\}) \equiv (\mu_1 \leftrightarrow \neg\mu_2), \mu_1 \not\models \mu_2, \mu_2 \not\models \mu_1$. *Then* $\Delta_{\mu_1 \vee \mu_2}(\{K_1, K_2\}) \equiv \Delta_{\mu_1}(\{K_1\})$.

A majority operator states that if an information has a majority audience, then it will be the choice of the group. Unlike the majority operator, an arbitration operator tries to satisfy each belief base as possible. Alternatively, there exists a more intuitive way to define IC merging operators: IC merging operator may correspond to a family of pre-orders on possible words.

Definition 3 (Syncretic Assignment [15]**).** *A Syncretic Assignment is a function mapping a belief set* E *to a total pre-order* $\leq_E$ *over interpretations such that for any belief sets* E, E_1, E_2 *and for any belief bases* K_1, K_2 *the following conditions hold:*

1. *If* $\omega \models \bigwedge E$ *and* $\omega' \models \bigwedge E$, *then* $\omega \approx_E \omega'$.
2. *If* $\omega \models \bigwedge E$ *and* $\omega' \not\models \bigwedge E$, *then* $\omega <_E \omega'$.

3. If $E_1 \equiv E_2$, then $\leq_{E_1} = \leq_{E_2}$.
4. $\forall \omega \models K_1 \; \exists \omega' \models K_2 \; \omega' \leq_{\{K_1, K_2\}} \omega$.
5. If $\omega \leq_{E_1} \omega'$ and $\omega \leq_{E_2} \omega'$, then $\omega \leq_{E_1 \sqcup E_2} \omega'$.
6. If $\omega <_{E_1} \omega'$ and $\omega \leq_{E_2} \omega'$, then $\omega <_{E_1 \sqcup E_2} \omega'$.

A *majority syncretic assignment* is a syncretic assignment which satisfies the following condition: 7. If $\omega <_{E_2} \omega'$, then $\exists n \omega <_{E_1 \sqcup E_2^n} \omega'$. A *fair syncretic assignment* is a syncretic assignment which satisfies the following condition: 8. If $\omega <_{K_1} \omega'$, $\omega <_{K_2} \omega''$ and $\omega' \approx_{\{K_1, K_2\}} \omega''$, then $\omega <_{\{K_1, K_2\}} \omega'$.

We have the following representation for merging operators:

Proposition 1 [15]. *A merging operator Δ is an IC merging operator (resp. an IC majority, an IC arbitration operator) iff there exists a syncretic assignment (resp. a majority syncretic assignment, a fair syncretic assignment) that maps each belief set E to a total pre-order $\leq_E$ over Ω such that $mod(\Delta_\mu(E)) = min(mod(\mu), \leq_E)$.*

2.3 Examples of IC Merging Operators

In the sequel, we give a model-theoretic definition of merging operators.

Example 1 [20]. Let us consider the academic example of a teacher who asks his three students which among the languages SQL (denoted by s), O_2 (denoted by o) and $Datalog$ (denoted by d) they would like to learn. The first student wants to learn only SQL or O_2, that is, $K_1 = (s \vee o) \wedge \neg d$. The second one wants to learn either $Datalog$ or O_2 but not both, i.e., $K_2 = (\neg s \wedge d \wedge \neg o) \vee (\neg s \wedge \neg d \wedge o)$. For the last, the third one wants to learn the three languages: $K_3 = (s \wedge d \wedge o)$.

With respect to Example 1, we have three propositional variables: s, d and o. The set of all possible outcomes/interpretations is $\Omega = \{\omega_1, \ldots, \omega_8\}$, where $\omega_1 = \neg s \neg d \neg o$, $\omega_2 = \neg s \neg d o$, $\omega_3 = \neg s d \neg o$, $\omega_4 = \neg s d o$, $\omega_5 = s \neg d \neg o$, $\omega_6 = s \neg d o$, $\omega_7 = s d \neg o$ and $\omega_8 = s d o$. Slightly abusing the notation, we will consider the interpretations as a conjunction of its literals. We will show two examples of operators commonly associated with belief merging: the *max* and *leximax* operators. First, we will assume that we utilise a distance between interpretations.

Definition 4 (Distance measure [14]**).** *A distance measure between interpretations is a total function d from $\Omega \times \Omega$ to $\mathbb{N}$ such that for every $\omega_i, \omega_j \in \Omega$, (1) $d(\omega_i, \omega_j) = d(\omega_j, \omega_i)$, and (2) $d(\omega_i, \omega_j) = 0$ iff $\omega_i = \omega_j$.*

In the first works on model-based merging, the distance used was the Hamming distance between interpretations [5], but any other distance may be used as well. The Hamming distance between interpretations characterizes the number of propositional variables at which the corresponding values are different. For example, the Hamming distance (denoted d_H) between $\omega_1 = \neg s \neg d \neg o$ and $\omega_6 = s \neg d o$ is $d_H(\omega_1, \omega_6) = 2$. Another example of a well known distance measure is the drastic distance [13], denoted by d_D, which is defined as $d_D(\omega_1, \omega_2) = 0$, if $\omega_1 = \omega_2$; $d_D(\omega_1, \omega_2) = 1$, otherwise.

Now we define the distance between an interpretation ω_i and a belief base K as follows: $d(\omega_i, K) = \min_{\omega_j \models K} d(\omega_i, \omega_j)$. The distance between an interpretation ω_i and a belief base K is the minimum distance between ω_i and the models of K.

Example 2. Regarding Example 1, the Hamming distance between each interpretation w.r.t. K_1, K_2 and K_3 is showed in Table 1. For instance, $d_H(\omega_1, K_1) = min(d_H(\omega_1, \omega_2), d_H(\omega_1, \omega_5), d_H(\omega_1, \omega_6)) = min(1, 1, 2) = 1$.

Table 1. The Hamming distances of K_1, K_2, K_3 and E.

Ω	$d_H(\omega, K_1)$	$d_H(\omega, K_2)$	$d_H(\omega, K_3)$	$d_{H\,max}(\omega, E)$	$L_\omega^{d_H, E}$	$d_{H \oplus \mathbf{P}}(\omega, E)$
$\omega_1 = \neg s \neg d \neg o$	1	1	3	3	$(3, 1, 1)$	1
$\omega_2 = \neg s \neg d o$	0	0	2	2	$(2, 0, 0)$	0.666
$\omega_3 = \neg s d \neg o$	2	0	2	2	$(2, 2, 0)$	0.8884
$\omega_4 = \neg s d o$	1	1	1	1	$(1, 1, 1)$	0.7032
$\omega_5 = s \neg d \neg o$	0	2	2	2	$(2, 2, 0)$	0.8884
$\omega_6 = s \neg d o$	0	1	1	1	$(\mathbf{1, 1, 0})$	0.5551
$\omega_7 = s d \neg o$	1	1	1	1	$(1, 1, 1)$	0.7032
$\omega_8 = s d o$	1	2	0	2	$(2, 1, 0)$	0.7772

Definition 5 (*max* **operator** [16]). *Let E be a belief set, d a distance measure and ω an interpretation. We define the distance between an interpretation and a belief set as $d_{max}(\omega, E) = \max_{K \in E} d(\omega, K)$. Then we have the following pre-order: $\omega_i \leq_E^{d, max} \omega_j$ iff $d_{max}(\omega_i, E) \leq d_{max}(\omega_j, E)$. The operator $\Delta_\mu^{d, max}$ is defined by $mod(\Delta_\mu^{d, max}(E)) = min(mod(\mu), \leq_E^{d, max})$.*

This operator is very close to the minimax rule used in decision theory [21]. The minimax rule tries to minimize the worst cases while $\Delta_\mu^{d, max}$ tries to minimize the more remote distance. The idea of this operator is to find the closest possible interpretations to the overall belief set [15]. The results of *max* merging operator w.r.t. Hamming distance for Example 2 are in the fifth column of Table 1.

Theorem 1 [15]. *$\Delta_\mu^{d, max}$ satisfies the postulates (IC0)-(IC5), (IC7), (IC8) and (Arb), but violates (IC6) and (Maj).*

$\Delta_\mu^{d, max}$ is said to be an IC arbitration quasi-merging operator since it only violates (IC6) in (IC0)-(IC8).

Definition 6 (*leximax* **operator** [14]). *Let $E = \{K_1, \ldots, K_n\}$ be a belief set. For each interpretation ω we build the list $(d_1^\omega, \ldots, d_n^\omega)$ of distances between this* *interpretation and the n belief bases in E, i.e., $d_i^\omega = d(\omega, K_i)$. Let $L_\omega^{d,E}$ be the list obtained from $(d_1^\omega, \ldots, d_n^\omega)$ by sorting it in descending order. Let $\leq_{lex}$ be the lexicographical order between sequences of integers, i.e., $(x_1, \ldots, x_n) \leq_{lex} (y_1, \ldots, y_n)$ if (1) for all i, $x_i \leq y_i$ or (2) there exists i such that $x_i < y_i$ and for all $j < i$, $x_j \leq y_j$. We define the following pre-order: $\omega_i \leq_E^{d,leximax} \omega_j$ iff $L_{\omega_i}^{d,E} \leq_{lex} L_{\omega_j}^{d,E}$. The operator $\Delta_\mu^{d,leximax}$ is defined by $mod(\Delta_\mu^{d,leximax}(E)) = min(mod(\mu), \leq_E^{d,leximax})$.*

The aim of this operator is to capture the "arbitration" behavior of $\Delta_\mu^{d,max}$ with the gaining of the logical postulate **(IC6)**. The idea behind this operator has been used in social choice theory [19], where leximin functions have been employed instead.

Theorem 2 [15]. $\Delta_\mu^{d,leximax}$ *satisfies the postulates **(IC0)-(IC8)** and **(Arb)**, but violates **(Maj)**.*

3   T-conorms

In this section we will describe some notions about T-conorms which will be employed in the remaining of this work. With regard to the *max* operation, the merging compares only the highest value of each interpretation to take a decision. The maximum can also be viewed as the disjunction logic operator, i.e., $(a \vee b) = max\{a, b\}$, and that is a T-conorm in the fuzzy logic literature.

Definition 7 (T-conorm [12]**).** *A binary function $\oplus : [0,1] \times [0,1] \to [0,1]$ is a T-conorm if it satisfies the following conditions: (i) $\oplus\{a,b\} = \oplus\{b,a\}$ (Commutativity); (ii) $\oplus\{a, \oplus\{b,c\}\} = \oplus\{\oplus\{a,b\}, c\}$ (Associativity); (iii) $a \leq c$ and $b \leq d \Rightarrow \oplus\{a,b\} \leq \oplus\{c,d\}$ (Monotonicity); and (iv) $\oplus\{a,0\} = a$ (Neutral Element).*

Every T-conorm has an absorbent element, also called annihilator, which is the natural number 1, i.e., $\oplus\{a,1\} = 1$ (in this case, 1 can also be associated as an implicit veto). A T-conorm is called strict if it is continuous and strictly monotone (i.e., $\forall x, y, z \oplus \{x,y\} < \oplus\{x,z\}$ whenever $x < 1$ and $y < z$). A T-conorm is called nilpotent if it is continuous and if each $a \in]0,1[$ is a nilpotent element. An element $a \in]0,1[$ is called a nilpotent element of $\oplus$ if there exists some $n \in \mathbb{N}$ such that $\oplus \underbrace{\{a, \ldots, a\}}_{n} = 1$. Besides, for all T-conorm $\oplus$, $\oplus\{a,b\} \geq max\{a,b\}$ [7,11]. Remember that for any $a, b \in \mathbb{R}$, $]a,b[= \{x \in \mathbb{R} : a < x < b\}$.

Definition 8 (Basic T-conorms [12]**).**   *The following are the four basic T-conorms:*

- *Maximum T-conorm: $\oplus_M\{x,y\} = max(x,y)$.*
- *Probabilistic sum T-conorm: $\oplus_P\{x,y\} = x + y - x \cdot y$.*
- *Łukasiewicz T-conorm: $\oplus_L\{x,y\} = min(x+y, 1)$.*

- *Drastic sum T-conorm:* $\oplus_D\{x,y\} = 1$, *if* $(x,y) \in]0,1] \times]0,1]$; $max(x,y)$, *otherwise.*

These four basic T-conorms are remarkable for several reasons. The drastic sum $\oplus_D$ and the maximum $\oplus_M$ are the largest and the smallest T-conorms, respectively (with respect to the pointwise order). The maximum $\oplus_M$ is the only T-conorm where each $x \in [0,1]$ is an idempotent element (recall $x \in [0,1]$ is called an idempotent element of $\oplus$ if $\oplus\{x,x\} = x$). The probabilistic sum $\oplus_P$ and the Łukasiewicz T-conorm $\oplus_L$ are examples of two important subclasses of T-conorms, namely, the classes of strict and nilpotent T-conorms, respectively (more details in [10]).

Definition 9 (Strength between T-conorms [10]). *For two T-conorms $\oplus_1$ and $\oplus_2$, if we have $\oplus_1\{x,y\} \leq \oplus_2\{x,y\}$ for all $x,y \in [0,1]$, then we say that $\oplus_1$ is weaker than $\oplus_2$ or, equivalently, that $\oplus_2$ is stronger than $\oplus_1$, and we write in this case $\oplus_1 \leq \oplus_2$.*

We shall write $\oplus_1 < \oplus_2$ if $\oplus_1 \leq \oplus_2$ and $\oplus_1 \neq \oplus_2$, i.e., if $\oplus_1(x_0,y_0) < \oplus_2(x_0,y_0)$ for some $x_0,y_0 \in [0,1]$. The drastic sum $\oplus_D$ is the strongest, and the Maximum $\oplus_M$ is the weakest T-conorm, i.e., for each T-conorm $\oplus$ we have $\oplus_M \leq \oplus \leq \oplus_D$. Between the four basic T-conorms we have these strict inequalities: $\oplus_M < \oplus_P < \oplus_L < \oplus_D$. Many families of T-conorms can be defined by an explicit formula depending on a parameter λ. We now give a quick overview of them.

Definition 10 (Schweizer-Sklar T-conorms [22]). *The family of Schweizer-Sklar T-conorms $(\oplus_\lambda^{SS})_{\lambda \in [-\infty,\infty]}$ is given by $\oplus_\lambda^{SS}\{x,y\} = \oplus_M\{x,y\}, if \lambda = -\infty; \oplus_P\{x,y\}, if \lambda = 0; \oplus_D\{x,y\}, if \lambda = \infty; 1 - (max(((1-x)^\lambda + (1-y)^\lambda - 1),0))^{\frac{1}{\lambda}}, otherwise.*

This family of T-conorms is remarkable in the sense that it contains all four basic T-conorms. When $\lambda = 1$, $\oplus_1^{SS} = \oplus_L$. For the rest of the parameters we have the following strict inequalities: $\oplus_\infty^{SS} > \cdots > \oplus_1^{SS} > \oplus_0^{SS} > \oplus_{-\infty}^{SS}$.

Definition 11 (Frank T-conorms [3]). *The family of Frank T-conorms $(\oplus_\lambda^F)_{\lambda \in [0,\infty]}$ is given by $\oplus_\lambda^F\{x,y\} = \oplus_M\{x,y\}, if \lambda = 0; \oplus_P\{x,y\}, if \lambda = 1; \oplus_L\{x,y\}, if \lambda = \infty; 1 - log_\lambda \left(1 + \frac{(\lambda^{1-x}-1)(\lambda^{1-y}-1)}{\lambda-1}\right), otherwise.*

The Frank family comprehends a series of T-conorms between the Łukasiewicz and the probabilistic sum T-conorms (for $\lambda \in [2,\infty[$). The Frank family has the following strict inequalities: $\oplus_\infty^F > \cdots > \oplus_2^F > \oplus_1^F > \oplus_0^F$.

Definition 12 (Yager T-conorms [27]). *The family of Yager T-conorms $(\oplus_\lambda^Y)_{\lambda \in [0,\infty]}$ is given by $\oplus_\lambda^Y\{x,y\} = \oplus_D\{x,y\}, if \lambda = 0; \oplus_M\{x,y\}, if \lambda = \infty; min((x^\lambda + y^\lambda)^{\frac{1}{\lambda}},1), otherwise.*

It is one of the most popular families for modeling the union of fuzzy sets. The idea is to use the parameter λ as a reciprocal measure for the strength of the logical operator "*or*". In this context, $\lambda = 0$ expresses the least demanding (i.e., largest) "*or*", and $\lambda = \infty$ the most demanding (i.e., smallest) "*or*". The Yager T-conorms comprehends a series of T-conorms between the drastic and the maximum T-conorms. When $\lambda = 1$, $\oplus_1^{\mathbf{Y}} = \oplus_{\mathbf{L}}$. The Yager family has the following strict inequalities: $\oplus_0^{\mathbf{Y}} > \oplus_1^{\mathbf{Y}} > \oplus_2^{\mathbf{Y}} > \cdots > \oplus_\infty^{\mathbf{Y}}$.

Definition 13 (Sugeno-Weber T-conorms [26]**).** *The family of Sugeno-Weber T-conorms* $(\oplus_\lambda^{SW})_{\lambda \in [-1,\infty]}$ *is given by* $\oplus_\lambda^{SW}\{x,y\} = \oplus_P\{x,y\}, \text{if } \lambda = -1; \oplus_D\{x,y\}, \text{if } \lambda = \infty; min(x + y + \lambda xy, 1), \text{otherwise}.$

Note that $(\oplus_\lambda^{\mathbf{SW}})_{\lambda > -1}$ are increasing functions of the parameter λ. The Sugeno-Weber family has the following strict inequalities: $\oplus_{-1}^{\mathbf{SW}} < \oplus_0^{\mathbf{SW}} < \oplus_1^{\mathbf{SW}} < \cdots < \oplus_\infty^{\mathbf{SW}}$.

4   Belief Merging with T-conorms

In this section we will present the contributions of this paper by analyzing the rationality of T-conorms merging operators through their logical postulates. We will also consider some additional logical postulates during this process.

Definition 14 ($\oplus$ operator). *Let* $E = \{K_1, \ldots, K_n\}$ *be a belief set,* $\oplus$ *a T-conorm, d a distance measure and* ω *an interpretation. Let* $M = max(\{d(\omega, \omega') \mid \omega, \omega' \in \Omega\})$. *We define the distance between an interpretation and a belief set as* $d_\oplus(\omega, E) = \bigoplus_{K \in E} \left\{ \dfrac{d(\omega, K)}{M} \right\}$. *Then we have the following pre-order:* $\omega_i \leq_E^{d,\oplus} \omega_j$ *iff* $d_\oplus(\omega_i, E) \leq d_\oplus(\omega_j, E)$. *The operator* $\Delta_\mu^{d,\oplus}$ *is defined by* $mod(\Delta_\mu^{d,\oplus}(E)) = min(mod(\mu), \leq_E^{d,\oplus})$.

Example 3. The results for the probabilistic sum T-conorm operator w.r.t. Hamming distance for Example 1 are in the seventh column of Table 1. The resulting pre-order $\leq_E^{d_H,\oplus_P}$ is $\omega_6 \leq_E^{d_H,\oplus_P} \omega_2 \leq_E^{d_H,\oplus_P} \{\omega_4, \omega_7\} \leq_E^{d_H,\oplus_P} \omega_8 \leq_E^{d_H,\oplus_P} \{\omega_3, \omega_5\} \leq_E^{d_H,\oplus_P} \omega_1$.

Observe that for any T-conorm the presence of the annihilator 1 on the evaluation of ω_1 works as an implicit veto for that interpretation; if an interpretation has the highest distance value for an agent, that interpretation has to be rejected by the group. It brings a principle of equality where the worst scenarios inside a group need to be avoided. In other words, the use of T-conorms as a merging operator presupposes that there exists a consensus among the agents stating that if a choice is the worst for an agent, then this choice has to be the worst for the group. Now, we will show what logical properties the merging operators with T-conorms satisfy in the general case:

Theorem 3. *Let $\oplus$ be a T-conorm. $\Delta_\mu^{d,\oplus}$ satisfies (IC0)-(IC5), (IC7) and (IC8). $\Delta_\mu^{d,\oplus}$ does not satisfy (Maj). The postulates (IC6) and (Arb) are not satisfied in general.*

This result is very similar to that for the *max* operator (Theorem 1). The difference comes from the fact the **(Arb)** is not satisfied in general for all T-conorms.

The first important concern when dealing with T-conorms is the presence of the annihilator 1. The first logical postulate that we need revisit is **(IC6)**. This postulate corresponds to the following syncretic assignment: 6. if $\omega <_{E_1} \omega'$ and $\omega \leq_{E_2} \omega'$, then $\omega <_{E_1 \sqcup E_2} \omega'$. It states if an interpretation ω is strictly more preferable than an interpretation ω' for a belief set E_1 and if ω is at least as preferable as ω' for a belief set E_2, then if one joins the two belief sets, we have ω will be strictly more preferable than ω'. Note that the presence of an annihilator is sufficient to falsify this condition. Consider that ω is equivalently preferable to ω' for a belief set E_2 ($\omega \approx_{E_2} \omega'$) and that $d_\oplus(\omega, E_2) = d_\oplus(\omega', E_2) = 1$. For any E_1, we will have $d_\oplus(\omega, E_1 \sqcup E_2) = d_\oplus(\omega', E_1 \sqcup E_2) = 1$, that is, $\omega \approx_{E_1 \sqcup E_2} \omega'$, which falsifies the condition 6 (and **(IC6)**). To overcome this issue, we will consider a weaker version of the logical postulate **(IC6)** with the presence of the annihilator 1: **(IC6-1)** Let $d_{op}(\omega_i, E_2) \neq 1$, for $i = 1, 2$. If $\omega_1 <_{E_1} \omega_2$ and $\omega_1 \leq_{E_2} \omega_2$, then $\omega_1 <_{E_1 \sqcup E_2} \omega_2$.

This weaker version of postulate **(IC6)** considers the principle when the annihilator 1 is safe to be used without falsifying it. The second important condition we will consider comes from the social choice theory, and it is related to egalitarianism between agents. It was proposed by Hammond [9] and it is known in the literature as the Hammond Equity condition [23]. This condition can be expressed as follows: If agent i is worse off than agent j both in ω and in ω', and if i is better off himself in ω than in ω', while j is better off in ω' than in ω, and if furthermore all others are just as well off in ω as in ω', then ω' is socially better than ω. It can be translated to the belief merging framework as

Definition 15 (Condition Hammond Equity [8]). *(HE) Let $E = \{K_1, \ldots, K_n\}$. If $\exists i, j \in \{1, \ldots, n\}$ such that $\omega <_{K_i} \omega'$, $\omega' <_{K_j} \omega$, $K_i \prec_\omega K_j$, $K_i \prec_{\omega'} K_j$ and $\forall l \neq i, j \ \omega \approx_{K_l} \omega'$, then $\omega' <_E \omega$.*

We say that K_i is better than K_j given ω, denoted $K_i \prec_\omega K_j$, if and only if $\exists \omega_1 \models K_i, \forall \omega_2 \models K_j, \omega_1 <_\omega \omega_2$. When distance-based merging operators are considered, this condition is equivalent to:

Definition 16 (Condition Hammond Equity [8]). *(HE) Let d be a distance measure. A merging operator op satisfies the Hammond Equity condition iff for any belief set $E = \{K_1, \ldots, K_n\}$, if $\exists i, j \in \{1, \ldots, n\}$ such that $d(\omega, K_i) < d(\omega', K_i) < d(\omega', K_j) < d(\omega, K_j)$ and $\forall l \neq i, j \ d(\omega, K_l) = d(\omega', K_l)$, then $d_{op}(\omega', E) < d_{op}(\omega, E)$.*

Intuitively, Hammond Equity is an egalitarian condition between two agents stating that an interpretation is more preferred than another if the inequalities between agents is lower. For instance, according to **(HE)**, the tuple $\omega = \left(\frac{1}{5}, 1, \frac{2}{5}\right)$ representing the satisfaction of three agents, is less preferred than the tuple $\omega' = \left(\frac{2}{5}, \frac{3}{5}, \frac{2}{5}\right)$. The reason is because the inequality between $\frac{1}{5}$ and 1 is greater than the inequality between $\frac{2}{5}$ and $\frac{3}{5}$. We can say that in this case ω' is more stable than ω.

The next egalitarian operator considered from the social choice literature is the Pigou-Dalton condition [6,8]. From the perspective of distance-based merging, it can be defined as

Definition 17 (Pigou-Dalton Condition). *(PD) Let d be a distance measure. An operator op satisfies the Pigou-Dalton principle iff for any belief set* $E = \{K_1, \ldots, K_n\}$, *if* $\exists i, j \in \{1, \ldots, n\}$ *such that* $d(\omega, K_i) < d(\omega', K_i) \leq d(\omega', K_j) < d(\omega, K_j)$, $d(\omega', K_i) - d(\omega, K_i) = d(\omega, K_j) - d(\omega', K_j)$ *and* $\forall l \neq i, j$ $d(\omega, K_l) = d(\omega', K_l)$, *then* $d_{op}(\omega', E) < d_{op}(\omega, E)$.

Pigou-Dalton restricts Hammond Equity for the cases where the difference between interpretations has the same value. This condition cannot be applied in the previous example of $\omega = \left(\frac{1}{5}, 1, \frac{2}{5}\right)$ and $\omega' = \left(\frac{2}{5}, \frac{3}{5}, \frac{2}{5}\right)$, since $\frac{2}{5} - \frac{1}{5} \neq 1 - \frac{3}{5}$. If we consider an interpretation $\omega'' = \left(\frac{2}{5}, \frac{4}{5}, \frac{2}{5}\right)$, we can compare ω with ω'', and according with **(PD)** the interpretation ω'' should be preferred. Intuitively, **(PD)** is an egalitarian principle which favors a better distribution of satisfaction between interpretations when the sum of the total amount is equal for both interpretations. Weaker versions of Hammond Equity and Pigou-Dalton conditions excluding the annihilator 1 are defined respectively as

(HE-1) If $\exists i, j \in \{1, \ldots, n\}$ such that $d(\omega, K_i) < d(\omega', K_i) < d(\omega', K_j) < d(\omega, K_j)$ and $\forall l \neq i, j$ $d(\omega, K_l) = d(\omega', K_l) \neq 1$, then $d_{op}(\omega', E) < d_{op}(\omega, E)$; and

(PD-1) if $\exists i, j \in \{1, \ldots, n\}$ such that $d(\omega, K_i) < d(\omega', K_i) \leq d(\omega', K_j) < d(\omega, K_j)$, $d(\omega', K_i) - d(\omega, K_i) = d(\omega, K_j) - d(\omega', K_j)$ and $\forall l \neq i, j$ $d(\omega, K_l) = d(\omega', K_l) \neq 1$, then $d_{op}(\omega', E) < d_{op}(\omega, E)$.

The justification for this restriction is the same applied to **(IC6)**: if for any $l \neq i, j$ $s_d(\omega, K_l) = s_d(\omega', K_l) = 1$, then we have $d_\oplus(\omega, E) = d_\oplus(\omega', E) = 1$ for any T-conorm $\oplus$, and consequently falsifying both postulates. The last egalitarian property we want to consider comes from the literature of liberal egalitarianism [2,4,17], a theory of justice which seeks to combine the values of equality, personal freedom and personal responsibility. It is called Harm Principle (or Principle of Non-Interference).

Definition 18 (Harm Principle Condition). *(HP) For all* $\omega_1, \omega_2, \omega_1', \omega_2' \in \Omega$, *suppose* $E = \{K_1, \ldots, K_n\}$, *a distance measure d and* $\omega_1 <_E^{d, op} \omega_2$. *Consider* ω_1', ω_2' *such that* $\exists i \in \{1, \ldots, n\}$, $d(\omega_1, K_i) < d(\omega_1', K_i)$, $d(\omega_2, K_i) < d(\omega_2', K_i)$ *and* $\forall j \neq i$ $d(\omega_1, K_j) = d(\omega_1', K_j)$, $d(\omega_2, K_j) = d(\omega_2', K_j)$. *If* $d(\omega_2', K_i) > d(\omega_1', K_i)$, *then* $\omega_1' <_E^{d, op} \omega_2'$.

In distributive justice theory, this condition embodies the idea that "an individual has the right to prevent society from acting against him in all circumstances of change in his welfare, provided that the welfare of no other individual is affected". In the distance-based merging framework, it can be seen as considering that an interpretation ω_1 is more preferred than ω_2, and if occasionally an agent i has an increase of the distance value in ω_1 and ω_2, resulting in ω_1' and ω_2', ω_1' will be preferred to ω_2' if the distance of i in ω_1' is still lower than the distance of i in ω_2'. In other words, we can say that a single agent does not have the power of interference in the choice of the group when occurring an increase of distance measure (we can also see the non-satisfaction of the condition as a kind of veto power of agents). The equality emerges from the fact that no specific agent has the power to interfere in the decision of the group. Finally, we can continue with the analysis of logical postulates for each specific T-conorm.

Theorem 4. $\Delta_\mu^{d,\oplus_M}$ *satisfies (Arb) and (HP), but it does not satisfy (IC6-1), (HE-1), (PD-1) in the general case.* $\Delta_\mu^{d,\oplus_P}$ *satisfies (IC6-1) and (PD-1).* $\Delta_\mu^{d,\oplus_P}$ *does not satisfy (Arb), (HE-1) and (HP) in the general case.*

One interesting point to highlight is the fact of a T-conorm being strict implies the satisfaction of the condition **(IC6-1)** (e.g., $\oplus_P$ is a strict T-conorm).

Theorem 5. *Let $\oplus$ be a strict T-conorm, then $\Delta_\mu^{d,\oplus}$ satisfies (IC6-1).*

Below, we have results for the other basic T-conorms operators.

Theorem 6. $\Delta_\mu^{d,\oplus_L}$ *and* $\Delta_\mu^{d,\oplus_D}$ *do not satisfy (IC6-1), (Arb), (HE-1), (PD-1) and (HP).*

The drastic sum T-conorm is not continuous, which implies that little changes in the variables can change drastically the result and this reflects the loss of some important logical properties. The Łukasiewicz T-conorm is a nilpotent T-conorm; in this case, the presence of a nilpotent element reflects the loss of some properties.

Theorem 7. *Let $\oplus$ be a nilpotent T-conorm, then $\Delta_\mu^{d,\oplus}$ does not satisfy (IC6-1), (HE-1), (PD-1) and (HP) in the general case.*

The nilpotent element works as a sort of annihilator and then inherits all the problems discussed above, even with these restrictions with the annihilator are applied. In the sequel, we will investigate deeper the behavior of T-conorms through some parameterized T-conorms to see in what conditions we can achieve egalitarian properties for the propositional belief merging. First, we will consider the Schweizer-Sklar T-conorms.

Theorem 8. $\Delta_\mu^{d,\oplus_\lambda^{ss}}$ *satisfies (IC6-1) and (PD-1) when $\lambda \in]-\infty, 0]$. Let $n \geq 3$ be the number of different propositional variables in the belief set E.* $\Delta_\mu^{d,\oplus_\lambda^{ss}}$ *satisfies (Arb), (HE-1) and (HP) when $-\infty < \lambda \leq -\lfloor \frac{2n}{3} \rfloor$.*

Regarding the results of Theorem 8, the interval $[1, \infty]$ comprises strictly increasing T-conorms from the Łukasiewicz T-conorm ($\oplus_1^{SS}$) to the drastic sum T-conorm ($\oplus_\infty^{SS}$). It is clear that all these conditions are falsified in this interval (since all T-conorms in this interval are weaker than Łukasiewicz T-conorm). Schweizer-Sklar T-conorm is strict for the interval $]-\infty, 0]$, therefore it satisfies **(IC6-1)** in this case. Considering this interval yet, we have that any Schweizer-Sklar T-conorm satisfies **(PD-1)**; and additionally satisfies **(Arb)** and **(HE-1)** when $-\infty < \lambda \leq -\left\lfloor \frac{2n}{3} \right\rfloor$, where n is the number of propositional variables in the belief set. Intuitively, as we decrease the parameter λ, we strengthen these conditions of egalitarian properties in the Schweizer-Sklar T-conorm.

Note that when the parameterized T-conorm gets closer to maximum T-conorm, it has stronger egalitarian properties (e.g., Harm Principle). When it gets closer to drastic sum and Łukasiewicz T-conorms, it tends to lose its logical properties. Now consider the Frank T-conorms:

Theorem 9. $\Delta_\mu^{d,\oplus_\lambda^F}$ *satisfies* **(IC6-1)** *and* **(PD-1)** *for* $\lambda \in]0, \infty[$. $\Delta_\mu^{d,\oplus_\lambda^F}$ *does not satisfy* **(Arb)**, **(HE-1)** *and* **(HP)** *in the general case.*

We observed previously that T-conorms converging to the maximum T-conorm tend to satisfy properties as **(Arb)**, **(HE-1)** and **(PD-1)**, while T-conorms converging to probabilistic sum T-conorm satisfy only **(PD-1)**. When the Frank T-conorm is considered, the convergence to Łukasiewicz T-conorm $(\oplus_\infty^F = \oplus_L)$ from probabilistic sum $(\oplus_1^F = \oplus_P)$ still implies the satisfaction of **(PD-1)**. Besides, considering this convergence of Frank T-conorm to the maximum T-conorm, we can have an additional result for the interval $[0, 1]$ (from $\oplus_0^F = \oplus_M$ to $\oplus_1^F = \oplus_P$). Let $\lambda \in]0, 1]$.

Theorem 10. *Let* $n \geq 3$ *be the number of different propositional variables in the belief set* E. $\Delta_\mu^{d,\oplus_\lambda^F}$ *satisfies* **(Arb)**, **(HE-1)** *and* **(HP)** *when* $0 < \lambda \leq 10^{-n}$.

The limit of $0 < \lambda \leq 10^{-n}$ is rather loose, but it is a statement that there is an interval between maximum and probabilistic sum in the Frank T-conorm where **(Arb)**, **(HE-1)** and **(HP)** are satisfied. In the sequel, we will see the Yager family of T-conorms.

Theorem 11. *Let* $n \geq 3$ *be the number of different propositional variables in the belief set* E. *For* $\lambda \in [2, \infty[$, $\Delta_\mu^{d,\oplus_\lambda^Y}$ *satisfies* **(Arb)** *when* $\lambda \geq \left\lfloor \frac{2n}{3} \right\rfloor$.

Yager T-conorms comprise from drastic sum $(\oplus_0^Y)$, passing through Łukasiewicz T-conorm $(\oplus_1^Y)$, to maximum T-conorm $(\oplus_\infty^Y)$. Unlike the previous parameterized T-conorms, Yager T-conorms are nilpotent for $\lambda \in]0, \infty[$, which does not result in satisfying **(IC6-1)**, **(HE-1)**, **(PD-1)** and **(HP)** in the general case, but **(Arb)** can be still satisfied.

For the last, we analyze Sugeno-Weber family of T-conorms.

Theorem 12. *For* $\lambda \in]-1, \infty]$, $\Delta_\mu^{d,\oplus_\lambda^{SW}}$ *does not satisfy* **(IC6-1)**, **(HE-1)**, **(PD-1)**, **(HP)** *and* **(Arb)** *in the general case.*

Sugeno-Weber T-conorms are another class of nilpotent T-conorms. They range from drastic sum $(\oplus_\infty^{SW})$ to Łukasiewicz $(\oplus_0^{SW})$ and probabilistic sum T-conorms $(\oplus_{-1}^{SW})$. As it is nilpotent, the conditions **(IC6-1)**, **(HE-1)**, **(PD-1)** and **(HP)** do not hold in the general case for any λ. It is believed that the absence of convergence for maximum implies in the falsification of **(Arb)**.

5   T-conorms and the Leximax Principle

In this section, we will use the results of [24] to characterize an egalitarian property of some parameterized T-conorms. The Leximax principle will be the key to this analysis.

Leximax (LM): Let $E = \{K_1, \ldots, K_n\}$ be a belief set. For each interpretation ω, we build the list $(d_1^\omega, \ldots, d_n^\omega)$ of distances between this interpretation and the n belief bases in E, i.e., $d_i^\omega = d(\omega, K_i)$. Let $L_\omega^{d,E}$ be the list obtained from $(d_1^\omega, \ldots, d_n^\omega)$ by sorting it in descending order. For all $\omega, \omega' \in \Omega$, (1) if there exists a position $k \leq n$ such that $d_k^{\omega'} > d_k^\omega$; and (2) for every $j < k$, $d_j^{\omega'} = d_j^\omega$, then $\omega <_E \omega'$ (ω is more preferred than ω'). Otherwise, $\omega \approx_E \omega'$.

Basically, it is the same idea behind *leximax* operator (see Definition 6). Besides **(LM)**, we need some additional properties in order to make a result of characterization for the Leximax Principle: they are the Strong Pareto and Anonymity.

Strong Pareto (SP): Let $E = \{K_1, \ldots, K_n\}$. For all $\omega, \omega' \in \Omega$, if $\exists i \in \{1, \ldots, n\}$ $\omega <_{K_i} \omega'$ and $\forall j \neq i$, $\omega \leq_{K_j} \omega'$, then $\omega <_E \omega'$.

Strong Pareto is very similar to **(IC6)**. The difference is that **(SP)** compares each belief base $K \in E$ and **(IC6)** compares two belief sets and their union.

Anonymity (A): Let $E = \{K_1, \ldots, K_n\}$ be a belief set and $l_\omega^{d,E} = (d_1^\omega, \ldots, d_n^\omega)$ the list of distances between the interpretation ω and the n belief bases in E. For all $\omega, \omega' \in \Omega$, if $l_\omega^{d,E}$ is a permutation of $l_{\omega'}^{d,E}$, then $\omega \approx_E \omega'$.

Anonymity is equivalent to Commutativity (also called Symmetry). The first important characterization we need to consider is

Theorem 13 [24]. *A Syncretic Assignment $\leq_E$ satisfies **(HE)**, **(SP)** and **(A)** if and only if it satisfies **(LM)**.*

This theorem can be used in belief merging to assert that any merging operator satisfying **(HE)** and **(SP)** and **(A)** is equivalent to the *leximax* operator. We turn now to the link between parameterized T-conorm merging operators and the Leximax principle. It is known that every T-conorm $\oplus \geq max$ and despite *max* operator does not satisfy properties as **(HE)** and **(PD)**, some T-conorms can satisfy weakened versions of them.

This analysis shows that some T-conorms present a similar (weaker) behavior to the *leximax* operator. What we want to achieve is that those T-conorms can also follow some weaker versions of the leximax principle. We introduce a restriction to the Leximax principle, named Leximax principle free from annihilator 1.

Leximax free from 1 (LM-1): Let $E = \{K_1, \ldots, K_n\}$ be a belief set. For each interpretation ω we build the list $(d_1^\omega, \ldots, d_n^\omega)$ of distances between this interpretation and the n belief bases in E, i.e., $d_i^\omega = d(\omega, K_i)$. Let $L_\omega^{d,E}$ be the list obtained from $(d_1^\omega, \ldots, d_n^\omega)$ by sorting it in descending order. For all $\omega, \omega' \in \Omega$, (1) if there exists a position $k \leq n$ such that $d_k^{\omega'} > d_k^\omega$; and (2) for every $j < k$, $d_j^{\omega'} = d_j^{\omega} \neq 1$, then $\omega <_E \omega'$ (ω is more preferred than ω'). Otherwise, $\omega \approx_E \omega'$.

It is possible then to make a restricted characterization of the Leximax principle for a belief merging operator: **(SP**-1) Let $E = \{K_1, \ldots, K_n\}$ and d be a distance measure. For all $\omega, \omega' \in \Omega$, if $\exists i \in \{1, \ldots, n\}$ $\omega <_{K_i} \omega'$ and $\forall j \neq i$, $\omega \leq_{K_j} \omega'$ and $d(\omega, K_j), d(\omega', K_j) \neq 1$, then $\omega <_E \omega'$.

Corollary 1. *A belief merging operator Δ_μ satisfies (**HE**-1), (**SP**-1) and (**A**) if and only if it satisfies (**LM**-1).*

This characterization restricts the Leximax principle when the annihilator is excluded from the possible distance values of the agents. As a consequence, we have

Corollary 2. *Let $n \geq 3$ be the number of propositional variables in the belief set E. $\Delta_\mu^{d,\oplus_\lambda^{SS}}$ and $\Delta_\mu^{d,\oplus_\lambda^F}$ satisfy (**LM**-1) when $\lambda \leq -\left\lfloor \frac{2n}{3} \right\rfloor$ and $0 < \lambda \leq 10^{-n}$, respectively.*

These operators satisfy **(HE**-1), **(SP**-1) and **(A)** in those specific intervals. In other words, when the annihilator is not present in the merging, we can say that these T-conorms have a behavior similar to the *leximax* operator. The last consideration of this section is about the Harm Principle. Although Hammond Equity and the Harm Principle are conceptually distinct and logically independent, it was proved the following result:

Theorem 14 [18]. *A Syncretic Assignment $\leq_E$ satisfies (**HP**), (**SP**) and (**A**) if and only if it is (**LM**).*

It is possible to assert a different version of Corollary 1.

Corollary 3. *A belief merging operator Δ_μ satisfies (**HP**), (**SP**-1) and (**A**) if and only if it is (**LM**-1).*

We just make clear that **(HP)** and **(HE)** are not logically equivalent. It is known that under **(A)**, Harm Principle implies Hammond Equity but the converse is not true [1].

6   Conclusions

In this paper, we proposed to use T-conorms operators in the propositional belief merging. T-conorms are a generalization of the usual two-valued logical disjunction, i.e., the *max* operator. In belief merging, the *max* operator is equivalent to the minimax rule in the decision theory: it tries to minimize the worst cases among the agents. Indeed, T-conorms allow us to diversify the method of the minimax rule by applying generalized versions of the *max* operator.

The purpose of this work is to offer more diversity of merging operators and explore their logical properties. In order to deepen this analysis, we considered other logical properties related to egalitarianism, more specifically, the Hammond Equity, Pigou-Dalton principle and Harm Principle. These conditions are intended to express preference for a more egalitarian distribution among the agents. They are well known conditions presented in Economics and these principles state that a society is more stable when the distribution of income is more balanced among the individuals. Another important condition of egalitarianism is the Strong Pareto principle.

We make clear that we analyzed weaker versions of the logical properties; we restricted them since T-conorms have an absorbent element, also called annihilator (which is 1 for T-conorms). T-conorm operators can be seen as merging operators with an implicit veto power: any agent having an interpretation with distance value equal to 1 is capable to interpose the decision of the group.

We chose in this paper some of the most representative classes of T-conorms. First, we analyzed the four basic T-conorms: drastic sum, Łukasiewicz, probabilistic sum and maximum T-conorms. The lowest T-conorm *max* satisfies only the egalitarian properties (**Arb**) and (**HP**). The probabilistic sum falsifies (**Arb**) and (**HE-1**), but satisfies (**IC6-1**) and (**PD-1**). Łukasiewicz and drastic sum falsify all of them.

When analyzing the parameterized T-conorms, which are basically generalizations of some of the four basic T-conorms, we observed that strict T-conorms converging to the maximum tend to satisfy (**HE-1**), (**HP**) and (**Arb**), as found in the Schweizer-Sklar and Frank T-conorms. In fact, in these cases we have a close connection between (**HE-1**), (**HP**) and (**Arb**). The same idea does not follow from nilpotent T-conorms, since they do not satisfy (**HE-1**) and (**HP**). In general, all the parameterized T-conorms exposed in this paper satisfy (**PD-1**) in a determined interval, except the nilpotent T-conorms. For the postulate (**IC6-1**), we proved that it is satisfied by the class of strict T-conorms, while it is not the case for nilpotent ones. With respect to (**Arb**), Schweizer-Sklar, Frank and Yager T-conorms satisfy it in some specific intervals. Thus it is possible to have a nilpotent T-conorm as an arbitration quasi-merging operator.

References

1. Alcantud, J.: Liberal approaches to ranking infinite utility streams: When can we avoid interferences? Mpra paper, University Library of Munich, Germany (2011). http://EconPapers.repec.org/RePEc:pra:mprapa:32198
2. Alcantud, J.C.R.: Non-interference and continuity: impossibility results for the evaluation of infinite utility streams. Technical report, p. 13 (2011)
3. Butnariu, D., Klement, E.P.: Triangular norm-based measures and games with fuzzy coalitions, vol. 10. Springer Science & Business Media, New York (1993)
4. Cappelen, A.W., Tungodden, B.: A liberal egalitarian paradox. Econ. Philos. **22**, 393–408 (2006)
5. Dalal, M.: Investigations into a theory of knowledge base revision. In: Proceedings of the Seventh American National Conference on Artificial Intelligence (AAAI88). pp. 475–479 (1988)
6. Dalton, H.: The measurement of the inequality of incomes. Econ. J. **30**, 348–361 (1920)

7. Detyniecki, M., Yager, R.R., Bouchon-Meunier, B.: Reducing t-norms and augmenting t-conorms. Int. J. Gen. Syst. **31**(3), 265–276 (2002)
8. Everaere, P., Konieczny, S., Marquis, P.: On egalitarian belief merging. In: AAAI (2014)
9. Hammond, P.J.: Equity, arrow's conditions, and rawls' difference principle. Econ.: J. Econom. Soc. 793–804 (1976)
10. Klement, E.P., Mesiar, R.: Logical, Algebraic, Analytic and Probabilistic Aspects of Triangular Norms. Elsevier Science B.V., Amsterdam (2005)
11. Klement, E.P., Mesiar, R., Pap, E.: On the order of triangular norms: comments on "a triangular norm hierarchy" by e. cretu. Fuzzy Sets Syst. **131**(3), 409–413 (2002)
12. Klement, E.P., Pap, E., Mesiar, R.: Triangular Norms. Trends in logic, Kluwer Academic Publ. cop., Dordrecht (2000). http://opac.inria.fr/record=b1104736
13. Konieczny, S., Lang, J., Marquis, P.: DA^2 merging operators. Artif. Intell. **157**(1–2), 49–79 (2004)
14. Konieczny, S., Pino-Pérez, R.: Merging with integrity constraints. In: Fifth European Conference on Symbolic and Quantitative Approaches to Reasoning with Uncertainty (ECSQARU 1999). pp. 233–244 (1999)
15. Konieczny, S., Pino-Pérez, R.: Merging information under constraints: a logical framework. J. Log. Comput. **12**(5), 773–808 (2002)
16. Lin, J., Mendelzon, A.O.: Merging databases under constraints. Int. J. Coop. Inf. Syst. **7**, 55–76 (1996)
17. Lombardi, M., Miyagishima, K., Veneziani, R.: Liberal Egalitarianism and the Harm Principle. Mpra Paper. University Library of Munich, Germany (2013)
18. Mariotti, M., Veneziani, R.: 'Non-interference' implies equality. Soc. Choice Welf. **32**(1) (2008). http://dx.doi.org/10.1007/s00355-008-0316-x
19. Moulin, H.: Axioms of Cooperative Decision Making, Econometric Society monographs, vol. 15. Cambridge University Press, Cambridge (1988)
20. Revesz, P.Z.: On the semantics of theory change: arbitration between old and new information. In: Proceedings of the 12th ACM SIGACT-SIGMOD-SIGART symposium on Principles of database systems. pp. 71–82. ACM (1993)
21. Savage, L.: The Foundations of Statistics. Wiley, New York (1954)
22. Schweizer, B., Sklar, A.: Associative functions and statistical triangle inequalities. Publ. Math. Debrecen. **8**, 169–186 (1961)
23. Sen, A.K.: Choice, Welfare and Measurement. Harvard University Press, Cambridge (1997)
24. Tungodden, B.: Egalitarianism: is leximin the only option? Working papers, Norwegian School of Economics and Business Administration (1999). http://EconPapers.repec.org/RePEc:fth:norgee:4/99
25. Viana, H., Alcântara, J.: Propositional Belief Merging with T-conorms (proofs) https://db.tt/OZWSR0EO
26. Weber, S.: A general concept of fuzzy connectives, negations and implications based on t-norms and t-conorms. Fuzzy Sets Syst. **11**(1–3), 103–113 (1983)
27. Yager, R.R.: On a general class of fuzzy connectives. Fuzzy Sets Syst. **4**(3), 235–242 (1980)

Sufficientarian Propositional Belief Merging

Henrique Viana[(✉)] and João Alcântara

Department of Computer Science, Federal University of Ceará,
Fortaleza, Brazil
henriquev.iana@ifce.edu.br, jnando@lia.ufc.br

Abstract. In this paper, we will introduce the theory of sufficientarianism in belief merging. Originally, there are two main subclasses of belief merging operators: majority operators which are related to the theory of utilitarianism, and arbitration operators which are related to egalitarianism. We will show that sufficientarianism brings novelties to the area by satisfying new logical postulates different from those satisfied by majority or arbitration operators.

1   Introduction

Sufficientarianism [6] is a theory of distributive justice which aims at ensuring that each person has an adequate amount of benefits. For instance, we recognize the instrumental importance of having enough sleep, enough money and setting aside enough time. Obviously, this requires a criterion for how much is adequate. Typically, the criterion of adequacy is something like enough to meet basic needs, avoid poverty, or have a minimally decent life, which we refer commonly as the poverty line.

The principle accommodates the concern we normally have for people who are badly off in absolute terms. According to most versions, Sufficiency rejects others theories of distributive justice, such as utilitarianism (concerned with the sum total of happiness of a group) and egalitarianism (which wants to promote equality for all people in a group).

When we consider the area of propositional belief merging, which studies the fusion of independent and equally reliable sources of information expressed in propositional logic, we need to consider some aspects of rationality and distributive justice. Indeed, there are already some belief merging operators based on utilitarianism and egalitarianism [5,9,12], but a study of sufficientarian operators in the context of belief merging is still missing.

In this paper, we will consider two operators of the theory of sufficientarianism in the belief merging settings: the *headcount* and the *shortfall* operators. *Headcount* operator simply counts the number of people below the poverty line and aims at minimizing the number of people below this line. On the other hand, *shortfall* operator adds up each person's *shortfall* from the poverty line (or the

---

This research is supported by CNPq and CAPES.

N. Criado Pacheco et al. (Eds.): EUMAS 2016/AT 2016, LNAI 10207, pp. 421–435, 2017.
DOI: 10.1007/978-3-319-59294-7_35

amount that they need to reach the poverty line). The objective is also to minimize the amount of *shortfall* in a group. We will prove that these operators
have a different rationality from others previously defined for belief merging by
showing that they satisfy different logical postulates.

The paper is structured as follows. In Sect. 2, we will present some basic
notions of propositional belief merging. In Sect. 3, we will introduce the operators of sufficiency for belief merging and will explore their respective logical
properties. In Sect. 4, we compare the differences between the sufficientarian
and the egalitarian reasoning. Finally, in Sect. 5 we will conclude the paper. Due
to lack of space, the proofs have been omitted and can be found in [21].

2   Propositional Belief Merging

2.1   Preliminaries

We will consider a propositional language $\mathcal{L}$ over a finite alphabet $\mathcal{P}$ of propositional variables. An interpretation ω is a function from $\mathcal{P}$ to $\{0, 1\}$. The set
of all interpretations is denoted by Ω. An interpretation ω is a model of a
formula $\varphi(\omega \models \varphi)$ if and only if it makes it true in the usual classical truth
functional way. Let φ be a formula, $mod(\varphi)$ denotes the set of models of φ, i.e.,
$mod(\varphi) = \{\omega \in \Omega \mid \omega \models \varphi\}$.

A belief base K can be seen as a propositional formula φ representing
the beliefs of an agent. Let $K_1, \ldots, K_n$ be n belief bases (not necessarily different). We call belief set the multi-set E consisting of those n belief bases:
$E = \{K_1, \ldots, K_n\}$. We denote $\bigwedge E$ the conjunction of the belief bases of E, i.e.,
$\bigwedge E = K_1 \wedge \cdots \wedge K_n$. The union of multi-sets will be denoted by $\sqcup$.

A pre-order $\leq$ over Ω is a reflexive and transitive relation on Ω. A pre-order
is total if $\forall \omega_i, \omega_j \in \Omega, \omega_i \leq \omega_j$ or $\omega_j \leq \omega_i$. Let $\leq$ be a pre-order over Ω, we define
$<$ as follows: $\omega_i < \omega_j$ iff $\omega_i \leq \omega_j$ and $\omega_j \not\leq \omega_i$, and $\approx$ as $\omega_i \approx \omega_j$ iff $\omega_i \leq \omega_j$ and
$\omega_j \leq \omega_i$. We say $\omega_i \in min(mod(\varphi), \leq)$ iff $\omega_i \models \varphi$ and $\forall \omega_j \in mod(\varphi) \ \omega_i \leq \omega_j$.
Let E_1, E_2 be two belief sets. E_1 and E_2 are equivalent, noted $E_1 \equiv E_2$, iff there
is a bijection f from $E_1 = \{K_{11}, \ldots, K_{n1}\}$ to $E_2 = \{K_{12}, \ldots, K_{n2}\}$ such that
$\models f(K_{i1}) \leftrightarrow K_{i2}$.

2.2   Logical Properties

We employ a logical definition for merging in the presence of Integrity Constraints (IC), that is, we give a set of properties an operator has to satisfy to
have a rational behavior concerning the merging. Additionally, the result of the
merging has to obey a set of integrity constraints represented by a propositional
formula μ. We will consider merging operators Δ mapping a belief set E and an
integrity constraint μ to a set of interpretations that represents the merging of
E according to μ.

Definition 1 (IC merging operators [9]**).** *Let* E, E_1, E_2 *be belief sets;* K_1, K_2 *be belief bases; and* μ, μ_1, μ_2 *be propositional formulas.* Δ_μ *is an IC merging operator if and only if it satisfies the following postulates:*

(IC0) $\Delta_\mu(E) \models \mu$.
(IC1) If μ *is consistent, then* $\Delta_\mu(E)$ *is consistent.*
(IC2) If $\bigwedge E$ *is consistent with* μ*, then* $\Delta_\mu(E) \equiv \bigwedge E \wedge \mu$.
(IC3) If $E_1 \equiv E_2$ *and* $\mu_1 \leftrightarrow \mu_2$*, then* $\Delta_{\mu_1}(E_1) \equiv \Delta_{\mu_2}(E_2)$.
(IC4) If $K_1 \models \mu$ *and* $K_2 \models \mu$*, then* $\Delta_\mu(\{K_1, K_2\}) \wedge K_1$ *is consistent if and only if* $\Delta_\mu(\{K_1, K_2\}) \wedge K_2$ *is consistent.*
(IC5) $\Delta_\mu(E_1) \wedge \Delta_\mu(E_2) \models \Delta_\mu(E_1 \sqcup E_2)$.
(IC6) If $\Delta_\mu(E_1) \wedge \Delta_\mu(E_2)$ *is consistent, then* $\Delta_\mu(E_1 \sqcup E_2) \models \Delta_\mu(E_1) \wedge \Delta_\mu(E_2)$.
(IC7) $\Delta_{\mu_1}(E) \wedge \mu_2 \models \Delta_{\mu_1 \wedge \mu_2}(E)$.
(IC8) If $\Delta_{\mu_1}(E) \wedge \mu_2$ *is consistent, then* $\Delta_{\mu_1 \wedge \mu_2}(E) \models \Delta_{\mu_1}(E)$.

See [9] for explanations of these properties. Besides these logical postulates, two main sub-classes of IC merging operators have been defined from two postulates. They are the IC majority operator, which has been tailored to resolve conflicts by adhering to the majority wishes (utilitarianism), while IC arbitration operator has a more consensual behavior (egalitarianism).

Definition 2 (IC majority and arbitration operators [9]**).** *An IC merging operator is a majority operator if it satisfies* **(Maj)** $\exists n \Delta_\mu(E_1 \sqcup \underbrace{E_2 \sqcup \cdots \sqcup E_2}_{n}) \models$ $\Delta_\mu(E_2)$. *An IC merging operator is an arbitration operator if it satisfies* **(Arb)** *If* $\Delta_{\mu_1}(\{K_1\}) \equiv \Delta_{\mu_2}(\{K_2\}), \Delta_{\mu_1 \leftrightarrow \neg\mu_2}(\{K_1, K_2\}) \equiv (\mu_1 \leftrightarrow \neg\mu_2), \mu_1 \not\models \mu_2, \mu_2 \not\models \mu_1$. *Then* $\Delta_{\mu_1 \vee \mu_2}(\{K_1, K_2\}) \equiv \Delta_{\mu_1}(\{K_1\})$.

A majority operator states that if an information has a majority audience, then it will be the choice of the group. Unlike the majority operator, an arbitration operator tries to satisfy each belief base as much as possible. Alternatively, there exists a more intuitive way to define IC merging operators: IC merging operator may correspond to a family of pre-orders on possible words.

Definition 3 (Syncretic Assignment [10]**).** *A Syncretic Assignment is a function mapping each belief set* E *to a total pre-order* $\leq_E$ *over interpretations such that for any belief sets* E, E_1, E_2 *and for any belief bases* K_1, K_2 *the following conditions hold:*

1. *If* $\omega \models \bigwedge E$ *and* $\omega' \models \bigwedge E$*, then* $\omega \approx_E \omega'$.
2. *If* $\omega \models \bigwedge E$ *and* $\omega' \not\models \bigwedge E$*, then* $\omega <_E \omega'$.
3. *If* $E_1 \equiv E_2$*, then* $\leq_{E_1} = \leq_{E_2}$.
4. $\forall \omega \models K_1\ \exists \omega' \models K_2\ \omega' \leq_{\{K_1, K_2\}} \omega$.
5. *If* $\omega \leq_{E_1} \omega'$ *and* $\omega \leq_{E_2} \omega'$*, then* $\omega \leq_{E_1 \sqcup E_2} \omega'$.
6. *If* $\omega <_{E_1} \omega'$ *and* $\omega \leq_{E_2} \omega'$*, then* $\omega <_{E_1 \sqcup E_2} \omega'$.

A *majority syncretic assignment* is a syncretic assignment which satisfies the following condition: 7. *If* $\omega <_{E_2} \omega'$*, then* $\exists n\ \omega <_{E_1 \sqcup E_2^n} \omega'$. A *fair syncretic assignment* is a syncretic assignment which satisfies the following condition: 8. *If* $\omega <_{K_1} \omega'$, $\omega <_{K_2} \omega''$ *and* $\omega' \approx_{\{K_1, K_2\}} \omega''$*, then* $\omega <_{\{K_1, K_2\}} \omega'$.

We have the following representation for merging operators:

Proposition 1 [10]. *A merging operator Δ is an IC merging operator (resp. an IC majority, an IC arbitration operator) iff there exists a syncretic assignment (resp. a majority syncretic assignment, a fair syncretic assignment) that maps each belief set E to a total pre-order $\leq_E$ over Ω such that $mod(\Delta_\mu(E)) = min(mod(\mu), \leq_E)$.*

2.3   Example of Merging Operators

In the sequel, we give a model-theoretic definition of merging operators.

Example 1 [16]. Let us consider the academic example of a teacher who asks his three students which among the languages SQL (denoted by s), O_2 (denoted by o) and *Datalog* (denoted by d) they would like to learn. The first student wants to learn only SQL or O_2, that is, $K_1 = (s \vee o) \wedge \neg d$. The second one wants to learn either *Datalog* or O_2 but not both, i.e., $K_2 = (\neg s \wedge d \wedge \neg o) \vee (\neg s \wedge \neg d \wedge o)$. For the last, the third one wants to learn the three languages: $K_3 = (s \wedge d \wedge o)$.

With respect to Example 1, we have three propositional variables: s, d and o. The set of all possible outcomes/interpretations is $\Omega = \{\omega_1, \ldots, \omega_8\}$, where $\omega_1 = \neg s \neg d \neg o$, $\omega_2 = \neg s \neg d o$, $\omega_3 = \neg s d \neg o$, $\omega_4 = \neg s d o$, $\omega_5 = s \neg d \neg o$, $\omega_6 = s \neg d o$, $\omega_7 = s d \neg o$ and $\omega_8 = s d o$. Slightly abusing the notation, the interpretation $\omega_1 = \neg s \neg d \neg o$ may be viewed as $\omega_1(s) = 0$, $\omega_1(d) = 0$ and $\omega_1(o) = 0$. We will show three examples of operators commonly associated with belief merging: the *sum*, the *max* and *leximax* operators. First, we will assume that we utilise a distance between interpretations.

Definition 4 (Distance [9]). *A distance measure between interpretations is a total function d from $\Omega \times \Omega$ to $\mathbb{N}$ such that for every $\omega_i, \omega_j \in \Omega$, (1) $d(\omega_i, \omega_j) = d(\omega_j, \omega_i)$, and (2) $d(\omega_i, \omega_j) = 0$ iff $\omega_i = \omega_j$.*

In the first works on model-based merging, the distance used was the Hamming distance between interpretations [4], but any other distance may be used as well. The Hamming distance between interpretations characterizes the number of propositional variables by which they differ. For example, the Hamming distance (denoted d_H) between $\omega_1 = \neg s \neg d \neg o$ and $\omega_6 = s \neg d o$ is $d_H(\omega_1, \omega_6) = 2$. Another example of a well known distance measure is the drastic distance [8], denoted by d_D, which is defined as $d_D(\omega_1, \omega_2) = 0$, if $\omega_1 = \omega_2$; $d_D(\omega_1, \omega_2) = 1$, otherwise.

Now we define the distance between an interpretation ω_i and a belief base K as follows: $d(\omega_i, K) = \min_{\omega_j \models K} d(\omega_i, \omega_j)$. The distance between an interpretation ω_i and a belief base K is the minimum distance between ω_i and the models of K.

Example 2. Regarding Example 1, the Hamming distance between each interpretation w.r.t. K_1, K_2 and K_3 are shown in Table 1. For instance, $d_H(\omega_1, K_1) = min(d_H(\omega_1, \omega_2), d_H(\omega_1, \omega_5), d_H(\omega_1, \omega_6)) = min(1, 1, 2) = 1$.

Table 1. The Hamming distances from K_1, K_2 and K_3.

Ω	$d_H(\omega, K_1)$	$d_H(\omega, K_2)$	$d_H(\omega, K_3)$
$\omega_1 = \neg s \neg d \neg o$	1	1	3
$\omega_2 = \neg s \neg d o$	0	0	2
$\omega_3 = \neg s d \neg o$	2	0	2
$\omega_4 = \neg s d o$	1	1	1
$\omega_5 = s \neg d \neg o$	0	2	2
$\omega_6 = s \neg d o$	0	1	1
$\omega_7 = s d \neg o$	1	1	1
$\omega_8 = s d o$	1	2	0

One simple way of defining the overall distance between an interpretation and a belief set is to take the sum of the distances between all the interpretations of Ω and each knowledge base K_i.

Definition 5 (*sum operator* [9]). *Let E be a belief set, d a distance measure and ω an interpretation. We define the distance between an interpretation and a belief set as $d_{sum}(\omega, E) = \sum_{K \in E} d(\omega, K)$. Then we have the following pre-order:*
$\omega_i \leq_E^{d,sum} \omega_j$ *iff* $d_{sum}(\omega_i, E) \leq d_{sum}(\omega_j, E)$. *The operator $\Delta_\mu^{d,sum}$ is defined by* $mod(\Delta_\mu^{d,sum}(E)) = min(mod(\mu), \leq_E^{d,sum})$.

The result of $\Delta_\mu^{d,sum}$ can be considered as the "election" of the most popular possible choices among the integrity constraints [10].

Example 3. The results of sum merging operator w.r.t. Hamming distance for Example 2 are found in Table 2. The resulting pre-order $\leq_E^{d_H,sum}$ is $\{\omega_2, \omega_6\} \leq_E^{d_H,sum} \{\omega_4, \omega_7, \omega_8\} \leq_E^{d_H,sum} \{\omega_3, \omega_5\} \leq_E^{d_H,sum} \omega_1$.

Table 2. Hamming distances between Ω and E w.r.t. *sum*, *max* and *leximax* operators.

Ω	$d_{H\,sum}(\omega, E)$	$d_{H\,max}(\omega, E)$	$L_\omega^{d_H,E}$
$\omega_1 = \neg s \neg d \neg o$	5	3	$(3,1,1)$
$\omega_2 = \neg s \neg d o$	**2**	2	$(2,0,0)$
$\omega_3 = \neg s d \neg o$	4	2	$(2,2,0)$
$\omega_4 = \neg s d o$	3	1	$(1,1,1)$
$\omega_5 = s \neg d \neg o$	4	2	$(2,2,0)$
$\omega_6 = s \neg d o$	**2**	1	$\mathbf{(1, 1, 0)}$
$\omega_7 = s d \neg o$	3	1	$(1,1,1)$
$\omega_8 = s d o$	3	2	$(2,1,0)$

In the example above we have that $\omega_2 \approx_E^{d_H,sum} \omega_6$ (both are the most preferred interpretations), $\omega_4 \approx_E^{d_H,sum} \omega_7 \approx_E^{d_H,sum} \omega_8$ and $\omega_3 \approx_E^{d_H,sum} \omega_5$. Consequently, when $\mu = \top$, $mod(\Delta_\mu^{d_H,sum}(E)) = min(mod(\mu), \leq_E^{d_H,sum}) = \{\omega_2, \omega_6\}$.

Theorem 1 [9]. $\Delta_\mu^{d,sum}$ *satisfies the postulates (IC0)-(IC8) and (Maj), but violates (Arb).*

The operator $\Delta_\mu^{d,sum}$ is called an IC majority merging operator.

Definition 6 (*max* **operator** [13]). *Let E be a belief set, d a distance measure and ω an interpretation. We define the distance between an interpretation and a belief set as $d_{max}(\omega, E) = \max_{K \in E} d(\omega, K)$. Then we have the following pre-order: $\omega_i \leq_E^{d,max} \omega_j$ iff $d_{max}(\omega_i, E) \leq d_{max}(\omega_j, E)$. The operator $\Delta_\mu^{d,max}$ is defined by $mod(\Delta_\mu^{d,max}(E)) = min(mod(\mu), \leq_E^{d,max})$.*

This operator is very close to the minimax rule used in decision theory [17]. The minimax rule tries to minimize the worst cases while $\Delta_\mu^{d,max}$ tries to minimize the more remote distance. The idea of this operator is to find the closest possible interpretations to the overall belief set [10]. The results of *max* merging operator w.r.t. Hamming distance for Example 2 are in the third column of Table 2.

Theorem 2 [10]. $\Delta_\mu^{d,max}$ *satisfies the postulates (IC0)-(IC5), (IC7), (IC8) and (Arb), but violates (IC6) and (Maj).*

$\Delta_\mu^{d,max}$ is said to be an IC arbitration quasi-merging operator since it does not satisfy all the (IC0)-(IC8).

Definition 7 (*leximax* **operator** [9]). *Let $E = \{K_1, \ldots, K_n\}$ be a belief set. For each interpretation ω we build the list $(d_1^\omega, \ldots, d_n^\omega)$ of distances between this interpretation and the n belief bases in E, i.e., $d_i^\omega = d(\omega, K_i)$. Let $L_\omega^{d,E}$ be the list obtained from $(d_1^\omega, \ldots, d_n^\omega)$ by sorting it in descending order. Let $\leq_{lex}$ be the lexicographical order between sequences of integers, i.e., $(x_1, \ldots, x_n) \leq_{lex} (y_1, \ldots, y_n)$ if (1) for all i, $x_i \leq y_i$ or (2) there exists i such that $x_i < y_i$ and for all $j < i$, $x_j \leq y_j$. We define the following pre-order: $\omega_i \leq_E^{d,leximax} \omega_j$ iff $L_{\omega_i}^{d,E} \leq_{lex} L_{\omega_j}^{d,E}$. The operator $\Delta_\mu^{d,leximax}$ is defined by $mod(\Delta_\mu^{d,leximax}(E)) = min(mod(\mu), \leq_E^{d,leximax})$.*

The aim of this operator is to capture the "arbitration" behavior of $\Delta_\mu^{d,max}$ with the gaining of the logical postulate **(IC6)**. The idea behind the operator has been used in social choice theory [15], where were employed leximin functions instead. The results of *leximax* merging operator w.r.t. Hamming distance for Example 2 are in the fourth column of Table 2.

Theorem 3 [10]. $\Delta_\mu^{d,leximax}$ *satisfies the postulates (IC0)-(IC8) and (Arb), but violates (Maj).*

3   Sufficientarian Belief Merging

In this section, we propose a characterization of a sufficientarian merging operator, based on the IC merging operators postulates and the syncretic assignment.
Besides, we present three different sufficientarian merging operators, as well as
additional logical postulates and their relation with each operator.

The idea of sufficientarianism is commonly traced back to Harry Frankfurt's
doctrine of sufficiency [6], which inspired and motivated a number of versions
of sufficientarianism in recent works [7]. Frankfurt claims that the doctrine of
sufficiency aims at maximizing the number of individuals at or above sufficiency
(sometimes denoted as the poverty line in the literature). We can translate Frankfurt's claim into our framework's point of view as

Frankfurt Sufficientarianism (FS): An interpretation ω is at least as good
as another ω' if and only if the number of agents at or above sufficiency in ω is
at least as large as that in ω'.

We want to show in the following subsections that the sufficientarian principle
can be also a plausible tool in belief merging. Although it differs from utilitarian
and egalitarian operators [5], it still can exhibit some interesting properties. We
will focus on two different operators: *headcount* and *shortfall* [7,20].

3.1   The *headcount* Operator

One of the simplest measures is the *headcount* measure, which originally simply
counts the number of people below a poverty line:

The Headcount Claim: we should maximize the number of agents who secure
enough.

This principle assesses interpretations solely in terms of the number of agents
who have secured enough in each interpretation. Benefits to those who do not
reach the sufficiency do not improve the assessment of the interpretation. As
for the framework of belief merging with distance measure, we will consider the
distance measure between an interpretation and a belief base as the measure of
sufficiency.

Definition 8 (*headcount* operator). *Let $E = \{K_1, \ldots, K_n\}$ be a belief set, d
a distance measure, ω an interpretation and $s \geq 0$ a threshold. We define the
number of belief bases in E above s as $hc(\omega, d, E, s) = \#(\{K_i \in E \mid d(\omega, K_i) > s\})$,
where $\#(A)$ is the cardinal of the set A. Then we have the following pre-order:
$\omega_i \leq_E^{d,hc_s} \omega_j$ iff $hc(\omega_i, d, E, s) \leq hc(\omega_j, d, E, s)$. The merging operator Δ_μ^{d,hc_s} is
defined by $mod(\Delta_\mu^{d,hc_s}(E)) = min(mod(\mu), \leq_E^{d,hc_s})$.*

Note that when $s = 0$, we have $\Delta_\mu^{d,hc_0} \equiv \Delta_\mu^{d_D,sum}$, that is, the *headcount*
merging operator is equivalent to the distance-based merging with the drastic
distance and the *sum* operator.

Example 4. The results of *headcount* merging operator w.r.t. Hamming distance
and $s = 1$ for Example 2 are found in Table 3. The resulting pre-order $\leq_E^{d_H,hc_1}$
is $\{\omega_4, \omega_6, \omega_7\} \leq_E^{d_H,hc_1} \{\omega_1, \omega_2, \omega_8\} \leq_E^{d_H,hc_1} \{\omega_3, \omega_5\}$.

Table 3. *Headcount* of Hamming distances between Ω and E for $s = 1$.

Ω	$d_H(\omega, K_1)$	$d_H(\omega, K_2)$	$d_H(\omega, K_3)$	$hc(\omega, d_H, E, 1)$
ω_1	1	1	3	1
ω_2	0	0	2	1
ω_3	2	0	2	2
ω_4	1	1	1	0
ω_5	0	2	2	2
ω_6	0	1	1	0
ω_7	1	1	1	0
ω_8	1	2	0	1

In this example, for $s = 1$, the merging operator is counting the number of agents in which the Hamming distance value is greater than 1 in a belief base. The interpretations ω_4, ω_6 and ω_7 are the result of the merging (when $\mu = \top$). Note that the sufficientarian principle is only worried if the agents are below or equal the threshold s and not about their specific values (ω_4, ω_6 and ω_7 are equivalent, independently of their values).

To begin with our analysis around logical postulates of the sufficientarian operator, first we will discuss about the basic IC postulates.

Theorem 4. Δ_μ^{d,hc_s} *satisfies* **(IC0)–(IC1)**, **(IC3)-(IC8)**. *The postulate* **(IC2)** *is not satisfied in the general case. Additionally,* Δ_μ^{d,hc_s} *satisfies both* **(Arb)** *and* **(Maj)**.

When $s = 1$, the postulate **(IC2)** is satisfied (i.e., it is equivalent to $\Delta_\mu^{d_D, sum}$). The reason why **(IC2)** is not always true comes from the fact that even if an interpretation is not a consensus between agents, it can be a choice of the merging operator (e.g., the interpretation ω_4 in Example 4).

Let us take a closer look on postulate **(IC2)**: If $\bigwedge E$ is consistent with μ, then $\Delta_\mu(E) \equiv \bigwedge E \wedge \mu$. It states that the result of belief merging needs to be complete and sufficient the consensus among agents (if the consensus exists). This postulate corresponds to syncretic assignments 1 and 2 [10]: 1. If $\omega \models \bigwedge E$ and $\omega' \models \bigwedge E$, then $\omega \approx_E \omega'$; 2. If $\omega \models \bigwedge E$ and $\omega' \not\models \bigwedge E$, then $\omega <_E \omega'$. We argue that the sufficientarian principle is weaker than **(IC2)**, since the result of belief merging needs to be only sufficient w.r.t. the consensus among agents (if the consensus exists). Formally, we have

(IC2'): If $\bigwedge E$ is consistent with μ, then $\bigwedge E \wedge \mu \models \Delta_\mu(E)$.

In other words, there are some choices of the merging that are not the consensus of the group. The following corresponding syncretic assignments for **(IC2')** are:

1. If $\omega \models \bigwedge E$ and $\omega' \models \bigwedge E$, then $\omega \approx_E \omega'$;
2'. If $\omega \models \bigwedge E$ and $\omega' \not\models \bigwedge E$, then $\omega \leq_E \omega'$.

Definition 9 (Sufficientarian merging operator). *We call IC sufficientarian merging operator an operator satisfying (IC0), (IC1), (IC2') and (IC3)-(IC8), and a sufficientarian syncretic assignment an assignment satisfying conditions 1, 2' and 3-6.*

Theorem 5. *A merging operator Δ_μ is an IC sufficientarian merging operator iff it can be represented by a sufficientarian syncretic assignment.*

This representation can be also used for majority and arbitration merging operators.

Corollary 1. Δ_μ^{d,hc_s} *is an IC majority/arbitration sufficientarian merging operator.*

Interestingly, the *headcount* operator satisfies **(Maj)** and **(Arb)**. It is not a new result, since it was already proved in [11] that the operator $\Delta_\mu^{d_D,sum}$ and the family of full sense operators Δ_μ^{d,sum^n} [11] satisfy also this condition. Based on these results, we can say that each agent is relevant for the merging and the opinion of the majority is the priority. The arbitration property guarantees that two agents will have a more consensual behavior in their decisions.

To finish this first part we will bring some new logical postulates for this sufficientarian operator, which come from the literature of liberal egalitarianism [1,3,14], a theory of justice which seeks to combine the values of equality, personal freedom and personal responsibility. The first postulate we will discuss is the Harm Principle [1]:

Definition 10 (Harm Principle Condition) (HP). *For all $\omega_1, \omega_2, \omega_1', \omega_2' \in \Omega$, suppose $E = \{K_1, \ldots, K_n\}$, a distance measure d, a merging operator op and $\omega_1 <_E^{d,op} \omega_2$. Consider ω_1', ω_2' such that $\exists i \in \{1, \ldots, n\}$, $d(\omega_1, K_i) < d(\omega_1', K_i)$, $d(\omega_2, K_i) < d(\omega_2', K_i)$ and $\forall j \neq i\ d(\omega_1, K_j) = d(\omega_1', K_j)$, $d(\omega_2, K_j) = d(\omega_2', K_j)$. If $d(\omega_2', K_i) > d(\omega_1', K_i)$ then $\omega_1' <_E^{d,op} \omega_2'$.*

In distributive justice theory, this condition embodies the idea that "an individual has the right to prevent society from acting against him in all circumstances of change in his welfare, provided that the welfare of no other individual is affected". In the satisfaction merging framework, it can be seen as considering that an interpretation ω_1 is more preferred than ω_2, and if occasionally an agent i has a loss of satisfaction in ω_1 and ω_2, resulting in ω_1' and ω_2', ω_1' will be preferred to ω_2' if the satisfaction of i in ω_1' is still greater than the satisfaction of i in ω_2'.

In other words, we can say that a single agent does not have the power of interference in the choice of the group, when occurs a loss of satisfaction (we can also see the non-satisfaction of the condition as a kind of veto power of agents). The equality emerges from the fact that no specific agent has the power to interfere in the decision of the group. A restricted version of **(HP)** was proposed in [14]:

Definition 11 (Weak Harm Principle Condition) *(WHP)*. *For all ω_1, ω_2, $\omega_1', \omega_2' \in \Omega$, suppose $E = \{K_1, \ldots, K_n\}$, a distance measure d, a merging operator op and $\omega_1 <_E^{d,op} \omega_2$. Consider ω_1', ω_2' such that $\exists i \in \{1, \ldots, n\}$, $d(\omega_1, K_i) < d(\omega_1', K_i)$, $d(\omega_2, K_i) < d(\omega_2', K_i)$ and $\forall j \neq i \ d(\omega_1, K_j) = d(\omega_1', K_j)$, $d(\omega_2, K_j) = d(\omega_2', K_j)$. If $d(\omega_2', K_i) > d(\omega_1', K_i)$ then $\omega_1' \leq_E^{d,op} \omega_2'$.*

The Weak Harm Principle assigns a veto power to agents in situations in which they suffer a harm and no other agent is affected. This veto power is weak as it only applies to certain welfare configuration (individual preferences after the satisfaction loss must coincide with group's initial preferences) and, crucially, the agent cannot force group's preferences to coincide with her own.

The counterpart of the Harm Principle, where a gain in the agent i's distance value is considered, it is called Individual Benefit Principle [1] and defined as

Definition 12 (Individual Benefit Principle Condition) *(IBP)*. *For all $\omega_1, \omega_2, \omega_1', \omega_2' \in \Omega$, suppose $E = \{K_1, \ldots, K_n\}$, a distance measure d, a merging operator op and $\omega_1 <_E^{d,op} \omega_2$. Consider ω_1', ω_2' such that $\exists i \in \{1, \ldots, n\}$, $d(\omega_1', K_i) < d(\omega_1, K_i)$, $d(\omega_2', K_i) < d(\omega_2, K_i)$ and $\forall j \neq i \ d(\omega_1, K_j) = d(\omega_1', K_j)$, $d(\omega_2, K_j) = d(\omega_2', K_j)$. If $d(\omega_2', K_i) > d(\omega_1', K_i)$ then $\omega_1' <_E^{d,op} \omega_2'$.*

The intuition is the same of Harm Principle, but now there is a decrease in agent i's distance value in ω_1' and ω_2'. This condition can be weakened too:

Definition 13 (Weak Individual Benefit Principle Condition) *(WIBP)*. *For all $\omega_1, \omega_2, \omega_1', \omega_2' \in \Omega$, suppose $E = \{K_1, \ldots, K_n\}$, a distance measure d, a merging operator op and $\omega_1 <_E^{d,op} \omega_2$. Consider ω_1', ω_2' such that $\exists i \in \{1, \ldots, n\}$, $d(\omega_1', K_i) < d(\omega_1, K_i)$, $d(\omega_2', K_i) < d(\omega_2, K_i)$ and $\forall j \neq i \ d(\omega_1, K_j) = d(\omega_1', K_j)$, $d(\omega_2, K_j) = d(\omega_2', K_j)$. If $d(\omega_2', K_i) > d(\omega_1', K_i)$ then $\omega_1' \leq_E^{d,op} \omega_2'$.*

Now we can relate *headcount* merging operator with the conditions presented above.

Theorem 6. Δ_μ^{d,hc_s} *satisfies (WHP) and (WIBP). The conditions (HP) and (IBP) are not satisfied in the general case.*

We highlight that the *sum* merging operator does not satisfy any of these properties. The *max* and *leximax* operators satisfy all four postulates. In this sense, the *headcount* operator has an intermediate behavior for these postulates when compared with the basic merging operators *sum* and *max/leximax*.

3.2   The *shortfall* Operator

Let us consider another measure of aggregation. The *shortfall* measure simply adds up each agent's total gap from the distance measure (where an agent?s *shortfall* is zero if her distance value is at or below s). The total *shortfall* operator simply adds up the *shortfall* from s across agents above s, and takes the unweighted sum to be the measure of the disvalue of the group [7]. Differently from *headcount* operator, which tries to minimize the number of agents above s, the *shortfall* is concerned with the total amount of deficit of the agents above s, and aims at minimizing it.

Definition 14 (*shortfall* operator). *Let $E = \{K_1, \ldots, K_n\}$ be a belief set, d a distance measure, ω an interpretation and $s \geq 0$ a threshold. We define the shortfall of belief bases in E above s in ω as $sh(\omega, d, E, s) = \sum_{d(\omega,K_i)>s} d(\omega, K_i) - s$. Then we have the following pre-order: $\omega_i \leq_E^{d,sh_s} \omega_j$ iff $sh(\omega_i, d, E, s) \leq sh(\omega_j, d, E, s)$. The merging operator Δ_μ^{d,sh_s} is defined by $mod(\Delta_\mu^{d,sh_s}(E)) = min(mod(\mu), \leq_E^{d,sh_s})$.*

We can see that this approach is prioritarian for those satisfaction values above s. The relative overall goodness of an interpretation is judged on the basis of a sum of different agent's well-being where it is determined by the disvalue of an agent's *shortfall* from s.

Example 5. The results of *shortfall* merging operator w.r.t. Hamming distance and $s = 1$ for Example 2 are in Table 4. The resulting pre-order $\leq_E^{d_H,sh_1}$ is $\{\omega_4, \omega_6, \omega_7\} \leq_E^{d_H,sh_1} \{\omega_2, \omega_8\} \leq_E^{d_H,sh_1} \{\omega_1, \omega_3, \omega_5\}$.

Shortfall operator is sensible for the variations of satisfaction values. In the above example, we can see this change with respect to interpretation ω_1. The total *shortfall* of ω_1 is equal to 2 and it is equivalent to ω_3 and ω_5. Regarding the *headcount* operator in Example 4, the interpretation ω_1 is more preferred than ω_3 and ω_5, because only one agent has the distance value above the $s = 1$, against two agents for ω_3 and ω_5. With respect to logical postulates some alterations also occur.

Theorem 7. *Δ_μ^{d,sh_s} satisfies (IC0), (IC1), (IC2'), (IC3)–(IC8) and (Maj). The postulates (IC2), (Arb), (HP), (WHP), (IBP) and (WIBP) are not satisfied in the general case.*

Table 4. *Shortfall* of Hamming distances between Ω and E for $s = 1$.

Ω	$d_H(\omega, K_1)$	$d_H(\omega, K_2)$	$d_H(\omega, K_3)$	$sh(\omega, d_H, E, 1)$
ω_1	1	1	3	2
ω_2	0	0	2	1
ω_3	2	0	2	2
ω_4	1	1	1	0
ω_5	0	2	2	2
ω_6	0	1	1	0
ω_7	1	1	1	0
ω_8	1	2	0	1

The *shortfall* merging operator is an IC majority sufficientarian operator. The difference between *headcount* and *shortfall* operators appears when some egalitarian and libertarian conditions are considered, as in the loss of logical postulates **(Arb)**, **(WHP)** and **(WIBP)**. This arises and can be explained by the sensibility to changes in an agent's distance value.

4   A Humanitarian Principle

In this section, we will present some logical postulates which characterize the behavior of the sufficientarian merging operators. We consider them as representatives of a humanitarian principle and, in light of this principle, we show that *shortfall* operator is more just than *headcount* operator.

We will include some positions in the general category of egalitarian perspectives of distributive justice presented in [19]. Some families of egalitarian properties were defined in this work and we will use a particular one, modified to fit in to our framework of belief merging.

Weak Povertymax for s (WPM-s): Let $E = \{K_1, \ldots, K_n\}$, d be a distance measure and $s \geq 0$. For all ω, ω', if (1) there exists a $k \leq n$ such that $d(\omega', K_k) > d(\omega, K_k)$ and $d(\omega', K_k) > s$; (2) every position i that $d(\omega, K_i) > s$ implies $d(\omega', K_i) \geq d(\omega, K_i)$, then $\omega \leq_E^{d, op_s} \omega'$.

Weak Povertymax differs from the *leximax* principle by giving priority to the agents above the threshold s, while the leximax gives absolute priority to the worst off agent (also referred as equality promotion [19]).

Leximax (LM): Let $E = \{K_1, \ldots, K_n\}$ be a belief set. For each interpretation ω we build the list $(d_1^\omega, \ldots, d_n^\omega)$ of distances between this interpretation and the n belief bases in E, i.e., $d_i^\omega = d(\omega, K_i)$. Let $L_\omega^{d,E}$ be the list obtained from $(d_1^\omega, \ldots, d_n^\omega)$ by sorting it in descending order. For all $\omega, \omega' \in \Omega$, (1) if there exists a position $k \leq n$ such that $d_k^{\omega'} > d_k^\omega$; and (2) for every $j < k$, $d_j^{\omega'} = d_j^\omega$, then $\omega <_E \omega'$ (ω is more preferred than ω'). Otherwise, $\omega \approx_E \omega'$.

We argue that **(WPM-s)** can be seen as a humanitarian condition, since it tries to favor a group of agents instead of prioritizing a unique agent. The agents below the threshold (s) are not considered essential for the group's choice. By way of illustration, **(WPM-s)** implies that the loss of a single agent satisfaction value s outweighs any gain of any number of agents above s.

We need to make an important observation about **(WPM-s)**. Its corresponding definition in [19] considers that the relation between ω and ω' is indeed a strict preference (the consequence is that ω is more preferred than ω'). Here in this work, we stated the definition of the axiom as ω is at least as just as ω' ($\omega \leq_E^{d, op_s} \omega'$).

Now, consider the following new condition:

Weak Absolute Priority of those Above s (WAPA-s): Let $E = \{K_1, \ldots, K_n\}$, d be a distance measure and $s \geq 0$. For all ω, ω', if there exist j, k such that (1) $s \geq d(\omega, K_j) > d(\omega', K_j)$; (2) $d(\omega', K_k) > d(\omega, K_k) \geq s$; (3) for $i \neq j, k$, $d(\omega, K_i) = d(\omega', K_i)$, then $\omega \leq_E^{d, op_s} \omega'$.

With the addition of Strong Pareto and Anonymity [19], we can achieve an important result.

Strong Pareto (SP): Let $E = \{K_1, \ldots, K_n\}$. For all $\omega, \omega' \in \Omega$, if $\exists i \in \{1, \ldots, n\}$ $\omega <_{K_i} \omega'$ and $\forall j \neq i$, $\omega \leq_{K_j} \omega'$, then $\omega <_E \omega'$.

Strong Pareto is equivalent to the logical postulate **(IC6b)** defined in [5]: **(IC6b)** If $\Delta_\mu(K_1) \wedge \cdots \wedge \Delta_\mu(K_n) \not\models \bot$, then $\Delta_\mu(\{K_1, \ldots, K_n\}) \models \Delta_\mu(K_1) \wedge \cdots \wedge \Delta_\mu(K_n)$.

Anonymity (A): Let $E = \{K_1, \ldots, K_n\}$ be a belief set and $l_\omega^{d,E} = (d_1^\omega, \ldots, d_n^\omega)$ the list of distances between the interpretation ω and the n belief bases in E. For all $\omega, \omega' \in \Omega$, if $l_\omega^{d,E}$ is a permutation of $l_{\omega'}^{d,E}$, then $\omega \approx_E \omega'$.

Theorem 8 [19]. *If a Syncretic Assignment satisfies* **(WAPA-s)**, **(SP)** *and* **(A)**, *then it satisfies* **(WPM-s)**.

In conclusion, by taking into account the humanitarian concern, this principle shows that there are alternatives to the *Leximax* principle of justice. Such an egalitarian position deals with both the claim of equality promotion and the humanitarian perspective. Hence, we have the following results for the *headcount* and *shortfall* operators.

Theorem 9. Δ_μ^{d,hc_s} *and* Δ_μ^{d,sh_s} *satisfy* **(WAPA-s)**, **(SP)**, **(A)** *and* **(WPM-s)**.

At a first view, both *headcount* and *shortfall* operators share the same humanitarian reasoning presented in the Weak Povertymin for s, but we can strengthen the assumptions of the proposed formulation in order to distinguish them. We will do this by restricting the preference relation: the conditions will conclude now that one interpretation is strictly more preferred than another one (instead of the relation of "at least as preferred"):

Strong Povertymin for s (SPM-s): Let $E = \{K_1, \ldots, K_n\}$, d be a distance measure and $s \geq 0$. For all ω, ω', if (1) there exists a position $k \leq n$ such that $d(\omega', K_k) > d(\omega, K_k)$ and $d(\omega', K_k) > s$; (2) every position i that $d(\omega, K_i) > s$ implies $d(\omega', K_i) \geq d(\omega, K_i)$, then $\omega <_E^{d,op_s} \omega'$.

The same restriction is applied for **(WAPA-s)**:

Strong Absolute Priority of those Above s (SAPA-s): Let $E = \{K_1, \ldots, K_n\}$, d be a distance measure and $s \geq 0$. For all ω, ω', if there exist j, k such that (1) $s \geq d(\omega, K_j) > d(\omega', K_j)$; (2) $d(\omega', K_k) > d(\omega, K_k) \geq s$; (3) for $i \neq j, k$, $d(\omega, K_i) = d(\omega', K_i)$, then $\omega <_E^{d,op_s} \omega'$.

We achieve the following result:

Corollary 2. *If a Syncretic Assignment satisfies* **(SAPA-s)**, **(SP)** *and* **(A)**, *then it satisfies* **(SPM-s)**.

We can now distinguish *headcount* and *shortfall* operators:

Theorem 10. Δ_μ^{d,sh_s} *satisfies* **(SAPA-s)**, **(SP)**, **(A)** *and* **(SPM-s)**.

The result is not true for the *headcount* operator. This is explained by the fact that the *shortfall* operator can distinguish two different interpretations above s, while the *headcount* treats them equally.

5   Conclusion

In this paper, we proposed to investigate another theory of distributive justice called sufficientarianism. It is a prioritarian approach which is concerned with alleviating the inequalities among groups of agents who have not reached a sufficient condition. It is an alternative to the egalitarianism, where the inequalities are remedied by giving absolute preference to the worst off agents in a group. The sufficientarian claim considers not only one, but everyone in the group of the less favored agents. It is important since it brings a more humanitarian approach to the distributive justice. In the literature, these inequalities are calculated using Poverty index measurement. We applied two of them: the *headcount* operator and the *shortfall* operator.

A characterization of the principle of sufficientarianism was proposed for the area of belief merging. Furthermore, we showed that sufficientarian merging operators may satisfy additional logical postulates, e.g., the headcount operator satisfies **(WHP)** and **(WIBP)**.

A point of discussion in this work was about conditions for a humanitarian distribution of justice. We found that the *headcount* operator is weaker than *shortfall* with respect to a property called Povertymax, which is a humanitarian alternative to the leximax principle. The shortfall operator establishes a strong version of Povertymax.

As a future work, we plan to research on other poverty measures indexes. There are in the literature important measures as Sen index, the Foster-Greer-Thorbecke index, Gini index, Theil index, Lorenz curve, etc. [2,18]. A further investigation into this issue is envisaged.

Another point which is argued by some authors against sufficientarianism is the necessity of a threshold (e.g., the poverty line). It is possible to avoid this fixed value and work with other parameters, as for example the mean of the utilities (each interpretation would have its own mean value). The consequences of this representation as well as its rationalization and intuition deserve more attention and a deeper analysis.

References

1. Alcantud, J.C.R.: Non-interference and continuity: impossibility results for the evaluation of infinite utility streams. Technical report, p. 13 (2011)
2. Allison, P.D.: Measures of inequality. Am. Sociol. Rev. **43**(6), 865–880 (1978). http://www.jstor.org/stable/2094626
3. Cappelen, A.W., Tungodden, B.: A liberal egalitarian paradox. Econ. Philos. **22**, 393–408 (2006)
4. Dalal, M.: Investigations into a theory of knowledge base revision. In: Proceedings of the Seventh American National Conference on Artificial Intelligence (AAAI 1988), pp. 475–479 (1988)
5. Everaere, P., Konieczny, S., Marquis, P.: On egalitarian belief merging. In: AAAI (2014)
6. Frankfurt, H.: Equality as a moral ideal. Ethics **98**(1), 21–43 (1987)

7. Hirose, I.: Axiological sufficientarianism. In: Fourie, C., Annette, R. (eds.) How Much is Enough? Sufficiency and Thresholds in Health Care (2014)

8. Konieczny, S., Lang, J., Marquis, P.: DA^2 merging operators. Artif. Intell. **157**(1–2), 49–79 (2004)

9. Konieczny, S., Pino-Pérez, R.: Merging with integrity constraints. In: Hunter, A., Parsons, S. (eds.) ECSQARU 1999. LNCS, vol. 1638, pp. 233–244. Springer, Heidelberg (1999). doi:10.1007/3-540-48747-6_22

10. Konieczny, S., Pino-Pérez, R.: Merging information under constraints: a logical framework. J. Logic Comput. **12**(5), 773–808 (2002)

11. Konieczny, S., Pino-Pérez, R.: On the frontier between arbitration and majority. In: KR, pp. 109–120 (2002)

12. Konieczny, S., Pino-Pérez, R.: Logic based merging. J. Philos. Logic **40**(2), 239–270 (2011)

13. Lin, J., Mendelzon, A.O.: Merging databases under constraints. Int. J. Coop. In. Syst. **7**, 55–76 (1996)

14. Lombardi, M., Miyagishima, K., Veneziani, R.: Liberal egalitarianism and the harm principle. MPRA paper, University Library of Munich, Germany (2013). http://EconPapers.repec.org/RePEc:pra:mprapa:48458

15. Moulin, H.: Axioms of Cooperative Decision Making, Econometric Society Monographs, vol. 15. Cambridge University Press, Cambridge (1988)

16. Revesz, P.Z.: On the semantics of theory change: arbitration between old and new information. In: Proceedings of the 12th ACM SIGACT-SIGMOD-SIGART Symposium on Principles of Database Systems, pp. 71–82. ACM (1993)

17. Savage, L.: The Foundations of Statistics. Wiley, New York (1954)

18. Sen, A.: On Economic Inequality. Clarendon Press, Oxford (1973)

19. Tungodden, B.: Egalitarianism: is leximin the only option? Working papers, Norwegian School of Economics and Business Administration (1999). http://EconPapers.repec.org/RePEc:fth:norgee:4/99

20. Vallentyne, P.: Sen on sufficiency, priority, and equality. In: Contemporary Philosophy in Focus: Amartya Sen, p. 138 (2010)

21. Viana, H., Alcântara, J.: Sufficientarian Propositional Belief Merging (proofs) https://db.tt/d7fpHB3g

AT 2016: Algorithms and Frameworks

The Argumentative Mediator

Carles Sierra[1]([✉]), Ramon Lopez de Mantaras[1], and Simeon Simoff[2]

[1] Artificial Intelligence Research Institute (IIIA-CSIC), Barcelona, Spain
{sierra,mantaras}@iiia.csic.es
[2] Western Sydney University, Sydney, Australia
s.simoff@westernsydney.edu.au

Abstract. In this paper we introduce a negotiation mediator in a multi-agent context. When negotiation fails, a mediator can interact with the parties, find out about their goals, ontologies, and arguments for and against negotiation outcome, and suggest solutions based on previous experience. An algorithmic schema to be instantiated with particular argumentation, semantic alignment and case-base reasoning techniques is presented. The proposal is neutral with respect to which particular technique is selected. An example illustrates the approach that is framed in the existing body of literature on argumentation and mediation.

1 Introduction

Achieving an agreement in disputes and deals is a process by which two or more parties reach a mutually acceptable outcome. The focus of this work is in consensual dispute resolution, where the parties themselves make the decision about the process and the outcome. Among the consensual dispute resolution processes, this work addresses mediation – the confidential process where an independent and neutral third party assists the disputants to negotiate and reach a decision about their dispute. Unlike arbitration or expert appraisal, the mediator *cannot impose* a binding solution upon the parties.[1] However, if the parties do not reach a solution and a case goes to an arbitration, the documented intermediate solutions and parties positions through the mediation process can be provided in assistance to the arbitration process.

Through *problem interpretation and reframing capabilities* as well as through various facilitation strategies and procedures, mediators are able to assist negotiating parties to explore the negotiation issues in depth and reach acceptable joint decisions, in many cases, among the best feasible solutions that benefit all negotiating parties under the given circumstances. The long term goal of this work targets the integrative "value creating" mediation strategies [31], which, in addition to interest-based mediation, consider alternative approaches, where the mediator and the parties involved go beyond the "zero sum" view, arguing about the solutions, sometimes reconsidering the original problem in order

---

[1] The Institute of Arbitrators and Mediators: http://www.iama.org.au/mediation.htm.

© Springer International Publishing AG 2017
N. Criado Pacheco et al. (Eds.): EUMAS 2016/AT 2016, LNAI 10207, pp. 439–454, 2017.
DOI: 10.1007/978-3-319-59294-7_36

to create more potential solutions and, if possible, to expand resources under negotiation. In line with the above, from the four categories of contemporary mediation approaches - evaluative, facilitative (also known as interest-based), transformative and narrative [23], we consider *transformative* (or *deliberative*) *mediation*, where the mediator's function is to persuade disputants to transform their respective perceptions of and responses to the dispute or conflict [23]. The motivation for this work is the transformative view, first expressed in [9], that conflict is primarily related to human interaction rather than just conflict of interests of self-interested individuals, aiming only at maximising their individual gain. In some sense, we view mediation as a process of creating value in disputes in line with [28]. We are further motivated by the developments of the cognitive negotiation theory, which focused on what negotiators are likely to do rather than what they should do [44].

Through the process mediators have to remain neutral and to move parties through various impasse-points in the negotiation. How to get to the "win-win" solution or convince the parties to revisit their stance is the know-how that distinguishes a successful mediation *process* and a competent mediator. Designing such evolving process is essential for designing a skilful computerised mediator. In [40] we formulated the issues facing the development of an automated mediation agent. The paper formulated the necessary and sufficient conditions for a mediation to take place and demonstrated the validity of those conditions on examples from the area of international relations. The title of the paper — "Mediation = Information Revelation + Analogical Reasoning" summarised, respectively, the two intertwined sets of requirements towards computational automated mediator: (a) capabilities to seek and utilise relevant information, and (b) capabilities to "think out of the box", i.e. to approach the problem that has stalled negotiation from a fresh perspective, if necessary, reframe it and present to negotiating parties the new solution, possibly unseen by them when remaining within their "original boxes".

Subsequently, the authors have focused on the development of the computational ability to "think out of the box."[2] In Sect. 4 in [40] we have introduced a high level view of the MediaThor mediating agent, which utilises past experiences and information from negotiating parties to mediate disputes and change positions of negotiating parties. The realisation of MediaThor required the specification of the mental models $\mathcal{M}^t$ of the agents at time t, introduced in [40] and the mechanisms for aligning of/agreeing on the ontologies of the dispute they used. The architecture of the mediator, presented in [2], implemented MediaThor's case-based reasoning (CBR) approach to mediation integrating analogical and common sense reasoning, achieving both the ability to utilise experience with cases in different domains and the ability to structurally transform the set of issues of the dispute for a better solution. The above mentioned problem reframing has been implemented as a combination of case-based reasoning and common sense reasoning with structure mapping.

---

[2] Not to be confused with the term "computational thinking" as introduced and discussed in [48].

This paper continues the development of an automated mediation agent within the 'curious negotiator' framework [39]. The automated mediator MediaThor presented in [40] and [2] generates the solution and presents it to the negotiating parties. Both works [2,40] are focused on solution construction aspects of mediation, based on the information revealed by the negotiating agents, including their goals and reservations. An acceptable solution was constructed in a single CBR cycle. What if one of the negotiating agents does not accept the solution proposed by the mediator and *argues* against it? What if both agents argue against parts of the solution and the mediator has to support the proposed solution with arguments relevant to the stance of each negotiator? These questions, related to the dynamics of the mediation process, were beyond the scope of both works [2,40]. They are the focus of the developments presented in this paper.

The contribution of this paper includes the integral analysis of the interplay of mediation and argumentation and the development of a high-level computational model of the transformative mediation process. Specifically, Sect. 3 presents five aspects of mediation, where structured argumentation offers means for realising automated mediation process. These are the overarching five principles for building an automated mediator, which uses argumentation through the mediation process for extracting additional information about the position of the negotiating agents, finding solutions and justifying them. The section then presents the high level modifications of the formal models of negotiating agents and the cases in the case base of the mediating agent, and the suitability of bipolar argumentation frameworks. Sections 4 and 5 present a high level view of the way a computational mediator can use argumentation and a case study which demonstrates how that works.

2 Computational Mediators

Early work on computational mediation has recognised the role of the mediator as a problem solver. The MEDIATOR [25,26] focused on case-based reasoning as a single-step for finding a solution to a dispute resolution problem. The case-based cycle of the MEDIATOR operated within a single domain. In the example with the Israel-Egypt dispute, the similarity was sought within political disputes that involved land and military force (see details in [26], p. 512). The selection of the closest case was biased towards the similarity of the arguments thrown in the dispute rather than the object of the dispute. The mediation process was reduced to a one-step case-based inference, aimed at selecting an abstract "mediation plan". The work did not consider the value of the actual dialog with the mediated parties.

Computational capabilities for problem restructuring in negotiation and mediation has been investigated in [41] as means for manipulating mediated parties in order to change their perceptions of the issues. The PERSUADER operated within the game theory paradigm, applied to labor management disputes. It deployed mechanisms for problem restructuring that operated over the goals and the relationships between the goals. It used means to manipulate the utility values of negotiating parties. To some extent this work is a precursor of another game-theoretic approach to mediation, presented in [47] and the interest-based negotiation approach in [32].

Manipulative mediation of human parties involved in dispute resolution has been attempted in the area of decision support systems. The Family_Winner [3] treats the dispute resolution process as a series of "mutual trade-offs" aiming at modifying the initial preferences of the parties in order to converge eventually to a feasible and mutually acceptable solution. Further, this line of works considered the incorporation of the notion of fairness in the mediation strategies [1].

MArCo is a theoretical framework, presented in [42], which stands aside of the mainstream works on computational mediation. It recognises that the computational system has to analyse the ongoing interaction and have the capability to identify a conflict and to mediate it. It does not necessarily aim at achieving conflict resolution per se. MArCo mediation framework is geared towards conflict control strategy, which attempts to reduce the negative consequences of conflict, rather than solely looking for a negotiation outcome that resolves the conflict. The mediator is oriented towards facilitating group development, hence the goal of the mediation is to suggest courses of action that provoke articulation and reflection [42].

Notable is the recent series of publications about the computational mediators AutoMed [13,14] and AniMed [29,30] for multi-issue bilateral negotiation under time constraints. Common to this family of game-theoretic creatures is that the solution space is known and that the mediator can offer either specific complete instances out of this space (AutoMed) or incremental partial solutions which are subsets of the solution set (AniMed). The later offers a better interaction interface. Similar to the mediator proposed in the 'curious negotiator' [39], both mediators monitor negotiations and intervene when there is a conflict between negotiators.

One of the reasons why negotiation may end up in a need for mediation is that in real settings information only about negotiation issues is not sufficient to derive the outcome preferences [46]. An exploratory study [36] of a multiple (three) issue negotiation setting suggest the need for developing integrative (rather than position-based) negotiation processes which take into account information about motivational orientation of negotiating parties. Incorporation of information beyond negotiation issues has been the focus of a series of works related to information-based agency [17,18,38] and the LOGIC framework [37]. These works are part of our broader series of works which consider the incorporation of information extracted from the illocutions of the negotiation dialogue as well as information provided by external information mining agents in response to a query from a negotiating agent. The research in value-focused thinking [24], value-based argumentation frameworks [5], interest-based negotiation [33] and interest-based reasoning [46] considers the treatment of information related to the preferences of parties involved in negotiation and decision making, in addition to the concrete negotiable matter (aspect, issue). These are the fundamental objectives, values, concerns, goals and desires, labeled as *interests* - any kind of motivational information that leads to a preference [46].

Before getting into the technical aspects, it is worth mentioning that the award of the 2002 Nobel Peace Prize to Jimmy Carter recognises the role of successful mediation in contemporary world.[3] Distinct element of Jimmy Carter's mediation strategies is the intertwining of the settlement-centred strategies, in which the mediator is highly manipulative in order to bring the parties to a resolution, proposed by the mediator, and relationship-centred (transformative) where the mediator assists parties in building mutual trust and understanding, and developing mutually-acceptable solutions on their own. Both types of mediation strategies involve elements of argumentation [35].

3 Unfolding Argumentation in the Mediation Process

Below we consider the aspects of mediation, where computational argumentation offers means for realising computational mediation.

I. *Mediation is a fluid and evolving process* [23]. Argumentation offers the machinery, which will enable the evolution of the process. It is very unlikely that the mediator is an "oracle", who knows the overall solution set at the beginning of the process. The mediator constructs the alternative solution sets with the help of the information extracted from the interaction with the negotiating parties. In real world a solution may emerge as a result of a change of the problem space. This is in fact what a skilful mediator does. This implies that the mediator will need to convince negotiators that the problem space needs to be and can be changed.

II. *The mediator should be capable to justify (explain) its suggestions.* Argumentation offers such justification mechanism. The approach in mediation can be analogous to the approach developed in argumentation-based machine learning [7], where an inductive learning algorithm is extended to use part of the data to form explanatory arguments for the outputs.

III. *The mediator should be capable to develop, adjust or extend an agreed ontology.* The agreed ontology, established at the beginning of the mediation session, may evolve as a result of the mediation process. Argumentation offers means to justify changes in the agreed ontology. The ontology is both means in the mediation and argumentation process (it is essential in the

---

[3] Though Jimmy Carter as a President launched a number of controversial weapons programs, see "The Nobel Peace Prize 2002 - Presentation Speech." [http://www.nobelprize.org/nobel_prizes/peace/laureates/2002/presentation-speech.html] for the supportive argument about his contribution as a mediator. Whilst Jimmy Carter's mediation between Israel and Egypt (the Camp David Accords) is a well-known classics, less known are his other numerous successes. For example, in 1994 his mediation resulted in a four-month cease-fire agreement in Bosnia at the height of the ethnic violence in the Balkans, and a pledge from all sides to resume peace talks, which eventually led to a peace agreement between Croatia, Bosnia, and Serbia in 1995. In 2008, his mediation led to the re-establishment in 2009 of relations at the level of charge d'affaires between Colombia and Ecuador.

implementation of analogy in [40]) or can be the object of the argumentation when mediator develops the ontology on which both parties agreed, or attempt to change it.

IV. *The mediator should be capable to extract information (intelligence) and use it in the mediation process.* Such information comes from the mediation process and from external sources. Argumentation can provide information about the process, encoded in the arguments, and can trigger external information queries.

V. *The mediator should be capable to combine different argumentation systems.* Each of the negotiators, involved in the mediation process most likely will have, loosely speaking, a collection of arguments in support of their position. If mediation allows argumentation, then the mediator will need to combine these argumentation systems in an argument that supports its proposed solution.

We develop further the mediation approach, introduced in [40] and developed further in [2]. In layman terms, the approach views the problem solving process in mediation as a combination of analogous reasoning and *information revelation*,[4] and part of the mediator's strategy is guiding the process of information revelation. The framework assumes that negotiating agents α and β are willing or are required to achieve a mutually beneficial agreement; that α and β are seeking or will accept mediation; and a mediating agent μ is available, hence, the set of agents involved is $A = \{\alpha, \beta, \mu\}$.

A mediator analyses the way negotiation parties have built their views on the disputed issues [22], i.e. the *sets of arguments* or *argumentation systems* that underpin their respective positions when negotiation stalled. This is in accordance with the view that negotiation can be conceptualised as a problem-solving enterprise in which *mental models* guide the behaviour of negotiating parties [45]. The mental model[5] $\mathcal{M}^t$ at time t, introduced in [40], denotes the internal model (representation) of the agent of the problem about which it negotiates. It represents the knowledge of an agent about a dispute, including the *arguments that support her stance Γ^t*; about the views of the other parties on that dispute that the agent is aware and the expected outcomes. This knowledge is internal to the agent and is being updated as the process progresses, so t will go from t_1 when the mediation starts to t_n when the mediation ends. At each time instant the ontology, goals and arguments may get modified due to the interaction.[6] We thus modify the mental model $\mathcal{M}^t$ presented in [2], and

---

[4] The utilisation of information in negotiation is central to the 'curious negotiator' framework [39].

[5] The term was introduced by Craik in [16] to label the models of reality that the mind forms and uses to anticipate events; we follow the terminology introduced and used in [2,40].

[6] In a previous work [40] we introduced *reservations* as those constraints that an agent requires the solution to satisfy. Here we will consider reservations as properties of the solution that the agent is never giving up and thus simply consider them a special kind of goal.

include the agent's set of arguments as $\mathcal{M}^t = \{o^t, G^t, \Gamma^t\}$, where o^t, G^t, Γ^t denote the agent's ontology, goals, and set of arguments at time t, respectively. We also extend the case-base format in [2], so that each case c_i in the case base is described by $c_i = \{o_i, A_i, G_i, \Gamma_i^{t_1}, \Gamma_i^{t_n}, S_i\}$, denoting respectively the finally agreed ontology of the dispute, the participating agents, the (consistent) union of their goals at time t_n, their joint argumentation system at the beginning and at the end of the mediation, and the final solution itself.

In this work we reuse Dung's theory of argumentation[7] [20], as it reduces argumentation to a completely abstract system consisting of a set of "atomic" arguments and (a set of) binary relation(s) over these. For example, such an atomic argument can be represented in a rule-based fashion as a pair $\{Antecedent, Consequent\}$, where $Antecedent$ is a set of premises. Dung's original work [20] follows the majority of argumentation frameworks, which consider only conflicts between arguments, represented by a single type of binary relation — "attack", "defeat". In order to use argumentation, the mediator, will have to create an acceptable (by both parties) sets of arguments for each proposed solution that it offers. The concept of acceptability is well explored and developed in [20] in a setting abstracted from the nature of the arguments, and interaction between the arguments limited to the "attack" relation. However, this limitation on the relations is counter-intuitive to the way we operate. Indeed, a seres of recent works from Cayrol and Lagasquie-Schiex [10–12] strongly argue in favour of modeling *bipolarity* in argumentation, when the argumentation system supports both *defeat* and *support* relations. This distinction has been supported by studies in cognitive psychology which have shown that the two kinds of preferences are completely *independent* and are processed separately in the mind [10]. For instance, it is not clear how an "attack"-based argumentation system will help our mediator μ to handle a situation when negotiating agent α advances an argument that confirms premises used by an argument provided earlier to μ by negotiating agent β. We adapt and extend bipolar argumentation frameworks, developed by Cayrol and Lagasquie-Schiex [10–12] as they reuse the principles, properties and algorithms of Dung's framework. We also consider mechanisms for building a "common" argumentation system acceptable to both α and β and mechanisms for merging argumentation frameworks as discussed in [15].

Every argument coming from α and β is a piece of information available to the mediator μ. Dubois and Prade's analysis of bipolarity of information for the needs of knowledge representation [19] supports the need for separate treatment of support relation, so that μ can assess such piece of information as a positive or negative with respect to another argument.

Definition 1. *An Argumentation System $AS = \langle \mathcal{A}, \mathcal{R} \rangle$ is defined by a set of arguments $\mathcal{A} = \{a_i | i \in \mathbf{N}^+\}$ and a set of binary relations between arguments $\mathcal{R} = \{r_k\}_{k \in K}$ where $r_k = \{(a_i, a_j) | a_i \in \mathcal{A}, a_j \in \mathcal{A}, i, j \in \mathbf{N}^+\}$.*

---

[7] For a broader and detailed overview of the state-of-the-art in argumentation the reader is referred to the editorial [4] to the special issue on argumentation of the Artificial Intelligence journal and to the recent collection of chapters [34].

For Dung's framework $\mathcal{R} = \{attack\}$; for bipolar argumentation frameworks $\mathcal{R} = \{attack; support\}$. We recall the three postulates for the automated mediator, formulated in [40]:

Postulate 1. *An automated mediator μ should start interaction with extracting information about the position of the parties on the negotiation;*

This information is formulated as a collection of arguments $\mathcal{A} \subset \Gamma^t$.

Postulate 2. *An automated mediator μ should develop an independent "grand view" of the problem, which is more comprehensive than the individual views of α and β;*

Postulate 3. *An automated mediator μ should operate from the initial stance that α and β are willing to achieve a mutually beneficial agreement and will accept mediation by μ.*

In this paper we have committed to deliberative mediation, hence, we add the following postulate for the automated mediator.

Postulate 4. *An automated mediator μ should be capable of developing an argumentation system AS_μ^t supporting the proposed solution, which is acceptable under agreed semantics by α and β.*

For instance, this may be achieved by the incorporation of the argumentation systems AS_α^t and AS_β^t in line with the ways proposed in [15], or with the *ArgMed* algorithm, presented in next section.

4   The Argumentative Mediator - Integrating CBR and Argumentation

In this section we present in layman terms how the mediator can use argumentation. At t_1 the mediator μ requests α and β for their respective ontologies of the dispute $o_\alpha^{t_1}$ and $o_\beta^{t_1}$. If $o_\alpha^{t_1}$ and $o_\beta^{t_1}$ are not the same, μ aligns these ontologies through *argumentation*[8] with α and β into the agreed ontology $o_\mu^{t_1}$. This step can adapt the methodology of the DILIGENT argumentation process in ontology engineering [43] and elements of the argumentation based approaches for ontology alignments presented in [6,27]. Further, μ provides to α and β the agreed $o_\mu^{t_1}$. The mediator μ requests the goals $G_\alpha^{t_1}$ and $G_\beta^{t_1}$ from α and β in terms of the working ontology $o_\mu^{t_1}$. If $G_\alpha^{t_1}$ and $G_\beta^{t_1}$ do not conflict, then $S^{t_1} = G_\alpha^{t_1} \cup G_\beta^{t_1}$. If there is a conflict then μ requests the argumentation systems that agents want to make public at time t_1, $AS_\alpha^{t_1} = \langle \mathcal{A}_\alpha, \mathcal{R}_\alpha \rangle$, such that $\mathcal{A}_\alpha \subseteq \mathcal{A}_\alpha^{t_1}$, $\mathcal{R}_\alpha \subseteq \mathcal{R}_\alpha^{t_1}$ and $AS_\beta^{t_1} = \langle \mathcal{A}_\beta, \mathcal{R}_\beta \rangle$, such that $\mathcal{A}_\beta \subseteq \mathcal{A}_\beta^{t_1}$, $\mathcal{R}_\beta \subseteq \mathcal{R}_\beta^{t_1}$, and merges them into $AS_\mu^{t_1}$. Next the mediator queries the CBR system. The query includes structural and semantic compositions of $o_\mu^{t_1}$, $G_\alpha^{t_1}$, $G_\beta^{t_1}$, and $AS_\mu^{t_1}$, with capability to retrieve

---

[8] See [21] for a compact overview of the area.

cases analogous to the current conflict/dispute and not necessarily in the same problem domain. If the solution is not accepted by the parties the process iterates until a solution is accepted or no progress can be made. During the process agents α and β update their mental models.

Algorithm 1. *ArgMed*

Require: $A = \{\alpha, \beta\}$ the set of agents
Ensure: S a solution to the conflict
1: $t = t_0$
2: $S^t = \emptyset$
3: **repeat**
4:    $t = t + 1$
5:    get $o_\alpha^{t'}$ $\{o_\alpha^{t'} \sqsubseteq o_\alpha^t$ if $t' \leq t\}$
6:    get $o_\beta^{t'}$ $\{o_\beta^{t'} \sqsubseteq o_\beta^t$ if $t' \leq t\}$
7:    $o_\mu^t = agree(o_\alpha^t, o_\beta^t)$ {via [6, 27, 43]}
8:    send o_μ^t to α and β
9:    $G_\alpha^t = get(\alpha, G_\alpha^t|_{o_\mu^t})$ {goals aligned to o_μ^t}
10:    $G_\beta^t = get(\beta, G_\beta^t|_{o_\mu^t})$ {goals aligned to o_μ^t}
11:    **if** $conflict(G_\alpha^t, G_\beta^t)$ **then**
12:        get AS_α^t
13:        get AS_β^t
14:        $AS_\mu^t = merge(AS_\alpha^t, AS_\beta^t)$
15:        $S^t = Adapt(CBR(o_\mu^t, G_\alpha^t, G_\beta^t, AS_\mu^t))$
16:    **else**
17:        $S^t = G_\alpha^t \cup G_\beta^t$
18:    **end if**
19: **until** $accept(\{\alpha, \beta\}, S^t)$ or $S^t = S^{t-1}$ {repeat until the agents agree or there is no progress}
20: **if** $accept(\{\alpha, \beta\}, S^t)$ **then**
21:    $memorise(o_\mu^t, \{\alpha, \beta\}, G_\alpha^t \cup G_\beta^t, AS_\mu^{t_1}, AS_\mu^t, S^t)$
22:    **return** S^t
23: **else**
24:    **return** $\emptyset$
25: **end if**

The solution sets in the case base can include two types of solutions - those that are directly applicable and those that require reframing of the problem. For example, in the case of resource disputes, the equal division of the resource between the disputing parties is a directly applicable solution. Reconsideration of the resource, as a collection of different structural parts, can lead to splitting the resource in different sets of its parts. This is restructuring of the problem; the solution in this case is offering different sets to the disputing parties.

5   Case Study: The Orange Dispute Revisited

We show the interplay of argumentation and case-based reasoning in the mediation process following an extended version of the Orange Dispute, introduced in [25] and considered in [40]. Two sisters need an orange each and there is one orange left, hence, they negotiate. The sisters are the negotiation agents α and β. Negotiation stalled at t_1 and the mediating agent μ intervenes, following the *ArgMed* procedure of previous section. In order to show the approach we extend the formulation of the orange dispute scenario with additional facts, that contribute to the rationale about why each sister wanted the orange — the set of arguments which each sister has, some of which or all can be used in support of having the orange, namely:

- α is expecting a business visitor to come for an afternoon tea. α plans to prepare an *orange chiffon cake*, as its interesting history[9] can be a good conversation starter. The recipe requires both *orange zest* and *orange juice*. She plans to serve it with a Calvados cocktail, which also requires orange juice. As the orange is a large one, α believes the juice of the orange will be sufficient for both.
- β has a flu. She wants to immediately start treatment as her timely recovery is critical due to forthcoming performance on stage over the weekend. She follows treatment with natural remedies, so she plans to take *orange juice* for the high concentration of vitamin C.

We represent the narrative in terms of propositions that constitute the argumentation knowledge bases $\Gamma_\alpha^{t_x}$ and $\Gamma_\beta^{t_x}$ which are part of the mental models $\mathcal{M}_\alpha^{t_x}$ and $\mathcal{M}_\beta^{t_x}$ of α and β, respectively, for $t_1 \le t_x \le t_n$. We denote by a_i, b_i and m_i the propositional symbols representing the facts in $\Gamma_\alpha^{t_x}$, $\Gamma_\alpha^{t_x}$ and $\Gamma_\mu^{t_x}$. The sets of arguments $\Gamma_\alpha^{t_1}$ and $\Gamma_\beta^{t_1}$ are shown in Tables 1 and 2.

Table 1. The set of arguments $\Gamma_\alpha^{t_1}$ that α has at t_1

$a_1 = \alpha$ plans to impress the business visitor
$a_2 = \alpha$'s selection of a cake with interesting history is part of the plan
$a_3 = \alpha$'s selection of the accompanying drink with interesting history is part of the plan
$a_4 =$ the orange chiffon cake has an interesting history, dating back to 1927
$a_5 =$ Calvados has an interesting history, dating back to Napoleonic times
$a_6 =$ accompanying drink matches selected cake
$a_7 =$ the recipe of the orange chiffon cake requires orange *zest* and *juice*
$a_8 =$ the recipe of the Calvados cocktail requires orange *juice*
$a_9 =$ one large orange is sufficient for both the cake and the cocktail
$a_{10} = \alpha$ knows the visitor likes citruses and citrus flavour
$a_{11} = \alpha$ respects her sister β commitment to performances
$a_{12} = \alpha$ needs an orange

---

[9] Harry Baker (1883–1974), a Los Angeles insurance agent turned caterer, is said to have invented the original chiffon cake in 1927. Baker kept the recipe secret for 20 years, baking the popular creation for the Hollywood elite. Finally, in 1947, he sold the recipe to Betty Crocker's parent company, General Mills, which released it to the public in 1948, naming it "the first really new cake in 100 years".

Table 2. The set of arguments $\Gamma_\beta^{t_1}$ that β has at t_1

$b_1 = \beta$ plans immediately to take measures against the flu to restore her health
$b_2 = \beta$ needs timely recovery
$b_3 = \beta$ aims to be ready for the performance over the weekend
$b_4 =$ orange *juice* is an excellent natural source of vitamin C
$b_5 = \beta$ prefers treatment with natural remedies
$b_6 = \beta$ likes cakes with orange flavour
$b_7 = \beta$ needs the juice of an orange

Step t_1: When negotiation between α and β stalled at t_1, the mediator μ, following the *ArgMed* procedure, requests from α and β their respective ontologies of the dispute $o_\alpha^{t_1}$ and $o_\beta^{t_1}$. In this case $o_\mu^{t_1}$ is a replica of either of $o_\alpha^{t_1}$ and $o_\beta^{t_1}$, as they are aligned, representing orange as a dividable resource with peel, pulp and juice, as shown in [40]. The mediator μ received from α and β their goals $G_\alpha^{t_1} = \{a_{12} - \text{need a full orange}; a_1 - \text{impress a business visitor}\}$ and $G_\beta^{t_1} = \{b_7 - \text{need the juice of a full orange}; b_2 - \text{need timely recovery}\}$. The working ontology $o_\mu^{t_1}$ recognises the divisibility of the orange, hence the conflict in the two goals is in the requirement for the orange juice. As $conflict(G_\alpha^{t_1}, G_\beta^{t_1}) = True$, μ requests the argumentation systems $AS_\alpha^{t_1}$ and $AS_\beta^{t_1}$.

The argumentation systems are described in terms of *support* and *attack* relations: $\mathcal{R} = \{r_k\}_{k \in \{supp, att\}}$.

$AS_\alpha^{t_1} = \langle \mathcal{A}_\alpha^{t_1}, \mathcal{R}_\alpha^{t_1} \rangle = \langle \{a_1, a_3, a_5, ..., a_{10}, a_{12}\}, r_{supp} = \{(a_6, a_9), (a_5, a_3), (a_3, a_1), (a_{10}, a_{12}), (a_8, a_9), (a_9, a_{12}), (a_{12}, a_1)\} \rangle$

$AS_\beta^{t_1} = \langle \mathcal{A}_\beta^{t_1}, \mathcal{R}_\beta^{t_1} \rangle = \langle \{b_1, ..., b_5, b_7\}, r_{supp} = \{(b_1, b_3), (b_2, b_3), (b_3, b_7), (b_4, b_7), (b_5, b_7), (b_7, b_2)\} \rangle$

The operator $merge(AS_\alpha^{t_1}, AS_\beta^{t_1})$ returns the merged argumentation system $AS_\mu^{t_1}$, in which μ finds out that argument b_7 attacks both a_7 and a_8. Arguments b_7 and a_{12} mutually attack each other as shown in Fig. 1a. This means $S^t = \emptyset$, which result triggers the case base retrieval and case adaptation operator

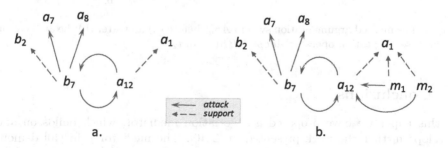

Fig. 1. The merged argumentation system $AS_\mu^{t_1}$ before (a) and after (b) the application of the case adaptation operator $Adapt(CBR(\cdot))$ in t_1.

$Adapt(CBR(o_\mu^{t_1}, G_\alpha^{t_1}, G_\beta^{t_1}, AS_\mu^{t_1}))$ of μ. As a result of this operation, μ adds to $AS_\mu^{t_1}$ two new arguments: $m_1 = $ *the recipe of the almond pound cake with orange glaze requires only orange zest* and $m_2 = $ *the recipe of limoncello does not require orange juice*, which both support a_1, and attack a_{12} as shown in Fig. 1b. μ returns to α and β the following solution $S^{t_1} = \{m_1, m_2, b_7, b_2, a_1\}$.

Step t_2: The operator $accept(\{\alpha, \beta\}, S^{t_1}) = false$, meaning that S^{t_1} has not been accepted, triggers the beginning of the next step. During this step α uses argumentation to inform μ that m_1 does not have an interesting history. There are no changes in the agreed ontology: $o_\mu^{t_2} = o_\mu^{t_1}$. The mediator μ receives from α and β their revised goals $G_\alpha^{t_2} = G_\alpha^{t_1} \cup \{a_2\}$ and $G_\beta^{t_2} = G_\beta^{t_1}$, and the updated argumentation systems $AS_\alpha^{t_2} = \langle \mathcal{A}_\alpha^{t_1} \cup \{a_2, m_1, m_2\}, \mathcal{R}_\alpha^{t_1} \cup \{\{r_{supp} = (a_2, a_1)\}, \{r_{att} = (a_2, m_1), (a_2, m_1)\}\}\rangle$ and $AS_\beta^{t_2} = AS_\beta^{t_1}$. The operator $merge(AS_\alpha^{t_2}, AS_\beta^{t_2})$ returns the merged argumentation system $AS_\mu^{t_2}$, shown in Fig. 2a, in which μ finds out that its suggestion m_1 and m_2 is attacked by a_2, which in turn supports a_1. This results in $S_1^t = \emptyset$, which triggers the case base retrieval and case adaptation operator $Adapt(CBR(o_\mu^{t_2}, G_\alpha^{t_2}, G_\beta^{t_2}, AS_\mu^{t_2}))$ of μ. As a result of this operation, μ replaces m_1 and m_2 in $AS_\mu^{t_2}$ with two new arguments: $m_3 = $ *the recipe of the orange Santiago tart requires only zest and has an interesting history* and $m_4 = $ *crema de limoncello does not require orange juice*, which both support a_1 and a_2, and attack a_{12} as shown in Fig. 2b. μ returns to α and β the following solution $S^{t_2} = \{m_3, m_4, b_7, b_2, a_1, a_2\}$.

The proposed solution S^{t_2} satisfies the goals $G_\alpha^{t_2}$ and $G_\beta^{t_2}$ of α and β, and $accept(\{\alpha, \beta\}, S^{t_2}) = True$. Consequently, the operator $memorise(o_\mu^{t_2}, \{\alpha, \beta\}, G_\alpha^{t_2} \cup G_\beta^{t_2}, AS_\mu^{t_1}, AS_\mu^{t_2}, S^{t_2})$ updates the case base of μ and this concludes the execution of $ArgMed$.

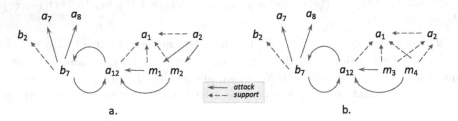

a.   b.

Fig. 2. The merged argumentation system $AS_\mu^{t_1}$ before (a) and after (b) the application of the case adaptation operator $Adapt(CBR(\cdot))$ in t_2.

6   Conclusions

In this paper we have proposed a negotiation mediator, which builds on and develops further the work presented in [2,40]. The mediator μ in [40] demonstrated the problem reframing capabilities and the case-based reasoning approach to implementing such capabilities [2]. These works assumed that α and

β provided all the information, requested by μ, and accepted the solutions provided by μ. Whilst both assumptions served the purpose of the work developed in [2,40], it is unlikely that these assumptions will hold in a majority of real world problems, which require mediation. The work presented in this paper demonstrates the next step towards the development of mediation agents, which can utilise argumentation in the mediation process. The proposed mediator follows an algorithmic schema to be instantiated with particular argumentation semantic alignment and CBR techniques. Similar to [40], the case study uses the popular Orange Dispute problem, extending the information about the reasons for the position of each party involved. This information is then utilised by the mediator in the subsequent cycles. The proposal is neutral with respect to which particular technique is selected.

The interplay between argumentation and the mediation process, presented in Sect. 3, has not discussed the time dependency of arguments. Arguments, for instance those related to specific legislation, may be valid until a new legislation is put in place and then become invalid. Capturing the time dependency of arguments and argumentation systems will require extensions of argumentation frameworks, like the ones proposed in [8], and modification of the description of each case c_i in the case base, the case-based reasoning cycle $CBR(\cdot)$ and the $Adapt(CBR(\cdot))$ operator.

Acknowledgments. This research has been supported by Generalitat de Catalunya project 2014 SGR 118.

References

1. Abrahams, B., Bellucci, E., Zeleznikow, J.: Incorporating fairness into development of an integrated multi-agent online dispute resolution environment. Group Decis. Negot. **21**, 3–28 (2012)
2. Baydin, A.G., López de Mántaras, R., Simoff, S., Sierra, C.: CBR with commonsense reasoning and structure mapping: an application to mediation. In: Ram, A., Wiratunga, N. (eds.) ICCBR 2011. LNCS, vol. 6880, pp. 378–392. Springer, Heidelberg (2011). doi:10.1007/978-3-642-23291-6_28
3. Bellucci, E., Zeleznikow, J.: Developing negotiation decision support systems that support mediators: case study of the Family_Winner system. Artif. Intell. Law **13**(2), 233–271 (2005)
4. Bench-Capon, T.J.M., Dunne, P.E.: Argumentation in artificial intelligence. Artif. Intell. **171**, 619–641 (2007)
5. Bench-Capon, T.J.M.: Persuasion in practical argument using value-based argumentation frameworks. J. Logic Comput. **13**(3), 429–448 (2003)
6. Black, E., Hunter, A., Pan, J.Z.: An argument-based approach to using multiple ontologies. In: Godo, L., Pugliese, A. (eds.) SUM 2009. LNCS (LNAI), vol. 5785, pp. 68–79. Springer, Heidelberg (2009). doi:10.1007/978-3-642-04388-8_7
7. Bratko, I., Žabkar, J., Možina, M.: Argument-based machine learning. In: Rahwan, I., Simari, G.R. (eds.) Argumentation in Artificial Intelligence. Springer US, New York (2009). doi:10.1007/978-0-387-98197-0_23
8. Budán, M.C.D., Gómez Lucero, M., Chesñevar, C., Simari, G.R.: Modeling time and valuation in structured argumentation frameworks. Inf. Sci. **290**, 22–44 (2015)

9. Bush, R.A.B., Joseph, F.: The Promise of Mediation: Responding to Conflict Through Empowerment and Recognition. Jossey-Bass Publishers, San Francisco (1994)
10. Cayrol, C., Lagasquie-Schiex, M.C.: On the acceptability of arguments in bipolar argumentation frameworks. In: Godo, L. (ed.) ECSQARU 2005. LNCS, vol. 3571, pp. 378–389. Springer, Heidelberg (2005). doi:10.1007/11518655_33
11. Cayrol, C., Lagasquie-Schiex, M.-C.: Bipolar abstract argumentation systems. In: Rahwan, I., Simari, G.R. (eds.) Argumentation in Artificial Intelligence, pp. 65–84. Springer, Heidelberg (2009). doi:10.1007/978-0-387-98197-0_4
12. Cayrol, C., Lagasquie-Schiex, M.-C.: Coalitions of arguments: a tool for handling bipolar argumentation frameworks. Int. J. Intell. Syst. 25(1), 83–109 (2010)
13. Chalamish, M., Kraus, S.: AutoMed - an automated mediator for bilateral negotiations under time constraints. In: Proceedings of the International Conference on Autonomous Agents and Multi Agent Systems, AAMAS 2007, Honolulu, Hawaii, USA. IFAAMAS (2007)
14. Chalamish, M., Kraus, S.: AutoMed: an automated mediator for multi-issue bilateral negotiations. Auton. Agents Multi-agent Syst. 24, 536–564 (2012)
15. Coste-Marquis, S., Devred, C., Konieczny, S., Lagasquie-Schiex, M.-C., Marquis, P.: On the merging of Dung's argumentation systems. Artif. Intell. 171, 730–753 (2007)
16. Craik, K.J.W.: The Nature of Explanation. Cambridge University Press, Cambridge (1943)
17. Debenham, J.: Bargaining with information. In: Jennings, N.R., Sierra, C., Sonenberg, L., Tambe, M. (eds.) Proceedings Third International Conference on Autonomous Agents and Multi Agent Systems AAMAS-2004, pp. 664–671. ACM Press, New York (2004)
18. Debenham, J.K., Simoff, S.: Negotiating intelligently. In: Bramer, M., Coenen, F., Tuson, A. (eds.) Proceedings 26th International Conference on Innovative Techniques and Applications of Artificial Intelligence, Cambridge, UK, pp. 159–172 (2006)
19. Dubois, D., Prade, H.: A bipolar possibilistic representation of knowledge and preferences and its applications. In: Bloch, I., Petrosino, A., Tettamanzi, A.G.B. (eds.) WILF 2005. LNCS, vol. 3849, pp. 1–10. Springer, Heidelberg (2006). doi:10.1007/11676935_1
20. Dung, P.M.: On the acceptability of arguments and its fundamental role in nonmonotonic reasoning, logic programming and n-person games. Artif. Intell. 77, 321–358 (1995)
21. Ermolayev, V., Davidovsky, M.: Agent-based ontology alignment: basics, applications, theoretical foundations, and demonstration. In Proceedings of the 2nd International Conference on Web Intelligence, Mining and Semantics WIMS 2012. ACM Press, New York (2012)
22. Gentner, D., Stevens, A.L. (eds.): Mental Models. Erlbaum, Hillsdale (1983)
23. Jarett, B.: The future of mediation: a sociaological perspective. J. Disput. Resol. 2009(1), 49–75 (2010)
24. Keeney, R.L., Thinking, V.-F.: A Path to Creative Decisionmaking. Harvard University Press, Cambridge (1992)
25. Kolodner, J.: Case-Based Reasoning. Morgan Kaufmann Publishers Inc., San Mateo (1993)
26. Kolodner, J.L., Simpson, R.L.: The MEDIATOR: Analysis of an early case-based problem solver. Cogn. Sci. 13(4), 507–549 (1989)

27. Laera, L., Tamma, V., Bench-Capon, T.J.M., Euzenat, J.: Agent-based argumentation for ontology alignments. In Proceedings of the Workshop on Computational Models of Natural Argument, CMNA 2006 (2006)
28. Letia, I.A., Groza, A.: Structured argumentation in a mediator for online dispute resolution. In: Baldoni, M., Son, T.C., Riemsdijk, M.B., Winikoff, M. (eds.) DALT 2007. LNCS, vol. 4897, pp. 193–210. Springer, Heidelberg (2008). doi:10.1007/978-3-540-77564-5_12
29. Lin, R., Gev, Y., Kraus, S.: Bridging the gap: face-to-face negotiations with automated mediator. IEEE Intell. Syst. **26**(6), 40–47 (2011)
30. Lin, R., Gev, Y., Kraus, S.: Facilitating better negotiation solutions using Ani-Med. In: The Fourth International Workshop on Agent-Based Complex Automated Negotiations (ACAN 2011), Taipei, Taiwan, May 2011
31. Mnookin, R.H., Peppet, S.R., Tulumello, A.S., Winning, B.: Negotiating to Create Value in Deals and Disputes. Harvard University Press, Cambridge (2000)
32. Rahwan, I.: Interest-based negotiation in multi-agent systems. Ph.D. thesis, University of Melbourne, Melbourne, Australia (2004)
33. Rahwan, I., Pasquier, P., Sonenberg, L., Dignum, F.: A formal analysis of interest-based negotiation. Ann. Math. Artif. Intell. **55**(3–4), 253–276 (2009)
34. Rahwan, I., Simari, G. (eds.): Argumentation in Artificial Intelligence. Springer, Heidelberg (2009)
35. Raiffa, H., Richardson, J., Metcalfe, D.: Negotiation Analysis: The Science and Art of Collaborative Decision Making. Belknap Press of Harvard University Press, Cambridge (2002)
36. Schei, V., Rognes, J.K.: Knowing me, knowing you: own orientation and information about the opponent's orientation in negotiation. Int. J. Confl. Manag. **14**(1), 43–60 (2003)
37. Sierra, C., Debenham, J.K.: The logic negotiation model. In: Proceedings Sixth International Joint Conference on Autonomous Agents and Multi-agent Systems (AAMAS 2007), pp. 1026–1033 (2007)
38. Sierra, C., Debenham, J.: Information-based agency. In: Proceedings of Twentieth International Joint Conference on Artificial Intelligence IJCAI 2007, pp. 1513–1518, Hyderabad, India (2007)
39. Simoff, S., Debenham, J.: Curious negotiator. In: Klusch, M., Ossowski, S., Shehory, O. (eds.) CIA 2002. LNCS (LNAI), vol. 2446, pp. 104–111. Springer, Heidelberg (2002). doi:10.1007/3-540-45741-0_10
40. Simoff, S., Sierra, C., López de Màntaras, R.: Mediation = information revelation + analogical reasoning. In: Meyer, J.-J.C., Broersen, J. (eds.) KRAMAS 2008. LNCS, vol. 5605, pp. 145–160. Springer, Heidelberg (2009). doi:10.1007/978-3-642-05301-6_10
41. Sycara, K.P.: Problem restructuring in negotiation. Manag. Sci. **37**(10), 1248–1268 (1991)
42. Tedesco, P.A.: MArCo: building an artificial conflict mediator to support group planning interactions. Int. J. Artif. Intell. Educ. **13**, 117–155 (2003)
43. Tempich, C., Studer, R., Simperl, E., Luczak, M., SofiaPinto, H.: Argumentation-based ontology engineering. IEEE Inetell. Syst. **22**(6), 52–59 (2007)
44. Thompson, L., Neale, M., Sinaceur, M.: The evolution of cognition and biases in negotiation research: an examination of cognition, social perception, motivation and emotion. In: Gelfand, M.J., Brett, J.M. (eds.) The Handbook of Negotiation and Culture, pp. 7–44. Standford University Press, Palo Alto (2004)
45. Van Boven, L., Thompson, L.: A look into the mind of the negotiator: mental models in negotiation. Group Process. Intergroup Relat. **6**(4), 387–404 (2003)

46. Visser, W., Hindriks, K.V., Jonker, C.M.: Interest-based preference reasoning. In: Proceedings of International Conference on Agents and Artificial Intelligence, ICAART 2011, pp. 79–88 (2011)
47. Wilkenfeld, J., Kraus, S., Santmire, T.E., Frain, C.K.: The role of mediation in conflict management: conditions for successful resolution. In: Multiple paths to knowledge in international relations. Lexington Books (2004)
48. Wing, J.M.: Computational thinking. Commun. ACM 49(3), 33–35 (2006)

Coalition Formation with Logic-Based Agents

Gianluigi Greco$^{(\boxtimes)}$ and Antonella Guzzo

University of Calabria, 87036 Rende, Italy
ggreco@mat.unical.it, guzzo@dimes.unical.it

Abstract. Coalition formation is studied in a setting where agents take part to a group decision-making scenario and where their preferences are expressed via weighted propositional logic, in particular by considering formulas consisting of conjunctions of literals only. Interactions among agents are constrained by an underlying social environment and each agent is associated with a specific social factor determining to which extent s/he prefers staying in a coalition with other agents. In particular, the utilities of the agents depend not only on their absolute preferences but also on the number of "neighbors" occurring with them in the coalition that emerged. Within this setting, the computational complexity of a number of relevant reasoning problems is studied, by charting a clear picture of the intrinsic difficulty of finding "agreements" in such social environments. Some restrictions leading to identify classes of tractable instances are discussed, too.

1 Introduction

Understanding how global behavior emerges from local interactions among individuals is a well-established topic of research in a number of different areas, including economics, finance, epidemiology, social psychology, and political science (see, e.g., [16]). Formally, this problem is often modeled and studied by assuming that a set of individuals/agents is given, each of them expressing some preferences over a set of possible alternatives, and by considering the question of how these preferences can be amalgamated in order to end up with some socially desirable outcome (see, e.g., [5,9,30]). In the paper, we specialize the problem to a setting where interactions among agents are constrained by an underlying social environment, which is modeled as an *interaction graph* whose nodes are the given agents and whose edges encode whether two agents (i.e., the endpoints of the edge) are influenced by each other. Accordingly, in this setting, the utility of the agents depend not only of their absolute preferences on the possible alternatives, but also on the number of neighbors agreeing with them. In particular, we assume that, in order to obtain higher worth than by staying all together, agents can group into *coalitions* (see, e.g., [19,32] and the references therein) each one selecting a possibly different alternative. Therefore, the utility of each agent actually depends on the neighbors occurring in the same coalition.

G. Greco's work was partially supported by a Kurt Gödel Research Fellowship, awarded by the Kurt Gödel Society and founded by the John Templeton Foundation.

© Springer International Publishing AG 2017
N. Criado Pacheco et al. (Eds.): EUMAS 2016/AT 2016, LNAI 10207, pp. 455–469, 2017.
DOI: 10.1007/978-3-319-59294-7_37

In order to encode the preferences of the agents with a compact representation language [20,22,29,35], we consider *weighted propositional logic* [15]. Following earlier group decision-making studies based on this logic (e.g., [28,34]), it is assumed that each individual expresses her preferences as a set of propositional formulas associated with numerical values. Given an interpretation σ assigning a truth value to each variable, the utility of the individual is defined as the sum of the values associated with the formulas satisfied by σ [15,34]. Actually, we depart from earlier approaches by considering formulas that consist of conjunctions of literals, only. Indeed, we show via a number of exemplifications that this language is powerful enough to model real-world application domains, while being conceptually simple and easy to manipulate.

The basic utilities associated with the agents will be then adjusted by considering the influence of the other agents. In particular, each agent will be associated with a specific social factor determining to which extent s/he prefers staying in a coalition with other agents. In fact, we model conformist agents which would like to stay with as many agents as possible. So, a tension will emerge between the number of agents staying together in the given coalition and the utility derived by the alternative on which such agents can agree. The paper studies the computational complexity of dealing with this tension, by conducting an analysis that is parametric w.r.t. the underlying semantics for aggregating the utilities of the agents belonging to the same coalition. On the one hand, the utilitarian semantics is considered, where the collective utility of a coalition is the sum of the utilities of the individuals, called the *utilitarian social welfare*. On the other hand, an egalitarian perspective is also considered. In fact, in a number of application domains, a "fair" approach would be more appropriate with the goal being to maximize the *egalitarian social welfare*, that is, the satisfaction of the least satisfied agent (see, e.g., [3,8]).

Organization. The rest of the paper is organized as follows. The setting to model social environments is discussed in Sect. 2 and some exemplifications are illustrated in Sect. 3. The computational complexity of a number of relevant reasoning problems arising in the framework are discussed in Sect. 4. Moving from the observation that in general such problems emerge to be intractable, some restrictions leading to identify classes of tractable instances are discussed in Sect. 5. A few final remarks are eventually illustrated in Sect. 6.

2   Formal Framework

In this section, we formalize a framework where rational agents can group into coalitions in order to find better agreements on the decision that has to be taken. In particular, the coalition formation process will be guided by constraints imposed by the topology of an underlying interaction graph, which is meant to encode the social influence phenomena occurring in a social environment.

2.1   Agents and Utility Functions

Throughout the paper, we assume that a universe $\mathcal{V}$ of propositional variables is given. An *interpretation* $\sigma : \mathcal{W} \rightarrow \{true, false\}$ over $\mathcal{W} \subseteq \mathcal{V}$ is a function assigning a Boolean value to each variable in $\mathcal{W}$. We denote by $\mathrm{I}(\mathcal{W})$ the set of all interpretations that are defined over $\mathcal{W}$. Intuitively, each propositional variable $X \in \mathcal{V}$ is meant to encode some specific alternative that is provided to the agents and on which they have to express their own preferences, so that its truth value w.r.t. an interpretation σ denotes whether or not the given alternative is selected, based on whether $\sigma(X) = true$ or $\sigma(X) = false$, respectively.

In more detail, we consider a framework where a set $\mathcal{A} = \{A_1, \ldots, A_n\}$ of *agents* is given. Each agent $A_i \in A$ is a associated with a *domain* $\mathrm{dom}(A_i)$ of propositional variables taken from $\mathcal{V}$ and with a utility function $u_i : \mathrm{I}(\mathcal{W}) \rightarrow \mathbb{Q}$ mapping any interpretation $\sigma \in \mathrm{I}(\mathcal{W})$ to the rational number $u_i(\sigma)$. With a slight abuse of notation, we denote the domain of the set $\mathcal{A}$ as $\mathrm{dom}(\mathcal{A}) = \bigcup_{i=1}^{n} \mathrm{dom}(A_i)$.

Example 1. Let us consider a very simple setting where two friends, say A_1 and A_2, have to express their preferences about the possibility of going to the cinema or to stay at home. We model the scenario with a propositional variable C, so that the interpretation σ_{cinema} (resp., σ_{home}) where C is mapped to *true* (resp., *false*) means that the agent goes to the cinema (resp., remains at home).

If A_1 prefers the cinema while A_2 would like to stay at home, then we can assume that the agents are equipped with the functions u_1 and u_2 such that:
$u_1(\sigma_{cinema}) = u_2(\sigma_{home}) = 1$ and $u_1(\sigma_{home}) = u_2(\sigma_{cinema}) = 0.$ ◁

Note that, in the above example, the maximum and minimum values of the utility functions are 1 and 0, respectively. This is not by chance, as we can always rescale the utility functions of the agents from a given set $\mathcal{A}$, in a way that they become *normalized*, formally, such that $\max_{\sigma \in \mathrm{I}(\mathrm{dom}(A_i))} u_i(\sigma) = 1$ and $\min_{\sigma \in \mathrm{I}(\mathrm{dom}(A_i))} u_i(\sigma) = 0$, for each agent $A_i \in \mathcal{A}$ (see, e.g., [20,28]). Unless stated otherwise, all agents are hereinafter assumed to be normalized.

2.2   Social Environments

The goal of the paper is to study the process of amalgamating the preferences of the agents in settings where they interact in a given social environment. In particular, by following a standard modeling perspective in the literature, a social environment is modeled as a network $\mathrm{IG}(\mathcal{A}) = (\mathcal{A}, E)$, which we call the *interaction graph* of $\mathcal{A}$, whose nodes correspond to the agents and whose edges encode their social interconnections which give rise to influence phenomena. The role of the interaction graph is to prescribe which agents can directly communicate with each other, by exchanging opinions and beliefs, and which *coalitions* of agents are allowed to form. Intuitively, coalitions are groups of agents among which some agreement on the possible alternatives can be find more easily.

In fact, for reasons that might range from physical limitations and constraints to legal banishments, certain agents might not be allowed to form coalitions with certain others (see, e.g., [13], and the references therein). Accordingly, a coalition

$C \subseteq \mathcal{A}$ of agents will be said to be *legal* if the subgraph of $\text{IG}(\mathcal{A})$ induced over the nodes in C is connected.

Example 2. Consider again the setting of Example 1, by assuming that another agent, say A_3, joins the group. Assume that $u_3 = u_1$, that is, A_3 prefers to go to the cinema. Assume that the interactions among the agents are formalized via the interaction graph $(\{A_1, A_2, A_3\}, E)$ where $E = \{\{A_1, A_2\}, \{A_2, A_3\}\}$. In this context, A_1 and A_3 are not related to each other, and hence they are not allowed to form a coalition. This means that, based on their preferences, a natural outcome would be that A_1 and A_3 both go to the cinema, but independently on each other (e.g., looking for a different film).   ◁

Now, while taking part to the coalition formation process, agents can be influenced by their "social" relationships, in that their own utility functions can be affected by the number of neighbors belonging to the coalitions they belong to. To define this influence, we first define the concept of neighborhood w.r.t. the underlying interaction graph. So, for each legal coalition $C \subseteq \mathcal{A}$ and agent $A_i \in C$, we define the neighbors of A_i that occur in C as the set $\text{neigh}(A_i, C)$ of all agents $A_j \in C$ such that there is an edge connecting A_i and A_j in $\text{IG}(\mathcal{A})$.

Belonging to a social environment, it makes sense to assume that the utilities of the agents depend not only of their absolute preferences but also on the number of neighbors occurring with them in the coalition that emerged. Accordingly, each agent $A_i \in \mathcal{A}$ is also implicitly associated with a rational number α_i with $0 \leq \alpha_i \leq 1$, which we call the *social attitude* of A_i.

In particular, for each interpretation σ over a superset of $\text{dom}(C)$, we define the following "adjusted" utility (indeed depending on C):

$$\hat{u}_i(\sigma, C) = \alpha_i \times \frac{|\text{neigh}(A_i, C)|}{|\text{neigh}(A_i, \mathcal{A})|} + (1 - \alpha_i) \times u_i(\sigma).$$

Note that an agent A_i with $\alpha_i = 0$ does not care of the agents belonging to the given coalition. Instead, with $\alpha_i = 1$, the agent would like to stay as much as possible together with all the neighbors in the interaction graph, by completely getting rid of the original utility function. Note that this approach is suited to model social agents that are "conformist" in their behavior, and it is fully consistent with traditional studies on opinion formation and diffusion in social environments based on influence models, such as the cascade, the tipping/threshold, and the homophilic models. Extending the analysis to "dissenter" agents, whose adjusted utility does not monotonically increase with the number of neighbors in the coalition, is an interesting avenue of further research.

Example 3. Let us continue our discussion about the running example over the set $\mathcal{A} = \{A_1, A_2, A_3\}$ of agents. Consider a setting where $\alpha_1 = \alpha_3 = 0$ while $\alpha_2 = 1$. In this case, agents A_1 and A_3 still act by maximizing their own internal preferences and, hence, they would like to go to the cinema. However, agent A_2 now completely overrides the original attitude to stay at home, with the attitude to join other agents. Then, given the interaction graph of Example 2 where $\texttt{neigh}(A_2, \mathcal{A}) = \{A_1, A_3\}$, there are four possible coalitions for A_2, such that, no matter of the given interpretation σ:

- $C^i = \{A_2\}$, with $\hat{u}_2(\sigma, C^i) = \frac{|\texttt{neigh}(A_2, C^i)|}{|\texttt{neigh}(A_2, \mathcal{A})|} = \frac{0}{2} = 0$;
- $C^{ii} = \{A_1, A_2\}$, with $\hat{u}_2(\sigma, C^i) = \frac{1}{2}$;
- $C^{iii} = \{A_2, A_3\}$, with $\hat{u}_2(\sigma, C^{iii}) = \frac{1}{2}$;
- $C^{iv} = \{A_1, A_2, A_3\}$, with $\hat{u}_2(\sigma, C^{iv}) = \frac{2}{2} = 1$.

In particular, note that for A_2 it is convenient to form a coalition with A_1 and A_3. This time, A_2 can act as a bridge between such agents, and therefore it is natural to expect that they go to the cinema all together.   ◁

2.3   Goals in the Aggregation Process

The final ingredient of the formalization is to define the objective functions that we would like to optimize for modeling the agreement process among the agents. To this end, we consider two classical approaches discussed in the literature, that is, the *utilitarian* and the *egalitarian* social welfare. In the former case we just look for maximizing the sum of the adjusted utilities, while in the latter a fair approach is considered where we maximize the utility of the least satisfied agent. More formally, for any given interpretation σ and coalition C, we will consider:

- the *utilitarian social welfare*, denoted by UT, where the utilities of the various agents are summed; hence, we define $\text{UT}(\sigma, C) = \sum_{A_i \in C} \hat{u}_i(\sigma, C)$;
- the *egalitarian social welfare*, denoted by EG, where we take care of the least satisfied agent; hence, we define $\text{EG}(\sigma, C) = \min_{A_i \in C} \hat{u}_i(\sigma, C)$.

Based on the above notions, we then say that an interpretation σ is UT-*optimal for C* if it has the maximum utilitarian social welfare $\text{UT}(\sigma, C)$ over all interpretations. The set of all UT-optimal interpretations is denoted by UT-OPT(C), and their utilitarian social welfare is denoted by UT-VAL(C). Similarly, σ is EG-*optimal for C* if it has the maximum egalitarian social welfare $\text{EG}(\sigma, C)$ over all interpretations. The set of all EG-optimal interpretations is denoted by EG-OPT(C), and their utilitarian social welfare is denoted by EG-VAL(C).

Example 4. Consider again the setting discussed in Example 3. For the coalition $C^i = \{A_2\}$, it is immediate to check that both σ_{cinema} and σ_{home} are (trivially) optimal interpretations, with respect to both the utilitarian and the egalitarian social welfare. Indeed, note that we just have $\text{UT}(\sigma, C^i) = \text{EG}(\sigma, C^i) = \hat{u}_i(\sigma, C^i) = 0$, no matter of the given interpretation σ. Consider instead the coalition C^{iv}. In this case, for the interpretation σ_{cinema}, we have:

$$\text{UT}(\sigma_{cinema}, C^{iv}) = \sum_{i=1}^{3} \hat{u}_i(\sigma_{cinema}, C^{iv}) = 1 + 1 + 1; \text{ and } \text{EG}(\sigma_{cinema}, C^{iv}) = 1;$$

whereas for the interpretation σ_{home} we have:

$$\text{UT}(\sigma_{home}, C^{iv}) = \sum_{i=1}^{3} \hat{u}_i(\sigma_{home}, C^{iv}) = 0 + 1 + 0 \text{ and } \text{EG}(\sigma_{home}, C^{iv}) = 0.$$

Therefore, it is immediate to check that σ_{cinema} is optimal with respect to both the utilitarian and the egalitarian social welfare, as we have already informally argued in Example 3.   ◁

In fact, in many practical real-world scenarios, one might want to study settings where agents can form a *coalition structure*, i.e., where they can partition themselves into a set Π of disjoint coalitions such that $\bigcup_{C \in \Pi} C = \mathcal{A}$.

Assessing which coalition structure might emerge in a given scenario is a fundamental problem in the study of multi-agent systems, which attracted much research in earlier literature (see, e.g., [19,32]). In particular, we are interested in those coalition structures Π that are optimal w.r.t. the utilitarian and the egalitarian social welfare, i.e., such that the values $\text{UT-VAL}(\Pi) = \sum_{C \in \Pi} \text{UT-VAL}(C)$ and $\text{EG-VAL}(\Pi) = \min_{C \in \Pi} \text{EG-VAL}(C)$, respectively, are maximized over all possible coalition structures.

Example 5. Recall by Example 4 that $\text{UT}(\sigma_{cinema}, \mathcal{A}) = 3$ and $\text{EG}(\sigma_{cinema}, \mathcal{A}) = 1$—indeed, just observe that $C^{iv} = \mathcal{A}$. Now, rather than assuming that all agents would like to stay all together, we assume that they form the coalition structure $\Pi = \{\{A_1\}, \{A_2\}, \{A_3\}\}$, i.e., each agent stays alone in Π. In this extreme case, we would have $\text{UT-VAL}(\Pi) = 2$, since we have already observed that the adjusted utility of agent A_2 is 0, by staying alone. Hence, we have $\text{EG-VAL}(\Pi) = 0$.

Eventually, the coalition structure where all agents stay together can be preferred to Π and it can be checked that such structure is the optimal coalition structure w.r.t. the utilitarian social welfare and the egalitarian social welfare.   ◁

In the above example, it emerged that it is convenient for the agents to stay all together. However, this is not in general the case, even when agents have some social attitude. An exemplification is discussed below.

Example 6. Let us go back to Example 1, where only agents A_1 and A_2 have been introduced. Recall that A_1 wants to go to the cinema, while A_2 wants to stay at home. By considering the social factors α_1 and α_2 (w.l.o.g., $\alpha_1 \leq \alpha_2$), and by assuming that the agents are connected in the interaction graph, we get:

- $\text{UT-VAL}(\{\{A_1\}, \{A_2\}\}) = \frac{\alpha_1}{2} + (1 - \alpha_1) + \frac{\alpha_2}{2} + (1 - \alpha_2)$;
- $\text{UT-VAL}(\{\{A_1, A_2\}\}) = \alpha_1 + (1 - \alpha_1) + \alpha_2$.

In particular, note that when staying all together, since $\alpha_1 \leq \alpha_2$, the maximum welfare is obtained if agents go to the cinema, so the adjusted utility of A_1 is 1 (resp., of A_2 is 0). It is immediate to check that, whenever $\alpha_2 < \frac{1}{2}$, the optimal coalition structure is $\{\{A_1\}, \{A_2\}\}$, where the two agents stay alone.   ◁

3   Further Exemplifications

In this section, we exemplify further possible applications of the general framework we have introduced for reasoning about social environments.

3.1 Voting and Influence Phenomena

Consider a scenario where a set $\mathcal{A} = \{A_1, A_2, A_3\}$ of agents have to decide whether they will vote for the Democratic Party. The agents are all friends of each other, so that the interaction graph $\mathrm{IG}(\mathcal{A})$ is a clique defined over them.

We consider two propositional variables: D and V. The latter is meant to encode whether the agent will vote (i.e., does not abstain), while the former is meant to encode whether the vote actually expressed is for the Democratic Party. Of course, it is meaningless to consider the interpretation σ^* where D is *true* and V is *false*. This is a kind of hard constraint, which can be easily encoded in our framework by assuming that $u_i(\sigma^*) = 0$, for each $A_i \in \mathcal{A}$.

Now, agents A_1 and A_2 are strongly inclined to abstain, so that $u_1(\sigma) = u_2(\sigma) = 1$, for the interpretation σ with $\sigma(V) = \sigma(D) = $ *false*. Moreover, they do not have any specific political preference, so that $u_1(\sigma) = u_2(\sigma) = \frac{1}{2}$ hold, for each other interpretation. On the other hand, agent A_3 is a Democrat, so that $u_3(\sigma) = 1$ if, and only if, $\sigma(V) = \sigma(D) = $ *true*—with all other interpretations being mapped to the value 0.

Concerning the social factors, assume for the moment that $\alpha_1 = \alpha_2 = \alpha_3 = 0$, so that $\hat{u}_i = u_i$, for each $A_i \in A$, and let us consider the support over all the agents for the interpretation σ^{dem} such that $\sigma^{dem}(D) = \sigma^{dem}(V) = $ *true*. It is immediate to check that $\mathrm{UT}(\sigma^{dem}, \mathcal{A}) = \frac{1}{2} + \frac{1}{2} + 1$, while $\mathrm{EG}(\sigma^{dem}, \mathcal{A}) = \frac{1}{2}$. Instead, for the interpretation σ with $\sigma(V) = \sigma(D) = $ *false*, we would have $\mathrm{UT}(\sigma, \mathcal{A}) = 1+1+0$, while $\mathrm{EG}(\sigma, \mathcal{A}) = 0$. This means that such an interpretation, where both A_1 and A_2 abstain, will be optimal with respect to the social welfare for $\mathcal{A}$. However, this is not optimal when considering the optimization of the egalitarian social welfare, since for A_3 it is definitely more desirable to vote for the Democratic Party—formally, we can check that σ^{dem} is EG-optimal for $\mathcal{A}$.

Finally, consider the scenario where $\alpha_3 = 0$ whereas $\alpha_1 = \alpha_2 = \bar{\alpha}$ is a fixed value strictly greater than 0. In this case, we have $\hat{u}_1(\sigma^{dem}, \mathcal{A}) = \hat{u}_2(\sigma^{dem}, \mathcal{A}) = \bar{\alpha} + (1 - \bar{\alpha}) \times \frac{1}{2}$, so that $\mathrm{UT}(\sigma^{dem}, \mathcal{A}) = 2 + \bar{\alpha}$, while $\mathrm{EG}(\sigma^{dem}, \mathcal{A}) = \frac{1+\bar{\alpha}}{2}$. As above, consider then the interpretation σ with $\sigma(V) = \sigma(D) = $ *false* and note that we would have $\mathrm{UT}(\sigma, \mathcal{A}) = 1 + 1 + 0$, while $\mathrm{EG}(\sigma, \mathcal{A}) = 0$. Hence, such an interpretation is no longer UT-optimal for $\mathcal{A}$, since $\mathrm{UT}(\sigma, \mathcal{A}) = 2 < 2 + \bar{\alpha} = \mathrm{UT}(\sigma^{dem}, \mathcal{A})$. In particular, in this case, the interpretation σ^{dem} is not only EG-optimal for $\mathcal{A}$, but UT-optimal for $\mathcal{A}$, too.

3.2 Influence in Large Networks

The proliferation of social networking services, such as FaceBook and Twitter, created novel and highly-dynamic forms of techno-social ecosystems where agents are deeply influenced by their social relationships. In a contest of this kind, consider an agent $A_1 \in \mathcal{A} = \{A_1, \ldots, A_{n+1}\}$ and an interpretation $\bar{\sigma}$ such that $u_1(\bar{\sigma}) = 0$—that is, $\bar{\sigma}$ is definitively the worse possible interpretation for A_1, whenever the agent does not take part to a group decision process. On the other hand, assume that all agents $A_i \in \mathcal{A} \setminus \{A_1\}$ are such that $u_i(\bar{\sigma}) = 1$. Therefore, we immediately have that $\mathrm{EG}(\bar{\sigma}, \mathcal{A}) = 0$ and that $\mathrm{UT}(\bar{\sigma}, \mathcal{A}) = \alpha_1 + n$. In particular, note that the adjusted utility function for A_1 when grouping all agents in $\mathcal{A}$ is such that $\hat{u}_1(\sigma) = \alpha_1$, which is greater than $u_1(\bar{\sigma})$ provided $\alpha_1 > 0$.

At the extreme opposite of being all together, consider the coalition structure Π where each agent stays alone. In this case, each agent $A_j \in \mathcal{A}$ can select the best possible individual interpretation (whose value is 1, as we are considering normalized agents), then getting $1 - \alpha_j$ as the resulting adjusted utility. Therefore, by looking at the sum of the utilities of the agents, we get the overall value UT-VAL(Π) $= \sum_{j=1}^{n+1}(1 - \alpha_j)$, so that being in isolation, whenever $\bar{\sigma}$ is selected, is convenient only if: $\sum_{j=1}^{n+1}(1 - \alpha_j) > \alpha_1 + n$. For instance, assuming that $\alpha_j = \alpha > 0$, for each $A_j \in \mathcal{A}$, we get that the above inequality reduces to asking that $n < \frac{1}{\alpha} - 2$. That is, for every sufficiently large value of n, provided that A_1 has some social attitude, it is never convenient to form the coalition structure Π where each agent stays alone. In fact, for a sufficiently large value of n, it can be checked that staying all together in the coalition $\mathcal{A}$ is optimal w.r.t. the utilitarian and the egalitarian social welfare.

4 Complexity Analysis

Now that we have entirely formalized the framework for reasoning about social environments, we move to analyzing the amount of computational resources that are intrinsically needed to reason about it. To this end, we consider the standard concepts taken from complexity theory, and we stress that such analysis is helpful to identify those questions that are likely to be efficiently answerable even over large environment and those are intrinsically intractable, formally **NP**-hard.

4.1 Computational Setting and Problems of Interest

In order to formalize the reasoning problems that will be analyzed, it is sensible to first discuss the specific encoding mechanisms we adopt to define the utility functions of the agents. By following well-known logic-based encoding approaches [15, 28, 34], we assume to this end that each agent $A_i \in A$ is transparently viewed as a finite set of pairs $\langle \varphi, w \rangle$, called *weighted formulas*, where φ is a *cube*, i.e., a formula built by using the Boolean connectives $\wedge$ and $\neg$, and where $w \in \mathbb{Q}$ is a rational number. Eventually, for any given interpretation σ, the utility $u_i(\sigma)$ is defined as the sum of all values w for the pairs $\langle \varphi, w \rangle \in A_i$ such that σ satisfies φ, shortly denoted as $\sigma \models \varphi$. Hence, A_i is just encoded by its associated underlying weighted formulas.

Example 7. For the running example discussed in Sect. 2, the utility function of agents A_1 and A_2 can be modeled by the set of weighted formulas $\{\langle C, 1 \rangle\}$, where the cube just consists of the propositional variable C meant to encode that the agents get 1 as their utility whenever the go to the cinema. Moreover, we have $A_3 = \{\langle \neg C, 1 \rangle\}$, which encodes that A_3 would like to stay at home.

For the example discussed in Sect. 3.1, instead, the utility functions of agents A_1 and A_2 can be modeled by the set $\{\langle \neg D \wedge \neg V, 1 \rangle, \langle V, \frac{1}{2} \rangle\}$, while the utility function of A_3 can be modeled as $\{\langle D \wedge V, 1 \rangle\}$.   ◁

Within this framework, we next embark on the study of a number of decision problems, being defined parametrically w.r.t. the specific kind of social welfare $X \in \{\text{UT}, \text{EG}\}$ we would like to consider. All these problems receive as input a set $\mathcal{A}$ of normalized agents, specified as above, plus a rational number γ:

X-CHECK: Given a legal coalition $C \subseteq \mathcal{A}$, does X-VAL$(C) \geq \gamma$ hold?
X-EXISTENCE: Is there any legal coalition $C \subseteq \mathcal{A}$ such that X-VAL$(C) \geq \gamma$?
X-CS-EXISTENCE: Is there any coalition structure Π such that X-VAL$(\Pi) \geq \gamma$?
X-MAXIMAL: Given a legal coalition $C \subseteq \mathcal{A}$, is C X-*maximal* for γ, i.e., such that
    X-VAL$(C) \geq \gamma$ and for which no coalition $C' \supset C$ exists with X-VAL$(C') \geq \gamma$?

Note, in particular, that the latter problem is meant to identify maximal coalitions on which good "agreements" can be found. Instead, the former problems reflect the concepts we have defined in our formal framework, so far.

4.2   Results and Technical Elaborations

We start our analysis by focusing on the problem X-CHECK.

Theorem 1. *For each* $X \in \{\text{UT}, \text{EG}\}$, X-CHECK *is* **NP**-*complete. Hardness holds on sets* $\mathcal{A}$ *of agents with* $\alpha_i < 1$, $\forall A_i \in \mathcal{A}$.

Proof
    (Membership) The problem UT-CHECK (resp., EG-CHECK) can be solved in polynomial time by a nondeterministic Turing machine that guesses an interpretation σ and then checks that UT$(\sigma, C) \geq \gamma$ (resp., EG$(\sigma, C) \geq \gamma$).
    (Hardness) Recall that deciding whether a Boolean formula in conjunctive normal form $\varphi = c_1 \wedge \ldots \wedge c_n$, where $c_1, \ldots, c_n$ are clauses, i.e., disjunction of literals, is a well-known **NP**-hard problem. Given a formula of this kind, consider a variable X not occurring in φ, and define $A_i = \{\langle \neg X, 1 \rangle\} \cup \{\langle X \wedge sc_1, 1 \rangle \mid sc_1$ is a conjunction of literals over variables in c_i and satisfying that clause $\}$ and consider the agent $A_{n+1} = \{\langle X, 1 \rangle\}$. Note that the role of X is to guarantee that all the agents are normalized. For an example, note if $c_1 = Y \vee Z$ holds, then, the conjunctions of literals included in A_i are $Y \wedge Z$, $Y \wedge \neg Z$, $\neg Y \wedge \neg Z$, and $\neg Y \wedge Z$. Moreover, note that these conjunctions are mutually exclusive.
    Let $\mathcal{A} = \{A_1, \ldots, A_n, A_{n+1}\}$ be a set of agents and assume that IG$(\mathcal{A})$ is the complete interaction graph over $\mathcal{A}$. Therefore, for any interpretation σ, we have UT$(\sigma, \mathcal{A}) = \sum_i \alpha_i + \sum_i (1 - \alpha_i) \times u_i(\sigma)$. Since we know that $\sum_{A_i \in \mathcal{A}} \alpha_i < |\mathcal{A}|$, we immediately derive that UT$(\sigma, \mathcal{A}) = |\mathcal{A}|$ if, and only if, X evaluates *true* in σ and σ satisfies all clauses in φ. Hence, UT-CHECK is **NP**-hard.
    In order to conclude, let us consider the egalitarian social welfare. Assume that φ is not satisfiable. Then, for each interpretation σ with $\sigma(X) = true$, there is at least an agent A_i such that $u_i(\sigma) = 0$ and, hence, $\hat{u}_i(\sigma, \mathcal{A}) = \alpha_i < 1$. Therefore, EG-VAL$(\mathcal{A}) \geq 1$ holds if, and only if, φ is satisfiable, which shows that EG-CHECK is **NP**-hard, too.   □

A similar result can be proven for X-EXISTENCE and for its counterpart to coalition structures, i.e., for the problem X-CS-EXISTENCE.

Theorem 2. *For each* $X \in \{UT, EG\}$, X-EXISTENCE *is **NP**-complete. Hardness holds on sets* $\mathcal{A}$ *of agents with* $\alpha_i < 1$ *(and* $\alpha_i \neq 0$ *if* $X = EG$), $\forall A_i \in \mathcal{A}$.

Proof

(Membership) The problem UT-EXISTENCE can be solved in polynomial time by a nondeterministic Turing machine that guesses a coalition $C \subseteq \mathcal{A}$ and an interpretation σ and then checks that $\text{UT}(\sigma, C) \geq \gamma$. With the same line of reasoning, it can be checked that EG-EXISTENCE belongs to **NP**.

(Hardness) Consider again the reduction we have exhibited in the proof of Theorem 1. Note that for each possible legal coalition $C \subseteq \mathcal{A}$, it is always the case that $\text{UT}(\sigma, C) \leq C$, because agents are normalized. Therefore, $\text{UT}(\sigma, C) \geq |\mathcal{A}|$ might hold only if $C = \mathcal{A}$. But, in this case, we know that checking whether there is an interpretation σ such that $\text{UT}(\sigma, \mathcal{A}) = |\mathcal{A}|$ is equivalent to checking whether a given Boolean formula in conjunctive normal form is satisfiable, which is a **NP**-hard problem. For the egalitarian social welfare, note that for each interpretation σ, coalition C and agent $A_i \in C$ with $C < |\mathcal{A}|$, it is the case that $\hat{u}_i(\sigma, C) \leq \alpha_i \times q + (1 - \alpha_i)$ with $q < 1$. Hence, $\hat{u}_i(\sigma, C) < 1$ holds, too. Therefore, given that $\alpha_i \neq 0$, for each $A_i \in \mathcal{A}$, $\text{UT}(\sigma, C) \geq 1$ might hold only if $C = \mathcal{A}$. But, again, we know that checking whether there is an interpretation σ such that $\text{UT}(\sigma, \mathcal{A}) \geq 1$ is equivalent to checking whether a given Boolean formula is satisfiable, which is a **NP**-hard problem. $\square$

Theorem 3. *For each* $X \in \{UT, EG\}$, X-CS-EXISTENCE *is **NP**-complete. Hardness holds on sets* $\mathcal{A}$ *of agents with* $\alpha_i < 1$ *(and* $\alpha_i \neq 0$ *if* $X = EG$), $\forall A_i \in \mathcal{A}$.

Proof

(Membership) The problem can be solved in polynomial time by a nondeterministic Turing machine that guesses a coalition structure Π and an interpretation σ_C, for each coalition $C \in \Pi$, and then checks that $\sum_{C \in P_1} \text{UT}(\sigma, C) \geq \gamma$ or $\min_{C \in \Pi} \text{EG}(\sigma, C) \geq \gamma$.

(Hardness) Consider again the reduction we have exhibited in the proof of Theorem 1 and the arguments in the proof of Theorem 2. Note that the inequalities $\sum_{C \in \Pi} \text{UT}(\sigma, C) \geq |\mathcal{A}|$ and $\min_{C \in \Pi} \text{EG}(\sigma, C) \geq 1$ can hold only if $\Pi = \{\mathcal{A}\}$. In both cases, hardness follows as we have observed that checking whether there is an interpretation σ with $\text{UT}(\sigma, \mathcal{A}) = |\mathcal{A}|$ or $\text{EG}(\sigma, \mathcal{A}) = 1$ is **NP**-hard. $\square$

To complete the picture of the complexity results, we now consider X-MAXIMAL for which a complexity increase occurs. Indeed, recall that **DP** is the class of all those problems that can be written as a conjunction of a problem in **NP** and a problem in the complementary class co-**NP**.

Theorem 4. *For each* $X \in \{UT, EG\}$, X-MAXIMAL *is **DP**-complete. Hardness holds on sets* $\mathcal{A}$ *of agents with* $\alpha_i < 1$ *(and* $\alpha_i \neq 0$ *if* $X = EG$), $\forall A_i \in \mathcal{A}$.

Proof

(Membership) Let $C \subseteq \mathcal{A}$ be the legal coalition provided as input, and recall that C is is X-maximal for γ if (C1) X-VAL$(C) \geq \gamma$, and (C2) there is no

legal coalition $C' \supset C$ such that X-VAL$(C') \geq \gamma$. We observe that (C1) can be checked in **NP**, as we shown in Theorem 1. Consider, then, the condition complementary to (C2), that is, that there is some legal coalition $C' \supset C$ such that UT-VAL$(\Gamma, C') \geq \gamma$. To verify whether the condition holds, we can just guess a legal coalition $C' \supset C$ and an interpretation σ, by subsequently checking that UT$(\sigma, C') \geq \gamma$ hold. This is feasible in **NP**, and hence (C2) can be checked in co-**NP**. Overall, the problem is in **DP**.

(Hardness) Recall that the problem receiving a pair (φ^1, φ^2) of Boolean formulas in conjunctive normal form defined over different propositional variables and asking whether φ^1 is satisfiable and φ^2 is not satisfiable is **DP**-hard.

Let $\mathcal{A}^1$ (resp., $\mathcal{A}^2$) denote the set of agents that can be associated with the formula φ^1 (resp., φ^2) based on the encoding discussed in the proof of Theorem 1. In particular, assume that the variable X used there to guarantee that all agents are normalized is replaced by the fresh variable X_1 (resp., X_2). Consider then the set of agents $\mathcal{A} = \mathcal{A}^1 \cup \mathcal{A}^2$ and note that $\mathcal{A}^1$ and $\mathcal{A}^2$ are defined over different propositional variables. Moreover, assume that IG$(\mathcal{A})$ consists of two cliques, one defined over the agents in $\mathcal{A}^1$ and the other defined over the agents in $\mathcal{A}^2$. That is, the agents in these two sets do not interact.

Now, by Theorem 1, we know that EG-VAL$(\mathcal{A}^1) \geq 1$ (resp., EG-VAL$(\mathcal{A}^2) \geq 1$) if, and only if, φ^1 (resp., φ_2) is satisfiable. Given that the two sets of agents are defined over different propositional variables, it can be checked that EG-VAL$(\mathcal{A}^1 \cup C) \geq 1$ with $\emptyset \subset C \subseteq \mathcal{A}^2$ if, and only if, $C - \mathcal{A}^2$ and both φ^1 and φ_2 are satisfiable. Hence, $\mathcal{A}^1$ is E.G.-maximal for 1 if, and only if, φ^1 is satisfiable and φ^2 is not satisfiable. That is, EG-MAXIMAL is **DP**-hard.

A more technical reduction based on the same kinds of ingredients can be then used to show the **DP**-hardness for the utilitarian social welfare, too.   □

5 Islands of Tractability

The results derived in the previous section are bad news concerning the possibility of dealing efficiently with the framework we have proposed for reasoning about social environment. This motivates the study of restrictions leading to identify classes of instances that are tractable.

The first natural restriction pertains the social factors associated with the agents in $\mathcal{A}$, since all results derived so far assume $\alpha_i < 1$, for each $A_i \in \mathcal{A}$, and $\alpha_i \neq 0$ when the egalitarian social welfare is considered. We now show that the problems are tractable, when they are confined over these extreme cases.

Theorem 5. *For each* X $\in$ {UT, EG}, *problems* X-CHECK, X-EXISTENCE, X-CS-EXISTENCE, *and* X-MAXIMAL *are tractable on sets* $\mathcal{A}$ *with* $\alpha_i = 1$, $\forall A_i \in \mathcal{A}$. *The latter three problems are also tractable for* $\alpha_i = 0$, $\forall A_i \in \mathcal{A}$, *if* X = EG.

Proof. For an agent $A_i \in A$, we have $\hat{u}_i(\sigma, C) = |\mathtt{neigh}(A_i, C)|/|\mathtt{neigh}(A_i, \mathcal{A})|$, since $\alpha_i = 1$. This means that for the agent, it is convenient to stay together with all the other agents in $\mathcal{A}$, by getting 1 as utility, no matter of the given interpretation and the semantics adopted for the social welfare.

Finally, for the egalitarian social welfare, note that if $\alpha_i = 0$, then by staying alone, agent A_i can always get the utility 1. Therefore, in this case, all problems are actually immaterial, but X-CHECK where the coalition is actually a-priori given and, in fact, intractability has already emerged (cf. Theorem 1).   □

Another interesting restriction is analyzed below about the language used for representing the utility functions, which similarly to the above case leads to a monotonic behavior and, ultimately, to tractability.

Theorem 6. *For each* X $\in$ {UT, EG}, *problems* X-CHECK, X-EXISTENCE, X-CS-EXISTENCE, *and* X-MAXIMAL *are tractable when negation is not allowed in the definition of the propositional formulas and all weights are non-negative.*

Proof. Consider the interpretation σ^* mapping each propositional variable to *true*. In the given setting, for an agent $A_i \in A$, it is immediate to check that $u_i(\sigma^*) = 1$, since the agent is also known to be normalized. Therefore, $\hat{u}_i(\sigma^*, C) = \alpha_i \times |\text{neigh}(A_i, C)|/|\text{neigh}(A_i, \mathcal{A})| + (1 - \alpha_i)$. Hence, the maximum is again achieved when all agents stay together, no matter of the given interpretation and the semantics adopted for the social welfare.   □

The final restriction we would like to analyze is a structural one. Indeed, many **NP**-hard problems in different areas such as AI, Database Systems, Game theory, and Network Design, are known to be efficiently solvable when restricted to instances whose underlying structures can be modeled via acyclic graphs. Below, we argue that this nice behavior still holds in our setting, with some further assumption in place. Formally, for any fixed natural number $h > 0$, we say that a set $\mathcal{A}$ is *h-bounded* if $|\text{dom}(A_i)| \leq h$ holds, for each $A_i \in \mathcal{A}$, and if an edge $\{A_i, A_j\}$ is in the interaction graph $\text{IG}(\mathcal{A})$ if, and only if, $\text{dom}(A_i) \cap \text{dom}(A_j) = \emptyset$.

At a high-level, the idea is to encode the problems in terms of *constraint satisfaction problems (CSPs)* [17], equipped with weighting functions, by establishing a one-to-one correspondence between solutions to the CSP and solutions to the problems of interest. The property of being h-bounded ensures that the construction is feasible in polynomial time; indeed, just note that, for each agent, we can explicitly enumerate in polynomial time the set of all possible interpretations. Moreover, it can be shown that the mapping preserves the structural properties of the original instance, so that the desired result derives from tractability results for CSPs (equipped with weights) over acyclic instances [26]. The proof is omitted due to space constraints. In fact, details are rather technical, but the line follows a template which is well-known in the literature [27].

Theorem 7. *Problems* UT-CHECK, UT-EXISTENCE, UT-CS-EXISTENCE, *and* UT-MAXIMAL *are tractable on h-bounded sets* $\mathcal{A}$ *such that* $\text{IG}(\mathcal{A})$ *is acyclic.*

Furthermore, by using standard technical machineries (see [27] and the references therein) the above result can be also extended to classes of interactions graphs that are *nearly acyclic*, formally, that have *bounded treewidth* [31]. However, note that the above results hold for the utilitarian social welfare only, and it is open whether they can be extended to the egalitarian social welfare, too.

6   Conclusion and Discussion

Social environments are usually modeled in the literature as networks, whose nodes correspond to the individuals and whose edges encode their social interconnections which give rise to influence phenomena, because of reasons ranging from similarity and social ties [1], to conformity [33], and to compliance [14], just to name a few. In particular, classical studies focuses their analysis on understanding how information diffuses over the newtwork by exploiting such phenomena (see, e.g., [7,10,12,23–25]).

In fact, richer models of social environments have been also proposed to study the process of opinion diffusion, rather than just information diffusion. In particular, they focused on how a given global opinion can emerge by amalgamating the information and the preferences of the single agents populating the network. An influential study in this contest goes back to the seventies [18] and postulated that each agent has to be equipped with a real number (for example, representing a position on a political spectrum or a probability assigned to a certain belief), which in each time step is updated to be a weighted average of that opinion with the current opinions of the neighbors. By doing so, the diffusion processes will converge to a state of consensus where all individuals hold the same opinion. In fact, this model has been more recently enriched by [2,4,6], by assuming that each agent is equipped with an innate opinion in addition to the expressed opinion, which is iteratively updated to minimize the disagreement with the innate opinion and the opinions expressed by the neighbors (see, also, [21]).

The paper position itself within this avenue of research, by studying the problem of assessing how a general consensus can be reached over a network and by considering a framework that goes beyond such earlier works, in that it deals with agents seen as thinking entities equipped with their own logical theories. Indeed, modeling the reasoning capabilities of the individuals as real numbers is a clear limitation from the knowledge representation viewpoint. In particular, we have proposed a framework where agents can form coalitions, i.e., we do not necessarily require that a general consensus is reached, and where their reasoning capabilities are encoded via weighted propositional formulas—formally, formulas consisting of conjunctions of literals only. On the one hand, a number of exemplifications have been provided to illustrate the expressiveness of the framework. On the other hand, a thorough complexity analysis has been conducted in order to precisely assess the amount of resources that are intrinsically needed to reason in the resulting setting. A natural avenue of further research is to implement the proposed framework, in order to apply it for reasoning on real social environments. In particular, when the goal is to optimize the utilitarian social welfare, it is not hard to envisage that the problem can be recast into a standard (weighted) MaxSAT problem [11].

References

1. Anagnostopoulos, A., Kumar, R., Mahdian, M.: Influence and correlation in social networks. In: Proceedings of KDD 2008, pp. 7–15 (2008)

2. Auletta, V., Caragiannis, I., Ferraioli, D, Galdi, C., Persiano, G.: Generalized discrete preference games. In: Proceedings of IJCAI 2016, pp. 53–59 (2016)
3. Bansal, N., Sviridenko, M.: The santa claus problem. In: Proceedings of STOC 2006, pp. 31–40 (2006)
4. Bhawalkar, K., Gollapudi, S., Munagala, K.: Coevolutionary opinion formation games. In: Proceedings of STOC 2013, pp. 41–50 (2013)
5. Bezáková, I., Dani, V.: Allocating indivisible goods. SIGecom Exch. 5(3), 11–18 (2005)
6. Bindel, D., Kleinberg, J., Oren, S.: How bad is forming your own opinion? Games Econ. Behav. 92, 248–265 (2015)
7. Borodin, A., Filmus, Y., Oren, J.: Threshold models for competitive influence in social networks. In: Saberi, A. (ed.) WINE 2010. LNCS, vol. 6484, pp. 539–550. Springer, Heidelberg (2010)
8. Bouveret, S., Lang, J.: Efficiency and envy-freeness in fair division of indivisible goods: logical representation and complexity. J. Artif. Intell. Res. 32, 525–564 (2008)
9. Conitzerm, V., Brandt, F., Endriss, U.: Computational social choices. In: Multiagent Systems. MIT Press, Cambridge (2012)
10. Carnes, T., Nagarajan, C., Wild, S.M., Van Zuylen, A.: Maximizing influence in a competitive social network: a follower's perspective. In: Proceedings of EC 2007, pp. 351–360 (2007)
11. Cha, B., Iwama, K., Kambayashi, Y., Miyazaki, S.: Local search algorithms for partial MAXSAT. In: Proceedings of AAAI 1997, pp. 263–268 (1997)
12. Cha, M., Mislove, A., Gummadi, K.P.: A measurement-driven analysis of information propagation in the flickr social network. In: Proceedings of WWW 2009, pp. 721–730 (2009)
13. Chalkiadakis, G., Greco, G., Markakis, E.: Characteristic function games with restricted agent interactions: core-stability and coalition structures. Artif. Intell. 232, 76–113 (2016)
14. Cialdini, R.B., Goldstein, N.J.: Social inuence: compliance and conformity. Annu. Rev. Psychol. 55, 591–621 (2004)
15. Coste-Marquis, S., Lang, J., Liberatore, P., Marquis, P.: Expressive power and succinctness of propositional languages for preference representation. In: Proceedings of KR 2004, pp. 203–212 (2004)
16. David, E., Jon, K.: Networks, Crowds, and Markets: Reasoning About a Highly Connected World. Cambridge University Press, Cambridge (2010)
17. Dechter, R.: Constraint Processing. Morgan Kaufmann Publishers Inc., San Francisco (2003)
18. DeGroot, M.H.: Reaching a consensus. J. Am. Stat. Assoc. 69, 118–121 (1974)
19. Elkind, E., Rahwan, T., Jennings, N.R.: Computational coalition formation. In: Multiagent Systems. MIT press (2013)
20. Escoffier, B., Gourvès, L., Monnot, J.: Fair solutions for some multiagent optimization problems. Auton. Agent. Multi-Agent Syst. 26(2), 184–201 (2013)
21. Friedkin, N.E., Johnsen, E.C.: Social influence and opinions. J. Math. Soc. 15, 193–206 (1990)
22. Gonzales, C., Perny, P., Queiroz, S.: Preference aggregation with graphical utility models. In: Proceedings of AAAI 2008, pp. 1037–1042 (2008)
23. Granovetter, M.: Threshold models of collective behavior. Am. J. Sociol. 83(6), 1420–1443 (1978)

24. He, X., Song, G., Chen, W., Jiang, Q.: Influence blocking maximization in social networks under the competitive linear threshold model. In: Proceedings of SDM 2012, pp. 463–474 (2012)
25. Kempe, D., Kleinberg, J., Tardos, É.: Maximizing the spread of influence through a social network. In: Proceedings of KDD 2003, pp. 137–146 (2003)
26. Gottlob, G., Greco, G., Scarcello, F.: Tractable optimization problems through hypergraph-based structural restrictions. In: Proceedings of ICALP 2009, pp. 16–30 (2009)
27. Gottlob, G., Greco, G., Scarcello, F.: Treewidth and Hypertree Width. In: Bordeaux, L., Hamadi, Y., Kohli, P. (eds.) Tractability: Practical Approaches to Hard Problems (2012)
28. Greco, G., Lang, J.: Group decision making via weighted propositional logic: complexity and islands of tractability. In: Proceedings of IJCAI 2015, pp. 3008–3014 (2015)
29. Lafage, C., Lang, J.: Logical representation of preferences for group decision making. In: Proceedings of KR 2000, pp. 457–468 (2000)
30. Lang, J., Xia, L.: Voting in combinatorial domains. In: Handbook of Computational Social Choice, pp. 1193–1195 (2014)
31. Robertson, N., Seymour, P.D.: Graph minors. II. Algorithmic aspects of tree-width. J. Algorithms **7**(3), 309–322 (1986)
32. Sandholm, T., Larson, K., Andersson, M., Shehory, O., Tohmé, F.: Coalition structure generation with worst case guarantees. Artif. Intell. **111**(1–2), 209–238 (1999)
33. Tang, J., Wu, S., Sun, J.: Confluence: conformity influence in large social networks. In: Proceedings of KDD 2013, pp. 347–355 (2013)
34. Uckelman, J., Chevaleyre, Y., Endriss, U., Lang, J.: Representing utility functions via weighted goals. Math. Logic Q. **55**(4), 341–361 (2009)
35. Uckelman, J., Endriss, U.: Compactly representing utility functions using weighted goals and the max aggregator. Artif. Intell. **174**(15), 1222–1246 (2010)

Boolean Matrix Approach
for Abstract Argumentation

Fuan Pu$^{(\boxtimes)}$, Guiming Luo, and Yucheng Chen

School of Software, Tsinghua University, Beijing, China
Pu.Fuan@gmail.com, gluo@tsinghua.edu.cn, chenyc14@163.com

Abstract. In this paper, we propose a Boolean matrix approach to encode Dung's acceptability semantics. Each semantics is encoded into one or more Boolean constraint models, which can be solved by Boolean constraint solvers. In addition, based on our Boolean matrix representations, we also propose a bit-vector-based approach to compute the grounded semantics, and the experimental results show that this approach can achieve a good performance.

Keywords: Boolean matrix · Abstract argumentation · Acceptability semantics · Encodings · Boolean constraints · Bit vector

1 Introduction

Argumentation theory is a formal discipline within Artificial Intelligence (AI) where the aim is to make a computer assist in or perform the act of argumentation. Dung's argumentation framework (AF) is a popularly used framework that covers general issues of argumentation [1]. It consists of a set of arguments and a binary relation that represents the conflicting arguments. It also provides a family of extension-based semantics for solving argumentation problems by selecting acceptable subsets (see [2] for an overview). However, finding extensions of these semantics could be a complex procedure when done without any computational help.

This paper introduces a Boolean matrices approach to encode and solve Dung's semantics, in which the subsets of arguments are represented by Boolean vectors (i.e., 0–1 vectors), the attack relation by a Boolean matrix (0–1 matrix). With some Boolean operations, such as logic AND, OR and NOT, Dung's semantics can be encoded as a finite set of Boolean constraints. Then, to find the extensions of a semantics is to find all assignments that satisfy these constraints. Moreover, based these encodings, we propose an efficient way to compute the grounded semantics by bit vectors, a high efficient and compact data structure. An experiment shows that our bit-vector-based approach can achieve a good performance for computing grounded extensions.

The research reported here was supported by the Fund NSFC61572279.

N. Criado Pacheco et al. (Eds.): EUMAS 2016/AT 2016, LNAI 10207, pp. 470–480, 2017.
DOI: 10.1007/978-3-319-59294-7_38

The paper is organized as follows. Section 2 recalls some necessary concepts. Section 3 introduces a Boolean matrix approach to represent arguments and attacks. Based on these representations, we encode Dung's acceptability semantics in Sect. 4. Section 5 describes a bit-vector implementation of our encodings to calculate the grounded semantics. Section 6 discusses related work and concludes.

2   Preliminaries

In this section, we briefly outline key elements of Dung's abstract AFs [1].

Definition 1. *An* argumentation framework *(AF) is a tuple* $\Delta \stackrel{\text{def}}{=} \langle \mathcal{X}, \mathcal{R} \rangle$ *where* $\mathcal{X}$ *is a finite set of arguments and* $\mathcal{R} \subseteq \mathcal{X} \times \mathcal{X}$ *is a binary relation on* $\mathcal{X}$, *called* attack relation. *For any* $S \subseteq \mathcal{X}$, *we denote by* $\mathcal{R}^-(S) \stackrel{\text{def}}{=} \{x \in \mathcal{X} : \exists y \in S$ *such that* $x\mathcal{R}y\}$ *and* $\mathcal{R}^+(S) \stackrel{\text{def}}{=} \{x \in \mathcal{X} : \exists y \in S$ *such that* $y\mathcal{R}x\}$.

The justified arguments are evaluated based on *extensions* (i.e., subsets of $\mathcal{X}$). The arguments in an extension are required to not attack each other (*conflict-freeness*), and attack any argument that in turn attacks an argument in the extension (defence).

Definition 2. *Let* $\Delta = \langle \mathcal{X}, \mathcal{R} \rangle$ *be an AF,* $S \subseteq \mathcal{X}$ *and* $x \in \mathcal{X}$. *(i)* S *is* conflict-free *iff* $\nexists x, y \in S$ *such that* $x\mathcal{R}y$ *(i.e.,* $S \cap \mathcal{R}^+(S) = \emptyset$, *or, equivalently,* $S \cap \mathcal{R}^-(S) = \emptyset$). *(ii)* S defends x *iff* $\forall y \in \mathcal{X}$ *if* $y\mathcal{R}x$ *then* $\exists z \in S$ *such that* $z\mathcal{R}y$, *(i.e.,* $\mathcal{R}^-(x) \subseteq \mathcal{R}^+(S)$).

Next, we introduces two useful functions for an AF, called *characteristic function* and *neutrality function*. The former applies to some set $S \subseteq \mathcal{X}$ and returns all arguments that are defended by S. The later returns all arguments that not attacked by S.

Definition 3. *Let* $\Delta = \langle \mathcal{X}, \mathcal{R} \rangle$ *be an AF. The* characteristic function *of* Δ *is* $\mathcal{F}_\Delta : 2^\mathcal{X} \mapsto 2^\mathcal{X}$ *such that, for any* $S \subseteq \mathcal{X}$, $\mathcal{F}_\Delta(S) \stackrel{\text{def}}{=} \{x \in \mathcal{X} : S$ *defends* $x\}$. *The* neutrality function *of* Δ *is* $\mathcal{N}_\Delta : 2^\mathcal{X} \mapsto 2^\mathcal{X}$ *such that, for any* $S \subseteq \mathcal{X}$, $\mathcal{N}_\Delta(S) \stackrel{\text{def}}{=} \overline{\mathcal{R}^+(S)}$, *where the bar on a set means the complement of the set relative to* $\mathcal{X}$.

We will omit the subscript Δ from $\mathcal{F}_\Delta$ and $\mathcal{N}_\Delta$ if there is no danger of ambiguity. Now, let us give two properties of the two functions.

Proposition 1. *Let* $\Delta = \langle \mathcal{X}, \mathcal{R} \rangle$ *be an AF. For any* $S \subseteq \mathcal{X}$, *the following holds:* *(i)* S *is conflict-free iff* $S \subseteq \mathcal{N}(S)$; *(ii)* $\mathcal{F}(S) = \mathcal{N}(\mathcal{N}(S))$.

Now, we can define extensions of an AF Δ under Dung's acceptability semantics, in terms of the fixpoints or the post-fixpoints of the functions $\mathcal{F}$ and $\mathcal{N}$ as below:

Definition 4. *Let $\Delta = \langle \mathcal{X}, \mathcal{R} \rangle$ be an AF, and a set $E \subseteq \mathcal{X}$. (i) E is a **conflict-free extension** (CF) of Δ iff $E \subseteq \mathcal{N}(E)$; (ii) E is a **stable extension** (ST) of Δ iff $E = \mathcal{N}(E)$; (iii) E is an **admissible extension** (AD) of Δ iff $E \subseteq \mathcal{N}(E)$ and $E \subseteq \mathcal{F}(E)$; (iii) E is a **complete extension** (CO) of Δ iff $E \subseteq \mathcal{N}(E)$ and $E = \mathcal{F}(E)$; (iv) E is a **grounded extension** (GR) of Δ iff E is the minimal (w.r.t. $\subseteq$) complete extension. Let σ be an acceptability semantics in $\{\text{CF}, \text{ST}, \text{AD}, \text{CO}, \text{GR}\}$, we denote the collection of all σ-extensions of Δ by $\mathcal{E}_\sigma(\Delta)$.*

A stable extension is a maximal (w.r.t. $\subseteq$) conflict-free extension. The existence of stable extensions is not guaranteed. If there exists a stable extension, it must be a complete extension (but not vice versa), and thus it is admissible. The grounded extension is unique and conflict-free (for proofs see [1, Theorem 25]). It can be computed by iteratively applying the characteristic function $\mathcal{F}$ from the empty set until we reach a fixed point. We summarize some properties of these semantics from [1,2] as below:

Proposition 2. *Let $\Delta = \langle \mathcal{X}, \mathcal{R} \rangle$ be an AF, and $S, E \subseteq \mathcal{X}$, then, (i) S is an admissible extension iff $S \subseteq \mathcal{N}(S)$ and $\mathcal{R}^-(S) \subseteq \mathcal{R}^+(S)$. (ii) S is an admissible extension iff $S \subseteq \mathcal{F}(S) \cap \mathcal{N}(S)$. (iii) S is an admissible extension iff $S \subseteq \mathcal{F}(S \cap \mathcal{N}(S))$. (iv) S is a complete extension iff $S = \mathcal{F}(S) \cap \mathcal{N}(S)$. (v) S is a complete extension iff $S = \mathcal{F}(S \cap \mathcal{N}(S))$. (vi) If S is the (unique) grounded extension, then S is included in each complete extension, i.e.,*

$$S \subseteq E, \forall E \in \mathcal{E}_{\text{CO}}(\Delta), \tag{1}$$

and arguments, attacked by S, are not included in any complete extension, formally,

$$\mathcal{R}^+(S) \nsubseteq E, \forall E \in \mathcal{E}_{\text{CO}}(\Delta). \tag{2}$$

They are also hold for stable semantics, if Δ has stable extensions, i.e., $\mathcal{E}_{\text{ST}}(\Delta) \neq \emptyset$.

3   Representing AFs via Boolean Matrices

Dung's argumentation theory is mainly based on set theory. This section shows that his theory can also be built on Boolean algebra via Boolean matrices. A Boolean matrix is a matrix with entries from the Boolean domain $\mathcal{B} = \{0, 1\}$, where 1 and 0 indicate the truth values **true** and **false**. Such a matrix can represent a binary relation between a pair of finite sets. In particular, we consider elements of $\mathcal{B}^{n \times 1}$ to be $n \times 1$ matrices, i.e., Boolean (column) vectors, which can represent subsets of finite sets. Now, let us present the Boolean matrix representations of argument sets and argument graphs.

Definition 5. *Let $\Delta = \langle \mathcal{X}, \mathcal{R} \rangle$ be an AF with $\mathcal{X} = \{x_1, x_2, \cdots, x_n\}$, and let $S \subseteq \mathcal{X}$. The subset S can be represented by a Boolean vector $\mathbf{s} \in \mathcal{B}^{n \times 1}$, whose row indices index the elements in $\mathcal{X}$, such that the entry $\mathbf{s}_i$ is 1 if $x_i \in S$; 0 otherwise.*

The attack relation $\mathcal{R}$ on $\mathcal{X}$ for Δ can be represented by an $n \times n$ Boolean matrix $\boldsymbol{A} \in \mathcal{B}^{n \times n}$, whose row and column indices index the elements of $\mathcal{R}$, such that the entry $\boldsymbol{A}_{ij}$ is 1 if $x_j \mathcal{R} x_i$; 0 otherwise. We call $\boldsymbol{A}$ as the attack matrix of Δ. It can be seen that $\boldsymbol{A}$ is the transpose of the adjacency matrix of the argument graph of Δ.

Clearly, $\mathbf{s}_i = 1$ indicates the presence and $\mathbf{s}_i = 0$ the absence of x_i in the set S. If $S = \emptyset$, then all entries of $\mathbf{s}$ are 0s, denoted by $\mathbf{0}^n$, and if $S = \mathcal{X}$, i.e., the universal set, then all entries of $\mathbf{s}$ are 1s, denoted by $\mathbf{1}^n$. To manipulate Boolean matrices, we need to define some operations on Boolean matrices. Before this, let us introduce some Boolean operations over Boolean domain $\mathcal{B}$. These operations are parts of Boolean algebra.

Definition 6. *A Boolean algebra is a four-tuple $\Lambda \stackrel{\text{def}}{=} \langle \mathcal{B}, +, *, \neg \rangle$, in which $\mathcal{B}$ is the Boolean domain, $+$ (logical OR) and $*$ (logical AND) are two binary operations, and $\neg$ (logical NOT) is a unary operation on $\mathcal{B}$, defined by, for two Boolean variables $a, b \in \mathcal{B}$,*

- *$a + b \stackrel{\text{def}}{=} 0$ if a and b have value 0; otherwise $a + b \stackrel{\text{def}}{=} 1$;*
- *$a * b \stackrel{\text{def}}{=} 1$ if a and b have value 1; otherwise $a * b \stackrel{\text{def}}{=} 0$;*
- *$\neg a \stackrel{\text{def}}{=} 0$ if a is 1, and $\neg a \stackrel{\text{def}}{=} 1$ if a is 0.*

The above operations are three basic operations in Boolean algebra. There are also two derived operations, which can be built up from the basic operations by composition:

- *$a \leqslant b \stackrel{\text{def}}{=} \neg a + b$, called logical implication. It is commonly written as $a \to b$.*
- *$a \equiv b \stackrel{\text{def}}{=} (a * b) + (\neg a * \neg b)$, called logical equivalence. It is 1 just when a and b have the same value, thus, it is always interpreted as the identity relation.*

All Boolean vectors of a given length form an element-wise Boolean algebra, that is, any n-ary Boolean operations can be applied to n-dimensional Boolean vectors at one time. Therefore, we can extend operations on Boolean variables to Boolean vectors:

Definition 7 (Operations over Boolean Vectors). *Let $\mathbf{s}$ and $\mathbf{t}$ be two $n \times 1$ Boolean vectors. We define the following operations over Boolean vectors, for $i = 1, 2, \cdots, n$,*

$$[\mathbf{s} + \mathbf{t}]_i \stackrel{\text{def}}{=} \mathbf{s}_i + \mathbf{t}_i, \quad [\mathbf{s} * \mathbf{t}]_i \stackrel{\text{def}}{=} \mathbf{s}_i * \mathbf{t}_i, \quad [\neg \mathbf{s}]_i \stackrel{\text{def}}{=} \neg \mathbf{s}_i,$$

$$[\mathbf{s} \leqslant \mathbf{t}]_i \stackrel{\text{def}}{=} \mathbf{s}_i \leqslant \mathbf{t}_i, \quad [\mathbf{s} \equiv \mathbf{t}]_i \stackrel{\text{def}}{=} \mathbf{s}_i \equiv \mathbf{t}_i$$

Note that each of the above operations over Boolean vectors actually realizes a set operation. The operations $+$, $*$ and $\neg$ over Boolean vectors realize the set union, intersection and complement operations. It has been shown that every finite Boolean algebra is isomorphic to some power set algebra, thus, set theory and Boolean algebra are essentially the same [3]. Table 1 illustrates some properties and axioms as applied to set theory. Since there is one-to-one correspondence

Table 1. The connections between set algebra and Boolean algebra

Set algebra	Boolean algebra	Set algebra	Boolean algebra
$\emptyset$	**0**	$S \cup T$	$\mathbf{s + t}$
$\mathcal{X}$	**1**	$S \subseteq T$	$\mathbf{s \leqslant t}$
$\overline{S}$	$\neg\mathbf{s}$	$S = T$	$\mathbf{s \equiv t}$
$S \cap T$	$\mathbf{s * t}$	$\mathcal{X} \cup S = \mathcal{X}$	$\mathbf{1 + s \equiv 1}$

between the subsets of $\mathcal{X}$ and the Boolean vectors in $\mathcal{B}^{n \times 1}$, in this paper, thus we may mix a subset and a Boolean vector whenever it is convenient.

Next, let us introduce an operation on Boolean matrix and Boolean vector, which multiplies a Boolean matrix with a Boolean vector, and returns a Boolean vector:

Definition 8. *Let* $\boldsymbol{A} \in \mathcal{B}^{n \times n}$ *be a Boolean matrix, and* $\mathbf{s} \in \mathcal{B}^{n \times 1}$ *a Boolean vector. The multiplication of* $\boldsymbol{A}$ *and* $\mathbf{s}$, *denoted by* $\boldsymbol{A} \odot \mathbf{s}$, *is a Boolean vector* $\mathbf{t} \in \mathcal{B}^{n \times 1}$ *defined by*

$$\mathbf{t}_i = \sum\nolimits_{j=1}^{n} \boldsymbol{A}_{ij} * \mathbf{s}_j \tag{3}$$

The multiplication of a Boolean matrix and a Boolean vector is completely analogous to the numerical matrix multiplication, except we use the Boolean operations $+$ and $*$ on the $\mathcal{B}$ instead of ordinary addition and multiplication, respectively. Similar to the numerical matrix multiplication, we can easily prove that the Boolean matrix multiplication also obeys distributive properties over matrix addition:

Proposition 3. *Let* $\boldsymbol{A} \in \mathcal{B}^{n \times n}$ *be a Boolean matrix, and* $\mathbf{s}, \mathbf{t} \in \mathcal{B}^{n}$ *two Boolean vectors. It holds that*

$$\boldsymbol{A} \odot (\mathbf{s} + \mathbf{t}) = \boldsymbol{A} \odot \mathbf{s} + \boldsymbol{A} \odot \mathbf{t} \tag{4}$$

Next, we will present a critical theorem, which provides a basis for characterizing Dung's acceptability semantics by means of Boolean matrix and vector multiplication.

Theorem 1. *Let* $\Delta = \langle \mathcal{X}, \mathcal{R} \rangle$ *be an AF with* $\mathcal{X} = \{x_1, x_2, \cdots, x_n\}$, *its attack matrix be* $\boldsymbol{A}$ *and a subset* $S \subseteq \mathcal{X}$. *Assume* $\mathbf{s}$ *to be the Boolean vector representation of* S *(w.r.t.* $\mathcal{X}$), *then it holds that:* (i) $\mathcal{R}^{+}(\mathbf{s}) = \boldsymbol{A} \odot \mathbf{s}$; (ii) $\mathcal{R}^{-}(\mathbf{s}) = \boldsymbol{A}^{\mathrm{T}} \odot \mathbf{s}$.[1]

The proofs of this theorem can refer to our previous work [4, Theorem 1]. A similar result also appeared in [5] almost simultaneously. By Definition 3, we can now write the Boolean matrix representation of the neutrality function as:

$$\mathcal{N}(\mathbf{s}) = \neg \mathcal{R}^{+}(\mathbf{s}) = \neg(\boldsymbol{A} \odot \mathbf{s}). \tag{5}$$

---

[1] Here, we consider $\mathcal{R}^{+}(\mathbf{s})$ and $\mathcal{R}^{-}(\mathbf{s})$ as Boolean functions, which map a Boolean vector to another Boolean vector.

By the relationship between the neutrality function and the characteristic function shown in Proposition 1, then we have

$$\mathcal{F}(s) = \mathcal{N}(\mathcal{N}(s)) = \neg(\boldsymbol{A} \odot \neg(\boldsymbol{A} \odot s)). \tag{6}$$

4 Encoding Dung's Acceptability Semantics

In this section, we encode Dung's acceptability semantics via Boolean algebra. Each semantics is encoded as a finite array of Boolean expressions (constraints) with a vector of Boolean variables. The goal is to find an assignment to the vector of all Boolean variables so that all constraints evaluate to 1, i.e., be *satisfied*. This is a typical Boolean constraint satisfaction problem. If no such satisfying assignment exists, then these Boolean constraints have no solution. Let $\Delta = \langle \mathcal{X}, \mathcal{R} \rangle$ be an AF with $\mathcal{X} = \{x_1, x_2, \cdots, x_n\}$, its attack matrix be $\boldsymbol{A}$, and Boolean vector s be a subset of $\mathcal{X}$.

Conflict-Free Boolean Constraints. Boolean vector s is conflict-free iff any of the equivalent Boolean constraints below are satisfied:

$$s * \mathcal{R}^+(s) \equiv 0 \qquad [\text{CF1}] \qquad\qquad\qquad s \leqslant \mathcal{N}(s) \qquad [\text{CF2}]$$

in which [CF1] follows from the definition of conflict-freeness, [CF2] follows from Proposition 1.

Stable Boolean Constraints. Boolean vector s is a stable extension iff any of the equivalent Boolean constraints below are satisfied:

$$s \equiv \mathcal{N}(s) \qquad [\text{ST1}]$$

where [ST1] follows from the condition ST in Definition 4.

Admissible Boolean Constraints. Boolean vector s is admissible iff any of the equivalent Boolean constraints below are satisfied:

$$\begin{cases} [\text{CF?}] \\ s \leqslant \mathcal{F}(s) \end{cases} [\text{AD1}] \qquad\qquad \begin{aligned} s &\leqslant \mathcal{N}(s) * \mathcal{F}(s) & [\text{AD3}] \\ s &\leqslant \mathcal{F}(s * \mathcal{N}(s)) & [\text{AD4}] \end{aligned}$$

$$\begin{cases} [\text{CF?}] \\ \mathcal{R}^-(s) \leqslant \mathcal{R}^+(s) \end{cases} [\text{AD2}] \qquad\qquad s \leqslant \mathcal{N}(s + \mathcal{N}(s)) \qquad [\text{AD5}]$$

where [CF?] can be one of any conflict-free Boolean constraints, [AD1] can be obtained from the condition AD in Definition 4, and [AD2], [AD3] and [AD4] follow from Proposition 2. [AD5] can can follow from [AD3]:

$$s \leqslant \mathcal{N}(s) * \mathcal{F}(s) \Leftrightarrow s \leqslant \neg(\boldsymbol{A} \odot s) * \neg(\boldsymbol{A} \odot \mathcal{N}(s))$$
$$\Leftrightarrow s \leqslant \neg(\boldsymbol{A} \odot (s + \mathcal{N}(s)))$$
$$\Leftrightarrow s \leqslant \mathcal{N}(s + \mathcal{N}(s))$$

Complete Boolean Constraints. Boolean vector s is complete iff any of the equivalent Boolean constraints below are satisfied:

$$\begin{cases} [\text{CF}?] \\ \mathbf{s} \equiv \mathcal{F}(\mathbf{s}) \end{cases} \qquad [\text{C01}]$$

$$\mathbf{s} \equiv \mathcal{N}(\mathbf{s}) * \mathcal{F}(\mathbf{s}) \qquad [\text{C02}]$$

$$\mathbf{s} \equiv \mathcal{F}(\mathbf{s} * \mathcal{N}(\mathbf{s})) \qquad [\text{C03}]$$

$$\mathbf{s} \equiv \mathcal{N}(\mathbf{s} + \mathcal{N}(\mathbf{s})) \qquad [\text{C04}]$$

in which [CF?] is a conflict-free Boolean constraints, [C01] can be encoded from the condition CO in Definition 4, [C02] and [C03] follow from Proposition 2, the proof of [C04] can refer to the proof of [AD3].

Next, let us provide a concrete example to show how to utilize these Boolean constraints to find extensions of a given semantics.

Example 1. Consider the AF $\Delta = \langle \mathcal{X}, \mathcal{R} \rangle$ shown in Fig. 1. Here, we consider to compute the stable extensions of Δ using [ST1]. Assume Boolean vector $\mathbf{s} = [s_1, s_2, s_3, s_4, s_5]^{\mathrm{T}}$, in which s_i is an unknown Boolean variable, then by the encoding [ST1], we have the following constraints:

$$\begin{bmatrix} s_1 \\ s_2 \\ s_3 \\ s_4 \\ s_5 \end{bmatrix} \equiv \neg \left(\begin{bmatrix} 0 & 0 & 0 & 0 & 0 \\ 1 & 0 & 1 & 0 & 0 \\ 0 & 0 & 0 & 1 & 0 \\ 0 & 0 & 1 & 0 & 0 \\ 0 & 0 & 0 & 1 & 1 \end{bmatrix} \odot \begin{bmatrix} s_1 \\ s_2 \\ s_3 \\ s_4 \\ s_5 \end{bmatrix} \right) \iff \begin{bmatrix} s_1 \\ s_2 \\ s_3 \\ s_4 \\ s_5 \end{bmatrix} \equiv \neg \begin{bmatrix} 0 \\ s_1 + s_3 \\ s_4 \\ s_3 \\ s_4 + s_5 \end{bmatrix}$$

Computing the stable extensions of Δ is to find out all assignments, which can satisfy all these Boolean constraints. It can be verified that there merely exists one solution $s_1 = 1$, $s_2 = 0$, $s_3 = 0$, $s_4 = 1$ and $s_5 = 0$, satisfying these constraints. Hence, Δ merely has one stable extension $\mathbf{s} = [1, 0, 0, 1, 0]^{\mathrm{T}}$, i.e., $\{x_1, x_4\}$.

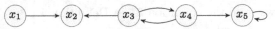

Fig. 1. A simple example of an abstract argumentation framework

5   Computing the Grounded Extension by Bit Vectors

This section introduces an efficient approach to compute the grounded extension based on our Boolean matrix representations. A grounded extension includes all arguments that are not attacked, as well as the arguments which are defended directly or indirectly by non-attacked arguments. The computation of the grounded extension is important. It can reduce the search space when it is used as an initial state to calculate the complete extensions and the stable extensions (see Proposition 2). For example, the grounded extension of the Δ in Fig. 1 is $\{x_1\}$, and it attacks x_2. Thus, we can assign $\mathbf{s}_1 = 1$ and $\mathbf{s}_2 = 0$ as an initial state to compute the complete and stable semantics. Then, the remaining problem is to search the assignments of $\mathbf{s}_3$, $\mathbf{s}_4$ and $\mathbf{s}_5$.

In Dung's set-based approach, the grounded extension can be computed by iterating the characteristic function $\mathcal{F}$ from $\emptyset$. Similarly, we can compute the grounded extension by iterating the Boolean-matrix-based characteristic function from $\mathbf{s}^{(0)} = \mathbf{0}^n$,

$$\mathbf{s}^{(k)} = \mathcal{F}(\mathbf{s}^{(k-1)}) = \neg\left(\boldsymbol{A} \odot \neg(\boldsymbol{A} \odot \mathbf{s}^{(k-1)})\right) \tag{7}$$

We have implemented this Boolean-matrix-based function by bit vectors, which are an array data structure that compactly stores bits. By this data structure, we can store a Boolean vector into a bit vector, and a Boolean matrix (an array of Boolean vectors) into an array of bit vectors on computers. The main advantages using bit vectors includes:

- Bit vectors are highly compact. For a Boolean vector with n variables, this data structure can store it using about n/w storage units, where w is the number of bits in one storage unit, such as a byte (8-bit), a word (32-bit), or a double word (64-bit).
- Bit vectors are effective at exploiting bit-level parallelism in hardware to execute bitwise operations rapidly. For example, given two bit vectors A and B with the same size n, denoting two sets, we can calculate their union and intersection using n/w simple bit operations each, as well as the complement of either, seeing the following C++ codes, where A[i] and B[i] represent a storage unit:

```
1 for (int i = 0; i < n/w; ++i) {
2     union_AB[i]        = A[i] | B[i];   // A + B
3     intersection_AB[i] = A[i] & B[i];   // A * B
4     complement_A[i]    = ~A[i];         // ¬A
5 }
```

Similarly, we also can compute the Boolean product of A and B using no more than n/w bit operations, where A is seen as a row vector, B as a column vector, and a Boolean value will be returned:

```
1 bool product(bitvector& A, bitvector& B) {
2     for (int i = 0; i < n/w; ++i)
3         // see Def. 8; if one of the bit in A&B is 1, returns true
4         if ( A[i] & B[i] > 0)
5             return true;
6     return false;   // otherwise, returns false.
7 }
```

Based on this implementation, we can easily implement the Boolean matrix-vector multiplication, by multiplying each row vector of the matrix with the column vector.

- Bit vectors allow some vectors of bits to be stored and manipulated in the register set with few memory access, and can maximally use the data cache. Therefore, they often outperform many other data structures on set operations.

We implemented the bit vectors using the **dynamic_bitset** class, from the Boost C++ Libraries.[2] The **dynamic_bitset** provides all of the bitwise operators, such as **operator&** and **operator|**, corresponding to set intersection and

---

[2] http://www.boost.org/.

Table 2. The average time (in milliseconds) for computing the grounded extensions over Barabasi-Albert benchmark and ICCMA2015 benchmark.

	Barabasi-Albert				ICCMA2015		
	60	250	500	1000	Small 1200–4200	Medium 1200–6600	Large 5000–9500
32-bit vector	<0.1	**4.0**	**10.5**	**24.0**	86.3	177.9	**500.4**
64-bit vector	<0.1	7.5	12.4	28.9	**74.2**	**154.2**	533.8
CoQuiAAS	<0.1	6.1	11.3	25.9	132.5	235.4	697.5
ArgSemSAT	10.0	69.7	158.8	346.4	1043.3	2372.1	11127.9

union operations. To test the efficiency of our approach, we run our implementation on a PC (2.4 GHz Intel Xeon processors, with 64 GB RAM, and the Linux distribution Ubuntu 14.04-64bits). We consider to execute our tests by using two benchmarks. The first benchmark argument graphs are from [6], where the authors randomly generate AFs according to the *Barabasi-Albert* graph models[3]. The Barabasi-Albert model generates arbitrary AFs and inserts for any pair (x, y) an attack from x to y with a given probability. The experiment is performed over 4 different test sets of Barabasi-Albert graphs with 60, 250, 500 and 1000 nodes, and each set having 100 cases. The second benchmark is from the ICCMA2015, which provides three test sets for grounded semantics, representing three levels of complexity: small, medium and large.[4] Each test set has 24 randomly generated AFs, with the number of arguments from 1200 to 4200 for the small test set, from about 1200 to 6600 for the medium test set, and from about 5000 to 9500 for the large test set. All tests are performed according to two types of storage unit: 32-bit word and 64-bit double word. We also compare our approach with two modern tools, CoQuiAAS [7] and ArgSemSAT [8], which receive the awards of "First Place" and "Second Place" of ICCMA2015, respectively. The average results are given at Table 2. The results show that the bit vector approaches (32-bit and 64-bit) and CoQuiAAS have a similar performance on Barabasi-Albert benchmark. However, the bit vector approaches have better performance than CoQuiAAS on ICCMA2015 benchmark, and the 64-bit vector approach outperforms the 32-bit vector approach. ArgSemSAT has the worst performance on both benchmarks.

By the way, the bit vector approaches can also be extended to verify whether a given set of arguments is an extension of Dung's semantics. We believe that it may be efficient, as all computation can be executed by bit operations.

6   Related Work and Conclusion

The first work using matrix approach to solve argumentation is presented in [9]. It considers to use adjacency matrices and their sub-blocks to determine the extensions of Dung's semantics according to some criteria based on the

---

[3] http://www.dmi.unipg.it/conarg/.
[4] http://argumentationcompetition.org/.

elementary permutation of matrices. This approach is quite different from ours. First, our approach does not use sub-blocks and the matrix permutation operations, but use Boolean matrices and Boolean operations to characterize Dung's semantics. Second, our approach is more intuitive than [9], as our approach is based on Boolean algebra, Dung's semantics are based on set theory, and both of them are naturally connected (see Table 1).

Recently, a Boolean matrix approach was proposed to formalize the basic concepts of Dung's argumentation [4]. In this paper, we enrich their work to encode Dung's acceptability semantics. Similar works also appeared in [5,10]. These works mainly aim to test whether a given set of arguments is an extension of a semantics. However, our approach can be used not only to verify an argument set, but also to find all possible argument sets (extensions). Moreover, our approach can equivalently encode each semantics into several Boolean constraint models, while the works in [5] and [10] just make one model for each semantics, and thus in some sense our approach has a stronger representation capability than their works.

We also propose a bit-vector-based implementation of our theory to calculate the single-status grounded semantics. The experimental results show that it can achieve a good performance compared to two other modern tools. In our future study, we will mainly concern on dealing with multi-extension semantics using our theory. A preliminary work has been done, in which we select a *Constraint Logic Programming over Boolean variables* (CLPB) as our solver to solve the Boolean constraint models. CLPB, provided by many Prolog systems, is an algebraically oriented Constraint Programming solver, and has abilities to handle any Boolean expressions (see [11] for a system description). We have submitted the codes to an online Prolog interpreter.[5] You can try our codes on your browser without installing any components on your system. Due to the space limit, we intend to elaborate these implementations in our future works.

References

1. Dung, P.M.: On the acceptability of arguments and its fundamental role in non-monotonic reasoning, logic programming and n-person games. J. Artif. Intell. **77**(2), 321–357 (1995)
2. Baroni, P., Caminada, M., Giacomin, M.: An introduction to argumentation semantics. Knowl. Eng. Rev. **26**, 365–410 (2011)
3. Givant, S., Halmos, P.: Introduction to Boolean Algebras. Springer Science & Business Media, Berlin (2008)
4. Pu, F., Luo, J., Luo, G.: Some supplementaries to the counting semantics for abstract argumentation. In: 2015 IEEE 27th International Conference on Tools with Artificial Intelligence (ICTAI), pp. 242–249. IEEE (2015)
5. Hadjisoteriou, E.: Computing argumentation with matrices. In: Schulz, C., Liew, D. (eds.) 2015 Imperial College Computing Student Workshop (ICCSW 2015). OpenAccess Series in Informatics (OASIcs), vol. 49, pp. 29–36. Schloss Dagstuhl-Leibniz-Zentrum fuer Informatik, Dagstuhl (2015)

---

[5] http://swish.swi-prolog.org/p/argmat-clpb.pl.

6. Bistarelli, S., Rossi, F., Santini, F.: Benchmarking hard problems in random abstract AFs: the stable semantics. In: COMMA (2014)
7. Lagniez, J.M., Lonca, E., Mailly, J.G.: CoQuiAAS: a constraint-based quick abstract argumentation solver. In: 2015 IEEE 27th International Conference on Tools with Artificial Intelligence (ICTAI), pp. 928–935. IEEE (2015)
8. Cerutti, F., Giacomin, M., Vallati, M.: ArgSemSAT: solving argumentation problems using SAT. COMMA **14**, 455–456 (2014)
9. Xu, Y.: A matrix approach for computing extensions of argumentation frameworks. CoRR abs/1209.1899 (2012)
10. Hadjisoteriou, E., Georgiou, M.: ASSA: computing stable extensions with matrices. In: System Descriptions of the First International Competition on Computational Models of Argumentation (ICCMA 2015) (2015)
11. Triska, M.: The boolean constraint solver of SWI-Prolog: system description. In: Kiselyov, O., King, A. (eds.) FLOPS 2016. LNCS, vol. 9613, pp. 45–61. Springer, Cham (2016). doi:10.1007/978-3-319-29604-3_4

A Target-Oriented Discussion Framework to Support Collective Decision Making

Jordi Ganzer-Ripoll[1], Maite Lopez-Sanchez[1],
and Juan Antonio Rodriguez-Aguilar[2]([⊠])

[1] Departament de Matemàtiques i Informàtica,
Facultat de Matemàtiques i Informàtica, Universitat de Barcelona,
Barcelona, Spain
jordi891@gmail.com, maite_lopez@ub.edu
[2] IIIA, Artificial Intelligence Research Institute, CSIC,
Spanish National Research Council, 08193 Bellaterra, Spain
jar@iiia.csic.es

Abstract. Argumentative debates are a powerful tool for resolving conflicts and reaching agreements in open environments such as on-line communities. Here we introduce an argumentation framework to structure argumentative debates. Our framework represents the arguments issued by the participants involved in a debate, the (attack and defence) relationships between them, as well as participants' opinions on them. Furthermore, we tackle the problem of computing a collective decision from participants' opinions. With this aim, we design an aggregation function to ensure that participants reach a coherent collective decision.

1 Introduction

As argued in [10,11], argumentative debates are a powerful tool for reaching agreements in open environments such as on-line communities. Nowadays, this is particularly true in our society due to the increasing interest and deployment of e-participation and e-governance ICT-systems that involve citizens in governance [14]. Not surprisingly some European cities are opening their policy making to citizens (e.g., Reykjavík [2], Barcelona [1]). Moreover, the need for argumentative debates has also been deemed as necessary for open innovation systems [12]. On-line debates are usually organised as threads of arguments and counter-arguments that users issue to convince others so that debates eventually converge to agreements. Users are allowed to express their opinions on arguments by rating them (e.g., [11]). There are two main issues in the management of large-scale on-line debates. First, as highlighted by [10,11], there is simply too much noise when many individuals participate in a discussion, and hence there is the need for *structuring* it to keep the focus. Second, the opinions on arguments issued by users must be aggregated to achieve a collective decision about the topic under discussion [4]. In this paper we try to make headway on these two issues.

Funded by Collectiveware TIN2015-66863-C2-1-R (MINECO/FEDER) and 2014 SGR 118.

N. Criado Pacheco et al. (Eds.): EUMAS 2016/AT 2016, LNAI 10207, pp. 481–489, 2017.
DOI: 10.1007/978-3-319-59294-7_39

Recently, argumentation has become one of the key approaches to rational interaction in artificial intelligence [5, 13]. Here, we propose to follow an argumentation-based approach that allows agents to issue arguments in favour of or against a *topic* under discussion as well as about other agents' arguments. Furthermore, we will consider that agents express their opinions about each other's arguments and the topic itself.

Within our multi-agent framework, we face the following collective decision problem: *given a set of agents, each with an individual opinion about a given set of arguments related to a topic, how can agents reach a collective decision on the topic under discussion?* To solve this problem, we propose: (1) A novel multi-agent argumentation framework, the so-called *target-oriented discussion framework*, to support discussions about the acceptance of a target proposal; and (2) A social choice function that aggregates agents' opinions to infer the overall opinion about the topic under discussion. Our aggregation function is based on combining opinions and exploiting dependencies between arguments to produce an aggregated opinion. Moreover, and most importantly, our aggregation function guarantees the resulting aggregated opinion to be *coherent*, namely free of contradictions.

1.1 Example

Next, we introduce a simple example to illustrate some of the presented concepts along the paper.

Example 1 (Flatmates' discussion). *Consider three flatmates (Alan, Bart, and Cathy) discussing about norm (N): "Flatmates take fixed turns for dishwashing at 10 p.m." and issuing the following arguments: a_1 = "10 p.m. is too late and should be changed"; a_2 = "Schedule is too rigid"; and a_3 = "Fair distribution". Notice that: arguments a_1 and a_2 attack N whereas a_3 defends it; and a_1 is in favour of a_2. Once all arguments and their relations are clear, flatmates express their opinions by accepting, rejecting (or not opining about) each argument: (1) Alan (Ag_1) gets up early 4 days per week, and so (as first row in Table 1 shows) he rejects norm N and accepts arguments a_1 and a_2. Nevertheless, he acknowledges and accepts argument a_3. (2) Bart (Ag_2) has spare time at night and is clearly pro norm N. Second row in Table 1 shows he accepts N and a_3, and rejects a_1 and a_2. Finally, (3) Cathy (Ag_3) is keen on routines so she rejects a_2 and accepts N, a_1, and a_3 (see third row in Table 1).*

Therefore, the question that arises is how to aggregate all these opinions so that a consensus is reached over the acceptance (or not) of this dish-washing norm.

Table 1. Flatmates' opinions in the discussion on the dish-washing norm.

2   The Target-Oriented Discussion Framework

The purpose of this section is to formally capture all the core elements of our argumentation framework.

2.1   Formalising Our Argumentation Framework

Our purpose is to provide an argumentation framework that allows one to capture both attack and defence relationships between arguments, as done in bipolar argumentation frameworks [3,8].[1] The motivation for including defence relationships is based on recent studies in large-scale argumentation frameworks involving humans (e.g., [11,12]). There, humans naturally handle both attack and defence relationships between arguments. Our notion of *discussion framework* aims at offering such expressiveness.

Definition 1. *A discussion framework is a triple $DF = \langle \mathcal{A}, \mapsto, \Vdash \rangle$, where $\mathcal{A}$ is a finite set of arguments, and $\mapsto \subseteq \mathcal{A} \times \mathcal{A}$ and $\Vdash \subseteq \mathcal{A} \times \mathcal{A}$ stand for attack and defence relationships that are disjoint, namely $\mapsto \cap \Vdash = \emptyset$. We say that an argument $b \in A$ attacks another argument $a \in A$ iff $b \mapsto a$, and that b defends a iff $b \Vdash a$.*

A discussion framework can be depicted as a graph whose nodes stand for arguments and whose edges represent either attack or defence relationships between arguments. Figure 1 shows our graphical representation of attack and defence relationships.

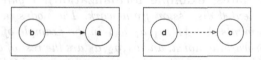

Fig. 1. Representation of an attack relationship $b \mapsto a$ and a defence relationship $d \Vdash c$.

Definition 2. *Let $DF = \langle \mathcal{A}, \mapsto, \Vdash \rangle$ be a discussion framework and $a \subset A$ one of its arguments. We say that an argument $b \in \mathcal{A}$ is a descendant of a if there is a finite subset of arguments $\{c_1, \cdots, c_r\} \subseteq \mathcal{A}$ such that $b = c_1$, $c_1 R_1 c_2$, $\cdots, c_{r-1} R_{r-1} c_r$, $c_r = a$ and $R_i \in \{\mapsto, \Vdash\}$ for all $1 \le i < r$.*

Definition 3. *A target-oriented discussion framework $TODF = \langle \mathcal{A}, \mapsto, \Vdash, \tau \rangle$ is a discussion framework satisfying the following properties: (i) for every argument $a \in \mathcal{A}$, a is not a descendant of itself; and (ii) there is an argument $\tau \in \mathcal{A}$, called the target, such that for all $a \in \mathcal{A} \setminus \{\tau\}$, a is a descendant of τ.*

---

[1] Nevertheless, there are notable differences, e.g., bipolar argumentation frameworks do not consider labellings (different opinions on arguments), nor their aggregation.

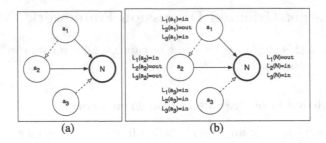

Fig. 2. Flatmates example: (a) TODF's associated graph; (b) *TODF* together with labellings.

Observation 1. *From the previous definitions we infer some properties that help us further characterise a target-oriented discussion framework: Attack and defence relations are irreflexive and non-reciprocal. Moreover, the target neither attacks nor defends any other argument. This distinguishes the special role of the target as the center of discussion to which attacks and supports are directly or indirectly pointed.*

Proposition 4. *Let $TODF = \langle \mathcal{A}, \mapsto, \Vdash, \tau \rangle$ be a target-oriented discussion framework and $E = \mapsto \cup \Vdash$. The graph associated with a TODF, $G = \langle \mathcal{A}, E \rangle$, is a directed acyclic graph, where $\mathcal{A}$ is the set of nodes and E the edge relationship.*

Proof. Straightforward from Definition 2 and Observation 1.

Example 2 (Flatmates' example formalization). *Figure 2(a) depicts the flatmates' target-oriented discussion framework. The nodes in the graph represent the set of arguments $\mathcal{A} = \{N, a_1, a_2, a_3\}$ in the example of previous section, where N is the dish-washing norm, and a_1, a_2, a_3 are the rest of arguments. Thus, N, the norm under discussion, is taken to be τ in our TODF. As to edges, they represent both the attack and defence relationships: $a_1 \mapsto N$, $a_2 \mapsto N$ and $a_1 \Vdash a_2$, $a_3 \Vdash N$ respectively.*

2.2 Argument Labellings

Agents encode their opinions about arguments through *labellings* [6,7]. An agent expresses its support to an argument by labelling it as *in*, rejects it with *out* labels, and abstains from deciding whether to accept it or reject it by labelling it as *undec*. This *undec* label also stands for the absence of an opinion.

Definition 5 (Argument labelling). *Let $TODF = \langle \mathcal{A}, \mapsto, \Vdash, \tau \rangle$ be a target-oriented discussion framework. An argument labelling for TODF is a function $L : \mathcal{A} \longrightarrow \{\text{in}, \text{out}, \text{undec}\}$ that maps each argument of $\mathcal{A}$ to one out of the following labels: in (accepted), out (rejected), or undec (undecidable).*

We note as $Ag = \{ag_1, \ldots, ag_n\}$ the set of agents taking part in a $TODF$, and as L_i the labelling encoding the opinion of agent $ag_i \in Ag$. We will put together the opinions of all the agents participating in an argumentation as follows.

Definition 6 (Labelling profile). *Let $L_1, \ldots, L_n$ be argument labellings of the agents in Ag, where L_i is the argument labelling of agent ag_i. A labelling profile is a tuple $\mathcal{L} = (L_1, \ldots, L_n)$.*

Example 3 (Flatmates' opinions). *Figure 2(b) graphically depicts Alan's, Bart's, and Cathy's labellings (noted as L_1, L_2, L_3 respectively), each one appearing next to the corresponding arguments in the $TODF$'s graphical representation in Fig. 2(a).*

2.3   Coherent Argument Labellings

Given an argument a, we will define:

- its set of attacking arguments as $A(a) = \{b \in \mathcal{A} | b \mapsto a\}$, and
- its set of defending arguments as: $D(a) = \{c \in \mathcal{A} | c \Vdash a\}$

Thus, the labelling of arguments in $A(a) \cup D(a)$ compose the indirect opinion on a.

Given an argument labelling L and a set of arguments $S \subseteq A$, we can quantify the number of accepted arguments in S as:

$$\mathtt{in}_L(S) = |\{b \in S \,|L(b) = \mathtt{in}\}|$$

and the number of rejected arguments in S as:

$$\mathtt{out}_L(S) = |\{b \in S \,|L(b) = \mathtt{out}\}|$$

Thus, given an argument a, we can readily quantify its accepted and rejected defending arguments as $\mathtt{in}_L(D(a))$ and $\mathtt{out}_L(D(a))$ respectively. Moreover, we can also quantify its accepted and rejected attacking arguments as $\mathtt{in}_L(A(a))$ and $\mathtt{out}_L(A(a))$ respectively. Now we are ready to measure the *positive* and *negative* *support* contained in the indirect opinion of a given argument as follows.

Definition 7 (Positive support). *Let $a \in \mathcal{A}$ be an argument and L a labelling on $\mathcal{A}$. We define the positive (pro) support of a as: $Pro_L(a) = \mathtt{in}_L(D(a)) + \mathtt{out}_L(A(a))$.*

Definition 8 (Negative support). *Let $a \in \mathcal{A}$ be an argument and L a labelling on $\mathcal{A}$. We define the negative (con) support of a as: $Con_L(a) = \mathtt{in}_L(A(a)) + \mathtt{out}_L(D(a))$.*

Notice that the positive support of an argument combines the strength of its accepted defending arguments with the weakness of its rejected attacking arguments in the argument's indirect opinion. As a dual concept, the negative support combines accepted attacking arguments with rejected defending arguments.

We now introduce our notion of coherence by combining the positive and negative support of an argument. We say that a labelling is coherent if the following conditions hold for each argument: (1) if an argument is labelled accepted (in) then it cannot have more negative than positive support (the majority of its indirect opinion supports the argument); and (2) if an argument is labelled rejected (out) then it cannot have more positive than negative support (the majority of its indirect opinion rejects the argument).

Definition 9 (Coherence). *Given a* $TODF = \langle \mathcal{A}, \mapsto, \Vdash, \tau \rangle$, *a coherent labelling is a total function* $L : \mathcal{A} \to \{\text{in}, \text{out}, \text{undec}\}$ *such that for all* $a \in \mathcal{A}$ *with* $A(a) \cup D(a) \neq \emptyset$ *it satisfies: (i)* $L(a) = \text{in} \implies Pro_L(a) \geq Con_L(a)$; *and (ii)* $L(a) = \text{out} \implies Pro_L(a) \leq Con_L(a)$.

Example 4. *Again, considering our example and its labellings from Fig. 2(b)* (L_1, L_2, L_3), *we note that just* L_1, L_2 *belong to the subclass of its coherent argument labellings* $Coh(TODF)$.

3   The Aggregation Problem

Definition 10 (Labelling discussion problem). *Let* $Ag = \{ag_1, \cdots, ag_n\}$ *be a finite non-empty set of agents, and* $TODF = \langle \mathcal{A}, \mapsto, \Vdash, \tau \rangle$ *be a target-oriented discussion framework. A labelling discussion problem is a pair* $\mathcal{LDP} = \langle Ag, TODF \rangle$.

Given an $\mathcal{LDP}$, our aim is to find how to aggregate the individuals' labellings into a single labelling that captures the opinion of the collective.

Definition 11 (Aggregation function). *An aggregation function for a labelling discussion problem* $\mathcal{LDP} = \langle Ag, TODF \rangle$ *is a function* $F : \mathbf{L}(TODF)^n \longrightarrow \mathbf{L}(TODF)$, *being* $\mathbf{L}(TODF)$ *the class of the argument labellings of* $TODF$.

Plainly, an aggregation function F takes a labelling profile representing all agents' opinions and yields a single labelling computed from the individual labellings. Such aggregation function is key to assessing the collective decision over the target.

Definition 12 (Decision over a target). *Let* $\mathcal{LDP} = \langle Ag, TODF \rangle$ *be a labelling discussion problem,* $\mathcal{L}$ *a labelling profile, and* F *an aggregation function for the* $\mathcal{LDP}$. *The decision over the target of the* $TODF$ *is the label* $F(\mathcal{L})(\tau)$.

The literature on Social Choice theory has identified fair ways of adding votes. These can be translated into formal properties that an aggregation function is required to satisfy [9]. Based on [4], here we formally state what we consider to be the most desirable property for an aggregation function that allows to assess the decision over the target of a target-oriented discussion framework. Thus, we consider an aggregation function $F(\mathcal{L})$ to be **Collective coherent** (CC) *iff* $F(\mathcal{L}) \in Coh(TODF)$ for all $\mathcal{L} \in \mathbf{L}(TODF)^n$, being $Coh(TODF)$ the subclass of coherent argument labellings.

Notice that if an aggregation function does not produce a coherent labelling, there is at least some argument whose collective label (direct opinion) is in contradiction with its indirect opinion. Thus, the aggregation would not be reliable.

4 The Coherent Aggregation Function

In order to define an aggregation function to compute the collective labelling, we first introduce notation to quantify the direct positive and negative support of an argument. Let $\mathcal{L} = (L_1, \cdots, L_n)$ be a labelling profile and a an argument. We note:

- The *direct positive support* of a as $in_{\mathcal{L}}(a) = |\{ag_i \in Ag \,|L_i(a) = \mathtt{in}\}|$; and
- The *direct negative support* of a as $out_{\mathcal{L}}(a) = |\{ag_i \in Ag \,|L_i(a) = \mathtt{out}\}|$.

Next, we define our chosen aggregation function: the *coherent aggregation function*. The main purpose of this function is to compute a coherent aggregated labelling, and hence fulfil the collective coherence property. that is, to yield a rational outcome that is free of contradiction.

Definition 13 (Coherent aggregation function). *Let $\mathcal{L}$ be a labelling profile. For each argument a the coherent function over $\mathcal{L}$ is defined as:*

$$CF(\mathcal{L})(a) = \begin{cases} \mathtt{in} & , IO(\mathcal{L})(a) + DO(\mathcal{L})(a) > 0 \\ \mathtt{out} & , IO(\mathcal{L})(a) + DO(\mathcal{L})(a) < 0 \\ \mathtt{undec} & , IO(\mathcal{L})(a) + DO(\mathcal{L})(a) = 0 \end{cases}$$

where DO (direct opinion) and IO (indirect opinion) functions are defined as:

$$DO(\mathcal{L})(a) = \begin{cases} 1 & , in_{\mathcal{L}}(a) > out_{\mathcal{L}}(a) \\ 0 & , in_{\mathcal{L}}(a) = out_{\mathcal{L}}(a) \\ -1 & , in_{\mathcal{L}}(a) < out_{\mathcal{L}}(a) \end{cases}$$

If $A(a) \cup D(a) = \emptyset$ then $IO(\mathcal{L}) = 0$, Otherwise:

$$IO(\mathcal{L})(a) = \begin{cases} 1 & , Pro_{CF(\mathcal{L})}(a) > Con_{CF(\mathcal{L})}(a) \\ 0 & , Pro_{CF(\mathcal{L})}(a) = Con_{CF(\mathcal{L})}(a) \\ -1 & , Pro_{CF(\mathcal{L})}(a) < Con_{CF(\mathcal{L})}(a) \end{cases}$$

Notice that to compute our CF on a single argument a we need to compute first the CF of its descendants. The acyclic characterisation of our $TODF$ prevents endless recursion.

Example 5 (Flatmates' discussion). *Back to our example involving a flatmates' discussion, we use the coherent aggregation function to obtain the aggregated opinion of the provided labellings (see Fig. 2(b)). Figure 3 shows the results of the aggregation and the decision over the target as produced by CF. We observe that the flatmates collectively accept arguments a_1 and a_3, whereas argument a_2 becomes undecidable. Finally, the decision over the norm is to accept it.*

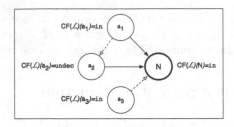

Fig. 3. Flatmates example: aggregated labellings (and decision over target N) computed by CF.

Proposition 14. *CF satisfies the collective coherence property.*

Proof. Let a be an argument such that $CF(\mathcal{L})(a) = \text{in}$. From Definition 13 we know that $IO(\mathcal{L})(a) + DO(\mathcal{L})(a) > 0$. Thus, there are three possibilities: (i) $DO(\mathcal{L})(a) = 1$ and $IO(\mathcal{L})(a) = 1$; (ii) $DO(\mathcal{L})(a) = 1$ and $IO(\mathcal{L})(a) = 0$; or (iii) $IO(\mathcal{L})(a) = 0$ and $DO(\mathcal{L})(a) = 1$. Since $IO(\mathcal{L})(a) \geq 0$ in all cases, this implies that $Pro_{CF(\mathcal{L})}(a) \geq Con_{CF(\mathcal{L})}(a)$, and hence CF satisfies the coherence property. The proof goes analogously for the case $CF(\mathcal{L})(a) = \text{out}$.

5   Conclusions and Future Work

This paper formalises the problem of taking collective decisions by proposing a target oriented discussion framework and a novel aggregation function that combines opinions. We show that such function satisfies coherence, a valuable social choice property.

We are currently studying other social choice properties, such as anonymity, non-dictatorship, or supportiveness. Regarding the operationalisation of our problem, we are also working on an algorithm for the computation of the decision over a target.

Finally, as for future work, we first plan to extend our Target Oriented Decision Framework (TODF) to permit loops, and hence ease rebuttal, a common feature of argumentation systems. Moreover we will also pursue to provide more fine-grained means of computing argument support.

References

1. City of Barcelona participation portal (2016). https://decidim.barcelona
2. City of Reykjavík participation portal (2016). http://reykjavik.is/en/participation
3. Amgoud, L., Cayrol, C., Lagasquie-Schiex, M.-C., Livet, P.: On bipolarity in argumentation frameworks. Int. J. Intell. Syst. **23**(10), 1062–1093 (2008)
4. Awad, E., Booth, R., Tohmé, F., Rahwan, I.: Judgment aggregation in multi-agent argumentation. CoRR, abs/1405.6509 (2014)
5. Trevor, J., Bench-Capon, M., Dunne, P.E.: Argumentation in artificial intelligence. Artif. Intell. **171**(10–15), 619–641 (2007)

6. Caminada, M.: On the issue of reinstatement in argumentation. In: Fisher, M., van der Hoek, W., Konev, B., Lisitsa, A. (eds.) JELIA 2006. LNCS, vol. 4160, pp. 111–123. Springer, Heidelberg (2006). doi:10.1007/11853886_11
7. Caminada, M.W.A., Gabbay, D.M.: A logical account of formal argumentation. Stud. Logica. **93**(2–3), 109–145 (2009)
8. Cayrol, C., Lagasquie-Schiex, M.-C.: On the acceptability of arguments in bipolar argumentation frameworks. In: Godo, L. (ed.) ECSQARU 2005. LNCS, vol. 3571, pp. 378–389. Springer, Heidelberg (2005). doi:10.1007/11518655_33
9. Dietrich, F.: A generalised model of judgment aggregation. Soc. Choice Welf. **28**(4), 529–565 (2007)
10. Gabbriellini, S., Torroni, P.: Microdebates: structuring debates without a structuring tool1. AI Commun. **29**(1), 31–51 (2015)
11. Klein, M.: Enabling large-scale deliberation using attention-mediation metrics. Comput. Support. Coop. Work **21**(4–5), 449–473 (2012)
12. Klein, M., Convertino, G.: A roadmap for open innovation systems. J. Soc. Media Org. **2**(1), 1 (2015)
13. Rahwan, I., Simari, G.R., Benthem, J.: Argumentation in Artificial Intelligence, vol. 47. Springer, Heidelberg (2009). doi:10.1007/978-0-387-98197-0
14. Weerakkody, V., Reddick, C.G.: Public Sector Transformation Through e-Government: Experiences from Europe and North America. Routledge, Abingdon (2012)

AT 2016: Applications

A Proposal for Situation-Aware Evacuation Guidance Based on Semantic Technologies

Holger Billhardt[1]([⊠]), Jürgen Dunkel[2], Alberto Fernández[1],
Marin Lujak[3], Ramón Hermoso[4], and Sascha Ossowski[1]

[1] CETINIA, University Rey Juan Carlos, Madrid, Spain
{holger.billhardt,alberto.fernandez,
sascha.ossowski}@urjc.es
[2] Computer Science Department, Hochschule Hannover, Hannover, Germany
juergen.dunkel@hs-hannover.de
[3] IA, Ecole des Mines de Douai, Douai, France
marin.lujak@mines-douai.fr
[4] Department of Informatics and Systems Engineering,
University of Zaragoza, Saragossa, Spain
rhermoso@unizar.es

Abstract. Smart Cities require reliable means for managing installations that offer essential services to the citizens. In this paper we focus on the problem of evacuation of smart buildings in case of emergencies. In particular, we present a proposal for an evacuation guidance system that provides individualized evacuation support to people in case of emergencies. The system uses sensor technologies and Complex Event Processing to obtain information about the current situation of a building in each moment. Using semantic Web technologies, this information is merged with static knowledge (special user characteristics, building topology, evacuation knowledge) in order to determine (and dynamically update) the most appropriate individualized evacuation routes for each user.

Keywords: Multiagent systems · Evacuation guidance · Context aware systems · Complex event processing · Semantic technologies · Smart buildings

1 Introduction

As cities are growing both in size and population, it is necessary to have reliable means to manage installations that offer essential services to the citizens (e.g., airports, stadiums, museums, and so on). Although there are already experts who design and manage such facilities, there is a lack of efficient operational tools and knowledge to explore their functional limitations in a principled manner, to identify potentially dangerous situations, and to support decision-making in case of emergencies.

Recommendations or guidelines about how to react in cases of emergencies obviously exist, but they can hardly be challenged or debated upon as they are often based on specific cases and experiences rather than strong general arguments. In practice, frequently it is up to human decision-makers to design and monitor an appropriate and

© Springer International Publishing AG 2017
N. Criado Pacheco et al. (Eds.): EUMAS 2016/AT 2016, LNAI 10207, pp. 493–508, 2017.
DOI: 10.1007/978-3-319-59294-7_40

timely course of action in response to a specific emergency situation. They do not adapt information to the context and the profile of each person, so the information they transmit might be useless. In large spaces, human coordinators are introduced mostly at a limited number of critical nodes of an evacuation network. Due to the lack of overall information, these coordinators usually direct all the evacuees to predefined evacuation routes not considering the real-time conditions of the building.

Recently, it was proposed that, by bringing together researchfrom the fields of Agent-Based Social Simulation (ABSS), Ambient Intelligence (AmI), and Agreement Technologies (AT), advanced methods and tools can be developed to address the aforementioned problem [1]. In particular, ABSS is useful for realistically modelling human crowds in large installations (taking into account both individual and herd behaviours). AmI techniques are adequate to model and simulate physical devices in smart spaces (sensors and actuators). Finally, AT are used to explore intelligent strategies for managing such installations as large-scale open distributed systems.

In this paper, we focus on the evacuation of installations of the aforementioned type in case of emergencies. In particular, we focus on smart buildings equipped with information processing, sensing and actuation facilities. In [2] a recommender system has been put forward that arranges personalized visits through a museum, based on user profiles and visitor location data provided by in-door localization techniques. Such situation-aware recommender systems can be considered as a special type of Context-aware Recommender Systems (CARS) that are discussed in detail in [3]. The present work aims at exploiting infrastructures of this type for evacuation purposes.

The objective of an evacuation is to relocate evacuees from hazardous to safe areas or the areas where the life-threatening risk is minimal, that is, providing them with safe routes to such areas. Present evacuation approaches are mostly static, based on pre-assigned evacuation routes. Frequently, no coordination is carried out except for pre-defined evacuation maps. There may arise dangerous situations caused, for instance, by herding and stampeding behaviours at potential bottlenecks. *Real-time* route guidance systems with *situation–aware* capabilities that dynamically determine and update evacuation routes based on the evolution of an ongoing emergency, can help reducing those risks. Furthermore, smart devices allow guidance to be *personalized*, taking into account, for instance, the specific circumstance of the elderly, disabled persons, or families. Finally, large groups of people may need to be evacuated so *scalability* issues are also of importance.

Our proposal concentrates on real-time situation-aware evacuation guidance in smart buildings. The system aims to assign efficient evacuation paths to individuals based on their mobility limitations, initial positions, respecting individual's privacy, and other evacuation requirements. In our approach, complex event processing and semantic technologies are the key technologies used to address this problem.

Section 2 describes in more detail the particular problem that we are addressing, and provides a brief overview of the technologies we use. Section 3 outlines the architecture of the system, and details the structure and dynamics of its key modules. We conclude the paper with Sect. 4, describing lessons learnt and future lines of work.

2 Evacuation Guidance in Emergency Situations

A pedestrian route recommender system for smart spaces that recommends the safest routes to pedestrians and simultaneously optimizes conflicting objectives of finding the social optimum and minimizing individual path travel times in steady state conditions while considering people flow and fairness was presented in [4]. The system considers the influence of stress on human reactions to the recommended routes and iteratively ponders user response to the suggested routes influenced by stress-related irrational behaviours until system acceptable routes are found. Moreover, the influence of affiliate ties and self-concerned individuals among evacuees was studied in [5]. Here, self-concerned and social group behaviour is modelled via individual and team reasoning. The recommended routes take into account the affiliate ties to guarantee evacuee's compliance with the routes.

The proposal we present in this paper applies a more lightweight approach for determining the evacuation routes for users. We rely on the existence of ara the extensive set of possible evacuation routes. This set should include multiple alternative paths for evacuating people from each possible location in the building. The routes may be determined by evacuation experts or through some automated process, which can be carried out offline or updated online if topology changes are produced during the emergency (e.g. new openings through broken walls). The way such potential evacuation routes are generated is out of the scope of this paper. The different evacuation routes are stored in an emergency ontology that, together with an ontology describing the topological structure of the building specifies the a priori knowledge of our system. In addition, situational knowledge about the current situation in each moment of the building and of the evacuees is generated in real-time through a network of sensors. The monitoring permits us to recognize the evacuees' behaviour with respect to the suggested routes and to perceive possible changes in safety conditions of the infrastructure. This dynamic knowledge is merged with the static knowledge about the infrastructure. In an emergency situation, semantic inference is used to select the most appropriate evacuation route for each individual in the building. Furthermore, the real-time monitoring allows the system to reroute evacuees in case of contingencies and, thus, to propose evacuation routes that are adaptive to unpredictable safety drops in the evacuation network.

In the following subsections we present the basic technologies used in our system.

2.1 Sensing Infrastructure

Our work assumes the existence of data provided by a smart infrastructure as well as by the users currently in the building.

Localization with Landmarks. A prerequisite for intelligent routing guidance is a detailed knowledge about the current location of all persons in the building: First, the routing system must know about the occupancy of each space in a building for calculating an appropriate route. Secondly, the precise position of each person is necessary for providing her with individualized routing recommendations taking her specific constraints into account.

496   H. Billhardt et al.

There are various technological approaches to localize persons in buildings:

- WIFI: The intensity of a WiFi signal can be measured to derive the distances to several access points. This allows calculating a person's position via trilateration. Unfortunately, WiFi doesnot yield good accuracy: the distance between a mobile phone and a WiFi access point is often rather large and may not be precisely estimated on base of the received signal, because the signal strength changes significantly with environmental conditions.
- RFID (Radio Frequency Identification) technology can also be used for indoor positioning. Persons equipped with passive RFID tags can be detected by RFID readers that are spread in the building. RFID technology has several drawbacks: First, it is rather expensive to equip a building with an adequate number of RFID readers. Second, it might be difficult to provide each person with a personal RFID tag.
- iBeacon technology has recently been introduced to support indoor navigation [6]. A beacon device uses Bluetooth LE to send in a configurable frequency a unique ID that can be read by any smartphone. Therefore, a beacon infrastructure is set up easily: Beacons are cheap enough to distribute many of them, so that they can form a much denser network in the building. Furthermore, no specific beacon readers are necessary, because usual smartphones are capable of reading and processing beacon signals.

Summarizing, beacon technology can provide a higher accuracy: there are as many readers as users, and each building section can be equipped with many beacons such that a dense network of landmarks is given. Furthermore, some of our former projects proved that beacons provide sufficient localization accuracy [7, 8]. Therefore, we applied beacon technology in our scenario, i.e. we assume that all sections of the buildings contain a sufficient number of beacons that cover completely the space in the building. In general, we use the term section to refer to spatial elements like rooms, floors, staircases, etc.

User Smartphones. From the point of view of information gathering, the personal smartphones of users play two different roles: they serve as readers for beacon signals and they can exploit their built-in sensors to derive more details about the current situation of its particular user.

- Beacon reader for localization: In smartphone operating systems such as iOS and Android, the capability of reading beacon signals is already integrated.
  Each room is equipped with several beacons with non-overlapping ranges. As soon as a user approaches a beacon within the predefined range the smartphone triggers an event carrying the beacon ID. Then the smartphone knows that it is near that beacon and can forward this information to a server that coordinates emergency situations.
- User activity recognition: The built-in sensors of a smartphone can be exploited to derive the current activity of its particular user. There exist several works on how to use phone-based sensors for performing activity recognition. For instance, the

authors in [9] applied different machine learning techniques to classify accelerometer data as certain activities. In our scenario, the current behavior of the users is crucial to detect panic situations, e.g. the situation that most persons in a room are running.

Besides, the smartphones serve as an individualized communication channel to each user to provide personalized routing guidance.

Further Sensors and Infrastructure. Further sensors are necessary for achieving situation awareness in the emergency recommender system. In particular, these sensors can be used to detect unexpected events in the building. For instance, smoke and temperature sensors could be used for fire detection. Furthermore, building operators can specify current incidents that could be detected automatically.

2.2 Complex Event Processing (CEP)

A key issue in emergency recommender systems is detailed knowledge about the current situation in the building. In this regard, in our scenario, an appropriate and individualized guidance for all people in the building requires information about: (i) the current position of each person and the occupancies of all sections in the building, (ii) the situations that can provoke panic, and (iii) the space safety for each constituent part of the evacuation network (made of building sections) that can be jeopardized by, e.g., fire or build-up smoke, or panic related herding and stampeding behaviors.

Apparently, such situational knowledge cannot be predefined. It can be considered as dynamic knowledge with a high change frequency and must be inferred by exploiting livedata. Usually, livedata is provided by sensors, which monitor their environment and produce a continuous stream of data. Each set of sensor data corresponds to a particular event in the environment.

Considering a solitary event is usually of no significance, because it represents just a single incident in the physical world. For instance, it is of no importance if a single person is running, but if all persons in a room are running it could indicate a panic situation. Complex event processing (CEP) is a software technology to extract the information value from event streams [10, 11]. CEP analyses continuous streams of incoming events in order to identify the presence of complex sequences of events, so called event patterns. The main goal of CEP is to extract a domain-specific meaning out of the observed streams of simple fine-grained and uncorrelated events. According to the key idea of CEP, a set of simple events must be correlated to a single complex event with a significant meaning [10]. For instance, a panic event can be inferred if the smartphones of nearly all persons in a certain section of the building emit a running event.

Event stream processing systems manage the most recent set of events in memory and employ "sliding windows" and temporal operators to specify temporal relations between the events in the stream (each event has a timestamp). The core part of CEP is a declarative event processing language (EPL) to express event processing rules. An event processing rule contains two parts: a condition part describing the requirements for firing the rule and an action part that is performed if the condition matches. The condition is defined by an event pattern using several operators and constraints.

An event processing engine analyses the stream of incoming events and executes the matching rules. Luckham introduced the concept of event processing agents (EPA) [10]. An EPA is an individual CEP component with its own rule engine and rule base. Several EPAs can be connected in an event processing network (EPN) that constitutes a software architecture for event processing. Event processing agents communicate with each other by exchanging events.

2.3   Knowledge Representation Using Ontologies

Ontologies are commonly used for knowledge representation in Artificial Intelligence. In the Semantic Web field, standard ontology languages have been recommended by the W3C, such as RDF, RDFS and OWL.

Resource Description Framework (RDF) is a model for knowledge representation. RDF models are directed graphs (semantic networks), where nodes represent concepts or individuals (instances) and arcs represent properties (or predicates). Using RDF terminology, a graph consists of a set of *subject-predicate-object* triples (statements), i.e. each triple represents an arc. *Subjects* and *predicates* are identified using IRIs[1], while *objects* can be represented by IRIs or literals (basic data types)[2].

There are several serialization formats for writing RDF. We use Turtle due to its simplicity and readability. In turtle, an RDF graph is written as a set of triples (the order is not important), each of them in the form <subject> <predicate> <object> ending with a dot. The following shows the turtle representation of the facts "Bob Smith is a security guard that is located in room1, which is connected to room2 and has a capacity of 50 people. Both, room1 and room2 are rooms and also sections.":

```
:bob             rdf:type          :SecurityGuard.
:bob             :locatedIn        :room1.
:bob             :name             "Bob Smith".
:SecurityGuard   rdfs:subClassOf   :Personnel.
:Personnel       rdfs:subClassOf   :Person.
:room2           rdf:type          :Section.
                 rdf:type          :Room.
:room1           rdf:type          :Section;
                 rdf:type          :Room;
                 :connectedTo      :room2;
                 :capacity         "50".
```

Note that the last three lines is a syntactic sugar where we can avoid repeating the same subject in consecutive triples by separating triples with a semicolon.

Semantic descriptions are given in standard ontology languages (e.g. RDF Schema, OWL), which extend RDF and are based on description logics (DL). This technique

---

[1] RDF syntax allows defining prefixes to ease IRIs readability. For example, *rdf:type* is the same as http://www.w3.org/1999/02/22-rdf-syntax-ns#type if we define prefix rdf = http://www.w3.org/1999/02/22-rdf-syntax-ns#. Here we use a default prefix (e.g. *:Room*).

[2] RDF also includes the concept of *blank node*, but we prefer not to mention it in this paper for the sake of clarity.

models knowledge in terms of TBox (terminological box) and ABox (assertional box). In general, the TBox contains sentences describing general concepts (e.g. Security Guard, Personnel, Section, etc.) and relations between them (e.g. *Security guards* are *Personnel*, *persons* are located in *sections*, *sections* have *capacities*, …). The ABox contains sentences about concrete individuals and their relations (e.g. *security guardBob* is *located* in *room1*, which has a *capacity* of 50 people and is *connected* to *room2*, *room1* and *room2* are *sections* and *rooms* etc.). TBoxes are normally reusable across different applications, while ABoxes typically represent particular cases.

RDF Schema (RDFS) extends RDF by defining a few IRIs with given DL semantics. Basically it introduces the notion of classes and instances (e.g. *:bob rdf:type :SecurityGuard*), as well as simple "subclass of" relations (e.g. *SecurityGuard* is a *subclass of Personnel* as shown in the previous example). In addition, RDFS introduces the concept of *property* (and *subproperty*), allowing specifying its *domain* and *range*. For example, the following sentences specify that *locatedIn* is a property whose domain is *Person* and range *Section*:

```
:locatedIn        rdf:type          rdfs:Property;
                  rdfs:domain       :Person;
                  rdfs:range        :Section.
```

Applying DL reasoning, in particular *subclass of* and *type* semantics, it can be checked that security guards are located in a section (e.g. "Bob is located in room1").

Web Ontology Language (OWL) extends RDFS with new primitives that allow creating more complex expressive ontologies. It is possible, for example, to specify cardinality and characteristics of properties (e.g. transitivity, symmetry, …), create complex classes (intersections, disjoints, …), etc.

Semantic representations provide the means to easily obtain inferred knowledge. For example, if we define a class *DisabledPerson* to represent people with at least one disability, then we can infer disabled people even though they have not been explicitly described as instances of that class.

For more complex reasoning tasks, we use rules on top of our OWL ontologies, which typically include new inferred knowledge into the A-Box. In particular, we use rules to determine the accessibility of certain sections in the building, and to select possible evacuation routes.

3 Emergency Management System

In this section we first present the architecture of the proposed emergency management system and describe the different components comprising it. Then, we give some details and examples of the CEP and Route recommender modules.

3.1 System Architecture

We propose a solution concept of an evacuation guidance system architecture that combines different CEP modules in order to provide situation awareness for evacuation route recommendation. An overview of this architecture is given in Fig. 1.

The general operation dynamics of the system is based on two modes: standard mode and evacuation mode. In standard mode, the system continuously monitors the current state of the building, trying to detect a possible emergency scenario. If such a situation is detected (e.g., an emergency event is detected through complex event processing), the system alerts some human operator who can activate an evacuation process and the system enters in evacuation mode. In this mode, the evacuation route recommendation module is executed, which provides individualized route guidance to the people that are currently in the building.

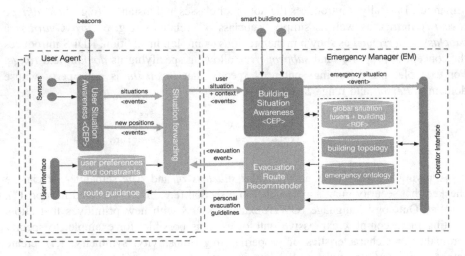

Fig. 1. Overall architecture of the evacuation guidance system.

The system consists of two main parts: User Agents (UA) and Emergency Manager (EM), as well as a set of Sensors located at different points in the infrastructure.

User Agent (UA). The user agent manages and stores all the information that is related to a particular user (a person that is currently located in the building under consideration). The UA is executed as an app on the smartphone of each user. We assume that people that enter the building have either downloaded and run such an app on their smartphones, or they have been provided with some Smartphone like device that runs the app when they entered the building.

The UA contains three parts: a preference module, a user situation awareness module and a recommendation interface. The *preferences and constraints module* allows the user to specify certain preferences or constraints regarding evacuation scenarios; e.g. disabilities that imply a restricted mobility of the person (wheelchair, blind, etc.). This information is entered during the configuration of the UA and is stored locally in form of RDF data.

The *user situation awareness* module exploits sensor data (from the smart phone and beacons installed in the building) and reasons about the behaviour and location of the user (through local CEP processes). The derived information is passed to the situation module in the EM. In order to assure privacy, the amount of information provided to external components is different in standard and in evacuation mode. In standard mode, only certain basic data about the user's situation are forwarded to the EM (e.g., location, running events). In case of the activation of an evacuation (e.g., the EM broadcasts an evacuation event to all user agents), more detailed events are detected and also the preferences and constraints regarding user mobility are passed to the EM. Thus, we consider that an emergency situation prevails upon privacy issues.

Finally, the evacuation mode will also trigger personalized navigation guidelines for evacuation through an appropriate interface. Thus, helping her to leave the building in the way it was suggested by the evacuation route recommender.

Emergency Manager (EM). The emergency manager is the central part of the system. A *building situation awareness* module combines and analyses the events provided from the individual user agents with data from smart building sensors and generates information about the global situation of the building. This information is stored in the data model as RDF data. In this process CEP is used to filter irrelevant information and to generate higher level events. Regarding user events, individual data is aggregated to detect events regarding groups of users as well as identifying the density of the distribution of users in the building.

When the building situation awareness module detects an emergency situation, an alert is sent to the operator interface. This interface allows, on one hand, to monitor the situation of the building and, on the other hand, to trigger an evacuation process and to execute control actions in such a process (e.g., specifying blockage of parts of the building). If an evacuation process is initiated, the system enters evacuation mode and the *evacuation route recommender* is executed. The module sends an evacuation event to all user agents informing them about the situation. Then it starts to calculate individual evacuation routes for all users. In this process, three types of data are used:

- Data regarding the *building topology*: Static information about physical elements in the building (e.g. rooms, corridors, floors, doors, etc.) and relations among them (e.g. room A is 10 m², is connected to room B and both are connected to floor F). As we said before, we use sections to logically identify physical spaces in a building. For instance, a room may be a section or a large hall could be represented through multiple sections. The sections are connected creating the graph of possible movements in the building.

- *Emergency ontology*: This static ontology contains general knowledge about emergency and evacuation scenarios, e.g., possible evacuation paths, the appropriateness of certain routes for people with limited mobility in emergency situations, the influence of certain events like fire and smoke on the security level of a section for evacuation purposes, etc.

- *Global* situation: Contains the current situation of the building itself including the people that are currently in the building. This information includes (i) the distribution of people in the building, (ii) momentary positions, evacuation preferences, and mobility constraints of each person, (iii) information on building sections that are blocked for evacuation, and the reason for blockage.

During evacuation, the global situation of the building is dynamically updated in order to reflect the situation in each moment. Also the route recommender continuously controls the viability of the current evacuation strategy. If changes occur that may violate that viability, then new evacuation routes may be selected for each user.

In the following we describe in more detail the CEP components, the knowledge bases and the principal functioning of the evacuation route recommender module.

3.2 CEP Components

Both agent types, User Agent (UA) and Emergency Manager (EM) analyse the incoming streams of events to understand the current situation.

CEP in the User Agent. The UA exploits sensor data and infers (i) the location and (ii) the behaviour of a single user. To explain the CEP component in more detail, we will assume that the UA monitors two types of explicit (or atomic) events to achieve this type of situation awareness:

- *beaconEvent(beaconID)*: a beacon with a certain ID[3] has been detected
- *accelerationEvent(velocity)*: the phone is moving with a certain velocity

The *beaconEvents* collected by a particular phone are used to derive the current position of its owner. The following CEP rule creates *enteringSection* and *leavingSection* events, meaning that the user is entering, respectively leaving a certain space. These events can be considered as complex (or materialized) events. They carry the ID of the user and the related beacon ID.

```
CONDITION: beaconEvent AS b1 → beaconEvent AS b2
           ∧ b1.id <> b2.id
ACTION:    CREATE enteringSection(userID, b2)
           CREATE leavingSection(userID, b1)
```

The rule describes the situation that a new *beaconEvent b2* has been read in the phone, where the beacon ID has changed. The symbol "→" indicates that event *b1* occurs before event *b2*.

Detecting a running user is another situation that must be forwarded to the Emergency Manager, because many running users can indicate a panic situation. An appropriate CEP rule checks if the average velocity of a user is higher than 5 km/h considering a time window of 5 s:

```
CONDITION: accelerationEvent As a [win:time:5sec]
           ∧ average(a.velocity) > 5 km/h
ACTION:    CREATE runningEvent(userID)
```

---

[3] Note that the *beaconID* is structured and includes, among other information, the ID of a certain section in the building.

If the condition matches, then the rule creates a *runningEvent* that contains the ID of the corresponding user.

CEP in the Emergency Manager. The CEP component in the Emergency Manager is responsible for deriving the global situation in the building. For instance, it could receive and analyze the following *atomic events*: produced by the CEP rules running on the users' smartphones.

- *enteringSection (userID, sec)*: a user with a given ID has entered section sec.
- *leavingSection (userID, sec)*: a user with a certain ID has left section sec.
- *runningEvent (userID)*: a user with a certain ID is running.

Another kind of situational knowledge describes the *global* situation. A first type of rules is calculating the occupancy of different sections in the building.

The following CEP rule calculates the number of persons staying in a certain section by counting all entries and exits in that section during the last 15 min:

```
CONDITION: (enteringSection AS e ∨ leavingSection As l)
                     [win:batch:15min] group_by (e.sec)
           ∧ e.sec = l.sec
           ∧ count(e) AS entries
           ∧ count(l) AS exits
ACTION:    CREATE occupancy(e.sec, entries - exits)
```

The second type of rules tries to infer a global behavior of the people currently staying in the building. For instance, the next rule intends to detect a panic situation in the building:

```
CONDITION: runningEvent AS r [win:time:1 min] group_by(r.sec)
           ∧ count(r) > r.sec.occupancy * 0.2
ACTION:    CREATE panicEvent(r.sec)
```

It groups all *runningEvent* according to a time-spatial window. The grouping criterion is defined by the section, where the *runningEvent* have occurred, and a time interval of 1 min. If more than 20% of the people staying in the section are running, a panic situation is indicated.

Note that also other situational events could be detected by appropriate CEP rules. For instance, a blocked staircase could be inferred, if numerous persons could not continue their recommended evacuation path along the staircase. Similarly, information from other sensors in the smart building can be exploited to derive certain important events. For instance, the data from temperature and smoke sensor can be used to detect a fire situation in a certain part of the building. There are appropriate CEP rules that derive such situations as well.

504   H. Billhardt et al.

3.3   Knowledge Bases

The knowledge used in our system is distributed between the User Agent and the Emergency Manager. All agents share the same common ontology (TBox) for representing the facts describing their knowledge.

User Preferences. In the UA, the user specified her personal preferences and constraints. The following facts written in RDF give an idea of a possible knowledge base content.

```
:user1              :accompaniedBy          :user2;
                    :hasDisability          :wheelchair.
```

We can distinguish between *preferences* (*user1* wants to stay in a group with *user2*) and *constraints* (*user1* uses a wheelchair).

Building Topology. The EM maintains detailed knowledge about the topology of the building. The following example shows how this knowledge can be described.

```
:room1          rdf:type            :Section;
                rdf:type            :Room;
                :connectedTo        :room2;
                :connectedTo        :staircase1;
                :capacity           "50".
:staircase1     rdf:type            :Staircase;
                rdf:type            :Section;
                :connectedTo        :room1.
:connectedTo    rdf:type            owl:SymmetricProperty.
:Staircase      rdfs:subclassOf     :Exit.
```

The RDF triples provide information about *room1*, which is connected to another *room2* and a *staircase1*. The room is a section and has a capacity of 50 people, which can be used to derive overcrowded situations. Furthermore, data about *staircase1* is given. Note that an OWL reasoner can infer the fact that *staircase1* is connected to *room1* by using the knowledge that *connectedTo* is a symmetric property.

Emergency Ontology. The following part of the EM ontology specifies knowledge necessary in *emergency situations*. The first fact informs that space *room2* cannot be used by wheelchairs. Then, an evacuation route is described. The route has a length of 50 m, it starts in *room1* and ends in *exit1* following a particular sequence of sections. In this example, we assume that for each section several evacuation routes are predefined providing different alternatives for the users. In the following subsection, we will show how an appropriate evacuation route can be selected for a particular user.

```
:room2      :notUsableFor   :Wheelchair.
:route1      rdf:type        :EvacuationRoute;
             :startsIn       :room1;
             :endsIn         :exit1;
             :length         "50";
             :path           (:room1 :staircase1 :room7 :exit1).
```

Global Situation. Finally, the EM knows about the current *situation* in the building. For instance, the following triples specify the locations of certain user, the current occupancy of sections and the certain emergency state (e.g. panic situation in *room2*).

```
:user1      :locatedIn          :room1 .
:room1      :occupancy          "40" .
:room2      :emergencyState     :panic.
:locatedIn :rdf:type            owl:FunctionalProperty .
```

The above facts are derived by appropriate CEP rules executed in the UA and the EM, as discussed in the previous section. The integration of events detected through CEP into the system knowledge is provided by a component that maps events to RDF facts. For instance, an *enteringSection(user1, room1)* event is mapped to the RDF fact *(:user1 :locatedIn :room1.)*. In this process, previous facts may have to be deleted. For instance, because the property *:locatedIn* is functional, a former *:locatedIn* assertion for the same user must be deleted from the knowledge base.

3.4 Evacuation Route Recommender Model

In this subsection, we show how to derive personalized evacuation routes from the knowledge base using semantic rules. The examples show, how evacuation experts could specify rules that can be used to determine personalized evacuation routes for users. The example rules are using a notation similar to Jena[4] rules.

First, one class of rules are used to block certain sections for particular users. If a *user* has the disability of being in a wheelchair, and a *section* is of type Staircase, then *section* is not accessible for that *user*:

```
(?user :hasDisability:Wheelchair)
(?sectionrdf:type   :Staircase)
    ->    (?section :notAccessibleFor ?user)
```

The former rule could be refined by not considering lightweight kids accompanied by adults. However, we opt here for keeping simple rules so as to convey the model operation rather than a detailed description.

If a user (*user1*) is accompanied by another person *user2*, then the restrictions hold for all persons in the group:

```
(?user1 :accompaniedBy ?user2)
(?section :notAccessibleFor ?user1)
    ->(?section :notAccessibleFor ?user2)
```

If a panic situation has been detected in a section, the section is restricted for access for any user (here *user*) who is currently located in an arbitrary section *Section 2*:

---

[4] jena.apache.org.

```
(?section1 :emergencyState :panic)(?user :locatedIn  ?section2)
notEqual(?section1,?section2)
        ->(?section1 :notAccessibleFor ?user)
```

Similar rules can be specified for restricting the access to sections due to other situational events (e.g., detected fire or smoke, etc.).

The following rule finds all evacuation routes that can be potentially used by a particular *user*, i.e. all routes that start in the same *section* where the *user* is located.

```
(?user :locatedIn ?section)(?routerdf:type :EvacuationRoute)
(?route :startsIn ?section)
        ->(?route :startingRouteFor?user)
```

But not all of these routes can be used by *user1* due to her personal restrictions. Therefore, another rule marks all routes that contain a section, which is not accessible for *user1*:

```
(?route :startingRouteFor  ?user)(?route :path  ?path)
(?section :notAccessibleFor ?user) listContains(?path,?section)
    ->(?route    :isNotPossibleFor  ?user)
```

Now, the next rule determines all routes that a *user* can really use in her current situation. Those are all routes for *user*, which are derived as her starting routes and which additionally are not marked as 'not possible'.[5]

```
(?route :startingRouteFor  ?user)
noValue(?route:isNotPossibleFor ?user)
        ->(?route :usableBy  ?user)
```

Finally, with an appropriate SPARQL[6] query the best evacuation route for each user can be searched by comparing the lengths of the evacuation routes.

```
SELECT ?user ?path ?minLength
WHERE {
?route :usableBy?user .
?route :length ?minLength .
?route :path  ?path .
    {
SELECT ?user (MIN(?l) AS ?minLength)
    WHERE {
?route :usableBy?user .
?route :length ?l .
    }GROUP BY ?user
    }
}
```

---

[5] Note that this rule must be processed in a subsequent reasoning step for guaranteeing that all 'not possible' routes have already been found by the preceding rules.

[6] SPARQL is a query language for RDF (https://www.w3.org/TR/sparql11-query/).

Semantic rules reflect the knowledge of domain experts. In contrast to traditional recommender methods such as Collaborative Filtering they don't need historical data, but are based on domain experts' expertise. Furthermore, they can easily integrate situational knowledge derived from the CEP rules (e.g., *?user1 :locatedIn ?room1*) with facts from the knowledge base (e.g., predefined evacuation routes).

4 Conclusions

In this paper we have presented a system for situation-aware evacuation guidance in smart building. The system provides an individual evacuation route recommendation to each user of a smart large installation. The proposal takes into account the current location and building state obtained through sensors and personal mobile devices, as well as human factors in emergencies.

We described the architecture and the main technologies proposed to implement the proposed system, namely, beacons and smartphones for obtaining live building information, CEP for efficient event processing, and knowledge representation and semantic reasoning for determining evacuation route recommendations. Although semantic reasoning may require high computational resources, we alleviate this fact by the use of efficient CEP technologies distributed in UAs and EM, whichefficiently provide a reduced set of high level facts describing current building situation.

In [4], we presented a distributed algorithm that calculates evacuation route recommendations through global optimization techniques, concentrating on the safety and fairness of the recommended routes. In this paper we have presented a more light-weight approach that uses semantic inference techniques to select appropriate evacuation routes out of a set of predefined routes. In contrast to other more automatic techniques, the proposed approach is based on domain experts' expertise. Thus, certain facts and particular conditions that are difficult to take into account in automatic methods may be taken into consideration when evacuation routes are calculated.

In an emergency situation, the system continuously monitors the evolution of the building's global state and recalculates recommended evacuation routes if necessary. Furthermore, the recommended evacuation routes can be personalized to each user, taking into account special mobility conditions or other restrictions. The information on such conditions is kept private (on users' smartphones) and is only revealed in case of an emergency situation.

In the future, we plan to test our architecture in a simulated scenario where we will evaluate the correctness of CEP rules and the route recommendation mechanismin different settings and comparing it to other approaches. Wealso consider an evaluation in a real world scenario in a University building.

Acknowledgments. Work partially supported by the Autonomous Region of Madrid (grant "MOSI-AGIL-CM" (P2013/ICE-3019) co-funded by EU Structural Funds FSE and FEDER, "SURF" (TIN2015-65515-C4-4-R (MINECO/FEDER)) funded by the Spanish Ministry of Economy and Competitiveness, and through the Excellence Research Group GES2ME (Ref. 30VCPIGI05) co-funded by URJC and Santander Bank.

References

1. MOSI-AGIL project (2016). https://www.gsi.dit.upm.es/mosi/
2. Hermoso, R., Dunkel, J., Krause, J.: Situation awareness for push-based recommendations in mobile devices. In: 19th International Conference on Business Information Systems (BIS) (2016)
3. Adomavicius, G., Tuzhilin, A.: Context-aware recommender systems. In: Ricci, F., Rokach, L., Shapira, B., Kantor, P.B. (eds.) Recommender Systems Handbook, pp. 217–253. Springer, New York (2011)
4. Lujak, M., Ossowski, S.: Intelligent people flow coordination in smart spaces. In: Rovatsos, M., Vouros, G., Julian, V. (eds.) EUMAS/AT -2015. LNCS, vol. 9571, pp. 34–49. Springer, Cham (2016). doi:10.1007/978-3-319-33509-4_3
5. Lujak, M., Giordani, S., Ossowski, S.: Distributed safety optimization in evacuation of large smart spaces. In: The 9th International Workshop on Agents in Traffic and Transportation (ATT 2016 @ IJCAI 2016) (2016)
6. Apple Inc.: iBeacons https://developer.apple.com/ibeacon/
7. Zimmermann, W.: Indoor navigation with iBeacon technology. Master thesis, Hannover University of Applied Sciences and Arts (2016). (in German)
8. Brown, M.: Introducing iBeacon Technology at SXSW 2015 (2015). http://www.sxsw.com/news/2015/introducing-ibeacon-technology-sxsw-2015
9. Kwapisz, J.R., Weiss, G.M., Moore, S.A.: Activity recognition using cell phone accelerometers. ACM SIGKDD Explor. **12**(2), 74–82 (2010)
10. Luckham, D.: The Power of Events. Addison-Wesley, Boston (2002)
11. Etzion, O., Niblett, P.: Event Processing in Action. Manning, Greenwich (2010)

Software Agents in Retinal Vessels Classification

Pablo Chamoso[1(✉)], Sara Rodríguez[1], Fernando De La Prieta[1],
Juan F. De Paz[1], Javier Bajo Pérez[2],
Juan Manuel Corchado Rodríguez[1], and Luis García-Ortiz[3]

[1] IBSAL/BISITE Research Group, Edificio I+D+I, University of Salamanca,
37007 Salamanca, Spain
{chamoso,srg,fcofds,fer,corchado}@usal.es
[2] Department of Artificial Intelligence, Technical University of Madrid,
Campus Montegancedo, Boadilla del Monte, 28660 Madrid, Spain
jbajo@fi.upm.es
[3] Primary Care Research Unit La Alamedilla,
Castilla and León Health Service (SACYL), Salamanca, Spain
lgarciao@usal.es

Abstract. This article presents a methodology for the classification of
retinal vessels based on agreement technologies and artificial vision. Some
studies have demonstrated a direct relationship between the information
gathered from retinal images and certain pathologies such as hypertension or diabetes. There are different works that present methodologies
based on image processing algorithms to extract that information, but
there is no globally accepted methodology to obtain the information
automatically, which is the objective of this work. The proposed methodology has been evaluated by one expert user and compared with other
existing free software with similar features.

Keywords: Agents · Agreement technologies · Retinal vessels · Visual
analysis · e-Health

1 Introduction

When trying to detect eye diseases, the information that is obtained from blood
vessels may be relevant. The blood vessels of the eye can be seen on retinal
images. Some of those diseases affect the morphology of the vessel tree itself,
such as retinopathy of prematurity.

Methods of digital image processing of fundus photographs have been proposed in recent years in order to improve the measurement of retinal vessel
parameters, and then find the association of those vessels with cardiovascular
diseases [1,2]. Nevertheless, there is no validated automatic methodology that
can obtain the necessary information and relate the extracted parameters with
pathologies.

In this work, we intend to extract different measurements that have been
proved to be related to pathologies. For example, the arteriovenous index

© Springer International Publishing AG 2017
N. Criado Pacheco et al. (Eds.): EUMAS 2016/AT 2016, LNAI 10207, pp. 509–523, 2017.
DOI: 10.1007/978-3-319-59294-7_41

(or just AV index) is a parameter that represents the relationship between the arteries caliber and the veins caliber, and it has been proved to be related to diabetic retinopathy.

To obtain the required information in an efficient way we propose the use of software agents for the execution of different artificial vision techniques is proposed. To this end, the first objective is vasculature segmentation, which provides the vessel structure apart from the retinal background. Agents must then collaborate to identify every vessel and classify them according to their type: vein or artery. This classification proved to be the most difficult step in previous works [3] because it is also a challenging task for human experts, given that the brightness of every image is always different.

Therefore, previous results for the vessel identification step are expected to improve with the tool that implements the proposed methodology. As the vessel identification step is obviously based on the vasculature segmentation step, every step is important for the final result. Agreement technologies (AT) and multi-agent systems (MAS) have been introduced because software such as the one proposed require high levels of intelligence, and all of them will have to negotiate to propose the most accurate result.

Once every blood vessel in the image has been detected and identified, interesting parameters related to its morphology, such as thickness, area or length, are extracted and saved in order to keep a complete database and find a relationship with illnesses in future works.

The proposed methodology has been implemented to be evaluated and the result is a software tool called ALTAIR (Automatic Image Analyzer to Assess Retinal Vessel Caliber). This is the second version (v2) of the software tool, which includes the MAS approach as the main modification (first version was a sequential application without agents [3]).

The remainder of this paper is structured as follows: a review of the current published works that led to the realization of this study is presented in the next section. Then, the proposed system is described, detailing separately the agent architecture and the image processing techniques that have been applied to extract the information from retinal images. The results obtained with this work are presented, followed by the conclusion and future work.

2   Background

Fundus examination is a non-invasive evaluation of the vascular damage caused by multiple factors. Images taken by a fundus camera provide a clear image of the retina.

As a result of various population studies carried out, a direct relationship has been found between the caliber of the retinal vessels and pathologies such as arterial [4], stroke [5], metabolic syndrome [6], etc.

The relationship between retinal blood vessels and pathologies is not a recent discovery; retinal images have been used and analyzed manually for decades [7]. Today, computer-based visual analysis is used to detect the vessel structure in retinal images. Different works, including [8,9], suggest the application of morphological methods like erosion or dilation [10], which are widely used when extracting different kinds of features from images with a previously known shape. Other works apply algorithms based on adaptive filtering techniques to highlight the vessels and detect them easily [11]. Methodologies such as [12] or that proposed in [13] for the detection of diabetic retinopathy, have also been proposed. These methodologies follow a four block analysis that includes a preprocessing step, a shape estimation step, a feature extraction step and a classification step. However, existing tools only apply one technique in every step, the results can be improved by combining more than one techniques in every step. A summary of the technologies applied by other methodologies for the analysis of retinal images can be found in [14].

Part of the medical team that collaborated in this study was previously involved in the development of another software tool (AVIndex [15]) which extracts information similar to that extracted with the software tool proposed in this work. However, the medical team realized that it was incomplete (information related to the area, length or vessel position was missing) and the analyzed area was not large enough to discover relationships with pathologies.

Artificial intelligence is usually applied to solve difficult problems, such as the detection and classification of the retinal vessels, to get the same or even better results than the ones an expert user would get by alone. Software agents have been widely used for decades as a solution to solve complex problems and more recently they have been used to solve e-health problems [16]. AT can be successfully applied in a large number of domains [17] to solve complex and dynamic runtime problems. This is the case of vessel identification, where agents have to determine the vessel type taking into account different parameters (defined by the retina morphology) and negotiate to reach a global agreement regarding their type.

3 Proposed System

The proposed system is based on a novelty methodology specifically designed and developed for the present work. Although this methodology follows a schema that is similar to the one followed by other developments and works, as shown in [14], the set of techniques applied in every state are novel. The steps to be followed when performing the analysis of the retina are sequential, but each of these steps can be carried out individually, even in parallel and using different techniques and algorithms. The proposed system follows an approach based on agents, in which the functionalities can be distributed and also carried out independently, but with a common goal. The schema that is followed by the proposed methodology uses eight states or steps as a basis for extracting the information. The output of the previous state is considered as the input for the next state, as can be seen in Fig. 1.

In order to carry out different analyses or studies linking the extracted information with the pathologies, the system must be able to associate that information with the patient in order to study the relationship with the patient's

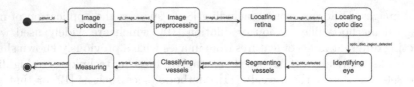

Fig. 1. State diagram.

clinical history. In this way, the first step of the system links the selected retina image with the patient.

The retinal images used in the current study have been taken by a commercial fundus camera whose model is irrelevant for the system, given that any fundus camera can be used to get the images. The reason for this is that the analysis only requires a suitable resolution (height from 600px) and the scale, relationship between pixels, and real measure, are features that all fundus camera manufactures should provide. One or more agent participates at every step of the process. When more than one agent executes one step for the same task, the input is the same, although each one can have its own output. In this case, agents will have to use agreement technologies to propose the output that is best suited for the desired result.

Agents have been developed by following the PANGEA specifications [19]. The communication between agents in PANGEA is based on the FIPA/ACL protocol. A diagram representing how agents take part in the system can be seen in Fig. 2.

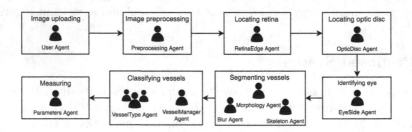

Fig. 2. Agents organized by stages.

First, the user must select the image to process and associate it to the patient. In the MAS, this action is executed by the **User Agent**. Then the system enters a state of "Image preprocessing" where the image is processed by the **Preprocessing Agent**. The image, usually RGB, is combined in a single layer image (grayscale) by using different filters. The result of this preprocessing step can be seen in the top middle of Fig. 3, where the original RGB image (a) is directly converted to grayscale (b) and converted by using a filtered combination (c). This combination mixes red (R), green (G) and blue (B) channels in a specific way to highlight the difference between blood vessels and the background to improve the analysis results.

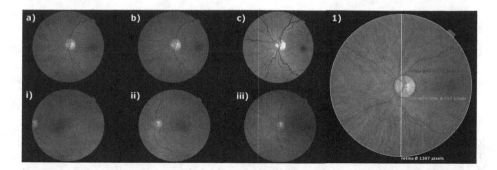

Fig. 3. Fundus retinography preprocessing and optic disc alignments. (Color figure online)

RetinaEdge Agent executes the retina location step. It is a very important step as it determines the image area (size and location) where the information is contained, which is the area to be analyzed. From that moment, all the analyses of the methodology are focused only in this area and processing time is significantly lower.

In order to detect the edge, the color of every pixel is analyzed to find a substantially color change that belongs to a blob big enough to be considered as the retina. This procedure is executed for every row, which detects both the top and the bottom points of the retina. The agent then does the same with the columns to detect horizontal retina limits.

The optic disc (or papilla) is another important element in the image that has to be located. All the blood vessels access the eye through the optic disc. Vessels inside the optic disc are too close to detect their morphology individually, so the analysis starts from its edge. The localization step is executed by the **OpticDisc Agent** and it is essential for the following steps.

Fundus images can be taken with the optic disc oriented in different ways: (i) with the optic disc in left or right side (Fig. 3(i)), (ii) with the macula centered (Fig. 3(ii)) or (iii) with the optic disc centered (Fig. 3(iii)). As we want to obtain as much information as possible, we are only considering the images with the optic disc in the middle because the region of interest (ROI) has no hidden parts.

The ROI where the analysis is executed is defined as the area from the optic disc border and its concentric circle whose radius is three times higher. With this definition, the analysis area will be different for every retina image as the size ratio of optic disc size can vary from 1:8 the retina size to 1:6 optic to retina size. Therefore, this is the radius value that has been established for all of them. An example of this relationship is shown in Fig. 3(1).

The optic disc is now located by applying pixel intensity, adaptive thresholding and morphologic filters to locate the lighter blob with the optic disc morphology. Its center of mass is defined as the middle of the circle that contains the optic disc. The result of every filter can be seen in Fig. 4.

Fig. 4. Visual analysis steps of algorithm for optic disc location.

Once the area containing all the information to extract is determined and the location of the optic disc is known, the eye side (left or right) can be determined. This information can be interesting when analyzing the results. The **EyeSide Agent** executes the algorithm of this step, which is very simple and consists of locating the macula, a taint that is always located in the image side closer to the external side of the face. Images are always taken with the fundus camera opposite the face so if the macula is in the left side of the image, it indicates that the image is associated with the right eye. If the macula is in the right side of the image, it means that an image of the left eye is being analyzed. As mentioned, the algorithm that the EyeSide Agent executes to detect the macula is very simple, so the analysis time is really low. The location of the optic disc is already known and the macula must be in one of the sides and approximately at the same height. For this reason, the grayscale image is divided into two new ROIs. The width of each ROI is delimited from the x-axis center of the optic disc and the retina border and the height of both ROIs is 1:4 of the retina height centered in the y-axis center of the optic disc. An example with both ROIs (ROI_1 and ROI_2) delimited is shown in Fig. 5(i). Once delimited, the algorithm compares the mean color of the two ROIs. The lowest one (0 = black; 255 = white) is the darker which means that the macula is in that ROI.

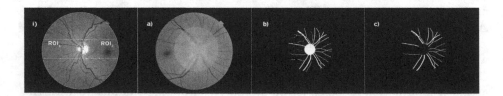

Fig. 5. Eye identification and vessel segmentation steps.

At this point of the methodology, the system knows all the information to segment the vasculature in the "Segmenting vessels" state, whose output will be the vascular structure separate from the background. This process requires the participation of more than one agent. More specifically, the Blur Agent executes different Gaussian filters so that blood vessels are mixed with the background. This will result in an image like the one shown in Fig. 5(a). The agent then detects the points of the new image with highest color difference from the same point in the grayscale image. It generates a binary image with those points (Fig. 5(b)), which is analyzed by the **Morphology Agent** to evaluate the morphology of every blob. This removes noise and results in a well-defined vessel structure as shown in Fig. 5(c). The **Skeleton Agent** can now extract the skeleton. Skeletonization is a widely known tool to describe binary images that captures the essential topology shape information of the object in a simple form. Every point of the skeleton is now analyzed by the agent to separate every single vessel. There are four kinds of points: (i) final, with just one neighbor, (ii) normal, with two neighbors, (iii) branch, with three neighbors, (iv) intersection, with four neighbors. This classification is really useful to identify single vessels from crossing vessels.

The information about blood vessels is then sent to the next step, where different VesselType Agents and one VesselManager Agent classify every blood vessel by its type: vein or artery. This step is detailed in the following subsection.

Once all the blood vessels have been detected and tagged, the **Parameters Agent** extracts all the parameters required to try the pathology relationship. These parameters represent the result of the tool, which generates the following information: veins length, arteries length, veins area, arteries area, veins thickness, arteries thickness and AV index. All measurements are in millimeters as a result of applying the fundus camera manufacturer scale.

3.1   Negotiation for Vessel Classification

Once blood vessels have been segmented and individually identified, the system proceeds with their classification as vein or artery. The only measurable parameter that differentiates veins and arteries in retinal images is the vessel color. The mean thickness of all the veins is usually higher than that of the arteries, but some arteries can be thicker than some veins, so thickness cannot be used to classify the vessels.

But vessel color cannot be the only parameter taken into account because color depends on the lightness of that area of the image (for example, all vessels close to the macula are usually darker), so the vessel's closest background color has to be measured too in order to evaluate the vessel type.

The retina morphology plays also an important role in this step of the methodology. All images should follow three basic rules: (i) there must be both veins and arteries; (ii) the number of arteries and veins must be similar (there is always at least a 40% of the total vessels that are veins or arteries, and the other % is associated to the other vessel type); (iii) both veins and arteries should be in the northern as well as the southern half of the image because they always follow that pattern.

The tool launches different VesselType agents, each one of which is associated with one area of the image as explained below, and one VesselManager agent. Each VesselType agent is responsible for obtaining both the vessel and the background tonality information (mean value). The negotiation between every agent now begins, coordinated by the VesselManager agent. An agreement must be reached to provide one result with the classification of every vessel as a vein or an artery.

In the classification of vessels is important to consider the different results obtained by the agents and including a complex process such as negotiation because according to medical experts and previous experience [5], a same image can produce different results. A negotiation, in which each agent can classify according its parameters and a final classification obtained, is necessary in the system. Each agent, meanwhile, could use the technique of classification for which it is implemented (traditional or own as in this case).

Agents in this tool were originally conceived as single actors, but within the MAS approach, a different method has become possible. The need for multiple-services and functionalities continues, but it has become a coordination problem. The vessel classification process can be conceived as a way to present the operational capabilities of a VesselType agent (or a collection thereof).

Communication between agents makes it possible to synchronize actions, send and receive knowledge, resolve conflicts in solving a task, etc. Meanwhile, negotiations can be described as social norms that impose a standard behavior for agents that avoid conflicts [20]. It is a process where each negotiator evaluates information from their own perspective, and there is a final decision made by mutual agreement. In this case there is a negotiation between VesselType agents to carry out a classification of the vessel according to its type (vein or artery). The process below describes the formalization of the negotiation process.

In this case, a trading strategy is carried out, where there are different proposals and a unilateral agreement in which a negotiator agent takes control to reach the final resolution, in this case the classification. There are several models of negotiation [18]. In this case it is centralized. There is a negotiation cycle in which VesselType agents start proposing a solution to the conflict, then discuss other possibilities, taking their preferences into account, and finally updating the storage solutions according to the final preferences.

This research proposes a coordination model that uses a cooperative MAS in which each agent is capable of establishing results dynamically in order to reach its objectives. Additionally, there should be a global mechanism that can optimally assign a final result to the agents so that they can work in a coordinated effort. The global mechanism considers the global objective of the group of agents. VesselType agents present a deliberative CBR-BDI (Case Based Reasoning - Belief Desire Intentions) [21] agent architecture to construct the negotiation model.

BDI architectures exhibit interesting properties that can deal with situations involving high level coordination among the agents available at a given time, and suggest the necessary extensions for this model, thus allowing the agents to engage in the correct social behavior.

The software presented in this study introduces a group of agents whose aim is to offer a classification vessel to the users. This group of agents is implemented by using the CBR-BDI model. The agent roles that have been identified within this study are (Fig. 6):

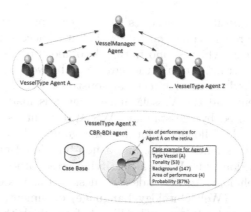

Fig. 6. Coordination problem between VesselType Agents and VesselManager Agent.

- **VesselType Agent:** This agent is in constant communication with the VesselManager Agent to obtain the classifications it requests within a defined area of the retina, and to know which VesselType agent group it is assigned to. An area will be a location within the retinal image with certain characteristics that may be appealing to the user. For example, within a given area there can be several vessels. The profile for the VesselType agent will be characterized by a set of variables specific to the agent (tonality, morphology, area, vessels, etc.).
- **VesselManager Agent:** An agent that assumes this role will be able to assign the final classification to take for VesselType Agents.

VesselType agents can generate a classification for the vessel identified in its area of performance independent of other agents, but depending on the resources and profile for each of them. The VesselManager agent will be responsible for assigning final classification vessels according to the best individual classification. The VesselManager agent will be responsible for assigning final classification vessels according to the best individual classification. This classification is chosen taking into account the probability of the cases of the base-cases stored for this vessel in the past. In other words, there may be certain individual restrictions for each agent that must be taken into consideration by the VesselType agents in order to generate a classification vessel; however, it is the VesselManager Agent who takes into account the restrictions for the entire group of agents in order to distribute and assign the final classifications. We can say that the VesselManager agent is like a coordinator that has access to the information on areas, previous classifications, tonalities, etc., stored in the system. The CBR-BDI agent, as suggested in [22], is assigned a cycle in which it will obtain its personalized optimal classification. The information stored is a data base of cases that considers the classification performed and the resources generated by each agent. This way the VesselManager agent ensures that the vessel classification process can at least be carried out.

There is a decomposition of services (in this case of classification services) to provide the required features; but after that it is necessary to address the structure of agreements which supports this decomposition, in order to make it adaptive. So, an important notion is the agreement between computational entities (agents) conceived as an architectural construct. The interaction between the VesselType agent and the VesselManager agent is made through a negotiation protocol inspired by the standard WS-Agreement used in web services [24–26]. In this case, the following information is going to be considered: Inputs, Outputs, Preconditions, and Results, and a non-functional parameter: classification process execution time. When a classifying vessel process is carried out in the system, a Morphology Agent sends a request to the VesselManager Agent, the query is an OWL (Web Ontology Language) document, which contains a set of service inputs, outputs and a deadline before which the required service should be provided:

$$query = <input, output, deadline>$$

The VesselManager agent, in order to determine a set of appropriate classification, analyzes the existing classifications of VesselType agents considering the Morphology Agent deadline. Each individual classification of a VesselType agent consists of a set of elements:

$$service = <serviceId, input, output, service - Duration, probability>$$

The VesselManager Agent selects the service, taking into account the success probability of the service and its execution time.

Internal Vessel Agents Agreements: Vessel Classification
In our proposal, arguments exchanged among VesselType agents are tuples of the form
$$Arg = \alpha, \beta, <S>,$$
where α is the conclusion of the argument, β is the value that the agent wants to promote, and $<S>$ is a set of elements that justify the argument (the support set).

The support set S can consist of different elements, depending on the argument purposed. For example, if the argument justifies a potential solution for a problem, the support set is (i) the set of features (premises) that match the problem to be solved, (ii) additional premises that do not appear in the description of this problem but have also been considered to draw the conclusion of the argument, and (iii) optionally, any knowledge resource used by the proponent to generate the argument (domain-cases, argument-cases or argumentation schemes). This type of argument is called a support argument. However, if the argument attacks the argument of an opponent, the support set can also include any of the allowed attack elements of our framework. These are distinguishing premises, counter-examples, or critical questions. A distinguishing premise is either a premise that does not appear in the description of the problem to be solved and has different values for two cases, or a premise that appears in the problem description and does not appear in one of the cases. A counter-example for a case is a previous case (i.e. a domain-case or an argument case), where the problem description of the counterexample matches the current problem to be solved and also subsumes the problem description of the case, but proposing a different solution. Also, as pointed out before, critical questions represent potential attacks that can defeat the conclusion of an argumentation-scheme. This other type of argument is called an attack argument.

The argumentation system that implements our framework has a specific structure of domain-cases and a concrete set of argumentation-schemes, depending on the application domain. An example of a case used by a VesselType agent could be the following (Table 1):

Table 1. Case example for VesselType agent

Case example for VesselType agent
Type Vessel {A}
Tonality {0}
Background {1}
Area of performance {4}
Probability {87%}

Argument-cases store the information about a previous argument that an agent had posed in a specific step of a dialogue with other agents. In argument cases we store a problem description that has a domain context consisting of the premises that characterize the argument. In this case, it is necessary to store all information related to the classification of the vessel, that is, tonality, background color, area of performance of the VesselType Agent, Type of classification result (in this case A-Artery or B-Vein), and the probability of success in the classification process.

4 Results

The proposed methodology includes different visual analysis techniques that agents use. A summary is shown in Table 2. The result of implementing this methodology is a multiplatform tool, called ALTAIR (v2), developed with Qt and OpenCV as shown in Fig. 7. The accuracy of this tool when analyzing the different existing components of the image has been assessed by processing a total of 200 images. Results for every analysis step are shown below in Table 3.

To assess whether the analysis is right or wrong, each image has been reviewed by an expert user. In the case of the retina edge location, optic disc location and eye side identification, the accuracy was excellent: 100%, 99.5% and 100% respectively.

For the evaluation of the segmentation stage, only main blood vessels were considered (generally there are at least 6–8 vessels thicker than the rest, and usually, at least 1 vein-artery pair in every eye quadrant). In the 200 images

Table 2. Visual analysis techniques used by agents.

Retina edge	Optic disc	Eye side	Segmentation	Classification
Pixel intensity	Pixel intensity	Pixel intensity	Pixel intensity	Pixel intensity
Morphologic filter	Adaptive thresholding	Adaptive thresholding	Adaptive thresholding	Adaptive thresholding
	Morphologic filters		Gaussian filters	Classifier
			Morphologic analysis	

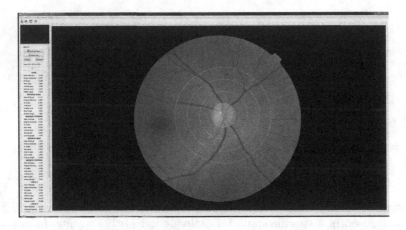

Fig. 7. Software tool screenshot (last step)

Table 3. Analysis results for every stage.

	Retina edge	Optic disc	Eye side	Segmentation	Classification
Right	200	199	200	1,316	1,119
Wrong	0	1	0	147	197
Total	200	200	200	1,463	1,316
Accuracy	100%	99.5%	100%	89.95%	85.03%

that were processed, the expert user marked a total of 1,463 main blood vessels and 1,316 were successfully detected, achieving a system accuracy of 89.95%.

Regarding the vessel classification as vein or artery, the most difficult step even for an expert user, the evaluation was performed considering only those main blood vessels that were successfully detected (1,316). In 1,119 cases, the classification of the system coincided with the classification performed by the expert user, which translates to an accuracy of 85.03%.

These results have improved the results obtained with the first version of ALTAIR [3] (without the MAS approach), where the segmentation achieved an accuracy of 80% and the system achieved an accuracy of 72% in the vessel classification step. The segmentation in ALTAIR v2 is much higher than the results obtained by the AVIndex tool, which only detects 50% of the vessels. In addition, in AVIndex, crosses and branches are not taken into consideration.

Another interesting issue to evaluate the tool that implements the proposed methodology (in this case, its usability), is the time spent in the analysis of every image. A slow tool could dissuade the user from using it. Timing results are shown in Table 4. All values are in seconds and they are the mean processing time for 10 images in every step of the methodology.

Table 4. Analysis time.

	Retina edge	Optic disc	Eye side	Segmentation	Classification	Total
Time (s)	0.9	1.2	0.3	2.2	1.4	6.0

The tool has been compared to an existing free software tool with similar characteristics [15]. The ALTAIR tool takes just 6.0 s until parameters are exported. The AVIndex tool takes 15.3 s to process the same images (steps cannot be evaluated because there is just one step and it is not an open source tool).

Clinical validation of the ALTAIR software tool and the results obtained have been published in [23], where the conclusion of the developed tool is that: (i) it showed a good reliability in the concordance inter observers, intra observer and inter device measurements; (ii) the tool is valid to show an association with vascular parameters, target organ damage and cardiovascular risk.

5   Conclusion and Future Work

A new methodology that improves the previous results has been presented by using different visual analysis techniques (a summary of the used techniques is shown in Table 2) and by using software agents with AI.

The proposed system follows a based agents approach in which the functionalities can be distributed and carried out independently, but with a common goal. Each agent can use different techniques of filtering, classification or segmentation among other. In this way, in a future work, using this approach it is possible to have several agents working in parallel on each step, and agents will have to deal with issues such as coordination, synchronization, etc.

So far, the only pathologies that have been demonstrated to be associated with the parameters measured and exported by the ALTAIR v2 software tool is organ damage and cardiovascular risk. This means that the measured values are right and these values do not depend on the user, because the evaluation showed a good reliability no matter who the user is.

Because of the large number of diseases and pathologies related to the blood vessels caliber and structure, future work will concentrate on finding the relationship of these types of pathologies with the parameters exported using the developed tool. Another CBR system will be implemented for this purpose.

In addition, different online services will be published to allow other users to use their images to increase the case database.

Acknowledgments. This work was carried out under the frame of the project with Ref. "TIN2015-65515-C4-3-R". The research of Pablo Chamoso has been financed by the Regional Ministry of Education in Castilla y León and the European Social Fund (EDU/310/2015).

References

1. Li, Q., Zhu, P., Huang, F., Lin, F., Yuan, Y., Gao, Z., Chen, F.: The relationship of retinal vessel diameters and fractal dimensions with blood pressure and cardiovascular risk factors. J. Am. Coll. Cardiol. **66**(16 S), 1–10 (2015)
2. McGeechan, K., Liew, G., Macaskill, P., Irwig, L., Klein, R., Klein, B.E., Wang, J.J., Mitchell, P., Vingerling, J.R., Dejong, P.T., Witteman, J.C., Breteler, M.M., Shaw, J., Zimmet, P., Wong, T.Y.: Meta-analysis: retinal vessel caliber and risk for coronary heart disease. Ann. Intern. Med. **151**(6), 404–413 (2009)
3. Chamoso, P., Pérez-Ramos, H., García-García, Á.: Supervised methodology to obtain retinal vessels caliber. ADCAIJ: Adv. Distrib. Comput. Artif. Intell. J. **3**(4), 48–57 (2014)
4. Tanabe, Y., Kawasaki, R., Wang, J.J., Wong, T.Y., Mitchell, P., Daimon, M., Yamashita, H.: Retinal arteriolar narrowing predicts 5-year risk of hypertension in Japanese people: the Funagata study. Microcirculation **17**(2), 94–102 (2010)
5. Yatsuya, H., Folsom, A.R., Wong, T.Y., Klein, R., Klein, B.E., Sharrett, A.R., ARIC Study Investigators: Retinal microvascular abnormalities and risk of lacunar stroke atherosclerosis risk in communities study. Stroke **41**(7), 1349–1355 (2010)
6. Wong, T.Y., Duncan, B.B., Golden, S.H., Klein, R., Couper, D.J., Klein, B.E., Hubbard, L.D., Sharrett, A.R., Schmidt, M.I.: Associations between the metabolic syndrome and retinal microvascular signs: the atherosclerosis risk in communities study. Investig. Ophthalmol. Vis. Sci. **45**(9), 2949–2954 (2004)
7. Daxer, A.: The fractal geometry of proliferative diabetic retinopathy: implications for the diagnosis and the process of retinal vasculogenesis. Curr. Eye Res. **12**(12), 1103–1109 (1993)
8. Zana, F., Klein, J.C.: Robust segmentation of vessels from retinal angiography. In: 1997 13th International Conference on Digital Signal Processing Proceedings, DSP 1997, vol. 2, pp. 1087–1090. IEEE (1997)
9. Fraz, M.M., Remagnino, P., Hoppe, A., Uyyanonvara, B., Rudnicka, A.R., Owen, C.G., Barman, S.A.: Blood vessel segmentation methodologies in retinal images-a survey. Comput. Methods Programs Biomed. **108**(1), 407–433 (2012)
10. Soille, P.: Principles and Applications. Springer Science & Business Media, Berlin (2013)
11. Chapman, N., Witt, N., Gao, X., Bharath, A.A., Stanton, A.V., Thom, S.A., Hughes, A.D.: Computer algorithms for the automated measurement of retinal arteriolar diameters. Br. J. Ophthalmol. **85**(1), 74–79 (2001)
12. Martinez-Perez, M.E., Hughes, A.D., Thom, S.A., Bharath, A.A., Parker, K.H.: Segmentation of blood vessels from red-free and fluorescein retinal images. Med. Image Anal. **11**(1), 47–61 (2007)

13. Ege, B.M., Hejlesen, O.K., Larsen, O.V., Møller, K., Jennings, B., Kerr, D., Cavan, D.A.: Screening for diabetic retinopathy using computer based image analysis and statistical classification. Comput. Methods Programs Biomed. **62**(3), 165–175 (2000)
14. Winder, R.J., Morrow, P.J., McRitchie, I.N., Bailie, J.R., Hart, P.M.: Algorithms for digital image processing in diabetic retinopathy. Comput. Med. Imaging Graph. **33**(8), 608–622 (2009)
15. García-Ortiz, L., Recio-Rodríguez, J.I., Parra-Sanchez, J., Elena, L.J.G., Patino-Alonso, M.C., Agudo-Conde, C., Rodríguez-Sánchez, E., Gómez-Marcos, M.A.: A new tool to assess retinal vessel caliber. Reliability and validity of measures and their relationship with cardiovascular risk. J. Hypertens. **30**(4), 770–777 (2012)
16. Furmankiewicz, M., Sołtysik-Piorunkiewicz, A., Ziuziański, P.: Artificial intelligence systems for knowledge management in e-health: the study of intelligent software agents. In: Latest Trends on Systems: The Proceedings of 18th International Conference on Systems, Santorini Island, Greece, pp. 551–556 (2014)
17. Ossowski, S., Sierra, C., Botti, V.: Agreement technologies: a computing perspective. In: Ossowski, S. (ed.) Agreement Technologies, pp. 3–16. Springer Science+Business Media, Dordrecht (2013). doi:10.1007/978-94-007-5583-3_1
18. Rodríguez, S., De Paz, Y., Bajo, J., Corchado, J.M.: Social-based planning model for multiagent systems. Expert Syst. Appl. **38**(10), 13005–13023 (2011)
19. Sánchez, A., Villarrubia, G., Zato, C., Rodríguez, S., Chamoso, P.: A gateway protocol based on FIPA-ACL for the new agent platform PANGEA. In: Pérez, J., et al. (eds.) Trends in Practical Applications of Agents and Multiagent Systems. AISC, pp. 41–51. Springer International Publishing, Cham (2013). doi:10.1007/978-3-319-00563-8_6
20. Castelfranchi, C., Miceli, M., Cesta, A.: Dependence relations among autonomous agents. In: Decentralized AI, vol. 3, pp. 215–227 (1992)
21. Corchado, J.M., Laza, R.: Constructing deliberative agents with case-based reasoning technology. Int. J. Intell. Syst. **18**, 1227–1241 (2003). doi:10.1002/int.10138
22. Corchado, J.M., Glez-Bedia, M., De Paz, Y., Bajo, J., De Paz, J.F.: Replanning mechanism for deliberative agents in dynamic changing environments. Comput. Intell. **24**(2), 77–107 (2008)
23. Garcia-Ortiz, L., Perez-Ramos, H., Chamoso-Santos, P., Recio-Rodriguez, J.I., Garcia-Garcia, A., Maderuelo-Fernandez, J.A., Gomez-Sanchez, L., Martínez-Perez, P., Rodriguez-Martin, C., De Cabo-Laso, A., Sanchez-Salgado, B., Rodríguez-González, S., De Paz-Santana, J.F., Corchado-Rodríguez, J.M., Gomez-Marcos, M.A.: Automatic image analyzer to assess retinal vessel caliber (ALTAIR) tool validation for the analysis of retinal vessels. J. Hypertens. **34**, e160 (2016)
24. Rahwan, I., Simari, G.: Argumentation in Artificial Intelligence. Springer, Heidelberg (2009)
25. Walton, D., Reed, C., Macagno, F.: Argumentation Schemes. Cambridge University Press, Cambridge (2008)
26. Heras, S., Jordán, J., Botti, V., Julián, V.: Argue to agree: a case-based argumentation approach. Int. J. Approx. Reason. **54**(1), 82–108 (2013)

Using Genetic Algorithms for Group Activities in Elderly Communities

Juan José Hernández[1], Angelo Costa[2], Elena del Val[1(✉)], Juan M. Alberola[1], Paulo Novais[2], and Vicente Julian[1]

[1] D. Sistemas Informáticos y Computación, Universitat Politècnica de València, Valencia, Spain
juahermo@fiv.upv.es, {edelval,jalberola,vinglada}@dsic.upv.es
[2] Centro ALGORITMI, Escola de Engenharia, Universidade do Minho, Guimarães, Portugal
{acosta,pjon}@di.uminho.pt

Abstract. This paper proposes a model for group formation in elderly communities using Coalition Structure Generation Problem implemented by Genetic Algorithms. The model parameters are physical requirements, preferences and social relationships, being the model able to learn from each execution and improve the future configurations. The results show near-optimal solutions to all proposed scenarios, beating greatly the computational time of CPLEX.

Keywords: Genetic algorithm · Group formation · Elderly activities

1 Introduction

Currently, collaboration is essential for successfully achieving any type of goal. We can simply observe the growing importance of concept of business teams in the literature. But this is not the only field where teams, groups, coalitions or partnerships are being used. For instance in education, educational organizations have shown a growing interest in shifting towards teaching paradigms that promote teamwork [1–3]; in sports competitions, it is well know the importance of building and managing a team to achieve success; and in other fields, such as science, many of the most important results arise from the formation of working groups and their collaboration.

In general, any task with hints of complexity require the collaboration of more than one individual. It is essential to current technology the ability of giving support to the needed processes of formation and management of groups or coalitions with the aim of maximizing the utility or expected benefit.

In this sense, agent technology, although still immature in some ways, allows the development of systems that support the formation and dynamic management of these teams. Many tasks cannot be completed by a single agent because of limited resources or capabilities, even if the task can be done by a single agent, the performance may be too low to be acceptable. In these situations, agents may

N. Criado Pacheco et al. (Eds.): EUMAS 2016/AT 2016, LNAI 10207, pp. 524–537, 2017.
DOI: 10.1007/978-3-319-59294-7_42

form groups to solve the problem or accomplish the task by cooperation. This work is focused on the formation of teams in order to do some specific task.

Traditionally, allocating agents into optimal groups has been a field of study for coalition formation [13,19,20]. Many coalition formation algorithms focus on optimally dividing coalitional payoffs [6,17,21], which are the resulting benefits from carrying on a task as a group.

Genetic Algorithms (GA) have also contributed to the state-of-art in group formation. They are general optimization and learning algorithms based on the evolutionary processes found in the nature. Candidate solutions for a problem form the genetic population of the algorithm, which gradually converges towards high quality solutions by applying genetic operators like mutation and crossover. GA's can be used as an implicit learning and adaptation mechanism in environments where dynamics and structure is also uncertain. This is perhaps what makes GA an adequate approach to group formation problems, since they can be used to learn and adapt both to the different needs and goals of the group's members.

In this sense this work proposes the use of GA in order to solve a specific problem of group formation. Concretely, the proposal has been used to analyse which is the best way to organize older people into activity groups in elderly communities (e.g. nursing homes, day-care centres). Different studies [4,5,7,10–12,14,15] have shown the benefits of a constructive group activities programme for the elderly, increasing their happiness levels and wellbeing. In most elderly communities exist the figure of activities manager, typically assumed by a psychologist or a registered nurse, whose task is to create a list of activities that please the elderly communities' users (care-receivers). An usual issue is the lack of novelty and low significance of the events, leading to bored and unengaged care-receivers. Caregivers should be able to arrange activities that relate to the care-receivers, e.g., likes, health condition, background. Exploiting the social interaction is key to keep a harmonious environment, thus it is essential to please the largest number of care-receivers [18]. The issue is that finding activities that please everyone is rather difficult and most of the activities that do that are ones that require little effort by the care-receiver (like watching television) defeating the goal of promoting active aging through playful psychological and physical activities.

One possible solution is to part the community into groups, being the participants related between them (likes, health condition, friendship), performing activities that are suited to them, optimizing the overall satisfaction of the community. The issue with this solution is that it is a hard problem to find suitable associations between the users. For instance, from the three areas (likes, health condition, friendship) the values can range from love to hate, thus one care-receiver may love another but hate every activity that the other likes, which may eventually lead to unhappiness of the care-receiver in the long term. By using technological helpers the task can be eased by performing the grouping task.

This idea emerged from an issue encountered in the iGenda platform [8,9]. When in a specific environment where the care-receivers were forced to interact with other care-receivers the iGenda was not able to provide events suggestions in a fashionable time. The complexity of the task and specificity was not initially foreseen thus the iGenda was not designed for this task. The aim of this paper is to treat this issue.

This paper is structured in the following way: Sect. 2 presents the proposed model and the problem definition; Sect. 3 presents the genetic algorithm design, with equations and examples that help to envision the development; Sect. 4 present the experiments and the results of 4 scenarios execution; and finally Sect. 5 present the conclusions.

2   Proposed Model

To make a proper planning of care-receivers allocated per activity during a long period of time (i.e., semester) several parameters should be considered: (i) the physical condition of care-receivers and the requirements of each activity to be performed; (ii) the preferences of care-receivers about activities, to improve their degree of satisfaction; (iii) the friendship relationships of each group.

The most of the nursing homes lack the appropriate number of staff, thus most of the staff is overworked. Another factor to be considered is that the number of activities the nursing homes can offer is limited, so residents have to repeat activities. The use of computational systems that facilitate the activities scheduling process may provide the help that institutions require, streamlining the list of possible activities and groups.

In this section, we describe our proposal for dividing care-receivers into groups to perform activities every day during a period of time using a Coalition Structure Generation Problem. The criterion to generate coalitions relies on physical and psychological aspects of each care-receiver (i.e., preferences, health, friendship, etc.) and the profiles of activities (i.e., physical requirements and the number of people per activity).

The Coalition Structure Generation problem refers to partitioning the components of a set into exhaustive and disjoint coalitions optimizing certain criteria. In our problem, the components of the set are the care-receivers that take part in group activities proposed by a senior residence centre and the criterion to optimize is a social welfare function of each coalition (i.e., the degree of matching between the profile of the care-receivers and the activity in which they participate).

Definition 1. *Let $E = \{e_i, \ldots, e_n\}$ be a set of care-receivers where each individual has a set of features that describes his/her profile. Let $G_j \in E$ be a subset of E called group.*

The profile of each individual is defined by the following features:

- *Physical status* refers to the physical condition of the individual and can take three values based on his/her medical profile: independent, partially independent, or dependent. Depending on the physical status, there are some activities that are most suitable for an individual. The physical status is known from the beginning and usually remains almost constant during his/her stay in the centre.

- *Preference of activities* refers to how appealing is an activity for an individual. This feature can take three values: appealing, neutral, or non-appealing. We assume that an individual does not have any preference until he/she participates in an activity. Upon the activity completion the feedback is collected about his/her preference.
- *Friendship relationships* represents the social network of the senior residence centre. Nodes represent the individuals and links are weighted bidirectional relations between individuals that take three values: non-friends (i.e., the individuals consider each other annoying), neutral (i.e., the individuals are indifferent with each other), or friends (i.e., the individuals are friends). Initially, information of friendship is not available. After each activity, individuals provide information about his/her relationships with other activity members.
- *Historical activity* the profile stores the sequence of activities already performed by the individual during the planned period. This information is used to avoid the repetition of activities during an specific period of time. Individual preferences, friendship relationships and historical activity profile will be considered in future group activity configurations.

Definition 2. *Let $A = \{a_i, \ldots, a_n\}$ be a set of activities planned for a period of time (i.e., several weeks or months depending on the requirements of the senior residence centre). Each activity is defined by a set of features.*

The features associated to an activity are the *type* and the *number of participants*. The activities are classified as psychological or physical. Psychological activities include table games, artistic expression, reading, or religious events, among others. Physical activities include dancing, walks, gardening or culinary lessons, among others. The number of participants is set between a minimum and maximum number of individuals.

We define $< G_j, a_i >$ as a group of individuals that participate in an activity. Given a group $< G_j, a_i >$, the value associated to group is given by a characteristic function $v(< G_j, a_i >) : 2^E \to \mathbb{R}$ that assigns a real-valued payoff to $< G_j, a_i >$. The value of a group $v(< G_j, a_i >)$ is calculated as a linear combination of functions that calculate different types of matching. We define the following functions, whose values ranges from 0 to 1:

- Function $phy(e_j, a_i)$ calculates the degree of match between the physical features of an individual $e_j \in G_j$ and the physical requirements of the activity $a_i \in A$.
- Function $act(e_j, a_i)$ calculates the match between the personal preferences of each individual $e_j \in G_j$ and the activity $a_i \in A$ care-receivers.
- Function $fri(e_j, X)$ calculates the degree of friendship of an individual $e_j \in G_j$ with other members of the group $e_k \in G_j : j \neq k$ considering the social network X.
- Function $his(e_j, a_i, d)$ penalizes the group if an individual $e_j \in G_j$ has performed the activity $a_i \in A$ in the last d days.

Given the above functions, the value of a group is calculated as:

$$v(< G_j, a_i >) = \sum_{e_i \in G_j} \alpha \cdot phy(e_j, a_i) + \beta \cdot act(e_j, a_i) + \gamma \cdot fri(e_j, X) + \theta \cdot his(e_j, a_i)$$

$$(1)$$

Note that parameters α, β, γ, and θ are defined to give more relevance to specific features in order to build groups.

Definition 3. *A group structure* $S = \{< G_1, a_i >, < G_2, a_j >, \ldots, < G_k, a_n >\}$ *is a partition of groups such that* $\forall i, j(i \neq j), < G_j, a_n > \cap < G_i, a_k > = \emptyset,$ $\bigcup_{\forall < G_j, a_n > \in S} < G_j, a_n > = E.$

The value of a group structure is denoted by $v(S)$, where $v(S)$ is an evaluation function for the group structure. In this work, we assume that the quality of each group is independent of other groups. Therefore, we can calculate the value of the group structure as:

$$v(S) = \sum_{<G_j, a_n> \in S} v(< G_j, a_n >)$$

$$(2)$$

The goal is to determine an optimal group structure for the organization of activities $\underset{S \in 2^E}{argmax}\ v(S)$.

It turns out that partitioning a set of elderly individuals into disjoint groups while optimizing a social welfare function corresponds to the formalization of coalition structure generation problems. In order to solve this problem, we propose the use of a genetic algorithm.

3   Genetic Algorithm Design

Genetic algorithms have been shown to be effective at finding approximate optimal solution, and, in some cases, optimal solutions to combinatorially explosive problems. To solve the coalition formation problem, we proposed a genetic algorithm (see Algorithm 1) that generates successive sets of solutions (generations), where each new generation inherits properties from the best solutions of the previous. Initially, the algorithm creates an initial random population of N individuals. Each individual is a solution to the problem (see Fig. 1). Therefore, the size of the chromosome is the number of residents. The chromosome gene order corresponds to the different care-receivers, and gene values correspond to the activity number a care-receiver is engaged. More than one care-receivers engaged in the same activity constitute a coalition.

The *fitness function* evaluates the quality of the solutions (i.e., the quality of the individuals). The fitness function in our problem corresponds to function that calculates the value of the group structure (see Eq. 3). However, not all the fitness values of the individuals are calculated in the same way. In the described

Care-receiver id	0	1	2	...			N
Activity id	14	7	7	...			10

Fig. 1. The encoding of a chromosome.

problem, there is a certain type of individuals that must be discarded for future generations, and therefore, they have a 0 fitness value. These individuals are those that are allocated to activities that exceed the maximum number of care-receivers or activities that do not reach the minimum required people.

$$v(S) = \begin{cases} \sum_{G_j \in S} v(G_j) & \text{if } \forall G_j \in S : min\_size < |G_j| < max\_size \\ 0 & \text{otherwise} \end{cases} \tag{3}$$

Genetic operators are applied over the individuals. The algorithm considers four genetic operators (see Fig. 2):

- Swap two different genes within an individual. This operator allows that two randomly selected participants from different activities swap his/her activities.
- Swap genes with a certain value for genes with another value within an individual. This operator allows to swap all participants of two activities selected randomly.
- Randomly replace genes with a certain value within an individual with a new, randomly chosen value. This operator allows to randomly change the activity of all the participants of a current coalition. This operator facilitate the inclusion of new activities.
- Swap genes with a certain value within an individual with genes with another value within another individual. This operator changes the activity of a group that is part of a planification with the activity of a group in other planification. This operator facilitate the inclusion of new activities.

The *genetic algorithm* is shown in Algorithm 1. A population consisting on a number of possible activities planifications is randomly generated. During each iteration (i.e., generation) of the algorithm, a randomly selected genetic operator is applied to each individual of the population and then, its fitness value is calculated according to Eq. 3. Once the genetic operators are applied, the new individuals are inserted in the new generation. The best N individuals remain in the new generation and the others are removed. The process ends when at least one of these situations occur: (i) the number of generations is exceeded; (ii) when there are a certain number of generations where there is none individual in the new generation that has a higher value of fitness than the best individual in previous generations; (iii) when the algorithm exceeds the time limit.

Example of operator 1

ind 1

0	1	2	3	4	...	39	40	41	42
2	19	4	12	12	...	11	4	4	9

ind 1'

0	1	2	3	4	...	39	40	41	42
2	19	11	12	12	...	4	4	4	9

Example of operator 2

ind 1

0	1	2	3	4	...	39	40	41	42
2	19	4	12	12	...	11	4	4	9

ind 1'

0	1	2	3	4	...	39	40	41	42
2	19	12	4	4	...	11	12	12	9

Example of operator 3

ind 1

0	1	2	3	4	...	39	40	41	42
2	19	4	12	12	...	11	4	4	9

ind 1'

0	1	2	3	4	...	39	40	41	42
2	19	16	12	12	...	11	16	16	9

Example of operator 4

ind 1

0	1	2	3	4	...	39	40	41	42
2	19	4	12	12	...	11	4	4	9

ind 1'

0	1	2	3	4	...	39	40	41	42
2	19	7	12	12	...	11	7	7	9

ind 2

0	1	2	3	4	...	39	40	41	42
1	7	7	2	9	...	7	5	3	2

ind 2'

0	1	2	3	4	...	39	40	41	42
1	4	4	2	9	...	4	5	3	2

Fig. 2. Examples of genetic operators.

Algorithm 1. The evolution algorithm

Generate an initial population of N random individuals
Evaluate the fitness of each individual of the population N
Select the best solution s
Number of generations k = 0
Number of generations without improving the solution q = 0
Temporal constraint t = 0
while ($k < max\_gen \wedge q < max\_gen$ without improving) **do**
  for ($j = 0; j < N; j + +$) **do**
    randomly apply one of the genetic operators over individual j
    evaluate the fitness value of j and j'
    insert j and j' in the new generation
  end for
  selection of N best individuals
  selection of the best individual s'
  if (s' ≤ s) **then**
    q++
  end if
  k++
end while

4 Experiments

In this section, we simulate five different scenarios in order to test the efficiency and performance of the algorithm proposed. For each scenario, we defined a population of individuals with different preferences in activities and friendship degree. We defined heterogeneous populations in which some individuals had a high friendship degree while others had a low friendship degree. Similarly, some activities were preferred by a high number of individuals while others were only preferred by few individuals. These five scenarios were configured as follows:

- *Scenario 1*: 43 individuals and 20 activities.
- *Scenario 2*: The 20 individuals with the highest degree of friendship and 20 activities.
- *Scenario 3*: The 20 individuals with the lowest degree of friendship and 20 activities.
- *Scenario 4*: 43 individuals and the 10 most preferred activities.
- *Scenario 5*: 43 individuals and the 10 few preferred activities.

In each scenario, groups of individuals were formed during 30 days in which the value of the group structure was calculated for each day, considering that each individual could carry out a single activity per day, and a penalization was introduced if the same activity was repeated in a three-days period. The size of each group ranged from 3 to 5 people per group. It must be pointed that some activities could be carried out by different group sizes while others must be only carried out by a specific number of group size. Note that an activity might have no individuals. The value of each group is calculated considering that each factor (physical condition, preferences, friendship, and previous activities performed) of the fitness function has the same weight.

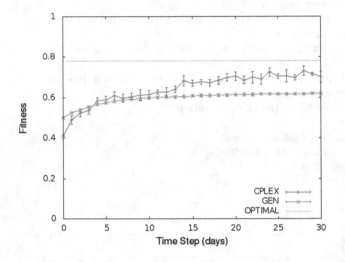

Fig. 3. Scenario 1.

In order to compare the efficiency of the genetic algorithm proposed, we also applied the commercial software *ILOG CPLEX 12.5*[1]. This software solves the problem as a linear programming problem [16] obtaining the best configuration for each day. In contrast, the computational time required to find the best configuration is expected to be high.

The execution of these two grouping strategies (*genetic algorithm* and *CPLEX*) was repeated 10 times for each scenario. Thus, each figure shows the 95% confidence interval, and Student's t-tests was performed to assess whether the differences among the strategies were significant. In addition, the upper bound of the highest value of the group structure is also represented as a continuous line above all the strategies. This upper bound represent an scenario in which all the preferences are known and any penalization is carried out.

4.1   Results

Figure 3 shows the results of the *Scenario 1*. As it can be observed in the figure, as the more information was considered for group formation, the higher the value of the group structure was.

---

[1] http://www.ibm.com/software/commerce/optimization/cplex-optimizer/   -   Last access: 25/07/2016.

Thus, both the *genetic algorithm* and *CPLEX* improved the performance during the 30 days, getting closer to the optimal. Although differences among both strategies were significant from day 15 on, the differences between the two strategies for all days that is lower than 0.1 in day 30, showing that the performance of the *genetic algorithm* algorithm is quite close to the *CPLEX*.

However, computational differences were notable. While the time required to obtain the optimal coalitional structure by the *genetic algorithm* was 14.21 s ± 0.41, the time required by *CPLEX* was 689.56 s ± 47.78.

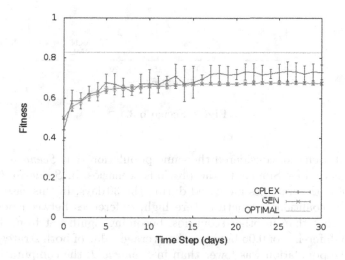

Fig. 4. Scenario 2.

In Fig. 4 we can observe the results of the *Scenario 2*. Similar to the previous scenario, the performance of both strategies increased during the 30 days as more information was considered. In contrast, the differences between the *genetic algorithm* and *CPLEX* were reduced and the average values in the day 30 were lower than 0.06. Regarding computational time, since the population was lower than in *Scenario 1*, the time required by both strategies was also lower. Despite this, the *genetic algorithm* performance was much better, requiring 0.68 s ± 0.01 to execute and iteration, while *CPLEX* required 3.76 s ± 0.12.

Figure 5 shows the performance of *Scenario 3*, which was similar to the previous scenario. Since this corresponds to a configuration in which individuals had a low degree of friendships, the values were low, and therefore, differences between both strategies were also few. Although these were significant from day 17 on, the difference between the average values of the coalitional structure obtained in day 30 by the *genetic algorithm* and *CPLEX* were lower than 0.04. In this scenario, computational consumption was similar to the *Scenario 2*, being 0.72 s ± 0.02 for the *genetic algorithm* and 3.84 s ± 0.18 for *CPLEX*.

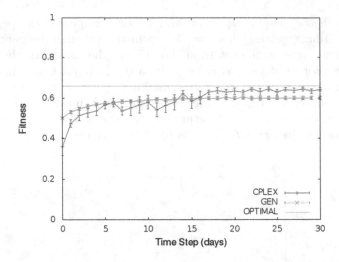

Fig. 5. Scenario 3.

The next scenario, considered the same population that *Scenario 1* but the half of the activities. Similar to the previous scenarios, in *Scenario 4*, the performance of both strategies increased during the 30 days. In this case, since the values of the coalitional structure were high, differences between both strategies were higher than in other scenarios, becoming significant from day 16 on, becoming a difference of 0.06 between the average value of both strategies in day 30. Since the population was lower than in *Scenario 1*, the computational time required by the *genetic algorithm* was lower, being $1.74\,\text{s} \pm 0.05$. In contrast, this is not relevant for *CPLEX*, whose computational time was $692.10\,\text{s} \pm 34.60$.

Finally, Fig. 7 shows the performance of the *Scenario 5* for the *genetic algorithm* and *CPLEX*. This scenario is similar to the previous one but the activities considered were those preferred by the lowest number of individuals. This caused that the values of the coalitional structures were lower compared to *Scenario 4*. In this case, the differences between both strategies in day 30 were around 0.03. Computational times were similar to the previous scenario, being $1.92\,\text{s} \pm 0.06$ for the *genetic algorithm* and $686.80\,\text{s} \pm 31.82$ for the CPLEX.

As a general conclusion, it is observed that the performance of the *genetic algorithm* was quite close to the *CPLEX*, which obtains the coalitional structure with the highest value possible since all the possibilities are explored. However, the average time required for obtaining the solutions were considerably different, requiring much more time for *CPLEX* as we can observe in Table 1. In addition, as it can be appreciated, as more complex scenarios are considered, more computational time is required, which would make some problems to become unmanageable at a reasonable time. In contrast, since the *genetic algorithm* provides quite optimal solutions in a response time much more lower, much complex problems could be managed (Fig. 6).

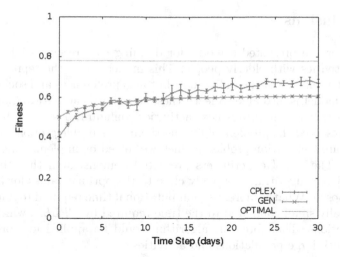

Fig. 6. Scenario 4.

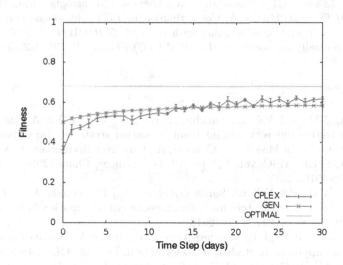

Fig. 7. Scenario 5.

Table 1. Time consumption (in seconds).

Strategy	Scenario 1	Scenario 2	Scenario 3	Scenario 4	Scenario 5
Genetic algorithm	14.21 ± 0.41	0.68 ± 0.01	0.72 ± 0.02	1.74 ± 0.05	1.92 ± 0.06
CPLEX	689.56 ± 47.78	3.76 ± 0.12	3.84 ± 0.18	692.10 ± 34.60	686.80 ± 31.82

5   Conclusions

In this paper, we presented a model for dividing care receivers into groups to perform activities with elderly people. This model allows the representation of physical requirements of the individuals but also preferences and social relationships. The model is also able to learn these features as activities are performed by care receivers and improves next activities configurations.

We represented the problem of finding the most suitable grouping as a Coalition Structure Generation problem, which we solved by implementing a Genetic Algorithm. The set of experiments presented demonstrated that the solution obtained by our algorithm was really close to the optimal values for all the scenarios proposed. What is more, the computational time required to find the solution was really small compared to the time required by *CPLEX*, which explores all the solutions. Therefore, our algorithm could be applied in more complex problems with large populations and activities.

Acknowledgment. This work has been supported by COMPETE: POCI-01-0145-FEDER-007043 and FCT - Fundação para a Ciência e Tecnologia within the Project Scope: UID/CEC/00319/2013. A. Costa thanks the FCT - Fundação para a Ciência e Tecnologia the Post-Doc scholarship with the Ref. SFRH/BPD/102696/2014. This work is also partially supported by the MINECO/FEDER TIN2015-65515-C4-1-R.

References

1. Alberola, J.M., del Val, E., Sánchez-Anguix, V., Julian, V.: A general framework for testing different student team formation strategies. In: Caporuscio, M., De la Prieta, F., Di Mascio, T., Gennari, R., Gutiérrez Rodríguez, J., Vittorini, P. (eds.) mis4TEL. AISC, vol. 478, pp. 23–31. Springer, Cham (2016). doi:10.1007/978-3-319-40165-2_3
2. Alberola, J.M., del Val, E., Sánchez-Anguix, V., Palomares, A., Teruel, M.D.: An artificial intelligence tool for heterogeneous team formation in the classroom. Knowl.-Based Syst. **101**, 1–14 (2016)
3. Alberola, J.M., del Val, E., Sanchez-Anguix, V., Julian, V.: Simulating a collective intelligence approach to student team formation. In: Pan, J.S., Polycarpou, M.M., Woźniak, M., de Carvalho, A.C.P.L.F., Quintián, H., Corchado, E. (eds.) HAIS 2013. LNCS, vol. 8073, pp. 161–170. Springer, Heidelberg (2013). doi:10.1007/978-3-642-40846-5_17
4. Ashe, M.C., Miller, W.C., Eng, J.J., Noreau, L.: Older adults, chronic disease and leisure-time physical activity. Gerontology **55**(1), 64–72 (2009)
5. Bal, S.K.: Leisure activity and risk of dementia scrabble, anyone? Canad. Fam. Phys. **50**, 51–53 (2004)
6. Blankenburg, B., Klusch, M.: On safe kernel stable coalition forming among agents. In: Proceedings of the 3rd International Joint Conference on Autonomous Agents and Multiagent Systems, vol. 2, pp. 580–587. IEEE Computer Society (2004)
7. Chang, P., Wray, L., Lin, Y.: Social relationships, leisure activity, and health in older adults. Health Psychol. **33**(46), 516–523 (2014)

8. Costa, Â., Castillo, J.C., Novais, P., Fernández-Caballero, A., Simoes, R.: Sensor-driven agenda for intelligent home care of the elderly. Expert Syst. Appl. **39**(15), 12192–12204 (2012). http://linkinghub.elsevier.com/retrieve/pii/S09574 17412006550

9. Costa, A., Novais, P., Simoes, R.: A caregiver support platform within the scope of an ambient assisted living ecosystem. Sensors (Basel, Switzerland) **14**(3), 5654–5676 (2014)

10. Freeman, S., Spirgiene, L., Martin-Khan, M., Hirdes, J.P.: Relationship between restraint use, engagement in social activity, and decline in cognitive status among residents newly admitted to long-term care facilities. Geriatr. Gerontol. Int. **17**, 246–255 (2016)

11. Guerin, M., Mackintosh, S., Fryer, C.: Exercise class participation among residents in low-level residential aged care could be enhanced: a qualitative study. Aust. J. Physiother. **54**(2), 111–117 (2008)

12. Haslam, C., Alexander Haslam, S., Knight, C., Gleibs, I., Ysseldyk, R., McCloskey, L.G.: We can work it out: group decision-making builds social identity and enhances the cognitive performance of care residents. Br. J. Psychol. **105**(1), 17–34 (2014)

13. Ito, T., Ochi, H., Shintani, T.: A group-buy protocol based on coalition formation for agent-mediated e-commerce. IJCIS **3**(1), 11–20 (2002)

14. Logan, S.L., Gottlieb, B.H., Maitland, S.B., Meegan, D., Spriet, L.L.: The physical activity scale for the elderly (pase) questionnaire; does it predict physical health? Int. J. Environ. Res. Public Health **10**(9), 3967–3986 (2013)

15. Minhat, H.S., Amin, R.M.: Sociodemographic determinants of leisure participation among elderly in malaysia. J. Community Health **37**(4), 840–847 (2011)

16. Ohta, N., Conitzer, V., Ichimura, R., Sakurai, Y., Iwasaki, A., Yokoo, M.: Coalition structure generation utilizing compact characteristic function representations. In: Gent, I.P. (ed.) CP 2009. LNCS, vol. 5732, pp. 623–638. Springer, Heidelberg (2009). doi:10.1007/978-3-642-04244-7_49

17. Ohta, N., Conitzer, V., Satoh, Y., Iwasaki, A., Yokoo, M.: Anonymity-proof shapley value: extending shapley value for coalitional games in open environments. In: Proceedings of the 7th International Joint Conference on Autonomous Agents and Multiagent Systems, vol. 2, pp. 927–934. International Foundation for Autonomous Agents and Multiagent Systems (2008)

18. Stumbo, N., Peterson, C.: Therapeutic Recreation Program Design: Principles and Procedures. Pearson/Benjamin-Cummings, San Francisco (2009)

19. Tsvetovat, M., Sycara, K., Chen, Y., Ying, J.: Customer coalitions in electronic markets. In: Dignum, F., Cortés, U. (eds.) AMEC 2000. LNCS, vol. 2003, pp. 121–138. Springer, Heidelberg (2000). doi:10.1007/3-540-44723-7_9

20. Yamamoto, J., Sycara, K.: A stable and efficient buyer coalition formation scheme for e-marketplaces. In: Proceedings of the 5th International Conference on Autonomous Agents, pp. 576–583. ACM (2001)

21. Zick, Y., Elkind, E.: Arbitrators in overlapping coalition formation games. In: The 10th International Conference on Autonomous Agents and Multiagent Systems, vol. 1, pp. 55–62. International Foundation for Autonomous Agents and Multiagent Systems (2011)

Using Argumentation Schemes for a Persuasive Cognitive Assistant System

Ângelo Costa[2], Stella Heras[1(✉)], Javier Palanca[1], Jaume Jordán[1],
Paulo Novais[2], and Vicente Julian[1]

[1] D. Sistemas Informáticos y Computación,
Universitat Politècnica de València, Valencia, Spain
{sheras,jpalanca,jjordan}@dsic.upv.es
[2] Centro ALGORITMI, Escola de Engenharia,
Universidade do Minho, Guimarães, Portugal
{acosta,pjon}@di.uminho.pt

Abstract. The iGenda framework is a cognitive assistant that helps care-receivers and caregivers in the management of their agendas. One of the problems detected in systems of this kind is the lack of user engagement. This engagement can be improved through the application of persuasion techniques in order to convince users to act in a specific way. According to this, this paper presents a new architecture that will allow the system to select and recommend activities that potentially best suits to the users' interests based on argumentation techniques.

1 Introduction

Ambient Assisted Living (AAL) is a subset area of Ambient Intelligence that is aimed to provide intelligent environments to elderly or disabled people. These people have certain needs (different from user to user) that have to be addressed distinctly from common people. Even though it is expected that intelligent environments conform to users, they are still constricted to the physical restrictions, sensors, and actuators that the environments possesses.

Due to medical and socio-economical advances, the life expectancy has been increasing over the last few years, i.e., in Portugal the life expectancy has increased 10% from 2004 to 2014, being in 2014 85 years old the mean age for both sexes [8]. In 1981 the ratio between the people between 15 and 64 years old was 5.5 and in 2011 is only 3.5, meaning that there has been a reduction of the people that are able to financially support elderly people [8]. Furthermore, the elderly population is left alone by their relatives during large periods of time,

A. Costa thanks the Fundação para a Ciência e a Tecnologia (FCT) the Post-Doc scholarship with the Ref. SFRH/BPD/102696/2014 and COMPETE: POCI-01-0145-FEDER-007043 project. This work is also supported by the projects TIN2015-65515-C4-1-R and TIN2014-55206-R of the Spanish government and by the grant program for the recruitment of doctors for the Spanish system of science and technology (PAID-10-14) of the Universitat Politècnica de València.

N. Criado Pacheco et al. (Eds.): EUMAS 2016/AT 2016, LNAI 10207, pp. 538–546, 2017.
DOI: 10.1007/978-3-319-59294-7_43

which gives rise to lack of socialisation and general help [3]. One solution may be the inclusion of technological devices that bring together the elderlies' relatives and other people, like friends.

The issue with the current applications directed to the elderly people is that they are not truly designed to the elderly, as most require intensive learning and more than advanced basic knowledge. Despite the shown interest, most abandon the application if they are not forced to use it, thus it is obvious that there is a need for appealing and understandable visual interfaces that engage the users. Also, people tend to trust the information that is presented by digital systems even if it is not true or incomplete, and when people realise that they were tricked they stop using the system [13]. Most recommender systems, for instance, tend to keep the information simple and hide the process behind the recommendation. However, several studies showed that when the control is given to the users (even if limited), and when the system can provide justifications, people tend to trust recommendations more [4,14]. Therefore, intelligent decision-support systems that can give understandable justifications for medical diagnosis and health-care recommendations have gained success in recent years. Recent work has investigated the role of argumentation theory in medical diagnosis and health care. In [2], authors present ongoing research on testing the effectiveness and usability of argumentation schemes, a well-known concept of argumentation theory, to improve the persuasion power of doctors and to enhance elderly diabetes patient's self-management abilities in chronic care. In [11], an argumentation-based approach to aggregate clinical evidence coming from multiple sources (randomised clinical trials, systematic reviews, meta-analyses, network analyses, etc.) and decide the best treatment is proposed. In [9], biomedical argumentation schemes are presented as logical programs to be able to automatically devise arguments from scientific texts. Also, the role of argumentation schemes to represent fallacious reasoning in public health has been analysed in [7].

In a previous work, we presented a persuasive module that has been integrated in a cognitive assistant framework, iGenda [5]. The proposed persuasive module improves user engagement generating arguments for the selection of activities that potentially best suits to the users' interests. These arguments where based on previous similar cases stored in a case-base database, which provided a justification only based on the information of the clinical guidelines used to recommend a specific activity. However, this was a basic argumentation feature that does not provide a way to generate more elaborated arguments and to determine the relation among arguments (e.g. specifying clearly how an argument can receive attacks). Furthermore, it is also important that users perceive the 'human-like' intelligence of the system, which is not only to be able to show experience-based arguments based on similar cases, but also arguments based on human common patterns of reasoning. Thus, in this work we investigate the role of argumentation schemes as knowledge resource to capture the way of reasoning that physicians and caregivers follow to recommend activities to patients.

2   The iGenda Framework

The iGenda is an AAL project, more precisely, a cognitive assistant platform [5]. Its aim is to provide assistance to the people in the elderly's sphere of people, e.g., family, relatives, health assistants, caregivers. This is achieved through its platform that manages daily activities that can be performed solo (like activities of daily living) or accompanied (like family visits or playing group games). The system provides automatic scheduling and conflicts management of events and user profiling and management [6]. Furthermore, it promotes active ageing by recommending activities (through direct scheduling) that impact physical or psychical aspects to keep the executers active and increase their happiness level.

Through its user mobile application, the iGenda is able to interact with their users and benefit from the sensors of the mobile device, like GPS or accelerometer, which may help iGenda by providing the platform with useful information about the current location and environment status. The iGenda visual interfaces divide into two strands: (i) the *care-receivers*, directed for the elderly, friends and relatives; and (ii) the *caregivers*, directed to health assistants, like registered nurses and physicians. The care-receivers will receive activities and perform them, creating a social network with other users, while the caregivers will attend to their assigned care-receiver's health status and assure that they are well and secure.

By using its recommendation module, the iGenda system periodically schedule activities that promote active living, selected from its *free time events* database. The events go through a filtering system that preselects activities that match the users medical condition (physical or psychological), the weather condition, and the available time. In its original version, iGenda gathers the events that outcome from the filter and uses a biased random function to suggest activities. However, the potential willingness of the user to accept a specific activity (based on his/her current social context - i.e. the specific user, the specific caregiver, their relation, etc. - and the knowledge of similar past experiences) was not taken into account. Then, the new persuasion module of iGenda enabled the provision of justification and argumentation about why each activity is recommended.

In this section, we provide an overview of the persuasive module of the iGenda tool, focusing on its knowledge resources (for a comprehensive explanation of the persuasive module see [5]) and on the operation of the module. This module allows the iGenda activities recommender system to collect the users' input and justify the recommendation provided in a way that emulates the humans way of reasoning. Therefore, when iGenda calls the recommendation module to recommend activities, the system tries to create one argument (or more) to support each activity and decide which one would be preferred by the user. Then, an internal argumentation process takes part to decide the activity that is better supported by its arguments.

2.1   Argumentation Framework

The persuasive module of iGenda implements the agent-based argumentation framework for agent societies presented in [10,12]. This framework takes into account the values that arguments promote (the preferences of the users), the users' preference relations (preference orderings over values), and the dependency relations between agents (the relations that emerge from agent interactions or are predefined by the system) to evaluate arguments and to decide which ones defeat others. In our system, agents can play the role of *patients*, *caregivers* (e.g. relatives, personal health assistants, friends), and *doctors*. In addition, in our system we have established the following typology of values, which represent preferences for activities that: are performed still, sitting, standing up, etc. (*Motion* Values); are performed indoors with or without movement, outdoors with or without movement, etc. (*Location* Values); involve socialise with others, or not (*Social* Values); are weather-dependent, or not (*Environmental Conditions* Values); and have immediate or direct impact on health, or not (*Health Conditions* Values).

In this work, we have adapted the knowledge resources of this framework to cope with the requirements of the iGenda domain: a database of *argumentation-schemes* and a case-base with *domain-cases*.

Argumentation schemes represent stereotyped patterns of common reasoning whose instantiation provides an alleged justification for the conclusion drawn from the scheme. Many authors have proposed different sets of these argumentation schemes, but the work of Walton [15], who presented a set of 25 different argumentation schemes, has been the most widely used by the AI community. AI researchers have appreciated the simplicity of Walton's schemes and the fact that these argumentation schemes have associated a set of *critical questions (CQs)* that represent potential attacks to the conclusion supported by the scheme. Thus, the schemes can be used to generate arguments that support each activity, and to guide the argumentation process by determining potential attacks to these arguments.

The most obvious pattern of human reasoning to recommend an activity to take care of elderlies' health is because an expert (e.g. a physician or a caregiver) thinks that it could improve the health of the user (probably following a well-stablished clinical guideline). This pattern of reasoning is captured by the *Argument From Expert Opinion* scheme of Walton's set. For illustrative purposes, we provide next an adaptation of this argumentation scheme for the iGenda application domain (we refer the reader to [15, Chap. 9] for the original version of the scheme). Note that critical questions 3 and 6 cannot be instantiated as potential attacks by the same nature of this recommendation domain, since all activities recorded in the iGenda database have a proposer by default (the doctor, caregiver or at least the system that created the activity).

Major Premise: Expert E (doctor, caregiver or expert system) is an expert on the area of expertise X where activity A belongs to
Minor Premise: Activity A is proposed by expert E
Conclusion: Activity A should be recommended in the current situation
CQ1: How credible is E as an expert source?
CQ2: Is E an expert on the area of expertise X where activity A belongs to?

CASE

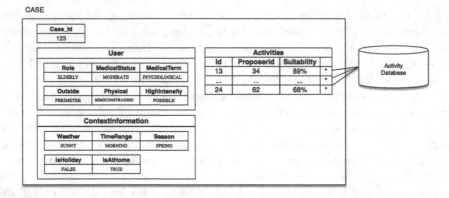

Fig. 1. Structure of a domain-case

CQ3: Did expert E recommend activity A?

CQ4: How personally trusted is E as an expert source?

CQ5: Is A consistent with what other experts have recommended?

CQ6: Is E's recommendation based on evidence?

Domain-cases represent previous problems and their solutions. The case-base of domain-cases stores previous experiences and their final outcome in the form of cases that can be retrieved and used later to select the best activity to recommend in view of past similar experiences. Domain-cases allow iGenda to generate basic experience-based arguments, and to store the new knowledge gained in each process, improving the system's recommendation skills. Figure 1 shows an example of the structure of a specific domain-case in our system. This domain-case is the representation of a set of previous activities that have been successfully recommended to the same kind of user. Each case has a set of attribute-value pairs (variables of any value type) that describe the characteristics of the user, the environmental context where the recommendation was provided, and the list of activities recommended. The characteristics of a user are a representation of users with the same attributes. These are their medical status (moderate, severe, mild, ...), their role (elderly, family, medical, ...), the medical term that defines them (psychological, physical, both, ...) and whether or not the user is allowed to go outside his/her house or just the perimeter. Besides the above, these characteristics also define if the user is physically constrained, semi-constrained or unconstrained and if the user is allowed to practice high intensity activities or not. The environmental context where the recommendation was provided is useful to be aware of the suitability of an activity regarding the environment. It's easy to conclude that an outdoor activity is directly dependent on the weather. The characteristics that are stored in the environmental context are: the weather, which is usually only important for outdoor activities, the time range when the activity was done, the season (there are activities that are more desirable than others regarding the season), whether the day was a holiday or not and, finally, if the user is at home or at other residence (hospital, holidays residence, ...).

Finally, the list of activities include the activity that was recommended (Id), the proposer of that activity (ProposerId) and a degree of suitability that represents if the activity was good or not for that case (Suitability).

Arguments that iGenda generates are tuples of the form $Arg = \{\phi, p, \langle SS \rangle\}$, where ϕ is the conclusion of the argument (e.g. the activity to recommend), p is the value that the argument promotes and $\langle SS \rangle$ is a set of elements that justify the argument (the support set). The support set $\langle SS \rangle$ is the set of features (*premises*) that represent the context of the domain where the argument has been put forward (those premises that match the problem to solve and other extra premises that do not appear in the description of this problem but that have been also considered to draw the conclusion of the argument) and any knowledge resource used by the proponent to generate the argument (domain-cases and argumentation schemes).

2.2 Recommendation Process

The recommendation process starts when iGenda has to schedule a new activity for the user. Then, the recommendation module is called to retrieve a list of candidate activities (those that match the requirements of the current situation) from the activities database. After that, the persuasion module executes the classical case-based reasoning cycle [1] (the Retrieve, Reuse, Revise, and Retain phases) to select from this list the best activities to recommend in view of past similar experiences. The design decisions adopted for each phase of this cycle were influenced by the proposed domain and the aim of providing flexibility.

The main goal of the *retrieval* phase is to obtain the set of stored domain-cases that are similar to the current situation. The module is able to work with heterogeneous activities with missing information and can also compute the similarity between them and the current context of the recommendation (user, schedule and environment). To implement the retrieval algorithm, we have adapted and tested several well-known distance measures (e.g. Normalised Euclidean, Tversky) in order to work with heterogeneous data. The most similar case or cases are selected by means of a k-nearest neighbour algorithm by using these distance measures.

In the *reuse* phase, for each activity selected by the recommendation module, the persuasion module looks at the set of retrieved cases if there are any whose activities list include the current activity under consideration. This would mean that the system has gained previous knowledge from a similar past recommendation experience and hence, the persuasion module can generate experience-based arguments that support the recommendation of a specific activity. In addition, a minimum *suitability threshold* is set to only take into account those previous cases that represent successful recommendation experiences (i.e. the activity recommended was enjoyable and useful for the user). If different cases can support the same activity or several different activities can be supported by the domain-cases retrieved, the experience-based arguments generated can be weighted by using the activities *suitability degree*.

Table 1. Argumentation scheme instantiation

Argument from expert opinion	
Elements of the scheme	Related data
Major premise	Proposer, area of expertise, activity proposed
Minor premise	Activity proposed
CQ1	Proposer reputation lower than a threshold or less preferably (computed from all recommendations provided by this proposer)
CQ2	Proposer area of expertise does not exactly match the required in this situation
CQ4	Trust degree between the user and the proposer lower than a threshold or less preferably (computed from previous interactions between them)
CQ5	Other different proposers that recommend different activities for this same situation (computed either from the iGenda database and/or from the retrieved domain-cases)

Regardless of whether the system has been able to generate experience-based arguments or not, the persuasion module tries to generate scheme-based arguments for each of the activities selected by the recommendation module. To do this, the module queries the iGenda database, which includes different tables to store information about patients, activities, doctors, caregivers, etc., and tries to retrieve the pieces of information that support the instantiation of the specific pattern of reasoning that each argumentation-scheme represents. Furthermore, any relevant data stored in the domain-cases retrieved can be also used to instantiate argumentation schemes. Table 1 shows these related data for the *Argument From Expert Opinion* example scheme. Thus, if any scheme can be instantiated, the module generates new scheme-based arguments to support the activity under consideration. Also, if a scheme is instantiated, the system also tries to retrieve data to instantiate their associated critical questions. In this way, attack arguments to the argument generated from the scheme can be also created.

Once all possible support and attack arguments have been generated to support each potential activity to recommend, an argument evaluation process is started to decide which of arguments hold or which are rebutted. The formal specification of this process is out of the scope of this paper and we refer the reader to [5, 10] for details. Finally, the system recommends the activity that it is deemed to be more suitable and persuasive for the user, which is that activity supported by more arguments and/or with higher weights (in the case of experience-based arguments). At the end of the recommendation process, when an activity is scheduled, the user must indicate to the system whether the activity proposed was actually performed and his/her degree of satisfaction with it. Then, the *retention* phase is executed, and the system can learn from the recommendation experience and store the degree of suitability of its recommendations.

To do this: (i) the system receives an input about the activity recommended; (ii) if the system was able to retrieve a domain-case that matches the current situation and the activity was in the list of activities associated with this case, the suitability degree of this activity is increased; (iii) otherwise, the activity is added to the list or, if no matching cases were found, a new domain-case is created to store the new knowledge acquired by iGenda.

3   Conclusions

Cognitive assistants try to enhance the user's well-being and quality of life managing his/her agenda, reminding appointments and events and becoming a constant helper. One of the main problems with applications of this kind is that users typically abandon the application if they are not engaged in some way to use it. This paper has presented an extension of the persuasive module included into the iGenda framework to improve user engagement through the generation of arguments for the selection of activities. As a future work, we want to test the complete iGenda framework in a real world scenario, with the new introduced features to support the activities recommendation. Moreover, the collected data about the users' experience would be useful to improve the iGenda framework and include new argumentation schemes to have a more powerful justification to the activities recommendations.

References

1. Aamodt, A., Plaza, E.: Case-based reasoning: foundational issues, methodological variations, and system approaches. AI Commun. **7**(1), 39–59 (1994)
2. Bigi, S.: Healthy reasoning: the role of effective argumentation for enhancing elderly patients' self-management abilities in chronic care. Active Ageing Healthy Living: Hum. Cent. Approach Res. Innov. Source Qual. Life **203**, 193 (2014)
3. Chao, S.F.: Changes in leisure activities and dimensions of depressive symptoms in later life: a 12-year follow-up. Gerontol. **56**(3), 397–407 (2014)
4. Chesñevar, C., Maguitman, A.G., González, M.P.: Empowering recommendation technologies through argumentation. In: Simari, G., Rahwan, I. (eds.) Argumentation in Artificial Intelligence, pp. 403–422. Springer Science + Business Media, New York (2009)
5. Costa, A., Heras, S., Palanca, J., Novais, P., Julián, V.: A persuasive cognitive assistant system. In: Lindgren, H., et al. (eds.) Ambient Intelligence- Software and Applications- 7th International Symposium on Ambient Intelligence (ISAmI 2016). Advances in Intelligent Systems and Computing, vol. 476. Springer, Cham (2016)
6. Costa, A., Novais, P., Simoes, R.: A caregiver support platform within the scope of an ambient assisted living ecosystem. Sensors (Basel, Switzerland) **14**(3), 5654–5676 (2014)
7. Cummings, L.: Reasoning and Public Health: New Ways of Coping with Uncertainty. Springer, Cham (2015)
8. Fundação Francisco Manuel dos Santos: http://www.pordata.pt/

9. Green, N.: Implementing argumentation schemes as logic programs. In: The 16th Workshop on Computational Models of Natural Argument. CEUR Workshop Proceedings (2016)
10. Heras, S., Botti, V., Julián, V.: Argument-based agreements in agent societies. Neurocomputing **75**(1), 156–162 (2012)
11. Hunter, A., Williams, M.: Aggregation of clinical evidence using argumentation: a tutorial introduction. In: Hommersom, A., Lucas, P.J.F. (eds.) Foundations of Biomedical Knowledge Representation. LNCS, vol. 9521, pp. 317–337. Springer, Cham (2015). doi:10.1007/978-3-319-28007-3_20
12. Jordán, J., Heras, S., Valero, S., Julian, V.: An infrastructure for argumentative agents. Comput. Intell. **31**(3), 418–441 (2015)
13. Marsh, S., Dibben, M.R.: Trust, untrust, distrust and mistrust - an exploration of the dark(er) side. In: Herrmann, P., Issarny, V., Shiu, S. (eds.) iTrust 2005. LNCS, vol. 3477, pp. 17–33. Springer, Heidelberg (2005). doi:10.1007/11429760_2
14. Staff, C.: Recommendation algorithms, online privacy, and more. Commun. ACM **52**(5), 10 (2009)
15. Walton, D., Reed, C., Macagno, F.: Argumentation Schemes. Cambridge University Press, Cambridge (2008)

AT 2016: Philosophical and Theoretical Studies

Characterising Polemical Disputes

Christian Lemaitre[1] and Pablo Noriega[2(✉)]

[1] Universidad Autonoma Metropolitana, Cuajimalpa (UAM-C), Mexico
christian.lemaitre@gmail.com
[2] IIIA-CSIC, Barcelona, Spain
pablo@iiia.csic.es

Abstract. We want to draw attention to "polemics", collective processes that are complex, unavoidable and not infrequently of substantial consequence in social, political and economical terms. We propose to address the topic from the perspective of agreement technologies in order to elucidate its inherent epistemic, argumentative and social coordination aspects. Our aim is to develop an analytical framework to describe the key components of actual controversies and eventually provide technological means to participate in an ongoing disputation. In this paper we take three modest steps in that direction: (i) we foray the topic and introduce some conceptual distinctions and terminology, (ii) we characterise a type of polemical dispute that we think is significant from a practical perspective and amenable to formal and computational treatment and (iii) we articulate some salient challenges we find pertinent for the agreement technologies community.

1 Introduction

In its everyday use, the word *polemic* (from the greek πολεμικός, "of war") usually refers to a verbal or written *battle* around a controversial issue. The attacks involved in polemics are commonly associated with pejorative meanings—hostile, virulent, caustic, sarcastic, scathing, even mordacious—while the process itself is labelled as chaotic, irrational even parasitic. Nevertheless, in spite of those quarrelsome, chaotic and unruly aspects of this form of social engagement, we would like to draw attention to the topic because polemical disputes perform epistemic, argumentative and social coordination functions that may be significant in economic, political and social terms.

Ours is a bottom-up approach in which we want to study actual polemical disputes. The real ones, however messy, that affect people. We do not intend to study them formally in the way that argumentation theory studies dialogues and disputation. We want to be able to *describe* them, to "make sense" of what goes on in a polemical dispute. We are not looking for a "prescriptive model" that determines which arguments are the most "solid" or how one should proceed to win. We see polemics as an agreement technology, consequently we want to understand the structure and dynamics of the dispute and represent that understanding in a way that can be communicated to those involved.

© Springer International Publishing AG 2017
N. Criado Pacheco et al. (Eds.): EUMAS 2016/AT 2016, LNAI 10207, pp. 549–564, 2017.
DOI: 10.1007/978-3-319-59294-7_44

Our proposal is guided by the will to develop *two complementary outcomes*: (i) A *descriptive framework* to make a polemic intelligible to those individuals who observe or participate in it and, (ii) the development of *technological artifacts* that facilitate the interpretation of an on-going polemic and eventually articulate and facilitate the participation in it.

In the next section (Sect. 2) we motivate our research proposal. We describe in very intuitive terms what we call a polemic by using examples and enumerating its distinguishing features. We argue also for the significance of the topic. In Sect. 3 we get more technical and propose a restricted understanding of polemical disputes, and finally, in Sect. 4, we identify some challenges that we believe are relevant for researchers and technologists concerned with persuasive disputation and its social use.

2   Motivation

Why study polemics? In a nutshell: because they are frequent, costly, technically challenging, inevitable and largely unexplored.

2.1   Polemics Are Frequent and May Have Substantial Value

An Illustrative Example. In order to motivate and illustrate some components of our framework, we will use a toy version of the polemic inspired by the London Shard Tower.[1]

> *Picture a polemic that starts when the city council of a large city—like London—with an emblematic location—like Hyde Park—announces that it has decided to sell the location to a group of foreign investors that want to build a one thousand meter tall skyscraper, the tallest ever. Let's call this proposal S.*
>
> *The* announcement *of S is officially made public (perhaps in the government gazette) and includes (i) the grounds (the city is broke; S will bring enough income to save the city finances and will foster local growth and employment; the city council is entitled to sell the land) and (ii) warrants (the list of norms and regulations that validate the entitlement) for the decision.*
>
> *The moment the public becomes aware of S, there is a strong and confusing social reaction both in pro and against it. There is a realisation that key information about the building project is lacking and several stakeholders— for instance, legislators, spokespersons for the judiciary system, city-hall*

---

[1] Manuel Appert & translated by Oliver Waine, "Skyline policy: the Shard and London's high-rise debate", Metropolitics, 14 December 2011. http://www.metropolitiques.eu/Skyline-policy-the-Shard-and.html.

> *employees, land developers, political and special interest groups and associations, citizens that find their interests affected—become involved in the debate.*
>
> *After a flurry of public statements, newscasts, editorials and* tweets, *the debate settles around a few* issues: *transparency of the decision, relevance of the purported warrants, actual economic benefits of the project, effect on the environment and the urban landscape, tradition and patriotic feelings, alternative solution to the financial problems of the city. Stakeholders adopt* positions *in favour or against those issues and propose and take different* actions: *for example, bring suit against officials for breaking a law, request environmental impact assessments, publish editorials and in-depth studies, convene demonstrations, . . .*

Although, this example is somewhat contrived, actual polemics are not all that different in flavour, content, structure and opacity. Some well-documented real cases are available, for example:

1. Contentious projects of public works that comport significant economic or social consequences. For instance, (i) the proposal to build the Franklin-Below-Gordon dam (cancelled in 1983 after a five-year polemic), (ii) the turbulent construction of Narita airport in Japan (1966–1982) or (iii) the construction of the Keystone Pipeline System in the US.
2. *NIMBY* (Not in my back-yard) opposition of residents of a city or neighbourhood to locating something perceived as unpleasant or hazardous (a prison, *fracking*) in their own neighbourhood, while raising no such objections to similar developments elsewhere.
3. Political quarrels associated with requests that involve major practical consequences for a polity. For example, (i) the Greek debt crisis or (ii) the Catalan claim to call a referendum.
4. Disputes over legislation that involve morally or socially sensitive issues, like the "Human stem cell" controversy, the "Same-sex marriage" debate and the dispute over the legal use of drugs.[2]

As these examples show, the social, economic and political significance may be substantial. Moreover, note also that actual polemics serve three inestimable functions: they serve as a means for reaching collective decisions, they are an epistemic device to discover the relevant aspects of a topic and provide grounds for the assessment of values, interests and conflicts. Finally, they serve to spawn and coordinate purposeful collective action.

---

[2] For detailed discussions of all the examples see *Wikipedia* articles on Franklin Dam controversy, Narita International Airport Construction, Keystone Pipeline, NIMBY, Greek government debt crisis, Catalan self-determination referendum 2014, Stem cell controversy, Same sex marriage, Arguments for and against drug prohibition.

2.2 Polemics Are Challenging

Polemics are situated processes and polemical disputation is more involved than the usual forms of disputation.

Notion 1. *A **Polemic** is a social process that involves several stakeholders who engage in* polemical disputation *by exchanging utterances that are linked to an objective reality and are uttered within a stable institutional framework.*¶

Notion 2. ***Polemical Disputation*** *is a form of disputation that has four aspects that, together, distinguish it from more classical forms of argumentation:*

1. Multiple players. *Thus, they involve several stakeholders (agents) with different (i) degrees of representation (individual actors, groups of individuals, organisations), (ii) legitimacy, entitlements and power, (iii) bindings (stable lobby groups, transitory task forces, volatile Twitter topics), and with (iv) multiple and often conflicting interests,*
2. Rich socio-cognitive interactions. *(i) Agents have individual motivations that reflect values, emotions, preferences, goals, ... (ii) they form expectations of the socio-cognitive effects of their actions, (iii) agents are not presumed to abide by any norms, social, legal or otherwise, (iv) agents are not presumed to be truthful, sincere, competent or consistent.*
3. No explicit interaction protocol. *Although agents interact with other agents through utterances (polemical moves) and a polemical dispute starts with an argument that becomes attacked and supported by other arguments, the process is rich: (i) at any moment of a polemic there may be several issues in dispute, (ii) argumentation threads intermingle, (iii) there are polemical moves that are labelled as "standard" rhetorical moves (threats, promises, information requests, declarations) but forces and effects may be not standard, hence agents not compelled to play standard dialogue games), (iv) there are moves whose effects are determined by the real-world context in which they are uttered, although not even these have unique, ostensible pragmatic effects (for instance a strike may be interpreted as "successful" even if it never takes place, or as "unsuccessful" even when it is supported because the number of followers is not large enough), (v) there are no explicit termination conditions.*
4. Actual. *That is, (i) utterances are exchanged in public, (ii) they affect and are affected by events and actions that take place in reality, (iii) they are sensitive to the passage of time.* ¶

2.3 Polemics are Useful

Since in spite of that inherent complexity polemics continue to take place, it must be that they serve a function that other forms of collective interaction do not or cannot serve better.

We can identify five uses of polemics that may have a positive value towards collective agreement:

(i) *Framing* a problem [16]. By choosing contentious issues and a given rhetorical strategy, a polemicist may influence the focus of attention of participants, the relevance of arguments, the set of values that bear upon the dispute and eventually the motivations of stakeholders.

(ii) A form of *empowerment.* For instance an NGO starts or jumps into a polemic in order to gain a public recognition or backing that isn't acknowledged and would otherwise be unlikely to receive.

(iii) A form to achieve *transparency.* A polemical confrontation may foster the revelation of hidden agendas, or may serve to demonstrate that there is nothing to hide.

(iv) *Avoid impunity or acquire protection.* By having the polemical issues exposed to the public, an authority or an opponent, are made accountable of their opinions and actions and reduce the risk of foul-play.

(v) *Shift public attention.* This may be a worthy strategy to gain time, leeway, or a better negotiation position; or a ruse to distract the attention of stakeholders, to avoid the proper assessment of an issue or to force the opponent to incur in costs.

Alongside these "constructive" uses, polemics may also serve spurious goals: (i) to avoid binding negotiation, (ii) to merely vocalise opposition, (iii) to create an opponent, (iv) to attach pejorative labels to someone, and (v) in its most devastating fashion, polemics may be used to obliterate the opponent [23].

Such inevitable presence will continue to produce some cost/benefit trade-offs related to the actual decisions that are fostered by the polemic, and also because of effort and time invested, and side effects to stakeholders in terms of unwanted public exposure, and distraction of attention and resources. Moreover, with new technologies for social participation, we are likely to see polemics that go beyond the classical constraints on time, territory, number of participants and cost of involvement.

2.4   The Topic is Almost Unexplored

There is abundant discussion of religious, philosophical and even scientific issues that are referred to as "polemical" but the focus of attention is in the issues themselves or the historical or anecdotal account of the polemic as such [7,11,20]. Our definition of polemical argumentation has some affinity with Churchman's "wicked problems" [6] and consequently some of its insights may be applied in our treatment. In addition to Dascal's classification of polemical moves [8] we have not come across any other examples of Polemics as the subject matter. Although the topic of Polemics as such is almost untouched from the perspective of formal argumentation theory, it does have—in the fashion we propose to address it—a strong connection with core notions of argumentation theory and specially with recent work of the ArgMAS community, as we shall see in (Sect. 4). Moreover, there are also strong affinities between our proposal and some environments for on-line argumentation support and specially with the efforts on argumentation mining as reported in [19]. These connections and affinities suggest opportunities in argumentation theory but also in the development of collective epistemology and social coordination.

2.5   The Use of Computational Models of Polemics

Currently, significant polemics like the ones mentioned in Subsect. 2.1, may become intelligible *ex-post*, off-line and generally through *ad-hoc* socio-economic-historical analysis. However the practical questions remain: While the polemic is unfolding, how can a regular citizen or a stakeholder make sense of what is in question? What is at stake? Who holds what position and why? And more importantly: What may this citizen do when given an opportunity to act upon the question?

The pertinence of our proposal is to provide elements to address those very questions. The *descriptive framework* outlined in Sect. 3 should provide "pegs" to identify, label and organise the contents of the polemic. Concomitantly, the *technological artifacts* suggested in Sect. 4 should make the actual "pegging process" (semi)-automatic. Together they aim to provide a rich visualisation of the unfolding polemic and furnish means to bring new cogent content into the polemic and its analysis.

3   Delimiting the Subject Matter

Recall that in the previous section we described a polemic as a situated process with several components (Notion 1), where a specific type of disputation (Notion 2) takes place. Now we want to narrow down the topic to a type of polemical dispute that we believe can be fruitfully formalised and tooled.

Notion 3. *A **Polemical Dispute** is a polemic that*

C.1 Takes place within an institutional environment that includes: (i) a set of explicit norms that forbid, allow or oblige certain actions under given circumstances, (ii) a set of established procedures that have to be followed in order to accomplish some results (for instance, procurement regulations, conflict resolution procedures, validation an environmental impact assessment, etc.), (iii) stakeholders with legitimate entitlements to participate in the polemic, and (iv) a legal system that takes care of the "official" interpretation of norms and evidence, and their enforcement.

C.2 Involves a set of entitled stakeholders who are able to introduce utterances ("polemical moves") in the dispute.

C.3 Utterances may be labelled with illocutionary particles and stand for arguments that may be organised into dialogues.

C.4 A polemical dispute starts with a "polemical proposal"; that is, a public declaration (Δ) that: (i) Has the dialogical structure of a promise (essentially that in that moment, the speaker commits to see to it that a certain goal is achieved according to a given plan). (ii) Is made by an entitled speaker. (iii) Is stated explicitly and communicated through appropriate *media that reaches incumbent stakeholders. (iv) Any change of the commit-ment is observable and binding.*

C.5 The dispute takes place only when one or more stakeholders oppose that original declaration and aim at having it withdrawn or modified.[3] ¶

3.1   The Institutional Framework

For our purpose of making polemical disputes intelligible, the institutional frame-work (*C.1* above) is significant for three main reasons:

 (i) It provides an ontology that is specific to the polemical dispute.
 (ii) It enables the possibility of an institutional debate that runs parallel to the polemical dispute and may serve to address in neutral, legal terms, the key contentious issues.
(iii) It prescribes the content and structure of the polemical proposal (Δ).

3.2   Three Levels of Abstraction and Their Relationships

As suggested in Fig. 1, we propose to understand a polemical dispute as a phe-nomenon that may be observed from three interrelated spaces: The polemi-cal proposal ($\mathcal{P}$), the controversy about that proposal ($\mathcal{C}$) and the relevant facts, events and actions in the physical world ($\mathcal{W}$). These are immersed in a core institution—the public policy framework—that restricts and conditions the polemic, which in turn is immersed in a wider institutional framework that conforms society and pertinent reality.

Level $\mathcal{P}$: The Polemical Proposal. This level consists of a declaration Δ by a legitimate stakeholder of the commitment to carry an action towards an osten-sible goal. It is conditioned by the public policy institution. It may evolve to $\Delta_1, \ldots, \Delta_n$, as a result of the controversy and may eventually be accomplished,

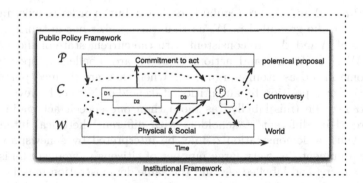

Fig. 1. A polemic as a three layer process within an institutional framework

---

[3] Notice that in spite of these additional conditions our notion of *polemical dispute* still applies to the four classes of polemics we mentioned in Sect. 2.1.

withdrawn or become unattainable. In our example, Δ is $\mathcal{S}$, which starts the polemical dispute and may evolve to a new $\mathcal{S}_1$, if some polemical moves or an institutional ruling force the city council to change it.

Level C: The Controversy. Contains utterances or polemical moves that are organised into *dialogues* which in turn give rise to *issues* and *positions* [29, 30].

In our example, a press release (in $\mathcal{W}$) may draw attention to the potential impact on the city skyline, thus causing polemical moves (in $\mathcal{C}$) that involve stakeholders like urban planners, architects and public figures into several "dialogues" around this issue. One dialogue over the profile of the tower; another one to elucidate the details of the financial aspects of the project, while an eristic dialogue may arise to bring the major down.

Level W: The World of Actual Individuals, Facts, Events and Actions. This includes, firstly, stakeholders who actively participate in the polemic, playing individual or collective roles, and have direct interests in the consequences of Δ and its derived effects in the world. Secondly, there are physical facts, events and actions that are of two kinds: those that are a consequence of exchanges in $\mathcal{C}$ and those that happen independently of $\mathcal{C}$ but become relevant for $\mathcal{C}$ because they are used in a dialogue. We recognise as elements of $\mathcal{W}$ those physical objects that may be reified as claims or dialogical moves: newspaper articles, expert opinions, impact assessment reports, putting someone in prison, a demonstration. Notice that passage of time is of significant consequence in a polemic because actions and commitments may depend on a timely execution (for example, procedures may impose deadlines).

3.3   Interrelationships Among Levels

The three levels are interrelated through a complex type of "counts as" relationship [13, 28].

1. *From $\mathcal{P}$ to $\mathcal{C}$.* Δ and Δ_n are regular speech acts but in order to exist in level $\mathcal{C}$, they need to be grounded in $\mathcal{W}$, so that the speaker has authority, and the contents of Δ and Δ_n are consistent with the current state of the world.
2. *From $\mathcal{W}$ to $\mathcal{C}$.* Events and actions α in $\mathcal{W}$ are labelled as speech acts ϕ that come into $\mathcal{C}$ as atomic arguments when they are deemed pertinent for a dialogue or a position by an entitled stakeholder. Notice, however that the same α may be (mis)labelled as more than one speech act ϕ_i in $\mathcal{C}$ when interpreted by different stakeholders with different rhetorical intentions in mind. Thus, a demonstration α may be interpreted by a newspaper as an atomic argument—a "very large number of citizens"—against the issue *size of the building* and labelled ϕ_1, and the same demonstration may be labelled ϕ_2 by the major as a failure of the opposition to prove enough popular support against $\mathcal{S}$.
3. *From $\mathcal{C}$ to $\mathcal{W}$.* As Searle and Sergot and Jones [13, 28] state, institutional actions (speech acts) may produce facts or events in $\mathcal{W}$, that in turn may

trigger other events that may be brought into the polemic as new speech acts. A threat by a prominent environmentalist to call for a demonstration (ϕ in C) is picked up by a reporter and published (α in W) and sympathisers react to the news by organising a march (β in W) that is brought into C as a new atomic argument ψ.

4. *From C to P*. There needs to be a valid claim κ (in C) that is consistent with Δ and is admitted by the issuer of Δ or another equally or more qualified authority. When κ is taken into account and properly declared, Δ is changed into a new proposal Δ_1 that leads the polemical dispute from then onwards. In our example, for instance, the major may be forced to modify the height of the tower because of public outcry, thus changing S into S_1.

3.4 The "Institutional" Debate

In Subsect. 3.1 we mentioned that the polemical dispute is embedded within an institutional framework governed by law and regulations that affect society in general. It establishes a due process and is overseen by a (judiciary) independent third party. This institutional framework *modulates* the progress of the polemical dispute by being aware of those matters that are brought to its attention and intervening in the polemical dispute when the due process and the institutional framework entitles it. Thus, there is an institutional debate $\mathcal{I}$ that is sort of "orthogonal" to the three levels just mentioned. It may be invoked at some point by authorities or any stakeholder but proceeds at its own pace. Not everything that transpires within it is reflected in the polemical dispute but its outcomes may.[4]

In terms of the polemical dispute, the most salient function of $\mathcal{I}$ is that some of its rulings, for instance ρ, may either force Δ to change or shield it from any change that is rooted on ρ and those arguments that, because of ρ, were settled in $\mathcal{I}$. For instance, in our example, an ecologist group may bring the city council to court—claiming, for example, that the project will affect an endangered species, based on environmental impact assessments—in hope of stopping the works. If the court finds the claim well grounded it will command the city council to stop the works and rule about compensations, otherwise, it may not accept other claims involving environmental impact.

3.5 Stakeholders

These are individuals (persons, groups of persons, organisations) that are affected or are interested in the polemical declaration. We may want to identify the role

---

[4] The relationships with the three levels are quite obvious. A fact in W may give grounds to any stakeholder for promote a request ρ to open a due process $\mathcal{I}$. Although ρ might not be reflected as such in the controversy C, at some point it is likely that utterances related with ρ will appear in C. Because level W is within the institutional framework, anything that happens in W and is relevant for the due process may be promoted into $\mathcal{I}$. The rulings of $\mathcal{I}$ (say ψ) will become public in W and may produce polemical moves in C.

some of them are playing when uttering a polemical move in order to assess their corresponding entitlements and potential power, responsibility or influence.

3.6   Arguments

Level C is populated by *polemical moves* that most of the time may be reified as arguments of classical argumentation theory.

Polemical moves can be "atomic", claims that correspond to a "brute" fact or action that takes place in level W or "non atomic", speech acts that have a structure that relates a claim (atomic or not) with its "backing".[5]

3.7   Dialogues

Since a polemic involves exchanges of dialectical moves akin to classical argumentation, we propose to reify the exchange of arguments in a polemic as dialogues, and thus may be associated to some standard *type*: eristic, deliberation, negotiation, enquiry, persuasion, information seeking [30].

However, such association is not unproblematic in polemical argumentation for two main reasons:

First, in classical argumentation theory, one assumes that each type of dialogue has an intended purpose and a socially (or formally) associated protocol that is coherent with that purpose. In particular, it is assumed that such purpose attaches a single illocutionary effect to the dialectical moves within the dialogue. Thus an information-seeking dialogue involves questions and answers, and a negotiation dialogue an exchange of offers and counteroffers with only two potential outcomes: withdrawal or acceptance of a final offer. That is not always the case in polemical disputes, because protocols are not enforced and moves may carry ambiguous or multiple illocutionary forces, and consequently multiple perlocutionary effects.

For instance, in our Hyde Park example, as in many real polemics, in a negotiation dialogue, an opposing party may utter the move "threat to convene a demonstration"; the role played by that party would lend the move a *prima-facie* rhetorical intention as a *promise to take a potentially damaging action*; however, its perlocutionary effect depends mostly on the credibility and expected impact of implementing the threat. Moreover, there is also the perlocutionary force of not actually fulfilling the threat but simply to exhibit power or to shift the context—means, jurisdiction, audience—of the dispute.

Second, the practical nature of polemics—and its intrinsic chaotic appearance—makes intervening dialogues to become *intertwined* and not always neatly interleaved. Walton [30] addresses the problem of dialogue shifting and

---

[5] We may use Toulmin's [29] argument structure that includes four types of components—a *claim* which is sustained by the other components: *grounds* (premises, atomic arguments, other claims), *warrant* (inference, pertinence, norm or regulation, ...) and *qualification* (certainty, number, power,...)—whose actual content depends on the type of dialogue.

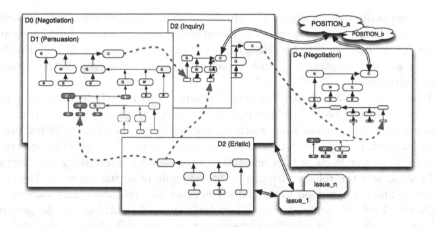

Fig. 2. Intertwining of dialogues. Claims sustained in one, may be used in other dialogues or become "commitments" for some stakeholders' position

embedding, features that are certainly part of this intertwining; however the structure of polemical arguments is richer because of the forward and backward branching connections between claims, the intervention of several parties in the different dialogues, the absence of clear termination conditions of dialogues, and new and concomitant dialogues that share claims or parties (Fig. 2).

This can be illustrated again in the Hyde Park polemic. Assume there is an eristic dialogue that involves slander against the major. As we illustrated in the previous example, the counter moves may have more than one perlocutionary effects and thus open new dialogues of different types. For instance: (i) to argue that the accusation is false (continuing the eristic dialogue or making the dialogue an information-seeking one); (ii) to haul the attacker into court (a threat of an institutional dispute, changing domain and stakes); (iii) to ignore the attack and distract attention by instigating news reports that accuse the attacker of ulterior motives (a new eristic dialogue); (iv) bring the dispute back to a pending dialogue by "leaking" a cooling of the investors' enthusiasm (shift attention to debate the financial distress of the city); (v) or negotiating, privately, a partial concession in exchange of a public apology.

3.8   Issues

We claimed that polemical argumentation is problematic because illocutionary vagueness, lack of compliance with standard dialogical protocols and involvement of multiple participants make it very difficult to keep track of the evolution and intermingling of active threads. Another feature that is intrinsic to polemical argumentation, the fact that most rhetorical moves are public, adds to this complexity. Paradoxically, it also provides a handle to cope with the richness of polemical dynamics. Indeed, the more stakeholders involved in the exchange, and the more exchanges, the clearer the *salience* of certain topics and the corresponding focus around certain claims. Thus, during some time interval, only a few claims—*issues*—draw the attention of participants and get more and longer argumentative threads. Roughly speaking, then, an issue is a claim that receives support or attacks. Active issues are the ones that centre the polemic at any given time.

Issues are easy to identify in actual polemics. In our Hyde Park example, the first issue may be the entitlement of the major to propose the project but it may shift to the ecological or aesthetic impact of the building, national pride, financial need, transparency of city dealings, and so on. The tell-tale aspects of an issue is that it belongs to a handful of topics that is limited by the original declaration and the relative frequency of the topic in a time-interval. Hence, a formal definition could be grounded on notions like *relevance* and *salience* of the topic. A relevance measure could be built from the ontology of the polemic and the number and length of arguments that include claims about the topic. A measure for salience should probably involve relative frequency of the topic and a way to reflect recency and latency of the topic.

3.9 Positions

Issues are not only easier to handle than their associated dialogical threads but they also reveal the "orientation" of individual stakeholders who have advanced an argument for or against each particular issue. Consequently an analysis of issue-stakeholder-orientation triads affords the possibility of obtaining "snapshots" of the strategic positioning of stakeholders during the polemic. Thus provide another handle to cope with the complexity of polemical dynamics.

Several stakeholders may hold the same position about a given relevant issue. This may provide grounds for alliances and agreements that transcend the particular issue. One way of anticipating or avoiding such alliances is to identify those "values" (ethical, social, utilitarian) behind issues and the positioning of potential allies or rivals with respect to the classes of issues that share similar values.

4 Areas of Opportunity

Polemics is a pertinacious topic that deserves to be studied from a multidisciplinary approach where agreement technologies could play a key part. These are lines of work that may be worth pursuing:

1. *Empirical study of actual polemics.* Few actual polemics have been studied by social scientists in a systematic way. Studies like [7, 20] have attempted to elicit heuristics that authorities may use in their communication strategies. Although focused in the cognitive behaviour of the citizens these studies bring to light the types of arguments that have been used and, to some extent, their evolution. Such studies have been performed off-line and have used only a fragment of the polemical moves, those that can be grasped from newspaper

accounts. We mean to support other types of empirical study, imposing a richer structure to the contents of the controversy—by looking into argumentation threads and their association with issues and positions—and draw contents from social media and other sources.

2. *A framework for the representation of polemical disputes.* Namely, an inventory of structures and features (arguments, dialogues, issues, positions; types of dialogues, types of warrants,...) that are common to all polemical disputes and the means to instantiate these in actual polemical disputes (argument mining, evolution of stakeholder positions,...). A representation framework that allows, from a descriptive perspective, to identify events and polemical moves, and their interrelationships as recurrent patterns or schemes; and, from an applications perspective, to bring support to socio-technical systems that may serve individuals to observe and participate in an on-line polemic.

3. *Argumentation* provides the formal core for the framework we propose. We propose to look for innovation on those features of polemical disputation that are specific or more complex than those of classical forms of argumentation. For instance,

   (a) The *dialectical shifts and dialogue embeddings* discussed by Walton [30] might be generalised or refocused in multilateral controversies, the passage of *time* and its influence in the validity and force of arguments is an unavoidable feature of polemical disputes, and different from what has been done so far in classical argumentation [27,29,30]; and, defeaslbe reasoning is inevitable [29,30]. For instance, in a recent paper, Walton et al. [32] propose a new deliberation model for open settings on the web. In this paper they extend the Deliberation Dialogue Framework (DDF) model of McBurney et al. [21].

   (b) *Rhetorics.* In Sect. 2 we touched upon the rhetorical richness of polemical moves. We see a good opportunity in the study of illocutionary regularities and dialogue schemata of rhetorical moves that are typically polemical. For example the threat to convene a demonstration or appeals to national sentiment [4]. Aside from the obvious lines of enquiry on illocutionary and perlocutionary aspects of these moves, we believe that one may find that classical fallacies take new shapes in online polemics and also that new classes of fallacies are being created. As we mentioned in Sect. 2, *Framing* [14,17] is a motivation for polemical disputes, hence a topic worth studying.

   (c) *New trends on Argumentation and Multiagent systems research.* The research challenges outlined in the *Dagstuhl Manifesto* [10], are now well established research topics that are quite relevant for the study of Polemics as we see it: argumentation and the semantic web [5,24,25,31]; argumentation and decision support in applications [15,26]; argumentation and multiagent systems (including multiparty dialogues and negotiation) [2,27]; and argumentation and social networks [15]. Noteworthy: (i) the use of AIF [5,24], core ontology in the design of multiuser open argumentation systems based in multiagent technology [3,31], and

(ii) two systems—based on visual maps about complex issues—for organising open deliberative discussion among large number of participants: *Debategraph* and *Deliberatorium* [15].[6]

4. *Understanding the institutional framework.* We noted that bringing a dispute into the legal system is a way of imposing an external arbitration to controversial issues. The descriptive framework should be able to capture these transformations so that observers may become aware of this type of changes during an ongoing dispute. For descriptive purposes, we expect to take advantage of recent work on normative MAS and electronic institutions and organisations to address this interplay [1,9]. We believe that the approach of Searle [28] to the constitutive concepts of an Institution can be useful to understand the highly complex relationship between levels of abstraction in a polemical dispute. For example the use of the collective assignment function: X counts as Y in context $\mathcal{C}$, (see for example [12]).

5. *Argumentation mining.* Given the type of results reported in *argumentation mining* [18,19,22], one may expect that the type of *official claim* Δ that triggers a polemic will possess a clean structure of warrants and grounds that is amenable to automated mining. This should constitute a good starting landmark for the identification of the ontology of the polemic, and consequently, of its issues, stakeholders and positions, of the threading of sub-dialogues and of the evolution of positions. Such subordinate contents should be mined from textual repositories in digital formats (from legal transcripts and press reports, to *tweets* and *facebook* posts) plus inputs that may be obtained from other sources (videoposts, TV newscasts, interviews), which may require some forms of human processing.

6. *Tools for the description of polemical disputes.*

   (a) *Functionalities*: (i) Extracting relevant information tokens from several web accessible sources: newspapers, official publications, blogs, *tweets*, and so on. (ii) "Map" the contents of a polemic as it unfolds, "tag" relevant information tokens in the ongoing polemic—issues, stakeholders, positions, argument structure, etc.,—and link tokens with rhetorical moves and with whatever entities in $\mathcal{W}$ are involved. (iii) Provide a graphical display of the evolving polemic.

   (b) *Integration.* Most likely those tools may become integrated into a hybrid on-line social system along the line of electronic institutions (and their extensions) because they afford, for example, the resource to a domain ontology, the isolation of polemical actions and reification of their polemical effects, the interleaving of utterances and localisation of contexts.

   (c) *Operation.* We envision an online organisation with agents (human-artificial) that specialise in different information processing tasks and delivers *ad-hoc* representations to stakeholders. We see at least two distinct modes of usage: (i) Off-line, mainly for "institutional debate" support, and for research (sociological, political and communication research; and for research in polemics and dialectics). (ii) On-line, for citizens, news

---

[6] http://debategraph.org/home.

people and different stakeholders to monitor evolution, identify players, issues, positions; to measure impact of particular actions; to assess per-locutionary effects of moves, etc.

5   Closing Remarks

Our intention in this paper was to motivate the topic of Polemics and give a taste of the type of formal and technical challenges that are open.

Our key concern is to develop the means to identify those elements that are relevant in a dispute and provide means to organise these. The first step in that direction is the development of the framework that we outline in this paper. Second, is to explore the construction of technological artifacts that may support identification and organisation of those relevant elements. Fortunately, many tools that could be useful for that purpose are already under development in fields like the semantic web, data mining, argument mining and several tech-niques of natural language processing. Finally, we want to apply these conceptual and technological tools to real controversies. We are aware of the complexity of that objective but we are aware also of the social significance of making sense out of the apparent chaos of a real polemic. Hence, there is a practical as well as altruistic objective: to empower citizens.

Acknowledgements. We received support of SINTELNET (FP7-ICT-2009-C Project No. 286370) and project MILESS (MINECO TIN2013-45039-P). We also wish to thank reviewers of the previous version of this paper, "Making sense out of polemics" (ArgMAS 2015).

References

1. Andrighetto, G., Governatori, G., Noriega, P., van der Torre, L.W.N. (eds.) Nor-mative Multi-agent Systems, vol. 4 of Dagstuhl Follow-Ups. Schloss Dagstuhl - Leibniz-Zentrum fuer Informatik (2013)
2. Bex, F.J., Reed, C.A.: Schemes of inference, conflict and preference in a computa-tional model of argument. Stud. Logic Grammar Rhetoric **36**, 39–58 (2011)
3. Bex, F., Lawrence, J., Snaith, M., Reed, C.: Implementing the argument web. Commun. ACM **56**(10), 66–73 (2013)
4. Bitzer, L.F.: The rhetorical situation. Philos. Rhetoric, 1–14 (1992)
5. Chesñevar, C., Modgil, S., Rahwan, I., Reed, C., Simari, G., South, M., Vreeswijk, G., Willmott, S., et al.: Towards an argument interchange format. Knowl. Eng. Rev. **21**(04), 293–316 (2006)
6. Churchman, C.W.: Guest editorial: Wicked problems (1967)
7. Cowan, S.: NIMBY syndrome and public consultation policy: the implications of a discourse analysis of local responses to the establishment of a community mental health facility. Health Soc. Care Commun. **11**(5), 379–386 (2003)
8. Dascal, M.: Types of Polemics and Types of Polemical Moves. Tel-Aviv University, Faculty of Humanities, Tel-Aviv (1998)
9. d'Inverno, M., Luck, M., Noriega, P., Rodríguez-Aguilar, J.A., Sierra, C.: Commu-nicating open systems. Artif. Intell. **186**, 38–94 (2012)

10. Dix, J., Parsons, S., Prakken, H., Simari, G.: Research challenges for argumentation. Comput. Sci.-Res. Dev. **23**(1), 27–34 (2009)
11. Dorschel, A.: Passions of the intellect: a study of polemics. Philosophy **90**(04), 679–684 (2015)
12. Herzig, A., Lorini, E., Troquard, N.: A dynamic logic of institutional actions. In: Leite, J., Torroni, P., Ågotnes, T., Boella, G., van der Torre, L. (eds.) CLIMA 2011. LNCS, vol. 6814, pp. 295–311. Springer, Heidelberg (2011). doi:10.1007/978-3-642-22359-4_21
13. Jones, A., Sergot, M.: A formal characterization of institutionalized power. Logic J. IGPL **4**(3), 427–446 (1996)
14. Kahneman, D., Tversky, A.: Prospect theory: an analysis of decision under risk. Econometrica: J. Econometric Soc., 263–291 (1979)
15. Klein, M.: How to harvest collective wisdom on complex problems: an introduction to the MIT deliberatorium. Center for Collective Intelligence Working Paper (2011)
16. Kuypers, J.A.: Framing analysis from a rhetorical perspective. Doing News Framing Anal.: Empirical Theoret. perspect., 286–311 (2010)
17. Lakoff, G.: Don't Think of an Elephant: Know Your Values and Frame the Debate. Chelsea Green Publishing Co., White River Junction (2004)
18. Lawrence, J., Reed, C., Allen, C., McAlister, S., Ravenscroft, A., Bourget, D.: Mining arguments from 19th century philosophical texts using topic based modelling. In: Proceedings of the First Workshop on Argumentation Mining, pp. 79–87 (2014)
19. Lippi, M., Torroni, P.: Argumentation mining: state of the art and emerging trends. ACM Trans. Internet Technol. **16**(2), 101–1025 (2016)
20. McAvoy, G.E.: Partisan probing and democratic decisionmaking rethinking the NIMBY syndrome. Policy Stud. J. **26**(2), 274–292 (1998)
21. McBurney, P., Hitchcock, D., Parsons, S.: The eightfold way of deliberation dialogue. Int. J. Intell. Syst. **22**(1), 95–132 (2007)
22. Mochales, R., Moens, M.-F.: Argumentation mining. Artif. Intell. Law **19**(1), 1–22 (2011)
23. Rabinow, P.: Polemics, politics and problematizations. An interview with Michel Foucault. In: The Foucault Reader, pp. 381–390. Pantheon Books (1984)
24. Rahwan, I.: Mass argumentation and the semantic web. Web Semant.: Sci. Serv. Agents World Wide Web **6**(1), 29–37 (2008)
25. Rahwan, I., Zablith, F., Reed, C.: Laying the foundations for a world wide argument web. Artif. Intell. **171**(10), 897–921 (2007)
26. Reed, C.: Wigmore, Toulmin and Walton: the diagramming trinity and their application in legal practice. http://tillers.net/reed diagramming trinity.pdf/ Downloaded 14 Oct 2006
27. Reed, C., Walton, D.: Argumentation schemes in dialogue. Dissensus and the Search for Common Ground (Proceedings of OSSA 2007) (2007)
28. Searle, J.R.: What is an institution. J. Inst. Econ. **1**(1), 1–22 (2005)
29. Toulmin, S.E.: The Uses of Argument. Cambridge University Press, Cambridge (2003)
30. Walton, D.: Dialogue Theory for Critical Argumentation. Benjamins, Amsterdam (2007)
31. Walton, D., Gordon, T.F.: The Carneades model of argument invention. Pragmatics Cogn. **20**(1), 1–31 (2012)
32. Walton, D., Toniolo, A., Norman, T.J.: Missing phases of deliberation dialogue for real applications. In Proceedings of the 11th International Workshop on Argumentation in Multi-Agent Systems, AAMAS2014, pp. 1–20. ArgMAS (2014)

Some Theoretical Results on the Relationship Between Argumentation and Coherence Theory

Yannis Dimopoulos[1]($\boxtimes$), Pavlos Moraitis[2], and Carles Sierra[3]

[1] Department of Computer Science, University of Cyprus, Nicosia, Cyprus
yannis@cs.ucy.ac.cy
[2] LIPADE, Paris Descartes University, Paris, France
[3] IIIA-CSIC, Barcelona, Spain

Abstract. This work provides initial results on the relationship between argumentation and Paul Thagard's coherence theory. We study the relationship, via appropriate transformations, between different types of coherent graphs (according to the values in the arcs) and different argumentation frameworks such as Dung's abstract argumentation framework, weighted argument systems or preference-based argumentation. The practical interest of our study is to show that coherence theory and argumentation can be mutually useful.

1 Introduction

This paper studies and provides initial results on the relationship between several models of argumentation and coherence theory.

Coherence theory, as proposed by Thagard [12], assumes that knowledge can be represented as a network where nodes represent claims, and valued edges linking nodes may be labeled with positive or negative values representing respectively the degree of coherence or incoherence between nodes. Every coherence graph is associated with a number called the *coherence of the graph*. Based on Thagard formalism, this can be calculated by partitioning the set of nodes N of the graph in two sets, A and $N \setminus A$, where A contains the accepted elements of N, and $N \setminus A$ contains the rejected ones. The aim is to partition N such that a maximum number of nodes linked by edges with positive values (weights) are in the same set (i.e. A or $N \setminus A$) while a maximum number of nodes linked by edges with negative values are in complementary sets (i.e. A, and $N \setminus A$). The values of edges belong to $[-1, 1] \setminus \{0\}$.

There have been different proposals to represent arguments and their relationships. An Abstract Argumentation Framework (AF) [5] can be considered as a pair of a set arguments and a binary attack relation defined on the set of arguments. Such a theory can be represented as an oriented graph where nodes represent the arguments and edges the attacks between them. In Weighted Argument Systems (WAS) [6] attacks are associated with a weight, indicating the relative strength of the attack. A key concept in this framework is the notion of an *inconsistency budget*, which characterises how much inconsistency we can tolerate when selecting the sets of preferred arguments (extensions). It means that

© Springer International Publishing AG 2017
N. Criado Pacheco et al. (Eds.): EUMAS 2016/AT 2016, LNAI 10207, pp. 565–579, 2017.
DOI: 10.1007/978-3-319-59294-7_45

given an inconsistency budget β, we are prepared to disregard attacks among the arguments up to a total weight of β. In Preference-based Argumentation (PAF), a preference relationship explicitly established between arguments, is used to rank sets of arguments.

Although argumentation and coherence theory strive to understand similar phenomena, such as making sense of contradictory information, their relation has not attracted much attention in the past. The need for a study of the relation between the two formalisms is also evident in the context of specific domains such as legal reasoning. Indeed, there are well established links between argumentation and legal reasoning on the one hand [10, 11], and legal reasoning and coherence on the other hand [1]. Another domain where the combination of coherence theory and argumentation may also prove beneficial, is the domain of argumentative debates. In this context, the coherence of the arguments that are used by the opponents during a debate could be taken into account. For instance, agents may decide to refrain from introducing arguments that decrease the strength of the coherence graph that corresponds to the arguments that has been exchanged in the course of that debate. E-justice or online dispute resolution are specific domains that could benefit from this kind of argumentative debates. Another application domain in which argumentation and coherence can be combined is that of policy analytics. Here the notion of coherence may serve as a measure of the impact of governmental policies on public opinion as it is expressed in social networks, by aggregating arguments supporting or attacking those policies.

As a first step in the direction of resolving these issues, this work provides the first formal results on the relation between coherence and argumentation.

In [8], coherence theory is used to understand the notion of norm adoption and a discussion on the relationship with AF is given although no formal account of this relationship is established. Here we contribute by giving some preliminary results on the relationship between optimal partitions and stable extensions in AF. In [9] argumentation dialogues are used to regain coherence when conflicts arise between agents. Argumentation is considered as a mechanism that permits the interaction between agents endowed with coherence theories. Here, differently from this work, we study the relationships between both approaches as alternative means of representing conflicting views.

In this paper we contribute to the study of the relationships between coherence theory and different argumentation formalisms. In particular we provide three results.

First, we transform classical argumentation theories into particular coherence graphs and show that the optimal partitions of these graphs correspond to stable extensions of the argumentation theory.

Second, we show that some coherent graphs can be understood as a WAS. More precisely, we consider a particular type of coherence graphs, those whose nodes represent atomic arguments, and that contain only maximally negative edges (i.e. -1). We prove that any subset A of arguments of such a coherence graph is an admissible extension with respect to the inconsistency budget β of a particular type of WAS.

Finally, we show that the maximal partitions of coherence graphs that contain edges labeled with $\{-1, 1\}$ can have an interpretation as extensions of PAF systems.

The paper is structured as follows. First, we provide some background knowledge on coherence and argumentation. Then, we study in order the relationship between coherence theory and Dung, WAS, and PAF systems. We conclude with a summary of the results and with the open lines for future work.

2   Background

2.1   Coherence Theory

The theory of coherence is a psychological motivational theory which understands coherence as an intrinsic domain independent motivation to agents. As any other motivational theory it aims at explaining the behaviour of agents at a high-level. We refer to Thagard's interpretation of the theory as he proposed a computational model for an otherwise long disputed concept.

Thagard presents the theory of coherence as a cognitive theory with roots in philosophy that interpret problem solving as the satisfaction of constraints over interconnected entities [12, 13]. The theory of coherence is then the study of associations among different pieces of information and the computation of how do they 'fit' together. Each piece of information puts constraints on other pieces of information; these constraints can be positive or negative. Positive constraints strengthen the connected pieces of information when considered together while negative constraints weaken them. In this theory, the cognitive process to be undertaken by an agent is to put together as many information pieces that have positive constraints while separating from these those that have negative constraints. In other words, coherent-based agents face an optimisation problem.

Several psychological processes can be understood in terms of coherence and constraint optimisation. These processes include stereoscopic vision, word perception, discourse comprehension, analogical mapping, and cognitive dissonance; see [14] for details.

Next we recall the basic definitions of coherence graph, constraint satisfaction and strength.

Definition 1 [7]. *A coherence graph is an edge-weighted undirected graph $g = \langle N, E, \psi \rangle$, where*

- ¬ *N is a finite set of nodes representing pieces of information*
- *$E \subseteq \{\{v, w\} | v, w \in N\}$ is a finite set of edges representing the coherence or incoherence between pieces of information and that we shall call* constraints
- *$\psi : E \to [-1, 1] \setminus \{0\}$ is an edge-weighted function that assigns a negative or positive value to the coherence between pieces of information, and which we shall call* coherence function.

The nodes of coherence graphs can be understood, from a knowledge representation perspective, as representing beliefs, desires, intentions, norms, or other cognitions an agent may have [7,9]. How the coherence values are computed depends on what sort of coherence we want to model. Thagard distinguishes among several types of coherence: deductive, explanatory, ..., and suggests different methods of computing these degrees. A coherence-based agent aims at determining which subset of the overall set of information pieces is to be accepted and which is to be rejected, that is, how to partition N into two sets containing accepted and rejected claims.

Definition 2 [7]. *Given a coherence graph $g = \langle N, E, \psi \rangle$ and a partition of N into (A, R), the set of satisfied constraints $C_A \subseteq E$ is given by:*

$$C_A = \{\{v, w\} \in E | v \in A \text{ iff } w \in A \text{ when } \psi(\{v, w\}) > 0,$$
$$v \in A \text{ iff } w \in R \text{ when } \psi(\{v, w\}) < 0\}$$

According to Thagard, Coherence-based agents perform a search process to find the *best* partition which is the one that maximises the strength as defined next.

Definition 3 [7]. *Given a coherence graph $g = \langle N, E, \psi \rangle$ the strength of a partition (A, R) is given by:*

$$Str(g, A) = \frac{\sum_{\{v,w\} \in C_A} |\psi(\{v, w\})|}{|E|}$$

The computation of the best partition does not tell us which one of the two sets is the one to accept, as the computation is symmetric, i.e. $Str(g, A) = Str(g, R)$. To determine which partition to accept an agent should use some ad-hoc criteria (e.g. greater number of nodes, greater average degree, etc.).

Thagard experimented with different computational implementations of coherence. Among them, ECHO [12] uses a neural network approach that, although does not guarantee convergence, has a good behavior on small networks. For very small networks like those in this work, a straightforward algorithm that enumerates all possible partitions is enough and is the algorithm we used.

A major question, left open by Thagard, is how to compute the degrees and links between pieces of information. Some works fill this gap proposing specific domain dependent functions, e.g. deductive relationships in [8]. We are assuming in this paper that these relationships are established and determined before our study can begin.

2.2   Some Specific Types of Coherence Graphs

From now onwards when we refer to the partition of a coherence graph we mean the best partition. We finally define the coherence of a graph as its strength assuming we would accept all its elements.

Definition 4. *Given a coherence graph* $g = \langle N, E, \psi \rangle$, *we define the* coherence *of graph* g, *noted* $Coh(g)$, *as the strength of the partition* $(N, \emptyset)$, *that is the partition with all nodes in N accepted,* $Coh(g) = Str(g, N)$.

Next definition is useful in some of the proofs later on.

Definition 5 (Subgraph). *Given two coherence graphs* $g = \langle N, E, \psi \rangle$ *and* $g' = \langle N', E', \psi' \rangle$ *we say that g' is a subgraph of g, noted* $g' \sqsubseteq g$ *iff* $N' \subseteq N$, $E' = \{\{v, w\} | v, w \in N', \{v, w\} \in E\}$ *and* $\psi' = \psi|_{N'}$, *where* $\psi|_{N'} : E' \rightarrow [-1, 1] \setminus \{0\}$, *with* $\psi|_{N'}(\{v, w\}) = \psi(\{v, w\})$.

In this paper we will use two particular types of coherence graphs. First, those where the links between nodes are all labeled with -1. This value expresses the fact that the two nodes are maximally incoherent. We call such graphs *negative unipolar* (or *neg-unipolar*). More formally:

Definition 6 (Negative Unipolar Coherence Graphs). *We say that a coherence graph* $g = \langle N, E, \psi \rangle$ *is negative unipolar (or neg-unipolar) if and only if for all* $e \in E, \psi(e) = -1$.

Second, those where the links between nodes are all labeled with -1 or 1. We call such graphs *Bipolar*. More formally:

Definition 7 (Bipolar Coherence Graphs). *Given a coherence graph* $g = \langle N, E, \psi \rangle$, *we say it is a* Bipolar Coherence Graph *iff (1) it is connected and (2)* $\psi(e) \in \{1, -1\}$ *for all* $e \in E$.

2.3 Argumentation Systems

An *argumentation system*, as introduced by Dung in [5], is a pair $\langle \mathcal{A}, \mathcal{R} \rangle$, where $\mathcal{A}$ is a set of *arguments*, and $\mathcal{R} \subseteq \mathcal{A} \times \mathcal{A}$ is an *attack relation*. The relation a *attacks* b, or b *is attacked by* a, is denoted by $a \mathcal{R} b$ or $(a, b) \in \mathcal{R}$.

In [5], different acceptability semantics were introduced. They are based on two basic concepts: *defence* and *conflict-freeness*, defined as follows:

Definition 8 (Defence/Conflict-freeness). *Let* $T = \langle \mathcal{A}, \mathcal{R} \rangle$ *be an argumentation system. Let* $A' \subseteq \mathcal{A}$.

- A' *is conflict free iff* $\nexists\, a, b \in A'$ *s.t* $(a, b) \in \mathcal{R}$.
- A' *defends* $a \in \mathcal{A}$ *iff* $\forall b \in \mathcal{A}$, *if* $(b, a) \in \mathcal{R}$, *then* $\exists c \in A'$ *s.t* $(c, b) \in \mathcal{R}$.

The basic idea behind these concepts is the following: for a rational agent, an argument a is acceptable if he can defend a against all attacks. All the arguments acceptable for a rational agent will be gathered in a so-called *extension*. An extension must satisfy a consistency requirement and must defend all its elements.

Definition 9 (Acceptability Semantics). *Let* $T = \langle \mathcal{A}, \mathcal{R} \rangle$ *be an argumentation system and* A' *a conflict free set of arguments.*

- A' *is an admissible extension iff* A' *defends every element in* A'.
- A' *is a preferred extension iff* A' *is a maximal (w.r.t set* $\subseteq$*) admissible set.*
- A' *is a stable extension iff it is a preferred extension that attacks any argument in* $A \setminus A'$.

In [6] the authors have proposed an extension of classical Dung's argument systems in which attacks are associated with a *weight* which indicates the relative strength of each attack. A key idea in weighted argument systems is that of an *inconsistency budget*, characterizing how much inconsistency we are prepared to tolerate. More formally:

Definition 10 (Weighted Argument Systems (WAS) [6]). *A weighed argument system is a triple* $W = \langle A, R, w \rangle$ *where* $\langle A, R \rangle$ *is a Dung-style abstract system and* $w : R \to \Re_>$ *is a function assigning real-valued weights to attacks.*

An *inconsistency budget* β characterizes how much inconsistency we are prepared to tolerate. Thus, accepting an inconsistency budget β means that we are prepared to disregard attacks up to a total weight of β. Dung systems implicitly assume an inconsistency budget of $\beta = 0$. An increasing number of extensions can be found for increasing values of β. We note a WAS system with budget β as $W^\beta = (\langle A, R, w \rangle, \beta)$.

Definition 11 [6]. *Let* $W = \langle A, R, w \rangle$ *be a weighted argument system. Given* $R \subseteq R$, *we define the* budget *of* R *as:*

$$wt(R, w) = \sum_{(a_1, a_2) \in R} w(a_1, a_2)$$

And the sets of links under budget β *as:*

$$sub(R, w, \beta) = \{R : R \subseteq R \text{ and } wt(R, w) \le \beta\}$$

3   Coherence Theory and Classic Argumentation (AF)

In this section we establish results on the relation of Dung classic argumentation [5] and coherence theory. Given a symmetric Dung system, i.e. $T = \langle A, R \rangle$, such that $(a, b) \in R$ *iff* $(b, a) \in R$, we define its associated coherence graph as $g_T = \langle A, R, \psi \rangle$, where $\psi(e) = -1$ for all $e \in R$. Obviously, g_T is neg-unipolar.

In the particular case we are considering in this work, namely arguments correspond to the nodes of a coherence graph and attacks to its arcs, it is reasonable to consider that the non-oriented negative arcs in a neg-unipolar graph correspond to symmetric attacks in the associated argumentation system.

The coherence graph g_T associated with a symmetric argumentation theory T is a classic undirected graph. A *bipartite* graph is a graph whose nodes can be divided into two disjoint sets A and B such that every edge connects a node in A to one in B. Clearly, if a coherence graph g is bipartite it admits an optimal partition (A, B) with $Str(g, A) = 1$. On the other hand, it is well known that a graph is bipartite iff it contains no odd cycles. The above leads to the following observation: A neg-unipolar graph g has a partition (A, R) with $Str(g, A) = 1$ iff it contains no odd cycles.

Clearly, the coherence graph g_T of a symmetric Dung argumentation theory T contains an odd cycle iff T contains an odd cycle. The next proposition states that an optimal partition of the coherence graph associated to a symmetric Dung theory without odd cycles induces two stable extensions for the theory.

Proposition 1. *Let $T = (\mathcal{A}, \mathcal{R})$ be a symmetric Dung theory, (A, R) an optimal partition of its corresponding neg-unipolar graph g_T, and $i(\mathcal{A}) \subseteq \mathcal{A}$ the set of nodes with degree 0. Then $A \cup i(\mathcal{A})$ and $R \cup i(\mathcal{A})$ are stable extensions of T iff T does not contain odd cycles.*

Proof. If T does not contain odd cycles, then g_T is a bipartite graph, i.e. there is an optimal partition (A, R) with $Str(g, A) = 1$. It suffices to show that $A \cup i(\mathcal{A})$ is a stable extension. First, $A \cup i(\mathcal{A})$ is conflict-free because otherwise $Str(g, A) \neq 1$. Now assume that A is not a stable extension because there is $b \in R$ such that there is no $a \in A$ with $\{a, b\} \in \mathcal{R}$. Clearly, b cannot have degree 0 because then $b \in i(\mathcal{A})$. Therefore, there must be $b' \in R$ such that $\{b', b\} \in \mathcal{R}$, which means that $Str(g, A) \neq 1$, and thus we get a contradiction. On the other hand, if T contains an odd cycle, g_T is not bipartite, and therefore the arguments of T cannot be partitioned in two sets that are conflict-free. Similar arguments hold for R.

We now study a relation between non-symmetric Dung frameworks and coherence theories based on a different coherence theory construction that is described in the next definition and used in the rest of this section.

Definition 12. *Given an argumentation framework $T = (\mathcal{A}, \mathcal{R})$, we define its corresponding coherence theory $g_T = \langle N, E, \psi \rangle$ as follows*

- $N = \mathcal{A} \cup \{x_{ij} | (a_i, a_j) \in \mathcal{R}\}$
- $E = \{\{a_i, x_{ij}\}, \{x_{ij}, a_j\} | (a_i, a_j) \in \mathcal{R}\}$
- $\psi(\{a_i, x_{ij}\}) = 1, \psi(\{x_{ij}, a_j\}) = -1, \forall (a_i, a_j) \in \mathcal{R}$

We say that a Dung argumentation theory $T = (\mathcal{A}, \mathcal{R})$ is *connected* if there is a directed path from any node in $\mathcal{A}$ to any other node in $\mathcal{A}$.

Proposition 2. *Let T be a connected Dung argumentation theory, and g_T its corresponding coherence theory. Any partition (A, R) on g_T such that $Str(g_T, A) = 1$ induces two stable extensions on T.*

Proof. Let $T = (\mathcal{A}, \mathcal{R})$ and let (A, R) be a partition of g_T with $Str(g_T, A) = 1$. We consider A, as similar arguments hold for R. Clearly, A contains a set of nodes $S \subseteq \mathcal{A}$ that correspond to arguments of $\mathcal{A}$. We show that this set $S = A \cap \mathcal{A}$ is a stable extension of T.

First observe that for each node $a_i \in S$ all nodes x_{ij} for arguments a_j s.t. $(a_i, a_j) \in \mathcal{R}$ must also belong to S, since $\psi(\{a_i, x_{ij}\}) = 1$ and $Str(g_T, A) = 1$.

The same holds for the nodes of $R \cap \mathcal{A}$. We first show that S is conflict-free. By way of contradiction, suppose that $a_i, a_j \in S$ and $(a_i, a_j) \in \mathcal{R}$. Then, A must contain the nodes a_i, a_j, x_{ij} with $\psi(\{x_{ij}, a_j\}) = -1$, therefore $Str(g_T, A) \neq 1$, contradiction.

We now prove that for all $a_j \in R \cap \mathcal{A}$ there is a node $a_i \in A \cap \mathcal{A}$ s.t. $(a_i, a_j) \in \mathcal{R}$. Since T is connected, there must be an argument $a_k \in \mathcal{A}$ s.t. $(a_k, a_j) \in \mathcal{R}$. If $a_k \in A$, the result holds. Assume that $a_k \in R$. Then there is a node $x_{kj} \in R$ s.t. $\psi(\{x_{kj}, a_j\}) = -1$ therefore $Str(g_T, A) \neq 1$, contradiction.

The above property leads to the following correspondence between the optimal partitions of the coherence graph of a Dung theory without odd cycles and its stable extensions.

Proposition 3. *Let T be a connected argumentation theory without odd cycles, and g_T its corresponding coherence theory. An optimal partition of g_T induces two stable extensions of T.*

Proof. Given g_T we construct an undirected graph g' as follows. For node a_i and all nodes x_{ij} connected to a_i with a positive link, we introduce a node a_i' in g'. A node a_i' is connected to node a_j' in g' if there is a node x_{ij} in g_T such that $\{a_i, x_{ij}\}, \{x_{ij}, a_j\} \in E$ for the nodes a_i, a_j that correspond to a_i', a_j'. Clearly, g' is isomorphic to (the graph that corresponds to) T, therefore does not contain odd cycles. Moreover, a bipartition of g' induces an optimal partition (A, R) of g_T with $Str(g_T, A) = 1$. Then the claim follows by Proposition 2.

4   Coherence Theory and Weighted Argument Systems (WAS)

In this section we study a relationship between coherence theory and weighted argument systems (WAS). We consider the particular case of *neg-unipolar* graphs. We consider that negative arcs linking nodes in a neg-unipolar graph represent symmetric weighted attacks of equal value (e.g. $w = 1$) between arguments in an associated weighted argument system. More formally:

Definition 13. *Given a neg-unipolar graph $g = \langle N, E, \psi \rangle$ we define the weighted argument system associated to g with inconsistency budget β as $W^\beta(g) = (\langle N, E, w \rangle, \beta)$ where $w(a, b) = w(b, a) = 1$ for all $(a, b) \in E$.*

When $\beta = 0$ the weighted argument system associated to a neg-unipolar graph corresponds to a symmetric Dung abstract argumentation system.

Based on the above we can define formally a $WAS(g)$ as follows:

Definition 14. *Given a neg-unipolar graph $g = (N, E, \psi)$ we define the weighted argument system of g as $WAS(g) = W^{2*|\Sigma\psi(e)|}(g)$.*

We need now to define a notion of *internal inconsistency* of a coherence graph which is simply the sum of the weights of its negative links. More formally:

Definition 15 (Internal Inconsistency (INC)). *Given a graph* $g = \langle N, E, \psi \rangle$ *the* internal inconsistency *of graph* g *is defined as* $INC(g) = |\Sigma_{\psi(e)<0}\psi(e)|$.

Based on the above notions we can now formulate a relation between coherence and weighted argument systems.

Proposition 4. *Let* (A, R) *be a partition of a neg-unipolar graph* $g = \langle N, E, \psi \rangle$. *Then* A *is an admissible extension of* $W^k(g)$, *where* $k = 2 * INC(\langle A, E|_A, \psi \rangle)$.

Proof. Clearly, A, as any subset of N, is an admissible extension. On the other hand the budget of A is the number of negative edges that link its nodes, i.e. $INC(\langle A, E|_A, \psi \rangle)$, multiplied by 2, since every undirected edge of g corresponds to a pair of directed edges in $W^k(g)$. □

It is then obvious that all admissible extensions of $WAS(g)$ are also parts of the possible bipartitions of the associated neg-unipolar coherence graph g.

We will now show that the strength of coherence graphs induces a ranking on the bipartitions of the nodes of neg-unipolar graphs that has an interesting meaning from an argumentation perspective. The following result shows that the order of the bipartitions induced by $Str(\cdot)$ of a neg-unipolar graph induces a ranking over Dung's stable extensions (i.e. for inconsistency budget $\beta = 0$ of the associated WAS).

Theorem 1 (Ranking of stable extensions). *Given a neg-unipolar graph* $g = \langle N, E, \psi \rangle$, *let* $P = \langle P_1, \ldots, P_n \rangle$ *be the partially ordered set (or poset), according to* $Str(\cdot)$, *of all possible partitions of* g *where* $P_i = (A_i, R_i)$. *Then, for any pair* $\mathcal{E}_i$ *and* $\mathcal{E}_j$ *of stable extensions of* $W^0(g)$, $INC(\langle N \setminus \mathcal{E}_i, E|_{N \setminus \mathcal{E}_i}, \psi \rangle) < INC(\langle N \setminus \mathcal{E}_j, E|_{N \setminus \mathcal{E}_j}, \psi \rangle)$ *if there are* k, l *such that* $P_k = (\mathcal{E}_i, N \setminus \mathcal{E}_i)$ *and* $P_l = (\mathcal{E}_j, N \setminus \mathcal{E}_j)$ *and* $k < l$.

Proof. Let $P = \langle P_1, \ldots, P_n \rangle$ be the partially ordered set, according to $Str(\cdot)$, of all possible partitions of the neg-unipolar graph $g = \langle N, E, \psi \rangle$. Let's consider two partitions $P_i = (\mathcal{E}_i, N \setminus \mathcal{E}_i)$ and $P_j = (\mathcal{E}_j, N \setminus \mathcal{E}_j)$ s.t. $\mathcal{E}_i, \mathcal{E}_j$ are stable extensions of $W^0(g)$. Following Definition 3 the strength of the partition P_i is $Str(g, \mathcal{E}_i) = Str(g, N \setminus \mathcal{E}_i)$ and the strength of P_j is $Str(g, \mathcal{E}_j) = Str(g, N \setminus \mathcal{E}_j)$. We must prove that $INC(\langle N \setminus \mathcal{E}_i, E|_{N \setminus \mathcal{E}_i}, \psi \rangle) < INC(\langle N \setminus \mathcal{E}_j, E|_{N \setminus \mathcal{E}_j}, \psi \rangle)$ if $Str(g, N \setminus \mathcal{E}_i) > Str(g, N \setminus \mathcal{E}_j)$ (i.e. $i < j$). Following Definitions 2 and 3 the strength of a partition P depends on the number of satisfied constraints namely (a) how many negative arcs are cut, splitting the linked arguments in the two subparts of a partition and (b) how many positive arcs are protected i.e. keeping the linked arguments in the same subpart of the partition. In our case the graph g is a neg-unipolar graph and therefore only negative arcs (i.e. for all e $\in$ E, $\psi(e) = -1$) exist between the arguments. That means that the number of not satisfied constraints only relies on the number of negative arcs that link arguments in any subpart of the partition.

As $\mathcal{E}_i, \mathcal{E}_j$ are stable extensions we know that $INC(\mathcal{E}_i) = INC(\mathcal{E}_j) = 0$. Thus there is no violated constraints (i.e. arguments linked by negative arcs). So the value of the strength of P_i (resp. P_j) depends exclusively on the number of not satisfied constraints (i.e. number of negative arcs) in $N \setminus \mathcal{E}_i$ (resp. $N \setminus \mathcal{E}_j$). As the total number of negative arcs is $|E|$, the lower the number of negative arcs appearing in e.g. $N \setminus \mathcal{E}_i$, the greater the number of satisfied constraints (i.e. negative arcs cut) and thus, according to Definition 3, the higher the value of $Str(g, N \setminus \mathcal{E}_i)$. Thus if $Str(g, N \setminus \mathcal{E}_i) > Str(g, N \setminus \mathcal{E}_j)$ that means that $INC(\langle N \setminus \mathcal{E}_i, E|_{N \setminus \mathcal{E}_i}, \psi \rangle) < INC(\langle N \setminus \mathcal{E}_j, E|_{N \setminus \mathcal{E}_j}, \psi \rangle)$. □

The above result implies an ranking on Dung's extensions according to the internal inconsistency of the arguments that are left out of the extensions. The following example illustrates this ranking.

Example 1. Consider the neg-unipolar graph g of Fig. 1 and its associated weighted argument system $W^{18}(g)$ (i.e. $18 = 2 * INC(g)$ with $INC(g) = 9$) in Table 1. On the left hand column of the table we see the partitions of the graph ranked according to their strength and on the right hand column the Dung's stable extensions (i.e. $\beta = 0$) of the associated weighted argument system $W^{18}(g)$.

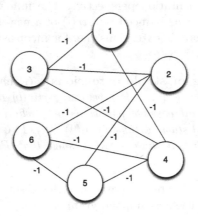

Fig. 1. A neg-unipolar graph.

The set of Dung stable extensions of $W^{18}(g)$ is $SE = \{\{2,4\}, \{3,6\}, \{3,5\}, \{1,6\}, \{1,5\}, \{1,2\}\}$. These extensions are ranked wrt the internal inconsistency of their complementary parts. So we can observe that (by abusing slightly the notation) for $\{2,4\}$ we have $INC[1,3,5,6] = 2*2 = 4$, for $\{3,6\}$ we have $INC[1,3,4,5] = 2*3 = 6$, for $\{3,5\}$ we have $INC[1,2,4,6] = 2*3 = 6$, for $\{1,6\}$ we have $INC[2,3,4,5] = 2*4 = 8$, for $\{1,5\}$ we have $INC[2,3,4,6] = 2*4 = 8$ and finally for $\{1,2\}$ we have $INC[3,4,5,6] = 2*4 = 8$.

Table 1. Partitions of graph in Fig. 1

Partitions	Strength	Ranking
[3, 5, 6], [1, 2, 4]	0.77	
[1, 3, 5, 6], [2, 4]	0.77	Rank 1 for [2, 4]
[1, 2, 6], [3, 4, 5]	0.66	
[3, 6], [1, 2, 4, 5]	0.66	Rank 2 for [3, 6]
[1, 3, 6], [2, 4, 5]	0.66	
[2, 4, 6], [1, 3, 5]	0.66	
[1, 2, 4, 6], [3, 5]	0.66	Rank 2 for [3, 5]
[3, 4, 6], [1, 2, 5]	0.66	
[1, 5, 6], [2, 3, 4]	0.66	
[1, 6], [2, 3, 4, 5]	0.55	Rank 3 for [1, 6]
[2, 3, 6], [1, 4, 5]	0.55	
[1, 2, 3, 6], [4, 5]	0.55	
[4, 6], [1, 2, 3, 5]	0.55	
[1, 4, 6], [2, 3, 5]	0.55	
[2, 3, 4, 6], [1, 5]	0.55	Rank 3 for [1, 5]
[1, 2, 5, 6], [3, 4]	0.55	
[3, 4, 5, 6], [1, 2]	0.55	Rank 3 for [1, 2]
[2, 6], [1, 3, 4, 5]	0.44	
[1, 3, 4, 6], [2, 5]	0.44	
[5, 6], [1, 2, 3, 4]	0.44	
[2, 3, 5, 6], [1, 4]	0.44	
[1, 2, 3, 5, 6], [4]	0.44	
[4, 5, 6], [1, 2, 3]	0.44	
[1, 4, 5, 6], [2, 3]	0.44	
[6], [1, 2, 3, 4, 5]	0.33	
[1, 2, 3, 4, 6], [5]	0.33	
[2, 5, 6], [1, 3, 4]	0.33	
[2, 4, 5, 6], [1, 3]	0.33	
[1, 2, 4, 5, 6], [3]	0.33	
[1, 3, 4, 5, 6], [2]	0.33	
[2, 3, 4, 5, 6], [1]	0.22	
[1, 2, 3, 4, 5, 6]	0	

5   Coherence Theory and Preference Based Argumentation (PAF)

In this section we present a relationship between coherence theory and *preference-based argumentation* (PAF) (see e.g. [2,3]).

Before recalling the definition of a PAF, we provide a quick reminder on notions related to *preference* relations. We use the symbol $\succeq\,\subseteq\mathcal{A}\times\mathcal{A}$ to denote a preference relation on the set of arguments $\mathcal{A}$. $\succeq$ is a *partial preorder* i.e. a *reflexive* and *transitive* binary relation. So $a \succeq b$ means that a is *preferred* over b (or a is at *least as good as* b). We also use $\succ$ for representing a *strict preference* relation. More precisely, a is *strictly preferred* over b and it is represented as $a \succ b$ iff $a \succeq b$ and $b \not\succeq a$. Finally, we use the symbol $\sim$ for expressing the *indifference* relation between a and b. We say that $a \sim b$ iff $a \succeq b$ and $b \succeq a$. We are now ready to define a *PAF* as follows.

Definition 16 (PAF). *A preference-based argumentation framework is a tuple* $PAF = \langle \mathcal{A}, Att, \succeq, \rhd\rangle$ *where* $\mathcal{A}$ *is a set of arguments,* $Att \subseteq \mathcal{A}\times\mathcal{A}$ *is an irreflexive and symmetric attack (or conflict) relation,* $\succeq\,\subseteq\mathcal{A}\times\mathcal{A}$ *is a preference relation on the set of arguments* $\mathcal{A}$ *and* $\rhd$ *is a defeat relation composed by Att and* $\succeq$. *Here we define a defeat relation* $\rhd$ *s.t.* $\forall a, b \in \mathcal{A}, a \rhd b$ *iff* $(a,b) \in Att$ *and* $a \succ b$.

It follows directly from the definition that if $(a,b) \in Att$ and $a \sim b$, then $(a,b) \notin \rhd$. We note that different ways of defining the *defeat* relation may lead to different *PAFs*.

Based on the definition of *PAF* given above we can now establish a relationship between a coherence graph g and a *PAF(g)* theory associated to it and defined as follows:

Definition 17 (Neg-unipolar graph-PAF relation). *Let* $g = \langle N, E, \psi\rangle$ *be a neg-unipolar graph, and* (A,R) *a partition of* g. *The PAF theory associated to* g *and* A *is* $PAF_g^A = \langle N, Att, \succeq, \rhd\rangle$, *where*

- $(a,b) \in Att$ *iff* $\{a,b\} \in E$
- $\forall a, b \in A$ $(a, b \in R)$ *it holds that* $a \sim b$
- $\forall a, b, a \in A$ *and* $b \in R$ *it holds that* $a \succ b$.

We can now interpret partitions of neg-unipolar coherence graphs in terms of extensions in PAF.

Proposition 5. *Let* $g = \langle N, E, \psi\rangle$ *be a neg-unipolar graph,* (A,R) *an optimal partition of* g *and* $i(N)$ *the nodes of* g *with degree 0. Then* $A \cup i(N)$ *is the unique grounded, preferred and stable extension of* PAF_g^A.

Proof. For any pair of nodes $a, b \in A$, it holds by construction that $a \not\rhd b$ and $b \not\rhd a$. Similarly for R. Therefore, A (and R) is conflict-free, and therefore $A \cup i(N)$ is conflict-free as well. On the other hand, the only attacks are from nodes in A to nodes in R, therefore PAF_g^A is acyclic. Therefore, its unique stable extension coincides with its grounded extension, so we need to show that $A \cup i(N)$ is a stable extension.

Since it has already been proved that $A \cup i(N)$ is conflict-free, it suffices to show that for any $a_i \in N \setminus A \cup i(N) = R \setminus i(N)$, there is some $a_j \in A$ s.t. $a_j \rhd a_i$. Clearly, there must be a node $a_k \in N$ such that $\{a_i, a_k\} \in E$, because otherwise $a_i \in i(N)$. If $a_k \in A$ the result holds. Otherwise, it must be the case that for all nodes $a_k \in N$ such that $\{a_i, a_k\} \in E$, it holds that $a_k \in R$. But then $Str(g, A \cup \{a_i\}) > Str(g, A)$ which contradicts the assumption that (A, R) is optimal. $\qquad \square$

Next, we introduce a relation between *bipolar coherence graphs* and *preference-based argumentation* (PAF).

Based on Definitions 7 and 16 we propose a PAF construction for bipolar graphs. To do this, we consider that a negative arc represents an attack (or conflict) between the linked arguments (similar to the case of neg-unipolar graphs) while a positive link represents a mutual support between the linked arguments.

Definition 18 (Bipolar graph-PAF relation). *Let $g = \langle N, E, \psi \rangle$ be a bipolar graph and (A, R) a maximally coherent partition such that $|A| \geq |R|$. Then we define the associated preference-based argumentation framework $PAF_g^A = \langle N, Att, \succeq, \rhd \rangle$ as follows:*

- $\forall \{a, b\} \in E$ *s.t.* $\psi(\{a, b\}) = -1$, $(a, b), (b, a) \in Att$
- $\forall a, b \in A$ $(a, b \in R)$ *if* $(a, b) \in Att$ *it holds that* $a \sim b$
- $\forall a, b$, $a \in A$ *and* $b \in R$ *if* $(a, b) \in Att$ *it holds that* $a \succ b$.

We can now interpret partitions of bipolar coherence graphs in terms of extensions in PAF.

Proposition 6. *Let $g = \langle N, E, \psi \rangle$ be a bipolar graph and (A, R) a maximally coherent partition such that $|A| \geq |R|$. Then A is the unique grounded, preferred and stable extension of PAF_g^A.*

Proof. Let (A, R) a maximally coherent partition and A be the accepted part s.t. $|A| \geq |R|$. Let also $Str(g, A)$ be the strength of this partition and C_A the set of satisfied constraints (see Definition 2). We have to prove that A is the unique grounded, preferred and stable extension of the associated PAF_g^A. We know by construction that $\forall a, b \in A, (a, b) \notin \rhd$. So A is conflict-free. The same holds for R. We also know by construction that $\forall a, b$, if $a \in A$ and $b \in R$, then $(a, b) \in \rhd$. We know that g is a connected graph so it holds that $\forall b \in R$ there exists at least a negative link coming from an argument $a \in A$ and therefore it holds that $\forall b \in R, \exists a \in A$ s.t. $(a, b) \in \rhd$. Otherwise, we could have an argument $x \in R$ that could be added to A so that we would have $A' = A \cup \{x\}$. By Definition 3 we know that $Str(g, A)$ is maximal which means that in that case we would have $Str(g, A) = Str(g, A')$ with $|A'| > |A|$. However this cannot be true because we know that the partition (A, R) is a maximally coherent partition. Contradiction. Thus A is also a maximal (wrt $\subseteq$) admissible extension and therefore it is stable extension. From the above we can also conclude that PAF_g^A is acyclic. Therefore A is also grounded and unique. $\qquad \square$

6   Conclusion

In this work we have presented a theoretical analysis of the relation between argumentation and Paul Thagard's coherence theory. We studied several connections between the two theories by defining transformations between coherence graphs and some well known argumentation frameworks (classical systems (AF), weighted argument systems (WAS), and preference based argumentation frameworks (PAF)). We showed that coherence theory can be interpreted as a weighed argument system (WAS) and that partition maximization generates a ranking of extensions. We also saw that some coherence graphs can be translated into PAF systems and its partitions interpreted as PAF extensions.

We would like to complete the study of links between the two fields, as we believe there are many interesting relations that are left unexplored. For instance, we plan to study the relationship between coherence theory and bipolar argumentation [4]. Furthermore, we would like to extend the notion of argument to sets of nodes of a coherence graph, i.e. sets of claims that are internally coherent. Moreover, a study of the computational aspects of both fields may reveal potential gains that can be obtained by applying algorithms from one field to the other. Finally, we reiterate that the ultimate goal of this line of research is to integrate argumentation and coherence in applications domains such as legal reasoning and policy analytics.

References

1. Amaya, A.: The Tapestry of Reason: An Inquiry into the Nature of Coherence and Its Role in Legal Argument. Bloomsbury Publishing, London (2015)
2. Amgoud, L., Cayrol, C.: A reasoning model based on the production of acceptable arguments. Ann. Math. Artif. Intell. **34**(1–3), 197–215 (2002)
3. Amgoud, L., Dimopoulos, Y., Moraitis, P.: Making decisions through preference-based argumentation. In: Brewka, G., Lang, J. (eds.) KR 2008, pp. 113–123. AAAI Press, San Francisco (2008)
4. Cayrol, C., Lagasquie-Schiex, M.C.: On the acceptability of arguments in bipolar argumentation frameworks. In: Godo, L. (ed.) ECSQARU 2005. LNCS (LNAI), vol. 3571, pp. 378–389. Springer, Heidelberg (2005). doi:10.1007/11518655_33
5. Dung, P.M.: On the acceptability of arguments and its fundamental role in non-monotonic reasoning, logic programming and n-person games. Artif. Intell. **77**(2), 321–358 (1995)
6. Dunne, P.E., Hunter, A., McBurney, P., Parsons, S., Wooldridge, M.: Weighted argument systems: basic definitions, algorithms, and complexity results. Artif. Intell. **175**(2), 457–486 (2011)
7. Joseph, S.: Coherence-Based Computational Agency. Monografies de l'Institut d'Investigació en Intel·ligència Artificial, vol. 45. CSIC, Madrid (2011)
8. Joseph, S., Prakken, H.: Coherence-driven argumentation to norm consensus. In: ICAIL, pp. 58–67. ACM (2009)
9. Pasquier, P., Rahwan, I., Dignum, F., Sonenberg, L.: Argumentation and persuasion in the cognitive coherence theory. In: Dunne, P.E., Bench-Capon, T.J.M. (eds.) COMMA. Frontiers in Artificial Intelligence and Applications, vol. 144, pp. 223–234. IOS Press, Amsterdam (2006)

10. Prakken, H., Sartor, G.: Logical Models of Legal Argumentation. Springer, Heidelberg (1997)
11. Prakken, H., Sartor, G.: The role of logic in computational models of legal argument: a critical survey. In: Kakas, A.C., Sadri, F. (eds.) Computational Logic: Logic Programming and Beyond. LNCS, pp. 342–381. Springer, Heidelberg (2002). doi:10.1007/3-540-45632-5_14
12. Thagard, P.: Coherence in Thought and Action. MIT Press, Cambridge (2002)
13. Thagard, P.: Hot Thought. MIT Press, Cambridge (2006)
14. Thagard, P., Verbeurgt, K.: Coherence as constraint satisfaction. Cogn. Sci. **22**(1), 1–24 (1998)

Author Index

Printed in the United States
By Bookmasters